New to the Fourth Edition

Brand New Chapter on Digital Communication—with Videos to Match

This edition of *Real Communication* comes with a new Chapter 2, "Communicating in a Digital Age." This chapter, with five accompanying videos available in LaunchPad, emphasizes technology's role in influencing our communication. Seeing the breadth of scholarship emerging in this area will help students to see the pervasiveness of digital media technologies in their communication and the importance of thinking about them more deeply.

Head to LaunchPad to watch the video that accompanies social information processing theory (p. 38).

A Focus on Real People in Real, New Careers

Real Communicator boxes, found in every chapter, highlight the value of communication skills in a variety of careers. New Real Communicators in this edition (strategic planner, digital media specialist, and the founder of a company that helps match tech entrepreneurs with investors, just to name a few) highlight emerging opportunities that students are likely to encounter in their job search.

Turn to p. 44 for a spotlight on Heather Wight, Independent Digital Media Specialist.

New Scholarship That Makes *Real Communication* the Authoritative Source

Substantial revisions in listening and group communication chapters, along with the appendix on mass and mediated communication, reflect changes in the field. Updated coverage of mediated communication technologies incorporates new research and practical advice on communicating via technology, including discussions of social networking, mass self-communication, and tailored persuasion.

Turn to p. 165 for new coverage of listening goals.

Fourth Edition

Real
Communication

AN INTRODUCTION

Dan O'Hair
University of Kentucky

Mary Wiemann
Santa Barbara City College

Dorothy Imrich Mullin
University of California, Santa Barbara

Jason Teven
California State University, Fullerton

bedford/st.martin's
Macmillan Learning

Boston | New York

For Bedford/St. Martin's

Vice President, Editorial, Macmillan Learning Humanities: Edwin Hill
Senior Development Director for Communication: Erika Gutierrez
Program Manager for Human Communication: Allen Cooper
Senior Development Manager: Susan McLaughlin
Marketing Manager: Kayti Corfield
Director of Content Development: Jane Knetzger
Development Editor: Catherine Burgess
Assistant Editor: Mary Jane Chen
Content Project Manager: Pamela Lawson
Content Workflow Manager: Jennifer Wetzel
Production Supervisor: Brianna Lester
Media Project Manager: Rand Thomas
Manager of Publishing Services: Andrea Cava
Project Management: Lumina Datamatics Inc.
Composition: Lumina Datamatics Inc.
Photo Researcher: Sue McDermott Barlow
Photo Editor: Angela Boehler
Text Permissions Researcher: Arthur Johnson
Permissions Manager: Kalina Ingham
Senior Art Director: Anna Palchik
Text Design: Kall Design
Cover Design: John Callahan
Cover Art/Cover Photo: Cover images: (top row): KidStock/Getty Images, JGI/Tom Grill/Getty Images, Sean De Burca/Getty Images, Sam Edwards/Getty Images; (second row): Klaus Vedfelt/Getty Images, Morsa Images/Getty Images, Paul Bradbury/Getty Images, Hero Images/Getty Images, David Schaffer/Getty Images; (third row): Ariel Skelley/Getty Images, Hero Images/Getty Images, TaPhotograph/Getty Images, Huntstock/Getty Images; (fourth row): Hill Street Studios/Tobin Rogers/Getty Images, PeopleImages/Getty Images, Hero Images/Getty Images; (fifth row): Copyrights @ Arijit Mondal/Getty Images, David Schaffer/Getty images, Hero Images/Getty Images
Printing and Binding: LSC Communications

Manufactured in the United States of America.

2   1   0   9   8

f   e   d   c   b

For information, write: Bedford/St. Martin's, 75 Arlington Street, Boston, MA 02116

ISBN 978-1-319-05949-1 (Paperback)
ISBN 978-1-319-07801-0 (Loose-leaf Edition)

Acknowledgments

Text acknowledgments and copyrights appear at the back of the book on page R-40, which constitutes an extension of the copyright page. Art acknowledgments and copyrights appear on the same page as the art selections they cover.

preface

Now is a fascinating time to teach human communication. The discipline as a whole is evolving at what seems like light speed, especially as scholarly research works to keep up with the profound changes wrought by technology. The field of interpersonal communication is evolving as new digital channels for communication develop; mediated communication has redefined the term *group* as organizations work in virtual spaces, generating new challenges for leadership and conflict management; and public speaking in mediated contexts is becoming a more crucial communication tool in too many professions to list. Our goal for *Real Communication* is to capture the dynamic and evolving nature of our discipline in a way that truly engages students while encouraging them to assess their own communication experiences and to consider the communication concepts at work in the world around them.

As scholars, we see communication concepts at work every day—in our interactions with others, in our online communication, in films and TV shows we watch, in the carefully choreographed language of political campaigns, and in both the subtle and blatant messages of advertising and marketing. But as instructors, we know that making these connections clear to students can be a challenge, especially in a course that requires us to cover diverse areas of the field in only ten to sixteen weeks. Perhaps the most disheartening comment we hear from students and colleagues—who find themselves pressed for time and depending on their textbook to cover the basics—is that the course materials do not reflect real life or the real world. As one student told us some years ago, "I just don't see myself or anyone like me in the book we used. It's filled with examples about fake people. It's not real."

This was the birth of *Real Communication: An Introduction,* inspired by our colleagues and students who reminded us that a truly effective book should give a cohesive view of human communication and that it should feel, well, *real*. We wanted to reimagine the human communication course and what an effective textbook for it might look like. The answer came in addressing the course challenges: we have to make it real, make it relevant, and help students make sense of the research. Books about hypothetical people will never drive home the point that effective, appropriate, and ethical communication can truly change our personal and professional lives.

To create a truly innovative and effective learning tool for the introductory course, we applied the strongest and most relevant scholarship—both classic and contemporary—to real and compelling people. We talked to students, instructors, and professionals from around the country, seeking personal stories about how they used what they learned in their communication course. We searched countless media sources and real-world locations for inventive and intriguing ways to illustrate communication concepts at work. We found our examples in the communication playing out in the world around us, whether in scenarios from reality television programs, mainstream movies, the national political scene, sporting and cultural events, or even visits to the grocery store. We involved instructors from all over the United States in reviews and discussion groups to get a true sense of what they want and need from a communication textbook. And as we followed up with students, both in our own classrooms and in focus groups around the country, we found them excited to engage with communication scholarship and practice key communication skills in their own lives, making the discipline *relevant* in a whole new way. In response, we designed in-text pedagogical features and other learning tools to match. Finally, throughout the process, we looked for opportunities to draw more clear-cut connections between the various parts of our exceptionally broad discipline. On the one hand, we created pedagogical callouts that draw students' attention to important connections between different areas of communication; on the other hand, we carefully tailored coverage in the text itself to highlight the ways that fundamental principles help us understand widely divergent aspects of communication. Perception, for example, merits its own chapter, but we also show how it informs conflict management, public speaking, and interpersonal and organizational communication. By taking this approach, we encourage students to see that the value of these concepts goes well beyond their "assigned" chapter.

The overwhelming response to our first edition told us that we were on to something—and the success of the second and third edition confirmed it. Over and over, we've heard from instructors and students that our approach—friendly, familiar, scholarly, and *real*—provides a solid foundation for understanding and appreciating the nuances of modern communication in a way that is thought-provoking, fun, and engaging. We are delighted to have heard from students who not only read our book but also keep thinking about what they've read long after they put it back on the shelf, applying the concepts they've learned to their own communication every day in both their personal and professional lives.

This positive response makes us even more excited about the new and improved fourth edition that you hold in your hands. This edition matches cutting-edge content with powerful digital tools. We have written a brand new chapter on digital communication (Chapter 2) to reflect the media environment of our students, who at this point are most likely digital natives. We've also created a brand new suite of videos to accompany this chapter, providing additional illustrative examples for complex or abstract concepts. All other chapters have been revised to include new scholarship, updated and realistic examples, and a focus on emerging technologies. We're also excited to offer LaunchPad, a powerful and easy-to-use learning platform, which combines the full e-book with curated videos and a video uploading tool, quizzes, activities, instructor's resources, and LearningCurve—an adaptive quizzing program.

Features

The very *best* coverage of human communication. All of the coverage you expect from a human communication textbook is presented here in compelling fashion: essential concepts and models of communication, digital communication, self, perception, culture, language, nonverbal communication, listening, interpersonal relationships, interpersonal conflict, small-group communication, organizational communication, public speaking, interviewing, and mass communication. But we've also included topics and research relevant in today's fast-changing world, topics often underrepresented in competing texts: cyberbullying, organizational ethics, physical ability and public speaking, learning disabilities and listening, culture and language, nonverbal cues, mediated presentations, interviewing guidance, and much more. And we consistently emphasize the concept of *competence* throughout, encouraging students to think about their verbal and nonverbal messages and the feedback they receive from their communication partners in the larger relational, situational, and cultural contexts.

Real Communication **is exactly that — real.** It incorporates stories, tales, and interviews with former communication students plus insights and examples derived from communication scholars into each of the book's boxes, examples, and features. These rich materials ring true because they *are* true. And the book invites readers in with numerous self-examination features that allow them to consider their own experiences, evaluate their own communication skills, and integrate their knowledge into improved, more effective behaviors.

Highlights *connections* among the different aspects of the course. On every page, *Real Communication* highlights ways that the different areas of our discipline support and inform one another. Marginal CONNECT notes throughout the book help students truly make sense of the human communication course — and the discipline. These unique callouts draw *concrete links* between coverage areas in different parts of the text — for example, explaining that understanding interpersonal conflict can lead to improved leadership in a small group, or that the steps students take to organize a speech can help them organize a group meeting.

Engaging examples — from pop culture and beyond — connect with students' lived experience. Today's students are interconnected as no generation has ever been. *Real Communication* harnesses this reality by illuminating communication concepts through students' shared experience of culture through novels, film, and TV; the viral language of the internet; the borderless interactions of online social networking; and the influence of current events in an age of round-the-clock news. This perspective informs the examples, features, and overall voice with which we introduce and develop knowledge of the discipline.

Learning tools and apparatus that help students understand, internalize, and practice communication concepts and skills.

▶ **Attention-grabbing opening and closing vignettes.** Each chapter of *Real Communication* is bookended with a topic that we think will resonate with students, from teams at Pixar working to represent their characters' nonverbal behavior to the significance of the diverse cast seen in *Hamilton*. At the end of each chapter, we revisit the opening story to show students how the principles and theories they have learned apply to the opening example.

▶ **Critical thinking boxes on ethics, culture, and technology.** From the ethics of résumé "padding" to insight into how the popularity of mobile communication apps differs across the globe to the use of robots in everyday life, the boxes in *Real Communication* offer students the opportunity to think critically about the ways in which communication concepts play out in a variety of situations.

▶ **Unique features that provide personal takes on communication.** In each chapter, Real Communicator boxes highlight how real people improved their lives by applying communication concepts. These interviews with real people explore the countless ways in which the application of communication concepts can help our careers, from digital media specialist Heather Wight thinking about how to adapt her communication to different clients and different audiences to admissions director Vanessa Gonzalez Lasso traveling to recruit international students. And throughout the text, What About You? self-assessments and marginal And You? questions prompt students to build self-awareness and assess their own communication in light of research.

▶ **Powerful study tools for student success.** The Real Reference study tool at the end of each chapter contains a focused overview of the chapter's key concepts and terms, linked to specific pages in the chapter. Before each Real Reference,

Things to Try activities encourage students to further explore the concepts and principles presented in the chapter. LearningCurve offers adaptive quizzes for each chapter as well as nearly three hundred videos (full-length speeches, key term videos, and more) that visually explain key concepts.

LaunchPad for *Real Communication* is a dynamic and easy-to-use platform that combines the e-book with carefully chosen videos, quizzes, activities, instructor's resources, and LearningCurve. LaunchPad — which can be packaged with *Real Communication* or purchased separately — allows instructors to create reading, video, or quiz assignments in seconds as well as upload or embed their own videos, YouTube clips, or custom content. Instructors can also keep an eye on their class's progress throughout the semester for individual students and for individual assignments. For easier access, LaunchPad offers deep integration with a number of course management systems, including Blackboard, Desire2Learn, Canvas, and Moodle.

LaunchPad comes fully loaded with powerful learning tools, including the following:

▶ **LearningCurve, an adaptive and personalized quizzing program, puts the concept of "testing to learn" into action.** Chapter callouts prompt students to tackle the game-like LearningCurve quizzes to test their knowledge and reinforce learning. Based on cognitive research on how students learn, this adaptive quizzing program motivates students to engage with course materials. The reporting tools let you see what students understand so you can adapt your teaching to their needs.

▶ **Video tools allow students to comment on videos you assign, or upload videos of their own.** We are increasingly inspired by the ways we hear instructors are using video in the classroom, which is why we are excited that Launch-Pad boasts a robust set of video tools. By using these tools, both students and instructors can upload videos or embed video from YouTube. They can then assess the video using time-based comments, which scroll as the video plays, and spark discussion with their classmates. Instructors can also create rubrics, which they can use to grade students' uploaded videos or which students can use for self-review or peer-review. A set of publisher provided speech rubrics are preloaded and editable.

▶ **Full-length student speech videos illustrate speech techniques and serve as speech models.** In addition to the two full-length speeches from the text, LaunchPad includes two polished, professionally shot, full-length speeches (on freeganism and becoming a socially conscious consumer), plus key "Needs Improvement" clips that help students recognize how to avoid common pitfalls. Each speech and clip comes with multiple-choice questions so that students can analyze the speaker's techniques and apply them to their own assignments. These four full-length student speech videos bring the grand total of full-length student speech videos to twenty-eight.

▶ **Nearly three hundred videos** visually explain important Communication concepts and show public speaking in action.

What's New in the Fourth Edition?

Our goal for this edition was twofold: to keep *Real Communication* at the forefront of the discipline with its engaging coverage and practical theory and to provide powerful digital tools to make student learning more individualized and immersive. The author team includes noted scholars and course coordinators who bring their formidable expertise, writing talents, and enthusiasm to the table. Through numerous author brainstorming sessions on every chapter, we discussed instructor and student feedback to make *Real Communication* even more current, authoritative, and dynamic. Some specific changes include the following:

▶ **A brand-new chapter on digital communication offers cutting-edge coverage that examines how we communicate now.** Combined with a suite of videos in LaunchPad, this new chapter incorporates exciting research and practical advice on communicating via technology, along with student-oriented topics like selfies, online privacy, and crowdfunding. Students are also introduced to challenges of digital communication that they may not immediately consider, such as digital disparities in the United States and around the globe, along with the influences of digital communication on mental health.

▶ **Revisions in the culture, listening, and group communication chapters reflect changes in the field.** The culture chapter (Chapter 6) has expanded its coverage of today's generations, such as millennials in the workplace and our newest generation, Generation Z. The listening chapter (Chapter 7) updates include biological factors in listening and the challenges of listening in digital contexts. Finally, the first group chapter (Chapter 10) explores how the nature of groups and relationships between their members can become more complex in online communities such as Reddit.

▶ **Updates to the Mass and Mediated Communication appendix encourage students to become more media literate.** In order to become competent media consumers, students need to build critical thinking skills to question the content they consume, its source, and its intended message. We've updated this full chapter appendix to reflect the changing nature and business models of media companies, with new coverage of mass self-communication and the role of media personalization in creating a polarized society.

▶ **Updated examples keep students reading and learning essential course concepts.** These include modern-day issues (from the Zika virus to Brexit) and familiar faces (from Jimmy Fallon to *The Bachelorette*) that illuminate theories for students.

Digital and Print Formats

For more information on these formats and packaging information, please visit the online catalog at **macmillanlearning.com**.

LaunchPad is a dynamic new platform that dramatically enhances teaching and learning. LaunchPad for *Real Communication* combines the full e-book with carefully chosen videos, quizzes, activities, instructor's resources, and Learning-Curve. Offering a student-friendly approach and an organization designed for easy assignability in a simple user interface, LaunchPad also allows instructors to create assignments, embed video or custom content, and track students' progress with Gradebook. LaunchPad can be ordered on its own or packaged with the print version of *Real Communication*. Learn more at **launchpadworks.com**.

The e-book for *Real Communication*, Fourth Edition, provides an affordable, tech-savvy option for students. With the same content as the print book, the e-book comes in a variety of formats. Find out more at **macmillanlearning.com/ catalog/ebook**.

Resources for Students

For more information on these resources or to learn about package options, please visit the online catalog at **macmillanlearning.com**.

The Essential Guide series **offers handy texts that give an overview of key communication areas within the discipline.** Titles include:

- *The Essential Guide to Intercultural Communication*
- *The Essential Guide to Rhetoric*
- *The Essential Guide to Presentation Software*
- *The Essential Guide to Small Group Communication*
- *The Essential Guide to Interpersonal Communication*

***Outlining and Organizing Your Speech* by Merry Buchanan (University of Central Oklahoma).** This student workbook provides step-by-step guidance for preparing informative, persuasive, and professional presentations and gives students the opportunity to practice the critical skills of conducting audience analysis, dealing with communication apprehension, selecting a speech topic and purpose, researching support materials, organizing and outlining, developing introductions and conclusions, enhancing language and delivery, and preparing and using presentation aids.

***Media Career Guide: Preparing for Jobs in the 21st Century* by Sherri Hope Culver (Temple University).** Practical and student friendly, this guide includes a comprehensive directory of media jobs, practical tips, and career guidance for students considering a major in communication studies and mass media.

***Research and Documentation in the Digital Age*, Sixth Edition, by Diana Hacker and Barbara Fister (Gustavus Adolphus College).** This handy booklet covers everything students need for college research assignments at the library and on the internet, including advice for finding and evaluating internet sources.

Resources for Instructors

For more information or to order or download these resources, please visit the online catalog at **macmillanlearning.com**.

Customize *Real Communication*. Add your own content or more of ours. Qualified adopters will have the ability to create a version of *Real Communication* that exactly matches their specific needs. Learn more about custom options at **macmillanlearning.com/catalog/other/custom_solutions**.

Instructor's Resource Manual. This downloadable manual contains helpful tips and teaching assistance for new and seasoned instructors alike. Content includes learning objectives, lecture outlines, general classroom activities, and review questions as well as suggestions for setting up a syllabus, tips on managing your classroom, and general notes on teaching the course. Also available in LaunchPad.

Computerized Test Bank for *Real Communication* by Al Golden (Joliet Junior College). The Computerized Test Bank includes multiple-choice, true/false, short answer, and essay questions keyed to various levels of difficulty. The questions appear in easy-to-use software that allows instructors to add, edit, re-sequence, and print questions and answers. Instructors can also export questions into a variety of formats, including Blackboard, Desire2Learn, and Moodle. The Computerized Test Bank can be downloaded from the Instructor Resources tab of the book's catalog page, and the content is also loaded in the LaunchPad question bank administrator.

Lecture Slides for *Real Communication* provide support for important concepts addressed in each chapter, including graphics of key figures and questions for class discussion. The slides are available for download from the Instructor Resources tab of the book's catalog page and are also available in LaunchPad.

NEW! iClicker, Active Learning Simplified iClicker offers simple, flexible tools to help you give students a voice and facilitate active learning in the classroom. Students can participate with the devices they already bring to class using our iClicker REEF mobile apps (which work with smartphones, tablets, or laptops) or iClicker remotes. We've now integrated iClicker with Macmillan's LaunchPad to make it easier than ever to synchronize grades and promote engagement — both in and out of class. iClicker REEF access cards can also be packaged with LaunchPad for *Real Communication,* 4e at a significant savings for your students. To learn more, talk to your Macmillan Learning representative or visit us at **www.iclicker.com.**

***ESL Students in the Public Speaking Classroom: A Guide for Instructors* by Robbin Crabtree (Loyola Marymount University) and David Alan Sapp (Fairfield University).** This professional resource provides support for new and experienced instructors of public speaking courses whose classrooms include linguistically diverse students. Based on landmark research and years of their own teaching experience, the authors provide insights about the variety of non-native English-speaking students (including speakers of global English varieties), practical techniques that can be used to help these students succeed in their assignments, and ideas for leveraging this cultural asset for the education of *all* students in the public speaking classroom.

***Coordinating the Communication Course: A Guidebook* by Deanna Fassett and John Warren.** This professional resource offers the most practical advice on every topic that is central to the coordinator/director role. Starting with setting a strong foundation, this professional resource continues on with thoughtful guidance, tips, and best practices on crucial topics such as creating community across multiple sections, orchestrating meaningful assessment, hiring and training instructors, and more. Model course materials, recommended readings, and insights from successful coordinators make this resource a must-have for anyone directing a course in communication.

Acknowledgments

First and foremost, we owe a great deal of gratitude to our families and friends who supported us and listened to us as we worked through ideas for the book, who made us laugh during bouts of writer's block, and who were understanding when we had to cancel plans to meet deadlines. Dan thanks his wife, Mary John; his son, Jonathan; and his daughter and son-in-law, Erica and Anders, and their daughter, Fiona. Mary thanks her husband, John; her daughter and son-in-law, Molly and Chad, and their children, William and Jackson; and her son and daughter-in-law, John and Andrea. Dolly thanks her husband, Charles, and their Aussie shepherds, Britney and Sky. Jason thanks his daughters, Magdalena and Julia, for their constant love and support. You will always remain our litmus tests for just how real our communication is across its many applications. In addition, we wish to credit and thank Gus Friedrich and John Wiemann, whose contributions to this book and our discipline are far too many to list. And, of course, we must thank our students and graduate student teaching assistants — including Daniel Bernard, Cory Cunningham, Kim Potts, Vanessa Gonzalez Lasso, Cynthia Inda, and Michel Haigh, among countless others — who continue to inspire us as teachers. We are grateful for the frank discussions that have opened our eyes to many of the challenges of this course from your point of view, and we are grateful for your helpful and thoughtful suggestions on examples.

We are likewise grateful to several colleagues who contributed to the first edition of *Real Communication*: Marion Boyer of Kalamazoo Valley Community College; Charee Mooney of Arizona State University; Celeste Simons of the University of Texas at Austin; Michele Wendell-Senter of the Art Institute of Washington; and Bobette Wolesensky of Palm Beach Community College.

We would also like to thank everyone at Macmillan Learning who helped make this book possible, including Vice President of Humanities Editorial Edwin Hill and Vice President of Content Management Catherine Woods. We owe a particular debt of gratitude to our editorial colleagues: Senior Program Director Erika Gutierrez for her leadership and passion for education; Senior Program Manager Susan McLaughlin for her support and enthusiasm for the project; Senior Development Editor Julia Bartz and Development Editor Catherine Burgess for their creativity, tenacity, constructive advice, calmness, and vision to create a book that truly reaches students; Assistant Editor Mary Jane Chen for her organization and competence, her creative ideas for our new cover and her dedication to the project; and Senior Media Editor Tom Kane for always managing all of our digital material with professionalism and grace. Additionally, without the production staff at Macmillan Learning, this manuscript would be nothing more than black words on white paper fresh from our printers (with quite a few typos to boot!). So we thank Content Project Manager Pamela Lawson for her calm dedication and superior organizational skills; and Senior Managing Editor Michael Granger. Also, we credit Senior Design Manager John Callahan; Senior Art Director Anna Palchik; our permissions specialists, Hilary Newman, Angela Boehler, and Kalina Ingham; and our very capable photo researcher, Sue McDermott Barlow. Finally, we wish to thank Macmillan Learning's extraordinary marketing staff for their incredible commitment and excitement about our book—and their willingness to share that excitement with others: Marketing Manager Kayti Corfield and Marketing Assistant Andie Aiken.

Finally, books simply do not happen without the feedback and suggestions of respected colleagues who read drafts of every chapter and tell us what works and what does not. Thank you for being part of this process: John Banas, University of Oklahoma; Allison Beltramini, Waubonsee Community College; Amy Burton, Northwest Vista College; Andrew Hermann, East Tennessee State University; Christine Hirsch, SUNY Oswego; Catherine Kelly, University of North Georgia; David Levy, University of Massachusetts, Boston; Carol Madere, Southeastern Louisiana University; David Myer, Jacksonville State University; Karen Nishie, Vanguard University; Andrea Pearman, Tidewater Community College; Evelyn Plummer, Seton Hall University; Elesha Ruminski, Frostburg State University; David Scott, Northeastern State University; Curt VanGeison, St. Charles Community College; and Brian Zager, Dean College.

Courtesy University of Kentucky

DAN O'HAIR is dean of the University of Kentucky College of Communication and Information. He is past presidential professor in the Department of Communication at the University of Oklahoma and past president of the National Communication Association. He is coauthor or coeditor of eighteen communication texts and scholarly volumes and has published more than ninety research articles and chapters in dozens of communication, psychology, and health journals and books. He is a frequent presenter at national and international communication conferences, is on the editorial boards of various journals, and has served on numerous committees and task forces for regional and national communication associations.

David Baldwin Photography

MARY WIEMANN is professor emeritus in the Department of Communication at Santa Barbara City College in California, where she was chairperson for eight years. Her books, book chapters, journal articles, student and instructor manuals, and online instructional materials all reflect her commitment to making effective communication real and accessible for students. A recipient of awards for outstanding teaching, she is also a communication laboratory innovator and has directed classroom research projects in the community college setting. She serves on the editorial board of the *Journal of Literacy and Technology* and has held a number of offices in the Human Communication and Technology Division of the National Communication Association. Mary uses her public speaking skills as a historical docent, and coaches and consults for nonprofits in her community.

Charles Mullin

DOROTHY "DOLLY" IMRICH MULLIN is a continuing lecturer in the Department of Communication at the University of California, Santa Barbara. Her published research is in the area of media policy and effects. Her current focus is on teaching communication to undergraduates. She specializes in large introductory communication courses, including research methods and theory, and has been recognized for her efforts with a Distinguished Teaching Award. She also trains and supervises the graduate student teaching assistants, working to develop and promote excellent teaching skills among the professors of the future.

Courtesy Gunsu Stephen Kim

JASON TEVEN, an award-winning scholar and teacher, is professor of Human Communication Studies at California State University, Fullerton. He has published widely in academic journals and is devoted to programmatic research and the social scientific approach to human communication, with research relating to credibility, caring, and social influence within instructional, interpersonal, and organizational communication contexts. His most recent scholarly activities include the examination of superior–subordinate relationships within organizations; communication competence; and the impact of personality traits on communication within the workplace and interpersonal relationships. One of his instructional innovations includes the development of an undergraduate teaching associate (lab director) program for the basic course in Human Communication.

brief contents

contents

Check out *Real Communication's* LaunchPad at launchpadworks.com for videos, quizzes, LearningCurve, and more.

 For videos and LearningCurve quizzing within LaunchPad, go to **launchpadworks.com**

 For videos and LearningCurve quizzing within LaunchPad, go to **launchpadworks.com**

CHAPTER 4 Verbal Communication 79

(top left) Quinn Rooney/Getty Images; (top center) oleg66/Getty Images; (top right) Mario Tama/Getty Images; (bottom left) Stockbyte/Getty Images; (bottom center) Photofusion Picture Library/Alamy; (bottom right) Neilson Barnard/Getty Images

For videos and LearningCurve quizzing within LaunchPad, go to **launchpadworks.com**

CHAPTER 5 Nonverbal Communication 105

Walt Disney Studios Motion Pictures/Everett
Collection, Inc/Courtesy Everett Collection

For videos and LearningCurve quizzing within LaunchPad, go to **launchpadworks.com**

CHAPTER 6 Communication and Culture 133

Theo Wargo/Getty Images

 For videos and LearningCurve quizzing within LaunchPad, go to **launchpadworks.com**

CHAPTER 7 Listening 161

sturti/Getty Images

For videos and LearningCurve quizzing within LaunchPad, go to **launchpadworks.com**

PART TWO   INTERPERSONAL COMMUNICATION

CHAPTER 8   Developing and Maintaining Relationships   185

Harry How/Getty Images

 For videos and LearningCurve quizzing within LaunchPad, go to **launchpadworks.com**

CHAPTER 9   Managing Conflict in Relationships 213

CSP_Reana/AGE Fotostock

For videos and LearningCurve quizzing within LaunchPad,
go to **launchpadworks.com**

PART THREE   GROUP AND ORGANIZATIONAL COMMUNICATION

CHAPTER 10 Communicating in Groups   237

For videos and LearningCurve quizzing within LaunchPad, go to **launchpadworks.com**

CHAPTER 11 Leadership and Decision Making in Groups 265

©Fox Network/Photofest

For videos and LearningCurve quizzing within LaunchPad,
go to **launchpadworks.com**

For videos and LearningCurve quizzing within LaunchPad, go to **launchpadworks.com**

PART FOUR PUBLIC SPEAKING

For videos and LearningCurve quizzing within LaunchPad, go to **launchpadworks.com**

CHAPTER 14 Organizing, Writing, and Outlining Presentations 345

The White House/Getty Images

For videos and LearningCurve quizzing within LaunchPad, go to **launchpadworks.com**

CHAPTER 15 Delivering Presentations 377

Popperfoto/Getty Images

For videos and LearningCurve quizzing within LaunchPad, go to **launchpadworks.com**

CHAPTER 16 Informative Speaking 405

Bryan Bedder/Getty Images

For videos and LearningCurve quizzing within LaunchPad, go to **launchpadworks.com**

CHAPTER 17 Persuasive Speaking 433

Gustavo Caballero/Getty Images

 For videos and LearningCurve quizzing within LaunchPad,
go to **launchpadworks.com**

APPENDIX A Competent Interviewing 463

Marco Brivio/AGE Fotostock

For videos and LearningCurve quizzing within LaunchPad, go to **launchpadworks.com**

APPENDIX B Mass and Mediated Communication   493

Geber86/Getty Images

▶ ✓ For videos and LearningCurve quizzing within LaunchPad,
go to **launchpadworks.com**

Real
Communication

Jimmy Fallon communicates his enjoyment of people both on and off *The Tonight Show Starring Jimmy Fallon.*

 LearningCurve can help you master the material in this chapter.

Go to **launchpadworks.com**.

Communication: Essential Human Behavior

Jimmy Fallon loves to connect with people. Not only does the host of *The Tonight Show* celebrate the famous stars on his show, but he is also renowned for engaging the non famous people he meets off the television set, posing with them for pictures and wishing them "happy birthday" or whatever celebration he comes across.

Unlike some other television hosts, Fallon never tries to ambush his guests or make them look bad. He seems to enjoy each of them thoroughly while playing a variety of games that reveal aspects of the celebrities' personalities not usually known by audiences. Fallon has even been called "cuddly and non-threatening" (Weinman, 2015, p. 58).

Many of the games Fallon plays are designed to get to know the guests better, especially things that are normally not talked about in initial relationships. With comics Tina Fey and Amy Poehler, Fallon played a "True Confessions" game; envelopes in front of each of the three contained one lie about them and one "true confession." Each person had to act as if the statement were true, even if the "lie" envelope had been chosen. Under one minute of questioning by the other two, the truth-teller/liar had to exhibit behaviors that would convince the others that he or she was telling the truth. Despite knowing one another fairly well (they have worked together on shows and films in the past), they were not always successful at discovering the lies (Mackie, 2015).

Fallon also comes across as someone willing to show his own "real" self. When actress Nicole Kidman appeared on his show and told the audience about their first meeting, his face turned pink in embarrassment, he fell behind his desk to hide his nervous laughter, and he admitted in a number of ways how insecure he felt when he blew a chance to date Kidman (Locker, 2015). Like many of us would in similar circumstances, Fallon couldn't believe that Kidman would be interested in him, and so he communicated awkwardly. Of course, we as the audience laugh *with* him, not at him, as most of us can relate to insecurities with our communication at times.

Jimmy Fallon has become a much-loved late-night host. His audiences vary in age, gender, and culture, but they all perceive openness and sincerity in how he communicates. He comes across as "one of them"—albeit a funnier version, in most instances.*

* Jimmy Fallon has a degree in communication from the College of St. Rose in Albany, NY.

After you have finished reading this chapter, you will be
able to

- Define the communication
  process

- Describe how communication
  functions

- Assess the quality or value of
  communication by examining
  its six characteristics

- Define what communication
  scholars consider to be competent communication

- Describe the visual representations, or models, of
  communication

- Describe why communication
  is vital to everyone

Communication is the process by which we use symbols, signs, and behaviors to transfer information. Almost everything that matters to us is "derived from and through communication" (Hannawa & Spitzberg, 2015, p. 3). Communication is so crucial that it has been described as "the process through which the social fabric of relationships, groups, organizations, societies, and world order—and disorder—is created and maintained" (Ruben, 2005, pp. 294–295). Successful communication allows us to satisfy our most basic needs, from finding food and shelter to functioning in our communities and developing meaningful relationships; it allows us to both produce and enjoy humor, as Fallon does. But because communication is such a natural part of our daily lives, we often fall for the commonsense "trap" when we believe that we can rely on our *own* common sense to guide us, even though we think that other people's common sense fails them miserably (Watts, 2011). (See Box 1.1 for the most common traps.) If we take communication for granted, communication breakdowns are all the more common. Throughout this book, you will come to realize that effective communication is not just common sense; it takes work, adaptation, and careful attention to the situation to be a good communicator.

Communication challenges exist in every profession and every personal relationship. For example, communication professor (and reserve police officer) Howard Giles claims that 97 percent of law enforcement practices involve communication skills (Giles et al., 2006). But police academies usually spend little time teaching those skills. Most citizens lack these crucial skills as well. One professor who teaches college-level communication classes to prisoners notes "the vast majority of my imprisoned students have been caged, in large part, because of their communicative illiteracy" (Hartnett, 2010, p. 68).

Become more literate communication-wise and it may even benefit your physical and emotional health. One study found that kindergartners who developed strong social skills were more likely to be living productive lives 20 years later (Jones, Greenberg, & Crowley, 2015). Another found that adolescents who enjoyed social friendships with five or more nondepressed friends lessened the probability of depression in their own lives by 50 percent (Hill, Griffiths, & House, 2015). In older adults, social connections have been found to decrease the odds of early death by 50 percent (Yang Claire et al., 2016).

In order to become effective communicators and enjoy all these benefits, we must develop an understanding of how our communication choices affect *others* and why *others'* communication choices affect *us* as they do. So in this chapter, we introduce you to this exciting discipline by looking at why we communicate, how we communicate, and what it means to communicate well. Then we examine ways of visualizing the communication process and consider the history of this rich field.

We Must Communicate: Functions Essential to Living

We communicate from the moment we are born. A baby's cry lets everyone within earshot know that something isn't right: he is hungry, is cold, or has a painful ear infection. Throughout our lives, we spend a huge amount of time communicating with others to ensure that our needs are met—though in more sophisticated ways than we did as infants. We talk, listen, smile, and nod; we write up résumés and go on dates. In these ways, we learn, express ourselves, form relationships,

communication is *not* just common sense

BOX 1.1

Everyone has ideas about what constitutes good communication. But just how correct are those ideas? Do your personal theories of communication match what social science tells us about the way we communicate? Consider the following questions:

▶ **Does talking equal effective communication?** Have you ever sat through a conversation in which a relative kept repeating the same boring stories, and you couldn't get a word in edgewise? Simply talking is not always effective on its own. To communicate effectively, you also need to be thoughtful about what you are saying, remain silent at times, and use listening skills and appropriate nonverbal behaviors.

▶ **Do body movements (often called "body language") constitute a language?** As you will learn in the nonverbal chapter, nonverbal behaviors are important and useful in effective communication, but there is no direct translation for what body movements mean. Because nonverbal communication can be interpreted in many different ways, it is not a true language.

▶ **Is more control necessarily better in communication?** Although we admire people who can articulate their point of view, if we think they are trying to trick us or force us, we resist what they are saying. A candidate's speech may be beautifully crafted with clever slogans, for example, but it still cannot make you vote for him.

▶ **Are most communication behaviors inborn and entirely natural?** Although we are certainly born with some ability to communicate, most of the skills we need to be effective communicators must be learned — otherwise, we'd go through life crying whenever we needed something. The best communicators never stop learning.

▶ **Is speaking well more important than listening?** If you talk and nobody listens, has communication taken place? No — because communication is a two-way street (even when you are just talking to yourself!), and listening is a crucial part of the process.

and gain employment. Communication thus **functions**, or works, to help (or not help) us accomplish our goals in personal, group, organizational, public, or technologically mediated situations.

There are usually multiple goals at play in any given situation. For example, you may want to host Thanksgiving this year to illustrate your adult status in the family, but your older sister may insist on keeping the holiday at her home out of tradition. You and she must try to make Thanksgiving happen (one goal) without alienating each other (another goal). These goals may be accomplished in different ways. You might ask your sister to alternate years hosting the holidays; you might drag your mother into it and ask her to advocate for you with your sister. You might even try to bully your sister into letting you host. (Of course, some of these strategies may be more effective than others!) Lastly, goals may change over time. For instance, you might initially have thought you wanted to host Thanksgiving but then realized your small apartment cannot comfortably fit your large family.

A long line of research conducted in a variety of contexts — including work groups, families, and friendships — has found that this goal-oriented

and you?

Consider a communication situation in which you played a part today. What was your communication goal? Were you up front and honest about your goal or did you keep your goal largely to yourself? For example, if you wanted to get your roommate to clean the mess in the kitchen, did you state this directly or did you complain about the mess without making a request?

communication serves one or more primary functions, such as *expressing affiliation, managing relationships*, or *influencing others* (Wiemann & Krueger, 1980). Let's consider each of these functions, keeping in mind that they are often intertwined.

Expressing Affiliation

Affiliation is the feeling of connectedness you have with others. You show how you want to be associated with someone by expressing liking, love, or respect—or, alternatively, dislike, hatred, or disrespect (Wiemann, 2009).

Obviously, it feels good to be loved and admired. But affiliation may also meet practical needs, as when you show respect for your boss, who can offer you stability and security in your job. Other times, affiliation may fulfill the need for companionship, intellectual stimulation, or a sense of belonging with a valued group of people.

Affiliation can be expressed in many different ways—verbally ("I love you") and nonverbally (a big hug), and through face-to-face or mediated channels (like sending text messages or using social networking sites). In fact, we are increasingly using media technologies to develop and maintain a positive sense of connection with each other (Walther & Ramirez, 2009), especially with people who are far away physically. A supportive text message from a friend can help you face a difficult personal situation with confidence. A simple "Like" on Facebook can show that you are a fan of your brother's new band.

Managing Relationships

All communication works (or not) within the context of **relationships**—the interconnections between two or more people. As mentioned earlier, communication allows us to express affiliation, and that can certainly be important in relationships. But relationships involve more than just affiliation—such as how intimately we get to know one another or how we handle conflict (as we will see in Chapters 8 and 9). We need effective communication to be able to manage these aspects of our relationships.

and you?

Have you ever been in a relationship in which you liked someone but at times felt a bit disconnected from the person? What messages did the person send (or not send) that gave you this feeling? How did you try to reestablish the connection?

Relationships also involve **interdependence**, meaning that what we do affects others and what others do affects us. For example, Jamie flips burgers to get a paycheck to help pay for college—that's her goal. Her boss depends on Jamie to do her job well and keep the business profitable. And the customers, who just want an inexpensive and quick lunch, depend on both of them. Jamie, the boss, and the lunch customers are interdependent. Jamie and her boss must communicate to get along well and yet keep their relationship professional. Similarly, Jamie and her boss use communication to establish a trusting and loyal relationship with their customers without getting to know each of them on a deeply personal level.

Communication is also important for managing relationships over time. Perhaps you made a best friend in kindergarten and you and he have remained close despite physical distance and the introduction of new friends and romantic partners into the mix. Verbal and nonverbal behaviors (see Chapters 4 and 5) likely had a big role in maintaining this relationship: you video chat with your friend once a month, keep up with each other on Instagram, and text him a special message on his birthday, reinforcing the relationship with laughs and words of encouragement. You've also likely lost friendships as time has passed. Perhaps you broke up with your high school sweetheart when the two of you went to separate colleges. Your phone calls and visits became less frequent and—when you did speak—you found your communication uncomfortable and strained. The kinds of verbal and nonverbal relational "work" you do in managing relationships may signal their health or demise, revealing how communication functions to establish and maintain your relationships happily or unhappily.

● **CONTESTANTS IN DEMANDING COMPETITIONS** know that it is impossible to achieve goals without cooperation and clear communication. © Fox Broadcasting/ Photofest

Influencing Others

Most communication is influential in one way or another. Some influence is intentional: a politician uses gestures strategically during a press conference to shape how voters perceive her. Other influence is unintentional: Michaela's lack of eye contact during an after-class meeting gives her professor the sense that she lacks confidence, but she's really just having trouble with her contact lenses.

The ability of one person, group, or organization to influence others and the way in which their interactions are conducted is called **control**. Unlike affection, which you can give and receive infinitely, control is finite: the more control one person has in a relationship or situation, the less the others tend to have. Distribution of control is worked out through communication—by how people talk with each other, what they say, and when they interact. This negotiation of control may seem like a power struggle at times. But it is a necessary aspect of every type of relationship: family, friends, romantic partners, colleagues, doctors and patients, teachers and students, advertisers and consumers.

→ **connect**

As you learn in Chapter 17, persuasive speaking is an attempt to influence others' attitudes, beliefs, or behaviors. It may seem as though the speaker has all of the control in the speaking situation, but this is not the case. The audience members can exert influence on the speaker through a variety of nonverbal cues (like eye contact and facial expressions) that may cause the speaker to alter his or her behavior.

● **FOR MOST LEARNING** environments to be successful, teachers should have more control than students in the classroom. Hero Images/Getty Images

How We Communicate

It's 8:45 A.M. in New York City. A woman walks up to a street vendor's cart, smiles and nods quickly at the vendor, and says, "regular." The man promptly prepares her a small coffee with milk and two sugars. He hands her the coffee; she hands him some money, says "thanks," and continues on her way.

With only two words spoken, an entire business transaction has been carried out to the satisfaction of both parties. But what exactly occurred? The characteristics of communication can explain.

real communicator

Real communicators — what job will you hold?

Did you come to college knowing exactly what you wanted to do for a career? Or are you discovering your interests as you investigate classes and programs? Wherever you are on your path to a successful career, we intend to help you throughout this text by showing you real people at work. The *Real Communicator* box in each chapter features someone who, in their profession, is using the skills they learned in an introductory class in communication like the one you are taking now. Some of these people also received a degree in communication; others enhanced their communication knowledge with advanced degrees in counseling, law, or business.

We detail the broad field of communication in Table 1.2 at the end of this chapter so that you can see the many areas of study. If you are asking, "But what do I *do* with those areas of study?" our *Real Communicator* box will help you answer that question by illustrating the breadth of careers available to you today. From sports management to acting, from marketing to advertising, from teaching to counseling — this diverse group of people will illustrate communication-related careers in action today. The flexibility of a communication degree also makes it ideally

situated for careers of the future, as existing careers evolve and new ones emerge to meet the demands of the digital age.

You might start a career search in one of the areas below; however, keep in mind that it might be a springboard to ever-changing and exciting careers of the future.

Advertising/Marketing/Public Relations (e.g., account executive, creative director, media sales, social media manager, public opinion researcher)

Communication Education (e.g., all educational levels, debate coach, drama director)

Electronic Media/Radio/Television Broadcasting/ Convergence Media Technology (e.g., community relations, news anchor, podcaster, comedy writer, talk show host)

Entrepreneurship/Innovation (e.g., small business creator, professional blogger, nonprofit start-up, event planner, consultant)

Print and Digital Journalism (e.g., media interviewer, reporter, editor, newscaster)

Organizational (e.g., human resource specialist, business manager, technical writer, labor negotiator, lobbyist, diplomat, legislative assistant)

Theater/Performing Arts/Dramatic Arts (e.g., performing artist, casting director)*

* Information from S. Morreale & A. Swickard-Gorman (Eds.). (2006). *Pathways to communication careers in the 21st century*. Washington, DC: National Communication Association; Natcom.org. (2016). *Why study communication? Pathways to your future*. Washington, DC: National Communication Association.

connect

As we discuss in Chapter 4, the most arbitrary symbolic behavior is language. There is no particular reason why the letters *t-r-e-e* should represent a very large plant form, but they do. And in Chapter 5, you learn that gestures serve a similar purpose. Holding up your thumb while clenching your other fingers stands for "good job" in U.S. culture, though you likely do not need to have this fact explained.

Characteristics of Communication

Communication has six defining characteristics: the *symbolic* nature of messages, the encoding and decoding of *shared codes*, the influence of *culture*, the sender's perceived *intentionality*, the presence of a *channel* or *channels*, and the *transactional* quality of the exchange of messages. That's quite a mouthful, so let's look at each characteristic more closely.

Communication Is Symbolic

Communication relies on the use of **symbols** — arbitrary constructions (usually language or behaviors) that refer to objects: people, things, and ideas. The stronger the connection is between symbol and object, the clearer the intended meaning, and vice versa. For example, our customer greeted the street vendor with a smile and a nod — behaviors clearly indicating the idea of "greeting."

A symbol can take on a new meaning if at least two people agree that it will have that meaning for them. A romantic couple might share a specific "look" that communicates their mutual affection; three friends might have a gesture that signifies an inside joke. Social groups, such as fraternities and sororities or sports teams, might use a handshake, password, or article of clothing to set themselves apart from others. We cover the use of such verbal and nonverbal symbols more deeply in Chapters 4, 5, and 6.

Communication Requires a Shared Code

A **code** is a set of symbols that are joined to create a meaningful message. For communication to take place, the participants must share the code to encode and decode messages. **Encoding** is the process of mentally constructing a message—putting it into a symbol that can be sent to someone. **Decoding** is the process of interpreting and assigning meaning to a message that gets received. If the relational partners are using the same code, they are more likely to encode and decode messages accurately and arrive at the shared meaning they want to communicate.

Speaking a common language is the most obvious example of sharing a communication code, though it is certainly not the only one. Baseball teams, for example, develop elaborate codes for various pitches and plays, which players communicate through hand gestures and body movements (removing a baseball cap, holding up three fingers and shaking them twice). Similarly, consider the emojis, texting, and chat room shorthand we all use when communicating through mediated channels—especially when we are in a hurry.

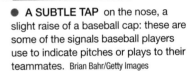

● **A SUBTLE TAP** on the nose, a slight raise of a baseball cap: these are some of the signals baseball players use to indicate pitches or plays to their teammates. Brian Bahr/Getty Images

Communication Is Linked to Culture

If you've ever traveled abroad, or even through the different neighborhoods of a large city, you know that communication is linked to culture. *Culture* refers to the shared beliefs, values, and practices of a group of people. A group's culture includes the language (or languages) and other symbols used by group members as well as the norms and rules about appropriate behavior.

Most people are members of several cocultures simultaneously. *Cocultures* are smaller groups of people within a larger culture that are distinguished by features such as race, religion, age, generation, political affiliation, gender, sexual orientation, economic status, educational level, occupation, and a host of other factors.

Consider Teresa, who identifies with a number of cocultures: she is an American, a Mexican American, a woman, a midwesterner, a lawyer, a wife and mother of two children, a person with an income over $100,000 a year, a Democrat, and a Christian. Each of these cocultures carries different meanings for Teresa and affects her communication—including the language she speaks (where and with whom), how she presents herself to others, how she evaluates her effectiveness, and how she interprets others' behavior (Chen & Starosta, 1996; Zarrinabadi, 2012).

Cultural identities can even form around interests and hobbies. For example, a music critic at Pitchfork.com might distinguish among rock, soul, and hip-hop and might even break those styles down further, using terms like *old school, freestyle, classic, punk, techno,* and *R&B*. For someone less involved or less interested in the music scene, such distinctions might seem unimportant—it's all just popular music. We uncover the cultural complexities of communication in Chapter 6.

Communication Can Be Unintentional

Some communication is *intentional*, such as messaging a friend to let her know you'll be away from your computer and using a mutually understood code (BRB!).

connect

As you learn in Chapter 6, culture can dictate communication norms, such as defining personal space. In Mediterranean cultures, for instance, men stand close together and frequently touch during conversation. But in North American cultures, the appropriate conversational distance is generally about three feet, and men seldom touch each other during social interaction, except when they shake hands in greeting.

● **TRANSACTIONS THAT OCCUR** on *Pawn Stars* involve more than just cash — buyers and sellers exchange words, tones of voice, eye contact, and facial expressions before a deal is made. © History Channel/Photofest

Other communication is *spontaneous* and therefore *unintentional* (Buck, 1988; Motley, 1990). For example, you communicate a message when you blush, even though blushing is an involuntary action. The distinction between the two types of communication can be described as the difference between *giving* information and *giving off* information (Goffman, 1967).

These distinctions are important: we tend to see involuntary (unintentional) messages as more honest and reliable because the person giving off the information does not have the opportunity to censor it. However, most spontaneous messages are ambiguous: Is your face red because you're embarrassed? Because you're angry? Because you had a hot cup of tea? Because you just ran up six flights of stairs? Other surrounding cues may give us more clues to the meaning, but in the end our final assessment can still be questionable. The most successful communicators are sensitive to the fact that both intended and unintended messages exert an impact on the people around them.

Communication Occurs Through Various Channels

Once the only means of communication — the only channel — was face-to-face contact. But as society became more sophisticated, other channels emerged. Smoke signals, handwritten correspondence, telegraph, telephone, email, and text messaging are all examples. A **channel** is simply the method through which communication occurs. We must have a channel to communicate.

Most people in technologically advanced societies use many channels to communicate, though they are not always proficient at adapting communication for the channel being used. Do you have a friend who leaves five-minute voice-mail messages on your cell phone as though speaking directly with you? Or do you have an aunt who shares deeply private information with all of her six hundred Facebook "friends"? We all need to identify the channel or channels that will work best for certain messages, at certain points in our relationships with certain people, and then adapt our messages accordingly.

Communication Is Transactional

"What do you want for it?" the pawnbroker asks the potential seller on the History Channel's reality television show *Pawn Stars*. A series of exchanges ensue before a decision to buy or sell is made. It is not just one way; every exchange involves not only the words spoken, but also tone of voice, eye contact, and facial expressions. That's because communication is a **transactional** process: it involves people exchanging messages in both *sender* and *receiver* roles, and their messages are interdependent — influenced by those of their partner — and irreversible. Once a message has been sent (intentionally or not) and received, it *cannot* be taken back, nor can it be repeated in precisely the same way. It is an ongoing process that can be immediate (as in a real-time conversation) or delayed (as in the case of a text message exchange). Some potential sellers on *Pawn Stars* even walk away from the shop (actually filmed on a movie set near the real shop in Las Vegas) and sell their item for even more on eBay.

As we illustrate throughout this book, whenever you communicate with others, you influence them in some way. Equally important, you are influenced *by* others. What you say to a person is influenced by what he or she says to you, and vice versa. In the end, every conversation or interaction you have changes you (and the other person), even if only in some small way, as it adds to your life experiences.

Assessing Communicative Value

To understand communication more fully, you assess the quality, or communicative value, of your communication. You do this by examining how well the communication demonstrates the six characteristics discussed earlier. If the symbols are well chosen, the code shared, and the messages sent as intended, the interaction has high communicative value, and misunderstandings are less likely.

For example, recall the coffee purchase described at the beginning of this section. The woman and the street vendor share a clear, if unwritten, code: in New York City, "regular" coffee means coffee with milk and two sugars. The code has a cultural meaning unique to New York. Even within the city, it is somewhat specialized, limited to street vendors and delicatessens. Had she said the same word to the counterperson at a Seattle's Best coffee shop on the West Coast — or even at the Starbucks just down the street — she might have received a perplexed stare in reply. See Table 1.1 for a more detailed breakdown of this transaction.

Communicating Competently

Communicating is inherently complex because people and situations vary. For example, the brilliant Apple entrepreneur Steve Jobs was known for his charismatic delivery in transformational presentations that introduced his new products (Ivic & Green, 2012), but he also was notorious for bringing employees to tears by belittling them for what he deemed a bad idea (Maycotte, 2015). Like many other people you may know, Jobs did not always adapt his talents to suit the needs of different people and situations.

In studying communication, our goal is to become competent communicators. We do not mean merely adequate or "good enough." Indeed, communication scholars use the term **competent communication** to describe communication that is effective and appropriate for a given situation, in which the communicators evaluate and reassess their own communication process (Wiemann & Backlund, 1980). We examine each of these aspects of competent communication in the following sections.

● **ALTHOUGH STEVE JOBS** was great in front of an audience, he was not always tactful with his employees. AP Photo/Paul Sakuma

Characteristic	Behavior
Communication is symbolic.	Both parties speak English.
Communication requires a shared code.	Both parties understand the meaning of "regular." Both parties understand the smile and nod greeting.
Communication is linked to culture.	Both parties are New Yorkers.
Communication need not be intentional.	The woman knows the meanings of her words and gestures; they are not ambiguous to the street vendor.
Communication occurs through various channels.	This example uses the spoken word, gestures, and eye contact.
Communication is transactional.	Both the man and the woman understand the messages they are sending and receiving.

TABLE 1.1

COMMUNICATION CHARACTERISTICS: ANATOMY OF A COFFEE SALE Approaching the study of communication through its characteristics will help you evaluate behaviors you encounter in terms of their communicative value. As you can see, the simple coffee sale described in the text is clearly communicative, meeting all six criteria.

● **PROTESTERS** often make their displeasure known by picketing when state or federal governments fail to effectively communicate plans to solve budget woes. Chip Somodevilla/Getty Images

Competent Communication Is Process Oriented

An old sports adage says, "It's not whether you win or lose; it's how you play the game." This means that the *process* (how you play) is more important than the *outcome* (who wins and who loses). In communication, an **outcome** has to do with the product of an interchange. In a negotiation, for example, the outcome may be that you get a good deal on a product or get a contract signed. Competent communication is also concerned with **process** — the means by which participants arrived at an outcome. Although outcomes obviously still play a role in a process analysis, *what* is said and *how* it is said have great significance.

When it comes to process, communicators who strive to create mutually satisfying outcomes are the most competent (Wiemann, 1977). A study of fathers and daughters, for example, found that the most satisfactory relationships involved a matching of needs and a balancing of control (Punyanunt-Carter, 2005). Asif, for example, hoped his daughter Laila would attend his alma mater. In the summer before Laila's senior year of high school, the two visited the university as well as several others. They worked together on her college applications and debated the merits of each school. Both Asif and Laila describe their relationship as satisfying and note that the process of searching for the right school made them even closer, even though Laila ultimately did not choose her father's alma mater.

Ethical considerations are a crucial part of the communication process. **Ethics** is the study of morals, specifically the moral choices individuals make in their relationships with others. Your personal values, along with your culture's values, provide guidance on how to construct your messages appropriately and how to analyze messages directed toward you (Casmir, 1997; Christians & Traber, 1997). Ethical concerns arise whenever standards of right and wrong significantly affect our communication behavior (Johansson & Stohl, 2012). For example, the communication of a political spokesperson who lies or twists the truth to garner a jump in the polls for a candidate is not competent, but rather unethical, manipulative, and exploitative.

Competent Communication Is Appropriate and Effective

Jim Parsons stars in the CBS series *The Big Bang Theory* as Dr. Sheldon Cooper, a theoretical physicist. Due to his self-centeredness, Sheldon is not a particularly skilled communicator despite his high intelligence and advanced degrees (Winston, 2014). Kaley Cuoco stars as Penny in the same series; despite her lack of higher education, she has more social awareness than Sheldon and the rest of the characters and shows a sensitivity to the wants and needs of others.

● **SHELDON AND PENNY** from *The Big Bang Theory* illustrate that educational intelligence does not always translate to social intelligence. AF archive/Alamy

If you've ever laughed at the inappropriateness of Sheldon's insensitivity to others, you already understand that for communication to be competent, it needs to be both effective and appropriate. You would not speak to your grandmother in the same way you talk to your friends; nor would a lawyer ask her husband to complete a task in the same way she would ask her office assistant. Competent, successful communicators adjust their behavior to suit particular individuals and situations; Sheldon does neither.

Appropriate Behavior

Singer Ariana Grande engaged in some donut licking captured on camera and found herself facing a

firestorm of criticism—she had not bought the donuts and they may or may not have been sold later to customers. To compound matters, she said, "I hate Americans. I hate America. That's disgusting" when an employee brought out a fresh tray of donuts. Though she apologized on social media and YouTube, saying she was sorry and blaming her struggle with childhood obesity and worry about the obesity epidemic in America, the singer clearly faced a problem herself for her inappropriate behavior.

Communication is appropriate when it meets the demands of the situation as well as the expectations of others present (whether physically or virtually). In almost all situations, cultural norms and rules set the standards for expectations. Although Ariana claimed she had learned a lesson and that she was young and would make mistakes, the problematic behavior was difficult to explain.

Sometimes even those whose profession it is to communicate, such as journalists, can be inappropriate. After the disastrous nightclub fire in Brazil several years ago that killed almost 250 people, reporters jockeyed for the "most dramatic-grieving-parent interview"; cartoons depicted young people going in one door of the club and coming out another escorted by death with a scythe (Xersenesky, 2013). Appropriate care and tact for the victims and their families were inappropriately ignored in the rush to share sensationalist stories.

Successful communicators know what is and is not appropriate in a variety of situations. Moreover, they have **behavioral flexibility**: the ability to use a number of different behaviors depending on the situation. So while you might love to talk about politics or your grades when you are with your friends, you might decide that these topics are not appropriate during Passover dinner at your aunt's house.

Effective Behavior

Behaving appropriately is not enough in itself. Competent communication must also be effective—it must help you meet your goals. This can be challenging, because it's not always easy to know what messages will work best—and you may have more than one goal (Canary, Cody, & Smith, 1994). For example, Travis and his fiancée, Leah, are arguing over whose family they will visit over the Fourth of July weekend. Travis has conflicting goals: he wants to see his family for the holiday but also wants Leah to be happy.

If you have some knowledge of your communication partner's expectations, you can more easily determine which messages will be more effective than others. If Travis knows that Leah would like to spend the holiday with her family because she wants to see her elderly grandmother, he might suggest that they spend the four-day weekend with his family but their weeklong August vacation with her family. In addition, prioritizing your goals can help you construct effective messages. If Leah knows that her grandmother is ailing, she may decide that going home for the Fourth is a more important goal than pleasing Travis. She can then tell him that she's sorry to let him down but that she absolutely must return home.

Communication behavior that is effective in one setting might not be suitable in others. For example, many students feel that their best teachers are those who are organized and logical (Kramer & Pier, 1999). But if your roommate handed you a detailed schedule of what you should do every day in your apartment during the upcoming semester, you might find this behavior strange and annoying.

Competent Communication Involves Ethical Decisions

Competent communicators must also weigh the ethics of the situation—what is the morally correct thing to do? Even though Dana knows that Bruce is cheating on her best friend, she must decide whether she should tell her. Or when Salvador

connect

One skill that can help you communicate appropriately is *self-monitoring*. As you learn in Chapter 3, the ability to monitor yourself and your environment for clues on how to behave is quite powerful. At a party, you can assess how formal or informal a situation is, what types of messages are considered acceptable or off-limits, and so on. Such knowledge allows you to tailor your communication to be competent in your environment.

● Ariana Grande's donut scandal and saying "I hate America" cost her a major singing gig at the White House. Denise Truscello/Getty Images

connect

The relational context usually determines how much information you are willing to share (or *self-disclose*) with another individual. In the relational chapter, you'll learn more about why it's competent to avoid telling your manager about the fight you had with your significant other but why it might enhance intimacy to share such information with your close friend or sibling.

knows that his best friend Han failed to pay his share of the utilities to his last roommates, should he reveal that to someone who asks if Han would be a good roommate? Sometimes appropriate and effective communication is complicated by the ethics of the situation and the relationship. Ethics is an important part of many communication curriculums (Swenson-Lepper et al., 2015) and serves to reinforce the credo of the National Communication Association (NCA, 1999).

Competent Communication Involves Communication Skills

Having exemplary skills in one area does not make someone competent overall: your mechanic may work wonders on your car, but that does not mean he can give you a great haircut. The same idea is true for great communicators: a politician who delivers a great speech may falter during a debate or interview; a social worker who conveys instructions clearly to her staff may have trouble clarifying her points during a meeting with the hospital board.

Communication skills are behavioral abilities based on social understandings that are used to achieve particular goals (such as asking for a raise, maintaining a relationship, or working on a team). Some of us may instinctively be better at communication than others, but all of us can benefit from experience and practice at developing our skills to find the best choice of words or the most appropriate tone of voice to use with our relational partners or work teams.

People who are judged as incompetent in some situations often do not know that they are unskilled; their inflated image of themselves seems to block their awareness (Dunning & Kruger, 1999). For example, suppose you see yourself as a great team player. During the evaluation at the end of a class project, you are surprised to learn that your teammates see you as "bossy." This feedback suggests that while you may be good at leading a team, you are less adept at working alongside others as an equal. The lesson? You may need to master some new communication skills to be a competent group member. In fact, having a number of skills increases your behavioral options, thereby boosting your odds of success in communicating with others.

The late-night show *Jimmy Kimmel Live!* has a recurring feature, "Lie Witness News," in which an interviewer asks people their opinions about things that never happened. Unaware of the ruse, people act as if they know all about a fictional band or a giant lizard attack on Tokyo (Dunning, 2014). The interviewees are unaware of their incompetence and jump to more wrong conclusions, all the while exhibiting more confidence (Williams, Dunning, & Kruger, 2013). On the other hand, people who are competent tend to underrate themselves (Ehrlinger, Johnson, Banner, Dunning, & Kruger, 2008). Apparently, it is difficult for many of us to make honest assessments of our own knowledge and skills; however, we must make the effort to do so in order to become more competent communicators.

Competent Communication Involves Using Technology

Communicating competently in face-to-face situations is complex. Adding technology to the mix can present even more challenges (Cupach & Spitzberg, 2011; Wright et al., 2013). So, can you measure the effectiveness and appropriateness of communication when you are on the phone or using a social networking site in the same way as when you are face to face? Research indicates that the answer is yes . . . and no.

As we've seen, competent communication must meet the goals of the communicators and be effective and appropriate for the situation. But our goals can sometimes

wired for communication

Email Etiquette: How *Not* to Communicate with Your Professor

> From: student@college.edu
> Sent: Tuesday, September 19, 2017, 11:42 A.M.
> To: professor@college.edu
> Subject: hey
> hey, sorry i missed class today . . . i had a little too much fun last nite had a rough time waking up ;)
> can you Email me your teaching notes ASAP? Thx.

think about this

Emails, when used effectively, are a valuable educational tool. They allow college students to ask questions outside of class and let professors provide instant feedback, making instructors more accessible than ever before. And while that's a great thing, many professors are complaining that some student emails are inappropriate.

Informal

Overly casual messages bother instructors and affect their perceptions of students' credibility (Stevens, Houser, & Cowan, 2009). Your message should be formal. It should open with a salutation ("Dear Professor Smith"), continue with a person/class identifier ("I'm Vera Yun in your 9:30 T/R conflict class"), and close with a proper signature ("Thanks in advance, Vera"). The rules of grammar, spelling, and capitalization all apply. There should be a clear subject line that should be appropriate to the content of the email (otherwise, your professor may reject your email as spam).

Inappropriate

The email shown here is wholly inappropriate for student–professor correspondence. There's a half-hearted attempt at an apology and a thinly veiled reference to being hungover on the day of class. Here, as with any communication, it's important to analyze your audience. There are some things you can say to your friends that you should not say to your professor. Review your draft before you send it; if you think you've written something that you think even *might* offend or be inappropriate, take it out!

Demanding

Many professors complain that student emails are becoming increasingly pushy in tone. Recipients of poor grades send nasty notes, absent students demand lecture notes, and many students send more than ten emails a day, expecting their professors to be available around the clock.

Some guidelines: Do not clutter in-boxes with a barrage of requests, and give recipients plenty of time to respond. Use the tools that your professor has provided, such as the course syllabus, assignment sheets, or notes posted on a website before you email; you may find that you already have what you need. And if you skipped class, do not ask your professor what you missed; that's what classmates are for.

1. What is the value of an effective and appropriate subject line in an email message? In what ways might the subject line influence your instructor's impression of the message and its sender?

2. Why might students tend to use email when a phone call or an office visit would be more appropriate? In what ways does the choice of communication channel influence the content and style of the message?

3. What are the advantages of email over other channels of communication when contacting a professor? How might a student capitalize on those advantages?

4. Have you ever received inappropriate emails? Have you sent any? What advice could you add to the advice given here to help others write appropriate emails?

be enhanced by the simultaneous use of more than one technology. For example, while chatting online or on the phone, many people locate information on the internet to share with a communication partner or to back up their own arguments (Walther, Van Der Heide, Tong, Carr, & Atkin, 2010; Lipinski-Harten & Tafarodi, 2012). If they were talking face to face with someone, this multitasking might be considered rude.

what about you?

Assessing Your Competence

Assessing your own competence is a useful step in understanding and improving your personal communication behaviors.

Complete the following questionnaire, evaluating your behavior with a long-standing partner in mind (e.g., close friend, family member, romantic partner). Rate each on the following scale: 5 = strongly agree; 4 = agree; 3 = undecided or neutral; 2 = disagree; and 1 = strongly disagree. Then add your responses and check the key for feedback on your competence.

_____ 1. I find it easy to get along with others.

_____ 2. I am "rewarding" to talk to.

_____ 3. I can deal with others effectively.

_____ 4. I am a good listener.

_____ 5. I will not argue with someone just to prove I am right.

_____ 6. I generally know how others feel.

_____ 7. I let others know I understand them.

_____ 8. I am relaxed and comfortable when speaking.

_____ 9. I listen to what people say to me.

_____ 10. I generally know what type of behavior is appropriate in any given situation.

_____ 11. I typically do not make unusual demands on my friends.

_____ 12. I am an effective conversationalist.

_____ 13. I am supportive of others.

_____ 14. I am sensitive to others' needs of the moment.

_____ 15. I pay attention to the conversation.

_____ 16. I am generally relaxed when conversing with a new acquaintance.

_____ 17. I am interested in what my partners have to say.

_____ 18. I am a likable person.

_____ 19. I am flexible.

_____ 20. I generally say the right thing at the right time.

74–100: You perceive yourself as highly competent; you are comfortable with your communication behavior and are usually both appropriate and effective in your communication.

47–73: You are competent at times but are sometimes unsure of what to say or do when you communicate with others. Sometimes you care more about being effective than appropriate; at other times, you worry more about being appropriate than being effective.

20–46: You frequently find yourself tense in communication situations, worried about how to adapt to your partner and the situation. You may be unconcerned or not tuned into the communication situation.

Note: your scores may change across situations (and with different people).

Information from J. M. Wiemann (1977).

The technology channels you use can also change others' perceptions of your communication competence. Texting a "thank you" might be an appropriate way to thank a friend for a compliment, but it probably will not impress your great-uncle Fred after he gives you a generous graduation gift. He will likely expect a handwritten thank-you note.

Choosing appropriate and effective channels for your messages is developed in more depth in Chapter 2.

Modeling Communication

As we've stated, the communication process is infinitely complex. For this reason, scholars have generated different models, or visual representations, of the process to help deepen our understanding of communication. Let's look at three such models: linear, interaction, and competent communication.

The Linear Model

In the **linear model** of communication (see Figure 1.1), a **sender** originates communication with words or actions constituting the **message**. The message is then carried through a channel (air and sound waves, written or visual, over telephone lines, cables, or electronic transmissions) or multiple channels. Along the way, some interference, called **noise**, occurs. Because of the noise, the message arrives at the **receiver** changed in some way from the original (Shannon & Weaver, 1949).

The linear model depicts communication as occurring in only one direction: from sender to receiver. So, although this model may be useful for showing how electronic signals (such as television and radio) are transmitted to the public, it does not show the receiver's role in interpreting meaning or in sending simultaneous feedback to the sender in a conversation. For this reason, scholars have dismissed the linear model as not particularly useful for understanding most kinds of communication, particularly interactive forms.

The Interaction Model

The **interaction model** shows communication as a two-directional process that incorporates feedback into communication between sender and receiver (see Figure 1.2). **Feedback** is a message from the receiver to the sender that illustrates how the receiver is responding. As with the linear model, noise may occur along the way.

FIGURE 1.1

LINEAR MODEL

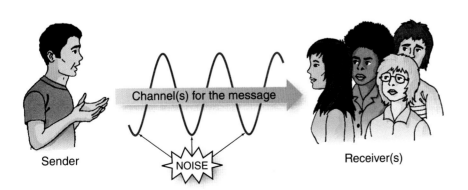

Sender   Channel(s) for the message   Receiver(s)

NOISE

FIGURE 1.2
INTERACTION MODEL

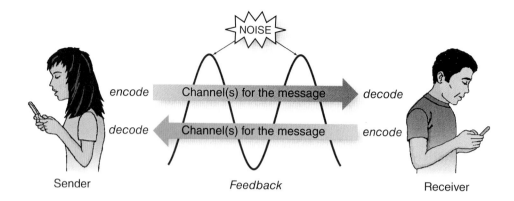

Feedback can be a verbal message (your friend invites you to a party on Friday night, and you reply, "About nine?"), a nonverbal message (your roommate is telling you about a movie, and you look up, smile, and nod while you are listening), or both (you frown while saying, "I do not think I understand"). Through feedback, communicators in the interaction model are both senders and receivers of messages.

Instant messaging is a good example of how the interaction model can be applied in mediated situations; you get feedback, but it's not in "real time." For example, while Gchatting, Melissa takes some time in composing her response to Howard's last comment; during the delay, Howard may log off, thinking that Melissa has lost interest.

The Competent Communication Model

Though the linear and interaction models describe some communication processes, neither captures the complexity of competent communication that we talked about in the preceding section (Wiemann & Backlund, 1980).

To illustrate this complex process, we developed a model of communication that shows effective and appropriate communication (see Figure 1.3). This **competent communication model** not only includes feedback but also shows communication

FIGURE 1.3
COMPETENT COMMUNICATION
MODEL

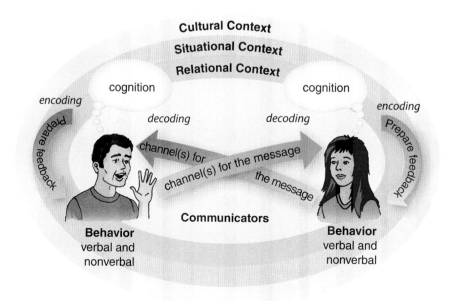

as an ongoing, *transactional* process: the individuals (or groups or organizations) are *interdependent*—their actions affect one another—and they exchange irreversible messages.

In this model, arrows show the links between communication behaviors by representing messages being sent and received. In face-to-face communication, the behaviors of both communicators influence each individual at the same time. For example, Cliff smiles and nods at Jalissa without saying anything as Jalissa talks about the meeting she hosted for her book club. Through these behaviors, Cliff is sending messages of encouragement while receiving her verbal messages. Jalissa sends messages about the book she chose for that week's discussion, as well as the foods she selected and prepared for the get-together. But she is also receiving messages from Cliff that she interprets as positive interest. Both Cliff and Jalissa are simultaneously encoding (sending) and decoding (receiving) communication behavior through verbal and nonverbal channels—and, increasingly, through digital channels.

This transaction changes slightly with different types of communication. For example, in a mediated form of communication—a Facebook posting or text, for example—the sending and receiving of messages may not be simultaneous. In such cases, the communicators are more likely to take turns, or a delay in time may elapse between messages. In mass media such as TV or radio, feedback may be even more limited and delayed—audience reactions to a TV show are typically gauged only by the Nielsen ratings (how many people watched) or by comments posted by fans on their blogs.

The competent communication model takes into account not only the transactional nature of communication but also the role of communicators themselves—their internal thoughts and influences as well as the various contexts in which they operate. There are four main spheres of influence at play in the competent communication model:

▶ The *communicators*. Two individuals are shown here, but many variations are possible: one person speaking to an audience of two hundred, six individuals in a group meeting, and so on.

▶ The *relationships* among the communicators (the relational context).

▶ The *situation* in which the communication occurs (the situational context).

▶ The *cultural setting* that frames the interaction (the cultural context).

Let's take a closer look at each of these influences.

The Communicators

The most obvious elements in any communication are the communicators themselves. When sending and receiving messages, each communicator is influenced by **cognitions**, the thoughts they have about themselves and others, including their understanding and awareness of who they are (smart, funny, compassionate), how well they like themselves, and how successful they think they are. We discuss this in depth in the self-concept/perception chapter (Chapter 3). For now, just understand that your cognitions influence your behavior when you communicate. **Behavior** is observable communication, including verbal messages (words) and nonverbal messages (facial expressions, body movements, clothing, gestures). Your cognitions are encoded into the messages you send, which are then decoded by your communication partner into his or her own cognitions, which influence the interpretation of your message and the preparation of feedback to you.

evaluating communication ethics

Friends who have More or Less than You

You know that students at your large state school come from all kinds of backgrounds and circumstances. You also know that you have it easier than some and try not to resent those who seem to have it easier than you. But your new roommate, Cameron, is beginning to frustrate you. Although you both think of yourselves as "ordinary middle-class guys," it's becoming clear that he comes from a more privileged background than do you. While you are taking out loans, along with help from your parents, to pay your tuition, Cameron's tuition is paid in full up front. And he is the only one of your friends who does not have a part-time job during the school year; his parents supply him with spending money on a regular basis.

He's a really nice guy, and you share a lot of the same interests, but he continues to suggest excursions — such as eating out or going to concerts — that you just cannot afford. When he notes that your favorite band is playing the local arena next weekend and that tickets are "only $75," you feel jealous and angry that he could be so clueless. What do you do?

think about this

1. What relational, situational, and cultural factors are involved in this ethical communication dilemma?

2. Is Cameron fully responsible for decoding these contextual cues? Do you have a responsibility here as well?

3. How might you construct a competent and ethical response to Cameron to help make him aware of your frustrations without insulting or alienating him?

and you?

Recall a communication situation in which you felt uncomfortable. Perhaps you were thinking that your partner disapproved of you or of what you were saying or doing. What were your thoughts (cognitions) about yourself? About your partner? What could you say or do to clarify the situation? What kind of feedback would be most effective?

This constant cycle can be seen in the following example: Devon knows that he's a good student, but he struggles with math and science courses. This embarrasses him because his mother is a doctor and his brother is an engineer. He rarely feels like he will succeed in these areas. He tells his friend Kayla that he cannot figure out why he failed his recent physics exam because he had studied for days. When he says this, his eyes are downcast and he looks angry. Kayla receives and decodes Devon's message, and because she prides herself on being a good listener and not reacting overemotionally, she encodes and sends a feedback message of her own: she calmly asks whether Devon contacted his physics professor or an academic tutor for extra help. Devon receives and decodes Kayla's message in light of his own cognitions about being a poor science student. He notices that Kayla made very direct eye contact, did not smile, and did not express sympathy. He concludes that she is accusing him of not working hard enough. He sends feedback of his own — his eyes are large and his arms are crossed and he loudly and sarcastically states, "Right, yeah, I guess I was just too dumb to think about that."

Because communication situations have so many "moving parts," they can vary greatly. More successful communicators often have a high degree of **cognitive complexity**. That is, they can consider multiple scenarios, formulate multiple theories, and make multiple interpretations when encoding and decoding messages. In this case, *both* Kayla and Devon could have considered other possible interpretations and responses to be more competent communicators.

The Relational Context

As we discussed earlier, from mundane business transactions to intimate discussions, all communication occurs within the context of a relationship. In the competent communication model, this relational context is represented by the inner sphere in Figure 1.3. A kiss, for example, has a different meaning when bestowed

● **THE MEANING** of a kiss changes depending on the context. A kiss between mother and child does not have the same meaning as a kiss between romantic partners. (left) Mango Productions/Getty Images; (right) Jose Luis Pelaez Inc/Getty Images

on your mother than it does when shared with your romantic partner. When you make a new acquaintance, saying, "Let's be friends" can be an exciting invitation to get to know someone new; however, the same message shared with someone you've been dating for a year shuts down intimacy. The relationship itself is influenced by its past history as well as both parties' expectations for the current situation and for the future.

A relational history is the sum of the shared experiences of the individuals involved in the relationship. References to this common history (such as inside jokes) can be important in defining a relationship, because such references indicate to you, your partner, and others that there is something special about this bond. Your relational history may also affect what is appropriate in a particular circumstance. For example, you may give advice to a sibling or close friend without worrying about politeness but might be careful with someone you have not known for very long. Relational history can complicate matters when you are communicating on social networking sites like Facebook. Your "friends" probably include those who are currently very close to you as well as those who are distant (e.g., former elementary school classmates). Even if you direct your post to one friend in particular, all your friends can see it, so you might be letting those distant relationships in on a private joke (or making them feel left out). Messaging a friend privately addresses some of these challenges.

Our communication is also shaped by our expectations and goals for the relationship. Expectations and goals can be quite different. For example, high school sweethearts may want their relationship to continue (a goal) but at the same time anticipate that going to college in different states could lead to a breakup (an expectation). Clearly, our expectations and goals differ according to each relationship. They change during the course of both short conversations and over the life span of a relationship.

The Situational Context

The situational context is represented by the middle sphere in the competent communication model and includes the social environment (a loud, boisterous party versus an intimate dinner for two), the physical place (at home in the kitchen versus at Chicago's O'Hare International Airport), specific events and situations

and you?

What relational, situational, and cultural contexts are influencing you as you read this book? Consider your gender, ethnicity, academic or socioeconomic background, and other factors. Have you studied communication or speech before? Have you taken a course with this professor before? What expectations and goals do you have for this book and this course?

connect

Organizations also develop their own cultures, which have a huge impact on communication. You might work for a company that encourages casual dress, informal meetings, and the ability to openly share thoughts with management. Or you might work for an organization that is more formal and hierarchical. Your communication needs to be adjusted to be competent in a particular *organizational culture*, a point we address in Chapter 12.

(a wedding versus a funeral), and even a specific mediated place (a private message versus a tweet). The situational context also includes where you live and work, your home or office decorations, the time of day or night, and the current events in the particular environment at the time (Mease & Terry, 2012).

For example, Kevin gets home from work and asks Rhiannon what's for dinner. If she shrieks, Kevin might conclude that she is mad at him, but if he considers the situational context, he might reinterpret her response. He might notice that his wife is still in her suit, meaning she just got home from a long day at work. He might notice that the kitchen sink is clogged; the dog has gotten sick on the living room rug; and the clean laundry is still sitting, unfolded, on the couch. By considering the situation, Kevin may calmly ask Rhiannon about these situational factors rather than get defensive and start an argument.

The Cultural Context

Finally, we must discuss the fact that all communication takes place within the powerful context of the surrounding culture, represented by the outermost sphere of the competent communication model. Culture is the backdrop for the situation, the relationship, and the communicators themselves. As you will learn in Chapter 6, the communication aspects of culture encompass more than nationality; culture also includes race, gender, religion, sexual orientation, group identities, and so on. This cultural mix can create tensions and challenges but also incredible opportunities (Sprain & Boromisza-Habashi, 2013).

Culture influences which of our messages are considered to be appropriate and effective and strongly affects our cognitions. For example, Hannah comes from a culture that shows respect for elders by not questioning their authority and by cherishing possessions that have been passed down in the family for generations. Cole, by contrast, was raised in a culture that encourages him to talk back to and question elders and that values new over old possessions. Both Hannah and Cole view their own behaviors as natural and may view the other's behavior as odd or abnormal. If they are to become friends, colleagues, or romantic partners, each would benefit from becoming sensitive to the other's cultural background.

Cultural identity—how individuals view themselves as members of a specific culture—influences the communication choices people make and how they interpret the messages they receive from others (Lindsley, 1999). Cultural identity is reinforced by the messages people receive from those in similar cultures. In our example, both Hannah's and Cole's cognitions have been reinforced by their respective friends and family, who share their cultural identity.

● **WHEN IT COMES** to interacting with parents and older relatives, different cultures teach different values. (left) Casarsa/Getty Images; (right) JackF/Getty Images

communication across cultures

Judging Sex and Gender

Upon learning that she would be replaced on the U.S. Supreme Court by John Roberts, retiring Justice Sandra Day O'Connor was pleased, but not completely. "He's good in every way," she responded, "except he's not a woman" (Balz & Fears, 2005). Appointed in 1981, O'Connor was the first woman ever to serve on the nation's highest court. Her disappointment that the court would once again include only one woman (Ruth Bader Ginsberg was appointed in 1993) would prove short-lived: within six years, the court would be one-third female.[1]

If justice is indeed blind, the sex (or race, ethnicity, religion, etc.) of individual justices should not matter. But there is some evidence that at least gender may affect the way judges come to decisions.

Consider the case of Savana Redding. A middle school student accused of supplying classmates with prescription-strength ibuprofen, she was stripped down to her underwear by two female school administrators searching for the pills. None were found. Feeling that her Fourth Amendment protection from unreasonable search and seizure had been violated, Redding and her family sued the school district, and the case eventually found its way to the Supreme Court. Judging from the comments made by justices during arguments, Savana's case looked bleak, as the justices did not seem to understand why the situation was such a big deal. Justice Stephen Breyer maintained it was normal in his experience to take off your clothes to change for gym (Lithwick, 2009). But Justice Ruth Bader Ginsberg took a very different view and spoke out both in the press and to her colleagues about how humiliating such an experience could be for a teenage girl at that sensitive age. The court eventually ruled that Redding's rights had indeed been violated, in an 8–1 decision. Today, the court's three female justices are often in agreement, but it remains unclear whether that is due to ideology (all three are fairly liberal), to gender, or to both (Liptak, 2013).

---

[1]Justice Sonia Sotomayor was appointed in 2009; Justice Elena Kagan was appointed in 2010.

think about this

1. Does it strike you as surprising that Ginsberg saw the case of Savana Redding differently than did her male colleagues? How might each justice's personal experiences — their specific relational and cultural context — influence their decisions?

2. Consider also the unique situational context of the Savana Redding case. Would justices have thought about it differently if she were a teenage boy? If she were older? Younger? If the drugs she was suspected of hiding were stronger than ibuprofen?

The Study of Communication

If you've never studied communication before, right now you might feel like you know more about messages and relationships and communication contexts than you ever thought you'd need to know! But there is still so much more to study that can profoundly affect your friendships, romantic relationships, group memberships, career, and overall success in life. You've seen that communicating well — effectively, appropriately, and ethically — is not an innate ability; it is a process we can all improve on throughout our lives.

So what's behind this discipline? What do communication scholars (like the authors of this book) do? Well, in democracies from ancient Greece to the United States, scholars realized early on that communication was the key to participation in government and civic life. **Rhetoric** (the art of speaking to inform, persuade, or motivate audiences) has been considered a crucial aspect of a well-rounded education from Aristotle to this day (Simonson, Peck, Craig, & Jackson, 2013). Throughout its history, communication has retained this rhetorical interest in language and social change (Goodnight, 2015).

Public speaking was taught in America's first universities, partly to reinforce the powerful effect that speaking out can have on society (Dues & Brown, 2004). A similar concern for the public's welfare lay behind the addition of professional journalism courses to university curricula early in the twentieth century. At that time, the sensationalistic excesses of the "penny press" highlighted the need for news writers who were trained in both the technical aspects of reporting and the ethical responsibilities of journalists in a free society.

Today, communication continues to be a dynamic and multifaceted discipline focused on improving interactions and relationships, including those between two individuals, among individuals of different cultures, between speakers or media producers and audiences, within small groups, in large organizations, and among nations and international organizations. (Table 1.2 illustrates some of the major areas of specialization and the focus of each.) The research in our field draws clear connections between these assorted types of relationships (Berger, Roloff, & Roskos-Ewoldsen, 2010). Furthermore, the principles of communication laid out in this chapter can be successfully applied to many different communication situations and contexts. For example, as technology advances, communication becomes more complicated, expansive, and sometimes unclear. For most of human existence, an interpersonal relationship was limited to face-to-face interactions, later enhanced by mediated communication via the written word and the telephone. But today, individuals strike up personal and business relationships through email, social networking groups, and phone contact across the globe, often without ever facing each other in person.

Thus, while the field of communication has traditionally been divided into the separate topic areas that are found in the different chapters of this book (interpersonal relationships, groups, mass media, etc.), rapidly changing technologies now make the boundaries of these topic areas more fluid. It is important that we understand how to accomplish appropriate and effective communication online and in our digital world, so we devote the next chapter to that task.

Throughout this book, we explore how communication skills, concepts, and theories apply to various communication situations and offer scholarship from five distinct areas of the discipline:

▶ *Basic Communication Processes.* All communication involves the basic processes of perception, verbal communication, nonverbal communication, intercultural communication, and listening. Skills that we develop in these areas inform the way we handle communication in a variety of contexts, from talking with friends to making presentations in front of a class or a large public audience to, more recently, the choice and use of digital channels to communicate. In the remainder of Part 1 of the book, you will learn how these basic processes affect every communication situation.

▶ *Interpersonal Communication.* As social animals, we human beings cannot avoid forming interpersonal relationships and interacting with other individuals. Interpersonal communication is the study of communication between **dyads**, or pairs of individuals. Most students find this study particularly relevant to their lives as they negotiate their friendships, romantic relationships, and family relationships. We investigate the exciting, nerve-racking, fun, confusing, tumultuous, and rewarding world of relationships and conflict in Part 2 of this book.

▶ *Group and Organizational Communication.* If you've ever tried to run a professional meeting, manage a class or work group, or plan a day trip for a

TABLE 1.2	

THE BROAD FIELD OF COMMUNICATION RESEARCH TODAY

Area of Study	Focus of Study
Argumentation and debate	Persuasion, reasoning, logic, and presentation
Communication technology and telecommunication studies	Development and application of technologies across communication contexts
Conflict management	Reducing adversarial messages in personal, organizational, and community contexts
Family communication	Communication between parents and children and between generations
Health communication	Communication messages of health care providers and patients
Instructional and developmental communication	Teaching effectiveness and life span communication
Intercultural communication	Communication rules and values across cultures and cocultures
Interpersonal communication	Basic two-person (dyadic) processes
Intergroup communication	Effects of communication within and between groups on social relationships
Journalism	Producing and analyzing written, visual, and auditory messages for public dissemination
Language and social interaction	Word acquisition and use in communication messages
Marketing	Communicating the value of products or services to customers
Mass communication and media studies	Designing and producing media messages and identifying and evaluating media effects
New media	Digital interactivity involving user feedback and on-demand access to content
Nonverbal communication	Nonlanguage codes that communicate
Organizational communication	Communication efficiency and effectiveness in business and other organizations
Political communication	Study of politicians, voters, and audiences and their impact on one another
Public relations	Message production designed to improve the image of individuals and organizations
Relational communication	Communication in close relationships, such as romances, families, and friendships
Rhetorical theory and criticism	Analyzing speeches and other public messages
Visual communication	Effectiveness of advertising and other visual media

Information from J. Bryant, & E. J. Pribanic-Smith. (2010). A historical overview of research in communication science (pp. 21–36). In C. R. Berger, M. E. Roloff, & D. R. Roskos-Ewoldsen (Eds.). (2010). *The handbook of communication science* (2nd ed.). Thousand Oaks, CA: Sage Publications, Inc.

bunch of friends, you know that as the number of people involved in a conversation, activity, or project increases, communication becomes more complicated. By studying interactions in groups and organizations, communication scholars help create strategies for managing the flow of information and interactions among individuals in groups. We'll explore this in Part 3 of the book.

▶ *Public Speaking.* Do not panic! We are going to provide a lot of help and guidance to assist you as you become a competent public speaker. Even if you have never had to speak in front of a group before, in Part 4 you'll learn not only how to research and develop a presentation but also how to connect with your audience on a personal level. We also offer tips on becoming a more critical audience member, whether you are engaged with a speaker in a lecture hall, a protest rally, or a professional conference.

▶ *Interviewing* and *Mass Communication.* Two appendices are included in this text to meet the specific needs of some introductory courses. Are you stressed about going for a job interview? Do you need help learning how to construct questions for a research project? The interviewing appendix can help you across a variety of interviewing situations. In the mass communication appendix, we explore the forces that shape media messages and the effects media messages can have on the attitudes and behaviors of audiences. Did you feel depressed after *Downton Abbey* aired its final episode? Do you get your news from a variety of sources, or usually just one? TV, radio, film, and many internet messages are important parts of American culture and our individual lives.

We are confident that this book will provide you with an enjoyable reading experience as well as help you improve your communication. As a result, your life, your work, your relationships, and your ability to speak out will all be enhanced.

back to ▶ Jimmy Fallon Connects with People

Uri Schanker/Getty Images

At the beginning of the chapter, we talked about how Jimmy Fallon feels comfortable with his audiences and his guests—and how they feel comfortable with him. Let's consider the importance of communication behaviors to his success on *The Tonight Show Starring Jimmy Fallon.*

▶ Fallon comes across as a "real" person; his first night on the show he introduced himself humbly by talking about his childhood, his wife and child, and even his parents in the audience (Stanley, 2014). Particularly memorable was his challenge to his doubters to "pay up." A few of those who said he'd never be the host of *The Tonight Show* came out to drop money on his desk: Lady Gaga, Kim Kardashian, Rudy Giuliani, Mike Tyson, and others.

▶ The ways in which Fallon presents guests varies in order to adapt to the particular guest and situation. He may conduct a traditional interview or play recurring games, or use a story or picture from the media. In one segment, he and comedienne/actress Amy Schumer looked through photos on each other's phones and tried to explain the embarrassing ones. In another, he and actress Melissa McCarthy competed in a lip synch battle.

▶ Some reviewers have criticized Fallon for what they perceive as his heavy drinking off the show. But others claim he just likes to have a good time and that he could not learn all the songs and dances he needs to for the show if he had a serious problem. Is Fallon simply adjusting to the context when he is out in the bars or engaging in inappropriate behavior?

▶ The show has all sorts of digital links, from Facebook to Twitter to replays on YouTube and Hulu. Interestingly, the format of the show has adapted to the way people use technology today. Show segments are timed to the DVR and musical performances; even a single joke can be easily posted online.

 **things to try** ▸ Activities

 **LaunchPad**
macmillan learning

1. LaunchPad for *Real Communication* offers key term videos and encourages self-assessment through adaptive quizzing. Go to **launchpadworks.com** to get access to:

✓ **LearningCurve**
Adaptive Quizzes.

▶ Video clips that illustrate key concepts, highlighted in teal in the Real Reference section that follows.

2. Think of someone (a family member, a celebrity, a politician, a friend, a professor) who exhibits competent communication in a particular context. What behaviors does this person exhibit that make him or her particularly effective? Would you want to model some of your own communication behavior after this person? Why or why not?

3. Keep a log of all the different channels (face to face, written, computer mediated, telephonic, others) that you use to communicate during the course of one morning or afternoon. Do you regularly communicate with a particular person via a specific channel? What channels do you prefer to use when sending different types of messages (long and short, positive and negative, business and personal, etc.)?

4. Describe two communication situations, one in which the communication was appropriate but not effective, and one in which the communication was effective but not very appropriate. Analyze these situations, considering the situation and relationship.

5. Consider a scene from a favorite film or novel. Imagine how it would change if you had not seen the rest of the film or had not read the entire novel. Would you come away from it with the same meaning if you did not understand the relational context between the characters or the situational context within the larger story?

 A Study Tool

Now that you have finished reading this chapter, you can:

Define the communication process:

▶ **Communication** is the process by which we use symbols, signs, and behaviors to exchange information (p. 4).

▶ Communication is much more complex than "common sense" (pp. 4–5).

Describe how communication functions:

▶ **Functions** explain how communication behaviors work (or do not work) to accomplish goals (p. 5).

▶ **Relationships** are the interconnections, or interdependence, between two or more people that function to achieve some goal (p. 6).

▶ Relationship **interdependence** means that what we do affects others, and vice versa (p. 7).

▶ There are three primary functions in communication:
  • Expressing **affiliation**, or feelings for others (p. 6)
  • Managing relationships (pp. 6–7)
  • Influencing others is to negotiate **control** in situations and relationships (p. 7)

Assess the quality or value of communication by examining its six characteristics:

▶ Communication relies on **symbols**, arbitrary constructions related to the people, things, or concepts to which they refer (p. 8).

▶ Communication requires a shared **code**, or a set of symbols, that creates a meaningful message; **encoding** is the process of producing and sending a message, whereas **decoding** is the process of receiving a message and making sense of it (p. 9).

▶ Communication is linked to *culture*, the shared beliefs, values, and practices of a group of people, and *cocultures*, smaller groups within a culture (p. 9).

▶ Communication may be *intentional* or *unintentional* (pp. 9–10).

▶ Communication requires a **channel**, the method through which it occurs (p. 10).

▶ Communication is a **transactional** process: you influence others while they influence you (p. 10).

Define what communication scholars consider to be competent communication:

▶ **Competent communication** is more **process** than **outcome** focused (pp. 11–12).

▶ **Ethics** is the study of morals (p. 12).

▶ Communication is appropriate when it meets the demands of the situation (p. 13).

▶ **Behavioral flexibility** involves knowing and using a number of different behaviors to achieve appropriate communication (p. 13).

▶ Communication is *effective* when it achieves desired goals (p. 13).

▶ Ethical communication is moral communication (p. 13).

▶ **Communication skills** are behaviors that help communicators achieve their goals (p. 14).

Describe the visual representations, or models, of communication:

▶ In the **linear model**, a **sender** originates the **message**, carried through a channel—perhaps interfered with by **noise**—to the **receiver** (p. 17).

▶ The **interaction model** expands on the linear model by including **feedback** between the receiver and the sender (pp. 17–18).

▶ The **competent communication model** is a *transactional* model incorporating three contextual spheres in which individuals communicate (pp. 18–19).

  • *Communicators:* **Cognitions**, thoughts communicators have about themselves, influence **behavior**, observable communication, and how the message is interpreted before preparing feedback. **Cognitive complexity** enables communicators to think about multiple and subtle nuances in messages (pp. 19–20).

  • *Relational context:* Communication occurs within the context of a relationship and is influenced by the relational history (pp. 20–21).

  • *Situational context:* The circumstances surrounding communication influence communication (pp. 21–22).

  • *Cultural context:* Cultural identity, how individuals view themselves as a member of a specific culture or coculture, influences communication choices (p. 22).

Describe why communication is vital to everyone:

▶ **Rhetoric** is the art of speaking well. Informed citizens become aware of the power of speaking out (p. 23).

▶ Interactions and relationships occur between **dyads**, groups, organizations, speakers and audiences, and mass and mediated contexts (p. 24).

Digital media provides avenues for students to express their feelings and share events or inspirations.

LearningCurve can help you master the material in this chapter.

Go to **launchpadworks.com**

2

Communicating in a Digital Age

A post appeared on Yik Yak in the University of Michigan area—an unidentified student planned to end his or her own life on April 30. Responses began pouring in addressed to "4/30": "The best is yet to come, but you'll only experience it if you stick around. . . ." "Carry on strong . . . I can tell you as someone who's attempted it that it's not worth it. No matter how hard things are, or how bad things seem, it gets better." "Breathe. You are loved. You are strong. You are amazing and beautiful. You can handle this. You can handle anything." In addition to the messages of support and encouragement came posts with suicide prevention hotline numbers and campus mental health services resources (Fotis, 2015). Within twenty-four hours, the campus social media director was able to assist the campus police in finding and assisting the troubled student (Griffin, 2015). Several campus departments also collaborated to begin a larger social media campaign with a message from the university: "Dear Wolverine: You have an entire community that supports you. You are *never* alone" (Fotis, 2015).

Yik Yak, a social media app that allows users within a five-mile radius to post and read anonymous text messages in real time, provided the student with a way to reach out to the immediate support of the larger UMich community. Other similar lifesaving Yik Yak stories emerged from other college campuses (Shahani, 2015). Some researchers argue that anonymity is valuable because it allows students to take risks with how they express their feelings, opinions, and identities (Junco, 2015). Of course, such anonymity also enables users to exchange gossip; spread false rumors; and ridicule, harass, and offend others. In the wake of bullying controversies, K–12 schools attempted to ban Yik Yak, so the company developed "geofencing" technology that disables the app on school grounds (Perez, 2014). With a reputation developing for nasty, juvenile posts, Yik Yak also began to filter messages so that full names could not be posted, and warnings popped up if someone tried to post "threatening" words (such as racial slurs). In an attempt to compete with the increasingly popular "personal" apps like Snapchat and Instagram (Machkovech, 2016), Yik Yak most recently introduced the ability to add a handle (username) to posts as well as a one-on-one chat feature.

Whether maintaining anonymity or embracing personal identity, Yik Yak is part of an ever-changing landscape of technologies that provide us with amazing digital communication tools—tools that we have at our disposal to help or hurt one another.

We have seen in the first chapter how we need to be both appropriate and effective to achieve competent communication. This process is complex enough when communicating face to face, but becomes even more complex when we consider the many channels of **mediated communication**, in which there is some technology that is used to deliver messages between sources and receivers. Mediated channels include the older versions, such as handwritten letters and the telephone as well as the wide array of digital media channels now available, such as the internet and smartphone applications. **Digital communication** is using electronic networks to transmit digital data, including text, images, video, or voice (Proakis & Salehi, 2007). Numerical codes are used to convert data into its digital form, but most of us do not do any of this encoding ourselves. We just upload and download our messages, and our networked devices—computers, tablets, smartphones—do all the work.

Digital forms of communication can foster social support, such as in the case of Yik Yak users helping to prevent suicide. This technology can also increase our productivity and our connectedness with friends and family. But with so many channels to choose from in sending and receiving messages, our communicative decisions can take us in many different directions. In this chapter, we examine how quickly technologies have changed, compare the qualities of digital and traditional communication, examine how digital communication can bring people together on a large scale, and highlight the challenges of digital communication that we need to overcome.

Digital Origins

When development began in the 1970s on a new protocol to allow diverse computer networks to interconnect and communicate with each other, a group headed by Vint Cerf and Robert Kahn never dreamed that digital communication would look like it does today. The early applications were for military communication and research uses. Even when they formed the Internet Society in 1992—with a mission to promote open development, evolution, and use of the internet for the benefit of people worldwide—Cerf and Kahn could not imagine the digital applications of their work over twenty-five years later (Haigh, Russell, & Dutton, 2015).

Then and Now

Changes have happened rapidly. In the early 1990s, a color photo of an illuminated Vatican manuscript from the Library of Congress took twenty minutes to load! Internet pioneer Walt Howe remembers: "We would start the download, go on coffee break, and return and marvel at the picture that had filled our screen" (Howe, 2016). By 2000, the internet had grown substantially, and speeds were much faster; however, users in the United States were still predominantly white, college-educated men who used dial-up connections to find information through online directories. Email was the prominent form of technology used to connect and collaborate, although internet users also participated in online "chat rooms" and shared music files through peer-to-peer services like Napster (Rainie, 2012). People were able to connect via mobile phones, but their communication was limited to talking or sending text messages that had to be clumsily typed with the phone's keypad.

● **TECHNOLOGY HAS EVOLVED** dramatically since the 1990s. While the internet was once a slow, dial-up connection available to a limited group of users, digital technology is now widespread, mobile, and accessible to an increasingly diverse population. (top left) Nita Winter/The Image Works; (top right) Hero Images/Getty Images

Fast-forward to today. Not only do almost all American adults use the internet, but over two-thirds have high-speed broadband access and stream music, videos, television shows, and full-length movies (Horrigan & Duggan, 2015). There is no longer a gender gap, and there is much greater race and income parity for both internet and mobile phone use (Rainie, 2015a). Although there is still a generation gap — younger adults use more digital communication than do older adults — older age groups are rapidly increasing in their access and usage (Perrin, 2015).

Web-based social networking sites (SNS) that began in the mid-2000s (Facebook in 2004, Twitter in 2006) have had steady growth for over a decade and now dominate the internet. Currently about two-thirds of adults use some form of social media (Perrin, 2015). Email is still a prominent way to connect with others, particularly in the workplace, but social media provide additional avenues for text-based messaging and information sharing.

Nearly all Americans now have mobile phone connections, and nearly two-thirds have smartphones that not only enable easy text messaging, but also provide access to the internet and an ever-increasing variety of social media apps (Smith, 2015). Because smartphones are also cameras, photo- and video-sharing via social media have also skyrocketed. A pervasive part of everyday life, we use our phones to schedule appointments, arrange transportation (e.g., Uber), evaluate restaurants and hotels (e.g., Yelp, TripAdvisor), find romance (e.g., Tinder, Bumble), and even ask Google or Siri to settle disputes about which movie won the Academy Award for Best Picture in 1966 (it was *The Sound of Music*). In fact, mobile phone use is so pervasive that some European cities have embedded blinking lights in the sidewalk in the hopes of alerting phone-gazers that they may be stepping into oncoming traffic (Schroeder & Berlinger, 2016)!

Ongoing Dynamic Changes

We have already seen that changes happened rapidly to get us to the era of smartphones and other devices; however, digital technologies are *still* constantly and quickly changing. For example, in 2010, Instagram was a mobile phone app limited to sharing small, square pictures. By 2015, Instagram users could upload pictures (of any size), as well as short videos and text, and could include hashtags (#) and link their uploads to other social media, such as Twitter, Tumblr, and Facebook (Facebook now owns Instagram; Stern, 2012). Getting numerous "likes" for

and you?

How has mobile phone technology changed for you in the last five years? What new social media apps do you use now that you did not have before, and which ones have you stopped using? How have these changes affected the way you communicate with your family members and friends?

what about you?

How Attached Are You to Social Media?

Consider your social media use (Facebook, Snapchat, Instagram, Twitter, etc.), and respond to each of the following statements on a scale from 1 ("strongly disagree") to 7 ("strongly agree"):

_____ 1. I use social media to interact with friends.

_____ 2. Social media provides a way for me to stay connected to people across distances.

_____ 3. I use social media because it makes staying in touch with others convenient.

_____ 4. Social media provides a way for me to keep in touch with others whom I care about.

_____ 5. Social media is one of the main ways I get information about major events.

_____ 6. Social media allows me to stay informed about events and news.

_____ 7. Social media is one of my primary sources of information about news.

_____ 8. I use social media as a way to de-stress after a long day.

_____ 9. I use social media to give myself a break when I have been busy.

_____ 10. Social media is an enjoyable way to spend time.

_____ 11. I seek advice for upcoming decisions using social media.

_____ 12. If I am unsure about an upcoming decision, I get input from friends on social media.

_____ 13. I get advice about medical questions on social media.

_____ 14. I feel affirmed when others comment on my posts.

_____ 15. When people respond to my posts in social media, I feel like they care about me.

_____ 16. It makes me feel accepted when people comment on my social media posts.

_____ 17. Sometimes I post things just to have a positive effect on other peoples' moods.

_____ 18. I post things on social media that I think will be helpful to my friends' lives.

_____ 19. I want to inspire other people with my social media posts.

_____ 20. I think it is important to share things on social media so those I care about stay informed.

To see where your bonds with social media are strongest, add your scores for each context:

Connecting with others (1–4): _____   Getting advice (11–13): _____
Staying informed (5–7): _____   Getting affirmation (14–16): _____
Relaxing/enjoying time (8–10): _____   Influencing others (17–20): _____

_____ TOTAL: Add your totals to get your overall attachment to social media (ASM) score.

Higher scores in multiple contexts mean that you have a greater overall bond with social media. The greater your attachment, the more likely you are to use social media to:

▶ share and re-share information (such as news and current events);

▶ advocate your entertainment preferences (such as movies), consumer choices (such as brand loyalties), and political support (such as for candidates) to others;

▶ interact with organizations (such as commenting on their websites) about products, services, and reputations.

You are also more likely to feel distress when separated from access to social media.

Information from R. A. VanMeter, D. B. Grisaffe, & L. B. Chonko (2015).

Instagram posts has become major currency for popularity among teenagers (Kircher, 2016). By the time you are reading this, the app will no doubt have morphed to allow other usage as well.

Part of the reason for such ongoing and rapid change is the competition for users among the various social networking sites, collaborative technologies, and phone apps. New innovations pop up all the time, each with new capabilities and features that challenge the previously popular ones. Vine, a video-sharing app, was a challenge to Instagram's picture-only platform, so it is not surprising that Instagram added video capability. Yik Yak's novelty was its anonymous messages and location-based interactions. Snapchat lets us share with our friends silly (and sometimes embarrassing) pictures, videos, and messages that then disappear. Services like Dropbox and Google Drive allow us to store and share documents "in the cloud" rather than having to send them back and forth as email attachments.

● **TECHNOLOGICAL INNOVATION** is successful when it helps people meet their personal and social needs. Tetra Images/Getty Images

But the more successful innovations are not just about technological gimmickry — they are meeting people's *communicative* needs and goals. Cloud storage services are effective when they enable us to more successfully share information and improve collaboration among work colleagues and classmates. Successful social media adapt in ways that enable us to create better social bonds (Kelly & Keaten, 2015). Yik Yak's addition of "handles" and the ability to "chat" was an attempt to make the app more personal (Newton, 2016). Snapchat added its Story feature to enable users to share a full day of "snaps" in a personal narrative. Instagram added its own similar Stories feature to meet that same need (Constine, 2016). Facebook, after repeatedly hearing from users how awkward it is to "like" someone's sad post, finally altered its long-standing "like" button to allow users to show a variety of emotional "reactions" (Chaykowski, 2016).

What changes will the future hold? Experts in internet, science, and technology research argue that we have had three digital "revolutions" so far: internet, mobile phone connectivity, and social media (Rainie, 2015b). They predict that the next revolution is an **internet of things**, in which the internet, artificial intelligence, and big data will be like "electricity" — less visible but everywhere, embedded in a multitude of screens, and the way we operate our homes and our environment as well as how we understand our emotions and bodies — all the things of our daily lives (Rainie, 2016).

Qualities of Digital Channels

When your grandparents were in high school, they probably passed handwritten notes to each other under their desks. You and your best friend likely texted each other on your phones. In both cases, you were using a discreet, quiet, text-based form of communication in order to elude the notice of your teacher while still being able to share messages with someone close. Handwriting and texting, therefore, have some things in common; however, texting also allows other people to be added easily to the conversation, and the devices we use to text can also send and receive lots of other kinds of messages — pictures, videos, social media posts — with the effect of reaching even more people. In this section, we discuss the aspects of digital channels that make them both similar to and different from more traditional forms of communication.

evaluating communication ethics

The Distracted Notetaker

You and Tania are close friends. You went to high school together and are now attending the same college. Although you are majoring in different subjects, you often take your general education classes together. You frequently compare lecture notes and study together.

In one of your classes, you notice that at every lecture, Tania props open her laptop and opens her notes file for the class. But she also opens an internet browser and logs on to Facebook to glance through her news feed. On another tab, she shops for flowers for her grandmother's birthday. When the professor starts lecturing, Tania clicks back to her notes and looks up at the front of the classroom. But this is only for a short time — after copying down the text that appears on the professor's PowerPoint slide, she is back to Facebook and flowers until the next slide appears on the classroom screen. Tania also snaps a quick selfie of the two of you sitting together and uploads it on Instagram with the caption, "Besties in Anthro!" She then checks her phone several times to see how many likes and comments her selfie is getting. It is difficult to stay attentive during lecture when you are watching the flickering of Tania's laptop and phone screens. But you try diligently to listen carefully to your professor and take detailed notes. You also participate in class discussion. You nudge Tania to get her to look up from her devices, but she just smiles and continues until there is a new PowerPoint slide to copy into her notes.

When it comes time to study for the midterm, Tania (as usual) wants to study together. "I don't understand this," she says, looking at her notes. "I've been to every lecture, but this still doesn't make sense. What do *you* think it means?" As you think about how to answer, Tania checks her phone for likes and comments.

1. How do you answer Tania? Do you share the detailed notes you took? Do you mention how she has been spending most of the term engrossed with her digital devices rather than paying attention?

2. How do *you* manage to pay attention in class while students have flickering laptop images nearby? If you take notes on a computer, how do you avoid the temptation to use your laptop for nonacademic uses during class, such as online shopping or social media?

3. Would it be reasonable for your professor to ban laptops in class so that all students get equal access to the information? Why or why not?

Synchronicity of Messages

When you talk with your roommate in your kitchen, you exchange messages in real time. When you reply to your professor's email, there is often a delay between your messages. According to **media synchronicity theory**, different channels of communication support different levels of **synchronicity**: the ability to allow people to communicate "at the same time with a shared pattern of coordinated behavior" (Dennis, Fuller, & Valacich, 2008, p. 576). Face-to-face communication, video chat, and telephone conferencing tend to be highly synchronous, whereas voice mail, fax, and "snail mail" are usually asynchronous. Texting, email, social media, and online discussion forums can be used *both* ways, depending on whether people reply quickly enough to coordinate a rapid, back-and-forth pattern of conversation.

For communication to be effective, there must be a good fit between the capabilities of the channels we choose and our communication needs and goals (Lam, 2016). When we need to convey new information to each other, such as classmates in a group project sharing their background research, asynchronous communication works very well. We benefit from the time we have to read and digest the information we receive, and we can compose and edit our messages before replying. That extra time to think about and carefully word our statements can also be beneficial for highly emotional messages, such as in romantic emails (Wells & Dennis, 2015). When we are trying to come to some mutual understanding or agreement, however, such as making a group decision or arranging social plans, then the give-and-take of synchronous media tends to be more effective. But scholars argue that the best choice in any given situation may actually involve using *multiple* channels, in order to take advantage of the capabilities of each of them (Lam, 2016). For example, suppose you are a member of the planning committee for your high school's alumni reunion event. You may meet face to face to get to know the other committee members and exchange ideas about the event, but you also each need to take time on Google Drive to look through last year's participant survey responses and add your feedback. When you suggest a new idea to the committee over email, you find yourself in a rapid exchange of emails as the committee members debate the pros and cons of the idea in order to decide how best to proceed.

Recognizing Expectations

The ability of some channels (e.g., texting) to enable both synchronous and asynchronous communication may set up complicated expectations and interpretations about the time it takes to respond to messages. The fact that we *can* engage in finger-flying text and social media exchanges makes many of us expect constant accessibility to others and immediate replies across many situations (Baron, 2008). This expectation often leads to uncertainty when we perceive a delay in someone's response time (is she mad at me, sick, tired, or just busy?). Uncertainty can lead to ruminating over the meaning of the delay as well as negative emotions, such as anxiety and anger (Tikkanen & Frisbie, 2015).

Our expectations also come from social norms for responding to digital messages; these differ depending on the medium and the particular communicators. For example, we do not tend to expect an immediate response for professional emails; however, if we do not receive a reply after a day has passed, we tend to evaluate the person negatively (Kalman & Rafaeli, 2011). Longer delays are often expected (and accepted) from high-status communicators, such as your boss or a valued client, but we still wonder about what the delay may mean (Tikkanen & Frisbie, 2015).

● ON *MAN SEEKING WOMAN,* Josh Greenberg struggles to compose the perfect text to a potential romantic partner, only to have to wait in agony for the response. © FX Networks/Photofest

Recognizing the Situation

If we know that our relational partner has to go to class or a meeting, we are not troubled even when a rapid-fire synchronous text exchange suddenly stops. When we have good feelings about a friend, we are more likely to assume that his or her delayed response was because they were unavailable (Frisbie, 2013). However, when a situation involves some risk, such as possible rejection by a new friend, then the uncertainty involved in asynchronous messages can lead to negative reactions. Researchers have found, for example, that parents who were waiting for a text message from their adolescent child had much greater anxiety if they were unsure of their child's safety (Tikkanen, Afifi, & Merrill, 2015). When they did not believe their child was at risk, they were much less concerned about the delayed response.

Recognizing the Benefits of Time

How many of us express ourselves with wit and charm, or care and sensitivity, without having to think first about what to say? One luxury of asynchronous media is that it gives us this opportunity. We can give more thought to the particular people who will be receiving our messages and tailor our communication accordingly. Scholars argue that we ought to take advantage of asynchronicity in digital communication to become more competent communicators—to create better personal impressions, engage in more appropriate self-disclosure, deliver more effective social support, and produce more successful persuasion (Tikkanen & Frisbie, 2015).

and you?

Have you ever experienced someone taking "too long" to respond to your post or text? How did you interpret what it meant? How did your interpretation affect your communication and relationship with the other person?

Media Richness and Naturalness

● **VIDEO CHAT TECHNOLOGY** helps stimulate the rich, natural visual and vocal cues found in face-to-face communication. Ariel Skelley/Getty Images

In addition to the timing of messages, digital channels vary based on how closely they allow us to approximate face-to-face communication. Video chat (such as via Skype or Facetime) allows us to see each other, use nonverbal gestures, and talk back and forth. Text-based messaging (such as Facebook chat, Twitter, discussion forums) has more limited visual and vocal cues. Before the explosion of digital technologies, many scholars had already argued that channels of communication had different levels of **richness** — the degree of visual, vocal, and personality cues that are possible as well as opportunities for feedback (Daft, Lengel, & Trevino, 1987). Early studies in business communication, for example, found that managers preferred more "rich" channels, such as face to face over paper-based written media or email, when faced with tasks that had a lot of uncertainty or required personal negotiations (Rice, 1993). Email tended to be preferred only for exchanging task-related information.

More recently, however, scholars have argued that the reason we often prefer digital media that are similar to face-to-face interaction is because they have more **naturalness** (Koch, 2005). For example, the visual and vocal cues and high-speed exchanges that are possible with video chat are a lot like the "natural" communication that humans have been using for ages — so much a part of our evolution that they require less cognitive effort to process. They also feel more personal — phone conversations and video chat were found to be the channels of choice for college students when they wanted to talk seriously with family members who lived far away (Smith, 2015). Arguably, the popularity of social media like Facebook, Instagram, and Snapchat involve their ability to share videos and photographs in addition to text (Kasoff, 2015). Even when not exchanging them synchronously, we are at least communicating with our real faces and voices.

Despite being drawn to more natural or rich media, much of our daily communication is also spent using solely text-based phone- or computer-mediated channels. **Social information processing theory** argues that although such mediated interaction lacks the nonverbal cues of natural spoken communication, we compensate for it by using other cues (Walther, 2011). The timing of responses is one important cue previously discussed, but research shows that we also adapt our language style (Baron, 2008) and use the keyboard itself in a variety of ways to clarify meaning, express emotion, and manage turn-taking (Riordan & Kreuz, 2010).

Visual emotional images (known as emoticons and emojis) can be text-based, like the wink face ;), or chosen from a wide variety of images provided by messaging and social media apps. Studies find that when they are added to a less natural medium like email, emoticons serve as markers of positive attitude or humor (Skovholt, Grønning, & Kankaanranta, 2014). They can also clarify intention when messages are ambiguous (Thompson & Filik, 2016), reduce the negative perception of criticism, and help us recognize sarcasm (Filik et al., 2015).

Other text-based cues are used to simulate changes in vocal tone. Studies find that we frequently repeat punctuation ("!!!!"), type in all caps ("SERIOUSLY?"), repeat letters for emphasis ("sweeeeet") or musical intonation ("happy birthday to youuuuuuu…"), or combine these techniques ("HEEEEELLLLLP!!!"; Riordan & Kreuz, 2010). In fact, the more emotionally laden our messages, the more likely we are to use such textual cues (Kalman & Gergle, 2014). Together with linguistic cues,

communication across cultures

think about this

Mobile Apps Compete for World Influence

For more than five hundred million people, one app has become the "go to" mobile phone app. Is it Google Search? YouTube? Facebook Messenger? No, it's called WeChat, and in China it is *the* primary way to send text messages as well as photos and videos (Pierce, 2015). In the United States, messaging apps like Facebook Messenger and Instagram Direct are becoming increasingly popular, but most text messaging is still primarily done using SMS (Short Message Service) through a person's mobile phone number. In other parts of the world, however, mobile phone services often do not offer unlimited texting as part of the costs of a data plan. So users turn to data-frugal internet-based mobile apps that accomplish the same messaging functions, and often much more. In Europe, for example, most people use WhatsApp (Goodwin, 2016). In addition to the cost savings, messaging apps like WhatsApp (now owned by Facebook) offer a much less cumbersome way to send photos and video, make it easy to create memes and graphics, and are integrated with social media apps. Of course, in order for these messaging programs to be useful, the people you wish to contact also need to be using the same apps.

For users of China's WeChat, easy messaging and social media use are just the beginning. WeChat is many apps within an app — it is used for everything from ordering dinner to hailing a taxi to playing video games to paying bills. "You can, for all intents and purposes, live your entire life within WeChat" (Pierce, 2015). WeChat has now also made huge strides in Africa, where many people's first use of the internet will be on mobile phones. According to Brett Loubser, the head of WeChat Africa, "They've missed the entire desktop, PC, laptop, whatever thing, and because of that, I think we're seeing innovation come out of Africa from a mobile perspective that is just leagues ahead of anywhere else on earth really" (van den Heever, 2016).

1. How likely is it that people in the United States will switch from phone-number-based texting to apps that integrate messaging with other social functions?

2. Does the proliferation of WeChat in China mean that we have already begun the technological revolution of the internet of things? Can you envision any downsides of one fully integrated app that you use for many aspects of life?

3. For the parts of the world that had never been reached by computers and the internet (such as much of Africa), how is smartphone innovation a "game changer"? What are the potential cultural impacts of this new access to technology?

---

these textual strategies help us convey our feelings as well as recognize and attend to the emotions of others. One study even found that during CMC chat, users were able to use such cues to recognize another person's bad mood and then respond in a "sociable" way that actually improved the person's mood (Tong & Walther, 2015).

Message Privacy and Control

There is an old adage: "Never put anything in writing that you don't want the whole world to know." These words of wisdom have been passed from grandparent to grandchild long before the internet, and yet they ring true perhaps more strongly today. That "confidential" email you sent to your coworker somehow ended up being read by your boss; the goofy selfie you thought was a private joke among friends got passed along to your whole school.

Digital channels differ as to how public or private our communication may be, and we have varying degrees of control over who sees our messages. Some digital channels are just inherently public (Kelly & Keaten, 2015). "Unprotected" tweets on Twitter are available to be seen by anyone, as are comments on YouTube. Other channels can be used much more privately, as in emails between colleagues or social media posts that can be seen only by friends or followers. What threatens even the "private" use of any of these media, however, is the fact that in so many cases our messages are *stored*, and therefore have **replicability** (Baym, 2015).

connect

Can you "hear" someone's voice in their text messages? How well do keystrokes and emojis make up for the lack of vocal cues or facial expressions in computer-mediated communication (CMC)? In Chapter 5, we discuss the importance of nonverbal messages and the many ways we use our faces, voices, and bodies to communicate with each other.

● **PRIVACY DIFFERS** across digital channels. Even when we think messages are private, it's possible that they can still be seen by others. JGI/Jamie Grill/Getty Images

connect →

Managing the kinds of information we share versus conceal is important to managing the closeness in our relationships (see Chapter 8). We often experience a tension in relationships between wanting to be *open* with others, while at the same time desiring to keep some things private or *closed*. We may also experience *turbulence* in our privacy boundaries when the people with whom we shared a secret ended up sharing the information with others.

In other words, because we post our status updates and videos via the internet or a smartphone, most messages are kept "in the cloud," which means they are on a networked computer server. Depending on who has access, the cloud enables our friends, family, and colleagues to retweet, share, or forward our messages to others (and you have to be pretty technically savvy to know how to delete messages permanently). Privacy settings on our social media apps give us some control over who gets to see what, such as whether we have to approve a photo before it can be shared. But if we do not give much thought to these settings, we are at the mercy of our own social networks (and the agreements we make with the social media apps themselves when we sign up) as to which of our messages could end up being widely distributed.

At times, we *wish* to be public. We post messages that we hope will get many "likes" or "shares" as a way to validate ourselves (O'Connor, 2014) or our products (Crum, 2015). We may use Facebook to keep all of our family and friends updated about a loved one's medical condition or memorialize someone after death. We share information and collaborate on work projects with fellow professionals. We promote our favorite bands and post criticisms of our favorite TV shows. But when we wish to keep messages private, we have to be mindful and careful. For example, we might need to remind others in a group email that we are including or excluding certain people ("Hi all, I'm copying Mom on this so that she's in the loop"). With social media in particular, we need to be aware of **context collapse**. Offline, we often communicate in distinct contexts (such as work versus home) and adapt behavior to different audiences (such as coworkers versus roommates). Online, however, multiple contexts are collapsed into one, and our different audiences are brought together—as Facebook friends, as Twitter followers (Davis & Jurgenson, 2014). This blurring of our social boundaries makes it difficult to keep audiences separated or exert control over who sees our posts (Baym & Boyd, 2012). So, if there are friends or followers you cannot trust not to breach confidences, you might take care *not* to share on social media (even "privately") the kinds of personal information that you would not want widely known.

In addition to variations in control over messages we *send* are the degrees of control we have over messages we *receive*. Whether as students, employees, or family members (or all of the above!), it can feel at times like we are constantly being bombarded by messages that need our attention (Baron, 2008). But most digital technologies allow us to know in advance who is calling, texting, emailing, or posting, and most of the time we can also see what they are calling, texting, emailing, or posting *about*. This gives us control over whose phone calls/texts to answer and which emails to read or delete. We can scroll past social media posts that are not interesting, share the ones that we like, and choose which forms of entertainment media to stream. In short, digital communication allows us to regulate our own social environment and manage our interactions with others (Baym, 2015).

The Power of the Crowd

What do you do when you have been treating a young boy with a mild but persistent cough, and he then suddenly coughs up an unrecognizable branch-like mass? If you are a doctor in our current age, you post a picture of the mass on SERMO, the online social media network exclusively for doctors. Dr. Easton Jackson, a primary care physician who found himself in this situation, asked for help with his patient and within 30 minutes the response posts from other doctors began to appear. Within hours, a cardiologist offered a diagnosis of a serious condition (plastic bronchitis), and others in the network began to discuss, argue, and eventually confirm the diagnosis with references to similar cases. Dr. Jackson referred his patient to cardiology even before any lab results had come back, and the cardiologists were able to save the boy's life (Pennic, 2015).

Inviting large numbers of people to help solve a problem via the internet is known as **crowdsourcing** (Howe, 2006). In this section, we explore several important ways that digital media enable us to use the "power of the crowd" to harness the talent, knowledge, creativity, and support of a diverse (and dispersed) population.

● **MEDICAL PROFESSIONALS** have benefited greatly from internet crowdsourcing. Using SERMO, doctors can get advice and feedback from colleagues near and far. Hero Images/Getty Images

Information Sharing

The medical network SERMO is just one of a multitude of online forums and social media apps that help people exchange information on a large scale. Not sure why your roses will not bloom? Post in a gardening forum. Need to find the best local gym? Ask in your community's Facebook page. We can crowdsource information on every topic from restoring cars to beekeeping to figuring out what is making that noise in your washing machine. We also rely on information from the crowd when we travel—to get reviews of restaurants, hotels, and tourist attractions (Wang, Xiang, & Fesenmaier, 2016). There are even apps that ask users to upload the most recent gas station prices in their area so that you can find the cheapest gas wherever you are driving.

Businesses also rely heavily on crowdsourcing. They maintain Facebook pages and broadcast messages on Twitter to gauge consumer response and generate "buzz" among their clients or fan base (VanMeter, Grisaffe, & Chonko, 2015). Organizations also increasingly seek to facilitate information-sharing *within* its own members. **Enterprise social media** are web-based platforms (not unlike Facebook) that allow workers to post and view organizational messages as well as edit files and otherwise engage with work teams on idea-sharing (Leonardi, Huysman, & Steinfield, 2013). All members of the organization can see the work that others are doing, and, because the information is stored, can search back to find key pieces of information or interaction.

Of course, the usefulness of crowdsourced information relies on people actually contributing—if no one in your community uses the local Facebook page, it will not be of much use. So the key is getting people involved, interested, and participating. Research shows that motivating factors include enjoyment (it's fun to contribute), recognition or status, collaboration on ideas, and building social connections with others (Roth, Brabham, & Lemoine, 2015).

Social Support

As we saw at the beginning of this chapter, digital media can be a powerful way to provide lifesaving social support quickly and on a large scale. In the case of Yik Yak, the support came from anonymous users; however, in many cases, the

strength of support comes from the *personal* ties we make with others. For example, "Buddy Check 22" groups have popped up all over Facebook for military units who served together in Iraq or Afghanistan. Named for a federal report suggesting that roughly twenty-two veterans commit suicide every day (Kemp & Bossarte, 2012), service men and women go online to check up on each other on the twenty-second day of each month. They also use these groups on an ongoing basis to help each other deal with the difficulties of returning home, including coping with post-traumatic stress disorder and separation from those whose bonds formed so tightly while serving together (Hauser, 2016). The veterans are engaged in **online peer-to-peer support** — people turning to others in a social network, rather than to professionals, to get help with personal, physical, and mental health problems (Ziebland & Wyke, 2012). These tend to be self-forming communities that develop in web-based forums or on social media by people who share a common experience or illness. The decision to participate in such a community can be a critical turning point in a person's life, which may be a start to better well-being even for someone suffering from severe mental illness (Naslund, Aschbrenner, Marsch, & Bartels, 2016).

Our online networks of friends, family, and acquaintances can also provide social support more broadly. Both strong and weak connections help build **social capital**, which refers to the valuable resources (such as information and support) that come from having connections and relationships among people (Williams, 2006). We feel good when we have "followers" and feel validated when they "like" or comment on our posts. We can also feel the emotions (positive and negative) of the people we care about and show our empathy in our replies (Lin & Utz, 2015). Emotion in social networks can even be "contagious," as there is evidence that happiness (or sadness) can be rapidly spread throughout massive social networks (Coviello et al., 2014; Kramer, Guillory, & Hancock, 2014). Social networking via Facebook in particular has been shown to increase the strength of what would otherwise be weak ties among acquaintances or friends who have moved to different geographic locations (Ellison, Steinfeld, & Lampe, 2007). And for first-year college students, research finds that maintaining a variety of online and mobile social networks helps them adjust to the multitude of stresses and changes they face (Smith, 2015).

and you?

How has your online social network helped you when you felt lonely or overwhelmed with the pressures of college? What kinds of messages did the members of your network send, and which ones were the most effective? How have *you* used social media to help your friends or family cope with stress?

● **CELEBRITIES SUCH AS** Tim Gunn and Rita Ora joined in to raise money for the ALS Association. The Ice Bucket Challenge was one of the most successful social media campaigns: the money raised has contributed to new findings in ALS research. (bottom left) Jackie Brown/Newscom; (bottom right) KGC-146/starmaxinc.com/Newscom

Social Causes

Kifleab Tekle was a beloved security guard at the Hockaday School in Dallas. When he retired after thirty years, the students wanted to help make his retirement special. So they used the website GoFundMe to see if they could raise a couple thousand dollars. There were so many alumni and parents who contributed that they were able to give Tekle a check for over $180,000. Also contributed were words of appreciation for his years of connecting, joking, and looking after them (Wanshel, 2016).

Raising public support and financial backing through online services is called **crowdfunding**. Some web-based services, such as GoFundMe, support charity or social causes, while others, like Kickstarter and Indigogo, raise money for entrepreneurial ventures, such as new products or creative art projects. Many fund-raising efforts are not successful, however, and the services usually take a percentage of the earnings. Even so, because they make it possible to solicit support for a cause on a large scale, they are increasingly popular (Vogt & Mitchell, 2016). Like most ventures, to be successful you have to put in a lot of work: identifying for others why it's important to support your project, presenting yourself as a credible person to be running it, designing an effective video or presentation, building a social media following (including your family and friends) before your "launch," and following up with contacts afterwards (Almerico, 2014).

In addition to crowdfunding web services, digital media can be used in other ways to rally people to social causes. The group "Organize" encourages hashtags on

real communicator

NAME: Heather Wight
OCCUPATION: Independent Digital Media Specialist
Courtesy, Heather Wight

My work changes all the time. For some projects, I am shooting videos, conducting interviews, and posting promotional messages on Facebook; for others, I am managing websites and responding to online customer comments. In some cases, I am doing all of these things! I am hired by clients to use digital media to market and promote their events and causes. I work with a partner, and together we plan the best strategies for each client. Every client is different, so we have to adapt to different personalities and goals and be creative and innovative.

We do social media promotions for small projects as well as large events. A local charter school had created an imaginative program to use vegetable gardening to teach children science. We made videos of the kids in the garden, interviewed them, and promoted the program on the internet to generate community support. On a larger scale, we digitally marketed a live music festival. There were fifty musical acts, and we had to coordinate with the social media managers and promoters for all fifty groups! We had to get all of our accounts linked up online and keep a close watch on what the artists were doing on social media. We then worked with their managers to get artists to cross-post their online messages with our event's social media posts and help promote the festival.

Sometimes, however, clients do things that have the potential to turn away sales. Our headliner at the festival had had an extramarital affair years ago that her fans were not happy about. It was old news, but we had to deal with that because so many negative comments got posted online about it. We tried to respond to the comments with a focus on how great her music is, but we had to be very sensitive about how we pushed that artist for the festival. But a good thing about digital media is that it allows us to change our plan *because* of online feedback. If we find out that people really like a certain aspect of an event, we can then push that. That way we are not wasting time and money pushing the wrong idea.

I learned from studying communication that it is important to be able to *think* about how you communicate with people — to get into the heads of your clients and customers and understand their views. We are aware that there are a lot of other marketing professionals out there wanting to replace us, so we need to be able to explain why we are the best fit. Every time we talk to a client, we provide them with reports about what we have accomplished — where they started and where they are now. It is interesting that although each client is different, there are some core elements that are the same — people want to avoid controversy and be loved by the community. We use digital media to help them achieve that.

Twitter (such as #organdonor and #donatemyparts) to spread support for organ donation and to solicit new donors (Bornstein, 2016). After the terror attacks in Paris in 2015, Facebook enabled people to put an overlay of the French flag over their Facebook profile pictures so that people could show empathy. Due to demand for more overlay choices, Facebook is now developing user-customized overlays for a variety of causes and charitable organizations (Opam, 2016).

One of the most successful social media charity campaigns has been the "ALS Ice Bucket Challenge." To raise funding for and awareness of amyotrophic lateral sclerosis (ALS), people challenged each other to post on Facebook a video of themselves dumping a bucket of ice water over their heads. Even celebrities joined in, and by the end of one summer, over $115 million had been raised for the ALS Association (Wolff-Mann, 2015). Starting a social media challenge may not often go as viral as this one, but the "share" and "retweet" functions of social media make it possible for compelling news events, programs, and causes to be spread rapidly through social networks.

Overcoming Digital Challenges

When Shannon started college, she was a bit intimidated. "My classes are hard," she thought. "I'm feeling overwhelmed by all the work, but everybody else seems to be just having a great time." Shannon made some new friends, but she missed her close friends who had gone off to other colleges. Whenever she saw the videos they sent her on Snapchat or photos they posted on Instagram, it seemed like they were dealing with the change just fine. Before college, Shannon used to rely on her grandmother for a smile and a pep talk whenever she needed encouragement. Now, she decided that she needed to teach Nana about Facetime. Like most college students, Shannon spent a lot of time on social media. Although she loved being in contact at almost every moment with her social network, she also sometimes felt very alone. In this section, we explore some of the challenges we face with digital forms of communication.

Digital Disparities

As we discussed earlier, digital media access has rapidly penetrated the U.S. (and global) population, and the numbers of users continue to grow across all demographic groups (Rainie, 2015a). Even Americans of lower socioeconomic status now typically have access to at least some digital technology, including the internet and mobile phones. However, there are still some important **digital disparities** in terms of regular access to broadband connections or the use of multiple digital devices. For example, although the majority of low-income Americans have a smartphone, that phone is often their sole digital device, which means that they are limited in their ability to do extensive internet searching or computer-based activities (such as writing papers for school; Rainie, 2015a; Schradie, 2013). Even among those with similar levels of access, there are differences in how they participate online—younger adults and those with higher incomes and education are the ones who take the most advantage of online technology (Perrin, 2015).

One difficulty for reluctant users is a lack of confidence when it comes to technology. We will see in the next chapter that the perception we have about our own skills and abilities has an important influence on our communication behavior. Those of us with computer, phone, or social media skills and experience could help others in developing their own skills—such as teaching Nana how to use Facetime. Of course, increasingly user-friendly websites and applications, along with more reliable and affordable internet connections, can also go a long way to increasing confidence and use across a diverse population.

Feeding Insecurities and Obsessions

Long before smartphones and social media, people have been concerned about connecting with friends, fitting in with social groups, and being popular. However, some media critics argue that digital technologies may feed our insecurities about these social needs (O'Connor, 2014), particularly for teens and young adults (Griffin, 2015). Although studies show that our online social networks are a source of support, they are also a source of idealized images with which to compare ourselves. Constant comparison with these seemingly ideal other lives can lead to a sense of isolation and poor well-being (Kross et al., 2013). Similarly, spending a lot of time online tracking the activities of others can lead to feelings of envy (Tandoc, Ferrucci, & Duffy, 2015). For our close ties, this can be a "benign" or harmless type of envy that motivates us to improve ourselves and be happy for our loved ones.

For weaker ties, however, our envy can become malicious and resentful and lead to depression (Lin & Utz, 2015).

In addition to poor mental health outcomes, a constant devotion to the praises and "likes" of people in our social media network may mean missing important things in our offline lives. Interviews of social media "trophy hunters" have revealed numerous stories of people trying so hard to get the perfect photo or video to post that they missed the enjoyment of the event itself (Grenny & Maxfield, 2015). For example, you might snap a photo of a beautiful sunset and then hurry away to post it without actually having spent time savoring it. While at a birthday dinner with family, you might post on Facebook where you are, tag the people you are with (even share what you ordered to eat), and then keep checking your phone to see what your likes and comments are, all the while not interacting much with the family members who are actually with you! Is it bad to share these moments on social media? Of course not. However, we need to recognize when we are so concerned about *documenting* the moment that we do not actually *live* in the moment.

How do we overcome the impulse to document everything online and focus on collecting social media likes? One of the most important things we can do is to be alert to what we are doing. A mother of a three-year reported: "I disciplined my son, and he threw a tantrum that I thought was so funny that I disciplined him again just so I could video it. After uploading it on Instagram I thought, 'What did I just do?' " (Grenny & Maxfield, 2015). Sometimes we just need to recognize what we are doing and remember to slow down, look around, and be part of what is happening around us. Another thing we can do is to take a break from social media for a few days or a week. Some of us may even need to take an indefinite break, as did novelist Ottessa Moshfegh, who closed her Facebook and Twitter accounts because her social network's constant drive for recognition "was making me hate everyone" (Wayne, 2016).

● **EVEN THOUGH SELFIES** may seem natural and spontaneous, research has shown that selfie-takers give much consideration to their photo and what it communicates to the people viewing it. Cindy Ord/Getty Images

● SNAPPING TOO MANY
PHOTOS of life's moments can make
us more concerned with *documenting*
life rather than *living* it. Apeloga AB/Getty
Images

Getting some distance can give us perspective and possibly help reconnect
with people face to face.

Cyber Attacks

You get an email telling you that your account may be in danger and that you
need to click to verify your account information and password. In all likelihood,
this is an attempt to get information from you that someone can use to steal
your identity (in order to rob your bank account or open credit cards in your
name) or get private information about your organization. You may think that
you are not important enough to be a target of cyber criminals, but hackers
frequently target individuals as a way to gain access to information about larger
organizations. The SANS Institute's Securing the Human program argues
that awareness and prevention are the keys to avoiding cyber attacks (SANS
Institute, 2016).

Phishing is an attempt to get information from you by using a digital message
that appears to be from a legitimate organization (such as your bank or your
school's technical support group). Sometimes an email or text may even appear
to be from a person you know. The messages often attempt to create a sense of
urgency and ask you to take immediate action. The idea is to trick you into giving
your password, opening an attachment, or clicking a link that will then send your
personal information to the criminal. So, whenever you get a message that seems
odd (even if it is from someone you know) or has attachments that you do not
expect—call them or message them separately (i.e., do not reply or click the links,
etc.) to verify the legitimacy of the message.

How about when using social media, such as Facebook or Instagram?
Unfortunately, cyber attackers can use the information that you post to steal your
identity. They can create an imposter site in order to solicit additional information
from your friends, including sending false requests from "you" to send money. Be
alert to odd requests that could indicate an imposter, such as requests to become

wired for communication

Selfies as Visual Conversation, Self-Promotion . . . and Self-Delusion

Sharing "selfies" (photos of yourself using the camera on your mobile phone) is a widespread phenomenon on social media. But isn't sending people pictures that we have taken of ourselves a bit narcissistic? Research suggests that selfies can actually be a "visual conversation" and serve as an important part of the language of relationships (Katz & Crocker, 2015). Indeed, selfie-takers report that one of the most prominent uses of their selfies is to update friends and family about their lives. From in-depth interviews with a number of young selfie-takers, researchers found that although selfies are typically designed to look spontaneous, they are often composed with thoughtfulness and deliberation (Katz & Crocker, 2015). Selfie-sharers give consideration to the platform (disappearing images on Snapchat versus lasting memories on Instagram) as well as to how the photo might come across to the people receiving it. They are aware of the potential for appearing vain, and so there must be a careful balance between trying to look good while not trying to look self-absorbed. The most valued selfies tend to be ones that tell a story about someone's life events and contexts rather than just emphasize the person's own face or body.

The sharing of selfies is not unique to the United States. A survey of American, British, and Chinese respondents revealed that almost all of them reported having shared a selfie at some point (Katz & Crocker, 2015). The few differences found were the frequency of selfies shared, with Americans doing so more often than the other two samples. Many in the American sample reported sharing upwards of twenty selfies in one day!

Although selfie-takers often give thought to how they present themselves, they may also be misleading themselves about how successful they are. Selfie-takers have been found to overestimate the positive nature of their own self-photos (Jacobs, 2016). In fact, they actually believe they appear more attractive in their own selfies than in photos taken of them by other people! One recent study found that when asking an external group of people to rate other people's selfies, the photos did not appear nearly as attractive and likable as the people themselves thought (Re, Wang, He, & Rule, 2016). Perhaps there *is* an aspect of narcissism to our selfies after all.

1. How much thought do you give to the selfies you take and share on social media? What is more important — capturing the life moment (where you are or what event is occurring) versus sending a flattering image of yourself? Can you do both effectively?

2. How do you evaluate the selfies that your friends and family members send to you? What makes some selfies come across as a person having fun or sharing a life moment, while others make the person seem to be self-absorbed or fishing for compliments and "likes"?

3. Should selfies be a reflection of someone's "true" self? Why or why not? How does the social media platform (Snapchat, Instagram, Facebook) make a difference in the appropriateness of the self-photo?

friends with someone you are already friends with. If you suspect anything odd, alert your friend and report the behavior directly to the social media website. You should also always be careful about the kinds of personal information that you reveal. Privacy control settings are important, but they change frequently and are often complex. Not unlike the old adage we discussed earlier about the danger of putting things in writing, the SANS Institute, as well as the information technology departments of many organizations, advise that you consider any information you post on social media as having the potential to become public (SANS Institute, 2016).

back to ▶ Yik Yak

Hero Images/Getty Images

At the beginning of this chapter, we saw how anonymous posts on Yik Yak helped support a college student on the verge of committing suicide. We also saw how this social media app in other contexts facilitated cruel messages and controversies about bullying. Let's consider Yik Yak in light of what we have learned in this chapter.

▶ Yik Yak is one of many constantly changing digital forms of communication. It is an application uniquely designed for smartphones (as opposed to computers), so that users can post messages based on their particular location. Such a capability is only possible given the current advances in digital technology.

▶ Yik Yak enables users to post messages fairly synchronously, responding in rapid succession in real time. After the initial suicidal post, quick response times were critical and provided immediate support and encouragement. But such synchronicity also means that Yik Yak users may not always give much time and thought to how to word their messages, and so they often end up insulting other users.

▶ The outpouring of support on Yik Yak for the suicidal student is an example of effective crowdsourcing. Students in the larger University of Michigan community were engaging in online peer-to-peer support to try to help the troubled student. They also used the incident more broadly to launch a campaign to raise awareness for suicide prevention.

things to try ▶ Activities

LaunchPad
macmillan learning

1. LaunchPad for *Real Communication* offers key term videos and encourages self-assessment through adaptive quizzing. Go to **launchpadworks.com** to get access to:

LearningCurve
Adaptive Quizzes.

▶ Video clips that illustrate key concepts, highlighted in teal in the Real Reference section that follows.

2. For twenty-four hours, live like you are in the "pre-digital" world of the early 1990s. You can use a computer, but no internet. You can use your cell phone, but treat it like it is a landline phone—use it only for phone calls and only from your home or office (no texting, no apps, no calling from your car, etc.). How do these restrictions change the way you communicate with your friends and family? What did you do instead to maintain contact? How did you feel without your apps?

3. Keep a diary for three days of your texting patterns. Make a note of when and with whom your texting is a serious of rapid, synchronous exchanges versus more delayed asynchronous messages. What kinds of conversations and tasks result in this difference?

4. Engage in crowdsourcing. Think of a question you have about something in your life (such as how to find internships in a particular career area or even something simple like which local eateries have the best prices). Do not do an internet search — post your question in an appropriate online forum or social networking site. How many responses did you get, and how quickly? How useful was the information that you received?

5. Take three different photos of yourself in a scenic place — try to make all of them as flattering to yourself as possible. In one photo, take a selfie and put yourself in the center as the focus. In another photo, take a selfie and put yourself at the side of the frame with the scenic background in the center. In the third photo, have someone else take the photo of you with the scenic background. Which photo would you feel most comfortable posting on Instagram or Facebook? Why? Which do you think would get the most positive responses (such as likes) from your followers/ friends? Why?

real reference ▶ A Study Tool

Now that you have finished reading this chapter, you can:

Describe the advances in digital technology that have changed communication:

▶ Digital technologies involve **mediated communication**, in which there is some technology that is used to deliver messages between sources and receivers. Specifically, **digital communication** is the transmission of digitally encoded data (text, images, video, voice) over electronic networks (p. 32).
▶ Developments changed rapidly from limited internet and mobile phone use for few Americans in the 1990s and 2000s to near total access today of a wide array of internet uses and smartphone applications (p. 32–33).
▶ Changes to digital technologies are ongoing and appear to be leading to an **internet of things**, in which digital technologies will be embedded in all aspects of our daily lives (p. 35).

Define the characteristics that distinguish different forms of digital communication:

▶ **Media synchronicity theory** argues that some channels enable greater **synchronicity**, the ability to communicate back and forth rapidly in a coordinated exchange of messages (p. 36).
▶ The effective use of synchronous or asynchronous channels depends on the fit between the channel and our communication goals, including our expectations about response times, our understanding of the situation, and the potential benefits of lag time (p. 37).
▶ Channels that afford greater **richness** allow for more visual, vocal, and personality cues. These channels also have more **naturalness**, in that they simulate the more biologically natural communication we experience when interacting with people's real faces and voices (p. 38).
▶ **Social information processing theory** explains how we use technology creatively to compensate for the lack of nonverbal cues of computer-mediated communication (p. 38).

- ▶ Digital channels vary as to how much our messages may be private or public. Messages that are stored have **replicability**, which means that they can be shared with larger audiences (p. 39).
- ▶ It is difficult to maintain control of messages on social media because of **context collapse**, the blurring of our social boundaries and combining of formerly separate audiences (p. 40).

Explain the ways in which digital communication brings people together on a large scale:

- ▶ When we invite large numbers of people on the internet to solve a problem or provide information, we are engaging in **crowdsourcing** (p. 41).
- ▶ **Enterprise social media** enable organizations in particular to allow workers to post and view organizational messages and engage with work teams on idea-sharing (p. 41).
- ▶ Social media can provide **online peer-to-peer support**, in which people rely on their social connections to help with personal, physical, and mental health problems. Online connections also build **social capital**, the broad set of resources that come from having connections and relationships with people (p. 42).
- ▶ Charity and social causes can be supported through **crowdfunding**, using websites and social media campaigns to raise public support and financial backing (p. 43).

Outline the challenges posed when communicating with digital media:

- ▶ Although access to technology is now more widespread than ever, some **digital disparities** remain in terms of access to multiple devices and ability to use digital media effectively (p. 45).
- ▶ Comparing ourselves to the idealized images presented in social media can lead to poor mental well-being. If we become driven to obtain "likes" and other forms of digital recognition, we may benefit from taking a "break" from social media (p. 45).
- ▶ Cyber criminals often try to get personal information from you by **phishing**, sending an "urgent" message that asks you to provide your password or open an attachment (p. 47).

The public image of Tiger Woods changed dramatically after a personal scandal rocked the top golfer's world.

 LearningCurve can help you master the material in this chapter.

Go to **launchpadworks.com**

chapter

3

Perceiving the
Self and Others

As one of the most successful professional golfers of all time, Tiger Woods was on top of his game and on top of the world. Enjoying the top world ranking for over thirteen years, he exuded confidence in his form and was one of the highest-paid athletes in any sport. Woods had a winning smile as well as a winning golf score. He had been easy with the media from an early age (he appeared on *The Mike Douglas Show* at age two). He enjoyed admiration from many when he and his father established the Tiger Woods Foundation to help inner-city children, and their $50 million Tiger Woods Learning Center helped underserved youth with programs for college access (GolfWeb Wire Services, 2006). What was not to love about Woods?

But the positive image of Tiger Woods took a severe hit in 2009, when attention turned to his personal life. A car accident following a marital row led to revelations that he had engaged in affairs for years with multiple women. The media—many claiming to have known about his double life for years—lost any sense of reverence for him in telling the tabloidlike stories (Smith, 2013). Faced with losses in the millions, company sponsors like Gatorade and Gillette dropped the now-unpopular Woods. The scandal had a wide effect on sports marketing, as companies became more hesitant to hire athlete spokespersons (Wertheim & Keith, 2015).

Over the next few years, Woods tried to repair his image. He acknowledged his infidelities and apologized to his wife and children. He asked for privacy for his family. He expressed his mortification, saying how sorry he was and asking his family and his public to forgive him. He promised corrective action: he entered a clinic for treatment and returned to his Buddhist religion, claiming that his behavior was due to his having lost his Buddhist roots. "Buddhism teaches me to stop following every impulse and to learn restraint," he said. "Obviously I lost track of what I was taught" (ISKCON News).

Woods partially repaired his tarnished public image with these strategies and slowly returned to the game and the public eye (Crouse, May 30, 2017). But Woods's age, injuries, and surgeries took a toll on his game; his own self-concept required adjusting to those realities and the uncertainty that he could ever return to his glory days (Hoggard, February 10, 2017).

After you have finished reading this chapter, you will be able to

- Describe how our personal perspective on the world influences our communication

- Explain how we use and misuse schemas when communicating with others

- Define the attributions we use to explain behavior

- Describe cultural differences that influence perception

- Identify how our self-concept — who we think we are — influences communication

- Describe how our cognitions about ourselves and our behavior affect our communication with others

ike Tiger, you present different "faces" to others at home, at work, in sports or through other activities. Different aspects of yourself are relevant in those different contexts, so your presentation of self necessarily varies. But whether you are managing your image in the public eye as Tiger Woods was, or just trying to look good to your boss, you have to consider the way that you and others notice, interpret, and understand your behavior. In communication terms, that means understanding perceptions.

Perception is a cognitive process through which we observe people and events, interpret our experiences, and form our own unique understandings. Those thoughts, or cognitions, influence how and what we communicate to others. They also affect how we interpret others' behaviors and messages. Thus, understanding the role that perception plays in communication is crucial to our success as communicators. In this chapter, we explore how our personal perspective on the world influences our communication, how we make sense of our experiences, how culture influences our perceptions, how we think about ourselves and others, and how these factors affect our communication behavior.

Perception: Making Sense of Your World

It is five o'clock on a Wednesday night, and a roomful of singles are gathered at the Comic-Con convention for an interesting event. Over the next two hours, each person will be introduced to twenty-five potential dates: "singles just like you," promises the website (newyorkcomiccon.com, 2016). The next day, each person logs in to the site and selects whom they liked. If a mutual "match" occurs, they receive each other's email and phone number.

Speed dating is popular in many metropolitan areas in the United States, England, and India. Organized on the premise that similarities will lead to attraction, the pool of potential love interests meet briefly to see if there is any "chemistry." But how much can one person learn about another in just a few minutes?

First impressions can generate quite a bit of information, but it is the *perception* of similarity rather than *actual* similarity that predicts attraction (Tidwell, Eastwick, & Finkel, 2013). Let's see how that plays out with Jill and Carter, two speed-dating attendees of the Comic-Con convention (usually in costume, of course, but taking a break for now from being Wonder Woman and Luke Skywalker). Jill tells Carter that she is twenty-nine, a public relations executive, was born in Milwaukee but now lives in Atlanta, and has a passion for *film noir* (in addition to *Star Wars*). Carter hears Jill but also notices that she is tall and attractive, makes steady eye contact, and has assertive mannerisms. He concludes (perhaps erroneously) that she is more serious and successful than he is. Carter feels a little intimidated by Jill and decides that they probably are not compatible despite the self-described similarities that put them into this dating pool.

Even during brief encounters — like Carter's meeting with Jill — we are bombarded with information: the other person's words, tone of voice, facial expressions, and degree of eye contact. Through **communication processing**, we gather, organize, and evaluate all these perceptions. Although we receive information through our senses, this is just the beginning of the process. How we interpret that information is unique to each of us, influenced by how we organize perceptions into our existing memory bases, called *schemas*.

Schemas: Organizing Perceptions

As you receive information, you strive to make sense of it. To do so, you consider not only the new information but also how it fits with information you already have. For example, in evaluating Jill, speed dater Carter makes associations with his own relationship experience and his assumptions about assertive women, guessing about her professional success. Carter is making sense of the interaction's many inputs through **schemas**, mental structures that put together related bits of information (Fiske & Taylor, 1991; see Figure 3.1). Once put together, these chunks of information form patterns that we use to create meaning. Schemas present various opportunities and challenges, as we discuss later.

● **WHEN OTHERS** approach you at an event, you immediately start forming opinions about them. How they are dressed, the sound of their voice, and their smile all play into whether you feel a connection with these potential partners. Daniel Zuchnik/ Getty Images

The Function of Schemas

Your schemas help you understand how things (like a job interview or a first date) work or should work. Communicators retrieve schemas from memory and interpret new information, people, and situations in accordance with those schemas. For example, imagine that during your walk across campus, a classmate approaches and says, "Hey, what's up?" An existing schema (based on memories of past encounters) tells you that you will exchange hellos and then, after some small talk, go your separate ways. When you recognize one component of a schema, the entire schema is activated and helps you to know what to say or how to behave in a particular situation. Thus, our perceptions of reality are constructed by the repeated social interactions we have with other people, a process known as **social constructivism** (Keaton & Bodie, 2011; Lindlof, 2008).

Schemas are fairly stable once they are established, but they can also change somewhat as you go through life perceiving new or conflicting bits of information about different people and situations. For example, the **interaction appearance theory** helps explain how people change their perceptions of someone, particularly their physical attractiveness, the more they interact (Albada, Knapp, & Theune, 2002). You probably have noticed that people become more or less attractive to you as you get to know them better. For example, you might find a colleague more attractive after you discover her quirky sense of humor or less attractive when you experience his short temper.

Challenges with Schemas and Perception

To send and receive messages that are effective and appropriate, you must be able to process information in a way that not only makes sense to you but is also accurately perceived by others. Schemas can help you do all of this. However, sometimes schemas can make you a less perceptive communicator; they may cloud your judgment or cause you to rely on stereotypes (discussed later in this chapter) or misinformation. Communication researchers note that schemas present several challenges to competent communication.

and you?

Think back to your first impressions of two different people, one whom you immediately liked and one who made a negative impression. What role might your schemas have played in these first impressions? Did these individuals remind you of other people you like or dislike? Did they exhibit traits that you have found attractive or unattractive in others?

FIGURE 3.1

CARTER'S SCHEMA ABOUT DAT-
ING AND RELATIONSHIPS Our
schemas affect our communication
and our relationships. Here is Carter's
schema for dating and relationships,
represented as a box containing
pieces of information from various
sources in his life.

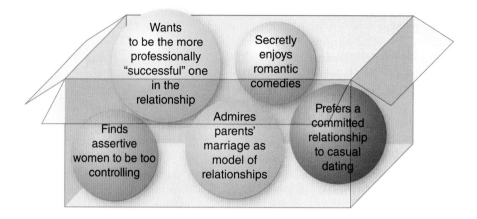

connect

If you have ever found yourself
saying "Uh-huh" at the wrong
time because you were not paying
attention during a conversation,
you know that listening and mindlessness are a bad combination.
In Chapter 7, you learn that competent listening involves being
an *active*, rather than *passive*,
participant in your communication
situations and requires you to
make mindful choices to decode
messages.

and you?

Think of an individual whom you
hold in very high regard, such
as a parent, a favorite professor,
a mentor, or a media pundit.
How might you have selectively
attended to some of this person's
qualities while ignoring others?
Could any of your perceptions be
distorted?

► *Mindlessness.* Schemas may make you a less critical processor of information by producing a state of **mindlessness**, during which you process
information passively. Mindlessness helps you handle some transactions
automatically; for example, you do not have to consciously think about
how to place an order every time you go to a restaurant. But mindlessness can create problems, too — including reduced cognitive activity (you
have fewer thoughts), inaccurate recall (you cannot remember simple
things), and uncritical evaluation (you do not question wrong or incom-
plete information; Roloff, 1980). The remedy for mindlessness is to pay
attention to your schemas, a process called **mindfulness**. Mindfulness
involves being aware of yourself and tuning out distractions to focus; it
has a variety of benefits, from higher test scores to reduced public speaking anxiety (Huston, 2010; Jacobs, 2013). Students who take notes in
class by hand (rather than on a laptop) have been found to be more
mindful — enhancing their learning by processing and reframing information in their own words (Mueller & Oppenheimer, 2014). Health benefits come from being mindful, too; being aware of and accepting your
own negative thoughts and emotions can reduce your psychological, emotional, and physiological stress (Daubenmier, Hayden, Chang, & Epel,
2014).

► *Selective perception.* Whereas mindlessness is passive, **selective perception** —
that is, choosing to attend to some things while ignoring others — involves
more active thought. If you listen to testimony at a trial, you may notice that
one witness will remember the exact time of the accident while another will
describe the color and make of the cars involved. They both saw the same accident but focused on and remembered different parts. Additionally, we often
selectively pay attention to the information that is consistent with our schemas.
In our speed-dating example, Carter hears what Jill says, how she says it, and
what she looks like. But other information, such as Jill's warm smile and easy
laugh, might escape his notice if it challenges his notion of what an assertive
person is like.

► *Distorted perception.* How much does a ten-pound bag weigh? People who feel
personally powerful repeatedly report that the bags feel lighter than those who
feel less powerful, despite the fact that the bags weigh exactly the same (Lee &
Schnall, 2014). If five people watch a televised debate between two political
candidates, they often have five different interpretations of what took place,

as each overestimates the greatness of his or her candidate's performance and undervalues the other candidate's arguments. In addition, we have a tendency to distort events based on vivid information. If you pay attention to sensational news stories, you may believe that you are at great risk of dying in a terrorist attack in the United States, whereas you actually have a much greater chance of being in a fatal car crash (Pomeroy, 2013). Similarly, if you are a heavy viewer of medical dramas like *Grey's Anatomy*, you are more likely to have unrealistic perceptions of important medical issues, particularly chronic illnesses such as cancer and cardiovascular disease, which can affect your decisions to seek or use proper medical care (Chung, 2014).

Attributions: Interpreting Your Perceptions

Our schemas help us organize the information we perceive about people; however, we also have a need to explain *why* people say what they do or act in certain ways. The judgments that we make to explain behavior are known as **attributions** (Jones, 1990). Consider the following exchange:

EMMA   I'm heading over to Mark's place to help him study for our midterm. He has really been struggling this semester.

CALEB   Well, he was never exactly a rocket scientist.

● AS VIEWERS WATCH *STAR WARS: THE FORCE AWAKENS,* they rely on schemas developed in Episodes I through VI to try to predict the lineage of the new character Rey, the talented scavenger from Jakku. Is the lightsaber she finds calling to her? Is she related to Luke Skywalker, or to Obi-Wan Kenobi? Why was she able to see the Knights of Ren in her vision? And where is her family?
© Walt Disney Studios Motion Pictures/Photofest

Emma might attribute Caleb's comment to his personality ("Caleb is obnoxious!") or to the situation ("Wow, something has put Caleb in a bad mood"). When we attribute behavior to someone's personality (or something within the person's control), we call that an *internal* attribution. When we attribute it to the situation (or something outside the person's control), that is an *external* attribution. How do we decide? If Emma considers her experience with Caleb and remembers that he is not usually so blunt or harsh about other people, she will likely attribute his behavior to the situation, not his personality.

Unfortunately, we are not completely rational in how we make attributions. The **fundamental attribution error** is a bias we have that causes us to overemphasize internal causes and underestimate external causes of behaviors we observe in others (McLeod, Detenber, & Eveland, 2001; Ross & Nisbett, 1991). For example, we might assume that "Mark failed the midterm because he was too lazy to study." The error works in the opposite way when we make attributions about ourselves. Owing to the **self-serving bias**, we usually attribute our own successes to internal factors ("I got an A because I'm smart") and attribute our failures to external effects ("I failed the midterm because my professor stinks"). Another bias is our tendency to focus on the worst things going on in the world around us. This **negativity bias** makes us think that other people's bad intentions must be responsible for our negative outcomes. There may be a biological basis for negativity; even babies as young as six months demonstrate that they see bad outcomes as caused by someone or something rather than a random chance (Hamlin & Baron, 2014). One study found that dangerous drivers (involved in more accidents and risky driving) had stronger negativity biases than safer drivers — and probably believed other drivers caused their accidents (Chai, Qu, Sun, Zhang, & Ge, 2016).

connect

Improving your perceptions is helpful in many communication situations. In Chapter 13, you learn how considering different aspects of an audience's demographic background can help you to target your message specifically to them (or know what to talk about in the first place).

Improving Your Perceptions

Making accurate perceptions can be challenging. For example, in the classic basketball film *Hoosiers*, Gene Hackman plays Hickory High basketball coach Norman Dale. Dale's small-town players are intimidated by the cavernous arena where they will be playing for the Indiana state championship. Though they know the court is regulation size, it looks enormous to them. Dale uses a tape measure to confirm the height of the basket and the distance from the foul line. Only then do they believe that the court is the same size as the one they play on in their gym. This restores their confidence.

The following suggestions can help you improve your perception abilities and thus become a better communicator.

▶ *Be thoughtful when you seek explanations.* Pause to give yourself time to evaluate. If someone's Facebook status update offends you, do not comment right away. Be mindful by taking a deep breath and thinking through your reaction so you can reduce negative perceptions and their effects (Partnoy, 2012).

▶ *Consider the perspective of the other person.* Look beyond your own explanation for what you observe. For example, your roommate, usually tidy, may have left your place a mess this morning. Rather than declaring that he is a slob, consider whether he felt ill last night or whether he needed to rush off to an exam.

▶ *Look beyond first impressions.* Do not rely completely on your first impressions; these often lead to inaccurate conclusions. Consider Meghan, who frequently comes off as loud when people first meet her. In fact, her manner springs from a love for meeting new people, so she enthusiastically asks questions while getting to know them. Hold off forming a judgment until you can gather further perceptions.

▶ *Question your assumptions.* Do not assume that you know what others think, feel, or believe based on their group affiliations or a host of other cultural factors. For example, many college students assume that most of their peers are busy getting drunk and having casual sex. Research shows, however, that many students are far less comfortable with these behaviors than they assume *other* students are (Reiber & Garcia, 2010). Thinking that everyone else in your demographic believes the opposite of you is a common perceptual error (Beiser, 2013).

▶ *Consider the channel or channels being used.* Do not assume that your sister is angry with you because she texts you often but hardly ever calls you. Perhaps she is more comfortable texting you about routine things in her life and chooses the phone for more intimate topics.

Perception in a Diverse World

A few generations ago, people may have gone months without coming into contact with someone from a different village or neighborhood. A wheelchair-bound child may have been unable to attend public schools. In parts of this country, white and black Americans were not permitted to sit at the same lunch counter. Today, people from all walks of life learn, work, and play together. And through technology, we can communicate with others across vast distances. A student in Louisville, Kentucky, can chat online with a student from Bangladesh. A salesperson in Omaha, Nebraska, may work full time with clients in Tokyo. In order to communicate effectively, we must stretch our perceptions to "see through the eyes, hearts, and minds of people from cultures" other than our own (Chen & Starosta, 2008). In this section, we do precisely that by examining the cultural context and perceptual barriers.

● **DO YOU SHARE** a cultural identity with any of these groups? Factors such as age, gender, race, religious beliefs, sexual orientation — even where you grew up — affect your own perceptions and the perceptions of others.
(top left) Digital Vision/Getty Images; (top right) The Washington Post/Getty Images; (bottom left) Tom Shaw/Getty Images; (bottom right) migstock/Alamy

The Cultural Context

Many students are fans of the FX series *Fargo,* a crime drama/comedy set in North Dakota. The locals are portrayed as people of few words, but friendly and polite — fitting our perceptions of people in small towns. Some are seemingly trapped in the small town and perceive no way of getting out or changing their lives; however, others happily go about their lives living as their families have for generations. In the TV series, violence comes to the snowy plains and collides big time with small-town values — and also with the Gerhardt clan, who have controlled the local crime scene for years.

As you likely know from experience, culture is an incredibly powerful context of communication: it has a profound effect on the way we perceive events, as well as ourselves and others. Think about how being from a big city versus a small town can shape your perceptions of people, crime, opportunities, and appropriate behaviors.

Consider your views about teenage crime; do you think it is due to their reckless behavior and emotional response? If you associate more crime with youthful age, think again; poverty is the real culprit. Poor people of all ages are more likely to commit crimes (Males & Brown, 2014). Now connect that research to the competent communication model in the first chapter. The ring that comprises the cultural context is made up of variables that make our perceptions unique: race, ethnicity, religion, politics, gender, sexual orientation, age, education, role, occupation, abilities/disabilities, geography, and even being wealthy or poor. These differences are known as *diversity* (Loden & Rosener, 1991). (Also see our discussion of cocultural variation in Chapter 6.) Your positive or negative perceptions of a show like *Fargo*

connect

To ensure that *diversity* is respected in professional situations, organizations (as well as the U.S. government) enact policies and codes of behavior to protect employees from hurtful, antagonistic communication regarding their race, religion, national origin, sexual orientation, age, and abilities. This type of derogatory communication, known as *harassment*, is discussed in Chapter 12.

● **TELEVISION SHOWS CAN PORTRAY** the cultural values for a specific population, such as the small-town values revealed in *Fargo*. © FX Network/Photofest

are linked to your perceptions about age, education, occupation, geography, religion, and a host of other factors. To communicate effectively and appropriately in today's world, you must possess an understanding of and appreciation for people who perceive others differently than you do. It is also important to understand the way your unique background affects your perceptions.

Perceptual Barriers

Karl Krayer is a communication consultant who does diversity training for corporations, schools, and other organizations. Based on his experience, Krayer notes that successful intercultural communication requires mindfulness, respect for others, and accurate perceptions of situations. "Resistance to cultural diversity usually boils down to ignorance," he says. "Once people understand other cultural groups better, it doesn't take long to see . . . people working cooperatively together for a common cause" (personal communication, May 19, 2004). In our diverse world, perceptual challenges can present barriers to competent communication, including narrow perspectives, stereotyping, and prejudice.

A Narrow Perspective

When the Zika virus broke out in Latin America, heart-wrenching pictures of babies with microcephaly (small head size) filled the news. Zika infections, largely spread by mosquito bites, were strongly linked to the microcephaly and attendant severe brain damage. Latin American health ministers recommended that women postpone pregnancy, and even Pope Francis (the head of the Catholic church) softened

communication across cultures

think about this

Perceptions of Hair Color: A Gray Area

Anne Kreamer looked at a photograph of herself standing alongside her teenaged daughter and suddenly came to a realization. She did not appear as her daughter's "faintly hip older friend," but rather as a "a schlubby, middle-aged woman with her hair dyed too dark." Inspired to authenticity, and with a bit of curiosity about what she really looked like, Kreamer decided to ditch the dye (Kreamer, 2006).

Gray hair is fraught with cultural meaning: for a woman, it might imply that she is past her prime. Many women worry that going gray will harm their careers (and there is some evidence that they are correct; Sixel, 2011). And although gray hair on men has long been considered "distinguished," the number of men choosing to cover their gray is rising (Daswani, 2012). Women typically begin dying their hair because they feel they are too young to be gray; however, some young women have dyed their hair gray to stand out and be different. Even young celebrities like Kelly Osbourne and Lady Gaga have experimented with gray hair. Instagram found a way to make it hip by using the hashtag #grannyhair — from the back, some might mistake a young gray-haired woman for her grandmother.

After Kreamer grew out her hair, she tried an experiment. She went to an online dating site and created profiles of herself with her new silver locks and with her hair colored brown. The gray-haired image drew more positive attention than the brown-haired one, even when she tried the same experiment in different cities. Kreamer theorizes that her authentic, natural look sent a signal that she was not hiding anything from the get-go and was actually an advantage in dating situations (Kreamer, 2007).

1. How do you perceive men or women with gray hair? Are your perceptions of someone changed if you know they are at an age when they would normally be gray, but obviously dye their hair?

2. Do our perceptions of gray hair carry the same meaning at age 30? 40? 50? 60?

3. Why might more men be opting to cover their gray? Have perceptions of age and masculinity changed, or are men simply more comfortable at a salon than they used to be?

the Church position against contraception, stating it would not be considered evil to avoid pregnancy in the face of this medical, not theological, problem (McElwee, 2016). Monica Roa, a Colombian lawyer and women's rights activist, countered that the ministers had a narrow perspective; the issue could not be reduced to one of contraception when many women in Latin America have poor access to contraceptives (including poor quality sex education) and live in countries with a high prevalence of rape (Roa, 2016). Solving the problem of the Zika virus would necessitate considering other cultural perspectives, including gender, religion, and cultural norms. Narrow perspectives would need to be broadened to combat this major health concern. Narrow perspectives exist among all countries and groups and are particularly problematic when members of the dominant group in a society are unaware of, or insensitive toward, the needs and values of others in the same society.

● **SUCCESSFUL INTERCULTURAL COMMUNICATION** requires overcoming perceptual barriers that can sometimes exist because of culture, gender, or religion. UniversalImagesGroup/Getty Images

Stereotyping

Schemas can be dangerous in a diverse society if we rely on them to make generalizations about groups of people. For example, **stereotyping** is the act of assuming that individuals have a set of attitudes, behaviors, skills, morals, or habits because they belong to certain groups. Stereotyping is applying a fixed or set type of group schema to people so that when you meet an individual from this group, you apply your set of perceptions of the group to that individual. You may not even be aware that you are doing this social stereotyping—researchers have been able to identify key brain regions that are activated by otherwise "hidden" stereotypes that are likely to manifest themselves in your behavior later on (Freeman & Johnson, 2016).

Stereotypes may be positive, negative, or neutral; they may be about a group to which you belong or one that is different from your own. If you have a negative stereotype about corporate executives, for example, you may think that they are all greedy and unethical, even though many (if not most) are hardworking, honest men and women who have climbed the corporate ladder. On the other hand, a positive stereotype might blind you to bad behaviors that do not conform to your ideas.

Such stereotyping plays a role in the way we perceive individual behaviors. In a study of the effects of friends' posts on Facebook (Walther, Van Der Heide, Kim, Westerman, & Tong, 2008), researchers found that for men, negative posts about their "misbehavior" (such as excessive drunkenness and sexual exploits) resulted in perceptions of greater attractiveness. But the same kinds of posts produced very negative judgments when posted about women. These negative impressions can reinforce double standards about the acceptability of certain behaviors among men versus women (Baile, Steeves, Brukell, & Regan, 2013). Gender stereotypes, indeed, run deep across contexts. Participants in one research study viewed only the heads of two social robots, one with longer hair and curved lips (feminine) and one with shorter hair and straight lips (masculine). Participants perceived the long-haired robot as more suited for household chores and caring for children and the elderly and the short-haired one as ready to repair technical devices or guard a house (Eyssel & Kuchenbrandt, 2012).

Prejudice

Negative stereotypes may lead to **prejudice**, a feeling of unkindness and ill will toward particular groups based on preconceived notions about those groups, often accompanied by feelings of superiority over those groups. In its most extreme form,

connect

As you learn in Chapter 6, stereotypes can lead to *discrimination* in which your thoughts about an individual or group lead to specific behaviors. So if you believe that all sorority members are poor students (and you dislike them because of your belief), you may discriminate against a Zeta Tau Alpha member in your study group, believing her incapable of handling the workload.

prejudice can lead to a belief that the lives of some people are worth less than those of others. Indeed, the institution of slavery in the United States flourished based on this belief. Even today, the cultural landscape of almost every nation is dotted with groups that advocate the notion of racial superiority. Your perceptions of group diversity are linked to your own age or race being represented in that group, and you are likely to expect discrimination from groups in which your race is not represented (Bauman, Trawalter & Unzueta, 2014).

Prejudice involves prejudging a person or persons negatively, usually without efforts to discover the relevant facts. Although we often associate prejudice with race and ethnicity, such snap judgments about people may also be based on any type of group membership like gender, social class, age, disability, or religion (or the lack of religion). Very small visual or communication cues can also trigger these prejudices.

Trying to confirm "facts" in our perceptions is often difficult. You might think that looking at the "facts" on video (think footage of riots or sports) would make you more objective; however, research finds that the more you look, the more likely you are to find evidence that confirms your preexisting perceptions (Granot, Balcetis, Schneider, & Tyler, 2014). We further discuss perceptual errors—and ways to remove them—in Chapter 6.

Cognitions About Ourselves

Imagine spending the first nineteen years of your life without an official first name. That is what happened to "Baby Boy" Pauson. His father disappeared, and his mother never got around to choosing a name for his birth certificate. People referred to him as Max (after his mother, Maxine), yet his official records still noted his legal name as "Baby Boy." Tormented and teased, Pauson perceived himself as an outcast and escaped through comic books, animation, and fantasy. It was only when he entered San Francisco's School of the Arts that he discovered that others valued his creativity and nonconformity. He found a lawyer who finally helped him create an official identity with the weighty name he had imagined for himself as a child—Maximus Julius Pauson (Eckholm, 2010).

For most of us, our name (or nickname) is an important element in our *cognitions*, or thoughts about ourselves. For example, many women who marry debate whether to change their last names: some feel that giving up the name might signify the loss of a personal identity; others see changing their name as a way to communicate their relationship status or signify a new family identity. We introduce ourselves using the names we prefer (our full name, a nickname, or a moniker like "Coach" or "Doc"), based on the way we perceive ourselves and want others to perceive us. Though you may not have struggled with your name, you—like all people—have certainly struggled with the challenge of understanding and projecting your identity in order to become a more competent communicator. Three important influences on our thoughts about ourselves are self-concept, self-esteem, and self-efficacy (see Figure 3.2). We discuss each of these in turn.

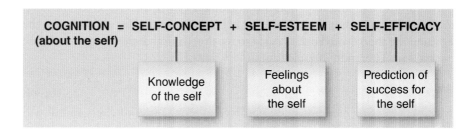

FIGURE 3.2

UNDERSTANDING COGNITION

COGNITION = SELF-CONCEPT + SELF-ESTEEM + SELF-EFFICACY
(about the self)

Knowledge of the self

Feelings about the self

Prediction of success for the self

what about you?

Need for Cognition Scale

Individuals have different perceptions about the thinking process. Some really enjoy grappling with complex ideas and innovating new ways of thinking, whereas others prefer to rely on familiar ways of handling people and situations. Consider the questions that follow and note how well they fit your experiences according to the following scale: 5 = extremely characteristic of you; 4 = somewhat characteristic; 3 = neither characteristic nor uncharacteristic; 2 = somewhat uncharacteristic; and 1 = extremely uncharacteristic.

Then add up your score and refer to the following analysis.

_____ 1. I prefer complex problems to simple problems.

_____ 2. I like to have the responsibility of handling a situation that requires a lot of thinking.

_____ 3. Thinking is my idea of fun.

_____ 4. I would rather do something challenging than something that requires little thought.

_____ 5. I look forward to situations in which I will have to think in depth about something.

_____ 6. I find satisfaction in deliberating hard and for long hours.

_____ 7. I prefer to think about long-term projects rather than small, daily ones.

_____ 8. I dislike tasks that require little thought once I have learned them.

_____ 9. The idea of relying on thought to make my way to the top appeals to me.

_____ 10. I really enjoy a task that involves coming up with new solutions to a problem.

_____ 11. Learning new ways of thinking excites me.

_____ 12. I prefer my life to be filled with puzzles that I must solve.

_____ 13. The notion of thinking abstractly is appealing to me.

_____ 14. I would prefer a task that is intellectual, difficult, and important to one that is somewhat important but does not require much thought.

_____ 15. I feel satisfaction after completing a task that required a lot of mental effort.

_____ 16. I usually end up deliberating about issues even when they do not affect me personally.

51–80: _High need for cognition._ You enjoy the thinking process and are self-motivated to apply your thinking skills to a variety of situations. You select important information and tend to be conscientious and open to new experiences.

33–50: _Medium need for cognition._ You find some satisfaction in expending mental effort but also find comfort in tasks that are established and predictable.

16–32: _Low need for cognition._ You enjoy completing less taxing, daily tasks that do not require a lot of reflection. You generally find thinking about difficult tasks unsatisfying. You prefer relying on your tried-and-true ways of thinking and you do not like to be presented with puzzles to solve.

Information from J. T. Cacioppo & R. E. Petty (1984).

● **ISIS KING,** former *America's Next Top Model* contestant, was the first transgender woman to compete on the show and became a public advocate for transgender youth.
Anthony Behar/Newscom/Sipa Press/New York/NY/USA

Self-Concept: Who You Think You Are

Six-year-old Coy Mathis has long hair, loves to wear pink dresses, and tears up when anyone refers to her as a boy. She was born biologically male but thinks of herself as female. Her parents and doctors agree that her gender identity is simply part of who Coy is as a human being (Frosch, 2013). So, who are *you*? You may describe yourself to others as a male, a female, a college student, a Latino, a Buddhist, a heterosexual, a biology major, an uncle, a mother, or a friend. But who you are involves much more.

As we discussed in Chapter 1, your awareness and understanding of who you are — as interpreted and influenced by your thoughts, actions, abilities, values, goals, and ideals — is your **self-concept**. You develop a self-concept by thinking about your strengths and weaknesses — thinking about yourself as active and scattered, as conservative and funny, as plain and popular, and so on. You also observe your behavior in a wide variety of situations, witnessing your own reactions to situations, and watching others' reactions to you (Snyder, 1979). From this, you form beliefs about how you tend to behave and how you expect to be treated in a variety of social situations. In addition to your cognitions and behavior, there is a growing body of research that attributes a variety of your behaviors to biological factors, particularly as they relate to sexual orientation (Garretson & Suhay, 2016). Your cultural experiences also influence both your brain and your behavior (Kim & Sasaki, 2014). In sum, your self-concept is a result of biology, cognition, and behavior.

Your self-concept powerfully shapes your communication with others. Because your perception of others is related to how you think of yourself, your self-concept can affect what you think of other people (Edwards, 1990). If attributes like honesty and wit are important to you, you will consider them important traits in other people. If you think that swearing makes you appear vulgar, you will likely think the same of others when they use foul language. When you interact with others, your self-concept comes into play as well. As we shall see when we discuss self-esteem and self-efficacy, your self-concept can affect how apprehensive you become in certain communication situations (McCroskey, 1997), whether you are even willing to interact with others (Cegala, 1981), and how you approach someone with a request (timidly or with confidence).

So while your self-concept strongly influences how and when you communicate with others, the reverse is also true: when you interact with other people, you get impressions from them that reveal what they think about you as a person and as a communicator. This information gets reincorporated into your self-concept. *Direct evidence* comes in the form of compliments, insults, support, or negative remarks. *Indirect evidence* that influences your self-concept might be revealed through innuendo, gossip, subtle nonverbal cues, or a lack of communication. For instance, if you ask a friend to evaluate whether you are promising enough to be a contestant on *America's Got Talent* and he changes the subject, you might get the impression that you are not such a great singer after all.

Our interactions with others, and their responses to us, often cause us to compare ourselves to others as we develop our ideas about ourselves. **Social comparison theory** (Bishop, 2000; Festinger, 1954) explains that we are driven to gain an accurate sense of self by examining our qualities and abilities in comparison to others. For example, if you are the least financially well-off among your friends, you may consider yourself as poor; given the same income and resources but a circle of less fortunate friends, you might think of yourself as well-off. Images in the media can have a similar effect. For example, if you compare your body shape with those of models in magazine photos, you might come to believe that you have flat hair, thin eyelashes, or short legs, even though the images of models are notorious for being altered or enhanced with image-editing software. The beliefs we develop about ourselves—our bodies, our personalities, our abilities—exert a powerful influence on our lives, our relationships, and our communication. Struggles with self-concept—the way we perceive ourselves—are closely related to the way we feel about ourselves, of course, so we next examine how these feelings relate to communication.

Self-Esteem: How You Feel About Yourself

Self-esteem refers to how you feel about your worth—your value as a person. Self-esteem consists of attitudes, the positive and negative feelings we have in a given situation about our abilities, traits, thoughts, emotions, behavior, and appearance. Self-concept and self-esteem are closely related: people need to know themselves before they can have attitudes about themselves. Consequently, many researchers believe that the self-concept forms first, and self-esteem emerges later (Greenwalk, Bellezza, & Banaji, 1988).

You have probably noticed that people with high self-esteem are confident in what they do, how they think, and how they perform. That is partly because these individuals are better able to incorporate their successes and good qualities into their self-concept as well as to accept their less positive attributes. This projection of confidence is evident in New Orleans Saints quarterback Drew Brees, who was born with a birthmark on the right side of his face that is now a very visible scar. Many people have asked about it (talk show host Oprah Winfrey thought it was a lipstick kiss when Brees appeared on her show), but he has no plans to remove it unless it poses a threat to his health. "It's just a part of who I am," Brees wrote in his book *Coming Back Stronger* (Brees & Fabry, 2011). Research shows that people with high self-esteem are more confident in their interpersonal relationships, too—perhaps because they tend to believe that being friendly is a positive trait that will cause others to be friendly in return (Baldwin & Keelan, 1999). In addition, perceived commitment from a romantic partner enhances self-esteem (Rill, Balocchi, Hopper, Denker, & Olson, 2009). Thus, individuals with high self-esteem may not feel a strong need for public displays of affection, feeling confident and secure in their relationship. By contrast, someone with low self-esteem might press their romantic partner to show affection in public, so others can see that "someone loves me!"

Research suggests that some people have low self-esteem, or a poor view of themselves, because they lack accurate information about themselves or they mistrust the knowledge they do possess. For example, you may feel that you are a poor student because you have to study constantly to keep up your grades in German class. Your German professor, however, might think you are a strong, hardworking student because of your efforts and improvement over the semester. Low self-esteem may also result from unreasonable comparisons to other people or to cultural stereotypes. If you are envious of another student in your German class, you may compare yourself to him, find yourself wanting, and feel hostile toward him along with your lowered academic self-esteem (Rentzsch, Schröder-Abé, & Schütz, 2015). If your self-concept about your body shape is based on comparisons with media personalities, that perception can affect your self-esteem. Indeed, exposure to images of body "perfection" in the media has been linked to negative body image and even eating disorders (Bishop, 2000; Hendriks, 2002; Jacobs, 2013). In fact, one study shows that men exposed to idealized male bodies in even brief music video clips reported decreased body and muscle tone satisfaction

and you?

Think about three characteristics that describe your self-concept and define who you are. Try to avoid characteristics that are obvious, such as "I am an Asian-American female." How did you come to believe these things about yourself? What types of direct and indirect evidence led you to these beliefs? Do your loved ones support the view you have of yourself?

● **SAINTS QUARTERBACK DREW BREES** has high self-esteem and no intention of removing his facial scar. Sean Gardner/Getty Images

connect

As you saw in Chapter 2, the many contexts of digital communication may make it more difficult to manage your social media profile. The control others exert over their own self-presentations make it easier for them (and you) to present only the glamorous sides of your life which distort perceptions.

(Mulgrew & Volcevski-Kostas, 2012). Similarly, comparing your life to the (supposedly) exciting lives presented by others on social media can have negative effects on your self-esteem (Chou & Edge, 2012). In contrast, becoming more "self-aware" by updating and giving thought to a positive presentation of your own social media profiles appears to enhance self-esteem rather than diminish it (Gonzalez & Hancock, 2011; Toma, 2013).

Self-Efficacy: Assessing Your Own Abilities

Actor Peter Dinklage won a Golden Globe Award for his portrayal of the complex Tyrion Lannister in HBO's popular original series, *Game of Thrones* (Kois, 2012); he received an Emmy nomination for the same role. But there was a time when such recognition seemed far off. Dinklage started his acting career while living in a rat-infested Brooklyn apartment without heat. Diagnosed with achondroplasia, a common cause of dwarfism, he tried to avoid roles as elves or leprechauns, fearing they would forever tie his talents to his stature. Ironically, it was his performance as Tom Thumb in a vaudevillian play that so impressed director Tom McCarthy that McCarthy rewrote a script for *The Station Agent,* casting Dinklage in the lead. A series of roles later, Dinklage earned the success he desired without playing parts that he felt would demean him — all because he believed he could "play the romantic lead and get the girl" (Kois, 2012).

Dinklage's experiences reveal the power of self-efficacy, which is the third factor influencing our cognitions about ourselves. Like Dinklage, you have an overall view of all aspects of yourself (self-concept) as well as an evaluation of how you feel about yourself in a particular area at any given moment in time (self-esteem). Based on this information, you approach a communication situation with an eye toward the

evaluating communication ethics

Ethics and the Self-Concept

You and your romantic partner, Peyton, have been together for three years and have supported each other through many ups and downs, particularly in your professional lives. Both of you have successful careers and have made sacrifices to help each other achieve personal and professional goals. Most recently, the two of you moved from Saint Louis to Washington, D.C., so that Peyton could accept a promotion with a large financial investment firm. Because you are able to work from a home office, you agreed to the move and were happy for Peyton. But it has been difficult: Peyton works long hours, and your entire family and most of your close friends are still in Saint Louis.

Peyton comes home early one afternoon to announce that the investment firm has offered another promotion, but the position requires travel from Monday to Friday two weeks out of the month. Peyton clearly feels good about this and talks excitedly about the increase in status and pay. Your immediate reaction is one of anger. You value harmony in your home and your relationships, and you value time spent with your partner. You believe that you are a flexible, reasonable person who appreciates joint decision making. You are hurt and cannot understand why Peyton seems to discount these aspects of your self-concept.

You are upset by the different ways that you and Peyton perceive the situation and the ensuing communication difficulties.

think about this

1. Consider the elements that make up your self-concept and your partner's. What do you each value about work, relationships, and other important matters?

2. How might your self-concept have affected how you perceived Peyton's message about the promotion? How might the message have affected your self-esteem?

3. Now take Peyton's perspective. How might your partner's self-concept have affected the way that the news of the promotion was shared with you? `

likelihood of presenting yourself effectively. This ability to predict actual success from self-concept and self-esteem is **self-efficacy** (Bandura, 1982). Your perceptions of self-efficacy guide your ultimate choice of communication situations, making you much more likely to engage in communication when you believe you will probably be successful and avoid situations where you believe your self-efficacy to be low.

Even though a person's lack of effort is most often caused by perceptions of low self-efficacy, people with very high levels of self-efficacy sometimes become overconfident (Bandura, 1982; Harris & Hahn, 2011). For example, some students believe that if they understood their professors' lectures well while sitting in class, then they would not need to study their notes much to prepare for exams. Those students are often shocked at how much information they do not remember when taking the test.

Self-efficacy affects your ability to cope with failure and stress. Feelings of low self-efficacy may cause you to dwell on your shortcomings. If you already feel inadequate and then fail at something, a snowball effect occurs as the failure takes a toll on your self-esteem; stress and negative feelings result, lowering your feelings of self-efficacy even more. For example, Jessie is job hunting but worries that she does not do well in interviews. Every time she goes to an interview but does not get a job offer, her self-efficacy drops. She lowers her expectations for herself, and her interview performance worsens as well. By contrast, people with high self-efficacy are less emotionally battered by failures because they usually chalk up disappointments to a "bad day" or some other external factor.

Perceptions of your self-efficacy may lead to a **self-fulfilling prophecy**—a prediction that causes you to change your behavior in a way that makes the prediction more likely to occur. If you go to a party believing that others will not pay attention to you or enjoy your company, for example, you will probably stand apart, not making any effort to be friendly. Others will not like you, so your prophecy is fulfilled. Self-efficacy and self-fulfilling prophecy are thus related. Low self-efficacy often causes you to exert less effort to prepare or participate than you would in situations in which you are comfortable and have high self-efficacy. When you do not prepare for or participate in a situation (such as at the party), your behavior causes the prediction to come true, creating a self-fulfilling prophecy (see Figure 3.3). One study of international soccer tournaments found that teams with a history of losing (even if the current players were not a part of the losing effort) were significantly less likely to win the penalty shoot-outs that decide

● **WHAT CAN WE** LEARN about the power of self-concept and self-esteem in our own lives from Peter Dinklage's success? © HBO/Photofest

> **connect**
>
> Self-fulfilling prophecies are deeply tied to verbal and non-verbal communication. If you believe you will ace a job interview because you are well prepared, you will likely stand tall and make confident eye contact with your interviewer (Chapter 5) and use appropriate and effective language (Chapter 4) to describe your skill set. Your confidence just may land you the position you want!

FIGURE 3.3

THE SELF-FULFILLING PROPHECY

Self-Fulfilling Prophecy (SFP)

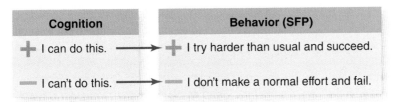

Cognition	Behavior (SFP)
➕ I can do this. →	➕ I try harder than usual and succeed.
➖ I can't do this. →	➖ I don't make a normal effort and fail.

Self-fulfilling prophecy imposed on others:

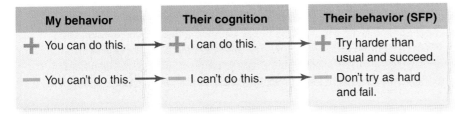

My behavior	Their cognition	Their behavior (SFP)
➕ You can do this. →	➕ I can do this. →	➕ Try harder than usual and succeed.
➖ You can't do this. →	➖ I can't do this. →	➖ Don't try as hard and fail.

a tied game (Jordet, Hartman, & Jelle Vuijk, 2012). Why? It is possible that the players choked under a high degree of performance pressure, unable to predict their own success from past performances. It is also possible that they hurried their preparation and thus created their own demise.

Self-fulfilling prophecies do not always produce negative results. If you announce plans to improve your grades after a lackluster semester and then work harder than usual to accomplish your goal, your prediction may result in an improved GPA. But even the simple act of announcing your goals to others—for example, tweeting your intention to quit smoking or to run a marathon—can create a commitment to making a positive self-fulfilling prophecy come true (Willard & Gramzow, 2008).

Assessing Our Perceptions of Self

Whenever you communicate, you receive feedback from people that allows you to assess your strengths and weaknesses. These assessments of self are important before, during, and after you have communicated. You evaluate your expectations,

---

real communicator

NAME: Lisa M. Turay, CSJ
OCCUPATION: Woman Religious, Women's Wellness Counselor
Courtesy Lisa Turay

Call me "Lisa." That's how I introduce myself to the mothers I counsel at our women's wellness clinic. I don't hide the fact that I'm a Catholic nun — Sister Lisa is clearly written on my name badge — but I like to give clients the choice to call me by either name. After all, focusing strongly on my status in religious life invokes a set of perceptions on the part of clients that they may or may not find comfortable. Given the highly personal and deeply emotional situations we discuss, it's important to establish an environment that's safe, compassionate, and accepting.

As I learned from my undergraduate communication courses and my graduate counseling ones, good counselors don't need to be "the same" as their clients or have had the same experiences; rather, they need to practice the communication skills of perspective taking and empathic listening. Using these skills, I'm able to help my clients get through some of the most stressful times in their lives: having babies, losing babies, and dealing with personal and family stresses.

Pregnant and postpartum (after-birth) women experience a wide range of physical and emotional changes. Imbalanced hormones coupled with physical challenges (like lack of sleep or impaired mobility) can be difficult. Postpartum women often need to be reminded to eat well, attend to personal hygiene, and sleep when the baby sleeps. They're often exhausted

and overwhelmed. I help these women adjust their sometimes-negative thinking about their current situations. There are so many schemas surrounding babies and parenthood. I sometimes have to help these women adjust negative thinking like, "I'm a bad mother because the baby keeps crying" or "I'll never sleep again." Seeing moms develop more realistic perceptions about parenthood — and begin to adjust to this new phase of life — is one of the most rewarding parts of my job.

Grief counseling is also a reality some mothers face. The loss of a pregnancy (particularly past the first trimester) and the death of a newborn are among the most difficult things a mother can face. Well-meaning friends and family members sometimes rely on mindless scripts of what to say in such situations. Too many times women hear, "Oh, you're young; you can have another child," when they're thinking, "Did I do something wrong? Am I fit to be a mother?" With active listening, caring eye contact, and unconditional positive regard, I provide these women with a safe space to grieve, ask questions, or simply be silent. They receive support and understanding as they deal with their grief.

When I can develop a therapeutic relationship that allows a woman to navigate through the life adjustment called "pregnancy" and all that it holds — I feel privileged and grateful to have been a part of it.

execution, and outcomes in three ways: self-actualization, self-adequacy, and self-denigration.

Self-Actualization

The most positive evaluation you can make about your competence level is referred to as **self-actualization** — the feelings and thoughts you get when you know that you have successfully negotiated a communication situation. At times like this, you have a sense of fulfillment and satisfaction from presenting yourself very well.

Self-Adequacy

Other times you may think that your communication performance was not stellar, but it was good enough. When you assess your communication competence as sufficient or acceptable, you feel a sense of **self-adequacy**, which is less intensely positive than self-actualization. You may feel a subsequent desire for self-improvement or you may feel content with being adequate.

Suppose that Phil speaks to his fraternity about its goals for charitable work in the coming year. He feels satisfied about his speech but realizes that with a little more effort and practice, he could have been even more persuasive. In this case, Phil's desire to be more than adequate is one of *self-improvement*.

In some circumstances, however, being *content* with your self-adequacy is sufficient. For example, Lilia has a long history of communication difficulties with her mother. Their relationship is characterized by sarcastic and unkind comments and interactions. But during her last visit home, Lilia managed to avoid getting into an argument with her mother. The two did not become best friends or resolve all their old problems, but Lilia was content to just avoid open conflict.

Self-Denigration

The most negative assessment you can make about a communication experience is **self-denigration**: criticizing or attacking yourself. This occurs most often when communicators overemphasize their weaknesses or shortcomings ("I knew I would end up tripping over my words and repeating myself — I am such a klutz!"). Most self-denigration is unnecessary, particularly when it prevents improvement. Hunter, for example, thinks that his sister is stubborn and judgmental and that he cannot talk to her. He says, "I always lose it with her, and I yell at her because there is nothing I can say that she will listen to!" Rather than just accepting the idea that nothing he says will ever "work," Hunter needs to assess the specific words and nonverbal behaviors (like eye rolling) that he might use with his sister when she "doesn't listen." He should identify communication behaviors he has used during positive interactions with his sister. In that way, Hunter can plan for communication improvement ("Next time, I won't raise my voice or roll my eyes. I'll look at and listen to her until she is finished talking before I say anything"). Thus, our assessments of our competence run from self-actualization on the positive end of the spectrum to self-denigration on the negative end.

● **SELF-DENIGRATING BEHAVIORS** can only hurt your performance, so the next time you feel like saying to yourself, "I will never be able to understand calculus," instead, try thinking, "Let's see if I can figure this out." Steve Debenport/Getty Images

Behavior: Managing Our Identities

As you have learned, you define yourself through your self-concept and your ideas about self-esteem and self-efficacy. But you also make decisions about how to share these internal viewpoints with others. This is manifested in your verbal and nonverbal behaviors.

We all have aspects of ourselves that we want to share and aspects that we would rather keep private. Many of the choices we make in our communication behavior, from the clothes we wear to the way we speak, are determined by how we want others to perceive us. In this section, we consider how we let the world know just who we think we are and how our communication with others can shape their perceptions of us.

Let's examine the process illustrated in Figure 3.4. At the core of this process is the self. The self has cognitions that consist of self-concept (knowing and understanding the self), self-esteem (evaluating the self), and self-efficacy (predicting the self's success)—all of which we have discussed. These cognitions influence our verbal and nonverbal behaviors, which consist of self-presentation and self-disclosure, two terms we will explain soon. Our behavior generates feedback from others, which leads to our assessments of self-actualization, self-adequacy, and self-denigration. These judgments of our performance then affect our cognitions. As you read about self-presentation, self-disclosure, and feedback in the coming pages, refer to this illustration to remind yourself of the roles these play in your interactions with others.

Self-Presentation

You let others know about yourself through **self-presentation**—intentional communication designed to show elements of the self for strategic purposes. You may tell your life story, your **narrative**, to communicate to others who you are, where you came from, or what you hope to be (Bochner & Ellis, 1992; Goffman, 1974). Your personal narrative may reflect your social and cultural values as well as contest those of others through the presentation of your experiences (Tovares, 2012).

We all tend to focus on self-presentation when we are being evaluated, formally or informally, by others (Canary & Cody, 1993). For example, you probably behave

FIGURE 3.4

THE SELF The self is composed of our cognitions, our behavior, and our self-assessments. These factors work together to affect our communication.

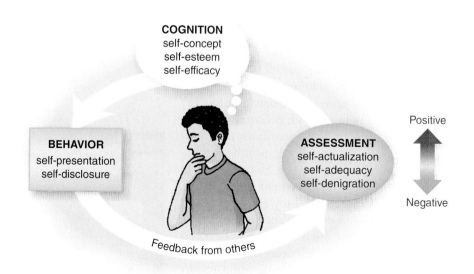

very differently when you are meeting your significant other's parents for the first time than when you are hanging out with your friends or your own family.

Self-presentation can take many forms. You can present yourself through face-to-face conversation, through a personal narrative as previously mentioned, through email, text messaging, Twitter, and Facebook. You may even have a preference for one of these channels when self-presenting. For example, many people use asynchronous channels (voice mail, delayed text messages) when they are unsure of the reaction they will get from the recipient (O'Sullivan, 2000). For example, after a heated argument with her boyfriend Lance, Julie wants to apologize. Because she is uncomfortable making this self-presentation to Lance over the phone or in person, she chooses to send him a text message when she knows he will have his phone silenced. Many students also prefer email over face-to-face or virtual office hours to interact with their professors (Li & Pitts, 2009). In fact, the most common reasons for choosing email or texting over face-to-face interaction is the ability to carefully construct our messages (Tikkanen and Frisbie, 2016) and to "shield" ourselves from any immediate negative feedback from the other person (Riordan & Kreuz, 2010).

To figure out how to present yourself in the best way, you have to pay attention to your own and others' behavior. **Self-monitoring** is your ability to watch your environment and others in it for cues about how to present yourself in a particular situation (Snyder, 1974). High-self-monitoring individuals try to portray themselves as "the right person in the right place at the right time." These people watch others for hints on how to be successful in social situations and try to demonstrate the verbal and nonverbal behaviors that seem most appropriate. For example, during class, a high-self-monitoring person may sit in a certain strategic position, get involved in discussions when others do so, gesture in a similar manner to others, and be silent when it is time to let others talk. These "sufficiently skilled actors" can display situation-appropriate communication behaviors. Low-self-monitoring individuals are not nearly so sensitive to situational cues. They communicate according to their instincts and feelings of the moment. They do not see the need to adapt to situations or people; rather, they feel that adjusting their style of communication would be "false." If low-self-monitor individuals anticipate a communication situation that is different from their own self-presentation style, they will either avoid the situation or accept the fact that their communication may not please all the parties involved.

and you?

Like Julie, you have probably encountered situations in which you chose to engage in either face-to-face communication or mediated communication (for example, text messaging, posting on Facebook, emailing). Why did you choose a particular channel? If you chose a mediated channel, did you feel safer from an unknown reaction as the research suggests? Why or why not?

● **PLACES OF WORSHIP** often have dress codes, whether they are explicitly stated or not. If you are a low self-monitor, preferring to ignore these rules and do things your own way, others may feel that you are being disrespectful and inappropriate.
Wathiq Khuzaie/Getty Images

Communicating successfully involves finding the appropriate level of self-monitoring for the situation and the people involved. It might seem like high self-monitors are the winners in social interaction, but this is not always the case. High self-monitors can drive themselves crazy by focusing on every little thing that they say and do (Wright, Holloway, & Roloff, 2007). They might also become manipulative in their carefully crafted efforts to impress people. Perhaps you have experienced social media users who brag about being at a great party, for the "benefit" of the people who are not there (Harmon, 2011). And consider those who ineffectually disguise bragging over social media by self-denigrating ("Can't seem to fit into those size two jeans, despite my daily workouts")—they have earned their own hashtag: #humblebrag.

By contrast, competent communicators will monitor their self-presentation just enough to present themselves effectively but without forgetting that communication involves others. They also know that you cannot control what *others* do around you that may affect your efforts to present yourself effectively—including what your friends post on your Facebook Timeline.

Self-Disclosure

Angelica is a stylish dresser, has a lovely apartment in Boston, eats out at nice restaurants regularly, and drives a new car. But she has a secret: she is drowning in debt, barely keeping up with her minimum credit card payments. She looks around at her friends; they are all the same age as she is and live similar lifestyles. She wonders if they make more money than she does or if they, too, are over their heads in debt. One night while she is having coffee with her best friend, Tonya, Angelica comes clean about her situation: she cannot go on their upcoming trip to Cozumel, she tells Tonya, because her credit cards are maxed out.

When you reveal yourself to others by sharing information about yourself—as Angelica has done with Tonya—you engage in **self-disclosure**. Voluntary self-disclosure functions to develop ordinary social relationships (Antaki, Barnes, & Leudar, 2005), but has more impact or creates more intimacy if it goes below surface information (Tamir & Mitchell, 2012). For example, telling someone that you like tofu is surface information; explaining why you became a vegetarian is deeper self-disclosure.

Self-disclosure can help you confirm your self-concept or improve your self-esteem; it can also enable you to obtain reassurance or comfort from a trusted friend (Miller, Cooke, Tsang, & Morgan, 1992). For example, Angelica might suspect that Tonya is also living on credit; if Tonya discloses that she is, her confession might reassure Angelica that it is OK to buy things she cannot afford on credit because everyone else is doing it. However, if Tonya reveals that she makes more money than Angelica, or that she manages her money more wisely, Angelica's self-concept may incur some damage. As you may remember from the first chapter, information you receive about yourself is termed *feedback*. The feedback Angelica receives from Tonya in response to her self-disclosure will also influence Angelica's perception of herself.

Managing Feedback

How you incorporate feedback into the self depends on several factors. One of the most important factors is your *sensitivity level* to feedback. Research demonstrates that some individuals are highly sensitive, whereas others are largely unaffected by the feedback they receive (Edwards, 1990), and at least some of this is hereditary (Gearhart & Bodie, 2012). Presumably, people who are more sensitive to feedback are more receptive to information about their abilities, knowledge, and talents. Low-sensitive people are less responsive to such information. For example, when Olympic short-track speed skater Apolo Ohno bombed at the

connect

The process we use to choose the information we are willing to share with others has long fascinated researchers. In Chapter 8, we examine the *social penetration theory*, which uses an onion as a metaphor to show how we move from superficial confessions to more intimate ones. Your outer "layer" might consist of a disclosure about where you are from; however, as you peel away the layers, your disclosures become more personal.

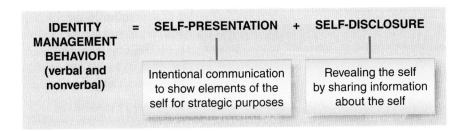

FIGURE 3.5

IDENTITY MANAGEMENT
BEHAVIOR

Olympic trials in 1998, he was not interested in hearing that his efforts were not sufficient. He was demonstrating a low sensitivity level to the advice and feedback from his coach, friends, and family. Ohno's father sent him to a secluded cabin for eight days to contemplate his career. After that, Ohno decided that he was ready to receive the feedback that he needed to improve his performance. He developed a higher sensitivity to feedback; won eight Olympic medals (Bishop, 2010); and finished the World Championships in the gold, silver, or bronze medal position eighteen times.

Managing feedback necessarily deals with how you handle both positive and negative comments. If you feel excluded by others, you might assume that you are unliked or unpopular. But if you consider how others feel in addition to your own feelings, you usually get better at seeing both sets of emotions in light of the situation. You are more likely to have a balanced reaction to feedback — and feel less defensive — which in turn leads to being more well liked by others (Cheung & Gardner, 2015). Figure 3.5 illustrates how self-presentation, self-disclosure, and managing feedback constitute the behavior segment of "the Self," seen in Figure 3.4.

Technology: Managing the Self and Perceptions

If you are wondering how your cousin Ned is doing, all you need to do is check out his Facebook profile — right? There you see photographs of his recent visit with his longtime girlfriend's family in Texas. You read funny status updates about his apartment hunt. And you see that others wrote on his Timeline to congratulate him on his recent promotion. Life is going well for Ned, so you send him a private message to let him know that you are glad for him. Would you be surprised if Ned responded to share that he is considering a breakup with his girlfriend, that he hates his job, and that he cannot afford a decent apartment because his student loans are crushing him? How is this possible (you wonder) when Ned's profile seems to indicate that his life is fulfilling and happy?

Social networking sites and other digital media, as we discussed in the previous chapter, allow you to control the presentation of self far more carefully than in face-to-face encounters (Choi & Toma, 2014). When you manage the self online, you can much more easily choose what to reveal and what to conceal. You can decide whether you will reveal your gender, ethnicity, and race as well as your religious or political preferences. What's more, you can edit, revise, and organize the information you disclose before the message goes out. In this way, you can present an image that is smart, charming, and eloquent, even if you tend to be nervous or timid in face-to-face communication. You can also use different media platforms to show yourself to the best advantage with different audiences — on LinkedIn, you present your "professional" self to potential employers, whereas you show your funny self to your buddies with selfies on Snapchat.

In Ned's case, he chose to present a self on Facebook that is carefree and happy — even though his current situation is quite the opposite. Of course, it is important to remember as a user of social media that if you can choose what to

wired for communication

Avatars: Virtual Personas and Perception

Thirteen-year-old Desmond, better known in cyberspace as Captain Obvious, modifies his avatar in the online role-playing game *Borderlands II*. He calls the character who wears an eye patch and a dockworker's skull cap "Butch." Desmond describes Butch as "psychotic." But when other players look at Butch, are they drawing conclusions about Desmond? Research suggests that they might be.

Avatars can be chosen as a way to draw attention to yourself, give others a glimpse of your interests, or capture some aspect of your personality (Suler, 2007). Researchers who looked at players in the massive online role-playing game *Second Life* suggest that avatars are "highly controlled information transmitters, well-suited to strategic self-presentation that can be used to communicate any of the selves" (Bélisle & Bodur, 2010). Put simply, specific cues in avatars communicate certain aspects of the self. For example, male avatars with long hair or stylish hairstyles were widely perceived as more extroverted, whereas those with jeans, gray shirts, long-sleeved shirts, or black hair were perceived as introverted. So when players choose specific attributes for avatars — from the way they look to what they wear — it is likely that they are making their choices in order to convey specific personal attributes.

Even if you did not design the avatar yourself, there is some evidence that your self-concept and behavior may be affected by the physical characteristics of an avatar randomly assigned to you; people who were assigned to more attractive avatars self-disclosed more and talked more intimately with others than those assigned less attractive avatars (Yee & Bailenson, 2007).

think about this

1. Does it surprise you that avatars can influence perceptions in such a way?

2. When you create an avatar — be it an elaborate skin on *Second Life* or a rudimentary stick figure for your online fan forums — how do you choose its attributes?

3. Does context matter? Do you think avatars function differently in different games or virtual environments?

and you?

Randomly select five Facebook friends or people you follow on Instagram or other social media. Consider the photos they post, their friends' posts about them, the things they like, and so on. What type of impression does their online activity make on you? What words would you use to describe these individuals? Do you believe they present themselves accurately?

present about yourself, so too can everyone else. As we discussed earlier, more time spent on social media seeing everyone else's seemingly "fabulous" lives can make you feel worse about yourself and your own life (Kross et al., 2013).

In addition, how *you* present yourself online may not be the only factor in how you come across to others. Statements made by your friends on Facebook, for example, can significantly affect people's impressions of you. One study found that when people post on their friends' Timeline positive statements about their friends' behavior, their friends' credibility and "social attractiveness" increased, compared to negative statements (e.g., about excessive drunkenness or sexual behavior); in addition, the perceived attractiveness of friends affected perceptions of self-attractiveness (Walther et al., 2008). Even the number and type of friends you have on Facebook can have an influence — if you have "too few" or "too many" friends, your reputation could suffer (Tong, Van Der Heide, Langwell, & Walther, 2008).

Darren Carroll/Getty Images

back to ▶ The Image of Tiger Woods

At the beginning of this chapter, we talked about how top golfer Tiger Woods struggled with reconstructing his public image after a personal scandal rocked his world. Let's reflect on how communication and perception scholarship can help us understand perceptions and image reconstruction.

▶ When a public figure's image is damaged, the economic and social ramifications can be huge. Public relations specialists and sports management professionals are usually called in to help repair their images, using strategies such as denial, evading responsibility, minimizing the event, reframing the event, attacking the accuser, taking corrective action, and expressing sorrow or mortification (Blaney, 2013). Some of these strategies may backfire; denial, for example, is not effective if later visual or written proof of culpability emerges. Tiger Woods employed the last two repair strategies. Would you have advised using others?

▶ Note that most professional athletes are not plagued by scandals and their lives do not make headline news. But we remember baseball great Alex Rodriguez's steroid scandal, Olympic swimmer Michael Phelps's pot smoking caught on camera, and the discovery of football darling Michael Vick's dogfighting. We fall for the *negativity bias*—remembering the scandals while forgetting about the many admirable athletes with happy, successful, and somewhat anonymous lives.

▶ Recent news stories (ESPN, 2016) portray Tiger Woods as a person haunted by his father Earl's death, unclear about how to behave to live up to his superstar image, and uncomfortable talking to women in clubs. The presentation of self is often at odds with internal feelings and self-perceptions. Do you think stories like this are just media attempts to help repair Woods's image or honest assessments of the complexity of his self-concept and his struggles to adapt?

things to try ▶ Activities

LaunchPad
macmillan learning

1. LaunchPad for *Real Communication* offers key term videos and encourages self-assessment through adaptive quizzing. Go to **launchpadworks.com** to get access to:

LearningCurve
Adaptive Quizzes.

Video clips that illustrate key concepts, highlighted in teal in the Real Reference section that follows.

2. Describe how you managed an impression of yourself in a face-to-face interaction and a mediated one. Describe your conscious preparations for this impression management and then describe the outcome. What contributed to your successful or unsuccessful management of self? Were the impression-management strategies you employed in the face-to-face interaction different from the mediated situation?

3. Take a look at the text of a presidential speech online at www.whitehouse.gov. After reading the complete speech, consider how the speech is characterized in various sources (blogs, liberal and conservative news sources, late-night comedy and satires). How do perceptions of the speech change from one source to another? Does your perception of the speech change as you consider the points of view of these various sources?

4. Think about a coculture (age, sexual orientation, socioeconomic status, race, religion, etc.) with which you identify. Make a list of stereotypes that are associated

with that group. In what ways do you conform to such stereotypes? In what ways do you not conform? Do you identify with more than one culture? If so, are there any stereotypes on your list that contradict each other? How might intersection of these cultures (e.g., being a white, Christian, thirty-year-old stay-at-home dad or a fifty-year-old Hispanic lesbian scientist) affect your perception of yourself as well as others' perceptions of you?

5. Watch some television programming or flip through a magazine that is typically geared toward a particular group. Pay close attention to the advertisements you see. Are they geared toward the groups that are expected to be watching the programming? If so, do you see instances in which the commercials allow for flexibility and mindfulness (e.g., any advertising geared toward women during football games)? If you are a member of the group being targeted during such programming, do you find yourself more or less persuaded by the message based on stereotypes about your group?

real reference ➤ A Study Tool

Now that you have finished reading this chapter, you can:

Describe how our personal perspective on the world influences our communication:

▶ **Perception** is the cognitive process that helps us make sense of the world (p. 54).

▶ **Communication processing** is how we gather, organize, and evaluate the information we receive (p. 54).

▶ Because we are constantly bombarded with information, we must sift through it to determine what is important and what to remember (p. 55).

Explain how we use and misuse schemas when communicating with others:

▶ **Schemas** are mental structures we use to connect bits of information together (p. 55).

▶ Schemas evolve as we select new information to help us understand how things work and how to act in various situations. (p. 54)

▶ **Social constructivism** explains that schemas are socially constructed perceptions of reality (p. 55).

▶ **Interaction appearance theory** explains how people change their perception of someone else as they spend more time together (p. 55).

▶ Schemas present three challenges to effective communication: 1) **Mindlessness** is a passive response to information which can be corrected by **mindfulness**, focusing on the task at hand; 2) **selective perception** allows our chosen observations to influence our thoughts; and 3) distorted perception involves schemas with inaccuracies (pp. 56–57).

Define the attributions we use to explain behavior:

▶ **Attributions** are our explanations for why someone says or does something (p. 57).

▶ The **fundamental attribution error** is our tendency to assume that another person's wrong behavior stems from an internal flaw, whereas the **self-serving bias** attributes our own failures to external causes. The **negativity bias** occurs when we focus on the negative over positive or neutral attributes (p. 57).

▶ Improve your perceptions by verifying them, being thoughtful, looking beyond first impressions, and questioning your assumptions (p. 58).

Describe cultural differences that influence perception:

▶ Effective communication depends on understanding how diversity, the variables that make us unique, affects perception (p. 60).

▶ A narrow perspective results in a failure to see beyond our own beliefs and circumstances and blinds us to alternative points of view (pp. 60–61).

▶ **Stereotyping**, or generalizing about people based on their group membership, limits our ability to see the individual and can lead to **prejudice**, ill will toward a particular group, and a sense of one's own superiority (pp. 61–62).

Identify how our **self-concept**—who we think we are—influences communication:

▶ We receive both direct and indirect evidence about the self (p. 64).

▶ We are more willing to interact in situations where we feel we have strengths and where our self-concept is confirmed by others (p. 64).

▶ We compare ourselves to others, even idealized images in the media, according to social comparison theory—often to our own disadvantage (p. 64).

▶ **Self-esteem** is how we feel about ourselves in a particular situation (pp. 65–66).

▶ **Self-efficacy** is the ability to predict our effectiveness in a communication situation. Inaccurate self-efficacy may lead to a self-fulfilling prophecy, whereby we change our behavior in ways that make our prediction more likely to come true (pp. 67–68).

▶ We assess our communication effectiveness through the lenses of **self-actualization** (high performance), **self-adequacy** (adequate performance), and **self-denigration** (poor performance) (p. 69).

Describe how our cognitions about ourselves and our behavior affect our communication with others:

▶ **Self-presentation** is intentional communication designed to let others know about ourselves. We often present the self through **narratives**, stories about ourselves or our experiences (p. 70).

▶ The tendency to watch our environment and others in it for cues as to how to present ourselves is called self-monitoring (p. 71).

▶ Sharing important information about ourselves is self-disclosure (p. 72).

▶ We can more easily control presentation of self online than in face-to-face encounters but that does not mean that everyone does it effectively (pp. 73–74).

Which of these pairs are partners?

chapter

4

Verbal Communication

Anne Kerry was walking to the bank in her San Francisco neighborhood when she ran into Scott, an old college friend, accompanied by another young man. "Anne," he said warmly, "I want you to meet my partner, Bryan." Anne was surprised—she had not realized that Scott was gay. She asked, "How long have you two been together?" Both men looked at her quizzically before they realized what she was thinking. "No," said Scott, "I became a police officer. Bryan and I work patrol together." "I was embarrassed," said Anne. "I didn't mean to misunderstand their relationship. I just figured that 'partner' meant love interest."

Like many words in the English language, *partner* has a variety of definitions and can give rise to ambiguity: Is the person you introduce with this term a business colleague, someone you play tennis with, or your "significant other"? Like Anne, many of us immediately jump to this definition: "Half of a couple who live together or who are habitual companions." People of all sexualities might use the term to reveal their committed state, particularly when they feel that they have outgrown the term *boyfriend* or *girlfriend,* or are unwilling to use the terms *husband* and *wife.* Yet some consider the use of "partner" a cowardly way to avoid revealing their sexuality in conversation (Qvist, 2013).

The labels we choose for our relationships have a huge impact on our communication. That is why some wedded gays and lesbians avoid the term *partner.* When Bob Buckley's partner, Marty Scott, needed medical treatment, Buckley was able to call him "my husband" and was immediately allowed to stay with Scott. Spouses are afforded this privilege, while partners are not (Jones, 2005).

chapter outcomes

After you have finished reading this chapter, you will be able to

- Describe the power of language — the system of symbols we use to think about and communicate our experiences and feelings

- Identify the ways language works to help people communicate — the five functional communication competencies

- Describe the ways that communicators create meaning with language

- Label problematic uses of language and their remedies

- Describe how language reflects, builds on, and determines the situational, relational, cultural and mediated context

As our opening vignette shows, the names used to describe our connections with others have power. This is true for all kinds of relationships. For example, calling your father "Dad" reveals less formality in your relationship than calling him "Father." In a stepfamily situation, calling your father's wife "Mom" indicates more closeness than using her first name. Choosing words can get complicated. That is why we dedicate this chapter to studying verbal communication, the way we communicate with language. **Language** is the system of symbols (words) that we use to think about and communicate experiences and feelings. Language is also governed by grammatical rules and is influenced by contexts.

Of course, nonverbal behaviors — pauses, tone of voice, and body movements — accompany the words we speak. Thus they are an integral part of our communication, and we examine them in Chapter 5. But we now focus on the nature of language, its functions, how it creates meaning, problems with language, and contexts that influence our use of language.

The Nature of Language

When thirteen-year-old "Genie" was discovered in California, the "wild child" had been chained in a small room with no toys and little food for nearly her entire life. Her abusive father gave her no hugs, no loving words, and no conversation. As a result, Genie never developed language. Medical doctors, linguists, and psychologists worked intensely with Genie for over seven years, hoping to give the girl a chance at life in a community with others. But despite their efforts, Genie never learned more than a few hundred words and was never able to form sentences of more than two or three words (Pines, 1997; "Secret," 1997). Genie's sad story highlights the complex nature of language: someone with Genie's background will never fully grasp that language is symbolic with multiple meanings, is informed by our thoughts, and is ruled by grammar. We explore the nature of language in this section.

Language Is Symbolic

What comes to mind when you see the word *cat*? A furry childhood best friend? Fits of sneezing from allergies? Either way, the word evokes a response because it is a *symbol,* a sign representing persons, ideas, or things. Words evoke particular responses because speakers of that language share meaning of the words (Davies, 2009). Thus when you share a common language, you can use words to communicate ideas and thoughts about particular subjects. Moreover, using words as symbols is a uniquely human ability (Wade, 2010).

Learning to use symbols appropriately is important to the development of self (Butler & Fitzgerald, 2010) and to later success with communication (Hirsh-Pasek et al., 2015). Thus families who have discussions around the dinner table are not only helping their children to develop healthy self-concepts, but also enabling them to use language successfully in later years.

Thought Informs Language

Jamal Henderson is applying to colleges. He keeps his father, Michael, involved in the process because he values his opinion. They both agree that Jamal should attend a "good college." But Michael feels hurt when Jamal starts talking seriously about urban universities in another state. He thinks his son has ruled out his own alma mater, the local campus of the state university system. Jamal and

Michael have different thoughts about what a "good college" is. Their language and thoughts are related in their own minds, and each thinks he is using the term appropriately.

Your **cognitive language** is the system of symbols you use to describe people, things, and situations in your mind. It influences your language (Giles & Wiemann, 1987) and is related to your thoughts, attitudes, and the society in which you live (Bradac & Giles, 2005). Michael may think a "good college" is close to home, is involved in the local community, and offers small class sizes. Meanwhile, Jamal may think a "good college" presents the opportunity to participate in research, go to football games, and study with people from other countries.

Our thinking affects the language we use—and the language we use influences our thoughts. If you tell yourself that a coworker is an "idiot," the word may influence your future impressions of him. If he is quiet during a meeting, you might conclude that he is ignorant about the subject under discussion, whereas if you see him as a "thinker," you may conclude that he is carefully evaluating the situation before speaking.

On a much larger scale, we can have visceral reactions to the words or names assigned to people and places. For example, children assigned linguistically low-status names (like Alekzandra instead of Alexandra) tend to be treated differently by teachers, are more likely to be referred for special education, and are less likely to be perceived as gifted (Rochman, 2011). Indeed, the city of Stalingrad in Russia was renamed Volgograd because of the strong, negative reaction to the name associated with the violent dictator, Joseph Stalin (Roth, 2013).

Language Is Ruled by Grammar

If you are a fantasy or science-fiction fan, you know that the language in today's video games and television must be more than the alien gibberish of old. It must have complete structures that consistently make sense. So Hollywood hires "conlangers"—people who construct new languages with complete grammatical structures that are spoken by Dothraki in the HBO series *Game of Thrones*, for example, or by BB-8 in *Star Wars* (Chozick, 2011). In case you were wondering, the droid BB-8's beeps and whistles are actually voiced by a human (Malara, 2015).

As your third-grade teacher likely told you, **grammar**—the system of rules for creating words, phrases, and sentences in a particular language—is important. Although good grammar does not always equal good communication, using correct grammar helps you communicate clearly. Because grammar has *phonological rules* governing how words should be pronounced (to-MAY-to versus to-MAH-to), others may not understand you if they do not recognize the pronunciation.

Similarly, grammar has *syntactic rules* guiding the placement of words in a sentence. If you shuffle the words in the sentence "I ran to the store to buy some milk" to "Store I to milk to ran the buy some," your meaning becomes unclear. Grammatical rules differ among languages. Native speakers of English, for example, must remember that the grammar of Romance languages (such as French and Spanish) requires a different syntax. In English, adjectives typically precede a noun ("I have an intelligent dog"), whereas in Spanish, adjectives follow the noun (*"Tengo un perro inteligente,"* literally translated as "I have a dog intelligent"). To communicate clearly in Spanish, an English speaker must adjust.

Excellent grammar on its own will not automatically make you an outstanding communicator. Telling your professor in perfect English that her style of dress is a sorry flashback to the 1980s is still offensive and inappropriate. Competent communicators must keep in mind the consequences of words as they see how they work, or *function*.

and you?

Have you ever found yourself in a situation where you are entirely sure that you are using a term precisely ("a good restaurant," "a fun party," "an affordable car") only to have someone wholeheartedly disagree? How did you handle this language challenge?

connect

As you learn in Chapter 14, it is important for speakers to choose clear and appropriate language when planning a speech. If your terms are confusing or inappropriate for the speaking occasion, your audience will quickly lose interest in what you are saying. This is true whether you are attempting to inform or persuade your listeners or even speaking in honor of a special occasion.

● WE LEARN HOW TO USE LANGUAGE at a young age from our family and peers as well as from television and other media. Elie Bernager/Getty Images

connect

Using language as an instrument of control is part of our *self-presentation*, discussed in Chapter 3. When you are on a job interview, you will want to use clear, professional language that highlights your skills (see Chapter 12). Similarly, when delivering a speech (see Chapter 15), your language should let your audience know that you are engaged with and informed about your topic.

The Functions of Language

One of the first phrases that eighteen-month-old Josie learned to use was "thank you." Had this toddler already mastered the rules of etiquette? Was she just picking up a habit from her parents? Or was she learning that certain phrases would help her get things she wants: a compliment, a smile, a cookie?

We all learn isolated words and grammar as we acquire language. Josie, for example, probably picked up the expression "thank you" from her parents, her older brother, or her babysitter. But to become a competent communicator, she must learn to use this and other symbols appropriately. If Josie uses "thank you" as a name for her stuffed bear, she is not using it appropriately, so she is not communicating effectively. **Communication acquisition** is the process of learning individual words in a language as well as how to use that language *appropriately* and *effectively* in various contexts. Just as Josie gets a smile from her parents for saying "thank you," using language competently helps us to achieve our goals.

Researchers have identified five competencies (Wood, 1982) for how language behaviors function: controlling, informing, feeling, imagining, and ritualizing. We all develop these competencies when we are young by interacting with family and peers and observing television and other media. These competencies remain important throughout our lives. For that reason, we now look at them more closely.

Using Language as a Means of Control

Language can be used as an instrument of *control*, to exert influence over others and our environment. Josie's use of the phrase "thank you" impresses her mother, who reassures her that using the term makes her a "good girl." Such appropriate use of language can make children seem cute, smart, or polite, giving them the ability to present themselves in a positive light. Recall from Chapter 1 that *control* is actually a neutral term; it is a crucial social skill when used in a positive way. As an adult, Josie will be able to use language to control her environment by negotiating a pay raise or bargaining with a car dealer. However, she will also need to avoid negative control strategies, such as whining, ridiculing, insulting, threatening, or belittling, as these do not contribute to productive, successful communication.

For someone who has been hurt, speaking out—harnessing the power of language—can actually restore a sense of control. College campuses struggle with ways to help students approach sexual encounters clearly (the "yes means yes" laws) and to deal with times when language fails to curb unwanted behavior—such as when one defendant labeled the sex a "special experience" rather than the rape it was (Orbe, Johnson, Kauffman, & Cooke-Jackson, 2014). In these instances, it is important to give victims a voice to talk about the atrocities and connect with others; language begins to help them regain a feeling of control over their lives (Edwards, Bradshaw, & Hinsz, 2014).

Using Language to Share Information

Have you ever asked a sick child to tell you "where it hurts," only to receive a vague and unhelpful answer? This is because young children are still developing the next functional competency, **informing**—using language to give and receive information.

As an adult, if you have ever been asked for directions, you know that providing people with information that they can understand and understanding the information they are conveying to you are equally important skills.

There are four important aspects of informing: questioning, describing, reinforcing, and withholding.

▶ *Questioning* is something we learn at a young age and use throughout our lives. Young children hungry for information about their world quickly learn the power of the simple, one-word question "Why?"

▶ *Describing* helps us communicate our world to others. Parents and teachers may ask children to repeat directions to their school or their home or to detail the specifics of a story they have heard.

▶ *Reinforcing* information can help us become competent listeners. We might take notes or simply repeat the information to confirm our comprehension.

▶ *Withholding* information or opinions may be appropriate in some situations. For example, you may withhold your opposition to your manager's plan because you want to keep your job. Or you may elect not to reveal a piece of information that might embarrass a friend.

Together, these four skills form the basis of the informational competency that we use to communicate throughout our lives.

Using Language to Express Feelings

Poets, writers, and lyricists are celebrated for using language to capture and express emotions. But most expressions of feelings are less elaborately composed than a Shakespearean sonnet or an angry protest song. In everyday conversation and correspondence, we use language to send messages to others expressing how we feel about ourselves, them, or the situation. Young children can say, "I'm sad," or cry or laugh to communicate feelings. As you mature, you learn how to express a more complex set of emotions—liking, love, respect, empathy, hostility, and pride—and you may even intensify emotion by using words like *obsessed* rather than *love/like*

connect

As indicated, sometimes competent language use means knowing when to withhold information or avoid topics. This is particularly important when developing and maintaining interpersonal relationships (Chapter 8). For example, strategic topic avoidance allows you to steer the conversation away from discussing your friend's recent painful breakup until she is ready to discuss it.

● **WE'VE ALL BEEN THERE:**
A tourist asks you for directions and you mutter, "Um, yeah, you go a little bit up this way and turn around that way. . . ." Zero Creatives/Image Source/Getty Images

![connect]

Using language to express feelings competently can be a powerful addition to your communication skills in a variety of settings. In a small group (Chapter 10), you might need to express your frustration with the fact that you are doing most of the work. In an organization (Chapter 12), you might save your company time and money by effectively sharing your concerns about a project.

(Goodman, 2013). The functional competency of expressing **feeling** is primarily relational: you let people know how much you value (or do not value) them by the emotions you express.

We all use language to express our feelings; however, to be competent, we must do so appropriately and effectively. Many people do not communicate their emotions well. For example, Elliot expresses frustration with his staff by yelling at them; his staff responds by mocking Elliot at a local pub after work. Instead, Elliot could have said, "I'm *worried* that we're not going to make the deadline on this project"; someone on his staff could have said, "I'm feeling *tense* about making the deadline, too, but I'm also *confused* about why you yelled at me." Sometimes, appropriate and effective communication means avoiding expressing feelings that we consider inappropriate or risky in a given situation (Burleson, Holmstrom, & Gilstrap, 2005). For example, when Abby's boyfriend suggests sharing an apartment next semester, Abby changes the subject to avoid admitting that she is uncomfortable taking that step.

Using Language to Express Creativity

What do Wonder Woman, "Veep" Selina Meyer, and Sherlock Holmes have in common? Each is the product of the imagination of a writer or storyteller. And regardless of whether they were conceptualized as part of a novel, comic book, screenplay, or television series, each character and his or her story are primarily expressed through language.

Imagining is a complex functional competency. It is the ability to think, play, and be creative in communication. Children imagine by pretending to be a superhero. Adults create a song, script a play, and coordinate special effects in a film — these all stem from imagination. On the job, imagining is the ability to use language to convey a vision for a project to your coworkers (such as architects explaining blueprints and models). In a debate, imagining enables you to think ahead of your opponent, to put words to each side of an argument, and to use language in logical and convincing ways.

Using Language as Ritual

When little Josie says "thank you" for her cookie, it is a sign that she is learning the fifth functional competency: ritualizing. **Ritualizing** involves the rules for managing conversations and relationships. We begin learning these rules as children: peekaboo games require us to learn turn-taking in conversations. When we learn to say "hi" or "bye-bye" or "please," we internalize politeness rituals.

In adulthood, ritualizing effectively means saying and doing the "right" thing at weddings, funerals, dinners, athletic events, and other social gatherings. Simple exchanges, like telling a bride and groom "congratulations" or offering condolences to a grieving friend, are some ways we ritualize language. However, our ritualizing is not always that formal, nor is it limited to big events. In our everyday lives we use ritual comments

● **WHILE A TOAST** might be the perfect way to wish a couple happiness at their wedding, some people use this language ritual poorly by telling embarrassing stories or inappropriate jokes. Corina Marie Howell/ Getty Images

to support one another in relationships, such as, "Have a great day, Honey!," "You're going to nail that speech," or even just "I'll text you later."

Language and Meaning

Imagine three-year-old Damon sitting in a house of worship with his parents. He is having a great time banging his plastic dinosaurs around until his mother grabs them away during a silent part of the service. Clearly upset, Damon calls her a nasty name. His mother's face turns bright red, and she escorts Damon out to the car. Damon associated his language with the concept of being unhappy; he was upset about his mom taking his toys, so he said the same word he had probably heard a family member use when that person was unhappy with someone.

Semantics involves the relationships among symbols, objects, people, and concepts; it refers to the *meaning* that words have for people, either because of their definitions or their placement in a sentence. Damon had probably observed reactions to the use of the nasty name, so he thought it carried power. What Damon had not learned was **pragmatics**, the ability to use his culture's symbol systems appropriately. He may have gotten a few laughs by using the language in front of his family at home, but he did not realize the inappropriateness of saying the word in other contexts. When you acquire language, you learn semantics; however, when you learn *how* to use the verbal symbols of a culture *appropriately*, you learn pragmatics. Understanding semantic and pragmatic meaning is dependent on discovering the multiple meanings of words and identifying their varying levels of abstraction.

Words Have Multiple Meanings

As we saw at the beginning of this chapter, a single word like "partner" can have many meanings. A dictionary can help you find the **denotative meaning** of a word—its basic, consistently accepted definition. But to be a competent communicator, you will also need to consider a word's **connotative meaning**, people's emotional or attitudinal response to it. Consider the word *school*. It has several denotative meanings, including a building where education takes place and a large group of fish. But the word can also carry strong connotative meanings, based on your attitudes toward and experiences with school: it might bring back happy memories of class birthday parties in second grade or make you feel anxious about final exams.

Obviously, choosing words carefully is important. Not only must you make sure the denotative meaning is clear (using the word *ostentatious* with a bunch of six-year-olds is not going to help you explain anything), but you also have to

and you?

What connotative meanings does each of the following words have for you: *religion, divorce, money, exercise, travel, dancing, parenthood*? Why do you have that reaction to each word?

● **THE WORD *SCHOOL*** has multiple denotative meanings: it is not only the place where students learn but also a group of fish. (left) MaxyM/ Shutterstock; (right) Comstock Images/Getty Images

be aware of the possible connotative meanings of the words you use (Cann, Kempson, & Gregormichelaki, 2009; Degani & Tokowicz, 2010). Consider the words people might choose at a party to introduce the person to whom they are married. They could say, "I'd like you to meet my *wife*," or ". . . my *spouse*" (or my *bride*, *lady*, *better half*). These terms denotatively mean the same thing—their marital partner. But connotatively, they might generate very different reactions. *Spouse* may have a positive connotation in some situations, such as in legal paperwork or a gender-neutral invitation ("spouses welcome"). But in a personal introduction, it may come across negatively, as too formal and lacking affection. Connotative reactions also depend on the people you are speaking to and your relationship to them—the same word may make your friends laugh but anger your family members.

Subtle differences in word meaning can even change your entire interpretation of an event. For example, your grandfather offers to give you $10,000 if you graduate with honors from college. Is his offer a bribe, a reward, or an incentive? How you perceive and process his offer depends on the meaning associated with the language used. You may resent your grandfather if you consider the money a *bribe*, feel proud if you earn your *reward*, or feel motivated by the *incentive*.

Abstraction

Language operates at many levels of abstraction, ranging from very vague to very specific. You might talk in such broad, vague terms that no one knows what you are staying ("Stuff is cool!"), or you can speak so specifically that people may think you are keeping notes for a court case against them: "I saw you at 10:32 P.M. on Friday, January 29, at the right-hand corner table of Harry's Bar with a six-foot-tall, brown-haired man wearing black jeans, boots, and a powder blue T-shirt."

The **abstraction ladder** (Hayakawa, 1964) illustrates the specific versus general levels of abstraction (see Figure 4.1). The top rungs of the ladder are high-level abstractions: these are the most general and vague. Lower-level abstractions

FIGURE 4.1

THE ABSTRACTION LADDER

Higher

ABSTRACTIONS

"You're useless."

"You never help out around the house."

"You keep forgetting to do your chores."

"The trash wasn't emptied last night, and it's your job to do that."

"I noticed you didn't take out the trash in the kitchen, the bathroom, or the bedroom. You agreed that taking out the trash every Monday and Thursday evening would be your job."

Lower

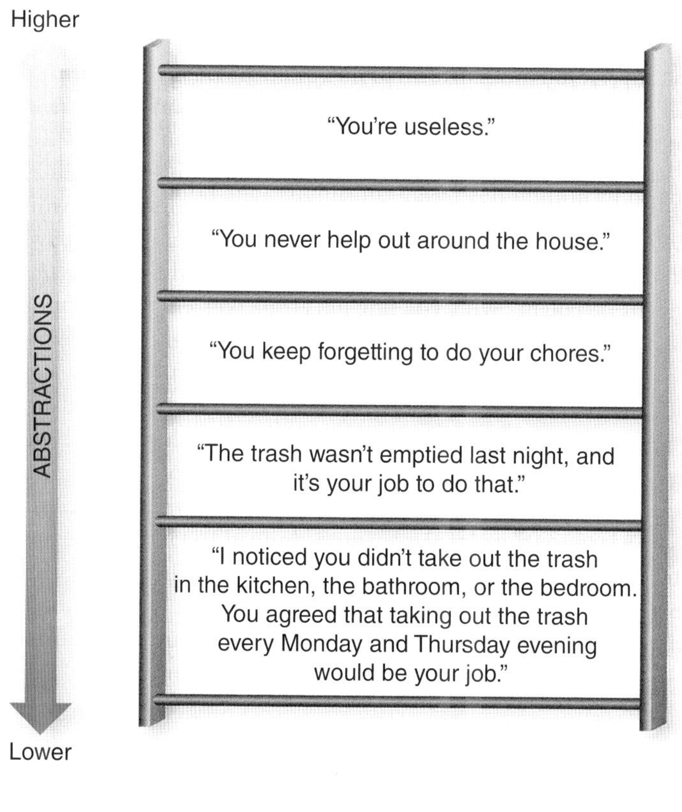

are more specific and can help you understand more precisely what people mean. "Let's watch something interesting on Netflix" is a high abstraction that allows a wide range of choices (and the possibility of some really bad movies). Saying, "I'd like to watch a historical drama tonight" (lower abstraction) is more likely to get you something you will enjoy, whereas naming the exact movie ("Let's watch *La La Land*") ensures satisfaction.

Although lower abstractions ensure clarity, high abstractions can accomplish certain communication goals. Here are a few examples:

▶ *Evasion.* Avoiding specific details is **evasion**—sometimes referred to as *lies of omission*. A teenager might tell her parents that she is "going *out* with *some friends*" rather than "going to a party at Nell's house with Fernanda, Justin, and Derek."

▶ *Equivocation.* **Equivocation** involves purposely using words that can be interpreted in multiple ways. These deliberately ambiguous terms can help us get out of an uncomfortable situation, as when a friend asks what you think of her new sweater — which you think is hideous — and you reply, "It's . . . *colorful.*"

▶ *Euphemisms.* **Euphemisms** are words or phrases with neutral or positive connotations that we use to substitute for terms that might be perceived as upsetting. For example, you might say that your uncle "passed on" rather than "died" or that your mother had a "procedure" rather than an "operation."

Problematic Uses of Language

"I think we're still in a muddle with our language, because once you get words and a spoken language it gets harder to communicate" (Ewalt, 2005). The famous primatologist Jane Goodall made this point when explaining why chimpanzees get over their disputes much faster than humans. They strike out at each other and then offer each other reassuring pats or embraces, and voilà, argument over. Not so with people: words can be really hard to forget.

As you have probably experienced, words can lead to confusion, hurt feelings, misunderstandings, and anger when we blurt things out before considering them (and their effects) carefully (Miller & Roloff, 2007). We sometimes engage in hurtful or hateful language, use labels in ways that others do not appreciate, reveal bias through our words, and use offensive or coarse language. And when we put thoughtless or hastily chosen words in emails or post them on Twitter or Facebook, they become permanent, and we may have great difficulty taking them back (Riordan & Kreuz, 2010).

Hateful and Hurtful Language

When Leonard Nimoy, the beloved Spock of *Star Trek* fame, died, the Westboro Baptist Church announced their intent to picket his funeral. They used offensive picket signs, such as "AIDS is God's curse." They associated Nimoy with other *Star Trek* stars who are openly gay (George Takei and Zachary Quinto) and "God-hating" (William Shatner, according to the WBC). Such language that offends, threatens, or insults a person or group based on race, religion, gender, culture, sexual orientation or other identifiable characteristics is **hate speech** (Waltman & Haas, 2011). Hate speech employs offensive words to deride the person or group, creating vividly negative images of groups in the minds of listeners while downplaying the unique qualities of individuals in those groups (Haas, 2012).

Other language choices may not be intended to offend individuals based on cultural factors but are nonetheless hurtful. For example, do sports fans have the right to jeer at the opposing team? Should they be allowed to yell at referees throughout the game? Although these behaviors are not technically against the law, they have communication effects and are often considered **hurtful language** — inappropriate, damaging, mean, sarcastic, or offensive (and many times untrue) statements that affect others in negative ways (Slagle, 2009).

Labeling

The literal definition of the term *feminist* is "an advocate for social, political, legal, and economic rights for women equal to those of men" (Dictionary.com). But who are these people who label themselves feminists? In our years of teaching undergraduates, we have heard plenty of students note that feminists are women who hate men and care only about professional success. But "there is no way to tell what a feminist 'looks' like. Feminists are young, old, women, men, feminine or masculine, and of varying ethnicities" (McClanahan, 2006). Feminists also hail from different religious backgrounds. When a group of Spanish Muslims approached city officials in Barcelona, Spain, about sponsoring a conference on Islamic feminism, one official responded with shock, noting that "Islamic feminism" must surely be a contradiction or an oxymoron (Nomani, 2005).

Labeling attaches a word or words to someone or some concept. The U.S. Department of Justice has recognized that labels such as "felon" and "convict" create vivid negative images in the mind of the listener that make it difficult for the persons to overcome. So they have decided to use "person who committed a crime" or a "person who was incarcerated" instead (*The New York Times* editorial, 2016). When we relegate everything about a person to a label like "felon," we lose the uniqueness of the individual person, we justify our detachment from him or her, and we reinforce our own in-group power by using negative terms for those labeled as in the out-group (Ruscher, 2001).

What these examples reveal is that the labels we choose for our beliefs affect how we communicate them to others (and how others respond). When we place gender, ethnic, class, occupation, or role labels on others, we ignore their individual differences (Sarich & Miele, 2004) and thus limit or constrict our communication. So if you think all feminists are liberal, secular, career-oriented women, you may miss out on the opportunity to understand the feminist views of your aunt, who is a stay-at-home mom, or your male neighbor, who is a conservative Jew.

and you?

Are you a feminist? What does the term *feminist* mean to you? If you hear someone called a feminist, what ideas or images come to mind?

● **WHAT DOES A FEMINIST** look like? Stereotypes may cause you to believe that the professional woman on the left is a feminist. But the woman on the right, Mukhtar Mai, is a feminist, too. A devout Muslim, she also supports and champions Pakistani rape victims. (left) Fuse/Getty Images; (right) RIZWAN TABASSUM/Getty Images

Biased Language

Some language is infused with subtle meanings that imply that a person or subject should be perceived in a particular way. This is known as **biased language**. For example, addressing an older person as "Sweetie" or "Dear" can be belittling, even if kindly intended (Leland, 2008). In particular, older individuals struggling with dementia are sensitive to language that implies that they are childlike ("Did you eat your dinner like a good boy?"), because they are struggling to maintain their dignity (Williams, Herman, Gajewski, & Wilson, 2009). In addition, there are many derogatory terms for women who engage in casual sex, though men who engage in similar behaviors in similar situations are afforded less derogatory labels (she is "easy"; he is a "player"). Such biased language perpetuates perceptions of women as less intelligent, less mentally healthy, and less competent than men in similar relationships or situations (Conley, 2011; Jacobs, 2012).

Your own biased position is often reflected in the language you use. For example, advocates for and against a state bill that would allow nurse practitioners, certified nurse midwives, and physical assistants to perform first-trimester aspiration abortions all argued for the "protection of women." Pro-life advocates wanted to protect the health of women against the imputed interests of the "abortion industry," while pro-choice advocates wanted to protect women against the interests of the "medical research industry" (Jesudason & Weitz, 2015).

Using biased language can also affect others' perceptions of you. For example, if you employ the vague "those guys" to describe coworkers in another department or a group of teens hanging out at the mall, others will likely see you as more biased than people who use concrete terms (e.g., "the attorneys in the legal department" or "the high school students at FroYo"; Assilaméhou & Testé, 2013).

When language openly excludes certain groups or implies something negative about them, we often attempt to replace the biased language with more neutral terms, employing what is known as **politically correct language**. For example,

connect

The federal government and organizations take derogatory labels that hurt and demean others quite seriously. Professional organizations typically provide employees with information regarding their *harassment* and *sexual harassment* policies, which are intended to protect employees from feeling threatened or attacked because of their race, religion, abilities, or other personal traits. We discuss this important issue in Chapter 12.

and you?

Has anyone ever labeled you in a way that truly irritated or offended you? What terms did they use? Are you aware of any biased language that frequently seeps into conversations among your friends, family, or coworkers? How might you address such biases?

---

evaluating communication ethics

Résumé Language

You have just graduated and are on the hunt for an entry-level position in marketing. You know that your résumé is strong in terms of your degree, relevant coursework, and good grades, but you are a bit worried that you may not have enough real-world experience. Since you had to work full time to pay college expenses, you could not afford to take the kinds of unpaid internships that look so impressive on a résumé; you waited tables all through college instead and graduated in five years instead of four.

You discuss these concerns with a friend who suggests making some changes in the language of your résumé. She suggests changing your entry date for college to make it look like you finished the degree in four years; that you cast your restaurant experience as a type of marketing internship in which you developed "people skills" and "sales skills" that helped you "analyze and synthesize" consumers and products; and, finally, that you use your cover letter to describe yourself as "a hard worker" with "proven creativity."

You are worried that some aspects of your résumé might not be impressive enough; however, you are not entirely sure that padding your résumé with vague language is the way to go. What will you do?

think about this

1. Is it crucial that an employer know how long it took you to earn your B.A.? Is it unethical to simply note the date you finished it?

2. Will you follow your friend's suggestion to use vague expressions like having "people skills"? How might you use more precise terms to describe yourself?

3. Rather than dressing it up as "marketing experience," how might you honestly use your restaurant experience to your advantage here?

the terms *firefighter*, *police officer*, and *chairperson* replace the sexist terms *fireman*, *policeman*, and *chairman*, reflecting and perhaps influencing the fact that these once male-dominated positions are now open to women as well. Critics of political correctness argue that such attempts at sensitivity and neutrality can undermine communication, as they substitute vague euphemisms for clarity when dealing with difficult subjects and place certain words off-limits (O'Neill, 2011). For example, calling someone "visually impaired" instead of "blind" may sound nicer, but it also is not clear about the severity of the person's lack of sight and may even suggest that there is some "shame" in being blind if we cannot speak of it openly. But others note that there is value in trying to be sensitive when we make choices regarding language.

Profanity and Civility

Comedians curse and audiences laugh; perhaps you have a relative who adds colorful words to his or her stories, which amuses your family members ("That's Uncle Mike for you!"). This was not the case for A. J. Clemente, who cursed on air during his first day as a broadcaster for the North Dakota NBC affiliate, KFYR. Clemente was ultimately fired despite apologies and excuses (Grossman, 2013) and never got another job in broadcasting. Recent years have seen an increase in swearing over mediated channels (Butler & Fitzgerald, 2011); some critics believe that public outrage over sex, violence, and profanity seems to have waned in recent decades (Steinberg, 2010). But another young producer/broadcaster, Van Tieu, learned a valuable lesson from Clemente: profanity in even a small market like Bismarck, North Dakota, was seen worldwide and not forgiven (Eck, 2016).

Profanity involves cursing (swearing) and other expressions considered taboo, rude, vulgar, or disrespectful. Such words get their social and emotional impact from the culture and can be perceived positively, neutrally, or negatively (Johnson, 2012) based on factors like the social setting (e.g., friends at home watching televised sports) or the relationship. For example, cursing in the workplace is not always perceived as negative if it could be expected under the circumstances, such as when everyone else does it or there is a great deal of job stress (Johnson, 2012). Additionally, students are not offended when their professors swear if they see the swearing as humorous, showing frustration, or emphasizing or elaborating on points (Generous, Frei, & Houser, 2015).

Regardless of whether profanity is viewed as rude, it should meet some standards of **civility**, the social norm for appropriate behavior. Crude, offensive, vulgar, and profane language can create uncomfortable and unproductive relationships and work environments (Johnson & Lewis, 2010).

● EVEN THOUGH HBO'S *LAST WEEK TONIGHT* can include lots of profanity from host John Oliver, the language is appropriate for the audience members who choose that media context. Frederick M. Brown/Getty Images

There are many ethical reasons to avoid using the problematic words summarized above, but you are probably thinking of situations from your own life that involve potentially problematic words in non-problematic ways. We are not telling you to boycott *Last Week Tonight*, the late-night talk and news satire program on HBO that involves lots of profanity, labeling of political and business groups, derogatory quotes, and even a sham religious organization (Our Lady of Perpetual Exemption); host John Oliver's behavior can be seen as alternately rude and hilarious. The news satire context — and the late-night audience — determine suitability. As we see next, our language choices should be monitored and made appropriate to the relational, cultural, and situational context.

Language Is Bound by Context

Imagine a scenario in which your cousin prattles on about her wild spring break in Miami. Now imagine that she is talking to your eighty-year-old grandmother . . . at your niece's fifth birthday party . . . in front of a group of devoutly religious family members. These contrasting scenarios illustrate how language is bound by contexts, such as the situation we are in, our relationship with the people present, the group identities of the participants, and the cultural factors at play. Does Grandma really want to hear about your cousin's behavior? Is it really OK to talk about this at a little kid's party? What about respecting the beliefs and sensibilities of your family members?

Communication accommodation theory (CAT) explains how language and identity shape communication in various contexts. CAT argues that competent communicators adjust their language (and also nonverbal behaviors, which we discuss in the next chapter) to the person, group, and context (Giles, Coupland, & Coupland, 1991; Shepherd, Giles, & LePoire, 2001; Soliz & Giles, 2010). Recent research also focuses on how people fail to accommodate or reluctantly accommodate in certain contexts, each choice impacting the effectiveness of their communication (Soliz & Giles, 2014). Context is particularly important to our study of language in three ways: language reflects, builds on, and determines context.

▶ *Language reflects context.* The language we use reflects who we are around, where we are, and what sort of cultural factors are at play—that is, the context we are in. In different contexts, we use different **speech repertoires** or "codes" — sets of complex language styles, behaviors, and skills that we have learned. For example, your professor probably has a "scholarly" speech style (useful when speaking about research with other academics) as well as a "teacher" language (useful when explaining concepts to undergraduates). When your professor talks to her students and shifts from her scholarly way of speaking to her teaching style, she is engaging in **code switching**, a type of accommodation in which communicators change from one repertoire or "code" to another as the situation or group warrants. Having several speech repertoires at our disposal allows us to choose the most effective and appropriate way of speaking for a given relationship, situation, group or cultural environment.

▶ *Language builds on context.* At the beginning of this chapter, we wondered about the difference between calling your stepmother "Mom" and calling her by her first name. It is an example of language building on context. If your stepmother raised you and is your primary maternal figure, you might well call her "Mom." But if your relationship with her is strained, you are close to your own biological or adopted mother, or your stepmother entered your life once you were an adult, you may prefer to call her Angie. As you develop relationships, you learn how people prefer to be addressed (and how you are comfortable addressing them) and adjust your language accordingly.

▶ *Language determines context.* We can also *create* context by the language we use. If your professor says, "Call me Veronica," one context is created (informal, first-name basis). If she says, "I'm Dr. Esquivel," you will likely have expectations for a more formal context. This influences your choice of speech repertoires—you are more likely to tell "Veronica" about your weekend plans than "Dr. Esquivel."

With these points in mind, let's consider how language works in different situations, in our relationships, in our groups, and in our cultures, as well as in mediated settings.

and you?

Consider the various situations you find yourself in over the course of a given day — at home, in the classroom, at a student activity, on the job, and so on. Do you have different speech repertoires for each situation? Does your language change further depending on who is present — your mother, your best friend, your professor?

Situational Context

Different situations (being at a job interview, in a court of law, or at your uncle's sixtieth birthday party) call for different speech repertoires. If you speak both English and Spanish, for example, you might speak English in the classroom or on the job but switch to Spanish with your family at home because it creates a special bond between family members (Gudykunst, 2004). With your friends on Instagram, it might even be "Spanglish."

You may also adapt your linguistic style to employ the particular slang, jargon, or grammar that fits a unique situation. These language accommodations may be ways to survive, manage defensiveness, manage identity, or signal power or status in different situations (Dragojevic, Giles, & Watson, 2013). For instance, police officers may adopt the street slang or foreign phrases used by citizens in the neighborhoods they patrol but use more formal, bureaucratic language when interacting with superiors, filling out reports, or testifying in court.

Similarly, you might decide to use **high language**—a more formal, polite, or "mainstream" language—in business contexts, in the classroom, and in formal social gatherings (as when trying to impress the parents of your new romantic interest). However, you would probably switch to more informal, easygoing **low language** (often involving slang, which we'll discuss later in the chapter) when you are in more casual or comfortable environments, such as watching a football game at a sports bar with your friends.

Our sex and gender can interact with the situation to affect our language use (Palomares, 2012). For example, women and men adapt their language use to

communication across cultures

Teaching Twain

It is considered a classic of American literature, a truly groundbreaking novel that thumbed its nose at convention when it was published in 1885 and continues to challenge ideas about race, relationships, and language more than a century later.

At a time when slavery was still fresh in American memory, Mark Twain's *The Adventures of Huckleberry Finn* told the story, in everyday language, of the unlikely relationship between a free-spirited white boy named Huck and a fugitive slave, Jim. Twain authentically constructed Jim and Huck's conversations, including their use of the "N-word."

Scholars and critics continue to argue about Twain's characters, as *The Adventures of Huckleberry Finn* is often banned or challenged by parents or school boards. One public school administrator called it "racist trash," saying its use of the N-word is offensive, no matter what the context or how teachers try to explain it (Howard, 2004). Yet others came to the book's defense, noting Twain's intention was "to subvert, not reinforce, racism" (Kennedy, 2003). One professor noted that the word must be seen in the context of the times and situation: "What was Twain supposed to do, call them African-Americans?" (Rabinowitz, 1995).

Teachers of American literature often find themselves struggling with self-censorship as they grapple with whether to speak the word aloud in class, since it may cause students to feel hurt and offended. One professor went so far as to create a revised edition of the work, replacing the N-word with the word *slave* to get students away from obsessing about it and to just let the stories stand alone (Bosman, 2011). But critics accuse the professor and publisher of censorship and sanitizing history. They call changing Twain's carefully chosen words to suit contemporary mores and eliminate hurt feelings "an abdication of a teacher's responsibility to illuminate and guide students through an unfamiliar and perhaps difficult text" (Nelson, 2011).

think about this

1. What meaning does the N-word carry for you? Does it seem appropriate to use it in a scholarly discussion? How do you feel about it being printed (or not printed) in this textbook? Does avoiding printing or saying the word give it more or less power?

2. If an instructor chose to use the word in class, how might he or she do so in a way that would be sensitive to students? Can students investigate the word's meaning and history without using it?

3. What is your opinion on the new edition? Are the editorial changes sensitive and helpful, or do they sanitize history?

same-sex versus mixed-sex situations. When women speak with other women, they tend to discuss relationships and use words that are more affection oriented (concerned with feelings, values, and attitudes). Men chatting with other men use more instrumentally oriented language (concerned with doing things and accomplishing tasks; Reis, 1998). Gender also comes into play in workplace situations. Occupations that have been traditionally defined as "masculine" or "feminine" often develop a job culture and language that follow suit. Male nursery school teachers (a traditionally "feminine job") and fathers doing primary childcare may use feminine language at work; female police officers (a traditionally "masculine" job) may adopt more masculine language on patrol (Winter & Pauwels, 2006).

● **THE FORMAL, HIGH LANGUAGE** that this young woman employs while at work with her colleagues differs from the more casual, low language that she probably uses when relaxing at home or socializing with friends. Ronnie Kaufman/Larry Hirshowitz/Getty Images

Remember that competent communicators should use the most effective and appropriate language in any given situation. That may mean putting aside gendered speech "appropriate" for our sex. For instance, a successful male manager uses language that reflects liking and respect when building relationships in the workplace, and a successful female manager uses direct language to clarify instructions for completing an important task (Bates, 1988).

Relational Context

Singer Beyoncé's "visual album" *Lemonade* (aired on HBO) is "an entire album of emotional discord and marital meltdown, from the world's most famous celebrity" (Sheffield, 2016). Her songs about betrayal and infidelity chronicle her relationship with husband Jay-Z. On the positive side, the language celebrates relationships with family and the "Lemonade Squad" of other black women seated on a front porch in solidarity with her (Mock, 2016). The words of *Lemonade* ring true because they reflect the positive and negative aspects of relationships. Beyoncé shows us how language can both reflect and create the relational context. Let's consider some examples.

Michelle and Chris have been dating for a few weeks. After a movie one night, they run into one of Chris's colleagues. When Chris introduces Michelle as his *girlfriend*, Michelle is surprised. She had not thought of their relationship as being that serious yet. The English language allows us to communicate the status of many of our relationships quite clearly: mother, brother, aunt, grandfather, daughter, and so on. But, as with the word *partner*, the language we use when communicating about other types of relationships can be confusing. Chris and Michelle are in the somewhat undefined state of "dating." When Chris uses the term *girlfriend* as a label for Michelle, this implies a more defined level of intimacy that Michelle is not yet sure she feels. Chris certainly had other options, but each has its own issues. For example, if Chris had said that Michelle is a *friend*, it might have implied a lack of romantic interest (and might have hurt Michelle's feelings). The English language has very few terms to describe the different levels of intimacy we have with friends and romantic partners (Bradac, 1983; Stollen & White, 2004).

● **IN BEYONCÉ'S LEMONADE** album, she sings about the ups and downs of relationships. Kevin Mazur/Getty Images

connect

The language we use in different relationships is often affected by unique *communication climates* or atmospheres that encompass relationships. This is certainly true when experiencing interpersonal conflict (Chapter 9). For example, if you and your brother experience a *supportive climate*, your conflicts will likely be characterized by careful, considerate words and an openness to hearing each other's thoughts.

Labels can also confer status and create understandings between and among individuals. If you say, "I'd like you to meet my boss, Edward Sanchez," you are describing both Mr. Sanchez's status and the professional relationship that you have with him; it tells others what language is appropriate in front of him. To indicate a more casual relationship, you might introduce him as, "Ed—we work together at Kohl's."

Cultural Context

Throughout this book, we remind you about the relationship between culture and communication (particularly in Chapter 6). Next we examine particular aspects of how the cultural context shapes our language, including the relationship among culture, words, and thoughts; the relationship between gender and language; and the impact of our region (where we grew up or where we live now) on our verbal choices.

Culture, Words, and Thought

Our language use may affect the way we think about the world. For years, researchers believed that if a culture did not have words for concepts, they would not be able to think about them in ways that other cultures could (Biever, 2004).

wired for communication

Speaking in Code

There is a large contingent of educators and parents who think the key to securing a good-paying job after college lies with learning a foreign language. Envisioning a future in which China leads the world's economy, they push school boards to teach Mandarin or enroll their children in extracurricular immersion courses (McDonald, 2012). But what if there were another language just as likely to lead to fruitful employment, one that applied to just about every existing and emerging industry that not only could be taught in schools but also learned at home for little cost? And what if that language, already in use around the world, was based primarily on English?

That language — well, technically, *those languages*, since there are many — is computer code. Code essentially refers to the directions given to a computer to make it do what you want it to do. The apps you use to play games on your phone, the programs that issue your credit card bill each month, the tools that small businesses use to manage supply chains and payroll, even the sensor that dings in your car when you forget to buckle up, all run on code. In every industry, from information tech to communications, manufacturing to agriculture, and food service to shipping, computers and code play a role. The most popular computer languages (like Ruby, Python, and C++) are "spoken" in just about every technologically advanced country, even though these languages are, by and large, based on English language keywords. Coding is not just for engineers or engineering majors. It is a skill that will benefit anyone in just about any job. *Huffington Post* CTO John Pavley points out that even for nontech types, coding can open doors to satisfying work. "[N]on-technical people can learn to code, which will open doors to better jobs and a richer understanding of the rapidly changing world around us" (Pavley, 2013).

Pavley likens the divide between those who can and cannot code to the low levels of literacy during the Dark Ages, when the written word, along with the power it conferred, was the provenance of only a small elite. Some even suggest making learning code an educational requirement along the lines of, or even in place of, a foreign language (Koerner, 2013). Multilingual education may take on a whole new meaning.

think about this

1. In communication terms, what kind of code is *code*? Is it a language like English or Mandarin?

2. Should schools require students to learn code the same way most schools require them to learn a foreign language?

3. Is the dominance of English in the programming world significant?

4. Consider your envisioned field of study and the career you hope to pursue after college. Do you think coding would be helpful for you?

The **Sapir-Whorf hypothesis** (also known as linguistic relativity theory), held that the words a culture uses (or does not use) influence the thinking (or lack of it) among people from that culture (Sapir & Whorf, 1956). But more recent investigations of languages and culture contradict this hypothesis; for example, the Herero people of southwest Africa use the same word for green and blue but have no difficulty distinguishing a green leaf from the blue sky (McWhorter, 2014). It seems that languages develop in response to the environment, efficiently capturing what is necessary to talk about to communicate effectively—but we do not have to have a word for something in order to think about it (Regier, Carstensen, & Kemp, 2016).

Our language may be connected to our thoughts, but probably in a different way from what Sapir-Whorf imagined. For example, have you ever tried to translate a joke from one language to another? It may end up not being funny because the wordplay does not quite work, or the circumstances do not relate very well in both cultures. Our words are tied to cultural concepts. These concepts may even play out in a language's grammar. Some languages (like Spanish, French, and German) assign a gender to objects. This is a bit of a foreign concept to many native speakers of English because English is gender neutral—English speakers simply say *the shoe*, whereas a Spanish speaker marks the word as masculine (*el zapato, el* being the masculine article); a French speaker marks the word as feminine (*la chaussure, la* being the feminine article). Marking an object as masculine or feminine changes a speaker's *mental picture* of the object. For example, German speakers describe a key (a masculine word in German) in traditionally masculine terms (*hard, heavy, jagged, metal, serrated,* and *useful*) whereas Spanish speakers describe a key (a feminine word in Spanish) in traditionally feminine terms (*golden, intricate, little, lovely, shiny,* and *tiny*; Wasserman & Weseley, 2009).

real communicator

NAME: Matt Burgess
OCCUPATION: Author and Creative Writing Instructor
Courtesy Matt Burgess

It took me a long time to find my voice. I went to college in New England, where I felt pressure to talk and write in a certain way, to employ more sophisticated terminology — like "employ" and "terminology." Between semesters, when I went back home to Jackson Heights, Queens, I felt the opposite pressure: to swallow all those high-diction words and spit game like I always had.

It was a no-win situation. Wherever I was, I felt inauthentic, as if I were hiding a vital part of myself. And that was especially hard when I first started writing fiction. So I split myself: my third-person stories were written in an academic register, which I mistakenly thought was more authorial; and my first-person stories were written so casually, in such a low-diction, that the characters lacked the complexity and intelligence of the people back at home I was trying to write about.

My problem was that I kept thinking I could only express myself using one voice at a time. But my voice is many voices: the classroom voice; the playground voice; the voice I use to speak to my friends, colleagues, students, and wife. Once I embraced the best parts of all of those voices, my writing became more vivid, more personal, and a whole lot more fun to create.

Since leaving college, I've published two novels (you should totally go buy them!). I've left Queens, too, and live in Minneapolis, where I teach creative writing in colleges, libraries, prisons, and literary centers. My main goal is to help students find their own unique voice(s) as writers, so that they can express themselves accurately, precisely, and genuinely. My journey with language has been deeply rewarding to me and continues to enrich my life. I hope that my readers and students will be able to say the same.

● **SKATEBOARDERS HAVE** their own jargon for their fancy flips and tricks. If you are not a skateboarder, an "ollie" might be a foreign concept. Michael Sharkey/Getty Images

and you?

What kinds of slang or jargon do you regularly use? How did you become familiar with these terms? And how would you go about explaining these terms to someone who is unfamiliar with them?

connect

Gendered language often affects mixed-sex small-group settings. Women are typically encouraged to build rapport, using affectionate language to keep the peace and share power (see Chapters 3 and 10). Men are rewarded for taking charge of a group and using direct, action-oriented language. Competent communicators must be aware of these differences in style in order to promote group communication that encourages all members to share and challenge ideas to achieve group goals.

Group Membership

Language also informs others about your affiliations and memberships. For example, **slang** is language that is informal, nonstandard, and usually particular to a specific age or social group; it operates as a high-level abstraction because its meanings are known only by its users during a specific time in history. A rock concert might be described as "wild," "awesome," or "lit"—each expression places the speaker in a particular time or place in the world. Teenagers might alert each other online that they have "GTG" (got to go) because of "POS" (parent over shoulder), and their parents are none the wiser. Slang is often intensified by adjectives that increase emphasis, such as *absolutely, completely, extremely, totally, wickedly,* or *massively* (Palacios Martínez & Núñez Pertejo, 2012). Slang evolves and changes over time, with some words disappearing and others enduring—a clear contradiction of the concept of language as static and uniform (Stamper, 2014).

Language can be used to strengthen group identity and shape relationships between the group and the individuals in those groups (Stubbe, 2012). Norms develop for what types of language (compliments, insults, etc.) are appropriate to the group (Hogg & Giles, 2012). By communicating group expectancies, group members are drawn together. When in-group members use aggressive language about out-group members, research finds it enhances the in-group identity and fosters intergroup competition (Burgers, Buekeboom, & Peters, 2015).

Another type of group language is **jargon**, technical language that is specific to members of a given profession or activity or hobby group. Jargon may seem abstract and vague to those outside the group but conveys clear and precise meanings to those within the group. For example, when a fan of the model game Warhammer 40K speaks of "kit bashing," other fans understand that the speaker is taking parts from two different models and mixing them together. The rest of us, however, would probably just stare blankly. Engineers, car mechanics, bakers, construction workers—even communication professors—use jargon that allows them to communicate clearly with those in their profession or group.

Some groups also engage in **gossip**—talk or rumor usually about the personal or private affairs of others. While often hurtful if spreading lies, and often thought of as a detestable character flaw, gossip has a positive side to it, too. Gossip can promote cooperation in groups by self-regulating; by talking behind each other's backs, members identify the cooperative types and ostracize the selfish ones (Feinberg, Willer, & Schultz, 2014). Some even call gossip a social skill. If we avoid gossip entirely, we are often socially isolated; however, by gossiping, we signal trust of the other by sharing secrets and developing rapport with and influence over others in the group (McAndrew & Dudley, 2016).

Gender and Language

Cultural factors deeply affect our thinking and perception of gender roles, which are often inscribed with "different languages" for the masculine and the feminine (Gudykunst & Ting-Toomey, 1988). The relationship of language differences to gender is both complex and tenuous when we also consider transgender individuals (Hancock, Stutts, & Bass, 2015), and thus the distinctions are not as pronounced as was found in the original research. Nonetheless, the idea that men and women speak entirely different languages remains popular fodder for comedy, talk shows, and pop psychologists, so let's identify what actual differences have contributed to that view.

Research has shown that women primarily see conversations as negotiations for closeness and connection with others, whereas men experience talk more as a struggle for control, independence, and hierarchy (Tannen, 1992). But either may use powerful, controlling language to define limits, authority, and relationships and less controlling language to express affection (Park et al., 2016). Let's look at a few examples.

▶ *Interruptions.* Male speakers are thought to interrupt others in conversation more than female speakers, but the situation and the status of the speakers are better predictors than biological sex (Pearson, Turner, & Todd-Mancillas, 1991). For example, female professors can be expected to interrupt male students more often than those male students interrupt female professors, owing to the difference in power and status. But when status and situation are neutral, men tend to interrupt women considerably more often than women interrupt men (Ivy & Backlund, 2004).

▶ *Intensifiers.* Women's speech patterns, compared with men's, contain more words that heighten or intensify topics: "so excited," "*very* happy" (Yaguchi, Iyeiri, & Baba, 2010). Consider the intensity level of "I'm upset" versus "I'm *really* upset."

▶ *Qualifiers, hedges, and disclaimers.* Language that sounds hesitant is perceived as being less powerful (often associated with women's speech). *Qualifiers* include terms like *kind of, sort of, maybe,* and *possibly. Hedges* are expressions such as "I think," "I feel," or "I guess." *Disclaimers* discount what you are about to say and can head off confrontation or avoid embarrassment: "I'm likely imagining things, but I thought I saw . . ." (Palomares, 2009).

▶ *Tag questions.* Another sign of hesitancy or uncertainty associated with traditionally feminine speech is the *tag question,* as in "That waitress was obnoxious, wasn't she?" Tag questions attempt to get your conversational partner to agree with you, establishing a connection based on similar opinions. They can also come across as threats (Ivy & Backlund, 2004); for example, "You're not going to smoke another cigarette, *are you?*"

▶ *Resistance messages.* There are differences in the way men and women express resistance in certain situations. On the job, women in positions of power use language similar to that of men in those positions. But in lower power positions, women use more indirect language to resist taking on more work—"I'm not sure I have time" rather than "No, I can't manage that now" (Primecz, Mahadevan, & Romani, 2016). In dating situations, women may resist sex by choosing vague or evasive language ("I don't have protection") over a direct *no* to save the feelings for their partner (Muehlenhard, Humphreys, Jozkowski, & Peterson, 2016). Both men and women need to evaluate the directness of their resistance messages (and those of others) to clarify meanings and intentions.

In summary, research has corroborated some differences in communication style due to sex (Kiesling, 1998), but many of those differences pale when we consider *gender* (the cultural meaning of sex), context, role, and task (Ewald, 2010; Mulac, Wiemann, Widenmann, & Gibson, 1988; Newman, Groom, Handelman, & Pennebaker, 2008). Additionally, studying language from a sex-difference approach can be misleading, because it treats women (and men) as a homogenous "global category," paying little attention to differences in ethnicity, religion, sexuality, and economic status (Crawford, 1995). In fact, recent studies focus on how we present our different "faces" in interaction (Tannen, 2009, 2010) and how language choices are more about negotiating influence (power, hierarchy), solidarity (connection, intimacy), value formation, and identity rather than about sex (Tannen, Kendall, & Gorgon, 2007). Decades of research find that we are less bound by our sex than we are by the language choices we make. Thus, regardless of whether we are male or female, we can choose to use language that gives us more influence or creates more connection—or both.

and you?

What are your personal thoughts on sex, gender, and language? Do you think men and women speak different languages? How do your thoughts and opinions match up with the research we have cited in this chapter?

● **IS THIS A SUB** or a hoagie? Perhaps a hero or just a plain old sandwich? StockFood GmbH/Alamy

and you?

Think back to where you grew up — whether in the United States or abroad. Are there any terms that you use that would cause confusion to others? Have you ever been in a situation where you have used a regional term that caused an embarrassing miscommunication?

Geography

Our editor from New Jersey assures us that even in such a small state, it makes a big difference if you are from North Jersey or South Jersey. (The status of people from the middle part of the state remains unclear, at least to us.) People in North Jersey eat subs (sandwiches that you buy at 7-Eleven or QuickChek) and Italian ice (a frozen dessert). The night before Halloween, when shaving cream and toilet paper abound, is Goosey Night or Cabbage Night. And "the city" is, of course, New York City. On the other hand, people from South Jersey eat hoagies (typically from a convenience store called Wawa) and water ice. The night before Halloween is Mischief Night. And going to "the city" means taking a trip to Philadelphia. (For the record, in the Bay Area of California, "the city" is San Francisco.)

As this example illustrates, even for speakers of the same language who grow up just fifty miles apart, local geography affects their language and their understanding of the world. Other examples are more extreme. Consider our friend Ada, who kindly shared an embarrassing moment with us (and is allowing us to tell you). When she came to the United States from Hong Kong, she knew she had to give up some of her Britishisms to communicate more effectively with her American-born classmates at Wesleyan University. This was never more apparent than when she asked a classmate for a rubber (to correct some mistakes in her notebook). She wanted an eraser; he thought she was asking for a condom. Needless to say, she was a bit perplexed by his response: "Maybe after class?"

Mediated Contexts

Have you ever sent an email or a text message that was misunderstood by the recipient? It has happened to all of us — and that is often because our emails, text messages, tweets, and other postings lack the nonverbal cues and hints we provide in face-to-face conversation. So if you text your spouse to say that you both have to spend Friday night with your slightly quirky Aunt Ethel, and he texts you back "Great," is he really excited? Is he being sarcastic? "Great" could mean either thing, but you cannot see his nonverbal reaction to know if he is smiling or grimacing and rolling his eyes. Communication in mediated contexts must be extra clear to be effective (DeAndrea & Walther, 2011) — a reason why many people now accompany their texts by some emoji to clarify the meaning. In addition, the speed and ease of using technology may change our language. For example, the ability to immediately tweet your thoughts and feelings from your smartphone may lead you to use more egocentric language (focused on the self rather than taking others' viewpoints) than if you are emailing, posting, or blogging over other electronic media (Murthy, Bowman, Gross, & McGarry, 2015).

Other characteristics of our online language can also influence communication. For example, people in computer-mediated groups who use powerful language, such as direct statements of their personal goals, are seen as more credible, attractive, and persuasive than those who use tentative language (hedges, disclaimers, and tag questions) (Adkins & Brashers, 1995). However, group-oriented language can be more persuasive and effective than language pushing personal goals. For example, one study of an international adolescent online forum found that students who were elected as "leaders" made references to group goals and synthesized other students' posts (Cassell, Huffaker, Tversky, & Ferriman, 2006).

Interestingly, sex and gender can influence the language you use with technology. In online games, for example, people who were assigned avatars of their own gender were more likely to use gender-typical language (more emotional expressions and tentative language if assigned a feminine avatar) than those assigned mismatched avatars (Palomares & Lee, 2010). Another study found that people infer a person's sex from language cues online (e.g., amount of self-disclosure, expression of emotion) and conform more to computer-mediated partners when they believe them to be male (Lee, 2007). And, in a sad parallel to gender language norms in face-to-face settings, a study of sexting among adolescents found that girls were judged negatively whether they sexted (e.g., "slut") or not (e.g., "prude"; Lippman & Campbell, 2014).

Technology affects language use in a broader way, too, when we see the proliferation of English as the language of the internet. Individuals in Salt Lake City, São Paulo, and Stockholm can all communicate digitally, often in English. Critics often claim that because English dominates the mass media industries, English speakers' values and thinking are being imposed on the non-English-speaking world. Nevertheless, many non-Western countries have benefited from this proliferation, with countless jobs being relocated to places like India and Hong Kong (Friedman, 2007). Every day brings increasing language diversity to the internet, and internet-based translators make it much easier to translate material into innumerable languages (Danet & Herring, 2007).

Despite the controversies surrounding English, the internet, and mass media, technology has, in some sense, created a language of its own. The language of text messaging and chat rooms frequently relies on acronyms (e.g., IMO for "in my opinion"), some of which people use in other contexts and some of which has even made it into the *Oxford English Dictionary* (Editorial, 2011). Acronyms are useful in texting because they enable rapid keystroking, yet their use has declined as new text applications fill in suggested words for us — even though we may be frustrated by "autocorrect" (Tagliamonte, 2016). These developments have resulted in speed of texting that makes this "fingered speech" more like spoken language (McWhorter, 2013). However, it is important to keep text language in its appropriate context. If your professor writes you an email asking about your recent absences from class, it is probably not a good idea to respond with "NOYB, IMHO" ("none of your business, in my humble opinion"). That would show not only a lack of respect for your instructor (obviously) but also a lack of understanding regarding context. Email etiquette calls for more complete sentences.

● **TEXTING YOUR FRIEND** "Coffee?" is a perfect way to schedule a quick get-together; however, if you are asking your professor to meet over a cup for career advice, it would be smart to send a more formal email. Blend Images/Veer

what about you?

Beliefs About Talk

As you have seen in this chapter, individuals value language as a way to gain control in conversations, share information, express feelings, be creative, and so on. Others, however, are more comfortable with fewer words, even silence.

Complete the following questionnaire about your own beliefs about talking and language use and rate the frequency that you engage in each behavior. Use the following scale: 5 = almost always; 4 = frequently; 3 = sometimes; 2 = not very often; and 1 = rarely. Then add up your scores and consider where you fall on the following continuum.

_____ 1. I enjoy meeting and talking with people.

_____ 2. In general, I consider myself quite a talker.

_____ 3. I do not mind initiating conversations with strangers.

_____ 4. I like to voice my opinion.

_____ 5. In general, I enjoy talking.

_____ 6. I enjoy small talk.

_____ 7. I like people who talk a lot.

_____ 8. When talking, I find myself trying to influence others' opinions and feelings.

_____ 9. I believe talk is one way to increase intimacy.

_____ 10. Small talk is an enjoyable use of time.

_____ 11. I do not mind taking responsibility for breaking the ice when meeting someone for the first time.

_____ 12. I talk more when I feel I am in control of a situation.

_____ 13. I feel uncomfortable with silences in a conversation.

_____ 14. In general, I like to be the first one to speak in a discussion.

_____ 15. I feel comfortable asking a stranger for information.

_____ 16. When in a discussion, I talk even if I am unfamiliar with the topic.

_____ 17. I enjoy going out to meet and talk with people.

_____ 18. I find myself turning on the radio or TV just to hear the sound of someone's voice.

67–90: You enjoy and value talk and are not apprehensive about talking; you see talking as a social experience and, as a rule, you are uncomfortable with silence.

43–66: You have a more measured approach to talk, using it to accomplish goals and meet the norms of the situation. You are comfortable with silence and more likely to adjust your rate of talking to that of your partner or partners.

18–42: You do not enjoy a lot of talk and prefer to use it with a purpose in mind. Silence is comfortable for you and you do not rush to fill it with words.

Note: Different cultures value talk in different ways (see Chapter 5), so it might be important for you to adapt your use of language or silence according to the situation. In addition, competent communicators remember that being appropriate and effective means talking up at times, being sociable with talk, but also knowing when to be quiet and let others talk.

Information from J. M. Honeycutt & J. M. Wiemann (1999); J. M. Wiemann, V. Chen, & H. Giles (1986).

back to ▶ Our Partners

Our discussion of the word *partner* and its various meanings showed that the labels we choose are powerful — and can complicate our communication.

▶ The word *partner* has several denotative meanings, as we discussed earlier. But it can also have powerful connotative meanings. Let's look at romantic couples who choose the term *partner*. When some people hear an individual refer to his or her "partner," they may assume the individual is gay or lesbian. And they may have positive, negative, or neutral reactions based on their cultural background. Others may wonder if the individual is trying to hide his or her marital or legal status. Still others may see *partner* as a term that marks equality in romantic relationships.

▶ Abstraction plays a role in the use of the term *partner*. If you introduce Cheryl as, "This is my partner," you have used a high-level abstraction, keeping your status and relationship vague. But if you introduce her as, "This is my business partner at 'Gardens for You,'" you have used a lower-level abstraction, clarifying the relationship at a specific company.

▶ Considering the relational, situational, and cultural context is one way to make the term *partner* less abstract and vague. If you let your chemistry professor know that your "partner" needs some help, the situational context allows your instructor to understand that you mean your lab partner rather than your romantic partner or the person you play tennis with. But consider the cultural context when introducing the love of your life to your elderly great-aunt. You might want to use a less ambiguous term, because your great-aunt may be of a generation that did not use the term *partner* to apply to a love interest.

things to try ▶ Activities

macmillan learning

1. LaunchPad for *Real Communication* offers key term videos and encourages self-assessment through adaptive quizzing. Go to **launchpadworks.com** to get access to:

✓ LearningCurve
Adaptive Quizzes.

▶ Video clips that illustrate key concepts, highlighted in teal in the Real Reference section that follows.

2. Take a look at a piece of writing you have produced (an essay, your résumé, or a private Facebook message to a friend). Do you use high or low levels of abstraction? Is your choice of language appropriate for the communication contexts involved? (For example, is your essay written in a way that is mindful of your relationship with your professor and the academic setting?)

3. Describe the similarities and differences you find in the language you use and the language a close friend or family member of the opposite sex uses over the course

of a single conversation. What did you notice? Were there any misunderstandings or power struggles in this conversation? How do your findings match up with what the research we presented tells us?

4. Examine the language you use in mediated communication. Are there subtle ways in which you and your communication partners negotiate influence and create connectedness? Are any language choices related to sex or gender? What differences do you find in the language you use in mediated contexts from the language you use in face-to-face contexts?

5. Make a study of your Facebook (or other social networking) pages. Compile a list of the types of language used, including acronyms. Do you ever misunderstand the language in posts from your friends? Have you ever used language that was misinterpreted? Are you ever offended by the posts or "shares" of your friends? Describe how you could post in the future to avoid problems due to language.

real reference ➤ A Study Tool

Now that you have finished reading this chapter, you can:

Describe the power of **language**—the system of symbols we use to think about and communicate experiences and feelings:

▶ Words are symbols that have meanings agreed to by speakers of a language (p. 80).
▶ **Cognitive language** is what you use to describe people, things, and situations in your mind (p. 81).
▶ **Correct grammar**, the rules of a language, helps ensure clarity (p. 81).
▶ Acquiring language and learning to use it effectively is the process of **communication acquisition** (p. 82).

Identify how language helps people communicate—the five functional communication competencies:

▶ As an instrument of **control** (p. 82).
▶ For **informing**, including four aspects: questioning, describing, reinforcing, and withholding (p. 83).
▶ For expressing **feelings** to let people know how we value them (p. 84).
▶ For **imagining**, communicating a creative idea (p. 84).
▶ For **ritualizing**, managing conversations and relationships (p. 84).

Describe the ways that communicators create meaning with language:

▶ **Semantics** refers to the meaning that words have; **pragmatics** refers to the ability to use them appropriately (p. 85).
▶ A **denotative meaning** is the accepted definition of a word; its **connotative meaning** is the emotional or attitudinal response to it (p. 85).
▶ The **abstraction ladder** ranks communication from specific, which ensures clarity, to general and vague (p. 86).
▶ Some communication situations may call for abstractions: **evasion**, avoiding specifics; **equivocation**, using unclear terms; or **euphemisms**, using substitutions for possibly upsetting terms (p. 87).

Label problematic uses of language and their remedies:

▶ **Hate speech** is language that offends, threatens, or insults a person or group based on race, color, gender, or other identifiable characteristics (p. 87), whereas **hurtful language** includes words or expressions that are considered inappropriate, pretentious, damaging, mean, sarcastic, or offensive to others (p. 88).

▶ **Labeling** ignores individual differences by using terms that stereotype people according to their group membership (p. 88).

▶ **Biased language** has subtle meanings that influence perception negatively (pp. 89–90); using **politically correct language** attempts to meet culturally appropriate norms (p. 89).

▶ **Profanity** involves expressions that are considered insulting, rude, vulgar, or disrespectful (p. 90).

▶ **Civility** involves language that meets socially appropriate norms (p. 90).

▶ **Communication accommodation theory** illustrates how people adapt their language and nonverbal behaviors to the person, group, or context (p. 91).

Describe how language reflects, builds on, and determines the situational, relational, cultural and mediated context:

▶ Different **speech repertoires** use the most effective language for a given situation (p. 91).

▶ Communicators change from one repertoire or "code" to another through **code switching** (p. 91).

▶ **High language** is the more formal, polite, or "mainstream" language, whereas **low language** is more informal and often involves slang (p. 92).

▶ The **Sapir-Whorf hypothesis** suggests that our words determine how we see the world; thus, speakers of different languages have different views of the world. Recent research confirms that our thoughts are not restricted by language (p. 95).

▶ **Slang** is a group's informal language; **jargon** is a group's technical language (p. 96).

▶ **Gossip** is talk or rumor about personal affairs of others, and sometimes serves to solidify group membership (p. 96).

▶ Assuming gender differences in communication is misleading, but interruptions, intensifiers, qualifiers, hedges, disclaimers, tag questions, and resistance messages are linked with feminine versus masculine speech patterns (p. 97).

▶ The culture of the geographical area affects language (p. 98).

▶ Although communication technology has made English the dominant world language and has created a global society, the internet also continues to create a language of its own (p. 99).

Color, dress, tone of voice, clothing, body shape, and movement are just some of the nonverbal behaviors that communicate complex emotions in the animated characters Anger, Disgust, Joy, Fear, and Sadness.

 LearningCurve can help you master the material in this chapter.

Go to **launchpadworks.com.**

chapter

5

Nonverbal Communication

When director Pete Docter set out to make the Pixar hit *Inside Out* (Docter & Del Carmen, 2015), he did his homework. In telling the story of 11-year-old Riley, who is uprooted from her life in Minnesota to move with her family to San Francisco, Docter envisioned Riley's complex emotions and how she would communicate these verbally and nonverbally in her new surroundings. Docter turned to two professors who specialize in emotion and expression: Paul Ekman and Dacher Keltner (Keltner & Ekman, 2015).

Based on Keltner's belief that emotions are "the structure, the substance, of our interactions with other people," Docter created a "headquarters" of five emotions in Riley to capture the complexity of emotions and how they are expressed and interpreted in interactions with others. Docter shows how expressing emotions effectively—even sadness—helps us handle important life circumstances, like moves, developmental changes, and the demands of others (Judd, 2015).

Throughout the move experience, Riley's parents want her to be happy. When she understandably has trouble adjusting to the change, they often say, "Where's my happy girl?" The forced smile that Docter constructs on Riley's animated face is instantly understood by any of us who have been pushed to show an emotion that we do not feel. What we witness in Riley and the personification of her emotions is the rich complexity of nonverbal behaviors that contribute to our communication with others. The colors, movements, clothing and voices of Anger, Disgust, Fear, Sadness, and Joy all represent important elements of nonverbal communication.

chapter outcomes

After you have finished reading this chapter, you will be able to

- Describe the power of nonverbal communication

- Outline the functions of nonverbal communication

- Describe the set of communication symbols that are nonverbal codes

- Illustrate the influence of culture, technology, and situation on our nonverbal behavior

nimators like the team at Pixar face a daunting challenge. They must make inhuman objects — whether a computer-generated "person" like Riley or the emotions, monsters, and imaginary friends in her mind — into believable, humanlike characters who can effectively communicate complex information and emotions both verbally and nonverbally.

In this chapter, we examine **nonverbal communication** — the process of intentionally or unintentionally signaling meaning through behavior other than words (Knapp & Hall, 2010). Nonverbal communication encompasses a variety of actions, such as gestures, tone of voice, and eye behavior, as well as all aspects of physical appearance. We begin by examining the nature and functions of nonverbal communication. Then we move to the nonverbal codes that convey messages without words and conclude with an examination of important influences on nonverbal communication.

The Nature of Nonverbal Communication

A deaf woman signs a message to a companion. A colleague writes a note to you on a pad of paper during a boring meeting. A man taps his watch to signal to a friend that it is almost time for lunch. In all three instances, communication occurs without a word being spoken. But not all of all these examples are actually nonverbal communication. Studying the essential nature of nonverbal communication reveals why.

Nonverbal Behavior Is Communicative

You communicate nonverbally when you convey a message without using any words. But you also communicate nonverbally when you use nonverbal behaviors *in addition* to words: when you smile, frown, or gesture as you speak or when you use a particular tone or volume while talking (Giles & LePoire, 2006). For example, as a kid, maybe you knew when your parents were angry with you because they called you by your full name while using "that tone."

Consider the examples we gave above. American Sign Language (ASL), a visual language with its own grammatical structure used by hearing-impaired individuals in the United States and English-speaking Canada, is still verbal communication. It may be *nonvocal*, because the communicators do not use their voices. However, it is still a language, because it uses hand signals (rather than spoken words) as symbols and has grammatical rules. The note that your colleague writes to you uses words, so it too is a form of verbal communication (written rather than spoken). Only the third example is nonverbal communication — tapping a watch signals meaning without the use of linguistic symbols. Yet this example reminds us that nonverbal behavior and verbal communication are connected. Had the friends not made a verbal agreement to meet for lunch, the act of tapping the watch might be confusing.

Nonverbal Communication Can Be Intentional and Unintentional

The best poker players think a great deal about nonverbal communication. They know how to bluff, or convince their opponents that they are holding a better (or worse) hand than is actually the case. A player who figures out an opponent's "tell" — a nonverbal signal indicating a good or bad hand — can profit from this knowledge if he, quite literally, plays his cards right. Mike Caro, a poker professional

● **GIVING SOMEONE** a big hug is an example of nonverbal communication, but communicating with someone using American Sign Language is not. (left) Simon Baker/Getty Images; (right) AP Photo/Al Behrman

and author of *The Body Language of Poker*, warns players not to look at the cards as they are laid out on the table. Players who look away from "the flop" have a strong hand, he explains. Those who stare at it—or at their cards—have a weak one. He also advises players to memorize their hand so opponents will not see them looking at their cards and glean cues from this action (Zimbushka, 2008).

Like poker players, we often send nonverbal messages unintentionally—we roll our eyes, laugh, slouch, or blush without meaning to. Unintended nonverbal behaviors like these are called **leakage cues**—nonverbal messages that "leak" out without our control and give people signs of what we might be thinking or feeling. Such behaviors can send powerful, unintended messages without us having much time to think through them (Capella & Greene, 1982). Great poker players know that they cannot completely eliminate these unintentional behaviors. That is why many of them wear sunglasses while playing: they want to mask their eyes so their opponents cannot pick up subtle and unintentional cues from their eye movements.

We often give leakage cues great significance in our interpretations. One study of presidential debates, for example, found that when listeners fixated on inappropriate nonverbal behaviors (e.g., rapid eye movements, "dismissive" tone of voice), they judged the candidates more negatively and paid far less attention to the substance of their arguments (Gong & Bucy, 2016). The interpretation of both intentional and unintentional nonverbal messages is difficult, however, because nonverbal behaviors can have so many different meanings, as we see in the next section.

Nonverbal Communication Is Ambiguous

Professional players like Caro might have a system for reading nonverbal behaviors, even if they know that it is more of an art than a science. That is because nonverbal communication is inherently *ambiguous*. Blinking, stammering, or hesitations in speech can indicate deception. But they can also indicate anxiety or uncertainty. In many cases, you can pick up clues about the meaning of behavior from the situational context. If your friend is sighing deeply and blinking rapidly as she heads off to her biochemistry final exam, she is probably anxious. But you cannot know for sure. Perhaps her boyfriend broke up with her twenty minutes ago and she just does not feel like talking about it. For this reason, it is best to regard her nonverbal behavior (and poker "tells") as clues to be checked out rather than as facts.

connect

You make sense of your world and decode nonverbal behavior through *schemas*, your accumulated experience of people, roles, and situations (Chapter 3). So if you catch your friend in a lie, you might suspect, on the basis of your relational history, that whenever he avoids eye contact with you, he is lying. But competent communicators must think beyond schemas when determining the meaning of nonverbal communication.

● **DOES THIS CARD PLAYER** have a good or bad hand? Who knows? His poker face reveals nothing. Pablo Blazquez Dominguez/Getty Images

People Trust Nonverbal Communication More Than Verbal Communication

Imagine you are grabbing lunch with your brother, talking a mile a minute about your exciting plans for after graduation. He is staring off into space. You wonder if you are boring him. But when you look closer, you notice that his face is ashen, he is not making eye contact with you, and he has not shaved in a few days. You pause and ask, "Hey, is everything OK with you? You seem . . . not yourself." Your brother looks up, somewhat startled, tries to smile, and says, "What? Oh! Yes, everything's great."

You have just experienced **channel discrepancy**, a situation in which one channel of communication says one thing and another seems to say something different. In this case, your brother's *verbal* communication says he is fine, but his *nonverbal* communication says he is not fine at all. So which message do you believe? In most cases, you will believe the nonverbal message. Like most of us, you assume your brother's nonverbal behaviors are leakage cues that he has less control over, so they must be more "reliable" indicators of how he is really" feeling. Indeed, studies show that you tend to give more weight to nonverbal behavior than to verbal behavior when you (or others) express supposedly spontaneous feelings (e.g., crying), when you assess others' motives (e.g., deception), when you are trying to express rapport with others (e.g., show liking), and when there are few versus many observable behaviors (Burgoon, Blair, & Strom, 2008; Hullman, Goodnight, & Mougeotte, 2012; Knapp & Hall, 2010).

However, just because we tend to place more stock in nonverbal communication does not mean that we are correct in our interpretation. Your brother might be fine, just as he says he is. Perhaps he is growing a "playoff beard" along with the rest of his hockey team and is thinking about the next day's game rather than listening to you talk about your plans. Even when we know others very well, we often fail to detect deception or read their nonverbal behaviors accurately (Knapp & Hall, 2010; Van Swol, Malhotr, & Braun, 2012; Vrij, 2006).

Functions of Nonverbal Communication

Now that we have established the essential nature of nonverbal communication, we discuss how it helps us interact effectively in relationships. We highlight the most important ways that nonverbal behaviors work on their own—and in combination with verbal behaviors—to affect communication (Burgoon, Floyd, & Guerrero, 2010).

Reinforcing Verbal Messages

Nonverbal behavior clarifies meaning by reinforcing verbal messages in three ways: repeating, complementing, and accenting. **Repeating** mirrors the verbal message through a clear nonverbal cue that represents the exact same idea. For example, you hold up three fingers while saying "three" or shake your head at a toddler while saying, "No." You can also reinforce verbal messages with **complementing**, nonverbal behavior that is consistent with the verbal message and often enhances it. For example, when you pat a friend on the back while saying, "You did a great job," you reinforce the message that your friend has done well.

Nonverbal behaviors are also used for **accenting**—clarifying and emphasizing specific information—in a verbal message. For example, suppose you want your friend to meet you at a local pub at 6 P.M. You make eye contact, touch the friend lightly on the forearm, and vocally emphasize "the one on *Victoria Street.*"

Substituting for Verbal Messages

Nonverbal cues can substitute for words. For example, a traffic officer's outstretched palm substitutes for the word *stop.* **Substituting** is common in situations where words are unavailable (e.g., communicating with someone who speaks a different language) or when speaking aloud would be inappropriate (e.g., at the symphony or during a religious service). Substitution cues signal information you would rather not say aloud (raising your eyebrows at your partner to signal you want to leave a party) or help you communicate when you do not know the words to use (pointing to the location of pain to your doctor; Rowbotham, Holler, Lloyd, & Wearden, 2012). Nonverbal cues can at times even be more powerful than words, such as when a big hug shows more support for a sad friend than any words you can think of.

Sometimes you may nonverbally substitute silence for words. If your roommate is driving you nuts with her constant talking (while you are trying to write a paper), you may become silent and look away from her when she asks for your input on last night's episode of *Twin Peaks* (Giles, Coupland, & Wiemann, 1992). Silence may also be a sign of deference (e.g., you do not express your opinion because the other has higher status); it may also signal defiance (e.g., you refuse to answer someone who angers you; Ng & Ng, 2012).

● **WHEN A TRAFFIC COP** holds out one hand, you know to stop; she does not have to scream, "STOP!" to get the intended effect. © Sandy Felsenthal/Corbis/VCG/Getty Images

Contradicting Verbal Messages

Nonverbal communication functions to **contradict** the verbal when the behavioral cues convey the opposite of the verbal message. Sometimes this is unintentional, as when you say that you are not upset but clearly look angry. Other times, contradicting behavior is intentional. For instance, Caroline sighs deeply to get Andy to ask, "What's wrong?" She can keep Andy engaged by refusing to answer or by tersely stating, "Nothing." Although such tactics can get Andy's attention, they are manipulative because they take advantage of his concern in order to serve Caroline's selfish purposes.

Contradicting behavior is also part of what makes joking around, teasing, and the use of sarcasm so powerful. When you roll your eyes and say, "Wow, that was a captivating lecture," you let your classmate know that, despite your words, you found listening to your professor about as interesting as vacuuming. Contradicting behavior can work positively as well. For instance, your friend calls to your beloved dog, "Come here, you smelly, ugly little monster!" Your friend's smile, high-pitch tone, and open arms reveal that your friend really thinks your dog is adorable.

Managing and Regulating Interactions

Nonverbal cues are used to manage impressions and regulate interactions of communicators in a variety of relationships and situations (Cappella & Schreiber, 2006). This **interaction management** function occurs from the first time you meet someone and continues throughout the life span of your relationship. For

and you?

Think of a personal example of a failed attempt at sarcasm. What do you think caused this communication breakdown? How might it have been avoided?

● **A SMELLY,** ugly little monster? Certainly not. Courtesy Stacey Propps

and you?

Have you ever ignored what someone said because the person's nonverbal behavior seemed to contradict the verbal message? Were you able to determine if the nonverbal communication was accurate?

example, you dress professionally for a job interview; your smile, firm handshake, and friendly tone convey your sincerity as you say, "This sounds like a wonderful organization to work for." The hiring manager's smiles and nods—or frowns and silence—in turn influence your behaviors back to her (Keating, 2006). Should you get the job, your nonverbal behaviors help you manage a tense situation with your boss by keeping a respectful distance and lowering your tone of voice. Additionally, nonverbal behaviors (like smiles and eye contact) help you manage your ongoing, everyday interactions with coworkers.

Nonverbal cues help us coordinate verbal conversation—they **regulate** the back-and-forth flow of communication. For example, if you pause after saying, "Hello" when answering your phone, you are offering the person on the other end a chance to self-identify and explain the purpose of the call. Face to face, you may hold your hand up while speaking to signal that you do not want to be interrupted or gesture broadly to indicate continued excitement about your topic (Cutica & Bucciarelli, 2011). Additionally, raising your hand in a face-to-face classroom setting lets your professor know that you have a question or information to share.

Filled pauses (e.g., "um," "er,") and *discourse markers* (e.g., "you know," "like," "I mean") help control the conversation by maintaining the speaking role while you are thinking about what to say. Although these markers themselves are verbal (words), they are used with nonverbal changes in vocal tone and the rate and rhythm of speech. For example, you might say in a halting voice, "I really thought . . . um . . . I mean . . . you know . . . that it wasn't such a big deal." These hesitations and discourse markers may also be used with nonverbal behaviors in an effort to share or rephrase opinions to turn the floor over to others (Laserna, Seih, & Pennebaker, 2014). You may remark, "You know, I think, um, what you're saying is . . .?"; you stretch out the "is," look them in the eye, and raise your eyebrows to signal them to fill in the answer.

If conversations are not regulated smoothly, there can be negative consequences. For example, if you successfully interrupt others when they are speaking, you may gain influence, but they may like you less. On the other hand, if you allow interruptions, others may perceive you as less influential (Farley, 2008). Naturally, the situational context plays a role. It is more serious to interrupt (or be interrupted) during a debate or a business meeting, whereas some interruption is acceptable during casual conversations with friends. Matching your regulation behaviors to those of your partner makes interactions go smoothly (Schmidt, Morr, Fitzpatrick, & Richardson, 2012).

Creating Immediacy

Nonverbal communication can also create **immediacy**, a feeling of closeness, involvement, and warmth between people (Andersen, Guerrero, & Jones, 2006; Prager, 2000). Immediacy behaviors include sitting or standing close to another person, turning and leaning toward the individual, smiling, making eye contact, and touching appropriately (Andersen, 1998; Andersen, Guerrero, Buller, & Jorgensen, 1998). Even adding "smiley face" emoticons to your email messages has been found to increase perceptions of immediacy and liking (Yoo, 2007).

and you?

Imagine that you are listening to a friend tell a long story in a face-to-face setting. How might you use nonverbal behaviors to regulate the interaction to show that you are listening or that you would like to interject a comment?

Immediacy behaviors help you form and manage impressions: closeness, eye contact, smiling, and gestures like hugs or light touches tell your romantic partner, your family members, and your close friends that you love and care for them and that you want to be near them. And while we are more aware of, and responsive to, the positive emotions of others (Campos, Schoebi, Gonzaga, Gable, & Keltner, 2015), our nonverbal displays of compassion (e.g., looking, touching, facial expressions) contribute to perceptions of honest sympathy, caring, and involvement with the other (Stellar, Cohen, Oveis, & Keltner, 2015).

In the professional world, multiple studies find that physicians, nurses, and staff who engage in immediacy behaviors have patients who are less fearful of them and more satisfied with their medical care (Richmond, Smith, Heisel, & McCroskey, 2001; Wanzer, Booth-Butterfield, & Gruber, 2004). And if you are a supervisor at work, you can combine positive messages with immediacy behaviors to enhance your likability and credibility (Teven, 2007).

Deceiving Others

The Transportation Security Administration (TSA) was formed after the terrorist events of 9/11 to prevent such tragedy in the future. Some training programs for TSA agents have focused on extensive interviewing of suspicious travelers to uncover inconsistencies in their personal accounts (Ormerod & Dando, 2015), while others have concentrated on suspicious nonverbal behaviors of emotions (e.g., nervousness, fear) shown in the face, the voice, and bodily movements (Bond, 2007).

Deception is the attempt to convince others of something that is false (O'Hair & Cody, 1994). If we are being honest, we might all admit to occasionally engaging in forms of deception. Sometimes we deceive to protect others, as when you tell your friend that no one noticed her stained shirt. Other times, we deceive out of fear, as when victims of abuse blame their injuries on falls or accidents. However, deception can have malicious and self-serving motives, as in the person who tries to get your Social Security number and other personal data in order to commit identity theft.

You may be drawn in by a solicitor who sounds warm and friendly; however, it is more likely that you will look for the opposite type of behavior when trying to sniff out a liar (Canary, Cody, & Manusov, 2008). People who appear anxious, who avoid making eye contact, who blink frequently, or who have frequent and awkward body movements seem deceptive (Leal & Vrij, 2008). However, research shows that although these cues make us more suspicious, they do not actually make us more accurate at detecting deception (Van Swol, Braun, & Kolb, 2013). This is partly because "honest" or "dishonest" demeanor is often inconsistent with whether people are actually telling the truth or lying (Levine et al., 2011). Liars often appear anxious only if they are concerned about the lie or about getting caught (Canary, Cody, & Manusov, 2008). On the one hand, if the lie is unimportant, liars may instead be relaxed and controlled. On the other hand, someone accused of lying may show nonverbal or physiological signs of anxiety even if he or she is not guilty. This is one reason why so-called lie detectors (and the newer brain scans) are not reliable measures of deception (Kirchner, 2013).

Did you ever lie to your parents? Research shows that if you did, the relationship you have with them probably enabled you get away with it. Almost 60 percent of parents accurately detected the lies of their young children but were

● **TSA AGENTS** look for signs of deception among airline travelers. Bloomberg/Getty Images

what about you?

Nonverbal Immediacy Scale

The following statements describe the level of involvement, warmth, and closeness (immediacy) that some people attempt to achieve when communicating with others.

Please indicate in the space at the left of each item the degree to which you believe the statement applies to you in a given conversation with a stranger. Please use the following five-point scale: 1 = never; 2 = rarely; 3 = occasionally; 4 = often; and 5 = very often.

_____ 1. I use my hands and arms to gesture while talking to people.

_____ 2. I touch others on the shoulder or arm while talking to them.

_____ 3. I use an excited voice while talking to people.

_____ 4. I look at or toward others while talking to them.

_____ 5. I do not move away from others when they touch me while we are talking.

_____ 6. I have a relaxed body position when I talk to people.

_____ 7. I smile while talking to people.

_____ 8. I make eye contact while talking to people.

_____ 9. My facial expressions show others I care about the conversation.

_____ 10. I sit close to people while talking with them.

_____ 11. My voice is warm when I talk to people.

_____ 12. I use a variety of vocal expressions when I talk to people.

_____ 13. I lean slightly toward people when I talk with them.

_____ 14. I am animated when I talk to people.

_____ 15. I express myself through facial expressions when I talk with people.

_____ 16. I move closer to people when I talk to them.

_____ 17. I turn my body toward others during conversations.

_____ 18. I nod in response to others' assertions.

Add your scores for 1–18 here: _____

67–90: You communicate a high level of immediacy in your nonverbal behavior. However, be careful not to exceed the comfort level of others, particularly strangers (i.e., watch out for people who shrink back, look away, or have negative facial expressions, as you may be getting too close or touching too much).

43–66: You communicate immediacy in many situations. Your nonverbal expressions of interest and warmth are likely to make new people in your life more comfortable, too.

18–42: You do not communicate immediacy behaviors very often. Consider increasing your nonverbal immediacy behaviors to help you manage impressions and initiate more satisfying relationships.

Information from V. P. Richmond, J. C. McCroskey, & A. D. Johnson (2003).

less accurate as the children got older (Talwar, Renaud, & Conway, 2015). By the time children are in their teens, parents are overwhelmingly confident they can tell if their children are lying; however, the parents are notoriously bad at it (Evans, Bender, & Lee, 2016). Do their children get better at masking their deception as they get older? Perhaps, but the context of the relationship makes parents think their kids just would not be liars! **Truth-default theory** points out that such context is important, and that people also have a general tendency to believe others without suspecting deception (Levine, 2014). This truth-bias may work well for us in many circumstances (we hope that we have good reason to trust each other!), but it poses a challenge when we need to be able to recognize a liar. For those whose job it is to detect deception, such as law enforcement, communication researchers are investigating the complexities of deception across many contexts. Their goal is to develop perceptual tools to help the intelligence community better detect deception and prevent tragedies like those of 9/11 (Dunbar, Jensen, Tower, & Burgoon, 2014).

and you?

When you attempt to deceive others (e.g., telling a friend you like her new boyfriend when you do not), are you aware of your nonverbal messages (altering your tone of voice or changing your eye contact)? What types of nonverbal indications do you look for in others in order to figure out if they are telling the truth?

Nonverbal Communication Codes

The difference between life and death in the postapocalyptic world of AMC's *The Walking Dead* may well hinge on nonverbal communication. Rick Grimes and his band of survivors struggle to maintain their humanity in the zombie world, forming a family of sorts to pursue their salvation (Ambrosius & Valenzano, 2016). The clan's ability to notice the nonverbal changes in Rick's former partner, Shane, are key to determining whether he remains a fellow-survivor or has become a threat to the group. They recognize a number of different **nonverbal codes** — the various *types* of symbols we have at our disposal for sending nonverbal messages. For example, Shane's voice becomes hard and erratic, he stares off into space, he shaves his head, and he becomes disheveled in appearance. The clan's ability to intercept and decode these behavioral codes will determine their survival.

In this section, we categorize nonverbal behaviors into codes or types for simplicity and clarity of discussion. But, as you saw in the last section, nonverbal behaviors seldom communicate meaning in isolation; clusters of nonverbal behaviors (hugs, smiles, eye contact) function together to regulate behavior or convey immediacy. The codes we examine here are gestures and body movements, facial expressions, eye behavior, voice, physical appearance, space and environment, touch, and time.

Gestures and Body Movements

At the conclusion of almost any type of performance, like a play or concert, the artists signal the end by coming onstage for accolades. Some do a quick head bow, while others bend deeply from the waist. Some do a deep curtsy, while others throw kisses or lace their hands together prayerfully. Then there is the arm (or arms) thrown above the head or palms outstretched toward the audience. In some instances, the whole cast comes out hand in hand to emphasize their equality and teamwork (Kaufmann, 2016). You may have heard body movements like bows called "body language," but the way you move your body is not a language at all — bowing has no specific, consistently understood definition. **Kinesics** is the use of gestures and body movements. When Eva motions toward Jane to include her in a conversation, or Rodney walks into an interview standing tall to project confidence — these are kinesic behaviors. And when your body movements are synchronized with others, people cooperate more and like one another more — even babies (Cirelli, Einarson, & Trainor, 2014).

There are five main categories of gestures and body movements that convey meaning nonverbally: illustrators, regulators, emblems, adaptors, and affect displays (Ekman & Friesen, 1969).

connect

Kinesics is important when delivering a speech, as your body movements should support your words. For example, illustrators help clarify a point for your audience; confident posture reassures your listeners that you are prepared and organized. Certain adaptors (like yawning), however, can leave the audience with the impression that you are bored with your own speech. We discuss these issues in Chapter 15.

real communicator

NAME: Octavia Spencer
OCCUPATION: Academy Award–Winning Actress
Jason Merritt/Getty Images

I've always wanted to work in the film industry, though I never dreamed it would be in front of the camera. But in 1995, I got a small part opposite Sandra Bullock in the hit film *A Time to Kill*, and I was on my way. Since that time, I've had a number of roles on stage, screen, and television.

What I do want everyone reading this interview to realize is that my success is tied to a number of the topics you're studying right now — particularly nonverbal communication. For example, pretty much anyone can read a script out loud, but *how* you read it is what counts in this industry. The tone of voice, the timing, the pause that is just long enough to get people to look up and pay attention — these are the keys to getting (and staying) employed!

Vocal cues alone are incredibly important in acting. When I was the voice of "Minny" on the audio version of the book *The Help* (Kathryn Stockett's *New York Times* bestseller), I had to study the appropriate accents, timing, and inflections to make my performance truly authentic. Later, when I played the same role for the film, I realized just how much more meaning and feeling I was able to communicate when I could use facial expressions and body movements to express my character.

Most of my roles are comedic and, let me tell you, acting in comedies isn't a barrel of laughs. It's incredibly challenging work. Facial expressions in particular have to be appropriate and come at just the right moment (otherwise, they aren't at all funny). Often there are ten different facial expressions I have to produce in less than one minute to show surprise, hurt, outrage, confusion, acceptance, determination, confidence, liking, disgust, and pleasure. Oh, and it has to appear natural, too.

In addition, the way I tilt my head or hold my body changes the information I'm trying to convey. For example, I played Dr. Evilini, a witch with dual personalities, on *Wizards of Waverly Place*. As one personality, my head was bent, and my voice low pitched with a diabolical, screeching laugh. The other personality had a normal voice, and I kept my body erect, though my eyes were always wide with expression. Because the show's target audience was primarily comprised of children, every movement was exaggerated to ensure its comedic value.

At the end of the day, I am truly grateful to be doing something that I absolutely enjoy—and none of it would be possible without a close study of nonverbal communication.

Illustrators reinforce verbal messages and help visually explain what is being said. Holding your hands two feet apart while saying, "The fish was *this* big!" is an illustrator. Illustrators can also be used to increase influence in relationships, as when we emphasize our words with pointing or sketch a thought in the air (Dunbar & Burgoon, 2005).

Regulators help us manage our interactions and the flow of conversation. Raising your hand and lifting your head, for example, indicate that you want to speak or ask a question. Raising your eyebrows usually indicates you want information from others (Flecha-García, 2010). We may try to get someone to stop yelling at us by putting our fingers in our ears, and we may wave our hand in quick circles in order to get a colleague to hurry up and "get to the point" in her presentation.

Emblems are the one type of gesture for which there *is* usually a dictionary-like meaning among the particular group or culture who uses them. Examples in the United States include the "thumbs-up" and "okay" signs. Their meanings are so clear that they can easily substitute for words. Emblems for "yes," "no," and "I don't know" are similar across cultures, but the meanings of most emblems vary greatly from one culture to another (Matsumoto & Hwang, 2013); the index finger and thumb touching one another to mean "okay" in the United States might be a vulgar insult in another country.

Adaptors satisfy some physical or psychological need, such as rubbing your eyes when you are tired or twisting your hair when you are nervous or bored. Usually not conscious behaviors, adaptors are used to reduce bodily tension (like shifting in your seat), but may be interpreted as anxiety or deception by some. Because they may be more frequent when someone is stressed, impatient, or bored, they are often interpreted as indicators of negative feelings (Goss & O'Hair, 1988).

Affect displays are nonverbal gestures that convey positive and negative feelings, moods, and emotions. Clinching your teeth and hitting your fist on the table may indicate your anger or frustration; a fist thrust high in the air may indicate joy when your team scores a touchdown.

Facial Expressions

Gestures are one way to convey emotion, but our faces are another. Consider the character Spock, the half-Vulcan, half-human science officer from *Star Trek* who suppresses his emotions at all costs in the pursuit of pure logic. Actors who have played Spock had their human eyebrows replaced with artificial "Vulcan" ones; because Spock's eyebrows—and eye expressions in general—appear less human, his emotions seem less human, too.

As humans, we are wired to use our faces to indicate emotions (Fridlund & Russell, 2006). Although the reasons behind our facial expressions might be difficult to ascertain, several specific expressions are common across all cultures (Ekman & Friesen, 1971). A smile, for example, usually indicates happiness; a frown, sadness; raised eyebrows, surprise; and wrinkled eyebrows, concern (see Figure 5.1).

Blind children, who cannot learn to mimic facial movements through sight, exhibit sadness, anger, disgust, fear, interest, surprise, and happiness in the same way that sighted people exhibit these feelings (Eibl-Eibesfeldt, 1973). These seven primary facial expressions are thus considered inborn, whereas most other expressions are learned from our culture (Gagnon, Gosselin, Hudon-ven der Buhs, Larocque, & Milliard, 2010). There is some evidence that pride also may be a universally recognized emotion (Tracy & Robins, 2008). These expressions are recognized across cultures, with agreement across cultures about which expressions are the most intense (Ekman et al., 1987).

Although most people are fairly adept at deciphering these common expressions of emotion, they are not necessarily experts at decoding all facial expressions (Bavelas & Chovil, 2006). Emotional intelligence (EI) is the ability to be aware of, identify, and manage your own emotions and the emotions of others by regulating their intensity and applying them to situations involving not just yourself, but others as well (Goleman, 1995). People with higher EI have a greater ability to interpret facial emotion, especially when facial cues do not match verbal ones (Wojciechowski, Stolarski, & Matthews, 2014). Increasing EI proves helpful in a number of situations; for example, increasing EI among young offenders helps them recognize emotions in others from their facial expressions—resulting in a reduction in subsequent

● **EVEN WITH THOSE** Vulcan eyebrows, Spock portrays little emotion. © Paramount Pictures/Courtesy Everett Collection, Inc

CROSS-CULTURAL PRIMARY
FACIAL EXPRESSIONS Research
shows that these seven expressions
of emotion exist in all cultures and are
inborn.

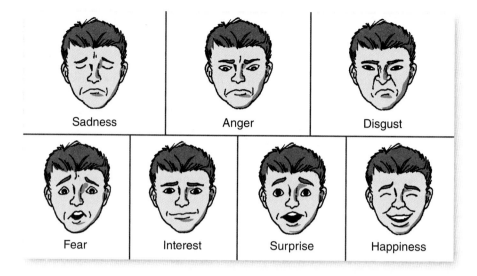

crimes (Hubble, Bower, Moore, & van Goozen, 2015). And there is evidence that reducing "screen time" (mobile phones, computers, etc.) for adolescents and having them instead interact face to face can improve their ability to read "real" people's facial expressions (Uhls et al., 2014).

Complicating our ability to accurately recognize facial expressions is the sheer number of expressions possible. The human face can produce more than a thousand different expressions (and as many as twenty thousand if you take into account all of the combinations of the different facial areas; Ekman, Friesen, & Ellsworth, 1972; Harrigan & Taing, 1997). Moreover, our emotions can be concealed by facial management techniques such as **masking**, when we consciously manipulate our faces to replace an expression that shows true feeling with one that shows the appropriate feeling for a given interaction. For example, you try your best to smile at customers at the restaurant where you work even though you are in a horrible mood and wish you were anywhere else (Richmond, McCroskey, & Payne, 1991).

Eye Behavior

Have you noticed your cereal box lately? If you have a Quaker Oats or Trix box handy, look at the man or cartoon rabbit gazing back at you. Researchers studying the eyes of cereal box characters found that making eye contact with even these nonhuman marketing figures inspires powerful feelings of connection—and subsequent sales (Musicus & Wansink, 2015). **Oculesics** is the study of the use of the eyes to communicate—and it is even more powerful when the communicators are both human.

Newborn infants (two to five days old) stare significantly longer at faces offering a direct gaze rather than an averted one. The babies orient themselves more often toward the face that makes eye contact with them. Babies as young as three months old smile less when adults avert their gaze, and begin smiling more when adults resume eye contact (Farroni, Csibra, Simion, & Johnson, 2002).

● **HAVE YOU EVER BOUGHT CEREAL** because you liked the character on the box? Making eye contact with even a cereal box character can make you feel connected. Kristoffer Tripplaar/ Sipa USA

There are some cultural variations in gazing with children. For example, European-American parents gaze more at their children, especially mothers with their sons, while Mexican-American parents spend less time making eye contact with their children. Accordingly, children gaze more directly at fathers in European-American homes than in Mexican-American homes (Schofield, Parke, Castañeda, & Coltrane, 2008), perhaps as a sign of respect for the cultural hierarchy in the family. Thus, children develop different norms and expectations for eye contact, which affect their subsequent nonverbal behavior.

The human gaze remains important beyond childhood, so you may find you need to adjust your eye behavior to a different cultural norm. For example, you use direct eye contact with a hiring manager in a job interview in the United States to make a stronger impression. In more personal relationships, you look at a friend differently than you look at your significant other and very differently from someone you dislike intensely. Even looking away from someone—gaze aversion—carries messages (e.g., disinterest, dislike, boredom, disagreement). Thus, your eye contact or the lack of it can send messages of liking, loving, attraction, or contempt (see Table 5.1).

Voice

When the University of Arizona opened the National Institute for Civil Discourse, they wanted to promote compromise and understanding among groups famously at odds with one another (Dooling, 2011). They quickly found out that it was not only the words used that stood in the way of civility, but also the vocal tone. Imagine yourself saying, "I respect your right to believe that" with a calm, balanced tone; now imagine saying the same words with a sarcastic tone while emphasizing the word *right*. You could communicate genuine respect in the first instance or disgust and intolerance in the second.

The vocalized sounds that accompany our words are nonverbal behaviors called **paralanguage**. **Pitch** in language involves variations in the voice (higher or lower) that give prominence to certain words or syllables. Vocal **tone** is a modulation of the voice, usually expressing a particular feeling or mood; you may notice your friend sounds "down" or hear the excitement in your teammate's revelry about your win. Vocal **volume** is how loud or soft the voice is—think of the softness of a whisper or the thunder of an angry shout.

In addition to pitch, tone, and volume, paralanguage also involves vocal alterations like voice quality, accents, and the rate and rhythm of speech, including pausing or hesitating. Voice qualities include hoarseness, nasality, smoothness, or deepness and may sound precise, clipped, slurred, or shrill. Uptalk makes statements into questions by raising the voice at the end of a statement ("It might be a fun idea?") and guttural flutter of the vocal cords called "vocal fry" lowers the voice deeply (Quenqua, 2012); both are associated more with female speech. We all have preferences about which voices are most attractive—angry, demanding voices are usually perceived as annoying—and whiny voices *really* annoying (Sokol, Webster, Thompson, & Stevens, 2005). Look no further than your favorite radio DJs or newscasters to examine the vocal qualities people enjoy the most. These individuals tend to have smooth voices and find a middle ground between precise and fluid speech. Pronunciation matters, too—and can identify individuals as coming from a particular region or another country. Thus, our Missouri readers may know that residents disagree on whether to pronounce their home state as "Missouruh" (which tags a speaker as being from a rural part of the state) or "Misoureeee," indicating a more urban environment. Interestingly, politicians often pronounce it both ways to cover their bases (Wheaton, 2012).

connect

Despite differing cultural norms regarding direct eye contact, it remains an important part of giving speeches and succeeding in job interviews in the United States. In both situations, eye contact signals respect for your audience and confidence in your abilities and preparedness. You learn more about the challenges of eye contact, and how to move past them, in Chapter 16.

and you?

How do you feel about making eye contact with others (fellow classmates or your professor) when speaking in the classroom? With strangers, when you lock eyes in the grocery store or on an elevator? When interacting with people who have higher status (such as a hiring manager or boss)?

TABLE 5.1

THE FUNCTIONS OF EYE CONTACT

Influences attitude change
Example: Looking at someone to get the person to trust you or comply with your wishes

Thanasis Zovoilis/ Getty Images

Indicates a degree of arousal
Example: Glancing across a crowded room to signal attraction or interest; looking at a customer attentively in the interest of receiving positive evaluations—and sales (Ford, 1999)

John Henley/ Getty Images

Expresses emotion
Example: Soft eyes of loving looks; frightened eyes of a startled person; hard eyes of an angry person

Vladimir Godnik/ Getty Images

Regulates interaction
Example: Looking more at a conversational partner when listening; regulating eye contact to assume or give up the speaking role (Wiemann & Knapp, 1999)

NicolasMcComber/ Getty Images

Indicates power
Example: Direct, prolonged gaze to convey dominance; avoidance of eye contact to signal submissiveness (Burgoon & Dunbar, 2006)

ColorBlind Images/Getty Images

Forms impressions
Example: Making eye contact with an audience to communicate confidence and sincerity

Frank Herholdt/ Getty Images

Information from Leathers (1997).

---

connect

Using vocalizations like "Uh-huh" can help others perceive you as an effective listener (Chapter 6). When a loved one discusses a difficult situation, you want to allow the person to speak and not constantly interrupt with your own words. Vocalizations tell your partner that you are listening and that you are actively engaged in the conversation.

In addition to the paralanguage we use while talking, we can use **vocalizations**—nonverbal utterances that give information about our emotional or physical state, such as laughing, crying, sighing, yawning, or moaning—think character Tina Belcher's moans of anxiety on *Bob's Burgers*. A loud statement becomes an alarming scream with more roughness in the voice (Arnal et al., 2015). Laughing along with others is a strong signal of liking; genuine laughter can be distinguished from fake laughter by its speed—genuine is faster than fake (Bryant et al., 2016). Like facial expressions, emotional vocalizations are well recognized across cultures (Sauter, Eisner, Ekman, & Scott, 2015).

Other vocalizations simply replace words or create nonword fillers in conversations. You might clear your throat to get someone's attention or use "Shhhh" to quiet a crowd. As mentioned earlier, when we are taking a moment to think, we may insert filled pauses like "umm's" and "ah's" into our conversation. We also frequently use **back-channel cues**, sounds that signal that we are listening or encouraging others to continue talking (such as "Mm-hmm," "Oh," "Uh-huh").

Physical Appearance

If you have ever seen a reality television makeover show, like *Love, Lust or Run*, you know that many people wish to alter their appearance to elicit positive changes in their personal and professional lives. Although what you wear—or the way you fix your hair or makeup—may not speak directly to your abilities or define you as a person, it communicates messages about you nonetheless. In fact, the initial impression your appearance makes may affect your future interactions with others (DeKay, 2009).

Most people in Western society are well aware of the significance of appearance. Research shows that society affords attractive people certain advantages. For instance, attractive students receive more interaction from their teachers (Richmond et al., 1991), and "good-looking" job candidates have a greater chance of being hired (Molloy, 1983; Shannon & Stark, 2003). Jurors find attractive defendants innocent more often (Efran, 1974), although discussion and deliberation can mitigate this bias (Patry, 2008). Appearance affects not only perceptions of attractiveness but also judgments about a person's background, character, personality, status, and future behavior (Guerrero & Floyd, 2006).

Perceptions about appearance and attractiveness are inferred not only from physical characteristics like body shape and size, facial features, skin color, height, and hair color but also from the clothing you wear, which can reveal quite a bit about your status, economic level, social background, goals, and satisfaction (Crane, 2000; Galak, Gray, Elbert, & Strohminger, 2016). In fact, your clothing choice can also speak to your communication intentions. When Queen Elizabeth II became the first British monarch to visit the Irish Republic after decades of discord, she wore a suit in emerald green, the proud color of the Emerald Isle. Clearly her choice signaled a hoped-for reconciliation (Dowd, 2012).

We also infer a great deal of meaning from **artifacts**—accessories carried or used on the body for decoration or identification. For example, the expensive Rolex watch that your uncle wears sends a very different message about wealth and status than a ten-dollar watch would. Other artifacts, such as briefcases, tattoos, earrings, nose rings, nail polish, and engagement and wedding rings, also convey messages about your relational status, your gender, and even how willing you are to defy conventions (Bellezza, Gino, & Keinan, 2014). Tattoos, for example, send a variety of messages. Some descendants of Holocaust survivors inscribe the concentration camp identification numbers of their ancestors onto their forearms to communicate their desire to remember their relatives and never forget the atrocities perpetuated by the Nazi regime (Brouwer & Horwitz, 2015; Rudoren, 2012). On a lighter note,

connect

Chapter 12 explains that the artifacts you exhibit in a professional setting both reflect and shape the organization's culture—its beliefs, values, and ways of doing things. Competent communicators must be mindful of the messages their artifacts send in light of the larger organizational picture.

research finds that men view a butterfly tattoo on the back of a sunbathing woman as a sign that she may be receptive to his romantic overtures (Guéguen, 2012).

Remember that perceptions of artifacts (and physical appearance in general) can change over time. To illustrate, when the late British politician Margaret Thatcher carried a handbag, it was at first perceived as a sign of weakness; however, with her rise to prime minister, the handbag came to be a symbol of tremendous power (Givhan, 2013).

Space and Environment

Have you ever put your jacket on a chair to claim it as "your" seat? Or moved away from a crowd to regain some personal space? You are sending nonverbal messages by using the spaces that surround you and your communication partners. We examine three factors here: proxemics, territoriality, and environment.

Proxemics

Ben's first job involved a coworker, Lucas, who was a close talker — a person who stands very near when speaking to others. "During shifts when I'd be on with this guy, I'd always have to try to find some excuse to be away from the counter," Ben said. "If we were behind the counter together, he'd talk so close that I'd end up completely backed into a corner, with the counter digging into my back, just hoping for someone to rob the place so there'd be an excuse to get out of the situation" (Edwards, 2013). Ben's intense discomfort with Lucas was due to **proxemics**, the way we use and communicate with space.

Professor Edward Hall (1959) identified four specific spatial zones that carry communication messages (see Figure 5.2). *Intimate* (0 to 18 inches) is usually reserved for spouses or romantic partners, very close friends, and close family members. *Personal* (18 inches to 4 feet) is the zone in which we feel comfortable communicating with friends, relatives, and occasionally colleagues. *Social* (4 to 12 feet) is the zone most comfortable for communicating in professional settings, such as business meetings or teacher–student conferences. *Public* (12 feet and beyond) is the zone that allows for distance between interactants at public speaking events or performances, for example.

FIGURE 5.2

ZONES OF PERSONAL SPACE
The four zones of personal space described by Edward Hall indicate ranges of comfort in our spacing with others.

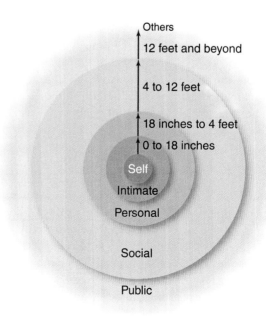

Others

12 feet and beyond

4 to 12 feet

18 inches to 4 feet
0 to 18 inches

Self

Intimate

Personal

Social

Public

Your personal space needs may vary from the foregoing space categories. They vary according to culture, too: how close or distant you want to be from someone depends on whom you are dealing with, the situation, and your comfort level. You might enjoy being physically close to your boyfriend or girlfriend while taking a walk together, but you probably do not hold hands or embrace during class. Gender also plays a role. Research says that groups of men walking together will walk faster and typically leave more space between themselves and others than women will (Costa, 2010). But regardless of your personal preferences, violations of space are almost always uncomfortable and awkward and can cause relational problems (Burgoon, 1978).

Proxemic messages are not limited to the real world. In the online virtual world *Second Life*, you create your own space in which you and your avatar move. Avatars use proxemic cues to send relational messages and structure interaction, much as people do in real life (Antonijevic, 2008; Gillath, McCall, Shaver, & Blascovich, 2008).

Territoriality

Closely related to proxemics is **territoriality** — the claiming of an area, with or without legal basis, through continuous occupation of that area. Your home, your car, and your office are personal territories. But territories also encompass implied ownership of space, such as a seat in a classroom, a parking space, or a table in a restaurant. Few people like anyone encroaching on their territory. Al Fawwar, an area covering less than a quarter mile, is the West Bank home of about seven

connect

Territoriality can have an impact on group communication, as we generally feel more in control of situations on our own turf (Chapters 10 and 11). Think about this the next time a professor breaks you up into random groups. Do you enjoy moving across the room from your usual seat, or do you prefer your group members to come to you? Chances are good that a new "territory" will affect your communication.

communication across cultures

What Nurses Wear

It might be strange to think that just a few decades ago, professional women with college degrees were expected to show up for work wearing nipped-waist dresses, frilly aprons, and white linen caps. For more than one hundred years, variations on this theme signified a woman trained in the medical profession. "The nurse's cap" was clearly and widely associated with the nursing profession. Well into the twentieth century, nurses' uniforms separated the nurses from the doctors (and in those years, the women from the men) in the health care field. But they also served as important signifiers. Prior to the opening of the first nurses' colleges in the 1830s, nursing was left largely to religious orders and untrained mothers, wives, and sisters. The adoption of a uniform — however odd it may seem today — served to provide status to these educated young women (Bates, 2012).

Such ensembles today are limited, for the most part, to Halloween costumes; however, most nurses still wear a uniform of sorts: usually a simple pair of hospital scrubs in any of a number of colors or prints. In contrast to the nurses' uniforms of yore, these simple and practical ensembles are mostly part gender-neutral. But even these seemingly nondescript items convey meaning. Research shows that the choice of color or print of scrubs can have an impact on patients' perceptions about a nurse's competence. Adults associate white scrubs with higher levels of professionalism, attentiveness, reliability, and empathy than colored or print scrubs (Albert, Wocial, Meyer, Na, & Trochelman, 2008).

Of course, uniforms are not limited to the nursing profession. Police officers, sports teams, military and paramilitary organizations, and many schools have dress requirements that are much more strict than those that govern what today's nurses wear to work. By dressing in uniform, members of these groups convey messages about who they are, what their role is, and to which group they belong.

think about this

1. Do you think that nurses' uniforms became less gendered as more men entered this traditionally female profession? Or do you think men began to think more seriously about the field as the frilly uniforms gave way to more androgynous scrubs?

2. Why do you think the color of nurses' uniforms had such an impact on adults' perceptions?

3. Why does the traditional nurse's uniform that indicated professional prestige years ago now seem so blatantly sexist?

4. The traditional nurse's uniform sent a very concrete message about the woman wearing it in terms of her job and her qualifications. What message, if any, do modern scrubs send?

evaluating communication ethics

The Job-Killer Tat

You are a few years out of college, working at a public policy think tank that specializes in childhood education research. It is a great position with lots of room for advancement and the ability to be active in an area that really interests you. What's more, the organization is growing rapidly and looking to fill new positions. When your manager mentions that they are seeking someone who can work with policymakers in the state capitol, and asks if you know anyone, you immediately think of your friend Dave. This position is essentially Dave's dream job. He is more than qualified, with a dual major in early childhood education and communication and experience as a freelance grant writer for nonprofit organizations. You pass Dave's résumé on to your manager and wish your buddy good luck.

When Dave shows up at your office for an interview, he is wearing a short-sleeved collared shirt that reveals the full arm sleeve of tattoos that he has been cultivating over the past ten years. You had mentioned to Dave that the office environment is very professional and that the position would require him to interact with lobbyists, lawyers, and lawmakers on a regular basis. You know that your boss will not think well of Dave's decision to bare his tattoos and not wear a suit. You are concerned that your boss will think you have wasted his time with a candidate who is less than serious. You take Dave's unprofessional appearance as an insult to your organization and worry that he has possibly made you look like a fool for recommending him. What do you do?

1. Why might Dave have failed to consider the professional context of the interview? Could his experience as a freelancer have changed his definition of "professional attire"?

2. If you could start over, would you give Dave clearer directions on how to dress? Or would you not recommend him at all?

3. Do you think Dave's failure to figure out what was appropriate attire ahead of time will keep him from being considered for this position, or others?

thousand people. The tiny public square in this camp has given the Palestinian refugees a sense of permanence and allowed them to have a marketplace, play area, and meeting ground (Kimmelman, 2014). Claiming this territory as their own makes them feel at home.

Territoriality operates in mediated contexts as well. Just as we do with physical spaces in the real world, we claim our social networking pages by naming them and decorating them with our "stuff," we allow certain people ("friends") access, and we "clean up" our space by deleting or hiding comments. Research shows that young people are more adept at managing their space on social media like Facebook than are their parents (Madden & Smith, 2010). Some clean up their online spaces regularly, deleting posts as often as they make them. Others take social media "vacations" or "breaks" or simply deactivate their accounts when they are not online so "friends" cannot post anything or tag them in photos while they are metaphorically not around (Boyd, 2010).

Environment

Any home designer or architect knows that humans use space to express themselves. The layout and decoration of your home, your office, and any other space you occupy tells others something about you. For example, the way you arrange your furniture can encourage interaction or discourage it; the décor, lighting, and cleanliness of the space all send messages about how you want interactions to proceed. Even the scent of a space impacts communication: customers stay in stores longer and rate the store higher if the aroma is pleasant (as in the scent of chocolate in a bookstore; Doucé, 2013). Professors who have neat, clean, attractive offices are rated by their students as more friendly, trustworthy, and authoritative (Teven &

Comadena, 1996). Prison architecture that is designed to offer more communal spaces and more campuslike cells can alter the way prisoners feel about the guards and how likely they are to be violent (Morris & Worrall, 2014).

Color also matters. Hollywood location scouts negotiated with Júzcar in southern Spain to paint all the bone-white Andalusian stone buildings baby blue to film the feature-length version of *The Smurfs* there. The blue color was so unique — and a clear nod to the popular movie — that tourists flocked there. Although the producers agreed to repaint the buildings white after the filming, the townspeople left them blue because the tourist trade had relieved their unemployment woes (Herman, 2013).

● **MANY PEOPLE** favor "their" spots, which can include a favorite table at the bar, a preferred spot in the lecture hall, or a usual seat in the car. © CBS/Photofest

The environment's power to affect communication may explain, in part, the success of shows like *Fixer Upper* and *Property Brothers*. In transforming dreary or cluttered spaces into warm and vibrant rooms, the best makeovers reflect not only a family's practical needs but also its unique personalities and interests. That is because the designers understand that environment communicates to others about who we are.

Touch

Touch is the first communication we experience in life. A newborn baby is soothed in the arms of her parents; she begins learning about herself and others while reaching out to explore her environment. **Haptics** is the use of touch to send messages. We hug our loved ones in happy and sad times, we reassure others with a pat on the back, and we experience intimacy with the caress of a romantic partner.

There are as many different types of touches as there are thoughts about and reactions for being touched. The intimacy continuum (Heslin, 1974) provides insights into how our use of touch reflects our relationship with a communication partner.

Functional-professional touch is used to perform a job. How would your dentist perform your root canal if he or she did not touch you? *Social-polite touch* is often a polite acknowledgment of the other person, such as a handshake. *Friendship-warmth touch* conveys liking and affection between people who know each other well, as when you hug your friends or offer your brother a pat on the back. *Love-intimacy touch* is used by romantic partners, parents, and children and even close friends and family members. Examples include kissing (whether on the mouth or cheek), embracing, and caressing. And *sexual-arousal touch* is an intense form of touch in sexual intimacy.

Another classification system for touch distinguishes among a dozen different kinds of body contact (Morris, 1977). Table 5.2 illustrates these types of contact in connection with the intimacy continuum.

Clearly, touch powerfully affects our relationships. It is one factor related to sustained liking in healthy marriages (Hinkle, 1999). Our reassuring touch also lets our friends know that we care and serves to regulate social interactions, as when beginning or ending an interaction with a handshake. However, not all touch is positive. Bullying behaviors like kicking, punching, hitting, and poking are inappropriate forms of touch, unless they occur inside a boxing ring.

and you?

Are you repelled by touches from strangers or those who are not your age (children or the elderly)? What about being touched by a colleague or a professor — someone you have a professional relationship with? Does it depend on the situation?

TABLE 5.2

HOW PEOPLE TOUCH

Type of Contact	Purpose	Intimacy Type
Handshake	Forming relational ties	Social-polite
Body-guide	A substitute for pointing	Social-polite
Pat	A congratulatory gesture but sometimes meant as a condescending or sexual one	Social-polite or sexual-arousal
Arm-link	Used for support or to indicate a close relationship	Friendship-warmth
Shoulder embrace	Signifies friendship; can also signify romantic connectiveness	Friendship-warmth
Full embrace	Shows emotional response or relational closeness	Friendship-warmth
Hand in hand	Equality in an adult relationship	Friendship-warmth
Mock attack	An aggressive behavior performed in a nonaggressive manner, such as a pinch meant to convey playfulness	Friendship-warmth
Waist embrace	Indicates intimacy	Love-intimacy
Kiss	Signals a degree of closeness or the desire for closeness	Love-intimacy or sexual-arousal
Caress	Normally used by romantic partners; signals intimacy	Love-intimacy or sexual-arousal
Body support	Touching used as physical support	Love-intimacy

Gauging the appropriate amount of touch for a given situation or relationship is also critical for communication. For example, dating partners usually expect touch; however, someone who wants constant hand holding, for example, can be perceived as needy or clingy. Withholding touch communicates a message of disinterest or dislike, which can damage a relationship, whether with a friend, a romantic partner, or a colleague. Obviously, it is important to adjust touch to individual expectations and needs (and culture, as we explain later in the chapter).

Time

Imagine that you are late for a job interview. If you are the interviewee, you have probably lost the job before you have had a chance to say a word — your lateness says you do not value the employer's time or the idea of punctuality. If you are the interviewer, however, it can be completely acceptable for you to keep the interviewee waiting — asserting your status by conveying that you have control. Many employers are well aware of how differences in time urgency and perspective among team members can affect the ability of the group to meet important deadlines (Waller, Conte, Gibson, & Carpenter, 2001). For many workers (and students, too), a deadline that seems to be immediate (as in this week rather than this year) puts an end to procrastination and gets them focused and started faster (Yanping & Soman, 2014).

Chronemics involves the use of time as a communicative message — the ways that you perceive and value time, structure your time, and react to time. Your *time orientation* — your personal associations with the use of time — determines the importance you give to conversation content, the length or urgency of the interaction, and punctuality (Burgoon et al., 1989). Spending time with others, for example, communicates concern and interest, as when good friends make plans to spend time together even when it is inconvenient.

connect

Are you punctual or habitually tardy? Do you evaluate others on their use of time? Does it vary when you are in friendship situations versus professional situations? In Chapter 12, we illustrate the ways to prepare for an interview so that your use of time is viewed positively.

In our personal lives, deciding the timing of a message can be tricky. How long do you wait after you have met a potential employer at a job fair to send an invitation to connect professionally on LinkedIn? How quickly do you respond to a text message from someone you met at a party? Right after you have left the party may seem too eager, but a day later may suggest you are not really interested. Research shows that we do use people's response rate (how quickly they return emails, texts, etc.) as an indication of interest and immediacy, but the situation and context also make a difference (Döring & Pöschl, 2009; Kalman & Rafaeli, 2011; Kalman, Ravid, Raban, & Rafaeli, 2006; Ledbetter, 2008).

and you?

What kind of message does it send if you are habitually late to class? What about showing up late to work? On the other hand, what kind of message do you send by showing up early for a party or to pick up a friend?

Influences on Nonverbal Communication

Pick any individual nonverbal behavior—let's say a kiss. A kiss can mean lots of different things in different places, between different people in different situations. A kiss is a friendly manner of greeting between the sexes and with friends of the same sex throughout much of southern Europe and Latin America. This is not necessarily the case in the United States and Canada, where kissing tends to be reserved for immediate family, romantic partners, or very close friends. In India, public kissing of any sort has only recently become acceptable (Harris, 2013). You might kiss your romantic partner differently in front of your family members than you would when you are alone. Indeed the very definition of *how* you kiss your partner might range from rubbing noses to exchanging saliva (Berliet, 2013). And if you are sending a text to your eight-year-old niece, you might end it with a big kiss, signaled by the emoji 😘. Clearly, culture, technology, and the situation all serve as powerful influences on our nonverbal behavior.

bontom/Shutterstock

Culture and Nonverbal Communication

When Mike and his friends visited a beach in Qingdao, China, they were surprised to see a woman emerge from the sea wearing gloves, a wetsuit, and a neon-orange ski mask. Another mask-wearing bather told them, "A woman should always have fair skin; otherwise people will think she is a peasant" (Levin, 2012). The tanning booths and self-tanning creams popular in the United States were clearly not important to beach lovers in China because different cultures view physical appearance differently. Relatedly, if you have ever traveled abroad, you may have been advised that certain nonverbal gestures that are entirely acceptable and quite positive in the United States (e.g., "A-OK" or "thumbs-up") are deeply insulting and crude in other parts of the world (Matsumoto & Hwang, 2013).

As these examples illustrate, nonverbal communication is highly influenced by culture. Culture affects clothing, touch, facial expressions, vocalizations, time orientation, and notions of physical attractiveness. For example, in the United States, people tend to make direct eye contact when speaking to someone, whether a colleague, a supervisor, or a professor. Similarly, in the Middle East, engaging in long and direct eye contact with your speaking partner shows interest and helps you assess the sincerity and truth of the other person's words (Samovar, Porter, & Stefani, 1998). However, in Latin America, Japan, and the Caribbean, such sustained eye behavior is a sign of disrespect.

Similarly, culture affects the use of touch. Some cultures are **contact cultures** (e.g., Italy; Williams & Hughes, 2005) and depend on touch as an important form of communication. Other cultures are **noncontact cultures** and are touch-sensitive or even tend to avoid touch. Latin American, Mediterranean, and Eastern European cultures, for example, rely on touch much more than Scandinavian cultures do. Public touch, linked to the type of interpersonal relationship

● **WHILE THE** "thumbs-up" is a friendly sign in America, it is considered rude and offensive in certain parts of the Middle East. Maridav/Shutterstock

that exists and the culture in which it occurs, affects both the amount of touch and the area of the body that is appropriate to touch (Avtgis & Rancer, 2003; DiBiase & Gunnoe, 2004; McDaniel & Andersen, 1998). Social-polite touch, for example, involves a handshake between American men but a kiss between Arabic men. And some religions prohibit opposite-sex touch between unmarried or unrelated individuals.

Clothing is one very visible cultural signal. Consider the business culture wherein your clothing often signals your conformity to the ideals of that business (Burgess-Wilkerson & Thomas, 2009). And if you are trying to assimilate into a new culture, you not only learn their language and customs but choose clothing that signals your adaptation to that culture as well (Yumiko, Camara, & Sorrells, 2012). Sex and gender also influence nonverbal communication. Larger eyes and rounded figures are associated with femininity as well as a series of clothing, makeup, and hairstyles; research on female political candidates finds that potential voters evaluate candidates less favorably if they have even a second's delay in determining their gender (Carpinella, Hehman, Freeman, & John, 2016). A particular nonverbal challenge for women politicians is to appear competent (usually a decisive masculine trait) yet attractively feminine.

Women usually pay more attention to both verbal and nonverbal cues when evaluating their partners and deciding how much of themselves they should reveal to those partners, whereas men attend more to verbal information (Gore, 2009). Women also engage in more eye contact, initiate touch more often, and smile more than men (Hall, 1998; Stewart, Cooper, & Steward, 2003). Such differences are not necessarily biologically based. For example, mothers may use more varied facial expressions with their daughters because they believe that women are supposed to be more expressive than men or because their childhood environment presented them with more opportunities to develop nonverbal skills (Hall, Carter, & Hogan, 2000). Adult gender roles may also play a part. Since women are expected to look out for the welfare of others, smiling—as well as other affirming nonverbal behaviors—may help women meet situational, gendered expectations (Hall et al., 2000). This may also help explain why women exhibit greater sensitivity to nonverbal messages. They tend to exhibit more signs of interest (such as head tilts and paralinguistic encouragers like "Uh-huh" and "Ah") and also decode others' nonverbal behaviors more accurately, particularly those involving the face (Burgoon & Bacue, 2003).

Mediated Nonverbal Communication

At a conference, our colleague Lori told us that she asked her students to submit their speech outlines via email by midnight on a Thursday. At 1:00 A.M., she received a frantic email from her student Aaron explaining that a computer malfunction had prevented him from sending his speech outline until then. As Aaron typically provided quality work and never missed deadlines, Lori was not concerned and did not intend to penalize him. So she simply wrote back "Got it" to quickly reassure him that she had received his outline. When she later saw Aaron in class, he said her short response made him worried that she was annoyed about his lateness. "If you had used a smiley face, I would have known you weren't upset," Aaron said. Like Aaron, many individuals expect others to use emoticons in mediated texts to help clarify meaning—whether to express emotion or to signal that something is a joke (Walther, 2006). As discussed in the digital communication chapter, emoticons can strengthen the intensity of a message, add or reduce ambiguity (was that *really* a joke?), or indicate sarcasm (Derks, Bos, & von Grumbkow, 2008). One study in Japan found that college students use positive emoticons as a "flame deterrent" — to try to prevent emotional misunderstandings that might upset others (Kato, Kato, & Scott, 2009).

When you speak with someone face-to-face, you have a number of nonverbal codes at your disposal. Even on the phone, where you have no visual cues, you can use *paralinguistic cues* (vocal tone, rate, pitch, volume, sighs) to offer information. But when you send an email or text message, many of the nonverbal channels you rely on (eye contact, paralanguage, etc.) are unavailable. However, people have developed a series of creative substitutions for nonverbal cues: capital letters to indicate shouting; creative use of font sizes, colors, and typefaces to provide emphasis; random punctuation (#@*&!) to substitute for obscenities; and animations, figures, diagrams, and pictures to add visuals to messages (Gayomali, 2013). Punctuation (or the lack of it) can help readers "hear" the intonation of what is being said (many people say that they "hear" their friend's texts or posts in that friend's "voice"). Timing is important in mediated situations, too (Kalman, Scissors, Gill, & Gergle, 2013); responding too

● **TECHNOLOGY ALLOWS** a father stationed abroad to witness his child's birth in the United States — via webcam. AP Photo/The Advocate Messenger, Clay Jackson

---

wired for communication

think about this

The Rich World of Emojis

Punctuation used to be the key to understanding emotion when we had only written words to go by. Adding a question mark (?) or exclamation point (!) communicated your uncertainty or excitement. A period (.) signaled the end of your thought. Punctuation in today's digital world does not suffice. Putting a period at the end of your text message can be associated with insincerity (Gunraj et al., 2016), and emoticons and emojis are an expected addition to texts, tweets, and posts. Emoticons are textual portrayals of emotions designed to clarify messages in the absence of nonverbal cues [:-), :-(, ;-)] and are fairly small in number. Emojis are Unicode graphic symbols; these seemingly unlimited icons have filled our online world. From the smiley face (☺) to an icon for sarcasm (😏), emojis enrich our nonverbal communication and help us send messages more rich in meaning in both personal and workplace applications (Skovholt, Grønning, & Kankaanranta, 2014). While tongue and wink emoticons can clarify sarcastic intent, for example (Thompson & Filik, 2016), emojis can communicate far more complexity in mobile communications and social media (Kralj Novak, Movak, Smailović, Sluban, & Mozetič, 2015) through color, animation, and complexity. There are emojis for sports, celebrations, personal interests, and religions — often animated.

In 2016, Facebook gave its users five more choices in addition to the "like" emoji: love, haha, wow, sad, and angry (Preimesberger, 2016), in an effort to help users clarify intent for their reactions to posts, pictures, or videos on its site. Marketers realize the power of emojis in online advertisements (Hof, 2016) by developing custom emojis for products. The next wave of emojis promises to include odor applications for online text chatting and voice-mail receiving (Xiang, Chen, Sun, Cheng, & Bove, 2016). The world of emojis continues to become richer in conveying the nonverbal messages previously absent in written text.

1. Do you think emoticons and emojis are useful in your digital communication? Are they overused?

2. Why does your digital communication need to clarify intent when nonverbal cues are absent? How often do you use emojis in your communication?

3. What do you think about odor emojis? Do you think the world of emojis can be overdone? What do you think might be an additional development of emojis?

slowly (or not at all) to an email or text can result in severe negative evaluations (Kalman & Rafaeli, 2011).

Mediated communication increasingly includes vocal signals in applications like Siri, the personal assistant on the iPhone, or Alexa, the voice of the Amazon Echo speaker. How to make these voices indistinguishable from human ones is a challenge, however—speech synthesis technology still struggles to make pleasant robotic voices (with correct stress, intonation, and sentiment) rather than disturbing, jarring ones (Markoff, 2016).

The Situational Context

Dancing at a funeral. Raising your Starbucks cup to toast your professor. Making long, steady, somewhat flirtatious eye contact with your doctor. Wearing a business suit to a rock concert. Do these situations sound strange or potentially uncomfortable? The situational context has a powerful impact on nonverbal communication. Recall from our model of competent communication from Chapter 1 that the situational context includes spheres like the place you are in, your comfort level, the event, current events, and the social environment.

Now imagine dancing at a wedding, toasting your friend's accomplishment, flirting with an attractive friend, or wearing a business suit to a job interview. In each instance, the situational context has changed. Situational context determines the rules of behavior and the roles people must play under different conditions. Competent communicators will always consider the appropriateness and effectiveness of nonverbal communication in a given context.

Two of the primary factors involved in situational context are the public–private dimension and the informal–formal dimension. The **public–private dimension** is the physical space that affects our nonverbal communication. For example, you might touch or caress your partner's hand while chatting over dinner at your kitchen table, but you would be much less likely to do that at your brother's kitchen table or during a meeting at city hall. The **informal–formal dimension** is more psychological and deals with our perceptions of personal versus impersonal situations. The formality of a situation is signaled by various nonverbal cues, such as the environment (your local pub versus a five-star restaurant), the event (a child's first birthday party or a funeral), the level of touch (a business handshake as contrasted with a warm embrace from your aunt), or even the punctuality expected (a wedding beginning promptly at 2:00 P.M. or a barbecue at your friend Nari's house lasting from 6:00 P.M. to whenever; Burgoon & Bacue, 2003). Competently assessing the formality or informality of the situation affects your use of nonverbal communication—you might wear flip-flops and shorts to hang out at Nari's, but you probably would not wear them to a wedding and certainly not on a job interview.

If your nonverbal communication does not appropriately fit the public–private and formal–informal dimensions, you will likely be met with some nonverbal indications that you are not being appropriate or effective (tight smiles, restless body movements, gaze aversion, and vocal tension).

and you?

Have you ever taken an online or distance-learning course? Were you happy with the instruction and the amount of interaction? It is challenging to both present and respond nonverbally in courses offered online. What are the most effective ways to do this, based on your experience?

back to ► Inside Out

At the beginning of this chapter, we considered how director Pete Docter uses elements of nonverbal communication to reveal complex emotions in the film *Inside Out*. Let's reconsider some of the ways nonverbal codes operate in this film.

▶ Color is a strong visual nonverbal cue, and the emotion characters in *Inside Out* are colored accordingly. For example, Disgust is portrayed with light-green skin, shoulder-length dark-green hair, long dark-green eyelashes, emerald-green eyes, a spring-green sleeveless dress, a mint-green belt with a dark-green buckle forming a "D," and forest-green tight pants. Anger is red, Fear is purple, Sadness is blue, and Joy is a sparkling golden yellow.

▶ Vocal pitch, tone, and pacing communicate how to interpret the words that are spoken. Fear has a trembling, hesitant voice, while Anger's voice is grouchy and gruff. Sadness speaks in a sighing monotone, in direct contrast to Joy's energetic, upbeat voice. Vocal cues can help or hurt us in getting our messages across. A grouchy, gruff voice may indicate anger but, like so many nonverbal cues, can be ambiguous—Is the person angry or just rushed and irritated?

▶ Some teachers have used *Inside Out* to help young students learn to identify and talk about their emotions (Leslie, 2016). While this is difficult to teach, grappling with emotions (recognizing their own as well as those in others) is an important skill for students to learn. So, for example, teachers can use a clip of Riley's first day at school to help students identify and express the emotions common to many of them. Asking questions like, "Have you ever felt sad (fearful, etc.)?" "What did you do/say?" "Did you ever have a time when that emotion made your life better?" "How do you know if your friend is sad?"

 **things to try** ▶ Activities

 **LaunchPad**
macmillan learning

1. LaunchPad for *Real Communication* offers key term videos and encourages self-assessment through adaptive quizzing. Go to **launchpadworks.com** to get access to:

   ☑ **LearningCurve**
   Adaptive Quizzes.

   ▶ Video clips that illustrate key concepts, highlighted in teal in the Real Reference section that follows.

2. Record a new episode of your favorite scripted television show. Try watching it with the sound turned all the way down (and closed captions turned off). Can you guess what is going on in terms of plot? How about in terms of what the characters are feeling? Now watch it again with the sound on. How accurate were your interpretations of the nonverbal behaviors shown? How successful do you think you would have been if it were an unfamiliar show, one with characters you do not know as well?

3. Shake up your clothing and artifacts today. Wear something completely out of character for you and consider how people react. If you normally dress very casually, try wearing a suit, or if you are normally quite put together, try going out wearing sweatpants, sneakers, or a T-shirt; if you are normally a clean-shaven man, try growing a beard for a week, or if you are a woman who never wears makeup, try wearing lipstick and eyeliner. Are you treated differently by friends? How about strangers (such as clerks in stores) or professionals (such as doctors or mechanics) with whom you interact?

4. Observe the nonverbal behaviors of people leaving or greeting one another at an airport or a train station. Do you think you can tell the relationship they have from their nonverbal behaviors? Describe the variety of behaviors you observe, and categorize them according to the codes and functions detailed in this chapter.

5. Try smiling (genuinely) more than you usually do — and with people you might not usually smile at. See what happens. Do you feel differently about yourself and others? Do others respond with more smiles of their own? (A group of thirty of our students tried this one day and reported back that they thought they had made the whole campus a happier place — though there were a few people they encountered who remained their solemn selves.)

6. Play with text-to-speech features on your computer. Compare the way the machine reads a passage of text to the way you would read it. Do you have a choice of voices from which to choose, and is there one you prefer? Would you rather listen to an audiobook performance by a noted actor or a computer-generated voice reading the same material?

real reference ▶ A Study Tool

Now that you have finished reading this chapter, you can:

Describe the power of nonverbal communication:

▶ **Nonverbal communication** is the process of signaling meaning through behavior other than words. It can be intentional or unintentional; **leakage cues** are uncontrolled nonverbal messages that give cues about our feelings, but can also be ambiguous (pp. 106–107).

▶ When **channel discrepancy** occurs, words and actions do not match, and nonverbal behaviors are more likely to be believed than verbal ones (p. 108).

Outline the functions of nonverbal communication:

▶ Nonverbal communication reinforces verbal communication in three ways: **repeating** (mirroring the verbal message), **complementing** (reinforcing the verbal message), and **accenting** (emphasizing a part of the verbal message; pp. 108–109).

▶ Nonverbal cues can be used for **substituting** or replacing words (p. 109).

▶ Nonverbal communication also functions as **contradicting** behavior, conveying the opposite of your verbal message (p. 109).

▶ Nonverbal cues also serve an **interaction management** function (p. 109) by **regulating** verbal interaction (p. 110).

▶ A feeling of closeness, or **immediacy**, can be created with nonverbal behaviors (p. 110).

▶ Individuals with good nonverbal communication skills may practice **deception**, with good or bad intentions (p. 111), when they attempt to use nonverbal behaviors to convince others of something that is false. However, according to **truth-default theory**, people tend to believe others without suspecting deception (p. 113).

Describe the set of communication symbols that are **nonverbal codes**:

▶ **Kinesics**, the way body movements send various messages, includes **emblems** (movements with direct verbal translations in a specific group or culture), **illustrators** (visually reinforcing behaviors), **regulators** (interaction management cues), **adaptors** (unconscious release of bodily tension), and **affect displays** (indications of emotion; pp. 113–115).

▶ Seven primary facial expressions are inborn and are recognizable across all cultures: sadness, anger, disgust, fear, interest, surprise, and happiness (pp. 115–116). **Masking** is a facial management technique whereby we replace an expression of true feeling with one appropriate for a given interaction (p. 116).

▶ **Oculesics** is the study of the use of the eyes in communication settings (p. 116).

▶ How we pause, the speed and volume of our speech, and the inflections we use are vocalized nonverbal messages called **paralanguage** (p. 117), including **pitch** (vocal variation that gives prominence to certain words or syllables), **tone** (vocal modulation that expresses feelings of moods), **volume** (how loud or soft words are spoken), and a variety of other factors.

▶ **Vocalizations** are paralinguistic cues that give information about the speaker's emotional or physical state, such as laughing, crying, or sighing (p. 118). **Back-channel cues** are vocalizations that signal encouragement for others to continue talking (p. 118).

▶ Physical appearance and **artifacts**, accessories used for decoration and identification, offer clues to who we are (p. 119).

▶ **Proxemics**, the way we use and communicate with space, depends on the cultural environment and is defined by four specific spatial zones: intimate, personal, social, and public (p. 120).

▶ **Territoriality** is the claiming of an area, with or without legal basis, by regular occupation of the area (pp. 121–122).

▶ The use of touch to send messages, or **haptics**, depends on the relationship with the communication partner (pp. 123–124).

▶ **Chronemics** is the perception of and use of time in nonverbal communication (p. 124).

Illustrate the influence that culture, technology, and situation have on our nonverbal behavior:

▶ **Contact cultures** are more likely to communicate through touch, whereas **noncontact cultures** may tend to avoid touch (p. 125).

▶ Gender influences communication with behaviors traditionally associated with femininity, such as smiling, often perceived as weak (p. 126).

▶ In mediated communication, capitalization, boldfaced terms, and emoticons are used as nonverbal cues (p. 127).

▶ Competent nonverbal communication relates to the situation; the **public–private dimension** is the physical space that affects our nonverbal communication, and the **informal–formal dimension** is more psychological (p. 128).

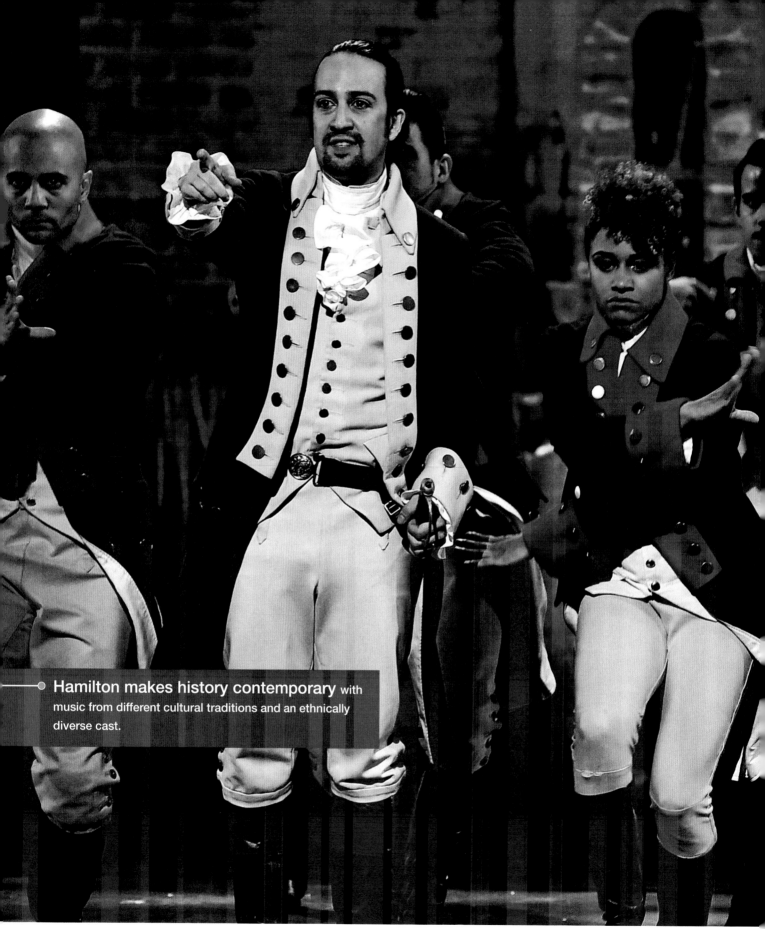

Hamilton makes history contemporary with music from different cultural traditions and an ethnically diverse cast.

 LearningCurve can help you master the material in this chapter.

Go to **launchpadworks.com**.

chapter 6

Communication and Culture

If you were trying to imagine the United States at the time of the American Revolution, would you envision George Washington singing hip-hop? The smash hit and award-winning Broadway musical *Hamilton* brings together an array of diverse cultural influences, including hip-hop, to tell the story of some of America's most famous historical figures. The costumes and set reflect the period, but the feel is contemporary (Gardner, 2015). The music and lyrics are a mix of styles that critics and fans alike have found exhilarating. Creator, composer, and lyricist Lin-Manual Miranda uses "complex raps married to traditional Broadway stylizations and repeated themes, with a little bit of Beyoncé and British pop thrown in for added effect" (Lawler, 2016). Even the inclusion of orchestral rock and "girl-group R&B" are nods to diverse cultural music genres.

Hamilton's casting is intentionally diverse. Miranda, himself a first-generation Puerto Rican American, originated the title role, and all the major characters, despite being white men historically, are played by actors of color. "Our cast looks like America looks now," Miranda boasts. "It's a way of pulling you into the story and allowing you to leave whatever cultural baggage you have about the Founding Fathers at the door" (Paulsen, 2015). Indeed, when Miranda first read Ron Chernow's biography of Alexander Hamilton (Chernow, 2004), he saw parallels between Hamilton's beginnings and the early years of rappers Jay-Z and Eminem. What others might have seen as very different cultural backgrounds, Miranda saw as common identities that were perfect for hip-hop music.

Alexander Hamilton himself is probably most famous for being killed in a duel by rival politician Aaron Burr. That too reminded Miranda of old-school rap rivalries: "It's a hip-hop story. . . . It's Tupac" (Piepenburg, 2016). But both Hamilton and Burr had many identities. They were both revolutionary fighters, lawyers, and statesmen. Hamilton was also an immigrant from the British West Indies and a child born out of wedlock. In the musical, Aaron Burr sings of him as "a bastard, orphan, son of a whore . . . and a Scotsman." And although Burr is often remembered as a murderer, Leslie Odom Jr., the actor who portrayed Burr on Broadway, gives Burr an additional identity: "None of us wants to be judged by our worst act on our worst day, and we consistently judge Burr for that," he said. "He was not a perfect man, but he's not a villain. He's a dude, just a guy" (Paulson, 2016).

After you have finished reading this chapter, you will be able to

- Define and explain culture and its impact on your communication

- Delineate important ways that cultural variables affect communication

- Describe the communicative power of group affiliations

- Explain key barriers to competent intercultural communication

- Demonstrate behaviors that contribute to intercultural competence

A s the musical Hamilton demonstrates, communication among individuals of different identities—whether race, class, immigrant status, or cultural tradition—can be messy, but it can also be exciting, challenging, enlightening, and enjoyable. To be part of any team, or to be a good neighbor and an informed citizen, you need to understand this essential communication process. Whether you are looking to learn how to better communicate with your older relatives, understand the way your roommate's faith plays out in her communication, or contemplate current national debates surrounding issues like immigration, this chapter aims to help you better understand cultural differences *and* similarities to increase your competence in intercultural encounters. We begin with an overview of culture. Then we explore cultural variations and group affiliations as well as the challenges and opportunities that intercultural and intergroup communication offers.

Understanding Culture

As you will recall from the communication competence model (Chapter 1), your encounters with others occur within overlapping situational, relational, and cultural contexts. **Culture** is a learned system of thought and behavior that belongs to and typifies a relatively large group of people. It is the composite of their shared beliefs, values, and practices, and it provides their rules for living in society (McDaniel & Samovar, 2015). Although we might commonly think of culture as a person's nationality, it applies to any broadly shared group identity. In this section, we investigate how culture is learned, how it is expressed through our communication, and why learning how to communicate in different cultures is so important.

Culture Is Learned

Culture is not something you are born with; it is something you learn through communication. As children, you observe the behaviors of your parents, siblings, and extended family members. For example, they teach you how to greet guests in your home, whether to make direct eye contact with others, and what words are polite rather than inconsiderate. Later you observe the behaviors of your teachers and your peer groups. You learn what types of conversational topics are appropriate to discuss with peers rather than adults; you learn the nuances of interacting with members of the same or opposite sex. You also listen to and observe television shows, movies, music videos, and advertising that reflect what your culture values and admires.

Through these processes, you acquire an understanding of what constitutes appropriate behavior as well as an overarching philosophy about how the world works. This philosophy is your **worldview**, the framework through which you interpret the world and the people in it (Samovar, Porter, McDaniel, & Roy, 2017). Your worldview includes deeply embedded ideas about spirituality and human nature (are people basically good?) as well as the more mundane aspects of life that you take for granted. For example, many of your nonverbal behaviors (like gestures, eye contact, and tone of voice) occur at an unconscious level (Hall, 1976). You have learned these behaviors so well that you may not even notice that you routinely make eye contact during conversation until someone fails to meet your gaze. Your use of language carries more obvious cultural cues; speaking Italian in Italy enables you to fully participate in and understand the Italian way of life (Nicholas, 2009). Language can also teach you the traditions of your culture as evidenced by prayers of your faith, folk songs of your grandparents, or patriotic oaths you make (such as the U.S. Pledge of Allegiance).

● **SOME WOMEN,** including Mayim Bialik of *The Big Bang Theory,* choose to dress in modest clothing to express their religious values. (left) Dinodia Photo/Getty Images; (right) Jen Lowery/Splash News/Newscom/Splash News/ Los Angeles/USA

Culture Is Expressed Through Communication

Just as we *learn* culture through communication, we also use communication to *express* our culture. Our worldview affects which topics we discuss in personal and professional settings as well as how we communicate nonverbally. It also affects the way we perceive others' communication.

In the United States (and many other cultures), a popular worldview often encourages the outward display of physical beauty—including body-hugging and skin-revealing clothing, particularly among women. This value is reflected in the messages we communicate. Media tabloids are filled with features on the latest celebrity "hot bodies"—whether in their bikinis at the beach (Sisavat, 2016a); in "sexy selfies" on Instagram (Sisavat, 2016b); or just out on the town showing bare legs, open shoulders, and cleavage (E!News, 2016). Even at the most "elegant" occasions, such as the Academy Awards, the gowns on the red carpet are known and often praised for their sleeveless, backless, and neck-plunging styles (The Fug Girls, 2016).

Showing skin has its limits, however. Complete nudity remains taboo both in the public square and in most mainstream media (apart from some pay-extra premium channels). And showing a lot of skin on an "imperfect" body can even generate controversy. Actress and writer Lena Dunham has done a lot of nearly nude scenes in her HBO show *Girls*. At first she found it empowering, but she admits that she sometimes struggles with nasty comments that are posted online about her body (Collins, 2016).

connect

You frequently communicate your worldview when you present yourself for strategic purposes (Chapter 3). For example, if you are meeting your significant other's parents for the first time or attending a job interview, you will likely present yourself in a manner that expresses key elements of your culture — perhaps bowing or shaking hands, using formal language, or dressing in a particular way.

and you?

Reflect on how you learned your general culture. In what ways was it directly imparted to you? What role did communication with parents, caregivers, siblings, and other important people in your life play in this process?

In many cultural traditions, worldviews about modesty and the exposure of the female body differ greatly. In India, women draped in traditional saris are often careful to cover their legs, but show their midriffs and navels. In many Muslim cultures, women are expected to cover themselves completely. American actress Mayim Bialik (*The Big Bang Theory*) has taken on the challenge of fitting into the culture of Hollywood while also observing modern orthodox Jewish traditions. Employing a "self-imposed red carpet dress code (nothing too short, nothing sleeveless)" (Blatter, 2016), Bialik argues that dressing modestly not only demonstrates her religious observances, but also her feminism.

Intercultural Communication Matters

The fact that people from different cultures perceive the world quite differently can lead to misunderstandings, anger, hurt feelings, and other challenges when they interact. This is why communication scholars invest a great deal of time and effort to study and write about **intercultural communication**, the communication between people from different cultures who have different worldviews. Communication is considered intercultural when the differences between communicators are substantial enough to create different interpretations and expectations (Lustig & Koester, 1993).

The answer to addressing intercultural misunderstanding is *not* to limit yourself to interactions with people who perceive things exactly like you. In this mobile society, you study, play, and work with people who are different from you on a number of levels. Let's now consider why studying intercultural communication matters so much.

A Diverse Society

The United States is a diverse country with a population that reflects a range of ethnic, racial, and religious backgrounds. Different regions of the country (and sometimes different neighborhoods in the same city) have distinct cultures as well. You have a unique cultural background and communication style that differ in some ways from those of others. So, to function as a member of such a diverse society, you need to be able to communicate appropriately and effectively with a wide variety of individuals. Two key parts of this process include understanding your own cultural expectations for communication and respecting those of others.

● **WHETHER YOU ARE** volunteering for the Peace Corps in another country or just going to a different part of your home state, it is important to be sensitive to cultural differences when communicating. Courtesy of the Peace Corps

Mobility

You and your family may have moved to a new community while you were growing up, or perhaps other families moved into your hometown. Whether due to shifts in the economy and employment (Henderson, 2016) or international immigration (Pew Research Center, 2015), the people around you are likely to be changing. As such, you must be ready to address cultural differences—not just between nations but also between regions, states, and cities. Even if you do not physically encounter many people from outside your community, you will almost certainly communicate with new people at some time or another through media.

Mediated Interaction

Clearly, mediated communication is changing the way we experience the world and broadening the range of people and groups with whom we regularly interact. As we discussed in Chapter 2, in the United States today, nearly 70 percent of American adults use high-speed internet at home (Horrigan & Duggan, 2015). About two-thirds of adult cell-phone owners access the internet via their smartphones or tablets (Smith, 2015). We communicate electronically more and more each year, and now more than one generation of adults worldwide are "digital natives" who have grown up with these technologies (Joiner et al., 2013; Prensky, 2012). Through the internet, we connect not only with far-off family and friends but also with individuals from around the country — or around the world — when we participate in online gaming, watch You-Tube videos, or comment on others' social media posts.

In addition to the newer media technologies, more traditional media also enable exposure to people from different cultures. Calls to customer service centers are answered in other parts of the country or on the other side of the world. Satellite radio stations bring international music and news right to your car. And television offers glimpses of cultures we might not be a part of — including British situation comedies on BBC America, soccer games broadcast from South America, and international films streamed via Netflix. American TV programming also has increasingly diverse casts.

Diverse Organizations

Any job you take will involve some degree of intercultural communication (Jones, 2013). A teacher may have students whose families are from different parts of the country or from other countries entirely; an entrepreneur must understand how different groups respond to her product and her marketing campaigns. Being aware of how culture affects communication is especially crucial to business communication across borders (Alon et al., 2016). During negotiations, for instance, you may need to know how hard to push a client to commit and when to be silent. The increasingly global reach of organizations also means that managers need to be effective leaders with increasingly multicultural workforces (Mor Barak et al., 2016; Carr-Ruffino, 2016).

Clearly, intercultural communication is important in your life as a student, as a citizen, and as a professional. The culture in which you live (or were raised) has particular ways of communicating in the world. We illustrate these now by examining seven cultural variations.

● **ARIANA MIYAMOTO IS ONE EXAMPLE** of a unique cultural background: born to an African-American father and Japanese mother, she has lived in both Texas and Japan. She was the first biracial woman to be crowned Miss Universe Japan Ethan Miller/Getty Images

and you?

How long have you lived in your current location? Are people in your community treated differently based on their status as a new or established member in the community? How might your response change based on your own level of involvement in the community?

Communication and Cultural Variations

It is one thing to notice cultural differences; it is quite another to be able to *explain* them. *Why*, for example, might it seem to Americans that Germans sound very blunt and direct as they speak, whereas the Japanese may seem indirect and talk around the point? Scholars have identified seven major communication variations[1] across cultures: high- and low-context cultures, collectivist and individualist orientations, comfort with uncertainty, masculine and feminine orientations, approaches to power distance, time orientation, and value of emotional expression (Hall, 1976; Hofstede, 1984, 2001; Matsumoto, 1989).

---

[1] Geert Hofstede referred to several of these variations as cultural *dimensions* — largely psychological value constructs that affect the way people think about and perform communication behaviors.

These seven variations are often treated like opposites, so you may think that your culture must be one or the other. However, these variations actually play out along a spectrum: your culture may be masculine in some ways and feminine in others. Also, within any culture, there is great variance among different groups in terms of where they fall on the spectrum. Finally, there are always differences among individuals as well—some people are more like their dominant culture than others. With these caveats in mind, let's consider each variation more closely.

High- and Low-Context Cultures

Our culture affects how direct we are in our use of language and how much we rely on other nonverbal ways to communicate. Individuals in **high-context cultures** (including Japan, Korea, China, and many Latin American and African countries) use contextual cues—such as time, place, relationship, and situation—to interpret meaning and send subtle messages (Hall, 1976; Hall & Hall, 1990). A Japanese person who disagrees with someone, for example, may say something indirect, such as "Maybe" or "I'll think about it," or she may not say anything at all. The communication partner must understand the message solely from clues of disagreement in the *context,* such as how the person is standing, whether the person is lower or higher status, and the fact that the person is silent (or hesitates to speak). People from a high-context culture may also prefer "richer" communication channels (such as face-to-face or video interaction) and oral agreements over text-based channels and

connect

If you are from a low-context culture, you may wonder how to decode communication from a high-context friend or colleague. The key lies in developing strong listening skills (Chapter 7). By participating in *active listening,* you can look for opportunities to select and attend to nonverbal messages or contextual clues that will help you understand the message your friend is encoding and sending.

real communicator

NAME: Vanessa Gonzalez Lasso
OCCUPATION: Marketing and Admissions Director
Courtesy Vanessa Gonzalez Lasso

If you had asked me who "I" am and what groups I belong to at the beginning of my college career, I could have answered you without a second thought: I'm Latina, I'm an American, I'm a first-generation college student, I'm studious, and I love to travel. But my experiences with intercultural communication — in college, and now in my job — really shook up these categories for me and taught me a great deal about communication with others.

My current job is with a college-preparatory high school in the United States that sponsors an international academy. The position requires a combination of marketing and intercultural skills. I work to attract students from many different countries to the academy, which is, as one might expect, culturally diverse. The school provides the opportunity for students to interact with others from all over the world through enriching classes and extracurricular activities. One program pairs the international students with the domestic students so that the former can become oriented to the school and the latter can learn more about another culture.

One of the most exciting parts of my job is the opportunity to travel internationally. Recently I visited schools in South Korea, Vietnam, Thailand, China, and New Zealand, where I participated in recruiting fairs and met with students and their families. As you might guess, I encountered several cultural variations. One that stood out to me was the different ways that students interact with their parents. In South Korea, students are expected to have a strong sense of independence by their early teens, including taking responsibility for their living arrangements and their studies with little parental oversight. In Vietnam, on the other hand, students are more closely watched over by their parents, who are concerned with guiding not only their academic success but also their overall happiness. When meeting students of both these cultures, I kept this information in mind so that I knew whether to bring the parents fully into the recruitment discussions or interact more directly with the student.

At the international academy, I also need to be sensitive and help students from high- and low-context cultures adapt (especially high-context cultural students, who are not always used to responding to blunt questions). Our teachers also need to adapt their methods to be sure their students understand them. It's incredible to watch such a diverse group grow comfortable with their surroundings and with their fellow students.

written contracts, where the opportunity to provide context is more limited.

A **low-context culture**, by contrast, values more direct language and relies less on situational factors to communicate meaning. The United States, Canada, Australia, and many northern European countries tend to have a low-context style. In the United States or Germany, for example, it might seem normal for someone to disagree by saying openly, "That's not right" or "I'm sorry, but I don't agree with what you are saying." Although people from high-context cultures would likely think such directness disrespectful, people from low-context cultures tend to believe it is rude to be unclear about what you think. In fact, researchers have found that Americans often find indirectness very confusing and may even interpret Japanese silence or a response such as, "I'll think about it" as agreement (Kobayshi & Viswat, 2010). Table 6.1 compares high- and low-context styles.

Collectivist and Individualist Orientations

An Arab proverb says that you must "smell the breath" of a man in order to know if he can be trusted. But in the United States, Americans get very uncomfortable when other people stand "too close" to them. Americans also tend to knock on a closed door before entering and usually ask the person inside if it is OK to enter or if she would like to join the group for lunch. But in Lesotho (a tribal culture in South Africa), people's rooms often have no doors at all; people go in and out freely, and if someone sees you, they may grab you and assume you want to have lunch with the group. Such differences in the value of personal space and independence versus belonging and group loyalty illustrate our second cultural value: collectivist and individualist orientations.

Individuals from **collectivist cultures** perceive themselves first and foremost as members of a group—and they communicate from that perspective (Triandis, 1986, 1988, 2000). Collectivist cultures (including many Arab and Latin American cultures as well as several Asian cultures, such as Chinese and Japanese) value group goals and emphasize group harmony and cooperation. Communication in such cultures is governed by a clear recognition of status and hierarchy among group members, and loyalty to the group and the honor of one's family are more important than individual needs or desires (Wang & Liu, 2010). In addition, collectivist communicators are generally concerned with relational support; they avoid hurting others' feelings, apologize, and make efforts to help others to maintain the group's reputation and position of respect (Han & Cai, 2010). For example, if an individual attending a business meeting discovers a financial error, she will not likely mention who made the error, nor will she call attention to her own success in discovering it. Instead, she will emphasize the group's success in correcting the error before it became a problem for the company.

● **INTERACTIONS BETWEEN** people from high- and low-context cultures require extra sensitivity to social cues. If you are preparing for a meeting with both American and Japanese business partners, it might be beneficial to research the cultural differences ahead of time. Robert Daly/Getty Images

and you?

To what degree do you identify with an individualist or collectivist culture? How might the answer to this question be complicated if the family you grew up with identifies strongly with one dimension but the larger culture in which you were raised strongly identifies with the other?

High-Context Cultures	Low-Context Cultures
• Rely on contextual cues and nonverbal signals for communicating meaning	• Rely on direct language for communicating meaning
• Avoid speaking in a way that causes individuals to stand out from others	• Admire standing out and getting credit
• Usually express opinions indirectly	• Construct explicit messages
• Usually express disagreement by saying nothing or being verbally vague	• Usually express disagreement clearly
• Prefer to make agreements using oral and visual channels that can provide more contextual cues	• Tend to make agreements in written contracts that lay out the terms explicitly

TABLE 6.1

A COMPARISON OF HIGH- AND LOW-CONTEXT CULTURES

Conversely, **individualist cultures** value each person's autonomy, privacy, and personal "space." They pay relatively little attention to status and hierarchy based on age or family connections. In such cultures, individual "self-esteem" is important, individual initiative and achievement are rewarded, and individual credit and blame are assigned. Thus, an individual who notes an error—even one by her superiors—will probably be rewarded or respected for her keen observation (as long as she presents it sensitively). The United States is a highly individualist culture—American heroes are usually those celebrated for "pulling themselves up by their bootstraps" to achieve great things or change the world. Other Western cultures, such as Great Britain, Australia, and Germany, are also at the high end of the individualism scale.

connect

Just because people from cultures like those in the United States and Ireland have a greater acceptance for uncertainty than others does not mean that they are entirely comfortable with the unknown. In fact, members of low uncertainty avoidance cultures will engage in *passive, active,* and *interactive strategies* to reduce uncertainty when dealing with a new relational partner (Chapter 8); similarly, they will seek opportunities to learn about a new organizational culture so that they can *assimilate* competently (Chapter 12).

Comfort with Uncertainty

Cultures also differ in the degree of anxiety that members tend to feel about the unknown. All cultures, to some degree, adapt their behaviors to reduce uncertainty and risk, a process called **uncertainty avoidance**. Cultures that are more anxious about ambiguity and unstructured situations are said to be high in uncertainty avoidance (Hofstede, Hofstede, & Minov, 2010). In these cultures (such as Greece, Peru, Italy, and South Korea), life is perceived as being inherently stressful and unstable, so communication is usually governed by a lot of formal and informal rules to provide stability and predictability. Although people may not necessarily follow the rules (the rules themselves can be stressful), they find comfort in their presence in their society (Minkov & Hofstede, 2014).

In contrast, cultures with a higher tolerance for ambiguity (like Denmark, the United States, the United Kingdom, and Singapore) are considered to be low in uncertainty avoidance (Hofstede, Hofstede, & Minkov, 2010). Their lower level of anxiety about the unknown means that these cultures express greater calm in the face of stress (Smit, 2015), have more optimism about relationships, are more tolerant of differences in communication styles, and have fewer formal rules for behavior (Minkov & Hofstede, 2014). They are also more likely to take organizational risks, such as changing jobs or starting businesses (Ashraf, Zheng, & Arshad, 2016).

Masculine and Feminine Orientations

The masculinity or femininity of a culture refers to the way an entire culture (including both men and women within the culture) values and reflects characteristics that have traditionally been associated with one sex or the other. Thus, a **masculine culture**—sometimes referred to as an *achievement culture*—places value on assertiveness, achievement, ambition, and competitiveness (Hofstede, Hofstede, & Minkov, 2010). Men and women in such cultures also usually make clear distinctions between the sexes, such as expecting more aggressiveness in men and more passivity in women. Mexico, Japan, and Italy tend to be high in masculinity.

Highly **feminine cultures**—sometimes referred to as *nurturing cultures*—place value on relationships and quality of life. Such cultures prize affection, friendliness, and social support between people over assertiveness. Scandinavian cultures (such as Sweden and Norway) as well as Chile and Portugal tend to rank high in femininity.

When discussing masculine and feminine orientations, remember that individual men and women *within* each culture vary in how they may value masculinity and femininity (Tripathy, 2010). For example, Japan ranks as a highly masculine culture, yet in recent years, many Japanese men have been embracing a less restrictive view of masculinity. Analysts note that these men may communicate in ways that are gentle, shy, or sensitive (Faiola, 2005).

Approaches to Power Distance

The *Divergent* movie series, based on a series of novels, has been very popular, especially among American teenagers. In these stories, a postapocalyptic society has been divided into factions based on citizens' human virtues, such as honesty or bravery. Heroine Tris must hide her diverse qualities for fear of being labeled "divergent" and therefore a threat to the social order. Part of the appeal of this series for American audiences is seeing how characters find where they fit in, while also ultimately helping to crumble the social divisions that the elites consider vital to a utopian society.

Divergent appears to be tapping into cultural ideas about the division of power among individuals, a concept known as **power distance**. In the United States, upward mobility is a value, children often challenge their parents, and underdogs become folk heroes. But in other cultures, social status is far more stratified and accepted. In India, for example, the caste system—formally outlawed in 1950 but still lingering in the country's culture—placed individuals, families, and entire groups into distinct social strata. That meant that the family you were born into determined with whom you could associate and marry and what job you could hold. Those born into the lowest tier (the untouchables) were considered subhuman, even contagious, and were ignored by higher castes of people. Individuals generally accepted their place in the caste system. Even today, the idea that one's social status is set in stone remains (Bayly, 1999).

Status differences in a culture result in some groups or individuals having more power than others. But a person's position in the cultural hierarchy can come from sources besides social class, including age, job title, or even birth order. In cultures with *high power distance* (like India, China, and Japan), people with less power accept their lower position as a basic fact of life. They experience more anxiety when they communicate with those of higher status. And they tend to accept coercion as normal and avoid challenging authority. In cultures with *low power distance,* (such as the United States, Canada, Germany, and Australia), people tolerate less difference in power and communicate with those higher in status with less anxiety. They are more likely to challenge the status quo, consider multiple options or possibilities for action, and resist coercion.

Figure 6.1 shows how different types of cultures vary in their value of power distance as well as how they differ on the other cultural dimensions of individualism and uncertainty avoidance.

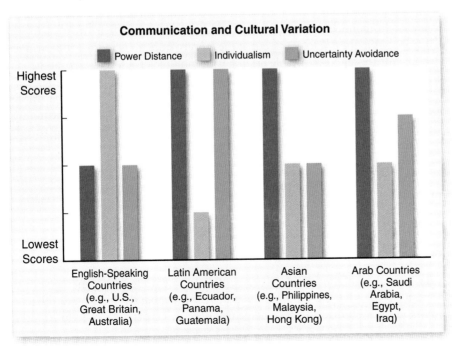

Communication and Cultural Variation

■ Power Distance   ■ Individualism   ■ Uncertainty Avoidance

Highest Scores

Lowest Scores

English-Speaking Countries (e.g., U.S., Great Britain, Australia) | Latin American Countries (e.g., Ecuador, Panama, Guatemala) | Asian Countries (e.g., Philippines, Malaysia, Hong Kong) | Arab Countries (e.g., Saudi Arabia, Egypt, Iraq)

FIGURE 6.1

COMMUNICATION AND CULTURAL VARIATION
Information from G. Hofstede, G. J. Hofstede, & M. Minkov (2010).

● **WAITING YOUR TURN** is typical for people in monochronic cultures; however, if you do not crowd in with the others in a polychronic culture, you may never get served. (left) Oli Scarff/Getty Images; (right) ROBERTO SCHMIDT/ Getty Images

Time Orientation

When you are invited to someone's home for dinner, when is it appropriate to arrive? Early, the exact time of the invitation, or twenty minutes (or even two hours!) later? **Time orientation**, or the way cultures communicate about and with time, is an important—yet frequently overlooked—cultural dimension (Hall, 1959).

Many Western European and English-speaking cultures (such as the United States and Great Britain) are extremely time-conscious. Every portion of the day is oriented around time—including time for meals, bed, meetings, and classes. Even sayings express the importance of time: *Time is money, no time to lose, wasting time* (Mast, 2002). But in many Latin American and Asian cultures, time is fluid, and the pace of life is slower. Arriving two hours late for an invitation is perfectly acceptable. An American businessperson might get frustrated and give up after spending six months working on a deal with a Japanese company, when the Japanese may be wondering why the Americans quit so soon when they were all just getting to know each other!

A key cultural distinction operating here is whether cultures are monochronic or polychronic (Hall & Hall, 1990). **Monochronic cultures** treat time as a limited resource. Such cultures (including the United States, Germany, Canada, and the United Kingdom) use time to structure activities and focus on attending to one person or task at a time; they value concentration on the task at hand and adherence to schedules. In monochronic cultures, people line up to wait their "turn"—to see a professor at office hours, to check out at the grocery store, to get into a concert. **Polychronic cultures** are comfortable dealing with multiple people and tasks at the same time. Seven or eight people all crowding around a stall and shouting out their needs at a *mercado* in Mexico is expected, not rude. Polychronic cultures (such as in Mexico, India, and the Philippines) are also less concerned with making every moment count. They do not adhere as closely to schedules, are less likely to make or attend to appointments, and change plans often and easily.

Even digital communication can be affected by such differences in the perception of time. People from monochronic cultures tend to expect more immediate replies to emails and emphasize the efficient exchanges of messages in organizations (Tikkanen & Frisbie, 2015).

Value of Emotional Expression

In the central highlands of Madagascar, Rakotonarivo Henri is dancing with the bones of his grandfather. Accompanied by five brass bands, Henri and others on this island in the Indian Ocean emerge from family crypts with cheerful emotion.

connect

In Chapters 15 and 17, we discuss the importance of connecting to your audience and appealing to their emotions (*pathos*). However, it is essential to understand your audience's comfort with emotional expression. You want to ensure that your verbal and nonverbal communication is logical, credible, and competent for the context while attempting to touch their hearts.

Amid joyful singing and dancing, they openly express their feelings to one another—and the dead—in a ritualistic ceremony called the *famadihana*, or the "turning of the bones." The ritual is meant to celebrate their ancestors, pass on the rituals and stories to the next generation, and publicly show how they love one another (Bearak, 2010).

One thing that people from all cultures share is the ability to *experience* emotion. But *expressing* emotions (including which emotions under which circumstances) varies greatly. In some cultures, overt emotional expression is associated with strength; in others, it is associated with weakness. Sometimes emotional expression is seen as chaos and other times as an identification of and processing of problems (Lutz, 1996).

● DURING *FAMADIHANA,* the Malagasy people of Madagascar embrace their ancestor's bones, literally, and love for each other and their culture, figuratively. Gideon Mendel/ Getty Images

We discussed in Chapter 5 the many ways we can show emotion nonverbally. But cultures also use *language* in different ways to express emotion. Many collectivistic cultures (e.g., Arab cultures) often use **hyperbole**—vivid, colorful language with great emotional intensity (and often exaggeration). Individualistic cultures (particularly English speaking) tend toward **understatement**, language that downplays the emotional intensity or importance of events (often with euphemisms; Wierzbicka, 2006). Consider, for example, the difference between describing a military battle by saying "the river ran red with the blood of the slaughtered" versus "there were a number of casualties." A particularly striking example of understatement comes from the United Kingdom and Ireland—three decades of bombings and violence by paramilitary groups in Northern Ireland is a period referred to simply as "the Troubles" (Allan, 2004).

We have seen that communication in different cultures varies along continuums in seven key ways. Yet within these broadly defined cultures, we all vary our communication in more specific ways based on the many groups to which we belong or with which we identify, as we see in the next section on group affiliation.

Understanding Group Affiliations

Ellen DeGeneres is an American, a woman, and a baby boomer. She is white. She is a Californian and also a southerner. She is a lesbian, a vegan, an animal rights activist, and an environmentalist. She is also a successful entertainer and very wealthy. All of these characteristics—and many others—form DeGeneres's unique identity. These attributes also make her a member of various groups. Some of these groups might be formal (as expressed by her affiliations with various animal rights groups). However, most are informal, reflecting the more general ways in which we all group ourselves and others based on particular characteristics. Thus Ellen is a member of the white community, the southern community, the wealthy community, the entertainment community, and so on.

You too have multiple aspects to your identity, including the many groups to which you belong. Of course, some of your group memberships may be more important to you than others; these group affiliations powerfully shape your communication—and affect how others communicate with and about you. In this section, we consider these facts by examining cocultural communication as well as social identity theory and intergroup communication.

● IN WHICH groups can Ellen DeGeneres claim membership? BSA/ ZOJ/Newscom/WENN/United States

what about you?

Cultural Values Assessment

We each have values about what is important and appropriate in interacting with others. Often these values reflect the larger culture in which we have been raised; however, our opinions may also vary widely as individuals. This scale should give you a sense of how closely your own values relate to the larger cultural differences discussed in this chapter. For each of the statements that follow, write the number that most closely matches your opinion: 5 = strongly agree; 4 = agree; 3 = unsure; 2 = disagree; and 1 = strongly disagree.

_____ 1. People should say what they think clearly and directly.

_____ 2. My own goals in life are not as important as my family's or community's hopes for me.

_____ 3. Change results in uncomfortable stress in life.

_____ 4. It is important to work hard to get ahead professionally, even if relationships might suffer.

_____ 5. Children should not be expected to provide for the old-age security of their parents.

_____ 6. It is important to plan carefully for the future.

_____ 7. People should keep their emotions to themselves.

_____ 8. If you disagree with someone, you should speak up.

_____ 9. People should take care of family before themselves.

_____ 10. Risk taking is foolish; it is better to follow the regular path.

_____ 11. People should try to be the "best" at whatever they do.

_____ 12. Students should feel free in class to disagree with their teachers.

_____ 13. It is important to be on time to appointments.

_____ 14. People should grieve quietly rather than make a big scene.

_____ 15. You should not have to guess what someone means.

_____ 16. If someone in my group or family fails, we all feel the shame.

_____ 17. I hate situations in which I do not know how I am supposed to act.

_____ 18. Men and women are just different; there is nothing wrong with that.

_____ 19. It is fine to question the views of people in authority.

_____ 20. You should make a schedule and keep to it.

_____ 21. Colorful language and exaggeration are signs of personal weakness.

Add your scores here to assess which way you lean in your cultural values:

1, 8, 15: _____ low context (9–15); high context (3–8)
2, 9, 16: _____ collectivist (9–15); individualist (3–8)
3, 10, 17: _____ high uncertainty avoidance (9–15); low uncertainty avoidance (3–8)
4, 11, 18: _____ masculinity (9–15); femininity (3–8)
5, 12, 19: _____ low power distance (9–15); high power distance (3–8)
6, 13, 20: _____ high time orientation (9–15); low time orientation (3–8)
7, 14, 21: _____ devalue emotional expression (9–15); value emotional expression (3–8)

Cocultural Communication

As we discussed in Chapter 1, **cocultures** are groups whose members share at least some of the general culture's system of thought and behavior but have distinct characteristics or attitudes that unify them and distinguish them from the general culture. As you saw in our example about Ellen DeGeneres and as Figure 6.2 shows, ethnic heritage, race (or races), gender, religion, socioeconomic status, and age form just a few of these cocultures. Other factors come into play as well: some cocultures are defined by interest, activities, opinions, or by membership in particular organizations (e.g. "I am a Republican" or "I am a foodie").

Our communication is intrinsically tied to our cocultural experience. For example, a **generation** is a group of people who were born during a specific time frame and whose attitudes and behavior were shaped by that time frame's events and social changes. Generations develop different ideas about how relationships work, ideas that affect communication within and between generations (Howe & Strauss, 1992). For example, Americans who lived through the World War II share common memories (the bombing of Pearl Harbor, military experience, homefront rationing) that have shaped their worldviews in somewhat similar—though not identical—ways. This shared experience affects how they communicate, as shown in Table 6.2.

Similarly, the interplay between our sex and our gender exerts a powerful influence on our communication. *Sex* refers to the biological characteristics (i.e. reproductive organs) that make us male or female, whereas **gender** refers to the social roles associated with being male or female. Gender is determined by the way members of a particular culture define notions of masculinity and femininity (Wood, 2011) as well as the traits, feelings, behaviors, and even appearance that are considered more typical of, or more appropriate for, one sex or the other

The Cultural Context

FIGURE 6.2

THE MULTIFACETED NATURE OF COCULTURES

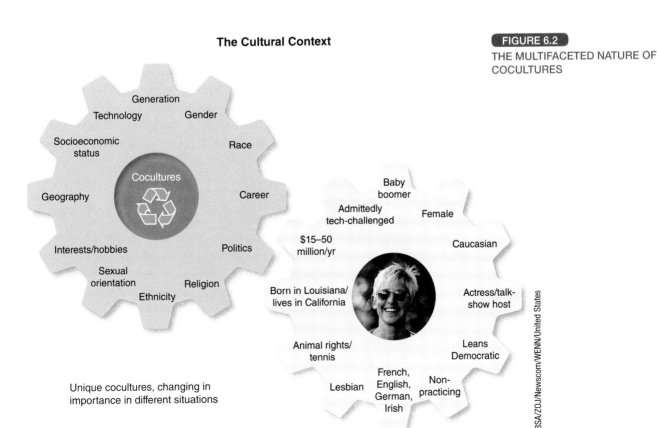

Unique cocultures, changing in importance in different situations

BSA/ZOJ/Newscom/WENN/United States

TABLE 6.2

GENERATIONS AS COCULTURE

Generation	Year Born	Characteristics Affecting Communication
Matures	Before 1946	Born before the World War II, this so-called silent generation lived through the Great Depression and World War I. They are hardworking, largely conformist, have strong civic instincts, and career focus.
Baby Boomers	1946–1964	The largest generation prior to millennial, products of an increase in births that began after World War II and ended with the introduction of the birth control pill. In their youth, they were antiestablishment and optimistic about the future; however, recent surveys show they are more pessimistic today than any other age group.
Generation X	1965–1980	Growing up during the post-Watergate, post-Vietnam malaise, this somewhat jaded generation is also savvy, entrepreneurial, and independent. They witnessed the fall of the Berlin Wall and the rise of cable television, home computing, and the internet.
Millennials	1981–2000	The first generation of the new millennium, this is the first group to fully integrate computers and mobile phones into their everyday communication. Raised by baby boomers, they are expressive, idealistic, and concerned about social and environmental issues.
Generation Z	2001–Current	The most culturally diverse of any generation, these digital natives were born into a media-rich, networked world and grew up with smartphones, social media, and digital multitasking. However, they also grew up with economic turmoil and global conflict and share with the older generations a deliberativeness about their futures.

Information from P. Taylor & S. Keeter (2010); B. Horovitz (2012); A. Williams (2015).

and you?

How masculine do you consider yourself? How feminine? How do these qualities align with your gender identity? Do others communicate with you in ways that support or criticize this aspect of yourself?

(Caplan & Caplan, 2016). Recall from Chapter 4, for example, that we can use differences in our language styles to express differences in gender identity (Tannen, 2009, 2010).

So are we destined to live our lives bound by the communication norms and expectations for our sex or gender, our generation, our profession, our hobbies, and our other cocultures? Hardly. First, as we see in the next section, we may not strongly identify with many of the groups to which we belong. Second, recall the concept of *behavioral flexibility* discussed in Chapter 1. Competent communicators adapt their communication skills to a variety of situations. For example, there are contexts and relationships that call for individuals of both sexes to adhere to a more feminine mode of communication (e.g. comforting a distraught family member), whereas other contexts and relationships require individuals to communicate in a more masculine way (e.g. using direct and confident words when negotiating for a higher salary). Similarly, a teenager who feels most comfortable communicating with others via text messaging or Facebook might do well to send Grandma a hand-written thank-you note for a graduation gift.

In addition, there is a great diversity of communication behaviors within cocultures (as well as diversity within larger cultures). For example, your grandmother and your best friend's grandmother may not communicate in the exact same style simply because they are both women, they were born in the same year, or they were both college graduates who became high school English teachers. Similarly, the group typically defined as African Americans includes Americans with a variety of cultural and national heritages. For some, their story stretches back to colonial times; others are more recent immigrants from Africa, the Caribbean, and elsewhere ("Census," 2010). Christians include a wealth of different denominations that practice various aspects of the larger faith differently. Christians also hail from different races and ethnicities, socioeconomic statuses, regions, political views, and so on. All of these intersecting factors affect communication within any given coculture.

Social Identity and Intergroup Communication

Clearly, our group memberships strongly influence our communication. This is because our group memberships are such an important part of who we are. According to **social identity theory**, you have a *personal identity*, which is your sense of your unique individual personality, and you have a *social identity*, the part of your self-concept that comes from your group memberships (Tajfel & Turner, 1986). We divide ourselves into "us" and "them" partly based on our affiliations with various cocultures. The groups with which we identify and to which we feel we belong are our **in-groups**; those we define as "others" are **out-groups**. We want "us" to be distinct and better than "them," so we continually compare our cocultures to others in the hope that we are part of the "winning" teams.

Studies in **intergroup communication**, a branch of the discipline that focuses on how communication within and between groups affects relationships, find that these comparisons powerfully affect our communication (Giles & Maass, 2016; Giles, Reid, & Harwood, 2010). For example, group members often use specialized language and nonverbal behaviors to reveal group membership status to others (Giles & Watson, 2013). A doctor might use a lot of technical medical terms

---

wired for communication

Online Gamers: Women Are Hardcore, Too

The stereotypical view of the gaming community — especially hardcore, excellent players — is that it is young and male. But industry reports note that nearly half of online gamers are female, and that the average female player is in her mid-40s (Entertainment Software Association, 2016). So what are women playing? And do they play differently than men?

Researchers have found that women play more casual games, while men play more competitive shooter and role-playing games (Trepte, Reinecke, & Behr, 2009). In the highly competitive massively multiplayer online (MMO) games, women make up only about 20 percent of the players. Men and women also report playing MMOs for different reasons — men are more motivated by achievement, whereas women are more motivated by social reasons. In fact, women are twice as likely as men to play with their romantic partner (Williams, Consalvo, Caplan, & Yee, 2009). And, although both men and women tend to underestimate how much time they spend playing, women are far more likely to lie about how often they play (Kahn, Ratan, & Williams, 2014).

Are these differences because women just are not as good as men at playing the games? Recent communication research has debunked this notion. In an overtime analysis of the actual game play of over nine thousand *EverQuest II* players and two thousand players of *Chevaliers' Romance III* (a Chinese game), researchers found *no difference* in performance — the characters played by women advanced in the game just as quickly as the characters played by men (Shen, Ratan, Cai, & Leavitt, 2016). Men's characters did often reach higher status levels, but that was a function of them having played the game for a longer time and being more accepted by other players into "guilds."

The researchers argue that many of the gaming differences between men and women may be due to a self-fulfilling prophecy. The stereotype of women being poorer players may contribute to a lack of acceptance by the gaming community and may encourage all but the most hardcore female players to avoid these games or limit their playing time.

think about this

1. Do you play live games online? Do you consider the gender of the players you compete against when you do? Do you choose to reveal your own gender when you play?

2. Do you or would you try online gaming with your romantic partner? Explain how you think your communication is (or might be) altered when you share games online.

3. Consider the discussion of gender as coculture in this chapter. Why do you think women are so much more likely to underreport the amount of time they spent playing?

connect

In Chapter 3, you learn that the *self-serving bias* holds that we usually attribute our own successes to internal factors and our failures to external effects. Because we want to feel good about our group memberships as well, we tend to make the same attributions. So if your sorority sister gets an A on a difficult exam, you may attribute it to her intelligence; if she fails, you may assume that the exam was unfair.

among nurses to assert her authority as a doctor, whereas sports fans use Facebook posts to support their fellow fans, team members, and coaches and to denigrate those of rival teams (Sanderson, 2013).

Our group identification and communication shift depending on which group membership is made **salient**—or brought to mind—at a given moment. For example, students often consider themselves in-group members with fellow students and out-group members with nonstudents. However, a group of students at different schools might identify themselves in smaller units. For example, suppose community college students consider themselves out-groups from students attending a four-year university. If all of these students discover that they are rabid fans of the *Hunger Games* trilogy or that they volunteered for the American Red Cross, they might see each other as in-group members while discussing these interests and experiences.

communication across cultures

The It Gets Better Project

Columnist Dan Savage was stewing. He had just heard about the suicide of an Indiana teenager, Billy Lucas, who had hanged himself in his grandmother's barn at the age of fifteen. Lucas, who may or may not have been gay, was perceived as gay by his classmates and bullied harshly because of it. Savage felt heartbroken and angry. So many gay teenagers experience bullying and harassment, and like other gay men and women, Savage had endured bullying during his teenage years. But in spite of it, he was now a happy adult with a fulfilling life that included a great career and a loving family. He was frustrated that Billy Lucas would miss out on those things. "I wish I could have talked to this kid for five minutes," Savage wrote in his column. "I wish I could have told Billy that *it gets better*. I wish I could have told him that, however bad things were, however isolated and alone he was, *it gets better*" (Savage, 2010).

It was too late to say those things to Billy Lucas. But Savage knew there were thousands more young people like Billy Lucas, teenagers who were gay or lesbian or simply unsure about their sexuality and who were being targeted and tormented. He knew that those teens are four times more likely to attempt suicide than others — and he believed that it was not too late to talk to them. So Savage and his partner sat down in front of their webcam and made a video. They talked about their own experiences at the mercy of bullies and about being isolated from their own parents when they first came out. But they also talked about what comes later: gaining acceptance, finding places where they were not alone, and building families and careers. They posted the video to YouTube and encouraged others to do the same. The It Gets Better Project was born.

Today, more than fifty thousand videos have been posted — from straight and gay people, celebrities, and ordinary people from all over the world — and the site has over a half million followers (It Gets Better, 2016). The project has also taken off internationally, bringing messages of hope and highlights of events and positive media coverage to LGBTQ youth on six continents.

Note: The project does not offer any solutions for dealing with bullies or advise students to engage in conflict with those who abuse them. It simply offers them a peer experience, to show them that they are not alone, and tries to show them that life will go on after the bullying ends.

think about this

1. Consider how the It Gets Better Project offers LGBTQ teens who are feeling isolated the opportunity to envision their lives as part of a coculture. Can the project help them find peers and role models?

2. Think about how technology allows individuals to connect with others who share narrowly defined interests or uncommon challenges. How can connecting with others who share these interests and challenges via the internet enrich their lives?

3. The Project is aimed at a very specific coculture — and yet, the videos posted come from people from all walks of life. Is it important for LGBTQ teens to hear messages of encouragement from outside the coculture? Do the messages posted have value for straight teens as well?

In addition, your group memberships are not all equally salient for you at any given time, and your communication reflects this. For instance, suppose you are a female Egyptian-American Muslim from a middle-class family and a straight-A student with a love of languages and a passion for outdoor adventure sports. When displaying who "you" are, you may emphasize your "student-ness" (by wearing your college insignia) and sports enthusiasm (by participating actively in sporting events). Your race, religion, and socio-economic status do not come as much to the forefront. But remember that other people treat you based on the groups to which *they* think you belong. So someone else might focus on other aspects of how you look or talk and see you primarily as "a woman," "a Muslim," or "an Egyptian."

The way in which others perceive your social identity, and how you perceive theirs, influences communication on many levels. Many corporate training sessions, for example, are now devoted to how to manage millennials. These young employees are assumed to have been heaped with so much praise by their baby-boomer parents that they now have (undeserved) self-confidence, are unable to accept criticism, and need lots of encouragement (Williams, 2015). But they also are praised for their can-do attitude, ability to multitask, and quest for meaningful contributions to society (Reshwan, 2015). Tips for managers, therefore, include making sure that you listen to their ideas (they are not used to being ignored), provide a fun but structured work environment (they are used to having activities coordinated around them), and give them lots of feedback that makes them feel their work is valued (Heathfield, 2016). Although these tips may be useful for many young recruits, a sizable portion of millennials do not actually identify with their generational label and reject the qualities ascribed to their so-called peers (Pew Research Center, 2015). So it may actually be problematic to make such sweeping assumptions about how best to communicate with an entire generation!

● **CARMELO ANTHONY'S TEARFUL RESPONSE** at the end of the 2016 Olympics gained him much media attention, perhaps because we are prone to criticize open displays of emotion from men. Jean Catuffe/Getty Images

Intercultural Communication Challenges

With all of the cultural variations that are possible in the individual and overlapping cocultures to which each person belongs, it is understandable that communication difficulties sometimes arise. Even with people you know well who are like you in many ways, you can sometimes experience difficulties during communication. Let's look at three of the more pressing intercultural challenges that communicators experience when interacting with others: anxiety, ethnocentrism, and discrimination.

Anxiety

"What if I say something offensive?" "What if I don't know how to behave?" "What if I embarrass myself?" These are just a few of the worries that people sometimes have as they approach intercultural communication encounters. Consider the experience of Allison, an American student about to set off on a semester abroad in China:

> Here I was, standing, in the check-out line of the Chinese market in Rockville, Maryland, listening to the cashier yell at me with an incomprehensible stream of syllables. This was after a rather harrowing

connect

In Chapter 15 on speech delivery, we offer practical tips to help you build your confidence and face the natural anxiety that accompanies a speaking opportunity. Many of these tips are also useful for overcoming anxiety in intercultural encounters. For example, Allison might visualize her success in navigating a foreign city in order to boost her sense of efficacy.

attempt to find groceries in the overcrowded store. A year of Chinese was not helping me as I stood in front of an entire display of green vegetables, trying to figure out which sign would lead me to my desired product. During all of this, my accompanying friend turned to me and said, "This is how crowded it will be wherever you go in China" (Goodrich, 2007).

You can probably imagine Allison's anxiety as she considered her upcoming adventure: If she felt uncomfortable navigating the market just a few miles from her dorm, how would she be able to communicate effectively several thousand miles away?

But for most of us, the more positive experiences we have with those who differ from us, the less intimidated we feel about communicating with someone from another culture. And the less intimidated we feel, the more competent our communication becomes. In fact, one study found that American students who took the risk and studied abroad perceived themselves as being more proficient, approachable, and open to intercultural communication than those who lacked overseas experience (Clarke, Flaherty, Wright, & McMillen, 2009). Even online interactions across cultures may ease anxiety and foster understanding. Digital tools such as Skype, email, and Google Docs enable students in globally connected classrooms to engage in international communication experiences even if physical travel is not feasible (Rubin, 2013).

Although anxiety may be a natural part of any new experience or interaction, it would be unfortunate to allow it to prevent you from experiencing the clear benefits and enrichment gained from intercultural experiences.

Ethnocentrism

In the fashion world, the gowns worn by prominent trendsetters are always big news. So, when the former first lady Michelle Obama wore a stunning Naeem Khan sheath to a state dinner, newspapers and bloggers were bound to comment. But the buzz the following morning was not over what she wore but on how to explain the color of the gown. Described by its designer as "a sterling-silver sequin, abstract floral, nude strapless gown," the dress was a color somewhere between peach and sand. The Associated Press initially described it as "flesh-colored," but changed it to "champagne" when one editor questioned: "Whose flesh? Not hers" (Phanor-Faury, 2010).

This is a simple and common example of **ethnocentrism**, a belief in the superiority of your own culture or group and a tendency to view other cultures through the lens of your own. Together with intercultural anxiety, ethnocentrism can inhibit our ability to have satisfying intercultural interactions and experiences (Neuliep, 2012). Ethnocentrism can make communication biased: we tend to communicate from the perspective of our own group without acknowledging other perspectives. The offense is often unintended, which further reveals the fact that we sometimes behave in ways that "normalize" one group and marginalize another—without even realizing it. Describing a peach-colored dress as "flesh" colored, for example, insinuates that light-colored skin is the default standard and that darker skin tones are therefore something "other" or different from the norm. It is also unclear. "While beige may be 'nude' for most white women," noted one commentator, "'nude' for me would be brown" (Phanor-Faury, 2010).

● **THE IDEA OF STUDYING** abroad may initially cause you anxiety, but positive experiences in a foreign country can make you a more competent and interculturally sensitive communicator. Ryan Sensenig/ Photo Agora

Ethnocentrism is not the same thing as ethnic or cultural pride. It is a wonderful and uniquely human experience to express feelings of patriotism or to experience a deep respect for your religion or ethnic heritage. Ethnocentrism arises when you express a bias on behalf of your own cocultures—when you treat others as inferior or inconsequential, or ignore them altogether. Carlos, for example, is a proud Catholic for whom the Christmas holidays have great religious meaning. He decorates his home with a nativity scene and sends Christmas cards to family and fellow Christians as December 25 draws near. But he also sends a separate set of "Season's Greetings" cards to his friends who do not celebrate Christmas. He thus shows respect for their traditions while still sharing his wishes for peace and goodwill with them.

Discrimination

Ethnocentrism can lead to **discrimination**—behavior toward a person or group based solely on membership in a particular group, class, or category. Discrimination arises when attitudes about superiority of one culture lead to rules and behaviors that favor that group and harm another group.

Recall from Chapter 3 that *stereotypes* about and *prejudice* toward a particular cultural group may result in discrimination, preventing individuals from understanding and adapting to others (Cargile & Giles, 1996). Yet seemingly positive stereotypes can have similarly discriminatory effects. For example, consider the "model minority" stereotype of Asian Americans that characterizes them as quiet, hardworking, studious, and productive. As Suzuki (2002) points out, these beliefs have led some employers to dismiss Asian Americans' complaints about discrimination in the workplace and have made government agencies and nonprofit organizations less inclined to support programs to assist lower-income Asian Americans since Asian communities seem largely self-sufficient.

Discrimination can be explained in part by research on intergroup communication. Studies show that we have a biased tendency to treat fellow in-group members better than we treat members of out-groups (Giles, Reid, & Harwood, 2010). In fact, we even *interpret* in-group behaviors more favorably than out-group behaviors. For example, if you discovered that someone in your sorority was caught cheating on an exam, you would likely explain the behavior as an unusual situation brought on by challenging circumstances. But if you heard about someone from another sorority (an out-group) cheating, you would be more likely to attach a personal explanation, such as, "She's dishonest."

● A BEAUTIFUL GOWN? Yes. A flesh-colored gown? Only if you are white and think ethnocentrically that white skin is the norm for "flesh." Brendan Smialowski/Getty Images

Improving Intercultural Communication

As with many worthwhile things in life, you can improve your intercultural communication with effort. The result can be positive changes in three areas:

▶ *Cognition (thinking).* Our thinking changes when we increase our knowledge about cultures and cocultures and develop more complex (rather than simplistic) ways of thinking about a culture. These moves reduce negative stereotypes and help us appreciate other points of view.

▶ *Affect (feelings).* When we experience greater enjoyment and less anxiety in our intercultural interactions, we feel more comfortable and positive about intercultural exchanges.

▶ *Behavior (actions).* When our thoughts and feelings are altered, our behavior changes, too. We develop better interpersonal relationships in work groups and perform our jobs better when we know what to say and not to say—do and not do. We thus act with greater ease and effectiveness in accomplishing goals.

How do you successfully make these changes? You don't need special training, but it will help to adopt some important principles as you communicate with people from other generations, faiths, ethnicities, and so on: mindfulness, openness to other cultures, effective intergroup contact, appropriate accommodation, and practice at using your skills.

Mindfulness

As you learned in Chapter 3, being *mindful* means to be aware of your behavior and others' behavior. In the intercultural context, mindfulness also means being "fully present" in the awareness of the cultural and intergroup aspects of the situation (Ting-Toomey & Dorjee, 2015). It involves becoming more conscious of your own thoughts and emotional reactions and understanding how these reactions may be rooted in your own culture. When someone stands a bit too close to you, for example, you might normally sense "something funny"; however, being mindful means recognizing the possibility of a cultural difference. Of course, not all uncomfortable interactions stem from cultural differences, but being mindful of the possibility gives you a wider range of effective ways to respond.

You should also ask yourself whether you might be interpreting another person's behaviors negatively or positively based on whether the individual shares your group memberships. Part of this mindfulness is practicing **intercultural sensitivity**, or mindfulness of behaviors that may offend others (Bennett & Bennett, 2004). When Luke, who is Catholic, married Caroline, who is Jewish, his mother insisted that the family pictures be taken in front of the church altar and religious statues in the garden outside. This was insensitive to Caroline's Jewish family. Had Luke's mother reflected on how she would have felt if her own religious beliefs had been disregarded in this manner, she might have behaved very differently. Being sensitive does not mean giving up your own beliefs and practices, but it does mean not forcing them blindly on others.

Openness to Other Cultures

In addition to being mentally engaged and sensitive to cultural differences, we can improve intercultural interaction by developing an "open heart" toward other cultures—a willingness to understand and appreciate their different practices (Ting-Toomey & Dorjee, 2015). Taking the time to learn culture-specific information can be a useful starting point. It can also prepare you to adapt—or not adapt—as you consider the factors that may be important in a particular situation.

But *how* do you go about learning about another culture or coculture and its members' communication preferences? Is it okay to ask group members questions or to seek clarification? Do you have to visit a foreign country to learn about that nation's culture? Do you need a close friend within a given coculture to understand aspects of that coculture's communication? We encourage you to ask respectful and earnest questions and to experience other cultures in whatever way you are able—whether that means trying foods outside of your own culture, studying the scriptures of another faith, or deciding to study abroad.

In fact, with all the technology available to you today, you can make contact through online communities and social networking groups even if you cannot personally travel around the world. For example, some students have taken to posting videos of themselves practicing a foreign language in order to elicit feedback from native speakers on the quality of their speech and accent. Such attempts to learn more about another culture's language or way of speaking can also be seen in YouTube videos in which American and British children attempt to swap accents and rate each other on how accurate they are.

and you?

Consider a time you felt competent in learning about another culture or coculture. What was the situation? How did you gain knowledge about the culture? Did this knowledge cause you to change your behavior or thoughts?

Effective Intergroup Contact

Learning about other cultures is a great start to improving intercultural communication. But many scholars also recommend spending time with members of other cultures and cocultures, virtually and face to face. **Intergroup contact theory** argues that interaction between members of different social groups generates a possibility for more positive attitudes to emerge (Allport, 1954; Pettigrew & Tropp, 2006). In other words, if you have contact with people who are different from you, you have a chance to understand and appreciate them better. Although contact theory has some support, researchers also find that mindlessly getting people from different groups together can actually backfire and reinforce cultural stereotypes (Paolini, Harwood, & Rubin, 2010). This happened in many U.S. cities during the 1970s and 1980s, when there was a highly controversial effort to racially integrate schools by busing children to schools on faraway sides of their cities. Even staunch proponents of the plan admitted that racial tensions became worse, not better (Frum, 2000).

Intergroup Biases

Part of the reason that intergroup contact can backfire is that there are cognitive biases that are often triggered when different groups get together. These are usually unconscious ways that we interpret interactions in a way that helps us to maintain our existing views about out-group members. For example, our intergroup schemas and stereotypes have a tendency to influence our perceptions—we see or hear what we want to see or hear. In other words, if you think teenagers are lazy, then regardless of how hard your fourteen-year-old cousin studies, you do not see the effort. Instead, you notice his eye-rolling or slumped shoulders and still perceive him as unmotivated. We may also engage in **behavioral confirmation**—when we act in a way that *makes* our expectations about a group come true (Snyder & Klein, 2005). Again, if you think your teenage cousin (like all teens) is lazy, you will more likely give him tasks that do not require much effort. When he, in turn, fails to put in a great deal of effort, you confirm to yourself, "See? I knew he wouldn't try very hard."

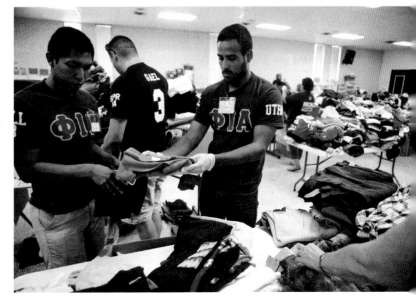

● **GOOD-QUALITY** contact with members of a campus fraternity could serve to counter the bias that frat brothers are nothing more than jocks or partyers. Marjorie Kamys Cotera/Bob Daemmrich Photography/Alamy

Overcoming Our Biases

So how do we make successful intergroup interactions more likely? First, intergroup researchers argue that we must have *good-quality contact* with out-group members, because negative contact can increase the perception of differences (Paolini,

Harwood, & Rubin, 2010). But good contact is not enough, because it makes it easy to explain away such positive interactions as unique to the individual or the situation. For example, if you believe that fraternity brothers are simply party boys and you wind up in a study group with a particularly hardworking member of Phi Sigma Phi, you can mentally create excuses: "Ben is the exception to the rule."

Researchers argue that we must have good contact *with people we think are "typical" of their group* (Giles, Reid, & Harwood, 2010). If you attended a few fraternity events and got to see Ben and several of his brothers more regularly in their fraternity setting, you might learn that many of them are serious students and that some of them are not even into the party scene. In addition, we may need extended *time* to interact, so that we can practice our intercultural messages and develop personal relationships. One recent study found that even the highly polarized groups of religious Jews and Palestinian Arabs showed significantly reduced prejudice toward each other after spending a year communicating online on student projects (Walther, Hoter, Ganayem, & Shonfeld, 2015).

Appropriate Accommodation

Another way to improve intercultural communication is to adapt your language and nonverbal behaviors. Recall from Chapter 4 that adjusting your language and style of speaking toward the people with whom you are communicating is a

---

evaluating communication ethics

That Is Not a Soy Substitute

You and your friend Greg share an apartment. Greg is a strict vegan and does not consume animal products, including meat, dairy, and even honey. You are not a vegan — in fact, you are not even a vegetarian — but you have always respected Greg's passion for animal rights and his hard work to become a veterinarian. Before you and Greg decided to move in together, you had a frank conversation during which he told you that he would be uncomfortable having animal products in the apartment and wondered if you would be willing to eat a vegan diet in your shared space. You thought Greg would make a great roommate and you wanted the situation to work out, so you agreed. Besides, you figured you could always grab a cheeseburger on campus.

The arrangement has worked out rather well. You barely think about the food restrictions, except for when Greg's girlfriend Amanda visits. Amanda is well aware of Greg's desires and views, but you suspect that she finds them to be ridiculous and insulting. Sometimes you even feel that she is trying to bait you into complaining about Greg's veganism so that the two of you can "gang up" on him in an effort to enact a change of behavior. You have tried to stay out of it, but one evening you arrive home to find Amanda alone in your living room, eating a container of pork fried rice — and we are not talking about a soy pork substitute. "Please don't tell Greg," she pleads. "I told him I'd hang out here until he's done with class tonight and I got hungry. I cannot eat any of that tofu stuff in your refrigerator so I ordered takeout. Besides, you must think that his restrictions on what we eat here are crazy . . . don't you?"

You feel annoyed by this conversation and want to mention it to Greg, but you also feel that Greg and Amanda's communication and discussions about personal practices and group affiliations are their business, not yours. What should you do?

think about this

1. How would this situation be different if it took place in a dorm and Greg were a randomly selected roommate? is it ethical for roommates to ask each other to follow food restrictions?

2. What if Greg's reasons for having food restrictions encompassed additional cocultural factors, such as religion? Would this be a more, less, or equally pressing reason for you to accommodate food restrictions in your home? Why or why not?

3. How might you structure an ethical response to Amanda or an ethical conversation with Greg based on the suggestions for improving intercultural communication provided in this chapter?

● **ALTHOUGH SQUATTING** to speak at eye level with a child is an appropriate accommodation, a senior adult may perceive this behavior as patronizing. Sitting may be more respectful. iconics/a.collectionRF/Getty Images

process called **accommodation**. On a simple level, you do this when you talk to a child, squatting down to make eye contact and using a basic vocabulary; police officers also do this when they adopt the street slang or foreign phrases commonly used in the neighborhoods they patrol. When speakers shift their language or nonverbal behaviors *toward* each other's way of communicating, they are engaging in **convergence**. We typically converge to gain approval from others and to show a shared group identity (Gallois, Franklyn-Stokes, Giles, & Coupland, 1988). Convergence usually results in positive reactions, because if I speak like you, it is a way of saying "I am one of you."

Accommodation is not an absolute, all-or-nothing goal: usually, it involves making small efforts to show that you respect others' cultural and communication behaviors and that you appreciate their efforts to communicate with you. Ramon makes efforts to speak English when he greets his customers at the restaurant where he works, even though it is not his native language and he struggles with it at times. Conversely, many of his regular customers who do not speak Spanish will greet him with the Spanish words they do know ("¡Hola, Ramon! ¡Buenos días!") and thank him for their meal ("¡Gracias!").

However, it is important to be careful not to **overaccommodate**, which means going too far in changing your language or changing your language based on an incorrect or stereotypical notion of another group (Harwood & Giles, 2005). For example, senior citizens often find it patronizing and insulting when younger people speak "down" to them (slow speech, increase volume, and use childish words; Harwood, 2000). For Ramon, if his customers were to speak slowly and loudly, or in poorly mangled attempts to communicate in Spanish, Ramon might think they were making fun of him.

Practice Using Your Skills

It is one thing to understand the principles involved in competent intercultural communication. But it can be another thing to put these ideas into practice. For example, you may stumble when you try to speak the language of another culture well enough to be understood. You may have difficulty expressing appreciation for another person's worldview when it just seems so "wrong." Communicators with fewer social skills have more difficulty managing the "different" interactions that intercultural situations demand, so you may need to practice the following skills (Arasaratnam, 2007):

▶ **Listen effectively.** You cannot be mindful unless you listen to what people say (and what they don't say). For example, if someone is speaking with a foreign accent, rather than just dismissing that person as too difficult to understand, you can make a conscious effort to avoid distractions and focus carefully on what he or she is saying (Dragojevic & Giles, 2016). Knowing when to talk and when to be quiet (so you can listen) is crucial to intercultural encounters.

▶ **Think before you speak or act.** When someone communicates in a way that seems strange to you—not meeting your gaze, for example, or speaking very directly—remind yourself to take a moment to think about whether his or her behavior is a cultural difference rather than evasion or hostility. Ask yourself what your own assumptions are about "normal" behavior.

▶ **Be empathic.** *Empathy* is putting yourself in someone else's place in an attempt to understand that person's experience. You are more likely to be able to learn about and appreciate another culture or group if you try to see the world through their eyes.

▶ **Do the right thing.** Stand up for someone who is being mocked for his or her race, religion, or sexual orientation. Fight for those who do not have a voice. You do not need to be wealthy, established, or powerful to do this. When a friend makes a remark that you see as culturally insensitive, respond with a simple reminder ("That's a rude statement," or "Oh, man, don't talk like that"). You will send a powerful message without chiding or berating your friend.

back to ▶ *Hamilton*

Theo Wargo/Getty Images

At the beginning of the chapter, we talked about the hit musical *Hamilton,* which depicts the complexity within and between cocultures in its telling of early American history. Let's revisit *Hamilton* to see how it both relates to and reflects some of the concepts described in this chapter.

▶ *Hamilton* reflects culture in the United States in terms of the diversity of the cast as well as the musical traditions. The popularity of rap music and hip-hop culture in the United States is celebrated and blended with the more traditional American musical conventions of Broadway. The story itself reflects American values of individualism and low power distance in its telling of the revolutionary war (Americans as the ultimate underdogs) and the development of a new country (including battles over the role of individual citizens). The acclaim of *Hamilton* also reflects some American individualism, as numerous awards have expressed appreciation for the achievement of individuals in the show, including particular performers, the composer, and the producer.

▶ *Hamilton* has also provided an avenue for contemporary audiences, including inner-city children of color, to develop an "open heart" for American history and an appreciation of a past culture that they might not otherwise be able to relate to. Composer Lin-Manual Miranda and producer Jeffrey Seller have even partnered with the Gilder Lehrman Institute of American History and the Rockefeller Foundation to bring children to see the show as well as to encourage them to compose their own modern musical interpretations of historical events (D'Orio, 2016).

▶ Think about social identity. African-American and Latino/a actors are playing historically white male figures, so conventional notions about race and ethnicity are upended in favor of understanding the complex motivations of the historical figures themselves. Burr and Hamilton may denigrate each other with negative references to their cultural groups ("orphan, son of a whore"), but they also share a common worldview as honored statesmen, even accepting and enacting the outlawed tradition of fighting in dual.

things to try ▶ Activities

1. LaunchPad for *Real Communication* offers key term videos and encourages self-assessment through adaptive quizzing. Go to **launchpadworks.com** to get access to:

LearningCurve
Adaptive Quizzes.

Video clips that illustrate key concepts, highlighted in teal in the Real References section that follows.

2. On a blank piece of paper, begin listing all the cocultures to which you belong. How many can you come up with? How do they overlap? If someone asked you to identify yourself by using only one of them, could you do it? Could you rank them in order of importance to you?

3. Make a list of all the places where you have lived or traveled. (Remember, this does not just mean "travel to foreign countries." Think about trips to other neighborhoods in your city or areas of your state.) Create a bullet-point list to describe the attitudes, customs, and behaviors of each place that seemed to typify the area. How was communication different in each area? How was it similar?

4. Many popular films in the United States are based on foreign language films from other cultures, such as *The Departed* (2006, based on the Hong Kong film *Infernal Affairs,* 2002), *The Tourist* (2010, based on the French film *Anthony Zimmer,* 2005), and *Let Me In* (2010, based on Sweden's *Let the Right One In,* 2008). Watch one such film as well as the original foreign language film that inspired it. What cultural changes to the story can you detect? How do the nonverbal behaviors of the actors differ?

5. Do a little virtual shopping in the toy department of an online retailer. Use the search options to see what kinds of toys the retailer suggests for girls versus boys. What do these suggestions say about culture, gender, and the ways in which children play? Do these nonverbal messages influence culture, or are they more of a reflection of culture?

real reference ➤ A Study Tool

Now that you have finished reading this chapter, you can:

Define and explain culture and its impact on your communication:

▶ **Culture** is a system of thought and behavior, learned through communication, that reflects a group's shared beliefs, values, and practices (p. 134).
▶ Your **worldview** is the framework through which you interpret people's behavior (p. 134).
▶ **Intercultural communication** is the communication between people from different cultures who have different worldviews (p. 136).

Delineate important ways that cultural variables affect communication:

▶ Individuals in **high-context cultures** use contextual cues to interpret meaning and send subtle messages; in **low-context cultures**, verbal directness is much more important (pp. 138–139).
▶ In **collectivist cultures**, people perceive themselves primarily as members of a group and communicate from that perspective; in **individualist cultures**, people value individuality and communicate autonomy and privacy (pp. 139–140).
▶ Our discomfort with the unknown (**uncertainty avoidance**) varies with culture (p. 140).
▶ **Masculine cultures** tend to place value on assertiveness, achievement, ambition, and competitiveness; **feminine cultures** tend to value nurturance, relationships, and quality of life (p. 140).
▶ **Power distance** is the degree to which cultures accept hierarchies among individuals (p. 141).
▶ **Time orientation** is the way that cultures communicate about and with time. In **monochronic cultures**, time is a valuable resource that is not to be wasted. **Polychronic cultures** have a more fluid approach to time (p. 142).
▶ Cultures differ in their expression of emotion. Cultures that embrace **hyperbole** use vivid, colorful, exaggerated language, whereas cultures that value **understatement** use language that downplays emotional intensity (p. 143).

Describe the communicative power of group affiliations:

▶ **Cocultures** are groups whose members share some aspects of the general culture but also have their own distinct characteristics (p. 145).
▶ A **generation** is a group of people born into a specific time frame (p. 145).
▶ **Gender** refers to the behavioral and cultural traits associated with biological sex (p. 145).
▶ **Social identity theory** notes that your *social identity is based* on your group memberships. We communicate differently with people in our **in-groups** versus **out-groups** (p. 147).

▶ Studies in **intergroup communication** examine how our group membership affects our interaction, and our social identity shifts depending on which group membership is most **salient** at a given moment (pp. 147–148).

Explain key barriers to competent intercultural communication:

▶ Anxiety may cause you to worry about embarrassing yourself in an intercultural interaction (pp. 149–150).

▶ **Ethnocentrism** is the belief in the superiority of your own culture or group (p. 150).

▶ **Discrimination** is biased behavior toward someone based on their membership in a group, class, or category. People often discriminate based on *stereotypes* and *prejudiced* views of other groups (p. 151).

Demonstrate behaviors that contribute to intercultural competence:

▶ Be mindful of cultural differences and develop **intercultural sensitivity**, an awareness of behaviors that might offend others (p. 152). Be open to learning about and appreciating other cultures (pp. 152–153).

▶ **Intergroup contact theory** suggests that interaction between members of different social groups can encourage positive attitudes. However, intergroup biases interfere with this process, such as seeing or hearing what you want to see or hear in group members. **Behavioral confirmation** is acting in a way that makes your expectations about a group come true (p. 153).

▶ Research supports the importance of **accommodation**, adjusting your language and nonverbal behaviors. **Convergence** is adapting your communication to be more like another individual's. If you **overaccommodate**, however, the interaction can be perceived negatively (p. 155).

▶ It is important to *practice* your intercultural skills (p. 156).

A doctor's ability to effectively listen to a patient can literally mean the difference between life and death.

sturti/Getty Images

 LearningCurve can help you master the material in this chapter.
Go to **launchpadworks.com**

chapter

7

Listening

Listening skills are crucial in medical care situations: doctors must probe patients for information and work with teams of other medical professionals whose expertise and perspectives can be valuable. In the college environment, health care issues are compounded by students living in close quarters, sharing personal items with ill roommates, and sharing bathrooms and food sources. Then there are mental health problems, sexually transmitted diseases, sports injuries, and injuries while under the influence of alcohol (Champion, Lewis, & Myers, 2015). When college students come into the health clinic, their problems may be due to a complex number of issues, so the team of health professionals must listen to them and one another to determine the correct diagnosis and treatment. When doctors do not listen to their patients, they are more likely to misdiagnose illnesses. These mistakes are costly; poor communication between doctors and patients is cited in at least 40 percent of medical malpractice suits (Landro, 2013).

But patients have listening responsibilities, too. They must listen carefully to any questions health professionals ask them in order to be able to respond clearly with the most relevant information about their current condition. They must be willing to disclose sometimes very personal facts about sexual or substance abuse that may be important. Communicating this information clearly can help the health professional listen more effectively as well. Patients must then carefully listen to all options and treatments and diligently follow the accepted treatment plan. When patients do not listen effectively, they are more likely to misunderstand the advice, increasing the likelihood of complications and hospitalizations.

Many hospitals, health care systems, and insurers are requiring doctors to receive special training to improve their communication skills, providing advice and skill-building exercises to help them to listen better to their patients and also to teach them to speak in ways that encourage their *patients* to listen more effectively (Landro, 2013). Candidates for admission at many of the nation's top medical schools must demonstrate effective communication skills in a series of short interviews that test their interpersonal skills and ability to work with others under pressure. Those who fail to listen well or who are overly opinionated are considered poor candidates (Harris, 2011).

If you have never thought about listening as a crucial communication skill for people on both sides of the medical situation, you are not alone. "I have demonstrated strong listening skills" does not often make a line on many résumés, like being able to speak Mandarin or build an app. Yet professors, employers, and medical professionals often affirm effective listening as a necessary and vital skill. In fact, scholars have even claimed that listening helps us achieve our most basic human need: to understand and be understood (Nichols, 2006).

Thus, all professions need listening skills that pay attention both to what is said aloud and to what information nonverbal cues add to the mix. Just as doctors can improve overall outcomes for their patients by listening effectively (Ranjan, Kumari, & Chakrawarty, 2015), you can improve your productivity, performance, and relationships with strong listening skills. As a bonus, you can help others, too. For example, when health care providers listen empathically, not only do they help patients reduce anxiety, but their patients are also more satisfied and compliant with treatments (Davis, Foley, Crigger, & Brannigan, 2008).

In this chapter, we examine the nature of listening—how we hear, process, come to understand, and then respond to others' communication. We learn why listening is so important and why we so often fail to listen effectively. We also describe tools and techniques you can use every day to become a more effective and competent listener.

How We Listen

Hearing and listening are not the same thing. Consider when you have music playing in your headphones or earbuds. You are *hearing* the music and lyrics, and you may sing along, but minutes later you forget what you heard. The music may help you to relax or pass the time, but you are not particularly focused on the songs playing. It is often just pleasant background noise to the other things you are doing, such as folding laundry. However, if you are really *listening* to the music, you do actively focus on it—you notice when and where the drum beats change; you attend to the cleverness (or lack of it) in the rhyming of the lyrics; you give thought to how the music is making you feel. You may learn from it, evaluate it, appreciate it. This difference works similarly when we communicate with others.

Hearing is the physiological process of perceiving sound, the process through which sound waves are picked up by the ears and transmitted to the brain. Unless there is a physical reason why hearing does not take place, it is an involuntary process—you cannot turn it on or off. Just like with music, when someone talks to you, you hear the sounds and words coming in. But sometimes the words go "in one ear and out the other," as the expression goes. It is a different matter to hear *and* decide which sounds and words you are going to notice. This is where listening comes in.

Listening is a multidimensional process of recognizing, understanding, accurately interpreting, and many times responding effectively to the messages you hear. It is much more than just hearing words or being able to recall information (Bodie, Worthing, Imhof, & Cooper, 2008; Janusik, 2005). Listening involves processing what others say and do, paying attention, understanding (Thomas & Levine, 1994), and then creating messages that respond to the speaker and are directed toward achieving goals (Bodie et al., 2012; Janusik, 2005; Wiemann, Takai, Ota, & Wiemann, 1997). Competent listening may also involve listening for the "unspoken," the things people only hint at in their communication that you must discover (Baab, 2014).

The Listening Process

The listening process occurs so quickly that we may think of it as automatic; however, listening involves three components: 1) affective listening involves having the motivation to pay attention; 2) cognitive involves selecting a specific message to pay attention to, focusing on it, and understanding it; and 3) behavioral involves responding verbally and nonverbally to let others know we have remembered and understood what they said (Bodie, 2012; Halone et al., 1998). We can develop and improve our listening skills by focusing on these three components.

Affective Component

Recall from earlier chapters that when you display your *affect*, you are showing the positive or negative feelings you have toward something—your attitudes. Similarly, the **affective component** of listening refers to your attitude toward listening to a person or message. For example, if you care about your roommate Brett, you are probably open to listening to him tell you how worried he is about his economics midterm. Being *willing* to listen is an important first step in listening effectively.

However, when you are not motivated to listen, you are prone to "tune out" or only listen halfheartedly. If Brett seems to worry or complain about exams all the time (especially if he gets good grades anyway), then you may not want to hear him go on and on about this again. Or perhaps you are jealous of Brett's good grades. There are many factors that can affect our motivation to listen, including preexisting schemas (see Chapter 3) that we have about a person, topic, or situation, and several listening challenges we explain later in this chapter.

Cognitive Component

The **cognitive component** of listening involves the mental processes of *selecting* messages to focus on, giving them our *attention*, and then trying to *understand* them. In the face of competing stimuli—your roommate Brett complaining about his economics midterm while your other roommates stream *Stranger Things* and you get multiple texts from your parents—you must choose one sound over the others, a process called **selecting**. You are more likely to select stimuli that you are motivated to listen to or that have features that grab your attention (such as volume or motion).

● **LISTENING TO A FRIEND** express concern about a personal issue involves both verbal and nonverbal skills not always necessary when hearing a song on your iPhone. (left) Samuel Borges Photography/Shutterstock; (right) Ariel Skelley/Getty Images

By **attending**, you alert your senses (such as your eyes and ears) to *focus* on the communication that you have selected. If you select Brett's voice (because it is louder or more important to you than the sound of *Stranger Things*), you concentrate on and try to remember what he is saying. Attending is not always easy; if your phone keeps chirping at you with new texts, attending to Brett's message may be more difficult.

Suppose Brett mentions a disagreement he had with his professor over the wording of an essay question on the midterm. He throws around phrases like "aggregate supply" and "reciprocal demand." You have never studied economics, so even if you are paying attention, you may barely understand a word he is saying. **Understanding**—making sense of messages—is a crucial step because it enables you to interpret meaning and make judgments. When you do not understand something, you need to listen more actively. You might even request that Brett repeat something or ask him questions about the economics terms or his situation (Husband, 2009). Understanding another's thoughts and feelings usually requires that you care about them enough to be responsive (Winczewski, Bowen, & Collins, 2016).

Behavioral Component

The third component involves *showing* the person that you understand and remember the information given—the **behavioral component** of listening. As a student, you know it is important to recall information from class during an exam but it also counts in personal listening situations. Showing that you **remember**,

---

communication across cultures

A Quick Lesson in Deaf Etiquette

The popular reality competition show *Project Runway* highlights twelve designers vying for the big prize: an opportunity to launch their own fashion line. In one recent season, Justin LeBlanc was one of those designers; he was ready and eager to work on the challenges doled out by host Heidi Klum and was grateful for the helpful advice of mentor Tim Gunn and the mostly constructive critiques of the show's three judges. But unlike his fellow competitors, Justin did not look Klum, Gunn, or the judges in the eye when they spoke. Instead, he watched his interpreter, who translated their words into American Sign Language (ASL) for him. LeBlanc is deaf; although he has a cochlear implant, he remains dependent on ASL for most of his communication.

Many people were surprised by how the show handled Justin's disability. For the most part, they ignored it by *listening to him*. The producers provided Justin with an interpreter and then, essentially, got out of the way. The interpreter sometimes appeared on camera but was never introduced or identified. Klum, Gunn, and the other contestants looked at Justin when speaking to him, even though he was focusing on their words through the interpreter's signs. The *Project Runway* cast and crew did not exclude Justin from the conversation and interaction; they got a lesson in deaf etiquette and truly listened to him (Marcus, 2013).

think about this

1. Do you think the hosts and judges of *Project Runway* had to learn to look at Justin rather than at the interpreter? Should the cast and crew have adapted their behaviors in any other ways?

2. What is the interpreter's role here? Should she have gotten some kind of billing or place in the story? Why or why not?

3. How did *Project Runway*'s treatment of Justin's disability compare with that of persons with disabilities on other television shows?

or recall information, contributes to perceptions of competence in interactions far beyond the classroom (Muntigl & Choi, 2010). If you do not recall what happened in your conversation with Brett, he might be annoyed later when he tells you about how his dilemma turned out and you stare vacantly at him.

Your verbal feedback and nonverbal reactions are behavioral responses that let others know you have received and understood their message. So when Brett wonders if he should talk to his professor, you nod your head and say, "Sounds like you think it's the best idea given the importance of this exam for your grade." This lets him know that you fully comprehend his concern. **Paraphrasing** is a particularly effective verbal response that can show what you have — or have not — understood. Paraphrasing involves rephrasing (not repeating) what you think the speaker has said. It also shows that you can recognize and elaborate on the other person's feelings, giving them some degree of legitimacy without suggesting an answer or solution (Fent & MacGeorge, 2006; Shotter, 2009). Just remember not to overdo paraphrasing; not only does the conversation become awkward, but also the other person may feel ridiculed (Weger, Castle, & Emmett, 2010).

Motivated listeners who attend, understand, and respond verbally and non-verbally — are called **active listeners.** These active listeners show that they both care and understand the other person; this level of responsiveness plays a key role in satisfying social interactions. **Passive listeners** do not show that they are listening; they may misinterpret messages, ignore them altogether, or need information and instructions repeated for them. It is no wonder that passive listeners are often regarded as less competent by the people around them. Some-times passive listeners get "caught" yet will not admit it. They are embarrassed about not listening carefully enough so purposely lie about it or engage in **con-fabulation**, where they fabricate and defend their distorted memories, unaware that the information is false. The goal, instead, is **listening fidelity**: the match-ing of our thoughts and another person's thoughts and intentions through com-munication (Beard, 2009; Fitch-Hauser, Powers, O'Brien, & Hanson, 2007; Powers & Bodie, 2003). Active listening plays an important role in achieving this goal.

Listening Goals

Tia had a meeting scheduled Monday morning with her colleague Farid to finish a presentation for an important client. But when Farid came to work, Tia noticed he was not his usual smiling self, and decided she needed to listen to whatever was bothering Farid before launching into their project. Like Tia, you probably find yourself in situations daily that require you to listen in different ways. With colleagues, professors, other students, family members, and friends, you probably spend a good deal of your time every day listening. Even when you are reading a text from a friend, you are also "listening" to the message sent. Clearly, listening remains a vital communication skill whether you are face to face or using mediated channels.

But how, exactly, should you listen? By adjusting your behavior to manage a relationship, analyze a situation, accomplish a task, or critically listen to others, you can listen more competently to accomplish these goals.

Relational listening accomplishes the work of maintaining your relationships. Also called *empathic listening,* the goal of relational listening is to understand and

what about you?

Assess Your Listening Goals

The following statements describe the ways some people think and behave when they are in various listening situations. Please indicate in the space at the left of each item how much you agree with the statement, using the following five-point scale: 1 = strongly disagree; 2 = disagree; 3 = unsure; 4 = agree; and 5 = strongly agree.

_____ 1. I enjoy listening to others because it allows me to connect with them.

_____ 2. I fully listen to what a person has to say before forming any opinions.

_____ 3. I get frustrated when people get off topic during a conversation.

_____ 4. I often catch errors in other speakers' logic.

_____ 5. When listening to others, I focus on understanding the feelings behind the words.

_____ 6. I try to withhold forming an opinion until I have listened to another person's entire message.

_____ 7. I find it difficult to listen to people who take too long to get their ideas across.

_____ 8. When listening to others, I notice contradictions in what they say.

_____ 9. I listen primarily to build and maintain relationships with others.

_____ 10. I wait until all the facts are presented before forming judgments and opinions.

_____ 11. I prefer speakers who quickly get to the point.

_____ 12. I have a talent for catching inconsistencies in what a speaker says.

_____ 13. When listening to others, I am mainly concerned with how they are feeling.

_____ 14. When listening to others, I consider all sides of the issue before responding.

_____ 15. I am impatient with people who ramble on during conversations.

_____ 16. Good listeners catch discrepancies in what people say.

Add your scores for the questions here:

Question *Score*

1, 5, 9, 13: _____ If greater than 15: You meet relational goals by focusing on the emotions and moods of the speaker.

2, 6, 10, 14 _____ If greater than 15: You are able to withhold judgment and fully listen to accomplish analytical goals.

3, 7, 11, 15 _____ If greater than 15: You accomplish task-oriented goals by trying to help the speaker quickly get to the point.

4, 8, 12, 16 _____ If greater than 15: Your ability to notice contradictions in a speaker helps you accomplish critical listening goals.

Note: If you score high on a number of these listening behaviors, you are able to adapt your listening to the person and situation, increasing your behavioral flexibility and competence.

Information from G. D. Bodie, D. L. Worthington, & C. C. Gearhart (2013).

appreciate how another person feels. It involves putting yourself in their position to assess their moods and communicating your empathy to them without judging. If Tia listens to what Farid says about how he is feeling and what may be bothering him, she lets him know she cares about him and values him as a person—not just for the work they have to accomplish.

Relational listening provides emotional support for someone in need or comforts someone when tragedy or disappointment strikes (Bodie, Vickery, & Gearhart, 2013; Gearhart & Bodie, 2011). Relational listening lets people know you share in their great joys or accomplishments by displaying nonverbal immediacy behaviors that communicate sensitivity and caring (Bodie & Jones, 2012). Relational listening also helps manage the emotions of people confronting adverse events and uncover erroneous assumptions contributing to their anxieties (Iedema, Jorm, Wakefield, Ryan, & Sorensen, 2009; Rehling, 2008).

Analytical listening involves taking in and organizing all of the pieces of information before making a judgment. Repeating or paraphrasing the ideas that you have heard and even taking notes when appropriate (such as at a meeting) are techniques that can help you to make sure you have a good sense of the situation and have considered all the possibilities. You may also group the pieces of information into categories or put them into an outline to help you organize how the ideas relate to or differ from one another. Analytical listening can help both Tia and Farid listen to clients thoroughly before they offer suggestions so that clients feel understood and validated. In addition, if Tia and Farid listen analytically, they will have fewer "do-overs" to correct mistakes or misperceptions about the clients' needs or wants.

Task-oriented listening does just that: focuses on the task at hand. Your primary goal is to understand the key or takeaway points of what is being said (also called *informational* or *comprehensive* listening). For example, when listening to directions or instructions, your goal is to process the information as efficiently as possible, so that you know exactly what you are supposed to do. Thus, clear, pertinent information is appreciated, and you may ignore or try to hurry people through extraneous details when they wander off track. Task-oriented listening can help others get to the point more quickly, but may be perceived as insensitive if the relationship is also important to you. If Tia tries to rush Farid when he starts to tell her what is bothering him, he probably will not feel validated by her; however, keeping Farid on topic when discussing their presentation might be necessary if they are to get it finished in time.

Critical listening focuses on evaluating information and finding any inconsistencies and/or errors in what is being said. Critical listening will also typically involve both analytical and informational listening at times because in order to criticize information, it helps to have first understood and organized all of the ideas or to have focused on the most relevant task-related points. Although valuable for saving time and money for individuals and organizations, critical listening runs the risk of sounding harsh or judgmental, depending on how you point out the inconsistencies or errors you discover. Tia and Farid can accomplish critical listening goals by evaluating the strengths and weaknesses of each other's ideas about their presentation without becoming defensive. In the end, they will be able to eliminate discrepancies and make a clearer and more compelling presentation.

The best listeners will adapt their listening goals to different persons and situations (Gearhart, Denham, & Bodie, 2014). For example, you may critically listen

connect

When listening for informational purposes, you may ask *primary* and *secondary questions*, which first seek information and then clarify the speaker's message (see the Interviewing Appendix). Secondary questions are particularly useful in job interviews because they show the interviewer that you are an engaged listener who desires to learn more specific information about the position and organization.

connect

As relationships develop, communication content changes, as do listening behaviors. When you are in the early stages of friendship with someone, you ask questions and seek information to help you discover things you may have in common. But in later stages, critical or analytical listening may become more important as you pursue a goal of connecting on a deeper level (Chapter 8).

TABLE 7.1

LISTENING GOALS

Type	Description	Strategies
Relational	Listening to assess and improve feelings in the relationship	Show empathy; demonstrate nonverbal immediacy
Analytical	Listening to gather and organize all pieces of information before judging	Paraphrase information heard; group or outline the ideas; withhold judgment initially
Task oriented	Listening to comprehend key points for accomplishing a task	Focus on task-specific information; keep speaker on track
Critical	Listening to evaluate information and uncover errors or inconsistencies	Evaluate accuracy and quality of statements, while avoiding sounding harsh

and you?

Consider the examples of listening goals we have given here. Are you able to adopt different behaviors in different situations to accomplish your goals? What if your goals are conflicting — how do you listen most effectively?

when evaluating a political candidate, relationally listen when consoling a friend, analytically listen when considering a complex situation, or engage in task-oriented listening when time is of the essence to get something done. In fact, meeting relational listening goals is often the way to make the other person comfortable in the listening situation; once the other person feels accepted and understood, it becomes possible to meet task, critical, and analytical goals (Keaton, Bodie, & Keteyian, 2015). So, to improve your listening skills, you need to actively work on them like any other skill (See Table 7.1 for strategies). It is easy to fall into thinking that it is a passive talent that cannot be developed. But from what we have demonstrated so far, this is not the case. You need to determine your goals and practice listening effectively to meet them.

The Value of Listening Well

As a young man, Dr. Ernesto Sirolli headed to Zambia to work with an Italian nongovernmental organization focused on building local agriculture. He had good intentions and dreams of helping the Zambian people, but every project his organization sponsored failed miserably. For example, Dr. Sirolli's team tried to teach the Zambian locals to grow tomatoes and zucchini. Just when the tomatoes were ripening to perfection, hundreds of hippos emerged from the river and ate absolutely everything. The Italians were shocked; the Zambians smiled knowingly and explained that this was why they didn't have agriculture. Sirolli's team learned a powerful lesson: instead of arriving in a community to tell people what to do, they should listen to them first (Sirolli, 2012). From this and similar experiences, Sirolli's team developed the Enterprise Facilitation model, which focuses on responsive, person-centered approaches to local economic development through listening to local people's needs, passions, dreams, abilities, realities, and prospects. As a result, more than two hundred fifty communities around the world have successfully implemented locally focused programs for economic development.

In every aspect of life—from arguing for a pay raise to helping a rural merchant establish a successful trade—listening well is essential to achieve success. Put simply, listening affects more than your ability to communicate: it enables you to live a productive, satisfying, and healthy life (Bodie & Fitch-Hauser, 2010). Let's look at a few specific examples.

Effective Listening Helps Your Career

Effective listening is valued and rewarded professionally. Listening is one of the most important skills that a college graduate can possess when seeking employment (Louthan, 2009; Wolvin & Coakley, 1991). Employers routinely report that effective listening is related to job satisfaction, performance, and achievement of the organization's goals (Flynn, Valikoski, & Grau, 2008; Gray, 2010; Welch & Mickelson, 2013). Employees who are good listeners are also considered alert, confident, mature, and judicious — qualities that result in professional rewards like promotions and pay raises. Employers also value employees who can listen effectively in diverse contexts. For example, a manager expects her assistant to listen carefully to instructions for a project as well as listen for irritation or confusion from a customer. Similarly, employees must listen carefully to others during teleconferences and WebEx meetings despite distractions like background noise or malfunctioning equipment (Bentley, 2000).

Moreover, to be strong leaders, established professionals need to listen to others, make others feel heard, and respond effectively to them (Stillion, Southard, & Wolvin, 2009). The CBS reality series *Undercover Boss* features CEOs who go undercover in their own companies. Unrecognized by employees, they listen more than anything — by asking questions, hearing about the reality of work life for people at all levels of the organization, and probing for insights into what works and what does not. In most instances, the CEO returns to make positive changes in the company's operations — and improve communication with the employees as well.

● **DAVE RIFE,** owner of a White Castle fast-food franchise, poses as a new hire in his own company so that he can listen carefully and take directions from a veteran employee. © CBS Photo Archive/Getty Images

Effective Listening Saves Time and Money

One reason that professionals value listening skills so much is that good listeners save time by acting quickly and accurately on information presented to them. Modern marketers, for example, "listen" to what customers are saying on Facebook, Twitter, YouTube, and other social platforms and respond immediately to their evaluations and interests, increasing sales and satisfaction (Foley, 2014). Similarly, in a classroom situation, you can comprehend more when you listen well (Rubin, Hafer, & Arata, 2000), so if you actively listen to your instructor's remarks about an upcoming exam, you can save time by studying more effectively.

Businesses lose millions of dollars each year because of listening mistakes alone (Rappaport, 2010). Repeated or duplicated tasks, missed opportunities, lost clients, botched orders, misunderstood instructions, and forgotten appointments can cost companies money — as can failing to listen to customers. One such example is when the makers of Tropicana orange juice changed its product packaging without researching what customer reactions would be. The company was deluged with irate letters and emails from customers. Company officials quickly responded and reverted to the recognizable label (an orange with a straw protruding from it), but they could have avoided the fiasco if they had listened to their customers before making the costly change (Wiesenfeld, Bush, & Sikdar, 2010).

Effective Listening Creates Opportunities

Good listeners do not just avoid mistakes; they also find opportunities that others might miss. A real estate agent who listens to what a young couple is looking for in their first home and comprehends their financial constraints will more likely find them the right home. An entrepreneur who listens to fellow diners at a popular restaurant complain that no place in town serves vegetarian fare might find an opportunity for a new business. Even writing a textbook like the one you are reading involves listening. As authors, we must listen to our peers (who help us decide what topics and scholarship to include), to students (who help us identify what

and you?

Can you think of a time when poor listening cost you something? Have you ever missed test instructions? Missed meeting a friend or a team practice? Do you think these lapses were due to ineffective listening on your part or that of your partner?

● **HOW WILL** your real estate agent help you find your dream home if he does not listen to and comprehend your desire for high ceilings and hardwood? Juice Images Ltd/Getty Images

examples and issues in the manuscript are most relevant), and to our editors (who help us make the material clear and engaging).

Effective Listening Strengthens Relationships

Have you ever had a friend who just talked about himself or herself without ever allowing you to share your own thoughts or concerns? Does your roommate or a colleague send text messages or check Snapchat while you're talking? They may be hearing, but they are almost certainly not listening. And your relationship may be suffering as a result.

In new relationships, the partners must listen competently to learn more about each other; failure to do this usually results in less attraction and more negative emotions (Knobloch & Solomon, 2002). As your relationships progress, listening remains a top priority. For example, you are more likely to self-disclose to a friend who you think is listening to you. Even when a friend verbally "ruminates"—talks again and again about the same issues—listening supportively can help the person feel more satisfied with the friendship (Afifi, Merrill, Denes, & Davis, 2013). Similarly, you can significantly reduce your partner's stress in a challenging situation by letting him or her talk through difficult events while you listen actively (Lewis & Manusov, 2009). Effective listening can help couples work through relational problems (Hendrix, LaKelly Hunt, Luquet, & Carlson, 2015), and is key to communicating care and support when a relational partner is suffering distress (Collins et al., 2014).

Though there is great value to listening well, competent listening does not happen easily, as the following listening challenges illustrate.

Listening Challenges

Fernando loved living in the big house on the edge of campus, but hated going to the required weekly meetings. Ashley would get overly excited about cleanliness in the kitchen and ignore everyone else. Gordon liked to make himself seem more important by giving orders to others without listening to the topics on the agenda. Fernando was intimidated by the whole bunch of them and tried to get away as quickly as possible, sometimes before they had even finished talking. Much like Fernando, we all fail to listen effectively at times—despite the established benefits of listening well. We may find ourselves unable to listen to someone or something that we find boring. We may have trouble focusing when we have a lot on our mind, are in a rush, or are coming down with a cold. We may want to be supportive, but feel we have heard the same complaint a hundred times. In this section, we discuss **listening barriers**, factors that interfere with our ability to hear, comprehend, and respond appropriately. We also offer advice for overcoming these barriers (Nichols, Brown, & Keller, 2006).

● **WHEN JURIES** weigh the evidence in a case, they must listen more comprehensively than they would during casual, everyday interactions with their families. Fuse/Getty Images

Environmental Factors

Loud noise, such as sounds we experience at sporting events and rock concerts or when working around heavy equipment, is only one environmental factor impairing our ability to listen (and sometimes hear; Cohen, 2013). Large groups present another difficulty, as they involve more people competing for your attention. Distractions in your environment — your phone signaling text messages, a baby crying, a train rumbling by your house — can also impair listening. Indeed, local transit systems can be as loud as a rock concert (about one hundred twenty decibels; Childs, 2009). In a classroom, the light from laptops and smartphones may flash in your eyes, impairing your ability to listen to the lecture. Even the temperature or air quality in a room can be distracting enough to affect our listening.

If you know that environmental factors will distract you from a listening situation ahead of time, you can take steps to eliminate distractions. For example, if there is a classroom on your campus that's always cold, even when it's ninety degrees outside, bring a sweater or jacket to that class. Avoid busy public places when planning for an intimate conversation. And if you must attend a lecture with a lot of rowdy people, get to the meeting early and pick a seat closer to the speaker.

● **SOME DISTRACTIONS,** like loud music or a large crowd, impair our ability to actively listen. Andrew Chin/Getty Images

Biological Factors

Lyz's brother Noah has Down syndrome and has never spoken a full sentence. Yet Lyz and her three sisters have each learned to listen to him in different ways. Catherine listens for nonverbal variations in Noah's grunts; Rebecca watches his hands and how they sign or react as she sings to him; Ruth listens through silence when Noah becomes rigid or relaxed; and Lyz listens to Noah by combining the advice of all her sisters. Rebecca tells Lyz, "Whenever you think you can't talk to someone, that just means you are deaf to the ways that they are making their voice heard. Everyone communicates; we just need to learn how to listen better" (Lenz, 2016).

Sometimes difficulty with listening lies with how others "talk," as in Noah's case; however, other times, the listener has a physical or medical issue. For example, our hearing ability declines with age, affecting our capacity to hear words as well as speech tone, pitch, and range (Bellis & Wilber, 2001; Villaume & Brown, 1999). Stereotypes of older adults portray them as unable to engage in normal conversation because of cognitive decline, but the real problem is often that they must work harder to distinguish sounds, especially in noisy places (Murphy, Daneman, & Schneider, 2006). Accidents, diseases, stress and anxiety, and physical differences can also cause varying degrees of hearing impairment — for anyone, not just elderly people (Roup & Chiasson, 2010).

● **LISTENING** is not reserved for those with the ability to hear. These two friends are sharing ideas through sign language. © vikki martin/Alamy

Still, hearing loss (even total hearing loss) does not mean that an individual cannot listen competently. Deaf individuals often speak of "listening with their eyes," and research notes that those who cannot hear physically are quite competent at decoding nonverbal behaviors revealing a speaker's emotions (Grossman & Kegl, 2007). Recent winner of *Dancing with the Stars* Nyle DiMarco is deaf and does not see it as a problem. "I've never wanted to hear," he says (Gomez, 2016). Like DiMarco, individuals who use American Sign Language as a primary language also listen to each other and encode and decode messages, as do any individuals speaking the same vocal language.

It is important to remember, however, that it is easy to make misattributions about listening when communicating with people who cannot hear well. Older people sometimes report being perceived as stupid or uncaring and feel blamed for "not trying hard enough" to listen when they are truly having difficulty

● **YOUR ABILITY** to accomplish tasks would undoubtedly be stretched too thin if you attempted to write a paper, browse websites, and carry on a texting conversation simultaneously. David Neil Madden/Getty Images

understanding your words. They often withdraw socially or pretend to hear, which usually makes things worse, in order not to have to endure people's frustrations at having to repeat things or speak louder (Heffernan, Coulson, Henshaw, Barry, & Ferguson, 2016). We may need to make accommodations to assist their ability to listen (such as facing them when we talk or reducing background noise).

Even someone with perfect hearing can face listening challenges. For instance, a person with *attention deficit disorder* (ADD) may have difficulty focusing on information and tasks, which can make listening challenging. People with high *sensory-processing sensitivity* (SPS) pay close attention to many fine details in a listen-ing situation (most of us filter out the fine details, focusing on the "big picture"). There are worries that high SPS listeners might become impatient and irritable in listening situations, missing some of the emotional impact of the speaker's words while being overwhelmed by details. Fortunately, many people with high SPS compensate effectively by recognizing their listening challenges and developing strategies to deal with their heightened sensitivity to behavioral cues (Gearhart, 2014). Similarly, people with *auditory processing disorder*, a learning disability that makes it difficult to process information they hear, must use strategies to focus on and understand spoken information: they might adjust to their environment, for example, by sitting in the front of the classroom or studying in the quietest sec-tion of the library. They might rely more heavily on written or visual cues when learning new information, use paraphrasing to confirm that they have received and processed messages correctly, and focus on only one listening task at a time.

Multitasking

Listening well can be nearly impossible when your attention is divided among many important tasks. **Multitasking**—attending to several things at once—is often considered an unavoidable part of modern life. We routinely drive, walk, cook, or tidy up while listening to music, talking on the phone, com-municating on social networking sites, or watching television.

We may believe we are giving fair attention to each task, but research shows that our ability to attend to more complicated chores suffers when we multitask. That's because our ability to focus is limited—we end up shifting our attention between various tasks, which decreases our efficiency and accuracy—even "rewires" our brain (Richtel, 2010). If you grew up surrounded by television, PlayStations, and iPods, you may be able to multitask better than people who grew up without such distractions. But regardless of age or experience, heavy multitaskers are less able to switch tasks efficiently and tend to be distracted by irrelevant pieces of informa-tion (Ophir, Nass, & Wagner, 2009). An additional downside is that their romantic partners can experience less relationship satisfaction (Roberts & David, 2016).

So what are realistic remedies for this listening barrier? One remedy is discipline: vow to silence your cell phone, log out of your social networking site, and refrain from texting for a specified period. Another remedy is to be mindful and considerate of others. You may think it is no big deal to text a friend during a classmate's presentation in your human communication course, but if the roles were reversed, you might take offense or wonder if you were boring your listeners (Mello, 2009; Stephens & Davis, 2009). This point goes for interpersonal interactions, too—if you are texting Rodney while having lunch with Alex, you might be sending Alex an unintended message that you do not value his company.

Motivational Factors

It can be hard to listen to a speaker whose presentation is lifeless or whose voice lulls you to sleep or even to a perfectly competent speaker presenting a boring topic. When something (or someone) seems overwhelmingly dull, we often wind up daydreaming about more interesting things like weekend events, an intriguing new stranger, or postgraduation plans. Nonetheless, boring information may still be important enough to warrant your attention. Your own overexcitement can also distract you from listening effectively, even if the speaker or topic is actually engaging. If you are consumed by thoughts of an upcoming vacation, for instance, you may have difficulty listening to a great class lecture.

You can still improve your listening skills in situations where you are experiencing boredom or overexcitement. First, become more conscious about the situation. Think about how *you* would deliver the information being discussed and how you would restructure it or give examples. As you do this, you may find yourself listening more attentively. Second, avoid daydreaming by taking notes. Third, relate information to your own life. To illustrate, if you are sick of listening to a friend complain for the hundredth time about her problems with her mother, imagine how you would feel in the same situation. Your interest in your friend's problem may perk up.

Negative Attitudes About Listening

You probably have not spent much time analyzing your attitudes and feelings about the act of listening (who has?). Yet sometimes our attitude is the very thing that causes our listening struggle. We may value talking more than listening, become

connect

Believe it or not, public speakers must listen to the audience to help the audience listen to the speech. Chapter 15 describes the importance of interacting *with* the audience rather than speaking *at* your listeners: Are they yawning, looking confused, laughing, or nodding in agreement? By watching for such verbal and nonverbal cues, competent speakers adjust elements of their speaking (rate, pitch, volume, etc.) to meet the audience's needs.

wired for communication

Don't Touch That Smartphone

The stack of phones in the middle of the table is buzzing. Three friends, gathered for an after-work drink at a local pub, are anxious. Mike, Jacob, and Elisse had all set their phones to vibrate. Only Karen sits smugly, looking over the menu with a bemused smile, knowing one of the others would soon give in. She had turned her phone off. There was no way she was paying for dinner tonight. "Phone Stack" is a game of sorts but also a response to the culture of multitasking and technology overload that has pervaded every aspect of our social lives. When a group goes out to dinner or for drinks, phones get stacked in the center of the table, the idea being that they are off-limits. The first person to give in gets stuck with the bill. The bigger the group, the higher the stakes (Tell, 2013).

Stepping away from the bings, beeps, and buzzes that connect us to our social networks is hard to do if you are worried that you might miss important information coming in on your smartphone. And although it may seem like you can easily attend to the people you are with *and* the people you are online with, you really cannot. According to cognitive researchers, the human brain does not really multitask — it just divides its attention. That means we are never really paying attention to more than one thing at a time; we are just constantly toggling between tasks (Wallis, 2006). Multitaskers are far less adept at filtering out extraneous information to focus on what is important (Richtel, 2010).

So when you pick up your phone to check the group chat, remember that you are actually ignoring the company of the people sitting beside you. Oh, and bear in mind that you might wind up picking up the tab, too.

think about this

1. Which is more rude: Ignoring a text or ignoring the person in front of you? Which communication transaction should take priority?

2. Does it bother you when people attend to other things — checking email, browsing the internet, and such — when you are speaking to them? Do you check your phone when you are out with friends?

3. Under what circumstances do you turn off your phone? Are there any times when you refuse to do so?

overconfident or lazy in our listening expectations, or consider listening a stressful experience.

Talking Seems More Powerful Than Listening

In many Western societies, people tend to think that talking is powerful, so *not* talking must be weak. By not valuing the power of listening, we neglect it. Michael listens to his wife only to plan what he is going to say next; he is not interested in what his wife has to say, only in making *her* listen to *him*. Katrina thinks she already knows what others will say; when her sister is speaking to her, she nods quickly and says, "Yeah, yeah, I know." If Michael and Katrina remembered that listening actually empowers us, they would be more effective communicators.

Listening well does not simply mean to stop talking. You have to adjust your speaking-to-listening ratio (talk less and listen more). If a desire to dominate a conversation creeps up on you, remind yourself that through the act of listening, you empower your communication partners to reveal their thoughts, insights, fears, values, and beliefs (Fletcher, 1999). In the long run, you may even exert more influence in your relationships because, as people come to think you understand and relate to them, they will give *you* more influence.

Overconfidence and Laziness

Randall walked into a status meeting certain that he knew everything that was going to be said. As he sat through the meeting only half listening to his colleagues tossing ideas around, his boss began asking him questions that he was unprepared to answer. Although confident individuals usually understand information better than their less confident peers (Clark, 1989), many people overestimate their abilities to retain and recall information. Thus, *over*confidence like Randall's frequently leads to laziness—failure to prepare or plan for a situation and then failure to pay attention during it.

Listening Apprehension

You may know that many people suffer from public speaking anxiety. But did you know that many people also struggle with concerns about listening? **Listening apprehension** (also called *receiver apprehension*) is a state of uneasiness, anxiety, fear, or dread associated with a listening opportunity. Listening to your boss reprimand you about your job performance, listening to someone else's personal problems, or listening to highly detailed or statistical information can trigger listening apprehension, which compromises your ability to concentrate on or remember what is said (Ayres, Wilcox, & Ayers, 1995). Students with high listening anxiety have lower motivation to process information in the classroom, which can affect their overall academic performance (Schrodt, Wheeless, & Ptacek, 2000). So it is important to assess your ability to listen effectively and to spend time developing your listening confidence.

Unethical Listening

As with other communication activities, you have ethical choices to make with listening situations. Some choices are positive and constructive, leading to more effective listening situations overall. Other choices are riskier; you may accomplish your own personal goals, but you may not contribute anything to the goals of others and could end up compromising your relationships or your job. Consider the potential damage that could be done with listening that is defensive, biased, self-absorbed, or faked.

real communicator

NAME: Tammy Lin
OCCUPATION: Physician
Courtesy Tammy Lin

As a physician specializing in internal medicine, I know I must listen closely to my patients — and they must also listen to me.

Listening to my patients' stories is a process of discovery. To make an accurate diagnosis and devise an effective treatment plan, I must search for as much information as possible about patients' health — such as what they eat and drink, what drugs (prescription and nonprescription) they take, what toxins they may have been exposed to, and what exercise they do (or don't do). This might seem like a simple question-and-answer method, but there are often roadblocks. For example, some patients are incredibly anxious when speaking with a doctor or are too embarrassed to give truthful answers (particularly about issues like diet, substance use, or mental health). Still other patients seem to withhold information to see how "good" I am at figuring things out on my own. In these circumstances, it's up to me to put the patient at ease by opening with generally "safe" questions and easing my way into more difficult topics. Building trust is vital. I focus on giving my full attention, not interrupting, and reassuring patients that I have most likely heard a version of whatever they are about to tell me. There are times when no treatment is needed other than listening to the patient. Providing a safe place to share their thoughts, followed by reassurance about their fears is all that is needed. Listening well is therapeutic.

My patients also have an obligation to be engaged listeners and honest participants in their own health care. Clearly, it's important that they listen in order to understand the options they have for treatment, and I encourage them to paraphrase (not repeat) the information I've shared. I encourage patients to ask me questions, saying no question is too silly or simple. When I give complex instructions, I encourage patients to take notes, or provide them with written materials they can bring home in case they have been distracted during their visit by stress or pain.

The next time you see your doctor, remember that for a physician to arrive at an accurate diagnosis and treatment plan, the patient must share all the information related to the health situation (current medications, recent life changes, etc.). Before your next visit, write down your questions. Don't be afraid to ask about anything you don't understand. Be prepared to listen to your doctor, and help your doctor listen to you.

Defensive Listening

Gillian constantly asks her friends about whether to stay with her romantic partner, Alex. But when they all point out how badly he treats her, Gillian argues with them, making up excuses for why she stays with him. Gillian is guilty of **defensive listening**, arguing with the speaker (sometimes with aggression) without fully listening to the message. She fends off her feelings of rejection by defending her behavior.

We have all been in situations where we ask for advice and get an unwanted response. But if you respond with aggressiveness and argue before completely listening to the speaker, you will experience more anxiety, probably because you anticipate not being effective in the listening encounter (Schrodt & Wheeless, 2001). If you find yourself listening defensively, consider the tips shown in Table 7.2.

Biased Listening

As we discussed earlier, we all engage in *selecting* which communicative messages to attend to while disregarding others. When you zero in on just the bits of information that support a particular point of view or attitude, you are engaging in **biased listening**. At times this may be beneficial, as when you decide to ignore your sister's

TABLE 7.2

STEPS TO AVOID DEFENSIVE LISTENING

Tip	Example
Hear the speaker out	Do not rush into an argument; wait for the speaker to finish stating their position before constructing your own.
Consider the speaker's motivations	The person may be tired, ill, or frustrated. Do not take it personally.
Use nonverbal communication	Take a deep breath and smile slightly (but sincerely) at the speaker; that may "disarm" the situation.
Provide calm feedback	After the speaker finishes, paraphrase what you think was said and ask if you understood correctly.

connect

Selective listening can also be influenced by our attributions—personal characteristics we use to explain other people's behavior. If you believe that your classmate Lara is lazy, you may listen only to messages that support your attribution. Competent communicators avoid selective listening by verifying their perceptions (see Chapter 3), seeking thoughtful explanations, and moving past first impressions to understand communication partners.

comment that you are the "preferred" child in the family and instead focus on her ideas for planning a happy upcoming holiday gathering.

But biased listening typically has negative implications. For example, if you really hate working on a group project with your classmate Lara, you may only pay attention to the disagreeable or negative things that she says. If she says, "I can't make it to the meeting on Thursday at eight," you shut off, placing another check in the "Lara is lazy" column of proof. However, you might miss the rest of Lara's message—perhaps she has a good reason for missing the meeting, or maybe she is suggesting that you reschedule. Similarly, you might only listen to the positive things your other classmate Micah says and thus end up with an inflated view of Micah's qualities.

A specific type of biased listening is **insensitive listening**, which occurs when we listen only to the words someone says, failing to pay attention to the emotional content. Your friend Adam calls to tell you that he got rejected from Duke Law School. Adam had mentioned to you that his LSAT scores made Duke a long shot, so you accept his message for what it appears to be: a factual statement about a situation. But you fail to hear the disappointment in his voice—even if Duke was a long shot, it was his top choice as well as a chance to be geographically closer to his partner, who lives in North Carolina. Had you paid attention to Adam's nonverbal cues, you might have known that he needed some comforting words.

To improve your communication, particularly when you are feeling apprehensive or defensive, you must take care to acknowledge your selective listening and pay attention to both the verbal and nonverbal aspects of a message. You must not close your ears to competing information just because it makes you uncomfortable.

Self-Absorbed Listening

Self-absorbed listeners hear only the information that they find useful for achieving their own specific goals. For example, your colleague Lucia may seem really engaged in your discussion about some negative interactions you have had with Ryan, your boyfriend. But if she is only listening because she is interested in Ryan and wants to get a sense of your relationship's vulnerability, then she is listening with her own self-interests in mind.

Self-absorbed listeners sometimes hurt others by the way they listen. *Attacking* is a response to someone else's message with negative evaluations ("That was a stupid thing to say!"). *Ambushing* is more strategic by listening specifically to find weaknesses in others—things they are sensitive about—and point them out at strategic or embarrassing times. So if Mai cries to Scott about failing her calculus final, and Scott is later looking for a way to discredit Mai, he might say something like, "I'm not sure you're the right person to help us draw up a budget, Mai. Math isn't exactly your strong suit, is it?" Self-absorbed listening can also be **monopolistic listening**, or listening to control the communication interaction. Monopolistic listeners listen for a pause in the conversation so they can cut in and keep the other from talking.

and you?

Do you know any people who engage in the unethical behaviors described here? Is it frequent behavior or a rare slip? How do these tendencies affect your interactions with those people? Do you ever find yourself engaging in such behaviors?

Pseudolistening

When you become impatient or bored with someone's communication messages, you may engage in **pseudolistening**—pretending to listen by nodding or saying "Uh-huh" when you are really not paying attention at all. While pseudolistening may help you keep up a polite appearance of listening, one of its downsides is that you can actually miss important information or offend your communication partner and damage the relationship when the pseudolistening is discovered. Pseudolistening is a common trope in television sitcoms—Homer Simpson nods absently (daydreaming about food or another inappropriate topic) even though he has not listened to a word his boss Mr. Burns has said. We may find it funny in sitcoms; however, in real life, implying that we have listened when we have not can have disastrous consequences: we miss instructions, neglect tasks that we have implied we would complete, and fail to meet others' needs.

● **WHAT MIGHT** Mr. Burns be saying here? Homer Simpson does not know, because he is pseudolistening. © Fox/Photofest

Listening Contexts

Chances are, you have recognized bits of yourself or your friends scattered throughout this chapter. We have all, at one time or another, felt defensive, nervous, bored, or lazy and found that we were less effective listeners because of it. But you probably do not feel that way all the time. You might find yourself to be a great listener in certain situations and weak in others. That is because, as with every other part of communication, our listening skills and abilities are affected by context (Bommelje, Houston, & Smither, 2003). In this section, we examine the ways in which the contexts of communication influence listening.

---

evaluating communication ethics

Listening When You're Sick of Hearing

You were happy to lend your friend Jamie a sympathetic ear as she worked through a difficult breakup earlier this year. You were by her side when her fiancé moved out; you took care of letting friends know that the romance had ended so she wouldn't have to go through the pain of telling them herself. You even served as a go-between for Jamie and her ex as they sorted through untangling their lives — helping look through paperwork and forwarding mail for her. And, of course, as a single person yourself, you were there to empathize as Jamie faced the prospect of heading back into the dating world. You agreed to be each other's date when attending parties with your coupled-up friends and made plans to check out a speed-dating party together as sort of a gag.

But now, only eight months after the breakup, Jamie is in the throes of a new romance with an attractive coworker. You cannot help but feel a bit jealous — you have been single for more than three years; it doesn't seem fair that Jamie should find love so quickly. What's worse is that Jamie insists on spending as much time as possible with this new love — often at the expense of time with you. You want to support and be happy for your friend, but you are finding it very difficult to listen to discussions about day hikes and movie nights and sports outings. You find yourself continually avoiding the subject of dating; as a result, you notice that Jamie seems less interested in talking to you. Somewhat relieved, you start to avoid talking to Jamie at all. You are not all that surprised when she suddenly asks you why you're mad at her. But you don't really know what to say. You know why you are avoiding your friend, but you're sort of embarrassed about your reasons. What should you say?

think about this

1. Should you tell Jamie the truth? Is it ethical to hide your true feelings from a friend? What might happen if you just say, "I'm embarrassed to say that I'm feeling a bit jealous"?

2. What are Jamie's ethical responsibilities here? Should she have been able to sense your sensitivity about the situation from the way you have responded?

3. What kinds of unethical listening behaviors might be at work here? Are you avoiding? Is Jamie ambushing?

The Relational and Situational Listening Contexts

The situation we are in can have a profound effect on our communication. When you are in an unfamiliar or uncomfortable place or at a formal event (such as a funeral, a wedding, or a professional conference), you may experience the sort of listening apprehension that we discussed earlier. And in some situations, such as a party, background noise can make it hard for you to listen. We have all been in a situation where there are so many people talking or loud music playing that we literally scream to be heard. It feels like it takes all our energy and concentration just to make out a conversational partner's words. Clearly, this kind of situational context can make listening more challenging.

The relational context can also create problems. Take your friend Yvonne. As great a friend as she is, you perceive her chronic lateness as a sign that she does not value your time or friendship. So when she tries to explain why she is late for this particular party, you hardly pay attention. You offer no empathy and do not think deeply about her message. Perhaps it is another excuse about car trouble or running into an old friend on her way to meet you. But maybe it is not—and there is something far more serious going on with Yvonne. The only way to find out is to listen actively.

The Cultural Listening Context

In various parts of the United States and abroad, you will encounter listening behaviors different from your own. As you travel or do business across the country or the world, you will likely find it necessary to understand and adapt to listening differences in a cultural context.

In Eastern cultures that value indirect styles of communication, like China and Japan, an effective listener will save face for the speaker. A listener would be expected not to question the speaker directly, to construct meaning and understanding from the context of the situation, and to accommodate the speaker's needs more than the listener's (Lustig & Koester, 2006). But in Western cultures, such as the United States and Canada, where speaking is more direct, the speaker usually

As you learned in Chapter 6, cultures vary in their comfort with emotional expression. Some cultures have a tendency toward *understatement* (downplaying emotion) whereas others favor *hyperbole* (exaggerating emotion). As a competent communicator, you must listen carefully to assess your partner's emotional state and needs based on this important cultural variation.

● **WHEN TWO PEOPLE** from different backgrounds address each other, they must be mindful of the culturally influenced behaviors and expectations that are at play. Jetta Productions/Getty Images

● **THE GANG** from *Family Guy* believes that listening — along with the verbal and nonverbal expressions that accompany it — is for women only! Everett Collection, Inc /Courtesy Everett Collection

tells the listener what he or she wants the listener to know, and the listener can ask direct questions without offending the speaker.

In addition to actual listening behaviors themselves, *perceptions* of appropriate listening vary among cultures. U.S. Caucasians are perceived as expressive listeners when they exhibit nonverbal facilitators (like nodding, saying "Mmm-hmmm," and the like) and use more questioning techniques to clarify and comprehend the speaker's message; U.S. Latinos and Asian Americans are perceived as somewhat less expressive; and African Americans are perceived as the least expressive listeners among these groups (Dillon & McKenzie, 1998). If you are comfortable or aware of the preferred listening style of your own culture only, miscommunication can occur. So Jennifer, a Colombian American, speaking with Jonathan, an African American colleague, might judge Jonathan as an ineffective listener if he is less expressive than she would hope as she complains about a difficult client. She needs to remember that culture — including gender — is at play in this situation.

Table 7.3 shows suggestions for communicating with people of different cultures.

TABLE 7.3

TIPS FOR COMMUNICATING ACROSS CULTURES

Tactic	Explanation	Example
Recognize cultural differences	Keep in mind that factors such as country of origin, religion, gender, educational level, and socioeconomic status play into our values and beliefs about communication. Learn about the person's background, and ask questions if appropriate.	If your future mother-in-law is a devout Catholic from France and you are a nonreligious person from St. Louis, you might want to learn more about French culture and Catholicism.
Clarify behaviors as appropriate	Be honest about your listening difficulty; observe context and nonverbal behaviors.	"I don't think I'm understanding you correctly. Can you say that in another way for me, please?"
Adjust to differences	Ask more questions if necessary; ask the speaker to work with you to understand more clearly.	"I can't seem to see the complete picture. Can you give me an example to help me understand better?"

A discussion of culture would not be complete without thinking about how your concepts of masculinity and femininity affect your perceptions of listening competence (Burleson et al., 2011). For example, men in the United States are usually discouraged from expressing intense emotions in public (Brody, 2000). This reluctance to react emotionally to information may give the appearance that men are not listening. Expectations about appropriate feminine behavior encourage women to exhibit *more* verbal and nonverbal feedback when listening, such as nodding and smiling more, and using more encouraging filler words ("Really?" "Oh, wow," "Right"). Females also report experiencing more listening apprehension than males (Sawyer, Gayle, Topa, & Powers, 2014). Most research indicates that an individual's role (e.g., being a parent) accounts for more listening differences than the sex of the listener does (Duncan & Fiske, 1977; Johnston, Weaver, Watson, & Barker, 2000). Nonetheless, listening stereotypes are still powerful and make their way into entertainment and advertising at every level. In the episode "I Am Peter, Hear Me Roar," *Family Guy*'s Peter decides to get in touch with his feminine side and calls his buddy Quagmire "just to talk." He wants to listen to what is going on with his friend and have his friend listen to him in turn. Quagmire is so uncomfortable with this situation that he slams down the phone!

The Technology Listening Context

Anish Patel could have walked across campus to attend his microeconomics course in person. But why bother, when the lecture is streaming live over the campus network? Instead of listening with his classmates in a crowded lecture hall, he watches on his laptop in the comfort of his own apartment (Gabriel, 2010).

Russell Hampton is both a father and the president of a book and magazine publishing unit of Walt Disney Company. When he was driving his daughter and her teenage friends to a play, he listened to their conversation about an actor in a Disney movie and tried to join in the conversation. Suddenly, the girls became very quiet. Russell could see his daughter texting in the rearview mirror and chided her for being rude and ignoring her friends. He later discovered that all three teens were texting each other — so that they could listen to one another without Russell listening to them (Holson, 2008).

As these two examples illustrate, technology can be both helpful and hurtful to the listening process. Anish Patel might listen more effectively in a classroom with the energy of live interaction and where questions can be asked and notes compared. But he might also be able to process the lecture more effectively by rewinding and listening again to sections of the lecture without distraction. Russell Hampton might be hurt that his daughter and her friends shut him out of their conversation; however, their texts give them a powerful way of listening to one another.

Listening to messages in various technological contexts requires a lot more effort than other forms of communication. And while college students still *prefer* face-to-face communication for accomplishing many communication goals (probably because it is easier to observe nonverbal behaviors), the channels they actually *use* are increasingly digital (Morreale, Staley, Stavrositu, & Krakowiak, 2015). Competent digital listeners have to work harder to accomplish effective listening by paying attention to capitalization cues, emoji, and the timing of responses; and when digital listeners enter an online chat, they should read the sequence of comments before blurting out a response to the first post they see.

The Doctor's Office

At the beginning of this chapter, we talked about the importance of good communication between doctors and patients as well as the costs of communication breakdowns in the health care field. Let's take a moment to revisit the nature of listening as it relates to patient–doctor interactions.

► All communication is transactional, and both parties—in this case, the doctor and the patient—are responsible for it. But the expense of lawsuits and malpractice insurance ultimately puts the pressure on the health care professionals to improve communication to avoid costly mistakes. That is why so many hospitals and insurance companies are providing training for doctors.

► Patients report that effective listening is not only an essential component of sharing information between doctor and patient, but that effective listening also acts as a healing and therapeutic agent—and even strengthens the doctor–patient relationship (Jagosh, Donald Boudreau, Steinert, MacDonald, & Ingram, 2011).

► Age may affect memory, but the situational context plays a role here as well. In a doctor's office, faced with concerns about our health and intimidated by unfamiliar medical terminology, we are more likely to experience listening apprehension, which will affect our ability to process information.

► Patients sometimes think they need to rush out of a doctor's appointment because "the doctor is busy." In this case, the relational context is negatively impacting communication. A doctor who implies that she is busy, or perhaps has more important patients to attend to, might leave a patient thinking that her case, or her illness, is less important or perhaps not as serious.

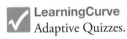 Activities

LaunchPad
macmillan learning

1. LaunchPad for *Real Communication* offers key term videos and encourages self-assessment through adaptive quizzing. Go to **launchpadworks.com** to get access to:

LearningCurve
Adaptive Quizzes.

Video clips that illustrate key concepts, highlighted in teal in the Real Reference section that follows.

2. Describe a time when you listened well. How do you know you listened well? Where were you? Who were you with? What were your goals? Did you adapt your listening to the situational, cultural, or relational context? What can you learn from this successful listening experience to guide you in future listening challenges?

3. Practice listening with your eyes as discussed in this chapter. When you go to your next class, observe your instructor or whoever is speaking. Form an overall

impression of the speaker from nonverbal cues, such as body movements, eye behavior, and tone of voice. What emotions do they suggest? Do they match the verbal message being conveyed?

4. As you become a more critical listener, inquire about inconsistencies when you observe them in conversation. For example, if your friend offers you verbal and nonverbal messages that contradict each other, let him or her know. Be careful to avoid being defensive here. Instead of saying, "You're sending me mixed messages," say, "I'm confused about what you mean. You said you were happy with the decision, but you frowned and sighed at the same time."

5. Practice listening styles that are less familiar to you. Some people do not paraphrase well; others are uncomfortable being person-centered. The best way to try this out is to look back at the chapter and think about the discussions that made you feel uncomfortable ("I could never do that"). Then give it a try in a context that might benefit you. For example, if you tend to be an empathic, person-centered listener in group meetings and your meetings always run late because of it, try being a more time-centered or action-centered listener.

6. Keep a log of how you "listen" with technology. Is it easier—or more difficult—for you to select, attend, remember, understand, and respond? Compare your experiences with friends. Do some of your friends or family prefer the technology or do they value face-to-face listening more?

real reference ➤ A Study Tool

Now that you have finished reading this chapter, you can:

Outline the listening process and goals for listening:

▶ **Hearing** is physiologically perceiving sound; **listening** is the process of recognizing, understanding, and interpreting the message (p. 162).

▶ The listening process involves three components (p. 163).

▶ The degree to which we are willing to listen is the **affective component** (p. 163).

▶ The **cognitive component** involves **selecting** (choosing one sound over others), **attending** (focusing on the message), and **understanding** (making sense of the message; pp. 163–164).

▶ The **behavioral component** involves communicating that we **remember** by giving feedback or **paraphrasing** their statements (pp. 164–165).

▶ **Active listeners** make choices about selecting, attending, and so on and are more competent than **passive listeners** (p. 165), who may engage in **confabulation** by fabricating facts to mask their defensiveness. **Listening fidelity** is the degree to which the thoughts of the listener agree with the intentions of the source of the message (p. 165).

People accomplish goals by listening in different ways:

▶ **Relational listening** is used to establish and maintain relationships (p. 165).

▶ **Analytical listening** is used to explore all ideas before making judgments (p. 167).

▶ **Task-oriented listening** is used to focus on clear and pertinent information quickly (p. 167).

▶ **Critical listening** is used to find inconsistencies or errors (p. 167).

▶ Competent listeners will adapt their listening goals to the person and situation (p. 167).

List the advantages of listening well:

▶ Listening well helps your career, saves time and money, creates opportunities, and strengthens relationships (pp. 168–170).

Identify challenges to good listening and their remedies:

▶ **Listening barriers** are factors that interfere with our ability to comprehend information and respond appropriately (p. 170).

▶ Text message alerts and crying babies are examples of environmental factors that impair our ability to listen (pp. 170–171).

▶ Hearing loss challenges can be overcome with understanding of nonverbal behaviors (pp. 171–172) and speaker accommodations. Processing challenges (e.g., ADD) are faced by many who have normal hearing (p. 172).

▶ **Multitasking**, attending to several things at once, limits focus on any one task (p. 172).

▶ A boring speaker or topic can be hard to follow, but overexcitement can be distracting (p. 173).

▶ Talking may be regarded as more powerful than listening (p. 174).

▶ Overconfidence may cause us to become lazy and not pay careful attention during communication (p. 174).

▶ **Listening apprehension**, anxiety or dread associated with listening, may hinder concentration (p. 174).

Identify types of listening that can have unethical consequences:

▶ **Defensive listening** is responding with aggression and arguing with the speaker, without fully listening to the message (p. 175).

▶ **Biased listening** is zeroing in on bits of information that confirm an existing point of view (p. 175).

▶ **Insensitive listening** occurs when we fail to pay attention to the emotional content of someone's message and just take it at face value (p. 176).

▶ Self-absorbed listeners listen for their own needs and may practice **monopolistic listening**, or listening in order to control the communication interaction (p. 176).

▶ **Pseudolistening** is pretending to listen while not really paying attention (p. 177).

Describe how various contexts affect listening:

▶ Different situations create different challenges (p. 178).

▶ The dynamics of the relationship changes how you listen (p. 178).

▶ The cultural context affects listening behavior (pp. 178–179).

▶ Technology is an increasingly important context for listening (p. 180).

Military families face many challenges when it comes to building a stable communication relationship, as they move repeatedly between reunion and separation.

Harry How/Getty Images

 LearningCurve can help you master the material in this chapter.

Go to **launchpadworks.com**

chapter

8

Developing and Maintaining Relationships

Mary Marquez is a U.S. Army wife. She is strong; she has to be. For a good part of the year, she manages her job, two teenage sons, the house with its bills and maintenance, and her relationships with other friends and family, all while missing—and worrying about—her husband, Justin. When Justin is home, Mary obviously wants to spend time with him. But as soon as she is feeling comfortable and connected, he is sent off to another part of the world, and she is on her own again.

Mary and Justin are like many families whose military-related separations put a strain on their communication and relationships (Houston et al., 2013). Justin and Mary often do not know when and where Justin will deploy; even when the deployment has been scheduled, dates often fluctuate. This uncertainty puts a strain on every member of the family, as they struggle between the independence they must have during the deployment and the connectedness they desire when they are all together (Merolla, 2010b). Some military spouses deal with it by not dealing with it at all—that is, by engaging in arguments about other matters or by shutting down communication completely. But Mary and Justin work on their communication. They hide notes for one another around the house while he is home. When he is away, they email frequently and plan times when they can connect online; during those online conversations they try to focus on "normal" things, like talking about their day or discussing a book they are both reading. Mary said these behaviors "made it feel more routine and made it feel like he wasn't so far away" (Sahlstein, Maguire, & Timmerman, 2009).

The distance and time zone differences can make connecting in real time difficult, though; when family members miss a connection, it can lead to hard feelings and misunderstandings. For example, one of Mary's friends described how disgruntled her husband became when she and the kids were not at home waiting for his call.

chapter
outcomes

After you have finished reading this chapter, you will be able to

- Explain key aspects of interpersonal relationships

- Describe why we form relationships

- List ways to manage relationship dynamics

- Describe the factors that influence self-disclosure

- Outline the predictable stages of most relationships

As you learned in Chapter 1, people need to be in relationships with other people; relationships help us meet many needs, such as companionship and intellectual stimulation—even contributing to our happiness, health (Waldinger, 2015), and ability to tolerate pain (Sullivan, Rickers, & Gammage, 2014). The military family we described here is no different. While there are many obstacles to meeting individual needs because of the changes in communication during deployment and reunion, there are many opportunities for the relationships to grow stronger through effective communication (Knobloch, Basinger, Wehrman, Ebata, & McGlaughlin, 2016).

In this chapter, we focus on interpersonal relationships. To understand these relationships, we need to be aware of the role communication plays in them. **Interpersonal communication** is the exchange of verbal and nonverbal messages between people who build relationships, share meanings, and accomplish social goals (Burleson, 2010). These relationships are constituted or formed by the communication people use as they develop their relationships, confirm their identities, and accomplish tasks (Manning, 2014). Interpersonal communication should not be confused with **impersonal communication**, which involves verbal and nonverbal messages that are not unique or designed to build a relationship; instead, they are instinctive or socially scripted responses based on people's social roles. For example, when you purchase coffee at the campus café, you (and the barista) exchange a set of commonly used messages ("I'll have a vanilla latte," "Here's your change"). There is no relational impact of these messages because they do not differ depending on who is on either side of the counter. But such encounters can *become* interpersonal if, for example, you disclose that you are buying that latte to treat yourself for doing well on a poli-sci midterm, and the barista shares that she is in that class, too. You engage in interpersonal communication when you communicate with each other as individuals. This happens, of course, in your most intimate relationships when you sit down to a heartfelt conversation with your significant other or when you catch up with your best friend. But you also engage in interpersonal communication when you get to know your professor during office hours, and when you chat with your new neighbor.

Interpersonal communication also takes place across digital channels. When you sympathize with a friend's injury on Facebook or send birthday or graduation congratulations to your cousin on Instagram, you send a message that reinforces your existing relationship. In fact, this mediated communication has the potential to become **hyperpersonal communication** in that it can exceed face-to-face relational development in speed, intimacy, and self-presentation (Walther, 1996). For example, when two people start getting to know each other on a dating site or app, it is possible they reveal more about themselves in this context more quickly than they would if they had met in a face-to-face setting. We now take a closer look at types of interpersonal relationships and the communication that takes place within them.

Types of Interpersonal Relationships

Martin asks Pete, "Do you know my friend Jake?" Pete responds, "I've met him once or twice." In two short sentences, we gain information about the relationships at play: to Martin, Jake is a friend; to Pete, he is just an acquaintance. We are all involved in multiple relationships, and we distinguish among them in countless ways: acquaintances, colleagues, coworkers, teammates, friends, family members, romantic partners, neighbors, and familiar passersby. Every person has a complex

Communication Standard	Examples
Openness	• Share feelings; talk openly when something is wrong • Talk about sensitive issues like sex or drugs
Structural stability	• Listen to and obey at least one family member • Deal with emotional issues at "safe" times
Affection	• Be loving and affectionate with one another, saying things like "I love you"
Emotional support	• Help each other; count on each other
Mind reading	• Know what is going on without asking • Understand how others feel
Politeness	• Never be rude or inconsiderate, or talk back
Discipline	• Have clear rules and know the consequences for breaking them
Humor or sarcasm	• Can tease other family members lovingly
Regular routine interaction	• Set aside time to communicate regularly
Avoidance	• Avoid topics that are too personal or painful

Information from J. Caughlin (2003).

TABLE 8.1

FAMILY COMMUNICATION QUALITIES

relational network or web of relationships that connects individuals to one another. In this section, we focus on four categories of relationships: family, friendship and social, romantic, and online.

Family Relationships

For some people, the term *family* refers to immediate relatives who live in the same household. For others, it means a more extended family that includes grandparents, aunts, uncles, and cousins. Still others use the term to describe groups of people with whom they are intimately connected and committed, even without blood or civil ties, like some fraternal organizations or religious communities. But for our purposes, a **family** is a social group bound by ties of blood, civil contract (such as marriage, civil union, or adoption), and a commitment to care for and be responsible for one another, often in a shared household.

Our first and most basic relationships are with family. From them, we learn communication skills and develop characteristics that affect how we interact with other people throughout our lives. ABC's award-winning *Modern Family* features three Los Angeles families—that of Jay Pritchett and those of his daughter Claire and son Mitchell. Jay and his second wife, Gloria, live with their son and her teenage son from a previous relationship; Claire and Phil Dunphy have three children; Mitchell and his partner, Cameron, have an adopted Vietnamese daughter. Although the mockumentary format delivers a lot of laughs, the communication relationships are very solid and serious. The diverse families manage their differences and are very involved in each other's lives (see Table 8.1). They teach their children the beliefs, values, and communication skills they need to face life's challenges, to feel loved and secure, and to achieve success both professionally and personally (Ducharme, Doyle, & Markiewicz, 2002). These messages are essential for enriching family life and positively developing younger family members (Guerrero, Andersen, & Afifi, 2013; Jackl, 2016; Mansson, Myers, & Turner, 2010).

● OPRAH WINFREY AND GALE KING'S decades-long friendship illustrates the benefits and joys that can result from a close, caring relationship. Frazer Harrison/Getty Images

connect

As you learn about interpersonal relationships, remember the competent communication model from Chapter 1. There is no one right way to communicate with friends, family, or romantic partners, because competent communication considers relational, situational, and cultural contexts. You may feel comfortable sharing personal information with your father; your friend Julie may not. You and your significant other may develop a communication style that simply would not work for your brother and his girlfriend.

and you?

What characteristics do you consider most important in your friendships? How do they compare to the characteristics mentioned in the research? Do your friends meet your expectations? As a friend, do you exhibit the characteristics you listed as most important?

Friendship and Social Relationships

As individuals grow and interact with people outside their families, they establish new, nonfamily relationships. **Friendship** is a close and caring relationship between two people that is perceived as mutually satisfying and beneficial. Friendship benefits include emotional support, companionship, and coping with major life stressors (Rawlins, 1992, 2008). Friendships are enhanced by sharing both positive and negative information with one another and by showing enthusiasm for the other's good news ("I'm so excited for you!"; Woods, Lambert, Brown, Fincham, & May, 2015). Children who form successful friendships with others perform better academically and demonstrate fewer aggressive tendencies than those who do not (Rawlins, 1994; Weisz & Wood, 2005). And secure, stable friendships and family relationships serve to enhance children's ability to process communication behaviors (Dwyer et al., 2010).

Although everyone has a personal opinion as to what qualities a friend should possess, research finds agreement on six important characteristics of friendship (Pearson & Spitzberg, 1990): availability (making time for one another), caring (expressing concern for well-being), honesty (being open and truthful), trust (being honest and maintaining confidentiality), loyalty (maintaining the relationship despite disagreements), and empathy (communicating understanding of feelings and experiences). The extent to which friends share these characteristics helps build the relational context of their relationship.

Some of the relationships you call "friendships" might be more accurately described as **social relationships**, relationships that are functional within a specific context but are less intimate than friendship. For example, you may have casual work pals with whom you can complain about your boss, people with whom you socialize in your pick-up hockey team, or a hair stylist you love to visit so that you can engage in celebrity gossip (Markoff & Sengupta, 2011). Indeed, it is likely that the majority of your six hundred Facebook "friends" are social acquaintances. Sometimes, these social relationships can become awkward when one partner assumes too much intimacy. For example, someone you barely know in your religious community might expect to be invited to your wedding, or you might encounter unease if you ask a few coworkers to go to happy hour in a corporate culture that discourages outside socialization (DeKay, 2012).

Romantic Relationships

What ideas, thoughts, and feelings come to mind when you think about romantic relationships? Do you think of romantic dinners, jealousy, butterflies in your stomach? Perhaps you think about sex or about commitment and love (Tierney, 2007).

Love can be used to describe feelings other than romantic ones, including our feelings for our families, friends, pets, or anything that evokes strong feelings of liking or appreciation (as in "I love the Chicago Bears" or "I love burritos"). But we typically define **love** within the context of relationships as a deep affection for and attachment to another person involving emotional ties, with varying degrees of passion, commitment, and **intimacy** (closeness and understanding of a relational partner). There are many types of love that can characterize different relationships—or even the same relationship at different times. For example, the love between Anna and Mario, married for fifty-seven years, is probably not the same as when they were first married. Studies involving hundreds of people revealed six categories of love: *eros* (erotic, sexual love), *ludus* (playful, casual love), *storge* (love that lacks passion), *pragma* (committed, practical love), *mania* (intense, romantic love), and *agape* (selfless, unconditional love; Hendrick & Hendrick, 1992; Lee, 1973). Some relationships may be characterized by only one of these types, whereas others may experience a number at once or different ones over time.

● **PARASOCIAL RELATIONSHIPS** have some of the characteristics of real relationships. Janice Peterson

wired for communication

Is This Relationship Real?

Do you ever imagine yourself in the arms of that romance novel hero? Do you feel a strong connection to your NFL team's quarterback? Can you not wait for the next weekly episode of *Keeping Up with the Kardashians*? Did you grieve when your favorite television drama "killed off" the character you had come to love? Perhaps you check a bodybuilder's Instagram feed a few times a week because you feel like you know her and want to catch up on what is going on in her life. Or maybe you seriously identify with your online gaming avatar and feel intimately aligned with others.

Parasocial interactions (PSIs), such as those described above, are one-sided relationships in which individuals extend emotional energy, interest, and time with celebrities or other media images who are completely unaware of their existence (Giles, 2002). Once thought of as simply an explanation for forming one-sided attachments with media figures (and perhaps even psychologically detrimental), PSIs are now thought to aid media consumers in their construction and presentation of their own mediated selves — and even as a way to construct their interaction with others in digital contexts (Chen, 2016; Shin, 2016).

Media users involved in PSIs feel they are actually in a relationship and respond as though they are. They feel loyal and attracted to the character; they are comforted by the "companionship" therein; and they often feel aided in their own lives by learning from the characters' perceived similar situations and behaviors (Bui, 2015). As our online communication continues to increase, parasocial relationships may become even more prevalent (Fox & Warber, 2013).

think about this

1. Do you or others you know have a parasocial relationship? How "real" do these relationships feel?

2. What are the benefits of having PSIs (e.g., for people who live alone)? What are the dark sides (e.g., stalking celebrities)?

3. What do you think of the PSIs children have with cartoon heroes or superheroes? Are they helpful or hurtful?

4. Is it possible that some parasocial relationships are just entertainment? Why or why not?

The complexities of romantic love can be astounding, but the desire to attain it is as universal as it is timeless. Indeed, researchers have found that the value of romantic relationships and the characteristics of happiness and warmth that comprise love and commitment between two people are fairly consistent regardless of culture (Kline, Horton, & Zhang, 2005). The value placed on romantic relationships is so powerful, in fact, that some singles complain that they are stereotyped and discriminated against because they do not share the "committed relationship ideology" of those pursuing romantic relationships (Day, 2016). It is not that those fighting the bias against "singlism" reject the importance of close relationships, just the necessity of *romantic* ones (DePaulo, 2015). In any case, scholars agree that it is not the mere fact of having a romantic partner that matters, but the *quality* of that relationship.

Studies show that closeness in romantic relationships comes with many benefits. For example, relational satisfaction leads partners to focus more effectively on goals and perceive more control and partner support in the achievement of their goals (Hofmann, Finkel, & Fitzsimons, 2015). Relational harmony also has important health benefits — both physical and psychological — as you can see in Figure 8.1 (Parker-Pope, 2010a). Romantic kissing in both marital and cohabiting partners reduces stress and improves relationship satisfaction (Floyd et al., 2009). In marital relationships, wives who report being happy with their marriage increase their husband's marital quality and life satisfaction significantly, giving credence to the familiar saying, "Happy wife, happy life" (Carr, Freedman, Cornman, & Schwarz, 2014).

However, research reveals that there is not one specific path to romantic satisfaction. Dating partners in both long-distance and geographically close relationships enjoy satisfaction by using compatible styles of humor and other coping skills to decrease relational stress (Hall, 2013; Vela, Booth-Butterfield, Wanzer, & Vallade, 2013). Same-sex couples in long-term, committed relationships share the same benefits of meaningful commitment (such as life satisfaction and general well-being) as heterosexual couples (Clausell & Roisman, 2009). Cohabiting unmarried couples who see themselves on a trajectory toward marriage enjoy similar satisfaction and well-being as married couples; however, those who have ambiguity about their path or the future of the relationship are more at risk for negative relational outcomes (Willoughby, Carroll, & Busby, 2012).

> **connect**
>
> One of the best ways to react with empathy is through *relational listening* (see Chapter 7). By paraphrasing your friend's words and using caring facial expressions and body movements (see Chapter 5), you encourage your friend to share what is on his mind — even if you have never had the experience that he is describing.

FIGURE 8.1

EFFECTS OF RELATIONSHIP HARMONY This figure represents some of the benefits that happy relationships might expect.
Information from: T. Parker-Pope (2010a).

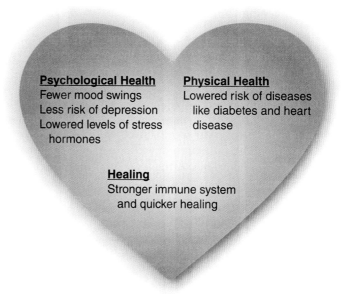

Psychological Health
Fewer mood swings
Less risk of depression
Lowered levels of stress
hormones

Physical Health
Lowered risk of diseases
like diabetes and heart
disease

Healing
Stronger immune system
and quicker healing

Different levels of intimacy may be desired in romantic relationships; what matters is not how intimate you are, but that your actual closeness meets your intimacy expectations and needs (Frost & Forrester, 2013). Over time, the harmony created in the relationship even contributes to health as partners age (Proulx & Snyder-Rivas, 2013). And the daily messages that partners share of kindness and generosity contribute to that harmony in the long term (Gottman & Silver, 1999). Married man Charles reflected this kind and generous consistency when he was asked how he and his wife were going to celebrate their twentieth wedding anniversary: "I like to think we celebrate our anniversary a little bit every day," he smiled.

Online Relationships

Tens of thousands of people around the world play and connect via online virtual worlds like *World of Warcraft* and *Second Life*. They create their avatars, explore their world, negotiate property trades with virtual currency, and participate in activities that result in what most of these players describe as at least one "real" friend (Welles, Rouse, Merrill, & Contractor, 2014). In fact, many of these players attend conventions, where they meet up in real life with friends made in the online games, illustrating the importance of the relationships they have formed within these online worlds (Schiesel, 2011).

For years, online relationships were considered impersonal, because technology lacks the richness of nonverbal cues found in face-to-face communication (Tidwell & Walther, 2002). But as we discussed in Chapter 2, mediated communicators take advantage of the lack of these cues to gain greater control over both their messages and their presentation of self. Recall that **social information processing theory** (Walther, 1996; Walther & Parks, 2002) argues that communicators use unique language and stylistic cues in their online messages to develop relationships that are just as close as those that develop face to face—but often take more time to become intimate. This hyperpersonal communication becomes even *more* personal and intimate than face-to-face interaction. Freed from the less controllable nonverbal cues (such as appearances or nervous fidgeting), online communicators can carefully craft their messages and cultivate idealized perceptions of each other (Walther & Ramirez, 2009). Indeed, relational partners often feel less constrained online

and you?

Do you have any relationships that exist strictly online? Do you consider these relationships different from other ones in your life? Are they more intimate or less?

● ROMANTIC COUPLES, regardless of sexual orientation, age, race, or ethnicity, enjoy similar benefits of being in a relationship: intimacy and commitment. (top left) Mike Powell/Getty Images; (top right) John Birdsall/The Image Works; (bottom left) Urikiri-Shashin-Kan/Alamy; (bottom right) Hola Images/Getty Images

evaluating communication ethics

think about this

Money, Family, and Paying the Bills

You have a good relationship with your parents, but money has also been a source of conflict with them. You are the first in your family to attend college and are working twenty hours a week (and full time during the summer) to contribute toward your living expenses and tuition. You have taken out a hefty amount of money in student loans as well. You know that money is tight for your parents and are grateful for the help that they can provide. Your mother, for example, sends generous packages of food, and your father and stepmother pay for your car insurance. But money is still a constant concern for you.

Recently, you discovered that you could qualify for a grant — money for college that does not need to be repaid — if you can prove that your income falls below a certain threshold. The only way to make that happen is to declare yourself independent from your parents' care. But that would have negative financial consequences for them, as they would no longer be able to claim you as a deduction on their tax return. When you discuss this with your father, he becomes so angry that he threatens to cut you off altogether — no more car insurance or place to live during your summer internship. He tells you that if you want to be independent, you should be completely independent.

Your relationship with your father has been affected no matter what you decide. If you declare yourself independent, you will lose his help and gain his wrath. But if you do not, you will have a lot of financial stress. Is there any way to repair your relationship with him?

1. Can you put yourself in your father's position? What are your responsibilities? His?

2. Consider the relationship information you have gleaned from this chapter; what family qualities should you emphasize and reinforce in your next conversation?

3. Based on the decision that you make regarding your independence, describe the communication skills you will use to manage the relationship most effectively.

(Caplan, 2001) and focus on validation and mutual support, which can lead to the development of rich and meaningful relationships both online and off (Antheunis, Valkenburg, & Peter, 2010; Tong & Walther, 2015).

Romances and friendships can frequently bud and be maintained through electronic media. More than one-third of U.S. marriages now begin as online matches (Cacioppo, Cacioppo, Gonzaga, Ogburn, & VanderWeele, 2013); although their initial interactions are entirely electronic—only meeting face-to-face after a series of messages, emails, and perhaps phone calls—the resulting relationships are more satisfying, and the individuals are slightly less likely to separate or divorce once married (Cacioppo et al., 2013). Even established couples maintain long-distance relationships by using electronic media; they tend to communicate greater intimacy than geographically close partners and are more likely to avoid conflict and problematic topics when communicating electronically (Stafford, 2010). Similarly, sharing photos, videos, and stories on Facebook, Twitter, or blogs allows us to share our lives with friends and family in other states and countries. And regular texting, video chats, phone calls, and email messages keep partners close and aware of each other's lives (Bergen, 2010; Maguire & Kinney, 2010; Mansson, Myers, & Turner, 2010; Merolla, 2010a).

Of course, a danger of communicating *solely* online with someone is that it can be difficult to detect whether the information posted is truthful. Photos can be altered and descriptions of one's experiences exaggerated. At the extreme, online relationships might even be outright false. Former Notre Dame linebacker Monti Te'o, and current linebacker for the New Orleans Saints, was the apparent victim of an elaborate relationship hoax. He thought he was developing a romantic relationship with a woman online who turned out to be a fake persona created by an acquaintance. When it was finally revealed, the hoax created a great deal of personal as well as public embarrassment and dismay (Zeman, 2013).

Why We Form Relationships

We have already established that romantic relationships are a universal desire, and additional research shows that individuals across cultures value a variety of relationships similarly (Endo, Heine, & Lehman, 2000; Landsford, Antonucci, Akiyama, & Takahashi, 2005). The reasons for forming specific relationships, however, are as individual and complex as each of us and rooted in unique needs and motivations, which may develop and change over time. In this section, we examine the factors of relationship formation, including proximity, attractive qualities, similarity, and personal and social needs.

Proximity

Would you be up for a Tweetup? For many working travelers, being alone in different cities is, well, lonesome. So they issue an open invitation on Twitter to anyone in the area to meet up for dinner or a drink—and people in the same area almost always show up. Similarly, through a website called Air Troductions, airline passengers can find others onboard who would like to chat during the flight (Quenqua, 2015). As practical as it sounds, one of the first criteria of relationship formation is simple **proximity**, or nearness. Think about how many of your friends you got to know because they sat next to you in elementary school, lived on the same dorm floor, or worked with you at Applebee's.

Physical proximity was once the most important factor in determining and maintaining relationships. If you were to move away from a neighborhood, switch schools, or change jobs, you would likely lose touch with old friends and eventually make new friends in your new surroundings. But modern technology allows you to interact regularly through mediated channels—*virtual* proximity with those who may be physically quite far away. Mobile phones provide communication proximity for those who might far apart from each other, as in urban China, where migrant workers keep in touch whether they are on the next farm or in the next province (Liu, 2015). Nonetheless, if people are not in physical proximity and fail to establish and maintain virtual proximity—for example, if they avoid social networking or do not have access to a computer, tablet, or smartphone—the chances of forming or maintaining relationships dwindle.

Attractive Qualities

An outgoing personality, sense of fun, intellectual prowess, or simply a warm smile: these are personal qualities that might attract you. As you have learned in earlier chapters, your physical appearance does play an important role in attracting others, especially in the very early stages of a relationship, when first impressions are formed. People who are considered beautiful or attractive are often perceived as kinder, warmer, more intelligent, and more honest than unattractive people and have earlier opportunities for dating and marriage (Canary, Cody, & Manusov, 2008).

But before you focus on physical attractiveness alone, remember two things. First, beauty is largely in the eye of the beholder, and individual tastes vary due to factors too numerous to discuss here (including cultural standards). For example, among the Padaung tribe of Southeast Asia, women wrap rings around their necks

connect

Although culture plays a powerful role in our ideas about physical attraction (Chapter 6), it is important to remember that we all have schemas about attractiveness (Chapter 3). So although you might find Jordan very attractive, your friend Cameron might not: Jordan may remind him of a previously awful romantic partner or bear a striking resemblance to his sister.

to push down their collarbones and upper ribs, giving the illusion of extremely long necks, considered a sign of beauty and wealth; Western standards of beauty are not the same. Second, our communication affects perceptions of beauty; repeated interaction with others alters our initial impressions of their physical appearance (Canary, Cody, & Manusov, 2008). Thus your ability to use verbal and nonverbal messages appropriately and effectively probably has a lot more to do with your perceived attractiveness than perfect clothing or the size of your jeans.

Similarity

and you?

Consider someone with whom you share a very close relationship. In what ways are you similar? Are those similarities what attracted you in the first place?

The notion that "opposites attract" is so common in popular culture that many people take it as an undeniable truth. But despite the popularity of the concept, research shows that attraction is more often based on the degree of *similarity* we have with another person, whether through shared hobbies, personality traits, backgrounds, appearances, or values (Gonzaga, Campos, & Bradbury, 2007). Shared taste in music, religion, and ethical views are the kinds of traits that are most likely to draw us to others (Launay & Dunbar, 2015). For example, consider close friends Liza and Cheryl. Liza is an African-American student from Denver, a literature major, and a tomboy who loves the Broncos. Cheryl is a white student from Boston majoring in engineering; she hates sports but follows fashion and rarely steps out of her dorm room without makeup. To an outsider, they seem like a mismatched pair. But ask either of them what they have in common, and they will roll off a list of similarities: both grew up in urban neighborhoods, attended all-girl Catholic high schools, love indie rock, and take great pride in their ability to quote J. R. R. Tolkien. As long as relational partners feel that they have much in common, as Liza and Cheryl do, they feel similar and attracted to one another.

Perceptions of similarity are tied to our perceptions of a person's attractive qualities. We are often attracted to those we think are about as physically attractive as we are. But it is our perception of similarity rather than actual similarity that is the stronger predictor of attraction (Tidwell, Eastwick, & Finkel, 2013). If we perceive that we use similar language terms and styles, we are attracted more strongly to that person (Ireland et al., 2011). And even if the other person is from another culture or ethnic group, we are more likely to perceive them as similar, as we interact with them more — practicing relational skills like self-disclosure and active listening that enable us to see many types of similarities in each other (Jin & Oh, 2010).

Personal and Social Needs

In addition to being attracted to each other for particular qualities we admire or share, we also form and maintain relationships in order to satisfy basic needs we have as human beings (Ramirez, Sunnafrank, & Goei, 2010). These needs include companionship, stimulation, and the fulfillment of goals.

Companionship

Humans feel a natural need for companionship and **inclusion** — to involve others in our lives and to be involved in the lives of others. Loneliness can be a major motivation behind some people's desire for a relationship. In fact, psychological problems such as anxiety, stress, depression, alcoholism, drug abuse, and poor health have all been tied to loneliness (Canary & Spitzberg, 1993; Segrin & Passalacqua, 2010). Unfortunately, beginning a romantic relationship just for the sake of not being alone or initiating a ton of friend requests on Facebook does not mean that you will not be lonely (Floyd, 2015). Finding a meaningful connection and creating an emotional tie with someone, such as helping a fellow

● **SENATOR JOHN McCAIN** cites communication with fellow prisoners of war, even if fleeting, as one of the factors that helped him to survive solitary confinement in Vietnam. Bettmann/Getty Images

student understand his class notes or providing water for a Race for the Cure participant, are ways of overcoming loneliness that can lead to high-quality relationships (Hawkley & Cacioppo, 2010).

Stimulation

All people have a need for intellectual, emotional, and physical stimulation (Krcmar & Greene, 1999; Rubin, Perse, & Powell, 1985). Nobody enjoys being bored, so we seek out diversions like television or music. Interactions with others frequently provide multiple types of stimulation at once, which can contribute to our relational satisfaction (Guerrero, Farinelli, & McEwan, 2009).

Consider the communication relationships you have formed with various people that provide stimulation over the course of a day. You might go for coffee with that classmate who makes you laugh. You stop your professor in the hallway to share an interesting story related to your class. You check up on Facebook and decide to hide updates from that person who always irritates you. And then you meet up with your significant other, who greets you with a warm hug after a long day. It is also possible, of course, for you to find multiple forms of stimulation in one person.

The innate need for stimulation is what causes many people to feel uncomfortable about solitary confinement in prisons. In fact, some states have dramatically reduced the number of inmates in solitary confinement and have found that assaults on staff have also been reduced (Associated Press, 2016).

Meeting Goals

In addition to our psychological needs to alleviate loneliness or obtain stimulation, we have mundane needs for achieving practical goals—getting through our daily tasks—as well as longer-term goals for achieving long-term plans. We often form relationships with people to help us or inform us or give us pep talks to meet these goals. For example, you might develop a relationship with a classmate because you need someone to help you figure out an assignment or give you advice about your major. If you have dreamed all your life about working in finance, you might seek relationships with influential people in that field through networking via your college alumni group or through an internship. We normally expect that relational partners will support our personal goals and interests, and they do—as long as those goals are seen as aligned with relational goals. However, if our personal goals are seen as a threat to the relationship (e.g., your partner wants the prestige of a job that would require spending lots of time traveling and away from you), support for our partner's personal goals diminishes significantly (Hui, Finkel, Fitzsimons, Kumashiro, & Hofmann, 2014).

Of course, people can form relationships to achieve manipulative goals as well, which is the argument that is put forward by those who feel that solitary confinement is justified. When particularly dangerous prisoners are kept in isolation, they are unable to form relationships that might help them to accomplish dangerous goals (such as gang memberships or terrorist networking; Sullivan, 2006).

Managing Relationship Dynamics

When it comes to relationship advice, you do not need to look far for what seems like "expertise." From Dr. Phil to *Essence* and *Cosmo* magazines, popular culture is brimming with advice on managing and maintaining healthy relationships. Thankfully, communication scholars explore the way we manage relationships in a far more scientific way. In this section, we rely on that scholarship to explore the dynamics of relationships as they constantly change, grow, and evolve throughout

and you?

Do you rely on different relational partners for companionship, stimulation, or goal achievement? Do you have relationships that fulfill all three needs?

● **CONFLICTS MAY** arise within a friendship based on the exchange of rewards and costs. JGl/Jamie Grill/Getty Images

our lives, specifically looking at costs and rewards, reducing uncertainty, and dialectical tensions (Knapp & Vangelisti, 2008; Solomon & Vangelisti, 2010).

Costs and Rewards

Every relationship has advantages and disadvantages for the parties involved. Your close friendship with Arturo may offer companionship and intimacy; however, you may also need to accept his negative feelings about your religious beliefs and invest time in working through difficult situations together. **Social exchange theory** explains this process of balancing the advantages and disadvantages of a relationship (Thibaut & Kelley, 1959). Relationships begin, grow, and deteriorate based on an exchange of rewards and costs.

Rewards are the elements of a relationship that you feel good about — things about the person or your relationship that benefit you in some way. There are *extrinsic rewards*, the external advantages you gain from association with another person (such as social status or professional connections); *instrumental rewards*, the resources and favors that partners give to one another (e.g., living together to save money); and *intrinsic rewards*, the personally satisfying rewards that result from an exchange of intimacy (e.g., intellectual stimulation or feelings of safety). **Costs**, by contrast, are the things that upset or annoy you, cause you stress, or damage your own self-image or lifestyle. If you find your relationship too costly (e.g., there is a lot of conflict, jealousy, or infidelity), you may decide to end the relationship (Dainton & Gross, 2008; Guerrero, La Valley, & Farinelli, 2008).

The social exchange of costs and benefits is inherently complicated. You might wonder, for example, what your friend Wendy sees in Joaquin. You do not think he is very attractive, and he does not often socialize with you and Wendy; both seem like costs to you. What you do not see is his kindness and generosity to Wendy in their private life and how his work ethic does not leave him much time for socializing — all benefits to Wendy. Be careful of disparaging Joaquin's behaviors, selectively remembering only the negative things about him (Visserman & Karremans, 2014). And resist wondering why Wendy doesn't dump Joaquin — the benefits of the relationship (including physical intimacy, intellectual stimulation, and individual security) might just outweigh your imagined or real costs.

Reducing Uncertainty

Although we weigh the costs and rewards in all stages of a relationship, we do not have much information to consider at the very beginning. We may have excitement at the prospect of a new friendship to enjoy or romance to explore, but the uncertainty about the other person is also uncomfortable. That is why we need to use various strategies to get to know one another.

According to **uncertainty reduction theory**, when two people meet, their main focus is on decreasing the uncertainty about each other (Berger & Bradac, 1982). The less sure you are of the person's qualities, the way the person will behave, or what will happen, the higher the degree of uncertainty. Uncertainty leads to discomfort, so to reduce that discomfort, you and your partner are motivated to learn what to say and do that is appropriate in your relationship. Your ability to predict one another's behavior, and the causes of that behavior, reduces uncertainty (Boucher, 2015). As two people — college roommates, coworkers, romantic partners — reduce the uncertainty between them, they uncover similarities, become better at predicting what the other will do or say, and thus develop more understanding and comfort.

what about you?

Assessing the Costs and Rewards of a Relationship

Think of a current romantic relationship (or, if you are not in one now, think of a past one). As you assess your partner's traits and behaviors, use a five-point scale for your answers: 5 = strongly agree; 4 = agree; 3 = neither agree nor disagree; 2 = disagree; and 1 = extremely disagree.

_____ 1. My partner laughs at my jokes.

_____ 2. My partner makes appropriate jokes or comments.

_____ 3. My partner is physically attractive to me.

_____ 4. My partner is affectionate.

_____ 5. My partner wears clothes I like.

_____ 6. My partner has a pleasing personality.

_____ 7. My partner and I have similar views about religion.

_____ 8. My partner and I have similar views about children.

_____ 9. My partner shares emotions appropriately.

_____ 10. My partner acknowledges my feelings.

_____ 11. My partner fits in with my friends.

_____ 12. My partner fits in with my family.

_____ 13. My partner and I share similar dreams for the future.

_____ 14. My partner and I enjoy similar hobbies and activities.

_____ 15. My partner and I agree about career paths.

_____ 16. My partner appreciates my racial and ethnic background.

_____ 17. My partner manages finances well.

_____ 18. My partner appreciates my political views.

_____ 19. My partner overlooks my shortcomings.

_____ 20. My partner is an interesting person.

Scoring: Add your scores together to get an informal assessment of how rewarding or costly you perceive your relationship to be. If you scored between 74 and 100, you perceive your relationship as very rewarding on a number of levels and are likely to value and maintain this relationship; if you scored 47–73, you see both costs and rewards in your relationship and are able to balance these effectively; if you scored 20–46, you perceive your relationship as having more costs than rewards, and you might consider ways to fix or end it.

Note: The importance of certain costs and rewards varies greatly from individual to individual, so the weightings (e.g., physical attraction or similarity of views) may vary.

In order to reduce uncertainty and increase the likelihood of a closer relationship, you must obtain information about your new relational partner. How do you get this information? Unless you can read minds, you have likely employed several different strategies, depending on the situation: passive strategies, active strategies, and interactive strategies.

connect

It is important to reduce uncertainty in all communication contexts. For example, in Chapter 13, we discuss audience analysis, which allows you to learn about the people who will listen to your speech. By understanding your audience's expectations, learning about their opinions of your topic, and carefully considering their demographics, you can reduce uncertainty and determine the most effective way to reach them.

Passive Strategies

Most college students who live on campus are faced with the prospect of sharing a small space with a stranger, and that can be frightening. So when Shawna heard about her new roommate, Ramona, she entered her name and hometown into Google. She quickly found Ramona on Facebook and learned that she is a concert pianist and an avid knitter who sometimes sells her creations through Etsy.com (see Antheunis, Valkenburg, & Peter, 2010).

Shawna engaged in a passive uncertainty reduction strategy. **Passive strategies** involve observing others in communication situations without interacting with them. You may also analyze their interactions with others when you believe they are not under a lot of pressure to conform to social roles. Without Ramona knowing it, Shawna had already found out quite a bit about her. Social networking allows us to monitor others with relative ease; however, we also use passive strategies in face-to-face situations whenever we observe others going about their day-to-day business.

Active Strategies

Active strategies let you obtain information about a person more directly by seeking information from a third party. For example, Shawna may discover that she and Ramona have one friend in common. In that case, Shawna might contact this individual to see how much she knows about Ramona. Does she party a lot? Is she neat or messy? Does she snore?

Active strategies can be particularly useful when the information you are seeking could be awkward for a new relationship. For example, Shawna might wonder if Ramona would be uncomfortable having significant others spend the night in their dorm room. Thus she might chat with the mutual friend to get a sense of Ramona's feelings to be prepared to discuss it when they arrive on campus.

Interactive Strategies

Sometimes you will need to find out important information about a relational partner through **interactive strategies**, that is, by speaking directly with that person rather than observing or asking others for information. When meeting for the first time (be it in person or virtually), Shawna might ask Ramona what kind of music she likes, what major she is pursuing, and why she chose this particular school. Although direct questioning reduces uncertainty, it also entails risks. If you ask questions that are perceived as too forward or inappropriate (e.g., "What are your political beliefs?"), you might push the person away.

Dialectical Tensions

and you?

Consider your relationship with your oldest friend or with a close family member. Evaluate the ways in which dialectical tensions have manifested themselves in that relationship over the years. Have these tensions shifted over time? Is there a particular tension that continues to crop up?

Weighing costs against benefits and reducing uncertainty are not the only challenges we face in developing relationships. In any relationship, it is common to experience contradictions or opposing feelings about your relational partner and about the relationship itself. When a love relationship becomes serious, for example, one or both partners might find themselves mourning their old, single lifestyle, despite the benefits of commitment.

Relational dialectics theory holds that contradictory feelings tug at us in every relationship, whether it is a newly formed friendship or a committed romantic partnership. These contradictions are called **dialectical tensions**, and they can be external (between the partners and the people with whom they interact) or internal (within their relationship). Of the many possible types, we focus on three internal tensions that dominate research: *autonomy* versus *connection, openness* versus *closedness*, and *predictability* versus *novelty* (Baxter & Simon, 1993). Note that dialectics exist along a continuum; they are not all-or-nothing trade-offs but rather ranges of options that need to be continually negotiated and adjusted (Baxter, Braithwaite, Bryant, & Wagner, 2004). These tensions are natural and normal—experiencing them does not indicate that your relationship is in trouble!

Autonomy Versus Connection

Identical twins Eva and Amelia have always done everything together—from their first breaths of air right on through their college education. As they grew older, loosening these bonds was a real struggle. Eva remembers bursting into tears at her bridal shower and explaining, "It's just that I've never had a party all to myself before" (see Hazel, Wongprasert, & Ayres, 2006).

● **THREE'S A CROWD** (sometimes). Perhaps no familial relationship plays out the delicate balance between autonomy and connection as clearly as that of multiple-birth siblings. Patti McConville/Getty Images

In all close personal relationships—family connections, romantic relationships, and friendships—there is a tension between independence (autonomy) and dependence (connection). In other words, we struggle because we want to be our own person while at the same time be fully connected to the other person. This tension can result in hurt feelings. Attempts to express autonomy can be easily misunderstood—children's attempts to express their own identities are often seen as acts of rebellion, whereas romantic partners risk alienating their loved ones when they pursue certain interests alone (Sahlstein & Dun, 2008). On the other hand, we can seem insecure when we try to force connectedness on our relational partners: if we drag our partners off to yoga class or a sporting event in which they have no interest, we are more likely to alienate them than to bring them closer.

So how might you bridge the gap between autonomy and connectedness? One strategy is to alternate time together and time apart. You might go to a spin class with your sister, who enjoys it, while your romantic partner enjoys a solo evening at home. On Saturdays, however, you and your significant other might try out different local kayaking spots—a shared passion that you engage in together. Or you might manage the tension with the physical space in your home—deciding the decor for the living room together but displaying your comic book memorabilia in your own office hideout.

Openness Versus Closedness

Every superhero from Batman to Superman knows about this tension. To become close, individuals reveal a part of their private selves that then becomes vulnerable. The tension comes as partners strive to find a balance between sharing information (openness) and desiring to keep some things private (closedness). The tension between Batman's duty to Gotham City and duty to his loved ones takes a toll on those relationships when he cannot tell them about his secret life as a superhero.

Without the excuse of a double life, most people need to disclose private information to those with whom they have relationships to facilitate a perception of involvement and deep understanding. Even when we account for cultural differences (see Chapter 6), relational intimacy is consistently advanced by self-disclosure (Chen & Nakazawa, 2009). But it is not always a good idea to reveal your every thought to your partner. Contrary to the notion that there should be "no secrets between us," some information might be better left unsaid. Telling your current romantic partner how you feel attracted to a celebrity is a good example.

Some relationships will alternate over time between one or the other ends of the spectrum, such as lots of openness during one phase of their relationship and more closedness at other times. Those who are willing to try to fulfill each other's needs for information while still maintaining their own privacy are more likely to manage this dialectical tension with satisfaction (Baxter, 1990).

● **FOR SOME,** the surprise of breakfast in bed might be enough to shake up the normal relational routine. For others, it might take zip-lining through a rainforest or backpacking across Asia. Cultura RM Exclusive/Matt Hoover Photo/Getty Images

Predictability Versus Novelty

Which is more important to relationships, safety and security or excitement and spontaneity? The third dialectical tension is where proponents of relational dialectics theory disagree with the concept of uncertainty reduction that we discussed earlier. Rather than accepting that uncertainty is inherently uncomfortable, dialectics researchers argue that people have a simultaneous need for stability through predictable relational interaction *as well as* a need for new and unexpected experiences in personal relationships. On the one hand, partners seek stable patterns of interaction: Colin and Casey, for example, enjoy the comfort of their evening routine of dinner and television, and their understanding of each others' typical reactions and emotions helps them to know how to support one another and avoid unnecessary upsets. At the same time, being able to almost finish each other's sentences can be too predictable, so some novelty in their interactions is also welcome. To break the predictability pattern, Colin might surprise Casey with an unexpected love note in the lunch she takes to work, or Casey might suggest a vacation in a place they would not usually consider.

Self-Disclosure and Interpersonal Relationships

Jorge recently moved to a small town where most of the residents have lived for most of their lives. In order to make friends in this tight-knit community, Jorge knows he needs to let others know about him to build relationships. He volunteers in order to give them general information about him as community-minded and generous; however, he will need to tell them other things directly (information about his family, his personal goals or his work history). As you have likely experienced in your own life, self-disclosure has a powerful impact on the development of interpersonal relationships (Samter, 2003). The process of choosing what information to disclose to others and when has long fascinated communication researchers and scholars who note that it is informed by issues as complex as personality type and individual tendencies (Hesse & Rauscher, 2013), situational and relational variables (Frisby & Sidelinger, 2013), and culture (Chen & Nakazawa, 2012). Keeping these variations in mind, we now examine the ways in which the decisions to divulge or withhold personal information affect relationships.

Social Penetration

In many relationships, a primary goal is to increase intimacy, or relational closeness. **Social penetration theory (SPT)** explains how partners move from superficial levels to greater intimacy (Altman & Taylor, 1973). SPT uses an onion as a metaphor to describe how relationships move through various stages: just as you might peel off layers of an onion to reach the core or center, a relational partner attempts to reach the most intimate thoughts and feelings at the other partner's "core" (see Figure 8.2).

According to SPT, each deeper layer contains information that is more private and therefore riskier to divulge to someone else. The outer layer represents aspects of the self that are obvious, such as our appearance, or are surface-level revelations, such as our social categories (male, college graduate, Texan). Successive layers become more private as partners assess the costs and benefits of the relationship and of disclosing information to each other. If costs exceed rewards, it is unlikely that the partners will move inward toward the more deeply concealed layers. Upon getting to know Jorge, for example, you might find that despite his boisterous exterior, he sometimes suffers from serious bouts of depression, which he manages with medication. But Jorge must choose to reveal this information: it is a part of him that only his closest, most trusted friends know, and he is likely to reveal it only as a relationship becomes more intimate.

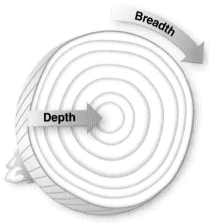

FIGURE 8.2

SOCIAL PENETRATION THEORY (SPT) MODEL According to the SPT model, relational partners peel away successive layers of information about each other as they move toward greater intimacy.

Managing Privacy

Jordana Narin describes a relationship that goes nowhere. Despite strong feelings for and physical intimacy with Jeremy, she never tells him how she truly feels nor calls him her "boyfriend." While they can talk about all sorts of things, they keep their feelings for one another private (Narin, 2015). **Communication privacy management (CPM) theory** explains that people believe they own the information they hold about themselves and make decisions about whether they will disclose or protect it (Petronio, 2004). CPM explains why Jordana will boldly share her religious or political beliefs but not her feelings for Jeremy, perhaps afraid that calling him her boyfriend will somehow ruin the relationship that they currently have. CPM theory also presumes that people set up boundaries among their friends and family members to control access to information and to manage the risks that may make them vulnerable (Petronio, 2004).

Two key features of relationships are central to privacy management. First, privacy management is affected by the dialectical tension of openness versus closedness, discussed earlier. You want to share information to increase intimacy with your partner, but it may be risky to do so, and keeping some information private is a worthy goal. Second, privacy management requires cultural, situational, and relational rules or expectations by which people must be willing to abide. For example, it would likely be considered impolite for you to ask your boss about his medical condition because that topic is far too private for a work context in many cultures, and you are unlikely to have that level of personal intimacy with your manager. Yet that type of disclosure is expected in close relationships (Derlega, Winstead, Mathews, & Braitman, 2008).

If there is a threat to your privacy boundaries (e.g., your trusted friend told your private information or feelings to someone else), you experience **boundary turbulence** and must readjust your need for privacy against your need for self-disclosure and connection (Guerrero, Andersen, & Afifi, 2013; Theiss, Knobloch, Checton, & Magsamen-Conrad, 2009). Boundary turbulence occurs in mediated situations, too. If you have personal information about someone

and you?

Do you post any personal information on social networking sites? What kind of information are you willing to reveal? What kind of information do you consider too private to share in mediated contexts?

real communicator

NAME: May Hui
OCCUPATION: Entrepreneur/Matchmaker
Courtesy May Hui

As a self-professed romantic, I love bringing people together. So after years of being a sales, marketing, and operations executive for a *Fortune* 500 company, I decided to use the relational communication principles I learned in college to help singles find a "match" and potentially develop a committed relationship.

Catch Matchmaking is not your average dating service; my partner and I create articles and YouTube videos to teach our clients the basics of interpersonal communication. This might seem surprising, but a lot of people do not know what to do on a date; either they have not had a lot of dating experience or they have had relationships that "went bad" and are afraid of another failure.

We interview clients personally about their preferences for religion, height, income level, common interests, goals, and values. We find that the profiles people create themselves are often abstract; they might say they are *adventurous*, but when we follow up, they may not mean what a "match" might (e.g., *adventurous* = climbing Mt. Everest or *adventurous* = trying a new

restaurant). We also coach our clients on the basics of self-presentation. Appropriate dress and grooming shows you care enough to make yourself attractive, and nonverbal behaviors like making eye contact, leaning in, softening your tone of voice, and smiling show warmth and interest in the other person.

We help our clients with questioning and listening skills, too. It is important to ask a lot of questions and get your date talking. Whoever talks more usually says the date was great, so it is often important to talk less about yourself to discover more details about the other person. Limit self-disclosure in the beginning, too; sex, religion, and politics are not the best topics for a first date. Neither are past relationships; do not complain about your past partner(s); give this new relationship a chance to start fresh.

I absolutely love what I am doing, particularly on days when I hear that two clients have become engaged! The communication classes I took are key to the way I run this successful business that brings me so much joy.

else, do you have the right to tweet that? What about inside jokes or pictures taken at a party—do you have the right to post them on Instagram? Judgments can be made about you based on what your "friends" do on Facebook (Walther, Van Der Heide, Kim, Westerman, & Tong, 2008), and you often alter the kinds of disclosures you make depending on whether you and your parents are Facebook friends (Child & Westermann, 2013; Mullen & Fox Hamilton, 2016) or whether you are messaging friends who are distant versus nearby (Waters & Ackerman, 2011). You can see how complex privacy management becomes in online communication.

Strategic Topic Avoidance

Certain topics are simply too sensitive for some people to confront openly. One or both relational partners can use **strategic topic avoidance** to maneuver the conversation away from potentially embarrassing, vulnerable, or otherwise undesirable topics (Dailey & Palomares, 2004). Just as in privacy management, there are topics we avoid because we are culturally trained to do so. For example, prior relationships, negative information, dating experiences, money issues, and sexual experiences are largely considered inappropriate for public communication (Baxter & Wilmot, 1985; Dailey & Palomares, 2004; Guerrero & Afifi, 1995). If a colleague at the office asks about the size of your recent bonus and you prefer not to share

and you?

What topics do you consider strictly off-limits? Are there topics you are willing to discuss with some people but not with others? How do you inform others of your unwillingness to discuss these topics?

this with him, you could say that it is none of his business. But research shows that you would be better off using a less direct avoidance tactic, such as keeping silent, deflecting, giving an unrelated response, lying, or simply ending the conversation (Dailey & Palomares, 2004).

Like other issues related to self-disclosure, there are ethical considerations regarding pursuing and avoiding topics. Is it appropriate for parents to disclose the private details of their impending divorce to their children? They may mean well (e.g., they may want to reduce uncertainty for their children), but they may use such strategies unethically (perhaps each parent argues for his or her own side of the story to be viewed in a better light). In addition, adolescent children may suffer emotionally and view the disclosures as inappropriate (Afifi, McManus, Hutchinson, & Baker, 2007).

Every relationship is unique and, as we have discussed, relational partners may experience different degrees of comfort with disclosure or avoidance at different times. For example, dating couples who are experiencing relationship dissatisfaction have been found to engage in more topic avoidance, often to create emotional distance (Merrill & Afifi, 2012). On the other hand, people in more satisfying relationships may also use topic avoidance, but they say they are trying to be sensitive to the other person's concerns and accommodate the other's needs (Dailey & Palomares, 2004). In other words, strategic topic avoidance can have benefits or detriments, depending on how and why the topics are being avoided.

Stages of a Relationship

In the CBC series *Heartland*, a family in Alberta, Canada, struggles to keep their ranch running and their relationships intact. Whether it is Tim reevaluating his current relationship when Janice returns, or the family banding together to find runaway Georgie, the episodes trace the growth and decline of relationships, challenged by significant relational events called **turning points** (Baxter & Bullis, 1986)—positive or negative events or changes that stand out in people's minds as important to defining their relationships (e.g., stories about "how we met" or detours such as negative disclosures).

A turning point can often move a relationship into a new "stage"—a different set of feelings and communication behaviors that partners demonstrate that are consistent with their level of intimacy (Knapp & Vangelisti, 2000). During each stage, communication patterns differ and assessments of costs and rewards determine whether the relationship will remain at the same stage, move to a closer stage, or shift to one further apart. Figure 8.3 outlines the relational stages we develop in the following sections.

Initiating Stage

In the **initiating stage** of a relationship, you make contact with another person, saying "Hello" or asking for a name. If you think about the number of new people you initiate with on a given day, you will not be surprised to learn that many relationships do not move beyond this stage. Just because you say "Good morning" to the woman who sold you a bagel does not mean the two of you will be chatting on the phone later today. But you will likely use your first impression of a person to gauge whether you are interested in moving forward with the relationship (Canary, Cody, & Manusov, 2008).

connect

It can be awkward to verbally indicate that you want a relationship to end or to move beyond the initiating stage. You would not tell a new classmate, "I don't like you. Stop talking to me." Luckily, nonverbal communication helps you address this issue. You can indicate like or dislike with facial expressions, posture, use of space, or touch (Chapter 5), hoping this individual properly decodes your message.

TYPICAL STAGES OF A RELATION-
SHIP It is normal to move between
and among stages in different relationships as we become more intimate or less intimate with others.

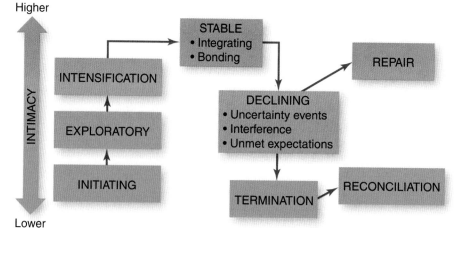

● **SUPERSTARS** Jay-Z and
Beyoncé Knowles have struggled
to maintain a stable relationship for
years; the strains and visibility of
being a celebrity couple contribute to
the challenges. Noel Vasquez/Getty Images

Exploratory Stage

In the **exploratory stage**, you are seeking relatively superficial information from
your partner. You make small talk, asking things like "Were you a fan of *Breaking
Bad*?" or "How many brothers and sisters do you have?" You are not likely to reveal
anything too deep or personal; you are still testing the waters, so to speak. You might
use a social networking site to seek information about the other person—pictures
and status updates from even years back—as you explore whether you want to
proceed (Van Ouytsel, Van Gool, Walrave, Ponnet, & Peeters, 2016). On the popular dating app Tinder, some have replaced "get-to-know-you" questions like, "How
was your weekend" with conversation starters like, "Suppose you were climbing
Everest . . ." Or on the dating service Bumble, where women must initiate all conversations, you may ask every match if he is a feminist (Johnston, 2016). Monitoring
strategies are also at work to reduce uncertainty in this stage. In addition to the
small-talk questioning we mentioned, you are likely to observe your partner closely
to learn more about his or her attitudes and behaviors. As in the initiating stage, you
will want to invest further in the relationship if the rewards seem high.

Intensification Stage

The **intensification stage** occurs when relational partners become increasingly
intimate and move their communication toward more personal self-disclosures.
This stage includes the use of informal address or pet names ("honey," "darling")
as well as "we" talk ("We're going to the concert on Friday night, right?" "Where
are we going for your birthday next week?"). Relational partners in this stage also
understand each other's nonverbal communication to a greater degree and often
share their affection with one another ("What would I do without you!"; Knapp &
Vangelisti, 2000).

Stable Stage

By the time partners reach the **stable stage**, their relationship is no longer volatile
or temporary. They now have a great deal of knowledge about one another, their
expectations are realistic, and they feel comfortable with their motives for being in
the relationship. Relationships reach the stable stage when uncertainty reduces to
the point where partners feel comfortable understanding each other's preferences
and goals (Goss & O'Hair, 1988).

Two substages occur here. First, we see relational partners **integrating** or
"becoming one." You and your roommate Dana now cultivate common friends,

develop joint opinions, and may share property. Second, people treat you as a pair—one of you would never be invited to a party without the other one (Knapp & Vangelisti, 2000). If the relationship progresses beyond integrating, **bonding** takes place when two partners share formal, public messages with the world that their relationship is important and cherished. Engagements, weddings, civil unions, and entering into legal contracts (such as buying a house together) are common ways to reveal a bonded romantic couple.

Life's challenges inevitably arise for partners in a stable relationship, so individuals will need to determine if the benefits of the relationship (such as intimacy or companionship) outweigh the costs that these challenges represent. When there are transgressions, forgiveness is an important factor in maintaining the romantic relationship (Kato, 2016). For a few tips on developing and maintaining stable relationships, see Table 8.2.

Declining Stage

Have you noticed your partner criticizing you more often, refusing to talk about issues important to you, getting defensive, or speaking with contempt? If these behaviors are occurring more often than positive behaviors in your relationship, you may be in a **declining stage**, when the relationship begins to come apart (Gottman & Silver, 1999). Three factors typically lead to this stage: uncertainty events, interference (concerning family, work, timing, money, or the like), and unmet expectations.

Uncertainty Events

Events or behavioral patterns that cause uncertainty in a relationship are called **uncertainty events**. They may be caused by competing relationships (romantic or platonic); deception or betrayal of confidence; fluctuations in closeness; and sudden or unexplained changes in sexual behavior, personality, or values (Planalp & Honeycutt, 1985). One or both partners are left wondering about the cause of the events and their significance for the relationship. If your romantic partner suddenly starts withholding information from you or a close friend begins engaging in activities that you find offensive, you will experience uncertainty. Uncertainty events may be sudden and very noticeable (e.g., betrayal of confidence), or they may be subtle and escape immediate attention (your sister gradually stops returning your phone calls).

Interference

When Patrick becomes involved in a serious romantic relationship, his best friend Dennis feels abandoned. Jason wants to get married, but Nora is not ready. Emma and Leigh find that financial troubles are straining their relationship.

These are just some of the many obstacles that may pop up in a relationship and interfere with its growth. Timing, the family or friends of one or both partners, and problems with work or money can all contribute to the decline of a relationship. Arguing over finances is a frequent reason for couples seeking therapy (Atwood, 2012), and a study of one thousand spouses found that 84 percent of married couples reported money as a culprit in marital distress ("Money," 2006). Romantic partners or even friends often view money differently because of upbringing, spending habits, and gender (Blumstein & Schwartz, 1983).

Unmet Expectations

Whenever people enter a relationship, they form ideas about what they think will or should happen; these expectations influence how we (and our partners) send and receive messages. Unrealistic expectations can create problems in a relationship: if Hannah believes that true love means never arguing, she might interpret her boyfriend Liam's criticism of her frequent tardiness as a sign that they are not meant to be together. Realistic expectations, by contrast, can increase relational satisfaction and improve interpersonal communication (Alexander, 2008). Luisa, for example, has learned that her friend Emily is never going to remember her birthday. It is not a sign that Emily does not care; she just is not good with dates. Instead, Luisa focuses on the kind things that Emily does for her, like sending her funny postcards from her business travel or watching Luisa's dogs when she has to leave town.

Repair Stage

A relationship in decline is not necessarily doomed to failure: partners may attempt to save or repair their relationship by changing their behavior, interactions, or expectations. If you have a strong commitment to someone else, particularly in a romantic relationship, you often perceive problems as less severe, so you are more likely to reduce conflict and potentially repair the relationship (Miczo, 2008). **Repair tactics** should include improving communication, focusing on the positive aspects of each partner and of the relationship itself, reinterpreting behaviors with a more balanced view,

communication across cultures

Grieving Relationships

The television images of the grieving parents and friends after a recent mass shooting brought it all back to Kai: the shock of the death of his own friend, shot by an alienated ex-student on the street of their college community. Kai's feelings of anxiety, anger, despair, and helplessness resurfaced, and he wished he could somehow help those gripped by sorrow as he had been helped a few years earlier (Herberman Mash, Fullerton, & Ursano, 2013). Experiencing the death of a loved one is not rare among college students; almost one in three will experience the death of a family member or friend during their time on campus (Balk, 2011). Most of these students are away from home and in a campus culture that is focused more on living than dying. How do they handle the death of a relationship?

In U.S. (and most Western) cultures, we honor the dead by eulogizing them — talking about them and the relationship we had with them — whereas in more community-based cultures (e.g., Africa, Asia), *not* talking about them is more common — though public expressions (e.g., wailing over the casket) illustrate grief emotions (Groot-Alberts, 2012). Yet, even in Western cultures, communication about death is painful and emotionally draining; most of the time, we do not know how to comfort ourselves or others experiencing grief. Listening to a grieving person means putting your own experiences and anxiety aside, realizing that you do not have to have had the same experience as the griever to be of help. You do not have to give advice, solutions, or cures — sometimes a simple touch and look of concern are what the griever needs.

Culture, personality, and gender all influence grieving styles (Doughty, 2009), as does family. Family communication patterns that encourage open and honest communication about grief contribute to feelings of personal growth as members deal with their sense of loss; less open family cultures are associated with more blame, panic, disorganization, and detachment from reality (Carmon, Western, Miller, Pearson, & Fowler, 2010). Kai counts himself as fortunate to have had family and friends who helped him through his grief. Like other people his age, Kai has found that his social network can also help in the grieving process. Visiting the Facebook profile of the deceased, looking at pictures to reinforce positive memories, and even writing online messages to his deceased friend have all been helpful coping mechanisms for his pain (Pennington, 2013).

think about this

1. Have you lost a relationship to death? If so, what have you done that helped you heal? If you have not experienced a loss yourself, describe what you think is helpful for others.

2. What cultural differences (including family, gender, country, religion) have you noticed in people's approaches to grieving?

3. Are there things you should avoid doing or saying when dealing with a grieving person? Are there things you should keep in mind when dealing with grief yourself?

4. Discuss with others what words and actions you think are appropriate or inappropriate when dealing with grief.

reevaluating the alternatives to the relationship, and enlisting the support of others to hold the relationship together (Brandau-Brown, & Ragsdale, 2008; Duck, 1984).

In short, partners hoping to repair a relationship must focus on the benefits of their relationship rather than laying blame (see Table 8.2); many tips for managing stable relationships also apply to repairing them. Relational partners should listen to each other, take each other's perspective, and remind themselves about the attractive qualities that sparked the relationship in the first place (e.g., how Talia can make Greg laugh and how Greg can make Talia feel at ease with her emotions). Partners may also try to increase their intimacy by offering more self-disclosures and spending quality time together (Blumstein & Schwartz, 1983). If a relationship is in serious decline, however, and seems beyond repair, the partners may need to seek professional help or outside support.

Termination Stage

Try as they might, not all relational partners stay together (hence the existence of sad songs and bad poetry). The **termination stage**, or end of a relationship, usually comes about in one of two ways (Davis, 1973). The first is *passing away,* which is characterized by a gradual fade as the relationship loses its vitality, perhaps because of outside interference or because partners do not make the effort to maintain it. Partners slowly stop texting, emailing, or calling so that termination is defined by silence (Brooks, 2015). Also, if partners spend less time together as a couple, communication and intimacy may decline, leading to dissatisfaction and a perception of different attitudes. Some romances and friendships deteriorate when one partner moves away; marriages and outside friendships may also change when children come into the picture.

The second way relationships often end is in *sudden death*—the abrupt, and for at least one partner, unexpected termination of a relationship. This might happen if your spouse or romantic partner has an affair, or if you decide that you can no longer tolerate a friend's emotionally manipulative behavior. There are times when continuing fights going nowhere seem to justify this definitive close to a relationship. While it

TABLE 8.2

STRATEGIES FOR MANAGING STABLE RELATIONSHIPS

Strategy	Examples
Remember what made you interested in the relationship in the first place	• Share inside jokes • Visit favorite places (a coffeehouse where you used to meet)
Spend quality time together	• Share your day-to-day activities • Explore new hobbies and interests
Share tasks and humor	• Plan finances and do chores together • Have inside jokes and laugh together
Be understanding	• Empathize with the other's concerns, dreams, fears, and so on • Try to see things from your partner's viewpoint
Express affection	• Proclaim how important your partner is ("You're a great friend" or "I love you") • Do something nice or unexpected for your partner without being asked
Have realistic expectations	• Do not compare your relationships to others • Accept your partner's strengths *and* weaknesses
Work on intimacy	• Offer supportive, positive messages, particularly during stressful times • Reinforce commitment by showing investment in the relationship (self-disclose, make future plans)

Information from L. K. Guerrero, P. A. Andersen, & W. A. Afifi (2013).

may seem mean, "ghosting" is an abrupt digital end to the relationship—essentially erasing digital evidence that the relationship existed (Hansen-Bundy, 2016; Pogensky, 2016). Others consider ghosting to occur in the stage previously explained, in which one party stops communicating with the other—particularly online—in the hope that they will "get the hint." If you are heavily involved in social media, you may experience more breakup distress as your networks learn of the end of your relationship (Lukacs & Quan-Haase, 2015). Communicating your desire to end a relationship can be difficult whether you do it face to face or online; examples of messages that are used for terminating romantic relationships are listed in Table 8.3.

Reconciliation

Is there any hope for a terminated relationship? Soap operas and sitcoms say so—and it is true in real life as well. **Reconciliation** involves attempts to rekindle an extinguished relationship. Attempting reconciliation entails a lot of risk—one partner might find that the other partner is not interested, or both partners might find that the problems that pushed them apart remain or have intensified. But there are a few tactics that can help the partners decide to reignite the relationship (O'Hair & Krayer, 1987; Patterson & O'Hair, 1992):

▶ *Spontaneous development:* The partners wind up spending more time together. Perhaps a divorced couple is involved in their son's school or two ex-friends find themselves helping a mutual friend.

▶ *Third-party mediation:* The partners have a counselor, friend or family member mediate the reconciliation.

▶ *High affect:* The partners resolve to be nice and polite to one another and possibly remind each other of what they found attractive about the other in the first place.

▶ *Tacit persistence:* One or both partners refuse to give up on the relationship.

TABLE 8.3

TERMINATION STRATEGIES FOR ROMANTIC RELATIONSHIPS

Strategy	Tactics	Examples
Positive-tone messages	Fairness	"It's not right to go on acting as if I'm in love with you when I don't feel that way."
	Compromise	"We can still see each other occasionally."
	Fatalism	"We both know this relationship won't work out anyway."
De-escalation	Promise of friendship	"We can still be friends."
	Implied possible reconciliation	"Perhaps time apart will rekindle our feelings for each other."
	Blaming the relationship	"We have to work too hard on this relationship."
	Appeal to independence	"We don't need to be tied down right now."
Withdrawal or avoidance	Avoid contact with the person as much as possible	"I'm not going to be able to see you this weekend." "I'll be away from my phone for a while."
Justification	Emphasize positive consequences of disengaging	"We should see other people since we've changed so much."
	Emphasize negative consequences of not disengaging	"We'll miss too many opportunities if we don't see other people."
Negative identity management	Emphasize enjoyment of life	"Life is too short to spend with just one person right now."
	Nonnegotiation	"I need to see other people — period!"

Information from D. J. Canary, M. J. Cody, & V. Manusov (2008).

▶ *Mutual interaction:* The partners begin talking more often following the dissolution, perhaps remaining friends after their breakup.

▶ *Avoidance:* The partners avoid spending time together and begin to miss each other.

If you think about couples in popular culture who have broken up and gotten back together—Connor and Oliver on *How to Get Away with Murder,* for instance—you can clearly see these strategies at work.

and you?

Have you ever been able to restore a relationship that you thought was irreparably damaged? Have you ever ended a relationship but secretly believed that you would repair it at some point in the future?

 **Mary and Justin**

At the beginning of this chapter, we met Mary and Justin, a couple struggling to maintain a close and functional family life during Justin's regular military deployment. Let's consider how they deal with the strains of time, distance, and uncertainty as we consider what we have learned in this chapter.

▶ Military spouses often take on the role of single parents, making new rules and routines for interaction with the children when their partners are gone. When the soldier returns, his or her unfamiliarity with these behaviors may strain communication. When Justin is home, he and Mary talk a lot about how they should guide and discipline their sons so that the boys experience consistency—and so that they manage the dialectical tensions of autonomy versus connection.

▶ Depending on what technologies are available (and when), families can talk every day or regularly to keep abreast of one another's lives. They can engage in activities together, even though they are far apart. Mary and Justin like to choose a book that they read independently and then discuss when they have time together. They also pray together at an agreed-upon time, even though they are not connected physically or electronically. These simple but meaningful activities help them to feel a sense of closeness despite the distance.

▶ Sharing family news—whether big ("Doug made the basketball team") or small ("Daniel was home from school today with a bit of a cold")—helps to keep Justin involved in the family's day-to-day activities. Mary and Justin's discussions of their daily lives help them to increase feelings of intimacy.

▶ All spouses may sometimes worry about how much to disclose to their partners. For example, Mary worries that if she discloses her exhaustion at dealing with their son's disrespectful behavior alone, Justin will feel guilty for not being there. However, research shows that healthy self-disclosure between spouses correlates with fewer health problems and higher marital satisfaction (Joseph & Afifi, 2010).

 **Activities**

📖 **LaunchPad**
macmillan learning

1. LaunchPad for *Real Communication* offers key term videos and encourages self-assessment through adaptive quizzing. Go to **launchpadworks.com** to get access to:

☑ **LearningCurve**
Adaptive Quizzes.

Harry How/Getty Images

Video clips that illustrate key concepts, highlighted in teal in the Real Reference section that follows.

2. List one family relationship, one friendship, and one romantic relationship in which you are or have been involved. For each of these relationships, list at least five self-disclosures you made to those individuals, and describe how each revelation advanced relational intimacy. Now list at least five self-disclosures you wish you had *not* made to each of these individuals. Did these inappropriate self-disclosures increase or decrease your intimacy? Reflect on these lists as you self-disclose in future relationships.

3. Consider a romantic relationship that has ended. Using the stages outlined in this chapter, create a time line of the relationship. Include significant turning points that encouraged the relationship to move into another stage as well as any stages that may have been skipped. Reflect on your level of satisfaction at each stage and note any changes you would have made at that point. If any stages were omitted from the time line, reflect on why. Based on your experiences in this relationship, did you or will you communicate differently with later romantic partners?

4. As a new romantic relationship begins, keep a journal of the communication events that occur. In this journal, indicate the stage you perceive the relationship to be in (based on the stages in this chapter). List key communication events that increase or decrease attachment in the relationship. Reflect on and include in your journal your level of satisfaction with the relationship and if and how you would like the relationship to proceed.

5. In small groups in your class, discuss how popular culture and films portray interpersonal relationships, considering specifically relationship stages. Discuss communication techniques that the characters might have used to produce different relationship outcomes. Analyze how accurately the communication behaviors of the characters themselves and those they use in their relationships reflect real-life communication episodes.

real reference ▶ A Study Tool

Now that you have finished reading this chapter, you can:

Explain key aspects of interpersonal relationships:

▶ **Interpersonal communication** is the exchange of verbal and nonverbal messages between people who are building relationships by sharing meanings and accomplishing social goals. **Impersonal communication** is role based, with little relational development or expressed emotion. **Hyperpersonal communication** takes advantage of digital channels to enhance intimacy in interpersonal relationships (p. 186).

▶ Our **relational networks** are complex webs of relationships. We have **family relationships**, **friendships**, **social relationships**, romantic partners, and relationships we establish and maintain online (pp. 187–188).

▶ **Love** is a deep affection for another person with varying degrees of passion, commitment, and **intimacy**, or closeness and understanding (p. 189)—and is important to romantic relationships.

▶ **Social information processing theory** explains that online relationships develop similarly to face-to-face contact; however, the process often takes longer to become more intimate (p. 191).

Describe why we form relationships:
- ▶ Relationship formation requires either physical or virtual **proximity**, or nearness (p. 193).
- ▶ Attractive physical, intellectual, and social qualities motivates relationship formation (pp. 193–194).
- ▶ Similarity often increases attraction (p. 194).
- ▶ Humans have a natural need for companionship and **inclusion**—a need to share our lives with others (p. 194).
- ▶ We form relationships for intellectual, emotional, and physical stimulation (p. 195).
- ▶ Relationships help us accomplish goals (p. 195).

List ways to manage relationship dynamics:
- ▶ **Social exchange theory** (p. 196) explains how we balance the advantages and disadvantages in our relationships.
- ▶ **Rewards** are what make you feel good about the relationship and may be extrinsic, instrumental, or intrinsic. **Costs** are aspects of the relationship that upset you (p. 196).
- ▶ According to **uncertainty reduction theory**, partners want to decrease the uncertainty through the use of **passive strategies**, which involve observing others without actually interacting (p. 198); **active strategies**, which involve seeking information from a third party (p. 198); and **interactive strategies**, which involve communicating directly with the person (p. 198).
- ▶ **Relational dialectics theory** holds that **dialectical tensions** are opposing or conflicting goals that always exist in a relationship (p. 198).
- ▶ Individuals may struggle to find a balance between independence and dependence, openness and closedness, and predictability and novelty (pp. 199–200).

Describe the factors that influence self-disclosure:
- ▶ **Social penetration theory** (SPT) explains how relational partners move toward intimacy through self-disclosure (p. 201).
- ▶ **Communication privacy management (CPM) theory** (explains how people perceive the information they hold about themselves and how they choose to disclose or not (p. 201). **Boundary turbulence** arises when violations make it necessary to readjust disclosure versus privacy (p. 201).
- ▶ **Strategic topic avoidance** is used to maneuver the conversation away from topics that make people feel vulnerable (p. 202).

Outline the predictable stages of most relationships:
- ▶ **Turning points** are events or changes important to relationship definition (p. 203).
- ▶ The **initiating stage** is the first contact (p. 203).
- ▶ In the **exploratory stage**, there is superficial communication (p. 204).
- ▶ More self-disclosure occurs in the **intensification stage** (p. 204).
- ▶ In the **stable stage**, expectations are accurate and realistic. We see partners **integrating**, or becoming one, and **bonding**, sharing messages about their relationship with the world (pp. 204–205).
- ▶ In the **declining stage**, **uncertainty events**, interference from outside the relationship, and unmet expectations take a toll (p. 205), though **repair tactics** may reverse the decline (p. 206).
- ▶ In the **termination stage**, the relationship fades away or is unexpectedly terminated by one partner (p. 207).
- ▶ **Reconciliation** is a way to rekindle relationships that have been terminated (p. 208).

Sibling conflicts give children and adolescents practice at developing skills for resolving differences later in life.

CSP_Reana/AGE Fotostock

 LearningCurve can help you master the material in this chapter.

Go to **launchpadworks.com**

chapter

9

Managing Conflict in Relationships

Taylor and Ashley are sisters. Both now in college, they keep in close contact and consider their bonds to be strong. When they were children, however, oh, how they could fight: "Maahhhm! Taylor knocked over my Lego tower!" "Well, Ashley started it!" They actually got along well most of the time, but could go from being best friends to fierce rivals in an instant: "Stop interrupting my story." "But *I* want to tell it." Later, in their teens, they still had heated arguments: "I can't believe you took my sweater!" "Well, you're always coming into *my* room and taking *my* stuff!"

How is it that these two bickering sisters could become close friends? Many experts argue that conflict can actually be good for young siblings, because it develops an important life skill: resolving differences (Markham, 2016). Through constructive conflict, children and teens can learn to negotiate, put themselves in someone else's position, develop patience, and tolerate others (Pickering & Sanders, 2015). Of course, they usually need help from parents and other adults to learn these skills. Rather than just taking over or punishing the girls for their conflict, Ashley and Taylor's parents used the opportunity to *coach* them. They steered them toward identifying what the real conflict was about (e.g., control, affection) and discussed the issue with them more broadly. They taught Taylor and Ashley how to communicate their feelings, rather than just complain. When the girls got older, their parents even motivated them to brainstorm ways to resolve conflict on their own (Raising Children Network, 2015).

No parent handles every family conflict effectively. In fact, some parents may do damage while dealing with their children's conflict. As they try to get to the bottom of who is "right," they may find themselves taking sides. If this happens regularly, siblings may perceive favoritism. This can lead to a much more serious rivalry lasting well into adulthood (Milevsky, 2016). When they have to deal with difficult issues, such as taking care of an aging parent or settling their parents' estate, old unresolved rivalries may resurface (Willens, 2016).

Taylor and Ashley recognize that conflict between them and in all families is unavoidable, but they feel fortunate to have learned strategies for resolving their disputes amicably and moving on. This benefits them not only in their birth families, but also as they form their own nuclear families, deal with tensions in the workplace, and manage differences among their friendship networks.

chapter outcomes

After you have finished reading this chapter, you will be able to

- Describe the factors that lead to productive conflict

- Identify conflict triggers in yourself and others

- Explain the forces that influence how people handle conflict

- Evaluate and employ strategies for managing conflict in different situations

- Articulate ways in which you can de-escalate and repair painful conflict

Dealing with conflict—be it with a sibling, a romantic partner, a colleague, a classmate, or an institution—can be hard. Some avoid it altogether, whereas others lash out aggressively, in person or via social media. But there is also a middle ground that falls between covering our ears and posting aggressive comments on Facebook. There are also lots of ways in which we may not only manage conflict but also grow and learn from it, as did Ashley and Taylor. In this chapter, we take a look at root causes of conflict and examine the ways in which we engage in conflict with others. We then consider productive ways in which to manage conflict and reconcile our relationships.

Understanding Conflict

You have undoubtedly had countless conflicts in your life. But just what is conflict, anyway? **Conflict** is not simply an argument or a struggle: it is an interaction between two or more interdependent people who perceive that they have contradictory goals or scarce resources. In other words, there is conflict when I believe that if you get what *you* want, I cannot have what *I* want. For example, consider Jake and Lori, who have been dating for several months and consider themselves a couple. Lori is frustrated with Jake because he seems to want to spend *all* their time together, when she wants time by herself or with her girlfriends. Jake is frustrated that Lori does not seem to want to spend very much time with him. They each perceive that their goal of wanting more or less time together conflicts with their partner's.

Scholars like to distinguish between conflict—which is inevitable and sometimes cannot be resolved—and **conflict management**, which refers to the way that we engage in conflict and address disagreements with our relational partners. Lori and Jake, for example, have many options for managing their conflict over the time they spend together. They could blame each other for their bad qualities ("Jake, you're too needy; you need to get over it," "Lori, you only think about yourself and not what matters to me"); or, they could try to understand each other's perceptions—why it seems to one that they are always together while the other feels that they rarely are. They could each try to prove that they are "right" by pointing out the literal numbers of hours or events that they have spent together; or, they could talk about the importance, for each of them, of feeling close versus valuing independence. They might even try to address the root of the conflict, such as differing expectations about relationships.

However they manage their conflict, Jake and Lori will experience important consequences on the health and strength of their relationship; unproductive conflict will hurt the relationship, but productive conflict can help it grow stronger. We look at those choices in the next section.

Unproductive Conflict

Unproductive conflict is conflict that is managed poorly and has a negative impact on the individuals and relationships involved. Which of Jake and Lori's choices do you think would be unproductive? If you guessed hurling accusations of neediness and selfishness, you are on the right track. Although any particular conflict strategy could be used in an unproductive way in a given situation, blaming the other person for the conflict, along with put-downs, personal attacks, and insults, most commonly result in negative relational impacts (Cupach, 2015). Unproductive conflict often escalates when one or both of the partners engage in negative nonverbal behaviors, such as rolling their eyes, sighing deeply, or using a sarcastic tone of voice (Yoo & Noyes, 2016).

There may be times when people *intentionally* engage in unproductive conflict. For example, if they want a romantic partnership to end or if they are seeking revenge against a friend who betrayed them, they may use hurtful conflict behaviors to accomplish their goals (Cupach & Carson, 2012). But the damage of unproductive conflict is not limited to relationships. Researchers have discovered that when conflict is handled poorly, those involved can experience a poorer sense of well-being at work (Sonnentag, Unger, & Nagel, 2013), as well as personal health problems, including sleep disruptions (Hicks & Diamond, 2011), elevated cortisol (a stress hormone; Priem, McLaren, & Solomon, 2010), hopelessness (Miller, Roloff, & Reznik, 2014), mood disorders (Segrin, Hanzal, & Domschke, 2009), heart disease, and immune deficiency (Canary, 2003).

Productive Conflict

Not all conflict is negative, however. In fact, conflict can be as valuable as it is inevitable. Conflict that is managed effectively is called **productive conflict**, and it is a healthy way for us to resolve disagreements in our relationships (Afifi & Coveleski, 2015). We do not always notice the conflicts that we handle productively, as when two people quickly reach a compromise over an issue (like whether to eat at Olive Garden or Pizza Hut), without argument or confrontation. But productive conflict can also take work. For Lori and Jake to constructively resolve their issue of how much time to spend together, they are going to need to listen to each other's perspectives and be able to empathize (Afifi & Coveleski, 2015). They will need to monitor their emotions and the verbal and nonverbal expression of their feelings (Cupach, 2015).

It is important to note that productive conflict does not necessarily mean a successful resolution of the dispute; however, even without resolution, productive conflict can still benefit both parties. Let's look at a few examples.

Productive Conflict Fosters Healthy Debate

To believe that conflict can be productive rather than destructive, you have to actively engage in it. There is no greater intellectual exercise than exploring and testing ideas with another person. And like a sport, it can get competitive, as evidenced by the popularity of debate teams in schools and the media fanfare surrounding political debates during major elections. In fact, active and lively debate allows us to exchange ideas, evaluate the merits of one another's claims, and continually refine and clarify each other's thinking about the issue under discussion. Debates on the floors of Congress, for example, allow representatives to go on record with their opinions on bills being considered and to try to persuade their colleagues to consider their positions. When government leaders fail to engage in such debates—when they evade questions or block a bill from going to debate on

connect

Few people enjoy conflict, but avoiding it can have negative consequences. In Chapter 10, we discuss *groupthink* — when groups focus on unity and conflict avoidance rather than openly discussing alternative solutions to problems. If your student organization president makes an irresponsible suggestion on how to spend funds and you and the others keep silent, conflict may be avoided — but at a cost.

● **EVEN WITH MATTERS** as simple as making plans for a Friday night, we can choose to be uncompromising and create unproductive conflict or we can discuss the options, reach an agreement, and have a great time together. conrado/Shutterstock

● **IN *THE AMAZING RACE*,** partners must deal with agreements effectively if they want to succeed. CBS Photo Archive/Getty Images

the floor of the legislature — they are formally engaging in the same kind of unproductive conflict avoidance that individuals use when they refuse to discuss difficult subjects. Conflict and healthy debate can also be a useful part of everyday life, as when a couple discusses and evaluates the pros and cons of buying a new car.

Productive Conflict Leads to Better Decision Making

Healthy debate serves a real purpose in that it helps individuals and groups make smarter decisions (Bradley, Anderson, Baur, & Klotz, 2015). By skillfully working through conflicting ideas about how to solve a problem or reach a goal, we identify the best courses of action. That is because a productive conflict provides an arena in which we can test the soundness of proposed ideas. Suggested solutions that are logical and feasible will stand up to scrutiny during the decision-making process, whereas weaker solutions are likely to be exposed as flawed. So by engaging in productive discussion about your conflict, the real costs and impact of, say, buying a hybrid car are revealed, and you are able to come up with a workable solution: you will continue driving your old car while sacrificing this year's vacation and dinners out to put an additional $350 every month into a special savings account toward the purchase of a secondhand hybrid car in one year.

Productive Conflict Spurs Relationship Growth

Differences of opinion and clashing goals are inevitable in any relationship. But how the partners *handle* the disagreements that arise determines whether their bond will grow stronger (Sillars & Canary, 2013). As two individuals — be they romantic partners, friends, roommates, or colleagues — work through their disagreements productively, they build on the relationship (Dainton & Gross, 2008). For example, contestant pairs on the CBS reality series *The Amazing Race* face many relational challenges as they travel around the globe completing obstacles and quests. Contestants may disagree with how their partner approaches a particular situation (like refusing to ask for directions when lost), or they may get frustrated if the partner loses an important document or forgets to ask the all-important taxicab to wait around until the end of a challenge. Yet most contestants manage to end their race without permanently damaging their relationships; many even cite the race as an experience that improved their communication during highly stressful and intense situations. How do these contestants' relationships survive and grow? Their commitment to each other and to a positive relational outlook may be key. Studies show that even under great stress, maintaining hopefulness about the relationship motivates partners to focus on relationship goals (rather than their own individual goals) and encourages cooperative, constructive ways to respond to their conflicts (Merolla & Harmon, 2016).

Conflict Triggers

▶ "He was drinking from the milk carton again. I caught him. It's so disgusting — I drink that milk, too, you know!"

▶ "Is there any point to making plans with Lynette? She always cancels at the last minute anyway."

▶ "I swear, my boss thinks I have no life outside of this organization. Why is he emailing me and texting me on weekends about my projects?"

Do any of these scenarios seem familiar? Everyone has a trigger that drives them absolutely mad when it happens, and conflict often ensues. The fact is that conflicts arise for a number of reasons. People often have differing goals, beliefs, or ideas; we face competition for scarce resources, such as money or time. We experience misunderstandings and, unfortunately, we lose our tempers. And sometimes we encounter people who are deceitful or uncooperative or who intentionally undermine our efforts to achieve our goals. In the following sections, we examine a few common conflict triggers.

Inaccurate Perceptions

Misunderstandings, including mistaken assumptions about the reasons for people's behavior, are a common—and regrettable—cause of conflict. For example, when Maureen calls her adult son Michael, she gets his voice mail. She is instantly furious, because she assumes that he knows she is calling but just cannot be bothered to talk with his mother. Michael, however, keeps his phone silent, because his work requires him to be in meetings that cannot be interrupted. When Michael is finally able to check his voice mail, he then gets furious at his mother's increasingly angry messages ("After all the trouble you gave me as a teenager, the least you could do is answer the phone when I call!"). He calls his mother back, but only to yell at her for not respecting his job. Maureen has an inaccurate perception of why Michael does not answer his phone, and Michael believes his mother does not respect his professional responsibilities, when really she just has no understanding of his schedule. Their lack of trust in each other's motives fuels their mistaken perceptions and triggers even more conflict. When they do talk, Maureen (believing her son does not value her) sounds mopey, irritated, and terse, and her negativity makes Michael want to avoid talking with her altogether.

Incompatible Goals

Since much communication is goal driven, conflicts are bound to arise when goals are perceived as incompatible (Canary, 2003). On *Grey's Anatomy*, for example, Callie and Arizona have had conflicting goals about the care of their daughter, Sofia. After their romantic relationship had broken up and Callie had entered another relationship, Callie wanted to move away and take Sofia with her. Arizona then fought for sole custody, and a nasty court battle followed. Whenever two separated parents both insist on full custody of a child, conflict ensues (and often in a courtroom) because they have set up their goals as completely contrary—they cannot both have full custody. Disagreements about such serious life decisions can make it extremely difficult to resolve conflict. However, if people are able to reframe their goals, such as both parents wanting to have a significant influence on the child's life, they might be able to negotiate an outcome without triggering such a battle. Arizona eventually appreciated the positives for Sofia and agreed to let Callie have her for alternating school years and Christmases. But even among relational partners who are in agreement on big life decisions, other goals are likely to come into conflict. For example, couples that are committed to having a family together may have conflicts about the timing, number, and rearing of children.

● **THOUGH CALLIE AND ARIZONA** each wanted custody of their daughter, could they have negotiated their opposing goals differently to avoid the court battle? © ABC/Photofest

connect

The best way to account for unusual behavior may be to ask if your perceptions are accurate. In Chapter 8, we discussed *interactive strategies* that help you to reduce uncertainty and get information directly from a person. You might tell a friend, "I sense that you're angry with me because your voice sounds terse. Am I right?" Such questions may eliminate unnecessary conflict by showing the other person that you are *listening* (Chapter 7) and allowing your friend to clarify perceptions.

Relational Transgressions

You are annoyed that your romantic partner flirts with an attractive person at a party. Your best friend gets angry at you because you lied about where you spent the weekend. Conflict often arises when we violate relational expectations or betray each other's trust. In fact, relational transgressions can trigger the most serious conflicts (Cupach, 2015). Infidelity, deception, broken promises, and disrespectful treatment are all typically perceived as violations of fundamental relational rules and can result in deeply hurt feelings and intense conflicts.

Many conflicts may also arise when our own relational insecurities lead us to *assume* that someone has wronged us. Was your partner really flirting or were you just feeling threatened because of the other partygoer's attractiveness? Even a friend's innocent comment about your hair ("It's really gotten long") might trigger conflict if you take the comment as a hurtful relational insult ("You never tell me I look nice!"). Fortunately, in the context of a healthy relationship, we often give our partner the benefit of the doubt or at least see such minor transgressions as unintentional (Vangelisti & Hampel, 2009). However, research shows that when we are dissatisfied in a relationship, we are more likely to be upset by transgressions and engage in more intense conflict (Aldeis & Afifi, 2015). We are also likely to think our *partner* makes more hurtful comments than we do ourselves (Young, Bippus, & Dunbar, 2015).

Provocation

Of course, not every conflict arises out of natural differences between individuals' goals or perceptions. The hard truth is that people can be uncaring or even aggressive at times. Although conflict is indeed a natural part of every relationship, many instances arise through **provocation** — the intentional instigation of conflict. A number of behaviors are used to spark intense negative reactions (Canary, 2003; Cupach, 2015). Examples include:

▶ *Aggression.* Aggressive behaviors range from verbal intimidation to physical violence. In addition to verbal conflict, aggression can provoke retaliatory aggression as well as fear and defensiveness.

▶ *Identity threats.* When someone insults you personally, it can threaten your identity. Such threats range from mild insults ("Man, you have a dirty car") to condescending remarks ("I'll go slowly so you can keep up") to attacks on one's values or religion and racial or ethnic slurs. Avoiding eye contact with a partner, failing to move closer to the other to show involvement, or using a superior tone of voice — all can communicate dislike for others that threaten their identity and decrease relational satisfaction (Spott, Pyle, & Punyanunt-Carter, 2010).

▶ *Lack of fairness.* When someone treats one person better than another or uses more than his or her fair share of resources — in families, workplaces, or living situations, for example — it commonly stirs up negative reactions.

▶ *Irresponsibility.* When someone you work with or depend on does not show up or performs their responsibilities in a careless way, their negligence provokes conflict. Feelings of anger and resentment occur, for example, when a lab partner fails to bring needed supplies or write his or her share of the lab report.

and you?

What kinds of behaviors provoke you the most? Are there times when you provoke conflict with others, perhaps even on purpose?

● **KANYE WEST'S** quick temper and aggressive behavior got him into scrapes on numerous occasions in his past. Kevin Mazur/Getty Images

Factors Affecting Conflict

We have just looked at triggers that can cause a conflict to crop up between people. But once a conflict arises, several specific forces can influence how the people involved handle the conflict. We examine these forces next.

Power Dynamics

When one person has power over another, that dynamic can cause one or both of the people to handle conflict unproductively. Power dynamics are often at play in the workplace, where your boss determines the nature of your work and can fire, promote, or transfer you. If you and your boss disagree about an issue at work, your boss may pull rank, saying something like "I'm in charge here." But power dynamics also come into play in more intimate relationships. For example, if you are dependent on your parents for tuition, shelter, food, or anything else, they may use that power to control your behavior, perhaps pressuring you to choose a specific school or major or making bold declarations about how you should spend your time.

In romantic relationships, unhealthy partnerships are often characterized by too much dependence of one partner on the other, control of one partner, and an inability to communicate boundaries, among other things (Canary, Cody, & Manusov, 2008). You can imagine what happens when conflict enters such an unbalanced relationship. In some cases, the partner with more power may engage in activities that make the other partner fearful and compliant, such as bullying or intimidating. Let's say that Chris and Amy are considering purchasing their first home together and that Amy is just starting a freelance writing career. Amy now relies on Chris's full-time job for health insurance and a stable income. In a relationship where power is balanced and healthy, Chris would be supportive of Amy's new venture and would want to come to a mutual decision about the size and type of home they purchase. But if the balance of power is skewed in Chris's favor—either because he is domineering or because Amy refuses to voice her opinions—Chris may engage in the tactics we have mentioned: saying, for example, "Well, I'm the one *paying* for the house," or "Fine, I guess we'll just keep throwing away money on rent," if Amy suggests that perhaps Chris's top-choice house is not what is best for them.

It is important to bear in mind that differences in power are not limited to material resources or emotional intimidation. A relational partner also has power over another if he or she controls the decision making in the relationship (Dunbar, 2004). When decision-making power is unequal, conflicts are more likely and relational partners tend to be less satisfied (Dunbar & Abra, 2010). But when decision making is perceived as equal, partners feel better able to voice their concerns and complaints, see problems as less severe, and have expectations for more positive outcomes (Worley & Samp, 2016).

Attitudes Toward Conflict

Some people love a good argument. They relish the opportunity to negotiate a new employment contract or debate friends on political issues. Studies show that those who have positive views about conflict spend time imagining conflicts with other people and planning out and rehearsing scenarios in order to achieve positive outcomes and relieve stress (Wallenfelsz & Hample, 2010). Others find conflict uncomfortable and believe it can only lead to hurt feelings or a damaged relationship. This discomfort might lead you to steer clear of conflict entirely or avoid it in situations when you do not think that you will argue very effectively, you do not consider the particular disagreement very important, or you do not believe that the current time or place is appropriate for having an argument.

connect

Cultural context has a strong impact on power dynamics. In Chapter 6, we discussed *high and low power-distance cultures*, which differ in their expectations and acceptance of the division of power among individuals and groups. In intercultural group settings — where members and leaders may have different attitudes about power dynamics — it's a good idea to discuss the dynamics openly to make conflict more productive and enhance group communication (see Chapter 11).

and you?

Think of an attitude you have about conflict that is making it difficult for you to talk productively about disagreements with someone in your life. For example, do you believe that discussing conflict will destroy your relationship? What steps might you take to begin letting go of this unproductive attitude?

● **YOUR ROOMMATE** keeps adding to her pile of dirty dishes in the sink and has not washed a single one in three days. Do you see this as an opportunity to talk about setting kitchen ground rules — or would you rather avoid conflict by washing the dishes so that you have space to clean your own? Gemenacom/Shutterstock

Some people take their negative views of conflict to the level of a destructive tendency called **taking conflict personally** (Hample & Dallinger, 1995). When we take conflict personally, we feel so threatened by it that we interpret most disagreements as personal insults or assault. We may also dwell on negative thoughts and feelings of persecution and, if we cannot avoid conflict altogether, may actually lash out aggressively or seek revenge (Miller & Roloff, 2014). Our attitudes about conflict, whether we embrace or detest it, have an important effect on how we deal with it.

Communication Climate

Another factor that affects how we handle conflict is the **communication climate** (Gibb, 1961) — the general "atmosphere" surrounding how we feel about our communication in different relationships. Suppose you are a member of The Groove Club, a local dance troupe that performs at elementary schools to get kids interested in dance. Daryl, who does the choreography, has featured Jalina as the lead dancer for the next show. This upsets you, because you wanted the lead role and feel that you have earned it. How your group handles this conflict will differ depending on whether your group's communication climate is *defensive* or *supportive*.

▶ **Defensive** climates are those in which the people involved feel threatened. It is an atmosphere of mistrust, suspicion, and apprehension, leading to efforts to control and manipulate others (Forward, Czech, & Lee, 2011). As a member of The Groove Club, if you express your disappointment through an evaluation of Daryl's unfairness ("You picked Jalina just because she's been your friend longer"), that will likely put Daryl on the defensive. Daryl will also contribute to a defensive climate if he emphasizes his own superiority ("You just don't understand my vision") and does not acknowledge your feelings ("Don't be such a baby about this"). Making matters worse would be manipulative questions from you, such as, "How's that ankle healing, Jalina?" or other strategic efforts to exert control, such as, "It's too bad that my mom now won't be able to pay for our costumes."

▶ **Supportive** climates involve communicators who are open to one another's ideas and feelings. Such climates involve neutral (rather than blame-filled) descriptions of the conflict situation and allow communicators to develop trust and cooperation toward a productive resolution of problems (Forward, Czech, & Lee, 2011). In The Groove Club, you could promote a supportive climate by expressing your honest disappointment ("I was really hoping to have a lead role this time") and describing your feelings ("I know Jalina is great, but I've been practicing so hard, and I thought I was getting really good too"). Daryl could help by showing empathy ("I can understand why you're so disappointed") and try to focus on the problem rather than just assert control ("Let me show you what I'm planning, and you may see why it fits Jalina better" or "Let's see if there's a part of the show where it would work to feature you").

connect

The differences among communication climates are often related to language and nonverbal communication (Chapters 4 and 5). In addressing conflict with a friend, you might raise your voice or speak sarcastically (defensive climate), or offer a reassuring touch and speak with a firm but understanding tone (supportive climate).

How do you move from a defensive climate to a supportive one? Your first task is to get a sense for which climate you are experiencing. Your gut instincts can be a credible guide here, but you can also make a formal assessment of the messages people are sending. How is your own communication contributing to this climate? Once you know the climate you are in, you can take steps to change your messages and move toward a supportive climate. Figure 9.1 shows how defensive kinds of messages can be reframed to help you find your way to supportive conflict climates.

Culture and Conflict

If we consider how important culture is to our identities and how pervasive conflict is in our lives, we can easily see that culture has an important influence on our conflict experiences. Differences in cultural values, beliefs, and attitudes can lead to conflict directly, and these differences can also affect how individuals perceive conflict, what their goals are for conflict, and how conflict is handled. We now examine the influence on conflict of our broad cultural orientations, as well as our cocultural group memberships.

● **WHEN EVERYONE WANTS** to be the star, it takes a supportive climate to make all of the performers feel appreciated, even if they did not get the lead role this time. Donna Ward/Getty Images

Cultural Orientation

Research in culture and conflict management often examines differences between individualist, low-context cultures and collectivist, high-context cultures. As you learned in Chapter 6, *individualist cultures* emphasize personal needs, rights, and identity over those of the collective or group, whereas *collectivist cultures* emphasize group identity and needs. In addition, you will recall that people rely more on indirect verbal messages and nonverbal communication than on what is actually said in *high-context cultures*. In *low-context cultures*, people are expected to be more verbally direct and say what they mean.

When applied to conflict, English-speaking and European cultures tend to take an individualist and low-context approach, whereas Latin American and Asian cultures are more collectivist and high context (Ting-Toomey & Oetzel, 2002). In the United States, for example, conflict is often viewed as a necessary way to work out problems and feel that specific conflict issues should be dealt with separately from relational issues. In Latin American and Asian countries, on the other hand, conflict is often perceived as having a negative effect on relational harmony, and conflict issues cannot be divorced from relationship issues. Indeed, cross-cultural research finds that people living in high-context cultures (e.g., India and Thailand) and

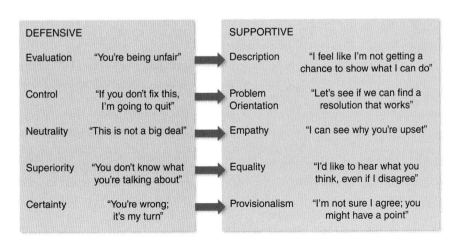

DEFENSIVE		SUPPORTIVE	
Evaluation	"You're being unfair"	Description	"I feel like I'm not getting a chance to show what I can do"
Control	"If you don't fix this, I'm going to quit"	Problem Orientation	"Let's see if we can find a resolution that works"
Neutrality	"This is not a big deal"	Empathy	"I can see why you're upset"
Superiority	"You don't know what you're talking about"	Equality	"I'd like to hear what you think, even if I disagree"
Certainty	"You're wrong; it's my turn"	Provisionalism	"I'm not sure I agree; you might have a point"

FIGURE 9.1

FROM A DEFENSIVE TO SUPPORTIVE CLIMATE

● IN *AMERICAN SNIPER,* wife Taya and her military husband Chris play out a common imbalance of communicativeness between females and males. © Warner Bros./Photofest

collectivist cultures (e.g., Ecuador) prefer to avoid conflict altogether, send indirect messages, or give in to the other person's wishes; people in low-context, individualist cultures (e.g., the United States and Ireland) prefer to engage in conflict and express emotions more openly (Croucher et al., 2012; Neuliep & Johnson, 2016). Efforts to restore relationships after conflict also differ cross-culturally. For example, in comparing the United States and China, researchers find that both cultures place a similarly high value on apology, but that forgiveness can be felt and shown much more subtly and mildly in China — in the United States, the relationship will have difficulty moving forward without the hurt being clearly restored (Zhang, Oetzel, Ting-Toomey, & Zhang, 2015). Understanding these important cultural distinctions can help us understand how confusion, frustration, and miscommunication can happen when conflict arises.

CoCultures

In the film *American Sniper,* Taya is worried about her Navy SEAL husband, Chris, who appears withdrawn and troubled following several tours of duty in Iraq. She asks him over and over if there is anything he wants to talk about. But stoic Chris simply does not want to talk. Although such nagging female–noncommunicative male stereotypes are standard in film and television, there is evidence to suggest that, in fact, women are more inclined to voice their complaints or criticisms, while men tend to avoid engaging in such discussions.

Differences between men and women reflect one important way that our cocultures affect how we deal with conflict. Recall from Chapter 6 that *cocultures* are the groups we belong to with unique characteristics that unify us and distinguish us from the larger general culture. These distinctions often play out in conflict situations. In a classic study of marital conflict, for example, women tended to criticize and attack their partner's character more than men, and men tended to "stonewall" (refuse to engage) more than women (Gottman, 1994). More recent research also suggests that sex and gender influence satisfaction level with regard to certain conflict management strategies. When women perceive that their dating partner is engaging in conflict avoidance, their satisfaction level decreases; however, avoidance does not tend to cause the same dissatisfaction in men (Afifi, McManus, Steuber, & Coho, 2009). In addition, although both men and women appear to value mutual resolutions in their romantic relationships, women's dogged persistence at finding a mutual resolution (rather than letting go of an ongoing conflict) is perceived very negatively by men (Worley & Samp, 2016).

Age is another cocultural difference that affects conflict. When faced with a potential argument, younger (under forty) and middle-aged (forty to sixty) adults are more likely to openly argue, whereas older adults (over sixty) prefer to use passive strategies, such as "letting it go" or waiting for the situation to change on its own (Blanchard-Fields, Mienaltowski, & Seay, 2007). These avoidance strategies appear to be beneficial, as older adults experience less negative emotion than their younger counterparts when they deal with social tensions passively (Birditt, 2013). Researchers argue that older people may have learned from experience to recognize when an argument is "just not worth it" and that they may be choosing the strategies that help them manage their own emotional well-being (Charles, Piazza, Luong, & Almeida, 2009). For younger and middle-aged adults, however, conflict situations may more often require direct confrontation (e.g., at work or in battles with parents), so passive strategies may be ineffective for them at achieving their goals. These confrontations can take a toll: by middle age, the increase in conflict

and you?

In what ways have gender differences influenced the conflicts you have experienced with people whose gender or gender identity is different from yours?

and interpersonal stress appears to have an especially negative impact on people's well-being (Darbonne, Uchino, & Ong, 2013).

When we think of conflict and culture or coculture, it is important to remember not to assume that all members of a culture or group reflect the extreme differences. It is also dangerous to assume that differences in culture mean irreconcilable differences in conflict. Competent communication in conflict means understanding and respecting differences while working to "expand the pie" for both parties. Even in the most uncomfortable and frustrating conflict situations, we can learn a great deal about others and ourselves through culture.

Communication Channel

As we discussed in Chapter 2, we have a variety of communication channels at our disposal, each with varying degrees of *synchronicity* (the ability to respond back and forth quickly), *richness* (the nonverbal cues available), and *privacy* (control over who gets access).

These qualities are important when it comes to conflict. If you have ever sent flowers and a card as a way of apologizing, left a voice mail on a weekend to let an instructor or colleague know you have missed a deadline, or delivered bad news via a text message, chances are you chose that channel as a way of avoiding engaging in face-to-face conflict. Indeed, one of the benefits of text-based forms of communication is that the lack of nonverbal cues can help us avoid emotional drama as well as give us time to consider what we say so we do not blurt out something we regret later (Tikkanen & Frisbie, 2015). Of course, there are also times when it is more appropriate to handle conflict face-to-face, such as when our nonverbal behavior can show empathy and support for a relational partner we may have hurt.

Choosing the wrong channel of communication can also itself cause conflict, such as when you post a picture on Instagram of your roommate's pile of dirty clothes rather than discussing this with him privately in person. With close friends or romantic partners, managing conflict through social media can come across as insensitive and even cowardly. Just ask those who found out that their relationship was over when their significant other's relationship status on Facebook changed from "In a Relationship" to "Single," or who saw that their friend had stopped following them on both Instagram and Snapchat. The physical distance that digital media provides also sometimes emboldens people to use more hostile or insulting language than they would use face-to-face. Even professional athletes, journalists, and celebrities who worry about maintaining a positive social image can find themselves embroiled in a hostile Twitter battle that ends up being discussed in the tabloids.

Digital channels are also an arena for even more aggressive conflict behaviors, such as **cyberbullying** — abusive attacks on individual targets conducted through electronic channels (Erdur-Baker, 2010). Researchers point out that traditional face-to-face bullying, although highly unpleasant, is also extremely intimate, and victims can find at least some place or time to get away and seek refuge. Cyberbullying, in contrast, makes use of text messages, emails, and social networking sites to deliver a nonstop stream of cruel messages or photos that may be visible to others for a long time (Patchin & Hinduja, 2011). The perpetrator

connect

A lack of nonverbal communication can pose problems when handling conflict via mediated channels (Chapter 5). If you text an apology to your friend, he cannot see your facial expressions to appreciate how sorry you are. Emojis do help display feelings (😊 !), but competent communicators must consider which channel of communication is the best for a particular message (Chapter 2). When dealing with conflict, it might be better to speak face-to-face or over the phone so that nonverbal behaviors such as tone of voice can be decoded.

● **THE COFOUNDER** of Wikipedia, Jim Wales, allegedly broke up with his girlfriend on his Wikipedia page. Perhaps that was not the best choice. Rick Friedman/Getty Images

wired for communication

think about this

Locking Down Trolls Versus Free Speech

Internet forums are, in a sense, a grand experiment in free speech. A trip to an open forum on just about any topic — from the new iPhone to the latest political campaign — is likely to yield astute critiques and interesting perspectives — as well as lots of irrelevant, incoherent, offensive, and inflammatory banter. Does the value of the open discourse outweigh the negative impact of vitriol? Editors at *Popular Science* decided that the negativity of trolls was overwhelming and shut down the comments section entirely on the magazine's website. Other organizations instead rely on moderators — commonly known as "mods" — who set strict rules for the forum, sometimes reviewing posts before making them public but mostly deleting them afterward. Webzine *Boing Boing* deletes posts that moderators find offensive. "It's fun to have disagreements," explains *Boing Boing* founder Mark Frauenfelder, "but if someone gets nasty, we will kick them out" (Niemann, 2014). Indeed, many moderators will ban repeat offenders for life. However, a recent study found that trolls can survive on a forum for a long time (and several hundred posts) before being banned (Cheng, Danescu-Niculescu-Mizil, & Leskovec, 2015). The researchers devised an algorithm to try to identify trolls earlier, based on their posting patterns and other people's responses to their comments (such as thumbs-down votes). Using data from three news sites, 1.7 million users and nearly forty million posts, they were able to accurately predict, based on the first ten posts, which users were likely to end up getting banned. Time will tell if such technology could be used effectively to weed out trolls before they cause too much damage. Other researchers suggest that the forum mods and members themselves are in the best position to deal with trolls — whether by recognizing troll behavior and not responding, turning the trolling behavior back on the trolls, or setting aside separate sections of the site for those who enjoy the vitriol to let loose (Coles & West, 2016).

1. Do you participate in internet forums? Do you prefer moderated or open forums? What makes you prefer one over the other?

2. Which is more important, a free-speech open forum or a managed, productive conflict? Do you think it is necessary to trade off one for the other?

3. Is it fair to ban someone for life from posting negative comments on a forum? How might moderators encourage better behavior and teach users effective ways to recognize and respond (or not respond) to troll-like comments?

and you?

Consider a recent conflict. What channel did you select to communicate with the other person? How did the communication channel affect the quality of the exchange? Did the channel you chose lead to a productive conflict or an unproductive one? Why?

may not even be known, and the torment can be difficult to escape (Dempsey, Sulkowski, Dempsey, & Storch, 2011). The problem has serious consequences, as victims often experience mental health problems, such as depression, loneliness, and low self-esteem; drops in academic performance and loss of relationships with peers at school; and a host of negative emotions, including fear, anger, embarrassment, sadness, and guilt (see Dehue, 2013). An extreme consequence, particularly among teens and preteens, can even be suicide.

Many online conflicts, including cyberbullying, are carried out among a small number of individuals; they usually know each other (even if only online). But digital channels of communication are also used to provoke conflict among a much broader and more anonymous audience. **Trolling** is the intentional posting of provocative and offensive messages to online forums or social networking groups in order to elicit from the participants a negative general reaction (Hardaker, 2010). Trolls may try to derail discussions by taking threads off-topic or bait users into arguments by posing ridiculous questions, using racial slurs, profanity, insults, or derogatory comments about group members (Cheng, Danescu-Niculescu-Mizil, & Leskovec, 2015). In the online gaming community, they also purposely disrupt teamwork or try to ruin the gaming experience of others (Thacker & Griffiths, 2012). Research reveals that trolls are often motivated by boredom, amusement, attention seeking, and revenge (Shachaf & Hara, 2010). Some also have the serious personality problem of a sadistic enjoyment of other people's distress (Buckels, Trapnell, & Paulhus, 2014). However, trolls are not always successful, and members of forums often recognize and expose these obvious attempts to stir up conflict (Coles & West, 2016).

Strategies for Managing Conflict

Let's consider a common, very simple scenario: you are sitting with your brother at the dinner table after a family meal. There is one last piece of Aunt Corinne's home-made chocolate peanut butter pie, and you and your brother both want it. Do you give up easily and just let him have it? Yell at him until he gives up (or until Dad takes it for himself)? Or suggest that you split the pie and each take half? We have different conflict strategies, or sets of goals and tactics that we can use to manage conflict (Guerrero, Andersen, & Afifi, 2013; Rahim, 1983). Some of us may feel most comfortable with one primary strategy or "style" that we employ in multiple situations, but often it works better when we are able to change our styles to fit the particular situation and parties involved.

● **SOMETIMES THE** competition for a lone piece of pie can mask larger emotional issues. Alan Richardson/Getty Images

In certain types of conflict, such as a competition for a piece of pie, the people involved can resolve the conflict — that is, bring it to an end — in just seconds. But when the conflict is more complex or when a seemingly simple disagreement is a symptom of a larger problem between people, resolving the situation will require more time and thought. If you are resentful of always having to share everything with your brother — your laptop, your Xbox, the family car, even attention from your parents — your conflict is bigger than a piece of pie. Resolving it may require a more involved approach, such as honest, lengthy dialogue about your resentments and possible ways for each of you to have more things you can call your own. The styles we use for managing conflict, whether simple or complicated, generally fall into one of three basic categories: escapist, competitive, or cooperative (see Table 9.1).

Escapist Strategies

People who do not like conflict often use **escapist strategies** — they try to prevent or avoid direct conflict altogether or, if they have to engage in it, get it over with as quickly as possible. There are two styles that both involve trying to escape conflict: avoiding and obliging.

Avoiding

When you are **avoiding**, you do not express your own needs and goals, even if you have a grievance. But before you think this is being selfless, note that avoiders also do not allow others to express *their* needs. Instead, when the potential for conflict arises, avoiders often hide from the person who is angry. When confronted, they may try to change the subject or offer to discuss the issue later ("Let's not spoil our nice dinner; we can put the pie back in the fridge and leave it until later"). Avoiding can be beneficial to a relationship in certain situations, such as when a confrontation might hurt the other person or when it would be better to postpone dealing with the conflict until a more appropriate time. Couples in long-distance relationships, for example, may benefit from conflict avoidance because it minimizes differences and maximizes positive interaction (Stafford, 2010). But avoidance strategies may be unproductive if they continually prevent people from dealing with issues that need to be addressed. Research has found that continual avoidance of conflict in families negatively impacts family strength and satisfaction (Schrodt, 2009; Ubinger, Handal, & Massura, 2013).

TABLE 9.1

CONFLICT STRATEGIES: THE PIE INCIDENT

Type		Description	Example Tactics
ESCAPIST Prevent or avoid having to deal with conflict altogether	Avoiding	Not addressing the conflict or either person's goals (nobody wins)	Postpone the pie debate ("Let's not have dessert now")
	Obliging	Giving in to the other person's goals to end the conflict quickly (you win/I lose)	Relinquish the pie ("You can have it")
COMPETITIVE Engage in conflict to pursue own goals	Direct fighting	Engaging in open conflict to assert and achieve personal goals (I win/you lose)	Claim the pie ("It's mine"; "Oh no, it's not"); argue for your right to the pie ("I deserve this pie")
	Indirect fighting	Using passive aggressive tactics to achieve personal goals without open conflict (I win/you lose)	Hint that you will do something bad if you do not get the pie ("It would be a shame if the pie ended up in the trash")
COOPERATIVE Engage in conflict to pursue mutual goals	Compromising	Negotiating to achieve a deal for each person to gain in part, lose in part (we both win and lose)	Share the pie; broker a deal ("I'll do the dishes if you let me have the pie")
	Collaborating	Addressing both self and other goals; finding a solution that achieves both (we both win)	Address underlying needs ("Pie means having something special; how else can we each feel special?")

Obliging

The other escapist style is **obliging** (also called accommodating or yielding). When you oblige someone, you give in to what he or she wants — that is, you let your brother have the pie. This is an escapist style because, like avoiding, it is a way to get out of having to engage in the conflict. The difference is that when you are obliging, you are at least somewhat concerned about the other person's goals — you would rather "lose" than have the other person be upset with you. Obliging strategies can be effective at preserving relational harmony, particularly when an issue is relatively unimportant (there will be other opportunities for pie) or when giving in shows that you recognize how much the issue really means to the other person (it is his favorite pie and he has had a tough day). Indeed, research shows that people who feel very close in their relationships tend to engage more in obliging than do more distant relational partners (Zhang & Andreychik, 2013). However, if you always give in, your brother may learn to exploit you (think about what happens when parents always give in to their child's tantrums!), or you may build up resentment at never getting your own needs met in the relationship.

Competitive Strategies

If you decide that you want the pie more than you want to avoid fighting with your brother, you might demand the entire piece for yourself, at your brother's expense. Such **competitive strategies** promote the objectives of the individual who uses them rather than the desires of the other person or the relationship.

Direct Fighting

Engaging openly in competition is **direct fighting** (also known as dominating or competitive fighting). Direct fighters see conflicts as "win or lose" battles — for me to

communication across cultures

Yours, Mine, and Both of Ours

The sight of a family lighting a menorah alongside their Christmas tree is not all that unfamiliar; nor is the story of one parent who quietly leaves behind his or her own religious faith and allows his or her spouse (and his or her spouse's family and congregation) to take the spiritual lead. Nearly four in ten American marriages are between spouses of different religious affiliations (Murphy, 2015). For these couples, navigating differences in religion can be fraught with conflict, ranging from inconveniences over holidays to misunderstandings with parents and extended families, to troubling arguments over inconsistent messages or values. How do they navigate these potential conflicts?

Many families simply attempt to embrace more than one religion. A number of interfaith nonprofit groups and schools have arisen to help couples plan interfaith weddings as well as help them raise children with an appreciation for both parents' faiths. Honeymoon Israel, for example, takes interfaith couples on trips to Israel to explore Christian, Jewish, and Muslim historic sites. Founder Avi Rubel says, "We don't care what you believe in. You married into our family, so you're in our family. We want couples to explore the issues on their own terms." (Miller, 2016). The Interfaith Family School in Chicago also helps couples who wish to raise children in both of their faiths, including counseling them on how to explain their faiths to their children and to their extended families. "For people who don't work at it — who don't really consciously come to agreement, it really won't work," says Jean, a Jewish woman who married a Roman Catholic. "Someone will feel slighted; someone will feel disrespected. We wanted both of us to be comfortable in our home. We wanted our children to have an identity that makes sense. I think we're achieving that, but it's not always easy" (Haines, 2014).

think about this

1. Is the kind of productive conflict attempted by interfaith organizations possible for people of all faiths? Why might having dual faiths be out of the question for some couples?

2. Is every mixed-faith relationship an exercise in compromise? What sorts of compromises do interfaith couples make? What other ways are there of managing conflicting faiths?

3. Think about the possible benefits of interfaith communities and organizations. Do you think it is possible to explore alternative faiths while still remaining true to your own? How do you handle disagreements about critical doctrinal differences?

win, you must necessarily lose. Winning arguments involves being assertive — voicing your positions with confidence, defending your arguments, and challenging the arguments of your opposition. Direct fighters are often effective at handling conflicts because they do not let negative emotions like anxiety, guilt, or embarrassment get in the way, and they stand up for what they believe is right. For example, people tend to openly challenge others when they feel the need to defend themselves from a perceived threat (Canary, Cunningham, & Cody, 1988). This would be a valuable strategy if the friend you came to a party with attempted to get behind the wheel of a vehicle after consuming alcohol. Drunk driving is a threat to your own, your friend's, and the public's well-being, and you would probably be well served to assert yourself competitively in this situation.

On the other hand, the direct fighting style has its downside, particularly for close relationships (Guerrero, Andersen, & Afifi, 2013). Part of the problem is that direct fighting often involves tactics that can be hurtful, such as threats, name-calling, and criticism. What begins as assertiveness can quickly move to **verbal aggressiveness** — attacking the opposing person's self-concept and belittling the other person's needs. For example, if you were to rudely assert to your brother "You're so fat — I would think you'd want to *avoid* pie," you may end up "winning" the pie, but you may well damage your bond with your brother. Indeed, research finds that parents' verbal aggression toward their children can negatively impact relationship satisfaction and is associated with nonsecure attachment styles among young adults (Roberto, Carlyle, Goodall, & Castle, 2009). When verbal aggression is used by

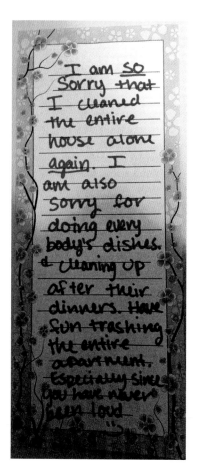

● **AN HONEST,** face-to-face discussion about apartment cleanup and chores is a much better way to solve this problem — chances are this note only made roommate relations worse.

supervisors toward their subordinates in the workplace, it can also negatively affect employee job satisfaction and commitment (Madlock & Kennedy-Lightsey, 2010).

Indirect Fighting

Competition does not always involve being openly assertive or aggressive. Many competitors instead use a "passive" style of aggression known as **indirect fighting** (Sillars, Canary, & Tafoya, 2004). Your brother might hide the pie so that you cannot find it or might leave a nasty note next to it that says, "I spit on this." With indirect fighting, people often want you to know that they are upset and try to get you to change your behavior, but they are unwilling to face the issue with you openly. In most situations, passive–aggressive behaviors come across as hostile and ineffective and usually end up being destructive to relationships. Studies have found that indirect fighting is associated with lower relationship commitment in friendships (Allen, Babin, & McEwan, 2012), reduced satisfaction in romantic partnerships (Guerrero, Farinelli, & McEwan, 2009), and even long-term distress in marriage (Kilmann, 2012).

Cooperative Strategies

Of course, one very practical way for you and your brother to manage the pie conflict is simply to split the last piece. That way, you at least both get some pie. Conflict styles that aim to benefit the relationship, to serve mutual rather than individual goals, and to produce solutions that benefit both parties are called **cooperative strategies** (Zacchilli, Hendrick, & Henrick, 2009).

Compromising

Splitting the pie is one particular cooperative conflict strategy called **compromising**. In a compromise, the goal is to find the "middle ground" between two (often extreme) positions. Each party gains something (half of the pie) but also gives up something (the other half). Compromises can be arrived at through trading, whereby one partner offers something of equal value in return for something he or she wants. For example, separated parents who must navigate joint custody arrangements might strike compromises regarding time spent with their children. The advantage of compromise is that it lets you and the other person both resolve conflicts by achieving some aspects of their goals. However, important relationships can suffer if the people involved are *always* making compromises. That is because compromising means giving up *some* of what you want, even though you are getting a little of something else in return.

Collaborating

To reach a truly win–win solution, in which both parties end up *fully* satisfied with the outcome, requires the **collaborating** strategy. Collaborators are problem solvers who creatively work toward finding ways to meet the goals of both parties. In order to see how this might be achieved, let's consider an issue more serious than pie, such as this conflict within a family: twenty-year-old Kieran wants to drop out of college to join the army. His mother is very upset and wants him to continue his education. A number of strategies can help them effectively collaborate.

First, it is important that the discussion *focus on issues*—remain centered on the matter at hand and steer clear of any personal attacks. If Kieran's mother boldly declares, "You are irrational and thoughtless. Who drops out of college with only one year left?" she is getting verbally aggressive and is not considering the fact that Kieran may well have very good reasons for his decision. Second, it helps to do some *probing*—asking questions that help you to identify each other's specific concerns.

evaluating communication ethics

The Accidental Relationship Counselor

You and your sister Ellen are close in age and very good friends. And while it was weird at first when Ellen began dating your best friend, Steve, you have now gotten used to them being together. They have been dating for three years. You still hang out with them, both individually and as a couple.

But lately you have been noticing that Ellen and Steve are not always together the way they used to be. Even though you all commute to the same college, Ellen seems to be making lots of new friends, joining campus clubs, and spending a lot of time away from Steve (and you). While you are happy to see your little sister spreading her wings, you worry about her future with Steve.

Making things more complicated, Steve is confiding in you his doubts about the relationship — he tells you that he thinks Ellen might be interested in other guys and asks if she has mentioned anyone in particular. He then mentions that there is a girl in one of his classes who he thinks might like him. Meanwhile, Ellen mentions that she is disappointed in the way Steve is handling college. When the three of you had lunch recently, Ellen publicly vented her frustration at Steve: "You still act like you're in high school. You have all the same friends, all the same interests. Don't you want something new?" As awkward as that encounter was, you feel even worse when Ellen later privately confides in you: "I feel like maybe it's time we broke up. What do you think?" You always knew that the day might come when Steve and Ellen split up, but you never imagined you would feel so caught in the middle. What will you do?

1. How can you maintain your relationships with Ellen and Steve even as their relationship is falling apart? Is it fair of them to involve you at all?

2. What outcomes are possible here? Can you provide advice to help them stay together? Should you?

3. What do you think of Steve mentioning another girl? Would it affect you differently if Ellen were just a friend, and not your sister?

If Kieran's mother asks probing questions ("Why do you want to join the army now when you're so close to graduating?"), she will get a better understanding of why and how he has come to this decision. Likewise, Kieran will get a better sense of his mother's feelings if he asks similar questions of her ("Why is it so important to you that I finish my degree now?").

Probing helps encourage another important aspect of collaboration — *disclosure*. Kieran, for example, might note that he is concerned about his career — the job market for college graduates in his major is completely flat, and so he sees the army as a great employment opportunity. His mother might play the role of *devil's advocate* — provide counterpoints and worst-case scenarios — and explain that he will still have to pay back all his college loans and that all that expenditure will have amounted to little if he does not finish. But Kieran's mother should also be disclosing. She might reveal her own fears ("What if you get hurt or killed?") as well as the hopes she had built for her son to have a college degree ("I want you to have the chance at success that I never had").

Finally, collaborating involves shifting the focus from what your positions are ("I want to leave college to join the army" and "I want you to stay and finish college") to addressing each other's *underlying needs*. Probing and disclosure may reveal that it is not just about a career opportunity for Kieran but also about his desire to serve his country, to do something noble and just with his life, or to fight for an important cause. His mother's needs may be about her wanting the best life for her son or about keeping him close to her. Once they identify and *respect* each other's needs, they can begin to find options and alternative solutions that may address many of them. For example, Kieran's mother might suggest that he join the Army Reserve instead, which would allow him to serve his country while still finishing school as well as ensuring a career if he wants to go on active duty after graduation. Kieran might also improve his correspondence skills and keep in regular contact with his mother, whenever feasible, while deployed.

what about you?

Self-Assessment on Conflict Management Strategies

Each statement that follows illustrates a strategy for dealing with a conflict. Rate each statement on a scale of 1 to 4, indicating how likely you are to use this strategy: 1 = rarely; 2 = sometimes; 3 = often; and 4 = always.

_____ 1. I explore issues with others to find solutions that meet everyone's needs.

_____ 2. I try to negotiate and adopt a give-and-take approach to problem situations.

_____ 3. I try to meet the expectations of others.

_____ 4. I argue my case and insist on the merits of my point of view.

_____ 5. When there is a disagreement, I gather as much information as I can and keep the lines of communication open.

_____ 6. When I find myself in an argument, I usually say very little and try to leave as soon as possible.

_____ 7. I try to see conflicts from both sides by asking questions like: What do I need? What does the other person need? What are the issues involved?

_____ 8. I prefer to compromise when solving problems so that I can just move on.

_____ 9. I find conflicts challenging and exhilarating; I enjoy the battle of wits that usually follows.

_____ 10. Being at odds with other people makes me feel uncomfortable and anxious.

_____ 11. I try to accommodate the wishes of my friends and family.

_____ 12. I can figure out what needs to be done in a given situation and I am usually right.

_____ 13. To break deadlocks, I meet people halfway.

_____ 14. I may not get what I want but it is a small price to pay for keeping the peace.

_____ 15. I avoid hurt feelings by keeping my disagreements with others to myself.

Scoring: The fifteen statements correspond to five prominent conflict resolution strategies. To find your most dominant style, total the points in the respective categories. The one with the highest score indicates your most commonly used strategy. The one with the lowest score indicates your least commonly used strategy. Try answering the questions for different situations, such as during work versus family conflicts. Do your scores change?

Total:

Collaborating: 1, 5, 7 _____

Competing: 4, 9, 12 _____

Avoiding: 6, 10, 15 _____

Obliging: 3, 11, 14 _____

Compromising: 2, 8, 13 _____

Information from R. Adkins (2006).

Could collaboration be achieved even in the case of chocolate peanut butter pie? If the pie is not that important, then compromising is probably the easiest cooperative strategy. But if the pie conflict is a reflection of underlying problems with competition or self-worth between you and your brother, then attempts to address each other's needs about "feeling special" or "deserving a treat" may lead you to think of mutually beneficial things you can do for each other that have nothing to do with pie!

Reconciliation

The Rolling Stones have been a successful rock-and-roll band for over fifty years. Many bands succeed in the music industry; however, few survive beyond a few years, given the pressures and strains of creative differences, close quarters while touring, and sometimes substance abuse. The Stones too have had their relational ups and downs, including explosive conflicts that have sometimes played out publicly. But they also took pains (and in some cases *years*) to reconcile their conflicts, and they still manage to record music and perform in concert together (Cohen, 2016). We now explore the forms of communication that have helped the Stones, as well as the less famous among us, to de-escalate conflict and push toward relationship reconciliation.

Apology

When guitarist Keith Richards was engaging in frequent bouts of debilitating heroin and alcohol use, lead singer Mick Jagger took leadership of the band. When Richards demanded more control, he and Jagger clashed over everything—recording contracts, stage sets, songs (Cohen, 2016). Jagger made attempts to go solo, and Richards felt betrayed. For years, they handled their conflict by alternating between avoidance and direct fighting. Neither strategy helped much in the long run—the band nearly split up several times, and Richards even published in his memoir very hurtful comments about Jagger (Richards & Fox, 2010). It was not until Richards apologized for these comments that the two were able to begin to repair their relationship (Gilmore, 2013).

To **apologize** is to admit wrongdoing and take responsibility for your own role in the conflict. It can often be difficult to apologize because it means swallowing your pride and confessing that you did something wrong. The apology may or may not be accepted, but when we hurt others, acknowledging it and expressing our regret and remorse can go a long way toward repairing the damage (Donnoli & Wertheim, 2012; Zhang et al., 2015). Jagger has remarked that Richards's apology was important for their fiftieth anniversary tour: "I think it was a good thing he got together with me and said that, and yes, it was a prerequisite, really . . . you can't leave [those things] unspoken" (Gilmore, 2013).

How do you know when it is time to apologize? Your friend or relational partner may well demand it from you directly, particularly if you have done or said something seriously hurtful (Theiss, Knobloch, Checton, & Magsamen-Conrad, 2009). Jagger actually requested an apology from Richards. But your own feelings of guilt might also be a good indicator—guilt is what makes us realize that we have behaved badly, which motivates us to confess and try to repair any damage we may have caused (Behrend & Ben-Ari, 2012). And studies show that you are more likely to be forgiven for relational transgressions or hurtful comments if you sincerely apologize (Bachman & Guerrero, 2006; Morse & Metts, 2011).

Some scholars argue that when relational breaches are very serious, only a "complete and heartfelt" apology from the offender offers any hope for the relationship to continue (Canary & Lakey, 2012). There are times, however, when the hurt is too deep for even a sincere apology to repair the damage. In that case, the relationship may end in separation. For it to continue, the offended partner often must be willing to accept the apology and begin to forgive the transgression.

connect

In Chapter 4, we discussed how to choose our words carefully, as they can often be misconstrued (especially when sent via technological devices!). If you are trying to heal a larger problem with a friend, you should aim to talk to the person face-to-face — and also think carefully about what you will say beforehand.

and you?

Consider the most serious situation you have faced in which you had to offer an apology. What events and feelings led up to your decision to apologize? How did you feel before the apology and after? Do you believe that the apology affected the outcome of the relationship? If so, how?

● **LETTING GO** of past hurts was essential for Keith Richards and Mick Jagger to continue their working friendship. Kevin Mazur/Getty Images

Forgiveness

To **forgive** is an emotional transformation, in which you "let go" and move beyond the conflict or "wrong" that you perceive another has done to you (Waldron & Kelley, 2005). It is not condoning, excusing, or forgetting someone's transgression but reducing the negative reactions to the transgression and engaging in compassion and kindness toward the other person (Toussaint, Owen, & Cheadle, 2012). After Richards's apology, both Jagger and Richards were able to put much of their turbulent past behind them and agree to work together again. However, the friendship between Jagger and Richards, once a close personal friendship, became more of a "working friendship." The two are united now mainly in their shared love of the performance and business of their music (Cohen, 2016). Indeed, scholars argue that forgiveness involves a renegotiation

real communicator

NAME: Anonymous
OCCUPATION: Police Officer

[*Note: Due to security reasons, the officer must remain anonymous.*] I'm a police officer in Chicago. Cops on TV are always running around with their guns drawn or tossing bad guys against brick walls; although I do some of that, of course, I'd say that over 90 percent of my job is spent communicating with people. And most of that time is about managing conflict.

In my first few years out of the academy, I responded to a lot of domestic disputes. Neighbors call in about other neighbors making too much noise; spouses and parents call in about fighting in the home. These are unproductive conflicts: screaming, destruction of property, and all too often violence. The first thing I do is use my eyes to see if physical injuries are apparent or if a crime has been committed. If so, it's a domestic violence situation, and I arrest the perpetrator, taking him or her to jail. The conflict is temporarily resolved. Most of the time, however, these calls are incidents of domestic *disputes*. A crime hasn't been committed. I can't make an arrest. And my job becomes much more difficult. Now I have to manage conflict — through mediation.

First, I don't use any challenging strategies. I stay nonaggressive (I am, after all, in someone else's home). I try not to lean forward, I stay out of

people's faces, and I speak in a monotone. I try to exude calmness, because everyone else in the place is freaking out.

One time, I had a man who simply wouldn't stop screaming at and about his wife: *I hate her! I hate her guts!* As calmly as possible, I asked, "You hate who?" He said, "*I hate my wife!*" I looked shocked and said, "Sir, you hate your *wife*?" I kept the questions coming. In the academy they call this verbal judo, the sword of insertion. In communication classes, it's called probing. I asked the man simple questions, getting him down to facts, getting him to think about things reasonably, as opposed to thinking about them emotionally.

Sometimes, I'll turn to one party and say, as respectfully as possible, "Listen, I know I don't have a right to ask you to leave your own house, but maybe there's a cousin's place you can go crash at for the night, or maybe you can go take a long walk and cool down." It's not a win–win or lose–lose resolution; it's a separation, a temporary one. It's an escapist strategy, a prevention of further unproductive conflict, a rain check on the situation until a better time, when heads are cooler. Often that's the best I can do. I've got other homes to go to, other conflicts to manage.

of the relationship, including new expectations and rules for future interactions (Guerrero, Andersen, & Afifi, 2013).

Forgiveness can enable relationships to survive that might otherwise destruct (Kato, 2016). But in addition to having relational benefits, forgiveness can also have health benefits. Research shows that forgiveness following interpersonal conflict can reduce the stress load on the heart (Lawler et al., 2003). Having a more "forgiving personality" is also associated with improved cardiovascular functioning (Toussaint & Cheadle, 2009) as well as greater overall mental health and physical well-being (see, e.g., Toussaint, Owen, & Cheadle, 2012).

Note, however, that there is evidence that *requiring* an apology or penance from another person before you are willing to forgive may actually have negative consequences. For one thing, the apology may never come, and you may be stuck hanging onto the bitterness. For another, withholding forgiveness until your "conditions" are met may be associated with relationship deterioration (Waldron & Kelley, 2005) and possibly even increased health risks (Toussaint, Owen, & Cheadle, 2012), compared to when you forgive because you feel it is the morally "right" thing to do (Cox, Bennett, Tripp, & Aquino, 2012). It is possible that some of the ongoing strain in the Rolling Stones is due to the forced nature of their reconciliation—not only in Jagger requiring Richards's apology, but in Richards himself apologizing mainly to please Jagger. Richards has said that he would have said "anything to get the band together" (Gilmore, 2013). It appears that being able to truly let go of the hurt is what provides the most optimism for relationship reconciliation.

back to ▶ Sibling Rivalry

At the beginning of this chapter, we talked about conflict between sisters Ashley and Taylor. Let's revisit their family now that you have explored both the good and the bad sides of interpersonal conflict.

▶ Few people get through childhood without some intimate familiarity with family conflict—either fighting as siblings or watching parents argue. But most of us manage to get through it, not necessarily unscathed, but without resorting to harming ourselves or others. Ashley and Taylor may have had unproductive conflicts, but they also learned, with help from their parents, how to manage conflict productively, an important part of growing up.

▶ In their childhood conflicts, both Ashley and Taylor tended to engage openly and use competitive conflict strategies. They each were pursuing their own goals in trying to "win" the arguments. However, as they grew older, they developed more cooperative strategies, learning to negotiate resolutions that benefited both of them. They also learned to respect each other's underlying needs for space, privacy, and fairness, which helped them collaborate on solutions.

▶ Siblings who do not learn to resolve conflicts effectively often hang onto their grievances into adulthood. Such relationships may become bitter rivalries characterized by defensive rather than supportive climates. Recurring conflicts may get triggered by relational transgressions, such as lying to each other or sharing private family matters with outsiders, or siblings may just decide to avoid each other altogether. However, reconciliation is possible, if siblings can take responsibility for their role in their family's discord and begin to forgive the grievances of the past.

 Activities

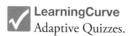
macmillan learning

1. LaunchPad for *Real Communication* offers key term videos and encourages self-assessment through adaptive quizzing. Go to **launchpadworks.com** to get access to:

✓ LearningCurve
Adaptive Quizzes.

▶ Video clips that illustrate key concepts, highlighted in teal in the Real Reference section that follows.

2. The engagement in and resolution of interpersonal conflict are often key factors in romantic comedies (like *Life as We Know It* and *When Harry Met Sally*), as well as in buddy-driven action films (such as *Shanghai Noon* and *The Other Guys*). Try watching a recent buddy movie or romance, and pay attention to the way in which the principal characters engage in conflict with one another. How does their conflict management lead to relationship growth?

3. For an interesting look at conflict and debate, you need not search further than the U.S. Congress. Debates on the floor of the Senate and House of Representatives are broadcast on C-SPAN and provide an interesting glimpse into the way that conflict and argument shape new laws and policy. In addition to observing how this process works, pay attention to the way that strict rules regarding time and etiquette keep the debate relatively diplomatic.

4. Read the advice section of an online magazine or listen to a psychological call-in show. Bearing in mind what you have read in this chapter, consider the nature of the interpersonal conflicts discussed. What are the precursors to the conflicts? What kinds of tactics does the columnist suggest using to manage and resolve the disagreements?

5. This week, if you have a disagreement with a friend, roommate, romantic partner, family member, or boss, identify *one* change you could make to manage and resolve the conflict more productively. For example, could you suggest a compromise? Look for a broader range of promising solutions to your disagreement? Apologize or forgive?

 A Study Tool

Now that you have finished reading this chapter, you can:

Describe the factors that lead to productive conflict:

▸ **Conflict** is a negative interaction between interdependent people, rooted in disagreement (p. 214).
▸ **Conflict management** refers to how relational partners address disagreements (p. 214).
▸ **Unproductive conflict** is conflict that is managed poorly and that has a negative impact (p. 214).
▸ **Productive conflict** is healthy and managed effectively. It fosters healthy debate, leads to better decision making, and spurs relationship growth (p. 215).

Identify conflict triggers in yourself and others:

▶ Many conflicts are rooted in errors of perception (p. 217).

▶ Incompatible goals can spark conflict (p. 217).

▶ Conflicts arise when relational rules are violated, such as engaging in infidelity, lying, or betraying trust (p. 218).

▶ **Provocation**, the intentional instigation of conflict, arises when one party demonstrates aggression, a person's identity feels threatened, fairness is lacking, or someone you depend on is acting irresponsibly (p. 218).

Explain the forces that influence how people handle conflict:

▶ Power dynamics affect relationships in which there is an imbalance of power (p. 219).

▶ Personal attitudes about whether conflict is good or bad influence whether people engage or avoid dealing with it (p. 219).

▶ People who take most disagreements as personal insults or an assault are engaging in a destructive tendency called **taking conflict personally** (p. 220).

▶ **Communication climate** may be **defensive**, in which people blame others and try to control them, or **supportive**, in which they show empathy and try to focus on the problem (p. 220).

▶ Cultural variations, such as individualism/collectivism and high or low context, and cocultures, such as gender or age, have a strong influence on conflict (pp. 221–223).

▶ Varying communication channels allow people in conflict situations to manage their emotions and messages in different ways (p. 223).

▶ The anonymity and distance of digital channels can provide an arena for **cyberbullying**, engaging in repeated abusive personal attacks, as well as **trolling**, posting intentionally offensive messages to provoke conflict in an online group (pp. 223–224).

Evaluate and employ strategies for managing conflict in different situations:

▶ **Escapist strategies** are used to stay away from direct conflict (p. 225). Walking away, changing the subject, or postponing conflict are tactics of **avoiding**, whereas giving in to the other person's wishes is **obliging**. Escapist strategies are good for quick resolutions but may leave issues unresolved (pp. 225–226).

▶ **Competitive strategies** promote the interests of individuals who see conflict as "win–lose" battles (p. 226). In **direct fighting**, people use assertiveness to argue openly to get their way, which can sometimes lead to **verbal aggressiveness**, or attacks on individuals personally (pp. 226–227). **Indirect fighting** involves using passive–aggressive tactics to express conflict without engaging in it openly (p. 228).

▶ **Cooperative strategies** benefit both parties (p. 228). With **compromising**, both parties give up something to gain something (p. 228). **Collaborating** involves finding a win–win solution that satisfies all parties. Collaborating involves focusing on issues, asking probing questions and playing devil's advocate, disclosing your concerns, and attempting to address each other's underlying needs (pp. 228–229).

Articulate ways in which you can de-escalate and repair painful conflict:

▶ **Apologize**, or openly take responsibility, for your own misbehavior (p. 231).

▶ **Forgive** in order to emotionally move past the conflict and let go of the bitterness and resentment (p. 232).

Team Rubicon, a group composed mainly of military veterans, uses skills from deployment to provide disaster relief.

Kirk Jackson, Team Rubicon

 LearningCurve can help you master the material in this chapter.

Go to **launchpadworks.com.**

Communicating in Groups

When a 7.0-magnitude earthquake devastated Haiti, Jacob Wood and William McNulty did not just watch television in horror. Instead, they made some phone calls and a couple of Facebook posts. Within three days, they and a small team of fellow veterans were on the ground in Port-au-Prince. As Marine Corps veterans who had served in both Iraq and Afghanistan, it was clear to Wood and McNulty that disasters and war zones had a lot in common: limited resources, collapsed infrastructure, a lack of information or communication, populations in chaos, and horrific sights and situations that can grind even the most earnest volunteer to a halt. It was also clear that the skills they had honed during their deployments—medical triage, decisive leadership, and the ability to quickly assess and respond to a situation as well as focus intently on the task at hand—were invaluable, especially during the first few days after a disaster.

Team Rubicon (TR), a veterans' service/disaster response organization founded by Wood and McNulty, has provided intense, immediate relief in places around the world, including Texas, Sierra Leone, Greece, Kansas, and Ecuador. It has assisted in the aftermaths of floods, earthquakes, hurricanes, tornadoes, and the Ebola virus. The summer of 2016 was one of its busiest: from providing reconnaissance for flood relief efforts in Louisiana to fighting wildfires in Montana, TR was on the scene. It has provided large-scale medical support for Syrian refugees, primarily in northern Greece where the refugee population is booming. The issue of refugee displacement is so great that even unilateral support can sometimes fall short. The group refers to its role as "bridging the gap" between disasters and the arrival of conventional aid (Team Rubicon, 2016). What TR has learned from handling disasters is that response time is the most critical component in saving lives during a crisis.

TR consists of more than fourteen thousand members, most of them military veterans, who mobilize quickly and deploy to disaster-stricken areas and regions on a moment's notice (Team Rubicon, 2014). But in the process of providing relief, Wood and McNulty found yet another gap they needed to bridge. Returning veterans often find it difficult to adjust to civilian life, a reality that was brought into sharp relief when close friend and TR founding member Clay Hunt took his own life in 2012. Once again proving that adaptability and focus are crucial to "bridging the gap," TR adjusted its mission to include veterans' services, including suicide prevention, career training, and leadership opportunities.

When three or more people come together, their interactions and relationships—and their communication—take on new characteristics. As you can see in our discussion of TR, groups can have a tremendous impact, both on individual members and on those with whom the groups interact. In this chapter, we learn more about group communication, how groups operate, and the factors that influence their communication.

Understanding Groups

Your family sitting down to dinner. A group of coworkers having a drink together at the end of a shift. Six exasperated parents sitting in a doctor's office with sick kids. Each of these examples involves multiple people engaged in some activity—and most of us would probably say that these are examples of "groups of people." But are they really groups? We now explore what it actually means to be in a group, in addition to understanding what types of groups exist and how those groups develop in the first place.

Characteristics of Groups

We consider a collection of individuals a **group** when there are more than two people who share some kind of relationship, communicate in an interdependent fashion, and collaborate toward some shared purpose. When we break that definition down, we can identify three key characteristics:

▶ *A shared identity.* Members of a group perceive themselves as a group. That is, they share a sense of identity: they recognize other members of the group, have specific feelings toward those individuals, and experience a sense of belonging. People may identify themselves, for example, as members of the student council, a park cleanup crew, a baseball team, or a string quartet.

▶ *Common goals.* Members of a group usually identify with one another because they have one or more goals in common. Goals may be very specific—coming up with an ad campaign for a new project or organizing a fund-raiser for your soccer team—or they might be more general, such as socializing. In either case, a shared sense of purpose helps define a group even when there is disagreement about specific goals or ways of achieving them.

▶ *Interdependent relationships.* Members of a group are connected to one another and communicate in an interdependent way. Simply put, the behavior of each member affects the behavior of every other member. This interdependence is fostered by the way that group members adopt specific roles and collaborate to accomplish their goals. When we develop relationships in a group, we obtain valuable feedback from our cohorts. This not only validates our identities within the group, but also serves to heighten the awareness of goals, and motivates us to perform up to the group's standard. When working alone, we are not given the valuable feedback that may be necessary to track our progress and evaluate our work.

Looking back at the examples at the beginning of this section, you can probably guess that your family or a group of coworkers constitutes a group. You share an identity with the other members and have feelings about them (for better or worse); you likely have common goals, and you are interdependent—that is, you rely on them, and they on you, for love, friendship, or professional accomplishments. This is not the case with the strangers in a pediatrician's office. They might share a goal (seeing the doctor), but they do not interact with each other interdependently, and they do not share an identity. Note that it is not the number of people involved or their location that determines whether people are communicating in groups. Four friends chatting over coffee at your local Starbucks constitute a group; so do twenty mothers who have never met but who contribute regularly to an online parenting forum. In both cases, the individuals are joined by shared goals, shared identity, and interdependence.

Types of Groups

Groups can take many forms. The most common among them are called **primary groups** — long-lasting groups that form around the relationships that mean the most to their members. Your family constitutes one primary group to which you belong; your friends are another.

In addition to primary groups, there are groups defined by their specific functions (for instance, support groups, study groups, and social groups). However, any one of these groups can perform multiple functions. Alcoholics Anonymous (AA), for example, is primarily a **support group** — a set of individuals who come together to address personal problems while benefiting from the support of others with similar issues. But AA is also a **social group**, as membership in the group offers opportunities to form relationships with others. And finally, as a group with a specific mission — to help members manage their struggles with alcohol and addiction — AA is also a **problem-solving group**.

Although all groups are to some degree social, some groups are more task-oriented than others. **Study groups**, for example, are formed for the specific purpose of helping students prepare for exams. Probably the most task-oriented and goal-driven type of group is the **team** — a group that works together to carry out a project or to compete against other teams. Sports teams are an obvious example. Teams are also common in large organizations or as subsets of other groups: an Army unit might select a few members to form a reconnaissance team; a community group might nominate a team of individuals to take charge of its annual fundraiser.

One of the more noteworthy and common types of teams in today's organizations is the **self-directed work team**, a group of skilled workers who take responsibility themselves for producing high-quality finished work (Colvin, 2012; Koepfer, 2015). In self-directed work teams, members control their own management functions, such as arranging their schedules; buying equipment; and setting standards for productivity, quality, and costs. They also conduct their own peer evaluations and coordinate their future plans with management. Their complementary skills and experiences enable the team to accomplish more together than any individual member could achieve independently (Katzenbach & Smith, 1993). These groups and teams, doing what is commonly referred to as collaborative work, are becoming commonplace, as studies indicate that this type of work has increased by more than 50 percent in the past two decades (Cross, Rebele, & Grant, 2016).

Perhaps the most dramatic impact of self-directed teams is the improved performance and cooperation of employees throughout the organization. Organizations are shifting their structural power and decision making from upper levels

and you?

In Chapter 8, we talked about family as an example of interpersonal relationships. Now think about your family as a group. What are the family's common goals? What do the members of your family see as the family's defining traits? How can a change in behavior by one family member affect other members?

● **MEMBERS OF A SUPPORT GROUP** may believe they are just coming together to benefit from the support of others, but support groups also act as social groups and problem-solving groups. John van Hasselt/Corbis/Getty Images

wired for communication

Smart Mobs: What Flash Mobs and Political Protests Have in Common

On a particular day each year, more than four thousand straphangers in New York City board mass-transit trains in their boxers, briefs, or bloomers for a coordinated "no pants subway ride" (Improv Everywhere, 2014). A seemingly spontaneous dance performance also erupted a few years ago among passengers at a train station in Shanghai — it was to celebrate the Chinese New Year and renew interest in Chinese folk traditions.

What do these stories have in common? They are both examples of smart mobs: large groups of individuals who act in concert, even though they do not know each other, and who connect and cooperate with one another, at least initially, via electronically mediated means (Rheingold, 2002). But smart mobs have two important additional characteristics that a generic social network lacks: a shared goal and a finite time frame (Harmon & Metaxas, 2010; also see www.smartmobs.com). Like all electronic social networks, smart mobs are grounded in a shared desire for communication and rely on affordable devices that offer instantaneous communication. Simply communicating is not enough to make a smart mob — there must be a tangible goal that is organized via mediated communication and achieved quickly and effectively.

There is a difference, of course, between a social movement and an absurd, pants-free subway ride. The latter is what has come to be called a flash mob — a form of smart mob in which people come together for a brief public act that may seem pointless or ridiculous. Even if the goal, often entertainment or artistic expression, seems not so smart, flash mobs are still smart mobs: through technology, the participants are organized and quickly mobilized to carry out their collective act. Political protests, on the other hand, are largely made up of activists who may already be connected and organized but use technology — including smart mob demonstrations — as tools for making their political or social goals more visible (Conover et al., 2013).

Social media–fueled revolutions in Tunisia, Egypt, and other Middle Eastern nations — sometimes referred to as "Twitter Revolutions" by media pundits — have bolstered the notion that electronic communications are somehow responsible for modern social movements. This is, most likely, an oversimplification: social movements are usually the culmination of frustrations that have been building for many years, which come to a pinnacle when activists begin to organize. Smart mobs utilize traffic as a means to allow their message to register with the greatest number of people (Rheingold, 2002). If a no-pants subway ride is held at 3 A.M., or if a Twitter revolution has a handle that is hard to remember, far fewer people would participate. The point of smart mobs is to generate community dialogue regarding artistic expressions or, more importantly, to express political or economic displeasure (Sutzl, 2016). Without the utilization of traffic paths, where people can see and then easily spread the message, smart mobs would not be nearly as effective.

1. Many social movements benefit from social networks, but is it fair to credit electronic communication with bringing about social change? How did groups like the American civil rights movement organize demonstrations? If these groups relied on technology, does that make them smart mobs?

2. In an effort to quell uprisings, some governments attempt to block citizens' access to the internet, yet protests continue. What does this say about the pervasive nature of electronic communication? What does it say about the role of electronic communication in causing and fueling action?

3. What is the social value of a flash mob? Is it just something fun that technology makes possible, or might there be important effects for the participants or the audiences?

---

to lower levels of management in efforts to implement change and growth and empower employees (Douglas, Martin, & Krapels, 2006). FedEx and Minnesota-based 3M are among an increasing number of companies that involve employees through work teams. (See Table 10.1 for tips on working in a self-directed work team.)

Action	Considerations
Define a clear purpose for the team	What are the team's goals — short term *and* long term?
Foster team spirit	Build a sense of energy, excitement, and commitment in your team by engaging in team-building activities and events, rewarding members who demonstrate commitment, and identifying new challenges for the team to take on.
Train	Working on a self-directed team may be a new experience for some members. See if your organization can provide training to help members understand and implement the defining practices of self-directed teams.
Clarify expectations	Make sure all members of the team understand what is expected of them in terms of their roles and performance. For example, what functions will each member serve? How, specifically, will the team define "success"?
Set boundaries	Articulate where the team's responsibilities begin and end. If necessary, remind members that they are working in the service of the organization and that they need to stay focused on their specific purpose.

TABLE 10.1

SELF-DIRECTED WORK TEAMS: TIPS FOR WORKING COLLABORATIVELY

Information from T. Capozzoli (2002); B. Nelson (2002); M. J. Rosenthal (2001).

Models of Group Development

If you have ever become wrapped up in a reality TV show such as *Survivor*, *The Biggest Loser*, or *The Amazing Race*, you know how fascinating and dramatic group interactions can be. In each of these shows, a season typically opens with the forming of a group: cast members start off as strangers but are quickly thrust into a group situation — sharing a living space and working together to accomplish certain tasks. As the season progresses, the group members bond, conflicts erupt, and alliances are forged. In fact, much of the drama in reality television stems from the tensions that arise between cast members as they struggle to work with — or against — one another (and of course, editing can heighten the drama even more). Researchers argue that as groups progress, they go through important *stages*, or changes over time, although not always as dramatically played out as the groups on television. Let's look at two different research perspectives on the stages of group development.

Stages of Group Development

The stage model (Tuckman & Jensen, 1977) states that as groups develop, they progress through five stages: forming, storming, norming, performing, and adjourning. The model proposes that these stages are linear — that is, groups go through them in order over time. Although the model was originally proposed for face-to-face groups, researchers have also applied these stages to how "virtual" teams develop online (Johnson, Suriya, Yoon, Berrett, & Fleur, 2002). Suppose you

● **GROUPS COME** in all shapes and sizes. Although volunteer builders for Habitat for Humanity might vary in size and purpose from a hip-hop dance group, both communicate in groups. Brendan Fitterer/Newscom/ZUMA Press/Spring Hill/Florida/U.S.

and you?

In college, you have probably had to work with others for discussions or for projects. What were the differences you experienced when you participated in these groups? Were the groups' goals better served with a team leader or when each member was given a specific task and had full authority over their segment of the project? What were the differences in the time it took to complete the task and the overall quality of the work?

connect ➤

Developing a relationship with a group is not so different from starting a new interpersonal relationship. In both contexts, we reduce uncertainty about our relational partners so that we feel secure and confident about roles, interactions, and so on. So whether you are beginning a new romance or forging a new student organization, you are likely using the passive, active, and interactive strategies that we discussed in Chapter 8.

just became a volunteer with your local affiliate of Habitat for Humanity, a non-profit organization that builds and repairs affordable homes for people in need. Let's look more closely at how your volunteer group might go through each particular stage:

▶ *Forming.* When a group first comes together, its members are unsure how to act around one another, nervous about how others perceive them, and unclear on their roles and the group's task. In this **forming** stage, group members try to figure out who will be in charge and what the group's goals will be. The primary purpose of this stage is for group members to learn more about one another and the group's objectives. Once individuals feel accepted, they can begin to identify with the group (Moreland & Levine, 1994). For example, when you meet for the first time in your Habitat for Humanity group, you will try to get to know each other and determine the types of shared goals you hold for how to be involved. Does everyone help with construction or do some volunteers do recruitment and fund-raising? How do you decide who gets to do what?

▶ *Storming.* After forming, group members move into the **storming** stage, in which they inevitably begin experiencing conflicts over issues such as who will lead the group and what roles members will play. Group members also begin to disagree on goals, tasks, and cliques, and other competitive divisions may even begin to form (Wheelan, 2012; Wheelan & Burchill, 1999). The group members must work on mending these differences and resolve conflicts if the group is to continue to function effectively. In your Habitat group, now that you are all more comfortable, you feel free to express preferences for doing different tasks and ideas for how you think the tasks can be done best. The follow-up discussion could become elevated as each person argues for her or his own ideas.

▶ *Norming.* During the **norming** stage, group members move beyond their conflicts, and norms emerge among members that govern expected behavior. **Norms** are recurring patterns of behavior or thinking that come to be accepted in a group as the "usual" way of doing things (Scheerhorn & Geist, 1997). During this stage, group roles also solidify based on individual member strengths, and a leader may emerge. In addition, group identity grows stronger as members realize the importance of their roles within the group and the need to cooperate to accomplish goals. In your Habitat meetings, you may find that your administrative skills have landed you the job of keeping track of the group's progress, while the members with construction experience discuss techniques for working with the latest environmentally friendly materials. You realize that your common purpose is to move forward on each housing and recruiting project and be proud representatives of the larger Habitat organization.

▶ *Performing.* Once the group has established norms, the action shifts to accomplishing their tasks. During the **performing** stage, members combine their skills and knowledge to work toward the group's goals and to overcome hurdles. This stage is characterized by high levels of interdependence, motivation, and clarity in delegation of team member tasks. You and your Habitat members now enact all the plans you have been working on, including doing the actual building and holding your recruiting events. You communicate collaboratively to support each other and are able to get things done.

▶ *Adjourning.* Many groups — though clearly not all — eventually disband. For groups whose project or task has come to an end, there is an **adjourning** stage (Tuckman & Jensen, 1977). The group members reflect on their accomplishments and failures as well as determine whether the group will disassemble or take on another project. Some groups choose to celebrate their achievements with a final get-together, or a **termination ritual** (Keyton, 1993). Members may also opt to maintain friendships even if they will no longer be working together. For many Habitat teams, the completion of a home for a needy person can be an emotional experience. The adjourning process in this context can bring great joy and pride as your group finishes its task successfully.

The Punctuated Equilibrium Model

Although the stage model represents a linear view of group development, other scholars have argued that groups do not necessarily follow sequential "stages" of development (e.g., Gersick, 1988). One argues that groups progress in a **punctuated equilibrium** process (Peng, Han, Wei, & Wang, 2015). This means that groups

and you?

Think about your experience as part of a group to which you no longer belong — a former job, your high school class, or a club from your past. Did the group go through all five phases described here?

real communicator

NAME: Bambi Francisco Roizen
OCCUPATION: Founder and CEO of an Entrepreneur and Investor Network
Courtesy Bambi Francisco Roizen

I have always been interested in innovation and entrepreneurship. Before I started my own company, I covered internet trends and investments as a columnist and TV correspondent. I closely followed technology stocks and reported about them for several cable TV business news networks. I also helped create *Capital Ideas*, a show about innovation. Today, my company aims to help great entrepreneurs find funding and help investors get in on the ground floor of tomorrow's leading companies.

Each project I've had a part in creating has always been the result of multiple coordinated efforts. When I was a journalist, I had an editor who made me dig deeper into stories, one who dotted my i's and crossed my t's, and yet another who helped my stories sing. As a TV correspondent, there was no chance of getting anything on air without writers, editors, producers, videographers, and interns working in harmony. In recent years, I've produced events for an audience of one thousand people. In one memorable instance, we had to make last-minute changes to a program that resulted in about ten people having to adjust and act accordingly: one person had to change the event brochure, another to change the event page and stage screens, another to inform talent on stage, another to inform the stage manager and stage crew, and so on.

One of the biggest challenges all teams face is maintaining trust in each member's abilities to execute and communicate effectively. I had an experience with one team member who could execute but preferred to work alone, and therefore had a brash way of communicating with others. This caused setbacks and anxiety and resulted in several team therapy sessions. We found there was lack of trust in this person's ability to rally others around a vision and get excited about a goal.

Teams need clear and consistent goals, directives, and timelines. A team also needs a leader, like a fleet needs a captain. The team leader sets the tempo and productivity pace, so if a manager is inconsistent in his or her expectations, and doesn't stay committed to a goal, teams may lose their focus, motivation, and energy. Yet productivity is never linear: there will come a time in every team when your project is near complete and a clunky bug appears. How do you reset the team's productivity? The team leader must create a plan to get everyone back on track by communicating with hope and coming up with steps to get the job done.

Teamwork is also important in my family. I have a household of eight. I live with my four sons, my husband, and my parents. We all contribute to the household by cooking dinner, taking kids to school and activities, and doing chores. On Thanksgiving, each child has a dish to prepare. My oldest makes the cornbread; my second oldest makes the stuffing; my third makes cranberry sauce, and when my youngest was three, he already had his contribution: whipped cream. Thanksgiving wouldn't be the same without a team effort.

● **THE TEAM MEMBERS** who make up Pied Piper in *Silicon Valley* find ways to procrastinate until it is necessary to buckle down and start coding. © HBO/Photofest

and you?

When you work independently, do you work in a linear fashion or does your pattern of activity resemble the punctuated equilibrium model? Does that behavior change when you work in a group? Can differing ideas of time frame and direction harm your group's objective?

experience a period of inertia or inactivity until they become aware of time, pressure, and looming deadlines, which then compel members to take action.

As a student, a pattern of procrastination followed by bursts of activity may sound familiar to you. Research confirms that it is common to procrastinate on class assignments, especially when working in groups when there is a perceived diffusion or share of responsibilities (Karau & Williams, 2001). Groups often procrastinate (and in reality waste time) until the critical halfway point of a project (Gersick, 1988). Then, when they hit this midpoint transition and realize that their original plan is not coming together, they focus their energy on completing the project and mobilizing their efforts. Groups go through this in a cyclical fashion, with long periods of inactivity followed by spurts of intense activity and change (Chidambaram & Bostrom, 1996); this pattern becomes almost a habit or routine (Gersick & Hackman, 1990).

Complexity of Group Communication

When you chat with an instructor in her office, you probably speak freely and informally. The two of you may exchange questions and comments rapidly, interrupt one another, and prompt each other for more information. But when you sit with that same professor in a classroom full of other students, the nature of your communication changes; you might be expected to raise your hand, defer to other students who are already speaking, or not ask questions at all.

What has changed? Why is the nature of your communication so different in the classroom from the way you converse in her office? In this section, we take a look at how complex group communication can be, depending on the number of individuals involved, their relationships, and their patterns of interaction.

Size of Groups

As you will recall from Chapter 1, dyadic communication refers to interactions between just two people (a dyad). When a third person joins the interaction, the dyad becomes a small group. Scholars generally agree that small-group communication involves at least three members (Bormann, 1990), with a maximum of fifteen to twenty-five members (Sosha, 1997). When a group expands beyond twenty-five members, it becomes a crowd or audience. Some communication scholars argue that in order to effectively perform tasks within classrooms or work projects, five to seven members may be optimum (Cragan, Wright, & Kasch, 2008). The basic logistics of communication — the need to take turns speaking and listening, for example — grow more complex the larger a group gets, creating the need for more structured exchanges among members. Specifically, the bigger the group, the more its communication takes on the following characteristics:

▸ *Interaction is more formal.* Group communication simply cannot work in the same kind of informal way that dyadic communication occurs because of the need to include more communicators in the discourse. Individuals participating in a group may feel the need to obtain permission to speak and may also be reluctant to interrupt a speaker. However, this can vary greatly in online communities. On Facebook, where our personal lives may be viewed by a large network of acquaintances, we often follow more formal norms for expressing ourselves and limit potentially inappropriate material, given the possible repercussions both personally and professionally. On sites like Reddit, Tumblr, and 4chan, where identities are largely anonymous, people often express themselves more openly and less formally since criticism is not personalized to our true identities.

▶ *Each member has limited opportunities to contribute.* Participants may want or be required by a leader to share "floor time" with other group members. Such time constraints can inhibit the quality and quantity of their contributions. Even without a formal leader, a few members tend to dominate much of the talk in larger groups, while the less assertive members tend to remain quiet. In mediated groups on Facebook, Reddit, and Tumblr, **moderators (mods)** are generally present to make sure no one commenter is monopolizing the discussion board. The mods' job is to uphold the "rules" of the site, which include keeping content relevant, getting rid of those who break the rules, and keeping servers refreshed and optimal. They hold virtual networks together and give members a sense of organization. However, in large online groups, there is still a tendency for a lot of members just to "lurk" (read posts but not post themselves), while certain members, usually those with more expertise on the topic, tend more often to contribute their ideas and reply to others' questions.

▶ *The communication becomes less intimate.* The greater the number of participants, the less comfortable they feel self-disclosing personal information or voicing controversial opinions. In large online communities, this hesitancy often depends on the norms of the groups—some are highly personal (such as cancer support groups) and some are controversial (such as fan groups). In very large social networks (such as Facebook), there is a tendency for members to avoid revealing "too much information" to such a broad, diverse audience.

▶ *The interaction consumes more time.* As more participants are invited to contribute or debate, and there are more possible opinions, the interaction takes longer to complete. Despite the drawbacks that come with longer debates, by increasing the number of opinions and contributions, we generally see a more diverse and complete outcome to discussions. In the online environment, there is an additional delay, in that group members may read messages and post replies at different paces.

▶ *Relationships become more complex.* As more participants are added, the relationships become more complex. In the dyad, of course, there is only one

connect

As you learned in Chapter 2, on social media platforms like Facebook the size of our groups is also complicated by *context collapse.* The diversity of participants in our network make it difficult to keep our audiences (such as work colleagues versus personal friends) separated, and so we must be more careful to post messages that are appropriate for all of our audiences to see.

● **WHEN YOU ARE** chatting with a professor during office hours, you are the focus of your professor's attention. However, in the classroom you have to respect that other students want to speak as well! (left) Bob Mahoney/The Image Works; (right) monkeybusinessimages/Getty Images

relationship—that between person 1 and person 2. But as shown in Figure 10.1, add another person, and you now have four potential relationships—between persons 1 and 2, 1 and 3, 2 and 3, and all three together. The number of relationships multiplies further with each additional participant. Again, digital channels of communication allow us even more complexity. Complete strangers or workmates we hardly know can respond to our opinions or give valuable feedback on our work that would have gone unnoticed and unused only twenty years ago.

The Formation of Cliques

As a group's size increases (up to twenty-five), small subgroups of individuals often begin to bond together within the group, forming **cliques** (or coalitions; Wilmot, 1987). Cliques are a common part of group life—they are a fixture in middle school and high school. You have your marching band kids, your football players, the art students, and so on. Many people think that they will escape cliques once high school ends, but this is rarely the case. In college, you might form cliques with others in your major, your dorm, or a particular organization. In office settings, members of cliques or coalitions typically sit next to each other in meetings, eat lunch together, share similar opinions, and support one another's positions.

When cliques take shape in a group, communication becomes more challenging because members are no longer dealing only with other individual members. Rather, they must navigate relationships and figure out how to communicate with entire subgroups. In addition, **countercoalitions**, in which one subgroup positions itself against another on an issue, can leave anyone who is not affiliated with a subgroup in a very awkward position. One example of the formation of cliques and countercoalitions can be seen in the self-described *social justice movement* on Reddit, an entertainment, social news, and networking site (an internet site with increasing numbers of users and visitors). In response to police shootings, LGBTQ community issues, and a new feminist movement, Reddit saw a huge increase in sub-Reddits (cliques) devoted to discussing perceived social injustices (/r/TheoryofReddit,

connect

As you learned in Chapter 6, we define ourselves by our group memberships, with a tendency toward favoring our *in-group* members and comparing ourselves to (and sometimes excluding) *out-group* members. Although it may be a natural tendency to form cliques with those who share our affiliations, competent communicators must remember to be inclusive of various groups and cocultures — particularly in team and organizational settings.

FIGURE 10.1
COMPLEXITY OF GROUP RELATIONSHIPS Each time a person is added to a group, the number of relationships increases substantially.

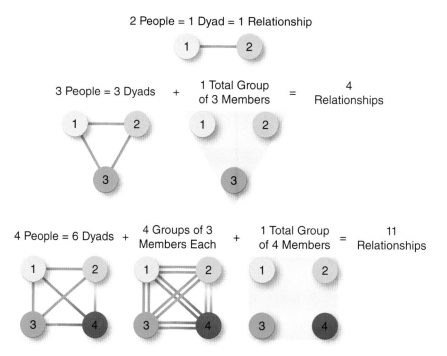

2016). In response to the movement, several counter sub-Reddits (countercoalitions) formed with the purpose of either debunking the evidence presented in social justice sub-Reddits or categorically denying their sincerity compared with real-world organizations with similar causes. Interestingly, in response, the social justice movement began creating new sub-Reddits specifically to undermine the countercoalitions. Like in many cliques, jargon and "inside jokes" were created that are undecipherable to anybody who is not a part of these specific sub-Reddits. Both sides remain very much opposed to one another, but are given a voice on Reddit to have legitimate discourse, even if discussions can sometimes become personal attacks or fallacious argumentation stemming from very emotional anecdotal topics. The tendency for members of groups to organize themselves into coalitions or cliques can have consequences for those who find themselves left out. **Social ostracism** is the exclusion of a particular group member (or members) — for example, when one clique or coalition limits the amount of information they share with a particular member and excludes him or her from group activities and the decision-making process (Kameda, Ohtsubo, & Takezawa, 1997). Ostracism can also occur in virtual groups, such as online work teams or Facebook friendship networks (Meagher & Marsh et al., 2017). In online environments, exclusion may occur through more subtle signals, such as reduced message frequency or an overall lack of responsive communication (Cramton, 1997; Williams et al., 2002). There are also instances when social ostracism is orchestrated aggressively by the group itself. As discussed earlier, online moderators have the power to strip a group member of his or her commenting power if that person has violated the group's illustrated rules. This usually entails a probationary period or a system of warnings.

Rejection by one's peers can lead to anxiety, anger, and sadness as targets of ostracism feel a decrease in belonging, control, and self-esteem (Williams, 2001; Wittenbaum, Shulman, & Braz, 2010). However, responses to social ostracism vary. Research on gender differences (Williams & Sommer, 1997), for example, has found that females who are ostracized are more likely to compensate, that is, work harder to be part of the group. Males, on the other hand, tend to engage in a practice called social loafing, which we discuss next.

Social Loafing

On many education and learning blogs, you can find students and instructors complaining about one of the most dreaded assignments of all time: the group project. At first glance, doesn't it seem that group projects should be easier than working solo? There are more minds with whom to try out ideas and share in the work. But what we all dread is having group members who do not pull their own weight. The fact is, in a group, people may become prone to **social loafing**—failing to invest the same level of effort in the group that they would put in if they were working alone or with one other person (Karau & Williams, 1993). In almost every group situation, from your high school yearbook committee to cutthroat competitions like *Survivor*, there are always a few individuals who manage to make it through to the end simply by keeping their heads low and letting their teammates do most of the work. Clearly, social loafing affects both participation and communication in groups (Comer, 1998; Shultz, 1999).

Despite the negative connotation of the word *loafing*, it is not always due to laziness. When a person fails to speak up because he or she feels shy around a lot of people, the person is engaging in social loafing. Social loafing also results from

● **AN OUTSIDER** of a clique can be or feel ostracized when he or she has not yet formed a bond with the rest of the group. Rob Blackburn/Getty Images

and you?

If you have ever been bullied or witnessed bullying, you know that social ostracism can be a powerful — and hurtful — force. But is excluding someone from communication always aggressive or malevolent? Consider situations in which you may have excluded a group member from communication, either in person or online. What were your motives, and how did it affect communication in the group?

the feelings of anonymity that can occur in larger groups, where it is more difficult for an individual member's contributions to be evaluated. Thus a member may put in less effort, believing that nobody will notice that he or she is slacking or, conversely, that he or she is working hard. If group members perceive an inequality in individual effort, conflict can and often does emerge, harming team morale. Social loafing even occurs in online groups and teams (Hagen, 2015): members of an online discussion group, for example, may post messages or photos that are unrelated to the group's topic or may not respond at all to a request for everyone's opinion on an idea. The repercussions of online loafing, like criticism, embarrassment, or lower-quality work are not as immediate or public and are thus easier to justify than face-to-face social loafing, where the consequences are quickly realized.

Scholars argue that there are several practices that can help to manage your group's productivity and prevent or reduce social loafing (Cox & Brobrowski, 2000; Latane, Williams, & Harkins, 1979; Van Dick, Tissington, & Hertel, 2009):

▶ *Establish objectives and performance goals.* Make the schedule clear to all team members so everyone is aware of deadlines. You may even consider putting everything in writing, akin to a contract, so that there is no confusion about who should be taking care of what.

▶ *Establish individual accountability.* At the beginning of a project, be sure that all team members understand that they are expected to carry out their duties responsibly. Also discuss how members will be evaluated and the consequences of social loafing or poor performance (Cox & Brobrowski, 2000).

▶ *Encourage team identity and ownership.* Early on in the process, promote team unity by coming up with a group name or symbol. Take the time to get to know each other and build social bonds and trust. This will help foster more team loyalty. Encourage team members to take pride and ownership in their work.

▶ *Stay in contact.* If a miscommunication occurs between members, be sure to discuss it right away. Ambiguity and confusion will only encourage members to become less connected with the group and more likely to engage in social loafing.

Group Networks

Just as a group's size and social relationships influence the complexity of communication within the group, so do networks. **Networks** are patterns of interaction governing who speaks with whom in a group and about what. To understand the nature of networks, you must first consider two main positions within them. The first is *centrality*, or the degree to which an individual sends and receives messages from others in the group. The most central person in the group receives and sends the highest number of messages in a given time period. At the other end of the spectrum is *isolation*—a position from which a group member sends and receives fewer messages than other members.

A team leader or manager typically has the highest level of centrality in a formal group, but centrality is not necessarily related to status or power. The CEO of a company, for example, may be the end recipient of all information generated by teams below her, but in fact, only a limited number of individuals within the organization are able to communicate directly with her. As you might imagine, networks play a powerful role in any group's communication, whether the group is a family, a sports team, a civic organization, or a large corporation.

what about you?

Are You a "Social Loafer"?

Do you exert less effort on a task when participating in a group than you would if you were performing it alone? If so, you may be a social loafer. A major complaint about group work involves dealing with free-riding behavior: resentment about group members who do not do their fair share or who even undermine the overall group goal. With your last group experience in mind, use the following five-point scale to determine if you were a social loafer: 5 = extremely like me; 4 = somewhat like me; 3 = neither like nor unlike me; 2 = somewhat unlike me; and 1 = extremely unlike me.

_____ 1. I arrived on time for group meetings and stayed until the end.

_____ 2. I showed enthusiasm about group activities.

_____ 3. I showed a positive attitude toward fellow group members.

_____ 4. I participated in planning the project/activity.

_____ 5. I volunteered for tasks appropriate to my expertise.

_____ 6. I contributed regularly to group discussion.

_____ 7. I put forth effort equal to or greater than that of my group members.

_____ 8. I delivered my contributions in a complete fashion.

_____ 9. My fellow group members perceived me as agreeable.

_____ 10. My fellow group members perceived me as thorough.

_____ 11. My fellow group members perceived me as dependable.

_____ 12. My fellow group members perceived me as conscientious.

_____ 13. I met all deadlines.

_____ 14. I asked for help from others when needed.

_____ 15. I supported the contributions of other group members.

_____ 16. I was open to suggestions from others.

_____ 17. I gave credit to others for their suggestions and contributions.

_____ 18. I made positive adaptations to the differences of group members.

_____ 19. I tried my absolute best.

_____ 20. I shared credit/blame for the outcome of our group.

_____ Add your scores together to get an informal assessment of social loafing.

74–100: You are *not* a social loafer. You carry your weight in a group and reinforce the contributions of others. People value you and your contributions.

47–73: You may be a social loafer in certain group situations. With your last group experience, you were probably frustrated but not sure how to make it better. In the future, be sure you are communicating support and involvement and show respect for others so that each person feels that he or she has a useful role to play.

20–46: Social loafer! In group situations, people are likely to see you as apathetic and may even resent you. Whenever you join a group in the future, you should work harder to do your fair share and show support for all your group members.

Information from B. Maiden & B. Perry (2011).

In some groups, all members speak with all others regularly about a wide range of topics. In others, perhaps only a few members are "allowed" to speak directly with the group's leader or longest-standing member about serious issues. In still other groups, some members may work alongside one another without communicating at all. There are several types of networks, including chain networks, all-channel networks, and wheel networks (see Figure 10.2; Bavelous, 1950).

Chain Networks

In a **chain network**, information is passed from one member to the next in a sequential pattern. Such networks can be practical for sharing written information: an email, forwarded from person to person along a chain, for example, allows each person to read the original information from other prior recipients. But this form of group communication can lead to frustration and miscommunication when information is spoken, since the messages can easily get distorted as they are passed along. Person A tells person B that their boss, Luis, had a fender bender on the way to work and will miss the 10:00 A.M. meeting. Person B tells person C that Luis was in an accident and will not be in the office today. Person C tells person D that Luis was injured in an accident; no one knows when he will be in. You can imagine that Luis will be in a full-body cast by the time the message reaches person G!

The "secret (gossip) game" is another good example of a chain network. The first person tells a "secret": "I watched a movie last night." Retold, this statement becomes, "Someone saw a film the previous evening," which is a slight change in meaning from what the original sender had intended. As each person tells the secret, the meaning changes slightly, until the original meaning is lost on those members receiving the message further down the line. The game ends with a completely different message being perceived by members of the network.

All-Channel Networks

In an **all-channel network**, all members interact with each other equally. When people talk about roundtable discussions, they are talking about all-channel groups: there is no leader, and all members operate at the same level of centrality. Such networks can be useful for collaborative projects and for brainstorming ideas; however, the lack of order can make it difficult for such groups to complete tasks efficiently. That is where wheel networks come in.

Wheel Networks

Wheel networks are a sensible alternative for situations in which individual members' activities and contributions must be culled and tracked in order to avoid duplicating efforts and to ensure that all tasks are being completed. In a **wheel network**, one individual acts as a touchstone for all the others in the group; all group members share their information with that one individual, who then shares the information with the rest of the group. Wheel networks have the lowest shared centrality but are very efficient (Leavitt, 1951).

FIGURE 10.2

GROUP COMMUNICATION
NETWORKS
Information from A. O. Scott (1981).

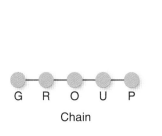

Chain

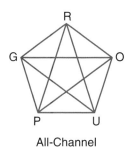

All-Channel

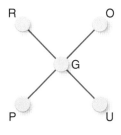

Wheel

● **THE COPYEDITING TEAM** in a newsroom works as a wheel network. All of the copy editors report to one copy chief, who regulates the copyediting style. MANDEL NGAN/Getty Images

Understanding Group Roles

When we communicate in groups, we tend to fall into particular roles, much like playing different parts in a play. These roles influence the process and outcomes of group interaction. Let's look closely at the various types of roles during group communication (Sapru & Bourland, 2015; Riddle & Martin, 1999; Benne & Sheats, 1948).

Task Roles

In some cases a role is defined by a task that needs doing, and a person is asked or appointed to fill it (or he or she volunteers). Such **task roles** are concerned with the accomplishment of the group's goals — specifically, the activities that need to be carried out for the group to achieve its objectives. For example, your role on a committee charged with organizing a campus Zumba party might be to post advertisements for the event in key locations around campus, in the student newspaper, and on the university website.

Task roles can also be specifically related to the group's communication; for instance:

▶ An *information giver* offers facts, beliefs, personal experience, or other input during group discussions ("When the College Republicans posted their ad in the student lounge, they had good attendance at their event").

▶ An *information seeker* asks for input or clarification of ideas or opinions that members have presented ("Jeff, are you saying you don't think we would get good attendance on a Thursday night?").

▶ An *elaborator* provides further clarification of points, often adding to what others have said ("I agree with Ellie about getting Spike to DJ the event — he has a huge following in town").

▶ An *initiator* helps the group move toward its objective by proposing solutions, presenting new ideas, or suggesting new ways of looking at an issue the group is discussing ("How essential is it that we schedule our event for the last Thursday of the month? If we moved it a week later, we wouldn't have to compete with the homecoming festivities").

▶ An *administrator* keeps the conversation on track ("OK, let's get back to the subject of when to schedule the event") and ensures that meetings begin and end on time ("We've got five minutes left; should we wind up?"). This role appears in online groups, too, where forum administrators (also known as moderators or masters) coordinate and sometimes screen the members' comments.

Social Roles

Some roles evolve to manage how people in the group are feeling and getting along with each other; such roles are called **social roles**. For example, in a college dormitory, one student might unofficially fill the role of "hall parent" — mentoring freshmen, listening compassionately to people's problems, and making everyone feel secure. Consider these additional examples of social roles:

▶ A *harmonizer* seeks to smooth over tension in the group by settling differences among members and working out compromises when conflict arises ("There is only one communal TV lounge per floor, so can we plan on reserving the first-floor lounge for people who want to watch the football game on Sunday, and leaving the second floor free for people who want to watch the Golden Globe Awards?").

▶ A *gatekeeper* works to ensure that each member of the group gets a chance to voice their opinions or otherwise contribute to discussions. ("Tonya, we haven't heard from you yet on the issue of overnight guests in our dorm. What are your thoughts?").

▶ A *sensor* expresses group feelings, moods, or relationships in an effort to recognize the climate and capitalize on it or modify it for the better ("I feel like tempers are getting a little short right now — maybe we ought to break for dinner, and meet back here in an hour to continue this discussion when we're all feeling less hungry?").

Each member in a group can play task and social roles, and the roles can be official or unofficial. For example, Evelyn is the dorm's resident adviser, officially tasked with maintaining harmony among the students who live there. But Mike is also an unofficial harmonizer because he has a knack for mitigating tensions between people. Mike also has a lot of ideas for events, so he frequently finds himself acting as an initiator during meetings. Members like Mike can move into or out of such personal or task roles depending on whether the role is needed and whether others in the group are willing to fill it.

Antigroup Roles

Unlike task and social roles, **antigroup roles** create problems because they serve individual members' priorities at the expense of group needs. You have probably seen evidence of these antigroup roles in the groups you belong to:

▶ A *blocker* indulges in destructive communication, including opposing or criticizing all ideas and stubbornly reintroducing an idea after the group has already rejected or bypassed it ("None of the dates any of you proposed will work for the party. It really needs to be five weeks from today, as I said earlier").

connect

Competent leadership can address problematic antigroup roles. As you learn in Chapter 11, a *directive leader* might lay out tasks to thwart a distracter; a *supportive leader* might thank each member for his or her contributions, preventing a recognition seeker from claiming the glory. Leaders have the power to affect norms and roles by encouraging group members to make productive contributions.

► An *avoider* refuses to engage in the group's proceedings by expressing cynicism or nonchalance toward ideas presented or by joking or changing the subject ("Well, whatever, I'm guessing it's not a big deal if this party doesn't even happen, right?").

► A *recognition seeker* calls attention to himself or herself by boasting or by going on and on about his or her qualifications or personal achievements ("I planned a gathering for a women's studies group last year, and it went really well. People still talk about it! So trust me on this one").

► A *distractor* goes off on tangents or tells irrelevant stories ("Does anyone know what happened on *Game of Thrones* last night? I missed it").

Antigroup roles obviously add to the dysfunction of a group (Wilson & Hanna, 1993). For instance, a *blocker* who acts superior to other team members and criticizes the members' ideas may harm group morale and productivity. To mitigate the impact of these antigroup roles, members can revisit the norms the group has established and make the changes needed to improve group communication (e.g., "All ideas get a fair hearing"). People fulfilling certain task or social roles can also help. For instance, if you are a gatekeeper, you can prompt an avoider to contribute her opinion on a proposal that the group has been considering. Research also indicates that positive and proactive responses to avoiders and blockers can help establish individuals as leaders in their organizations (Garner & Poole, 2009).

Role Conflict

Imagine that you work at a local retail store and you have been promoted to store manager. As part of your new role, you will have to manage staff members who are working as individual contributors at the store. In this new role, you will be managing several close friends you used to work alongside as regular staff. That is where things might get complicated: as manager, you will have to evaluate staff members' performance. How can you give a good friend a poor performance review and still remain friends?

Role conflict arises in a group whenever expectations for a member's behavior are incompatible (Baxter & Montgomery, 1996). Role conflict can make group communication profoundly challenging. For the manager who must evaluate a friend—especially a friend whose performance could be better—there is rarely a perfect option. You might give candid constructive feedback to your friend on his performance while trying to constrain the damage to your friendship by saying something like, "I hope you know I'm offering this feedback as a way to help you improve. As your friend and manager, I want to see you do well here." A less ethical approach, of course, would be to defer to your friend's feelings instead of to your responsibility as manager—essentially, to spare his feelings by giving him a better review than he deserves.

Status

Groups also form around—or are defined by—status. Status is like a social currency, unequally distributed within groups, which gives certain members more power than others. In some groups, status is formally defined by a clear hierarchy: the military, for example, operates on a hierarchy of leadership with officers outranking enlisted troops. But status is also informally conferred: a charismatic or especially competent military recruit may emerge as a leader and gain status among her peers even if she does not outrank them. That kind of perceived

and you?

Have you ever been in a leadership role in a group of friends? Have you ever been subordinate to a friend in a group situation? Did any conflict arise and, if so, how did you resolve it?

connect

Status is often pertinent in the workplace — especially between supervisors and supervisees. To settle well into a company's *organizational culture*, it is necessary to carefully foster this relationship. In Chapter 12, we give tips on how to interact with a supervisor or supervisee in a professional and courteous way.

status — based not on any kind of formal rules but instead on peoples' perceptions of one another — can be potent.

A number of factors have been shown to increase perceptions of status. For example, status can be gained through having access to material resources or information that other group members do not have (Poole & Hollingshead, 2005). Similarly, physical attractiveness has been known to enhance a group member's status (Webster & Driskell, 1978, 1983). Gender may play a role, too, as males have traditionally had higher status and participation rates and greater access to resources and information than females (Carli, 1999; Ellyson, Dovidio, & Brown; Smith-Lovin, Skvortz, & Hudson, 1986). Of course, as mentioned in the foregoing military example, people can also *earn* status through their own competence or communicative effectiveness as they participate in the group.

Within groups, those with higher status are given more opportunities to make contributions toward completing the task, their suggestions are often evaluated more positively, and they exert greater influence over lower-status members (Berger, Wagner, & Zelditch, 1985). Perceptions of higher status can lead to those group members' having greater influence even if they do not have any formal power. The "popular kids" at a high school, for example, may have more influence on school events than the elected student council.

Group Climate

In addition to the complexity of group interaction and the roles that group members play, group communication is also strongly affected by the overall "climate" or collective atmosphere in the group. Specifically, group members are affected by the level of the group's cohesion, the norms that emerge for their behavior, clarity of goals, and their differences as individuals. In the sections that follow, we explore each of these factors in more detail.

Cohesion

Cohesion is the degree to which group members bond, like each other, and consider themselves to be one entity. A cohesive group identifies itself as a single unit rather than a collection of individuals, which helps hold the group together in the face of adversity (Breslau, Setodji, & Vaughn, 2016). In fact, cohesion is an important factor in generating a positive group climate, in which members take pride in the group, treat each other with respect, develop trust, feel confident about their abilities, and achieve higher success in accomplishing goals. Such positive climates can also foster optimism and confidence in the face of obstacles. Cohesive teams have been recognized to exhibit better chemistry, commitment to goals, and more timely communication than their noncohesive counterparts (Franz, Leicht, Molenaar, & Messner, 2016). A self-confident, cohesive group tends to minimize problems, eliminate barriers, and cope well with crises (Folger, Poole, & Stutman, 2001). In general, cohesive groups perform better than noncohesive groups on decision-making tasks (e.g., selecting a course of action more quickly and making more informed choices; Carless & DePaola, 2000; Welch, Mossholder, Stell, & Bennett, 1998). Nonverbal communication is also influenced by group cohesion; Yasui (2009) found that cohesive group members often repeat and build on one another's gestures.

You can determine group cohesion in several ways. If you take a look at how the participants feel about their own membership in the group, you will see that the more satisfaction and fulfillment members feel, the more cohesive they are. Members of a cohesive group are also enthusiastic, identify with the purposes of

connect

In Chapter 4 we discussed *jargon*, vocabulary unique to a specific hobby or profession. Jargon helps build group cohesion because it connects members to one another. A group of police officers, for example, might speak about *perps* (perpetrators), *vics* (victims), *collars* (arrests), and *brass* (supervisors) — terms that their mechanic or physician friends would not use. This use of language helps officers bond as a group.

the group (Tekleab, Quigley, & Tesluk, 2009), and tell outsiders about its activities. Even positive, constructive argumentation (as opposed to verbal aggressiveness) can be a sign of group cohesion (Anderson & Martin, 1999). Finally, consider how well the group retains members. A cohesive group will retain more members than a noncohesive group.

Gouran (2003) offers several practical suggestions individuals can use for increasing cohesion and fostering a more positive group experience:

- ▶ Avoid dominating other group members.

- ▶ Stay focused on the tasks the group must accomplish.

- ▶ Be friendly.

- ▶ Show sensitivity to and respect for other members.

- ▶ Demonstrate that you value others' opinions.

- ▶ Cooperate with other members rather than compete with them.

Cohesion clearly offers groups tremendous benefits (Uysal, 2016); however, there is also a downside. Too much cohesion can actually cause the group to be unproductive. For example, if you and the other members of your study group enjoy each other's company so much that you talk and laugh together about everything *but* the course material, you will never get your work done, which will hurt your goal of doing well on the exam! In addition, if your group members wish to maintain their cohesion at all costs, they may fail to question or criticize each

communication across cultures

The International American Pastime

The typical Major League Baseball (MLB) team has a full roster of players and a substantial staff of coaches who work with players on specific skills. There is the general manager, a bullpen coach, a batting coach, and a bevy of trainers and coordinators. And, sometimes, there is a language coach.

In any given year, about a quarter of MLB players are foreign born (Lagesse, 2016). Many arrive in American locker rooms with much fanfare but few or no English skills. In order to succeed as part of a team, however, it is crucial that they be able to communicate with their teammates and coaches, both on and off the field. For Asian players — most drafted straight out of the Japanese leagues, like Ichiro Suzuki, Koji Uehara, and Nori Aoki — translators are essential. They have long accompanied players on the field during practices and assisted them in interviews. New MLB rules also allow them to accompany coaches onto the field during games for on-field conferences (Associated Press, 2014).

The rules may not help many Latino players; they do not usually have translators and instead try to rely on bilingual teammates. Some teams, such as the San Diego Padres, teach basic Spanish to their staff. "It's something I thought was important to make us efficient when dealing with players when we're going to the Dominican [Republic] or with our players who are just coming here and don't have command of the English language yet," said Padres Director of Player Development Randy Smith (Brock, 2010). MLB teams also target players long before they get to the big leagues: most teams have training academies in the Dominican Republic, and many have added classes emphasizing English and financial skills to help players better manage living in America (Lagesse, 2016).

think about this

1. How important is it to have all the players on a team speak the same language? Would having a single language policy increase group cohesion? What might the downsides of such a policy be?

2. What other cultural differences might inhibit communication on a professional sports team? How does multiculturalism and globalization affect other sports?

other's knowledge or ideas, even if they are incorrect. In this scenario, you could all end up with the wrong understanding of key concepts that will be on your exam. In the next chapter, we will also see that excessive cohesion and the failure to express disagreement play a key part in groupthink, a serious problem in the group decision-making process.

Norms

As we discussed earlier in this chapter, over time a group will develop norms. Norms emerge within the group and are imposed by members on themselves and each other; they may not be stated outwardly, but they direct the behavior of the group as a whole and affect the conduct of individual members. For example, at the dawn of the digital age, we found ourselves starting to rely on email more than paper copies of work. This paperless norm began a new age in group communication, with faster responses and more articulated feedback. Group members needed to adapt quickly to the changes in order not to feel ostracized and left behind. In a business environment (Uysal, 2016), norms might dictate the kinds of topics that can be expressed in a meeting: Should nontask-related conversation be interjected? Are jokes appropriate? In an online group, norms might evolve to govern the use of foul language, negative comments, or criticism. For example, a study showed that established members of an online anorexia support group allow new members to share pro-anorexic statements in order to establish that they are ill. In time, however, these members are initiated into the group norm that prohibits such unhealthy and negative statements (Stommel & Koole, 2010). In another context, leaders of quilting guilds have developed a unique norm enforcing strategy: they use what are called exemplar narratives (or stories of great work) to maintain the highest standards of quilting without offending members or calling anyone out personally (Launspach, 2016).

Some norms have a negative impact on communication. For example, suppose a group permits one member to dominate the conversation or tends to dismiss ideas before discussing their pros and cons. A group with these norms will have difficulty generating enough diverse ideas to make informed decisions. If you find yourself in a group with unproductive norms like these, consider modifying them—this is possible if you approach the task diplomatically (Brilhart & Galanes, 1992). The following three-step process can help:

1. *Express your loyalty and dedication to the group to show that you have the group's best interests at heart.* For instance, "I've been a member of this school committee for two years now and have hung in there during the tough times as well as the good times. I want to see us be the best we can be."

2. *Cite specific examples of the behavior you find harmful to the group's effectiveness.* To illustrate, "When we didn't take time to explore the pros and cons of the special-ed funding strategy that came up last month, we ended up making a decision that we regretted later."

3. *Ask other members for their opinions about the problem norm you have identified.* If others feel that the norm is still warranted, they may advocate keeping it ("Well, there are some situations where we don't have as much time as we'd like to consider the merits of an idea. During those moments, we need to be able to move ahead with a decision quickly").

Clarity of Goals

Think of the worst group meeting you have ever attended. How would you describe that meeting? Was the conversation disorganized? Unproductive? Confusing? Often such a poor communication climate is caused by the group's lack of a clear goal

connect

As you learned in Chapter 1, *goal achievement* is an important function of communication in all contexts. Just remember that although it is important for a group to keep the end goal in sight, competent communicators are flexible — they try to maintain interdependence while being open to various ideas on achieving goals. They also recognize that the goal itself may change as group members share ideas and present solutions to problems.

to begin with. To communicate productively and promote a positive atmosphere in any group, members need goal clarity: that is, they must understand what the group's purpose is, what goals will help the group achieve its purpose, how close the group is to achieving its goals, and whether the activities members are engaging in are helping the group move toward its goals.

Goals vary considerably from one group to another. For example, a team in one of your classes may have the simple goal of completing a fifteen-minute in-class exercise and reporting the results to the rest of the class. An urban beautification fund-raising committee may have the goal of collecting $4,000 for new landscaping at a neighborhood park.

One effective way to make sure your group has clear goals is to encourage the members to define them as a group. When members take part in establishing goals, they feel more committed to and excited about achieving those objectives. Research shows that a group is more likely to reach its goals when those goals are communicated in terms that are specific ("Raise $4,000 by the end of March"), inspiring ("Imagine our neighborhood becoming a community of choice for young families"), and prioritized ("We'll need to focus on this goal first and then this other one next"; O'Hair, Friedrich, & Dixon, 2007).

Once your group begins working toward its goals, encourage yourself and your fellow members to talk regularly about the decisions you are making and the actions you are taking to ensure that these all support progress toward the goals.

● **JUST AS ANY** Girl Scout troop sets personal and group goals for the cookie-selling season, your groups can productively divvy up responsibilities to make sure you achieve your aims. AP Photo/Matt Slocum

Individual Differences

Members of a group may share norms, goals, and cohesion with their fellow members, but they each also bring personal differences that can strongly affect the communication climate. We now examine how cultural factors and communication apprehension—which vary by individual—affect our ability to communicate in groups.

Cultural Factors

Cultural diversity can have a significant impact on group processes and outcomes (Thomas, Ravlin, & Wallace, 1996). When a group has culturally diverse members, that diversity can have benefits (such as enabling the group to produce a wide array of viewpoints) as well as challenges (including misunderstandings between members). For example, groups of students with international backgrounds are increasingly common in college classrooms. The nonnative language speakers are often more hesitant to speak or feel that their ideas are not being taken seriously (Crose, 2011). It can be helpful to break larger groups into smaller ones, and to have groups rely not only on face-to-face discussions, but also digital channels. Online forums, for example, allow members more time to understand and compose posts and provide a less intimidating environment to ask questions.

Diverse cultural values are also important. As we discussed in Chapter 4, cultures in English-speaking nations such as the United States, Great Britain, and Canada are largely individualist and low context, valuing personal accomplishment, self-esteem, and direct communication. As such, people in individualist cultures want their own opinions heard and appreciated, and they are likely to express them clearly and openly. In a collectivist and high-context culture, people value cooperation and group harmony as well as indirect expression.

and you?

Have you ever misunderstood another member of a group you were involved in because of cultural differences? If so, how did you and the other person deal with the misunderstanding?

connect

If you suffer from communication apprehension in groups, you are probably aware of the negative effects it can have on your social and professional life. Luckily, there are many practical strategies for dealing with apprehension, as we discuss in Chapter 15. Check out our tips on desensitizing yourself, visualizing your success, and taking care of yourself in anxiety-producing situations.

They allow group norms (rather than their own personal goals) to have a larger influence on their behaviors and thoughts (Triandis, Brislin, & Hul, 1988). Not surprisingly, this difference can present a challenge when members of these cultures are working together in groups. People from individualist cultures will likely more openly vocalize their disagreement with the others and try to persuade each other, whereas the collectivists may feel "bulldozed" as they stifle their own objections for the good of the group.

Communication Apprehension

The next time you are sitting in your communication classroom or logging on to a discussion forum in your online course, take a peek around. Is there someone who never speaks up or raises a hand? Perhaps you are assuming that this person has nothing to say or that he or she is a social loafer. Maybe you are right. But it is also possible that this individual feels uncomfortable participating in group conversation, even when his or her contribution would clearly help the group. People who are fearful or nervous about speaking up in groups are experiencing **communication apprehension (CA)**. This anxiety is particularly common in public speaking situations, but it can affect collaboration in groups as well. (We discuss CA more fully in Chapter 15.) Particularly in newly formed groups, individuals experiencing high levels of communication apprehension are less likely to participate; they produce and share fewer ideas with team members, make less significant contributions to the group discussions, and perceive group discussions as less positive than do members of the team with low levels of communication apprehension (Comadena, 1984; Sorenson & McCroskey, 1977). Team members experiencing communication apprehension are also less likely to be perceived as leaders (Hawkins & Stewart, 1991). Within the work environment, those with high levels of communication apprehension prefer to work independently, engage in more listening and observation than action during group interactions, respond less favorably to change and evolving task demands (Russ, 2012), and are much more likely to view participative decision making as valuable (Russ, 2013).

Simple techniques can help a group address communication apprehension among members. For example, to ease self-esteem problems, consider starting a group meeting by having each member tell the member to the left what he or she appreciates about that person. To neutralize status differences, have members sit in a circle, and invite lower-status members to speak before higher-status ones. To rebalance participation, suggest a norm that calls for everyone to weigh in on ideas presented in the group. Or look for members who are holding back and invite them specifically to contribute their views.

Online groups can ease some of the anxiety that individuals may experience while working in a team, but there still are online environments in which communication apprehension manifests. On the one hand, many online environments afford those with high communication apprehension more anonymity and less social risk (Ward & Tracey, 2004), and shy individuals tend to report less communication apprehension during discussions conducted online rather than face to face (Hammick & Lee, 2014). However, studies also reveal that shy and apprehensive college students on Facebook self-disclose less and are less self-expressive (Hunt, Atkin, & Krishnan, 2012), especially in larger, less-private groups (Green, Wilhelmsen, Wilmost, Dodd, & Quinn, 2016). In virtual work teams, members with greater apprehension contribute less (both in terms of quality and quantity) and are less likely to emerge as leaders (Charlier, Stewart, Greco, & Reeves, 2016). Even people who might normally not be apprehensive in groups may, if they perceive their views to be in the minority, find themselves holding back participation

evaluating communication ethics

Sketchy Behavior

You have recently formed a comedy troupe with four other friends: Calvin, Eddie, Meredith, and Sylvia. Your first live show with the group is in just a few weeks, and your group has written and rehearsed five sketches. But you and Calvin have had doubts about one sketch, written by Eddie and Sylvia, since day one. Rather than voice your concerns, you and Calvin have been trying to come up with an alternative sketch. During a late-night session, the two of you come up with an idea for a sketch that in your opinion outclasses the one you have been having problems with.

A few days before the show, the two of you have decided, independent of the other members, that the weaker sketch needs to be changed in favor of the one you have written. You are concerned about how this will look and have a nagging feeling the other members are going to perceive your writing of this sketch as a selfish way to push your work over that of your teammates, but you feel strongly that the new sketch will make the show a greater success. Calvin suggests that you present your sketch to Meredith, since she was not involved in writing either sketch. "If we convince Meredith that our sketch is the stronger one," Calvin reasons, "we'll be able to point to her opinion as a truly objective opinion — she's got no agenda."

You are pretty certain that Meredith will prefer your sketch, not only because you feel it is better but also because it features a role that Meredith would love to play. And you know that if you talk to Meredith beforehand, you will have a clear majority in favor of your sketch should the decision be put to a vote. But is this ethical?

think about this

1. What role did group communication play in this scenario? Might cliques have been involved? What were other communication options?

2. Is it unethical to attempt to gain Meredith's vote even if you honestly believe that it is in the best interest of the group?

3. What ethical implications arise from approaching Meredith with the new sketch? Should the sketch be presented to the entire team at the same time? Is it fair to tempt Meredith with a juicy role in exchange for her vote?

online in fear of negative reactions from others (Neubaum & Krämer, 2016). So regardless of the channel (traditional or online), communicatively apprehensive individuals are more reticent to participate in groups.

Assertiveness and Argumentativeness

Although people who experience communication apprehension are *less* likely to speak up in groups, there are also people whose traits make them *more* likely to speak up. Have you noticed when working on class projects that certain members of your group always seem to voice their opinions boldly or never seem to be afraid to speak out when they disagree with group members? These are likely to be students with assertive and argumentative personalities. **Assertiveness** refers to the use of communication messages that demonstrate confidence, dominance, and forcefulness to achieve personal goals. For example, you are being assertive when you openly tell your group members, "I want an A on this project and would like us all to work as hard as possible to make this happen." Some people have a greater tendency than others to use such assertive messages. **Argumentativeness** is a particular form of assertiveness, in which a person tends to express positions on controversial issues and verbally attack the positions that other people take (Infante & Rancer, 1982) — in other words, people who are argumentative tend, not surprisingly, to argue, and they often even enjoy it! But note that to be "argumentative" and not "aggressive" means that you refute the other people's *positions on issues* — you do not attack them personally!

What effect do assertive or argumentative people have on group interaction? Highly argumentative group members are likely to be more dominant and, hence, play a significant role in group decision making (Limon & La France, 2005). In meetings, for example, individuals who are more argumentative are perceived

and you?

Do you believe argumentativeness to be a trait of group leaders? In a group setting, have you ever experienced a member's argumentativeness to be a hindrance to the group's objectives? How might a group resolve conflicts created by an overly argumentative member?

● IN *GOOD GIRLS REVOLT* the group climate at *News of the Week* encourages communication apprehension among Patty Robinson and her female colleagues, as they struggle to be assertive and argumentative when working through group tasks. © Amazon/Everett Collection/ Courtesy Everett Collection

as more credible communicators (Infante, 1981); within small groups, they are more often perceived as leaders (Schultz, 1980, 1982). Interestingly, research has found that leadership appears to be most strongly associated with higher levels of argumentativeness *in combination with* lower levels of communication apprehension (Limon & La France, 2005).

You might think that group harmony would suffer when people openly assert or argue their positions, but argumentativeness can actually reinforce cohesion within a group (Anderson & Martin, 1999). This is because group members are advocating for the solutions that may be most helpful at accomplishing the group's tasks. Indeed, in most group situations, assertiveness and argumentativeness are perceived as constructive traits (Infante, 1987). It is important to remember, however, that we must distinguish these constructive forms of speaking up with the destructive tactic of "verbal aggressiveness" that we discussed in Chapter 9 as a negative, hostile way of handling conflict.

back to ▶ Team Rubicon

Kirk Jackson, Team Rubicon

At the beginning of the chapter, we were introduced to Team Rubicon, a team of military veterans who provide disaster relief. Let's consider what we have learned in this chapter, and how it applies to the experience of these inspiring veterans.

▶ The name "Team Rubicon" sends two messages. "Team" speaks to the small, cohesive nature of military units. "Rubicon" is taken from the phrase "crossing the Rubicon," a military metaphor that dates back to classical Rome and refers to making a commitment to a difficult course of action from which there is no turning back. By establishing its goals right in the group's name,

Team Rubicon makes both its goals and its means clear. Although the organization has many members, it consists of many small teams that are able to adjust plans and adapt tactics to administer immediate aid in the most dire of circumstances.

▶ The only people who can truly understand what combat veterans are going through are other veterans. Team Rubicon draws on this unique bond as well as the specialized skills of veterans; the group's impact comes in the form of small, platoonlike groups that share a goal and a purpose. That unity, identity, and cohesiveness mean a lot. "It is a brotherhood—or a sisterhood," explains Danielle Harrington, an army reservist and Team Rubicon volunteer who joined hurricane relief efforts in New York in 2012. "It is nice to be around like-minded people, who have the same values and the same ethos" (Hameed, 2012).

▶ In military organizations, roles are assigned to each group member with a clear hierarchy of leadership and designated task roles. These roles are easily adapted to emergency situations, when decisions must be made and actions taken quickly and effectively. That is a large part of Team Rubicon's success. But it is also true that the decisions involved in civilian jobs, higher education, and family life might seem unimportant or insignificant to men and women returning from life-and-death situations. This lack of purpose can be devastating for veterans, especially when coupled with depression or post-traumatic stress disorder.

things to try ▶ Activities

1. LaunchPad for *Real Communication* offers key term videos and encourages self-assessment through adaptive quizzing. Go to **launchpadworks.com** to get access to:

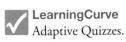

LearningCurve
Adaptive Quizzes.

Video clips that illustrate key concepts, highlighted in teal in the Real Reference section that follows.

2. Consider a group to which you belong—your communication class, your family, your religious community, and so on. Draw a chart that depicts members of the group and the patterns of communication among them. What kind of network does the group most closely resemble?

3. Read up on the history of some influential but now defunct music group (such as the Beatles, or Nirvana). Did the group go through all the stages of group development outlined in this chapter? How did the group determine roles and establish norms? How did members deal with conflict? How did the eventual disbanding of the group play out?

4. Consider the adjourning phase of group development for a group you were part of that disbanded—Scouts, a sports team, the school newspaper staff—and think about what aspects of the group made for the hardest good-bye from the group. Are high-performing groups hardest to leave? Groups with the clearest established norms? What sorts of closing rituals have you experienced?

5. The "secret (gossip) game," passing a message from person to person, is fun simply because of the inevitable message distortion that gets revealed at the end. Can you think of a time when a message was passed to you from an indirect source that you discovered to be blatantly wrong? Maybe it was bungled homework instructions or a wrong meeting time or place. Given these sorts of problems, what type of workplace might function best with a chain network?

6. Analyze the group dynamics from five of your favorite television shows. See if you can identify the various social and antigroup role types in each of the groups.

7. Next time you work in a group, pay attention to how the group works. Does the activity follow a linear model, or is the activity punctuated by periods of inertia and periods of intense activity? How does the group activity pattern differ from your own behaviors when you work alone?

real reference ▶ A Study Tool

Now that you have finished reading this chapter, you can:

List the characteristics and types of groups and explain how groups develop:

▶ A **group** is a collection of more than two people who have a shared identity, have common goals, and are interdependent (p. 238).

▶ **Primary groups** are long-standing and meaningful groups, such as family groups (p. 239).

▶ Specific-function groups include **support groups**, **social groups**, **problem-solving groups**, and **study groups** (p. 239).

▶ A **team** is a task-oriented group, and a **self-directed work team** is a group with responsibility for producing high-quality finished work on its own (p. 239).

▶ Groups often develop through five specific stages: **forming**, **storming**, **norming** (**norms** are recurring patterns of thought or behavior), **performing**, and **adjourning** (p. 242). A **termination ritual** takes place in the adjourning stage of group development, where the group chooses to celebrate its achievements with a final gathering (p. 243).

▶ Some groups show patterns of **punctuated equilibrium**, in which procrastination and inactivity are followed by bursts of intense activity and change (p. 243).

Describe ways in which group size, social relationships, and communication networks affect group communication:

▶ The bigger the group, the more interaction becomes formal, less intimate, more time-consuming, and complex and the less opportunity members have to contribute (pp. 244–245).

▶ **Moderators (mods)** are generally present to make sure no one commenter is monopolizing the discussion board (p. 245).

▶ **Cliques** (coalitions) — small subgroups — may emerge within larger groups, making communication more challenging. A **countercoalition** — a subgroup positioned against another subgroup — may leave unaffiliated members in an awkward position. Some members of cliques may also engage in **social ostracism**, when particular group members are ignored or excluded from participating in the group (pp. 246–247).

▶ Group members are often prone to **social loafing**, giving less effort and making other group members pick up their slack (p. 247).

▶ **Networks** are patterns of interaction governing who speaks with whom in a group. The member who sends and receives the most messages has the highest degree of centrality; at the other end of the spectrum is isolation (p. 248).

▶ In a **chain network**, information is passed from one member to the next rather than shared among members (p. 250).

▶ In an **all-channel network**, all members are equidistant and all interact with each other (p. 250).

▶ In a **wheel network**, one individual is the touchstone for the others (p. 250).

Define the roles individuals play in a group:

▶ **Task roles** involve accomplishment of goals and include information giver, information seeker, elaborator, initiator, and administrator (p. 251).

▶ **Social roles** evolve based on personality traits and members' interests and include harmonizer, gatekeeper, and sensor (p. 252).

▶ **Antigroup roles** put individual needs above group needs and include blocker, avoider, recognition seeker, distractor, and troll (p. 252).

▶ **Role conflict** arises when expectations for behavior are incompatible (p. 253).

▶ Group members with higher status have more power and influence within the group (p. 253).

Explain how a group's cohesion, norms, and individual differences affect group processes and outcomes:

▶ **Cohesion**, how tightly group members have bonded, helps hold the group together in the face of adversity and helps to create a positive climate (p. 254).

▶ Norms direct the behavior of the group, sometimes negatively, requiring modification (p. 256).

▶ Goals should be specific, arrived at by group decision, clearly defined, supported with the necessary resources, and able to be monitored (pp. 256–257).

▶ Individual differences can create communication challenges in groups—including cultural factors and varying levels of **communication apprehension (CA)**, or nervousness about speaking up. Group members also vary in their **assertiveness**—their tendency to use communication openly to accomplish their goals, and their **argumentativeness**—a trait characterized by advocacy for or defense of positions along with the refutation of the positions that other people take (pp. 258–259).

Captain Ray Holt may not have the easiest police squad to command, but his leadership skills make him a respected and effective head of the team.

© Fox Network/Photofest

 LearningCurve can help you master the material in this chapter.

Go to **launchpadworks.com**

Chapter

11

Leadership and Decision Making in Groups

Think back to the first season of *Brooklyn Nine-Nine*. Captain Ray Holt was finally in charge: as the new commanding officer, he arrived at his post intent on turning the precinct into one of the best in the NYPD. But he inherited a motley crew of officers. His two top detectives, the fiercely competitive Amy Santiago and the immature yet effective Jake Peralta, were continually at odds with each other. The mysterious Rosa Diaz did not even try to control her temper. Holt's old friend and new second-in-command, Sergeant Terry Jeffords, was on desk duty after suddenly — and comically — becoming risk-averse after the birth of his child.

But Holt was undeterred. He advised his staff of his high expectations: regulations were to be followed and paperwork properly filed. With his no-nonsense style and an imposing presence, he did not seem like a man to be trifled with. At first that did not stop the childish Peralta: when Holt insisted he wear a necktie, Peralta responded by wearing one around his waist.

Before long, however, Peralta was wearing that tie, Jeffords was back in action, and Diaz was managing to smile at juries during testimony. Holt earned their respect, loyalty, and even obedience, not by coercive power but by explaining himself. Later on in the series, after several years as captain under his belt, Holt learned to adapt the way he led his team. He was more participative, while his ability to express his vision to the other detectives held firm. He demonstrated a charismatic leadership style, even with the threat of murder, that inspired very productive police work (*Brooklyn Nine-Nine*, 2016).

After you have finished reading this chapter, you will be able to

- Explain how a leader's power, style, and personal qualities impact his or her effectiveness

- Identify how culture affects appropriate leadership behavior

- List the forces that shape a group's decision-making process

- List behaviors to improve effective leadership in meetings

- Describe the ways to assess group performance

What makes Captain Holt effective? His power? Experience? Decisiveness? In this chapter we continue our discussion of group communication by examining two additional processes that often emerge in groups: leadership and decision making. These two processes are tightly interrelated: a group's leader affects how the group makes decisions, and the decisions a group makes affect how the leader operates. When leadership and decision making work together in a constructive way, a group stands the best possible chance of achieving its goals. To understand how these processes influence a group's effectiveness, we begin by taking a closer look at group leadership.

Understanding Group Leadership

It is a word that is constantly tossed about in political campaigns, highlighted on résumés, and used in book titles and biographies. But just what is *leadership*? Scholars have grappled with the task of defining leadership for many years.

Two key terms that show up in many definitions are *direction* and *influence*. That is because in its most essential form, **leadership** is the ability to direct or influence others' behaviors and thoughts toward a productive end (Nierenberg, 2009). This capacity for influence may stem from a person's power or simply from group members' admiration or respect for the individual. Because influence involves power over others, let's take a look at power—what it is and where it comes from.

Sources of Power

If you have ever seen the classic Steven Spielberg film *Jaws,* you know that it is, on the surface, the tale of a small coastal town being terrorized by a nasty, man-eating shark. But at the heart of the tale is the interaction among a group of men, each of whom takes some responsibility for ridding the waters of the treacherous animal. There is the town's mayor, whose main priority is protecting the local economy. There is the town's new chief of police, who is thrust into the story when the first body washes ashore. Also playing a role are Matt Hooper, a young marine biologist who studies sharks, and Quint, the war-scarred local shark hunter. Over the course of the film, each man demonstrates leadership that is firmly rooted in the nature of the power he possesses.

Researchers have identified five types of power—legitimate, coercive, reward, expert, and referent (Abudi, 2011; French & Raven, 1959). These types of power are not mutually exclusive, however, and leaders may use several depending on what the situation entails.

> **Legitimate power** comes from an individual's role or title. The president, a work supervisor, and the coach of a team all possess legitimate power as elected or appointed leaders. In *Jaws,* the elected mayor of Amity Island, Larry Vaughn, has some degree of legitimate power as does Martin Brody, the chief of police, though his power is subordinate to the mayor's authority.

> **Coercive power** stems from a person's ability to threaten or harm others. A harsh dictator who keeps his people under threat of violence or economic hardship holds such power, but so does a boss who threatens to suspend or demote employees if they step out of line. In *Jaws,* the mayor—whose primary concern is protecting the town's tourist-dependent economy—uses this kind of power to influence or override decisions made by the police chief: he hired Chief Brody, and he can fire him.

▶ **Reward power** derives from an individual's capacity to provide rewards. For example, your boss might offer all the people in your department a paid day off if they work late three nights in a row on an important project. In the film, the mayor relies on reward power: hundreds of local fishermen set out to catch the shark in hopes of winning a cash prize.

▶ **Expert power** comes from the information or knowledge that a leader possesses. Expert power is divided in *Jaws.* Faced with any other kind of homicide, Brody's credentials as a former New York City police officer might have given him a fair amount of expert power, but as a newcomer without fishing experience, he gets little respect from the islanders. Matt Hooper, who studies sharks, fares a little bit better. But Quint, who has decades of shark-hunting experience, quickly emerges as the true expert, garnering the respect of his crewmates.

● **QUINT, CHIEF BRODY,** and Matt Hooper each bring something different to the shark-hunting mission and derive their power from different sources. © Universal Pictures/Everett Collection/ Courtesy Everett Collection

▶ **Referent power** stems from the admiration, respect, or affection that followers have for a leader. The popular kids in your high school may have had the power to influence other students' style of dress or way of behaving simply because others admired them. In *Jaws,* Quint demonstrates this kind of power: when he relays his story as a survivor of the USS *Indianapolis,* which sank in shark-infested waters during World War II, Brody and Hooper gain a new sense of understanding of, and admiration for, Quint's obsession with killing sharks.

As noted earlier, these types of power are not exclusive of one another; indeed, most leaders wield several, if not all, of these types of power. Consider the instructor for your course. He or she demonstrates legitimate power as your teacher but may also exercise reward and expert power, providing you with extra credit and offering valuable information, respectively. In *Jaws*, Quint demonstrates legitimate power as captain of his own vessel as well as expert and referent power. Note also that individuals gain power only if others grant it to them. That is true to some degree even of coercive power: for example, Brody could have chosen to quit his job early on rather than to acquiesce to the mayor. Thus group members often decide to allow a particular individual to lead them.

Shared Leadership

With so many sources of power, it is not surprising that in some groups, several individuals take on leadership roles, each drawing from different sources of power. Thus leadership can be shared by a few members of the group who divvy up the power and take control of specific tasks. Think of the U.S. presidential cabinet. Despite being the head of the executive branch, the president would be overwhelmed and ineffective without the help of Cabinet leaders in fifteen executive departments. The Secretary of State, for example, leads the State Department on matters of international relations, while the Attorney General handles law enforcement issues in the Department of Justice. Given the colossal size of the federal government, the power

and you?

Consider three groups to which you belong. Is there a clearly established leader for each group? If so, what type of power does this leader have? Do you find certain types of power more ethical or appropriate than others? Explain your answer.

communication across cultures

Gender Judo

Making up 50 percent of the population and 47 percent of the workforce (U.S. Census Bureau, 2012), women are outperforming men in terms of earning college and advanced degrees (National Center for Education Statistics, 2012; Perry, 2013). But when you look at the highest levels of corporate and public sector leadership, it is clearly still a man's world: in January 2017, a mere twenty-one of *Fortune* 500 CEOs were female, and there were only 104 women in the U.S. Congress (and 83 out of 435 in the U.S. House of Representatives). Leaving aside the reasons for the underrepresentation of half the population in corner offices, consider the communication challenges that women working in male-dominated industries face. What is it like to be the lone woman at the boy's club? And how do women overcome preconceived notions of masculine versus feminine leadership styles?

Some women have found that it may actually be effective to use traditionally feminine communication techniques when dealing with an entrenched masculine culture. Work–life legal scholar Joan C. Williams interviewed 127 highly successful women and found that adopting masculine communication styles often backfired. "If you're too feminine," Williams explains, "you're perceived as incompetent. But if you're too masculine, you're seen as difficult to work with." Williams suggests women engage in what she calls "gender judo" (judo being the Japanese martial art of the "gentle way," which involves overcoming your opponent by using his own momentum to overpower him) to remind men of the traditional feminine roles (like that of a mother, daughter, or teacher) with which they are comfortable and using those roles to exert authority. "Be warm Ms. Mother 95 percent of the time," explained one executive, "so that the 5 percent of the time when you need to be tough, you can be" (Williams, 2014).

think about this

1. How do Williams's suggested tactics reflect the concept of behavioral flexibility discussed in Chapter 3?

2. In which contexts do you think it would it be appropriate for women to rely on stereotypically feminine roles in order to lead effectively? In which circumstances might women need to be more traditionally masculine in their approach?

3. How much responsibility do *men* bear for ensuring that they communicate competently and ethically with their female supervisors, colleagues, and staff? Do workplaces need to become, essentially, more feminine?

---

connect

At the heart of the self-directed work team we described in Chapter 10, shared leadership goes beyond improving group member motivation to allow members to set standards for the group, conduct peer evaluations, bring in new members, and coordinate plans with management. The end result is often goal achievement and a sense of cooperation among members rather than divisive competition.

distributed to these cabinet leaders helps the president run government operations more smoothly.

When the talents and powers of each group member are leveraged through shared leadership, members feel more satisfied with the group process and more motivated to perform (Drescher & Garbers, 2016; Kanter, 2009; Serban & Roberts, 2016). As a result, the group is more likely to achieve its goals. Probably for these reasons, many businesses and professional organizations in the United States are moving toward a shared-leadership model, whereby people at lower levels of an organization carry out leadership and decision-making responsibilities (Krayer, 2010) and act in more entrepreneurial ways (Zhou, 2016).

Group Leadership Behavior

What is the best way to lead a group? Should you accept input from the members or rule with an iron fist? Do you focus mainly on the task at hand or help resolve relationship problems? It turns out that there is no one "best" style of leadership. Rather, scholars argue that effective group leaders, whether they are leading alone or sharing power with someone in the group, adapt their leadership behaviors to the needs of the group or the situation at hand. Five behavioral approaches are discussed here — directive, supportive, participative, laissez-faire, and achievement-oriented leadership — each of which works best under different conditions (Gouran, 2003; Pavitt, 1999). Like the sources of power discussed earlier, leadership behaviors are not mutually exclusive, and effective leaders will often employ several approaches depending on the situation.

Directive

A **directive leader** focuses on the group's tasks and controls the group's communication by conveying specific instructions to members. This style works best when members are unsure of what is expected of them or how to carry out their responsibilities. Directive leaders can move their group in the right direction by charting next steps in the group's tasks and clarifying the group's goals, plans, and desired outcomes. For example, the leader of a police squad—like Sergeant Olivia Benson on *Law & Order: SVU*—specifically instructs her team of detectives on how to handle their cases or follow complicated regulations.

● *LAW AND ORDER: SVU'S* Sergeant Olivia Benson never leaves her detectives hanging; she gives them specific and thorough directions for every step of a case. © NBC/Photofest

Supportive

A **supportive leader** attends to group members' emotional and relational needs. This style is especially helpful when members feel frustrated with their task or with each other. Supportive leaders might stress the importance of positive relationships in the group, reminding members of the group's importance, and expressing appreciation for members' talents and work ethic. Consider Tim Gunn of *Project Runway*. As a leader and mentor figure to the aspiring designers, he helps them not only visualize their designs and talk through their frustrations but also encourages team members to communicate with each other, listen to each other, and "make it work." He is always profuse in his praise; even when a particular design does not impress him, he is encouraging and positive in his criticism.

Participative

A **participative leader** views group members as equals, welcomes their opinions, summarizes points that have been raised, and identifies problems that need discussion rather than dictating solutions. This style works well when group members are competent and motivated to take on their tasks but also benefit from their leader's involvement and feedback. Participative leadership seems to be effective in early stages of the innovation process as well (Kesting, Ulhoi, Song, & Niu, 2015). Participative leaders do give assistance and support to group members; however, unlike directive or supportive leaders, they tend to guide and facilitate group discussion rather than giving direct instructions or motivational messages. Many online topic forums and blogs are moderated by participative leaders—they allow discussion among members of the group to take off in many directions, and they contribute right along with everyone else. But they also step in when needed to remind inappropriately contributing members of the purpose of the discussion or the accepted rules of discourse.

Laissez-Faire

The **laissez-faire leader**, whom some call a "hands-off" or delegating leader, gives up a large degree of power or control and gives that power to team members. This style is the absence of overbearing leadership—the leader trusts others to handle their own responsibilities, minimizes her or his own part in the group's discussions

and you?

What type of leader do you prefer when working in a group? Have you ever had a group leader you did not personally like but managed the group effectively? What type of leadership behavior did that person use? Why was it effective?

or work efforts, and provides feedback only when needed. History is replete with effective laissez-faire leaders. President Ronald Reagan was probably one of the most notable leaders with a hands-off style: he set policy for his presidency but stayed out of the way as his administration attended to the details. Successful Apple founder and CEO Steve Jobs was similarly effective at developing grand ideas and setting the tone, but expected his colleagues to carry out the particulars. Warren Buffet, one of the most successful financial investors and leader of a multinational conglomerate of businesses, is also known for his laissez-faire personality. He, like Reagan and Jobs, is a great visionary and clearly communicates his goals for the team and organization. But the laissez-faire type of leadership can be tricky to navigate: it is effective only if you can trust your people to do an effective job in your absence.

Achievement Oriented

An **achievement-oriented leader** (often referred to as path–goal leader) sets challenging goals and communicates high expectations and standards to members. This style works best when group members are highly skilled and eager to produce great accomplishments. In addition to setting lofty goals, such leaders encourage outside-the-box thinking, compare the group with other high-performing groups, and keep members focused on tangible outcomes. In the classic show *Parks and Recreation*, Leslie Knope has an achievement-oriented style of leadership. She identifies an ambitious goal and then does everything in her power to make it happen. Her ambition is often initially at odds with her apathetic coworkers and reluctant community. But her commitment, enthusiasm, and optimism are infectious, and she usually ends up inspiring everyone around her to help pitch in to make it happen.

Leadership Qualities

When leaders are able to adapt their styles to the needs of the groups they guide, they can enhance the productivity and satisfaction of group members in their day-to-day activities. But there are also leaders who have unique qualities that enable them to effect change on a larger scale—be it reforming a school; turning a small company into a huge, multinational corporation; coaching a winning sports team; or inspiring a massive social movement. We now examine some of these unique qualities.

connect ➤

All types of leaders — visionary, transformative, and charismatic — must have the ability to persuade others to their plan or way of thinking. They must be able to speak persuasively (Chapter 17) in a way that resonates with their audience.

▶ *Vision.* **Visionary leaders** are able to picture a new or different reality from what currently exists and consider the bigger, long-range picture of the group's or organization's future (Sashkin & Burke, 1990). They do not just consider how best to reach certain goals, but they also question the very goals themselves and are able to empower group members to take risks, explore possibilities, and develop creative ideas (Margolis & Ziegert, 2016; Uhl-Bien, 2006). Of course, when leading groups on a day-to-day basis, such questioning may stall the progress of basic tasks, but when attempting major reforms or trying to get to the root of serious problems, this kind of vision is a key ingredient of leadership effectiveness (Bennis & Nanus, 1985; Caridizahavi, Carmeli, & Arazy, 2016). For example, a principal at a failing high school might see her school functioning more effectively. She might envision students engaged in cooperative projects, a new computer lab, or mentoring partnerships with members of the surrounding business community.

▶ *Charisma.* Although vision may be important for many kinds of leadership, other leaders may be effective because they have an engaging personality and dynamic speaking style. **Charismatic leaders** are vibrant, likable communicators who generate a positive image among their followers. Their

what about you?

What Type of Leader Are You?

Leadership is the ability to direct or influence others toward a productive end. Leadership behaviors can vary from person to situation. Use the following five-point scale to rate which style of leadership you exhibit: 5 = extremely like me; 4 = somewhat like me; 3 = neither like nor unlike me; 2 = somewhat unlike me; and 1 = extremely unlike me.

_____ 1. I ask a lot of questions to find out what others know.

_____ 2. I usually know or find out the facts and delegate work to group members early on.

_____ 3. I have high expectations and expect everyone to contribute positively.

_____ 4. I watch the emotional reactions of group members to be sure I do not hurt anyone's feelings.

_____ 5. I think that my group members should be able to make their own decisions.

_____ 6. I ask questions and encourage others to participate so they will contribute their ideas.

_____ 7. I organize the group's notes and agenda, paying less attention to individuals.

_____ 8. I figure everyone should share responsibility for making the group successful.

_____ 9. If people are not participating, I will reach out to find out why.

_____ 10. I do not give a lot of feedback to group members; they should know what they are doing.

_____ 11. When a problem arises in a group, I present it and then sit back and listen to everyone's responses.

_____ 12. I am comfortable explaining the overall project and then assigning others to specific tasks.

_____ 13. I expect everyone to have high standards for success.

_____ 14. I pay attention to personal problems that may affect the working environment.

_____ 15. I find that group members will be more successful if I just check in on them occasionally.

Add up your answers for the question numbers that follow, noting the areas with the highest score:

_____ (1, 6, 11): You tend to be a participative leader.
_____ (2, 7, 12): You tend to be a directive leader.
_____ (3, 8, 13): You tend to be an achievement-oriented leader.
_____ (4, 9, 14): You tend to be a supportive leader.
_____ (5, 10, 15): You tend to be a delegating leader.

A mix of high numbers (12–15) indicates a diverse leadership style; as we point out in this chapter, adapting your leadership style to suit your group's needs is an essential leadership skill.

charisma can motivate people and make them respond receptively to their leader's ideas (Bono & Ilies, 2006; Hwang et al., 2015). Charisma has been found to have positive aspects on the communication climate of a group or organization (Zehir, Muceldili, Altingage, Sehitoglu, & Zehir, 2014).

● **ACTIVIST CELEBRITY** Michael J. Fox uses his vision and charisma to invigorate his foundation dedicated to research on Parkinson's disease. Michael Buckner/Getty Images

Without charisma, even leaders with exciting visions for the future may still find it difficult to motivate others to reach their goal. The high school principal might speak enthusiastically at a town meeting about her plans, compliment the community, and maybe even tell tasteful jokes. Her dynamism could help motivate her faculty, her students, their parents, and community leaders to embrace and work toward her goals.

▸ *Initiative.* **Transformative leaders** see change, adaptation, and growth as the means for groups and organizations to survive. They spark change not only by *having* a new vision but also by conveying that vision clearly to others, showing real passion for the work ahead, and energizing the group toward meeting the goals set forth in the vision (Dabke, 2016; Xu, Caldwell, Glasper, & Guevara, 2015). If the principal is able to improve the high school (i.e., to bring reality in line with her vision), she would have to ensure that her incentives or programs actually make students and teachers work harder and that the hard work results in higher levels of engagement and performance. Transformational leadership is an extraordinary form of leadership that causes followers to set and accomplish goals beyond their expectations (Northhouse, 2012).

Many of our most celebrated leaders, like Dr. Martin Luther King Jr. and Mahatma Gandhi, have demonstrated all three of these qualities. Dr. King, for example, had a clear vision for the United States and eloquently articulated it in his seminal "I Have a Dream" speech. He was also charismatic—a gifted writer and speaker with a magnetic personality and a presence that inspired Americans to join him in demanding equal rights for all citizens. And, finally, he was a transformative leader: he motivated those inside the movement to work hard for civil rights, while changing the way others thought about race, rights, and equality. In a similar vein, our effective high school principal may exhibit vision, charisma, and initiative as she successfully transforms her school.

Unethical Leadership

Competent leadership requires more than the ability to adapt your leadership styles to your group or exhibit the effective qualities of vision, charisma, and initiative. Competent leaders also hold both themselves and the group accountable for achieving their results, and they treat all group members in an ethical manner.

However, some leaders use unethical tactics to try to acquire and keep control over an entire group or individual members within a group. As you recall from Chapter 9, some people use verbal aggressiveness to try to get what they want or to "bully" others in online environments. Unfortunately, unethical leaders may also make use of such **bullying** tactics, which include harsh criticism, name-calling,

evaluating communication ethics

Leading the Interns

You are currently working as an editorial assistant at a reputable music magazine. Among your responsibilities is leading a group of summer interns. Reflecting back on how mind-numbing your own magazine intern experience was, your goal is to make theirs more rewarding.

When you were an intern, an assistant named Bradley always seemed to pass off his boring, most tedious work—filing, answering his boss's routine emails, and setting up appointments—to the interns, allowing him time to further his career in rock criticism. In order to be given a good recommendation, you did these tasks, even though what you really wanted to do was talk to writers, write or edit copy, and sit in on pitch meetings. You always resented Bradley, feeling that he had used you.

Now that you are an assistant, you wonder if Bradley actually had the right idea. You too aspire to be a music critic, and the mundane parts of your job are beginning to frustrate you (even though they are in the job description). Having to get lattes for your boss is keeping you from bolstering your portfolio. Yet here are young interns eager to do anything to get ahead, perhaps even taking over those menial tasks. You still want to make sure the interns have a worthwhile experience. What should you do?

think about this

1. Was Bradley wrong, or was he doing what any aspiring journalist would do to free up his time? Do you have a greater understanding for his struggle in light of your own position?

2. Is it OK to pawn your work off on unpaid college students, even if they are willing to do it?

3. Looking back at your own internship, is it possible that it was more valuable than you think? What might you have learned about the business while answering the boss's emails or filing?

gossip, slander, personal attacks, or threats to safety or job security (Smith, 2005). Bullying can also include offensive gestures, ignoring, withering looks, or even just a sarcastic tone of voice. In group situations, a leader might withhold needed information from group members, exclude them from meetings, or insist on unrealistic deadlines or expectations. Sometimes a positive social community or atmosphere at work can help control the negative effects of a leader's bullying (Francioli et al., 2015). Unfortunately, bullying tactics and unethical behavior can sometimes be more advantageous to a leader than ethical behavior. Take the 2016 U.S. presidential race, where the amount of mudslinging and number of ad hominem attacks far outstripped what had been seen in previous elections. With increased media coverage of the candidates and more polarized views among the American population, voters put more stock in candidates who seemed more honest and personally open. But rather than *reinforcing* their personal character to voters, Democratic and Republican candidates focused on *diminishing* the personal character not only of their opponents but also of their opponents' campaign staff, family, and other affiliates. It is highly unethical to dig up personal and irrelevant information to defame an adversary; however, presidential hopefuls in all races have found these tactics—characteristics of unethical leadership—to be a necessary means to an end in the race to the White House.

Although politicians' bullying behavior is aggressive and potentially harmful, it is, at least, transparent. There is little guessing as to what candidates want from their staff or why they use certain tactics. But some unethical leaders might use more sinister means to manipulate their subordinates. Consider, for example, a crime lord who speaks with sweetness and praise, but who also intimidates by hinting at violent consequences for anyone challenging his control in a particular community. On a smaller scale, a supervisor might manipulate employees by pretending to favor one employee's position while also making a "backroom" deal with an opposing employee. Such maneuvering reflects an unethical

connect

In many organizational contexts, bullying behaviors can escalate to illegal harassment, communication that hurts and offends, creating a hostile environment. Victims of bullying may find our tips in Chapter 12 helpful for dealing with such unethical behavior in a group, in an organization, or even in an interpersonal relationship.

● **MACHIAVELLIAN MOBSTER**
Don Corleone from *The Godfather* may seem like a calm family man; however, consider the consequences of not taking him up on one of his "offers you can't refuse." Everett Collection, Inc/Courtesy Everett Collection

leadership style known as **Machiavellianism**, named for sixteenth-century philosopher Niccolò Machiavelli, who advised rulers to use deceit, flattery, and other exploitative measures strategically to achieve their desired ends (Becker & O'Hair, 2007; Christie & Geis, 1970). This leadership style is centered almost exclusively on accomplishing goals regardless of the means (Rao, 2015). Machiavellian leaders in groups may, like bullies, have some success in exerting power and control but at a cost—they are liked less and have less credibility (Teven, McCroskey, & Richmond, 2006).

It is also important to be aware that the very talents and qualities mentioned earlier that make leaders effective can also be used for unethical purposes. Some leaders use their charisma or transformative power for self-serving purposes (O'Connor et al., 1995; Yukl, 1999) or in pursuit of a vision that is morally reprehensible. Consider Adolf Hitler and Osama Bin Laden. Both of these men held visions that were destructive and hateful. However, they possessed the personal charisma to motivate others to work toward their vision—resulting in some of the most notorious acts of evil in human history.

Culture and Group Leadership

As you recall from Chapter 6, culture can strongly shape the way people interact. We look now at culture, which proves to be a particularly powerful factor when leading a group.

Cultural Variations

Two additional leadership factors are the variations we see among cultures, such as whether they are high or low context or value high or low power distance. Recall that people from high-context cultures (such as Japan) tend to communicate in indirect ways, whereas those from low-context cultures (like the United States) communicate with more verbal directness (Hall, 1976; Ward, Ravlin, Klaas, Ploiyhart, Buchan, 2016). Imagine, for example, a manager tasked with keeping a team on target to meet a very tight deadline. A leader from a high-context culture might simply present a calendar noting due dates and filled with tasks and competing projects; she would rely on her team to get the point that the deadline is in trouble and expect team members to offer solutions. A leader from a low-context culture, on the other hand, would be more likely to clarify the situation directly: "I'm moving the deadline earlier by two weeks; that means you'll need to accelerate your work accordingly." The ways in which group members respond will also be influenced by culture: group members from a high-context culture might communicate in a similarly indirect way with their leader ("We have concerns about the new deadline"), whereas those from a low-context culture would be more direct ("Sorry, we can't make the new deadline").

Power distance is another cultural difference that affects how groups may communicate with their leaders (Lian, Ferris, & Brown, 2012). As we discussed in Chapter 6, *power distance* is the extent to which less powerful members of a group, be it a business organization or a family, accept that power is distributed

● **IN A LOW "POWER DISTANCE"** culture, meetings might feel like roundtable discussions, where everyone gets a chance to speak. In a high power distance culture, meetings are usually more hierarchical. (left) Peopleimages/Getty Images; (right) Klaus Vedfelt/Getty Images

unequally. In a high power distance culture, the members are not likely to challenge their leader's opinions or authority. This means that a leader who wants all members to offer their ideas at a meeting might need to make a special effort to encourage everyone to participate in the discussion. In contrast, in a culture with low power distance, members are likely to offer their opinions and disagree with the leader without much prodding.

Gender and Leadership

With a few key exceptions, research has provided little support for the popular notion that men and women inherently lead differently, although the idea has nonetheless persisted. For example, we might assume that men would have a masculine style of leadership, emphasizing command and control, whereas women would have a feminine style of leadership, emphasizing more nurturing relationship environments. However, meta-analyses (which examine the combined results from many different studies) have found that men and women do not differ in overall leadership effectiveness (Eagly, Karau, & Makhijani, 1995). In fact, one study (Rutherford, 2001) even notes that men and women's leadership styles are often dictated by factors *other* than sex and gender, such as the general communication style of the group or organization.

Decision Making in Groups

The blue skies above Cape Canaveral in Florida seemed to be ripped open when the Space Shuttle *Challenger* suddenly exploded shortly after liftoff in January 1986. One of the worst disasters in NASA history (the second being the explosion of the *Columbia* seventeen years later), it claimed the lives of seven astronauts. Investigation into the tragedy found that faulty fittings (called O-rings) had failed during takeoff, causing the explosion. But a large part of the blame for the disaster was laid on communication failures within NASA. Prior to launch, there had been concern among NASA engineers that the O-rings might fail in cold temperatures, but the shuttle launched in spite of these concerns.

How could a collection of such brilliant minds have committed such a grave error? Although faulty leadership may have played a role, there were many people involved in the exchange of information as well as in the final decision making. Indeed, decision making in a group is more complex than decision making by one leader or between just two people, and thus it is important to examine the forces that influence the group decision-making process. In the following sections, we examine each of these topics in detail, looking at the *Challenger* disaster specifically as an example of what can go wrong in group decision making.

Groupthink

The *Challenger* disaster is often pointed to as a classic example of **groupthink**—a problem in which group members strive to maintain cohesiveness and minimize conflict by refusing to critically examine ideas, analyze proposals, or test solutions (Janis, 1982). After the disaster, NASA engineers testified that the climate at NASA made them reluctant to voice their concerns if they could not back them up with a full set of data (McConnell, 1987). Indeed, the Rogers Commission (1986), which investigated the disaster, noted that had safety concerns been more clearly articulated—and had NASA management been more receptive to concerns raised by engineers from various departments—it is unlikely that *Challenger* would have launched that day.

Unity and cohesion are important for groups to operate effectively, but if these qualities are taken to an extreme—that is, if they become more powerful than members' desire to evaluate alternative courses of action—the group cannot generate enough diverse ideas to make smart decisions (Miller & Morrison, 2009; Park, 2000). This appears to have been the case at NASA in the 1980s. In a more receptive group climate, productive conflict over the O-rings might have revealed the problems that the engineers sensed but could not quite voice. The following are symptoms of groupthink that you should be aware of in your group interactions:

▶ Participants reach outward consensus and avoid expressing disagreement so as not to hurt each other's feelings or appear disloyal.

▶ Members who do express disagreement with the majority are pressured to conform to the majority view.

▶ Tough questions are ignored or discouraged.

▶ Members spend more effort justifying their decisions than testing them.

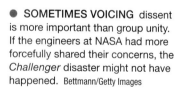

and you?

Thinking back to Chapter 10, how might cliques have played a role in the *Challenger* disaster? Could the fear of social ostracism have prevented scientists from voicing their concern over the faulty O-rings? Did role conflict play a part in NASA's disastrous groupthink?

● **SOMETIMES VOICING** dissent is more important than group unity. If the engineers at NASA had more forcefully shared their concerns, the *Challenger* disaster might not have happened. Bettmann/Getty Images

One important way to prevent groupthink is to encourage dissent among members and manage it productively (Breitsohl, Wilcox-Jones, & Harris, 2015; Klocke, 2007). In fact, some of the same practices for handling interpersonal conflict discussed in Chapter 9 can help you deal constructively with disagreements in a group. For example, frame conflicts as disagreements over issues or ideas, not as evidence of a weak character or a personal shortcoming in particular members. For example, when someone in the group expresses a dissenting viewpoint, rather than saying, "It's clear that you aren't as dedicated to our cause as I had hoped," you might say, "It looks like we have different ideas circulating about how to handle this new problem. Let's list these ideas and talk about the possible benefits and risks of each one." Indeed, in a study of an online cancer support community, researchers found that productive conflict can generate more supportive communication for members than simply expecting members to keep dissenting opinions private (Aakhus & Rumsey, 2010).

The Problem-Solving Process

Even if groups can avoid falling victim to groupthink, that does not necessarily mean they will arrive at good decisions. Some scholars argue that to make effective decisions, groups and their leaders should go through a multistep process (Dewey, 1933; Hirikawa & Gouran, 2006). To illustrate these steps, consider EcoCrew, a group of sixteen environmentally active students at a West Coast community college who wish to resolve environmental problems in their community.

Identifying the Problem

The EcoCrew group has scheduled its first meeting in the student union lounge. Susan, the group's founder, adopts a participative leadership style and invites each person to give his or her perception of the problem that the group will set out to address before debates or questions occur. Members pipe up with a number of issues and activities, such as eliminating plastic bags from campus shops and reducing littering on the beaches.

By inviting members to voice their concerns one at a time, Susan provides an opportunity for the group to identify and define several problems. After discussing the various proposed definitions of the problem, the group decides that litter, both on campus and on the nearby beach, is the most immediately troubling environmental issue.

Having defined the problem it wants to address, EcoCrew has gotten off to an effective start. According to researchers, many groups do not spend enough time identifying the problem they want to tackle (Gouran, 2003). Without a clear, agreed-on problem to address, a group cannot work through the rest of the decision-making process in a focused way.

Analyzing the Problem

Having decided to tackle litter cleanup as its primary mission, EcoCrew begins to analyze the problem. Susan suggests that each member carry a diary for a week and note how much litter they see, and where. When the group meets again the following week, all members agree that the two biggest litter problems in the area are on the beaches and in the wooded areas surrounding the campus parking lots. Several members note that the trash cans on the beaches are not being emptied often enough by city sanitation workers, causing trash overflow to be blown onto the beach by the ocean wind.

● **WRITING DOWN** any ideas that your team has can be a great way to get the creative juices flowing. Paul Bradbury/Getty Images

Generating Solutions

Once the EcoCrew team has identified and analyzed the problem, the next step is to come up with a solution.

The group engages in a technique called **brainstorming**, in which members of a group come up with as many ideas as possible without first judging the merits of those ideas. Someone must be sure to write down the ideas on a whiteboard, notepad, or laptop. The intent is to prompt fresh thinking and to generate a larger number of potential solutions than a group might arrive at if members evaluated each idea as it came up. As the EcoCrew members throw out idea after idea, the list grows dense with possibilities (see Figure 11.1).

Once the members have run out of new ideas, they will need to narrow down the list by defining the criteria that eventual solutions will have to meet. First, Susan reminds them that the primary goal is to reduce litter on the beach. One member, Wade, points out that the group has no funding, so they need to limit their efforts to tasks that have little or no cost. Another member, Larissa, notes that because their group has a relatively small membership, they should focus on things either that the group can manage on its own or in which the group could encourage nonmembers to participate. The group concludes that an acceptable solution must meet these key criteria.

Evaluating and Choosing Solutions

Once EcoCrew has generated its list of possible solutions, group members have to evaluate the pros and cons of each idea to consider how well it meets the criteria

connect ➤

Brainstorming and clustering can help you in both public speaking and small-group settings. When choosing a topic, both strategies allow you to generate ideas based on your interests, your audience's interests, and your time constraints (Chapter 13). In a group, brainstorming and clustering allow you to identify and discuss solutions from a variety of perspectives to ensure that the solution meets the needs of the group.

FIGURE 11.1

ECOCREW'S WHITEBOARD

- More trash cans!
  - Can we provide these?
  - Get the city to provide?
- Covered trash cans that keep litter in—wind-resistant?
- Increase city sanitation pickups!
  - Letter writing/email campaign?
  - Contact the mayor?
- Beach cleanup?
  - Massive volunteer beach cleanup event
  - Monthly volunteer beach cleanup
- Antilitter advertising? "Don't pollute!"
  - Flyers/posters would create more litter.
  - Permanent signs/billboards? $$$$

the members have defined. For example, one member, Kathryn, points out that the lack of funding makes replacing the garbage cans out of the question and would make an antilitter advertising campaign difficult, if not impossible. Wade notes that organizing a beach cleanup would cost next to nothing: they could all get together to pick up garbage and clean up the beach. Larissa adds that if they get the word out via social media, they could attract additional volunteers—and potential new members—from outside the group to participate. So the group decides to launch a monthly beach cleanup: this regular social event will raise awareness of the group, encourage nonmembers to participate and new members to join, and cost little to nothing.

Implementing the Solution

Implementing a solution means putting into action the decision that the group has made. For EcoCrew, this means enacting their plans for the regular beach cleanup. The group focuses first on logistics—setting dates and times. One member, Allison, volunteers to act as a liaison with the county sanitation department to see if it can provide trash bags and picks for the volunteers and to arrange for the sanitation trucks to pick up the trash once it has been bagged.

● **AFTER THEIR BEACH** cleanup, the EcoCrew team needs to assess the results. Michael Buckner/Getty Images

Larissa agrees to handle the social media outreach in order to turn the cleanup into a large community event; she arranges for her mother's sandwich shop to donate food, and posts updates on Facebook, Instagram, and Twitter about the end-of-day celebration for volunteers. Wade promises that he can get his roommate's band to entertain free of charge as well.

Assessing the Results

Once a group has implemented its agreed-upon solution, members should evaluate the results. Evaluation can shed light on how effective the solution was and whether the group needs to make further decisions about how to address the problem in the future. For EcoCrew, it will be helpful to assess the first event in terms of how well it met the three key criteria:

▶ Was the beach cleaner at the end of the day as a result of the group's efforts? Before-and-after photos of the beach reveal a very successful cleanup.

▶ Did the event wind up costing the members any money? Thanks to the donations of local restaurants and supplies provided by the county sanitation department, along with free advertising via social networks, the event cost the group absolutely nothing.

▶ Did the event attract volunteers from outside the group? Fifteen nonmembers participated in the cleanup, among them several schoolchildren who attended with their parents.

By revisiting these criteria, the group is able to adjust its plan for the following month's cleanup event. Kathryn volunteers to submit a brief story about the cleanup, along with photos, to the campus newspaper. Susan suggests holding a raffle at the next event, with half the proceeds paid out in prizes and half retained by the group, to get a small budget started to cover future ads and expenses.

and you?

Consider the six steps to problem solving we have just discussed. If the leader of EcoCrew had chosen a different leadership style, would this have affected how the problem-solving steps were carried out? If so, how? What has your experience been in solving problems in groups with different types of leaders?

connect

Planning a meeting can be similar to planning a speech, particularly regarding audience analysis (Chapter 13). In both contexts, you must be aware of the expectations and goals of others involved (your audience or attendees): Why are they present? Why should they listen to you? How is the meeting or speech relevant to them? In addition, you need to consider the situational context for the event (location, room setup, etc.) in both contexts to ensure that it will not inhibit communication.

Leadership in Meetings

EcoCrew was able to identify a problem, create a solution, and implement it very successfully. Much of the planning and implementation took place in meetings. Whether they are face-to-face, over the phone, online, or through a combination of media, meetings are an integral part of many group activities. But they are not always successful, and the failure of a meeting often rests on the shoulders of the group leader.

Consider Julia, a freelance website designer who is working on a new website for her biggest client, a skateboard manufacturing company. On Friday, Julia received an email from CEO Jacob asking her to phone in to a meeting to discuss marketing plans for the launch of the new site. Struggling with several competing deadlines, Julia dreaded spending time listening to parts of the project she had little to do with, but reluctantly confirmed that she could take part in the meeting the following Monday.

After spending Monday morning reviewing her design and outlining a few ways to tease it into the marketing campaign, Julia dialed into the meeting at the designated time, only to be placed on hold for twenty minutes. What followed was equally frustrating: Jacob spent an hour describing the site as a whole to the team of salespeople, who were entirely unfamiliar with the project. Julia — who had nothing to do with marketing or sales — sat miserably watching the clock.

Meetings can often be unproductive and frustrating. Ineffective meetings are one of the top time wasters cited by workers. According to one study, while executives spend as much as eighteen hours a week in meetings, 25 to 50 percent feel their time is wasted (Bailey, 2013). This does not have to be the case. Research underscores the value of meetings and shows that they can contribute to employee empowerment and information management in organizations (Allen, Lehmann-Willenbrock, & Sands, 2016). In this section, we analyze meetings from a communication perspective and consider how they can be best used to arrive at better decisions and solutions. We discuss how technology has changed meetings — and how it has not. Most important, we show that effective leadership is crucial to conducting effective and productive meetings.

Planning Meetings Effectively

Let's consider the reasons Julia found the meeting we just described so frustrating. First, it came at a bad time: she was struggling to meet deadlines and did not want to stop working to call into a meeting. Worse, it was probably not necessary for her to call in — Jacob was using the meeting to inform the sales team about the site as a whole, not to discuss Julia's design. Further complicating the issues were the meeting's late start, Julia's unfamiliarity with the sales force, and a medium — speakerphone — that limited her communication with the team. Put simply, the meeting was poorly planned.

Proper planning is crucial for successful meetings. Making a few decisions beforehand and taking steps to clarify goals and logistics for the team can lead to more effective decision making during the meeting itself. There are several steps that group leaders can take to plan meetings more effectively.

and you?

How do you feel about group meetings? Do you find them energizing, boring, or a waste of time? Consider an effective meeting and an ineffective meeting that you have attended. To what degree did the leaders plan appropriately, justify each meeting, and clarify the purpose? How involved were nonleaders? Was their involvement initiated by the leader, or prompted by other means?

▶ *Justify the Meeting.* Before calling a meeting, a group leader must consider what he or she wants to accomplish and assess whether a meeting is even necessary to meet that goal. The leader also needs to ensure that only those members whose presence is necessary in order to meet the goals or who would truly benefit from attending are invited. In addition, meetings can be avoided altogether or made smaller and more efficient by asking team members to contribute information ahead of time or simply picking up the phone to ask someone a question when one arises (Conlin, 2006).

▶ *Clarify the Role of Participants.* If a meeting is necessary, it is the responsibility of the leader to alert members in advance of the reason for the meeting and the roles of everyone who is to attend. Think back to Julia's situation. Her client, Jacob, wants to get his salespeople interested and excited about the launch of the website. Getting the sales force together to view the beta version and get feedback on it might seem like a good way to brainstorm ideas for marketing. But Jacob failed to think ahead about what he wanted to accomplish at the meeting and what Julia's role would be. He might have made a more efficient use of Julia's time by discussing elements of the design with her prior to the meeting or asking her to outline a few key features for him to use in the meeting without her actually attending.

▶ *Set an Agenda.* President Dwight D. Eisenhower noted, "I have often found that plans are useless, but planning is indispensable." Creating a plan is a crucial step in preparing for meetings, even if the plan itself is not followed to the letter in the end. An **agenda** is a plan for a meeting that details the meeting's subject, goal, logistics, and schedule. It also lists or includes as attachments any materials that participants would need to have read or reviewed in advance of the meeting so that everyone arrives with the appropriate background on the issue. Think of the agenda as a checklist—an essential component of meeting success (Gawande, 2009). A sample agenda for Jacob's meeting is provided in Figure 11.2.

OWIT, Inc.
Meeting on 4/25/18 at 12:00 P.M.

AGENDA

▶ Call to order (Westerfield—1 minute)
▶ Reading and approval of minutes from February 8, 2018 meeting (Westerfield—10 minutes)
▶ Establishing and reporting a quorum (Parliamentarian—2 minutes)
▶ Old business (Westerfield—10 minutes)
▶ Reports of standing committees
   ▶ Budget and finance (Jackson—5 minutes)
   ▶ Suspensions and reinstatements (Holloway—10 minutes)

▶ Reports of special committees
   ▶ 2020 conference (Holloway—5 minutes)
   ▶ Inviting new members (Barton—5 minutes)
   ▶ New land acquisition (Simpson—5 minutes)

▶ New business
   ▶ United Way golf tournament partnership (Barnhart—10 minutes)
   ▶ Next generation data management systems (Lane—15 minutes)
   ▶ Evaluation report for new printer vendor (Gutierrez—10 minutes)
   ▶ Reform performance evaluation system (Wilson—10 minutes)

▶ Comments from the group (10 minutes)
▶ Adjournment (Westerfield)

FIGURE 11.2

AGENDA FOR OWIT, INC. For meetings to run smoothly and on time, it is helpful to indicate who is responsible for presenting a particular portion on the agenda, and how much time the person has for that portion.

connect

To keep a group focused and productive, you must employ effective listening skills (Chapter 7). You might think that leaders should talk more than listen, but without informational, critical, and empathic listening skills, they miss opportunities to learn new information from others or to analyze ideas that might help the group achieve goals.

● **ALTHOUGH DR. MINDY LAHIRI** and her colleagues on *The Mindy Project* often disagree about how best to run their practice, they are able to work through disputes to manage a well-respected office known for strong patient care. Everett Collection, Inc/Courtesy Everett Collection

Managing Meetings Effectively

Planning ahead is an important step toward holding a successful meeting; however, leaders also need to be effective at running the meeting itself. It is the leader who is responsible for managing the discussion in ways that help the group communicate while remaining focused on the meeting's goals. The following steps can help.

▶ *Arrive Prepared.* Once a leader has done the necessary planning, he or she must then bring the group together, articulate the goals for the meeting, and present the agenda. It is also important for leaders to have at the ready any visual aids (such as PowerPoint slides or handouts) and supporting materials (such as data summaries or mission statements) that they may need to help guide discussion.

▶ *Set Ground Rules.* Rules provide the mechanism for snatching order from the clutches of chaos (Schwarz, 2016). Groups are each unique and will require different rules depending on their mission, composition, and purpose. So group leaders need to establish a set of ground rules that works for them. Examples include agreeing on the definition of important words and terms, deciding how they will share important information with outsiders, and deciding next steps.

▶ *Keep the Group Focused.* Participants often contribute relevant information during meetings but also often get off track. When a member brings up a topic that is not on the agenda or goes off on a tangent, the leader can bring the group back to the main focus of the meeting by politely interrupting and noting, "We're getting off the subject here" (Business Week, 2005).

▶ *Keep an Eye on the Time.* Nobody likes wasting time sitting through a long meeting when a short one would do. Group leaders need to be aware of time constraints to keep their meetings running efficiently and to respect the time pressures on the members. When large groups are involved or when the agenda includes many topics or issues, it can be helpful to impose time limits on certain components of the discussion. When a decision must be made, taking an informal vote on a decision—a tactic called a **nonbinding straw poll**—can help move the group forward.

▶ *Manage Distractions.* Unfortunately, even the best of us can easily become distracted. In particular, the use of cell phones during meetings can really harm group productivity: checking email, texts, or social media is inappropriate and often offensive to colleagues. Research shows that cell phone use impacts the way group members perceive individual communication competence (Tolman, 2012). Thus it is essential that the group comes up with a policy and enforces the rules regarding proper etiquette and behavior during its meetings, particularly in regard to cell phone use.

▶ *Manage Conflict.* As discussed earlier, productive conflict in groups can lead to good decisions (Kuhn & Poole, 2000; Nicotera, 1997). Leaders can facilitate this by encouraging members to ask clarifying questions, respectfully challenge one another's ideas, and consider worst-case scenarios. However, leaders need to curtail unproductive conflict, such as personal attacks and hostile comments. Leaders can also urge members to strive for **consensus** — group solidarity in sentiment, belief, or decision — rather than just allowing decisions to be made by majority vote. If everyone must agree on the final decision before it can be implemented, it can be a powerful way to enhance feelings of ownership and commitment from group members. One caution, however, is to be careful to encourage *genuine* consensus, rather than allowing group members to silence their opposition in order to preserve group harmony.

► *Summarize Periodically.* As a group explores and settles on decisions, it is important that the leader encourage someone in the group to summarize what is happening throughout the conversation. Summaries provide members with opportunities to confirm, correct, or clarify what has occurred so far. Summaries also help ensure agreement, formation of next steps, and how members are to carry out their designated tasks.

► *Follow Up.* Checking in with group members after the meeting has concluded can ensure that everyone came away with the same perceptions of what was decided and what each member must do to keep the group moving toward its goal. Depending on the nature of the group, a leader may follow up with a simple email or post the meeting's minutes to the group's online workspace. If group members are expected to reply or provide feedback, that is an important part of the follow-up communication as well.

and you?

Do you have experience with group conflict as either a group member or leader? If so, how was this conflict handled? Did conflict strengthen or weaken the communication between group members?

real communicator

NAME: Aaron Tolson
OCCUPATION: Dancer, Choreographer, Instructor
Courtesy Aaron Tolson

I jump feet first into my work. I am a tap dance instructor, performer, and choreographer, and—together with my voice—I use my feet to champion the art form, promote it worldwide, and share it with others.

As a teacher, I take the role of directive leader, as students come to me from all over the world for instruction on how to learn the art of tap. This type of dance is very popular throughout Europe and also in Russia and in Japan, so I have the pleasure of working with a varied group of international students. I read my classes for their learning style, observe their nonverbal behavior, and adapt my leadership approach accordingly. The pace and tempo of the classes vary, as well as my leadership behaviors. For example, I'm less sarcastic with older students and use more humor with younger groups.

I've been interested in dance since the age of ten. I also ran track. I was given a track scholarship to college, where I earned an undergraduate degree in communication. During my time there, I also focused on looking for opportunities to dance wherever I could. By my senior year, I landed a place in the New York Shakespeare Festival tap program, Funk U!

Having become a leader in the tap community, I was made national spokesman for SóDança, a professional dancewear company. Because I was chosen for my expertise, I appreciate the opportunity to try out their tap shoes and offer ideas to make them even better. In an effort to enhance and develop tap opportunities for aspiring dancers, I helped to create Speaking in Taps, a preprofessional company designed to teach youth, as well as Tap2You, a program that offers classes and tap competitions (which I started with a business partner, Derick Grant). Through all these endeavors, I strive to emphasize the rhythm, musicality, and timing of tap with a strong focus on performance and education. I hope to inspire others to do what I did: jump feet first into a dancing career.

● **RESEARCH INDICATES** that although group members work better face to face initially, individuals who are familiar with each other and established as a team also work productively with videoconferencing technology. B Busco/Getty Images

Using Meeting Technology Effectively

Technology has changed the nature of meetings in both positive and negative ways. Of course, the ability to set up virtual meetings through teleconferencing and internet videoconferencing makes it possible for groups to collaborate over long distances. Such virtual links can be critical for a team whose members regularly work in different locations or when matters cannot wait until everyone is next in the office. The ability to share information with team members quickly and efficiently via email and file sharing has even enabled teams to avoid some meetings altogether (Conlin, 2006).

However, is there a difference in performance or quality between face-to-face meetings and virtual meetings? Research indicates that face-to-face teams perform better initially. But once the group has been established, virtual teams actually do better at brainstorming, whereas face-to-face teams perform better on tasks that require negotiation or compromise (Alge, Wiethoff, & Klein, 2003; Salkever, 2003). In one study, virtual teams performed worse on a decision-making task when the task had an obvious correct solution (O'Neill, Hancock, Zivkov, Larson, & Law, 2016). Savvy team leaders, then, will bring their teams together for face time early in the process, if possible, so that team members can get to know one another and get a sense of the others' styles and personalities. But as the teams develop, electronically mediated communication—especially email—can often take the place of face-to-face group meetings.

Evaluating Group Performance

Groups that intend to work together and meet on a regular basis should evaluate their decision-making performance periodically (Krayer, 2016). By assessing how well the group makes decisions, achieves its goals, and solves problems, a group can identify and address areas needing improvement. Regular and consistent assessment helps ensure quality and improvement (Levi, 2017). When evaluating your group's performance, it is helpful to assess the group's overall effectiveness as well as the performance of individual members and leaders.

Scholars with extensive research on evaluating groups recommend assessing multiple aspects of a group's performance (Kowitz & Knutson, 1980; Levi, 2017). We focus on three: the informational, procedural, and interpersonal considerations.

Informational Considerations

Ask yourself whether your group is working on a task that requires everyone's expertise and insights. If not, the group may not actually need to be a group. Instead, one or two members might address the task on their own, allowing the group either to disband or to shift its attention to tasks that do involve everyone.

For tasks that require contributions from everyone, members of the group must evaluate how well they are doing on this front. Are they conducting needed research and inviting one another to share information during meetings? Do they know when they need to get more data before making a decision? How well do they analyze problems and generate creative solutions? By regularly assessing these aspects of information management, you can identify where your group is falling short and address the problem effectively. For example, if you learn that your group tends to rush to a decision without getting all the facts first, you might intervene to slow them down the next time ("I think we need to find out more about this problem before we take action").

Procedural Effectiveness

How well does your group coordinate its activities and communication? Key things to evaluate on this front are how the group elicits contributions, delegates and directs action, summarizes decisions, handles conflict, and manages processes. For example, do some members talk too much while others give too little input? If so, the group needs someone to improve the balance of contributions ("I think we should hear from other people on this subject"). Or does your group tend to revisit issues it has already decided on? If so, you can expect many members to express frustration with this time-wasting habit. A leader or another member can steer the group back toward its current task ("OK, what we've been talking about is . . ." or "I'm not sure revisiting this previous decision is helping us deal with our current problem.").

wired for communication

Robots Are Here to Stay

The notion of robots has been around for many years, some of the most famous being R2-D2 (*Star Wars*), Deep Blue (IBM's chess-playing bot), and Data (*Star Trek*). In recent years working robots have made the transition from science fiction to reality, making their entrance into society and the workplace in rapid fashion. Robots are already popular in the manufacturing sector and have become a key innovation for analyzing "big data." In a 2016 report by the World Economic Forum, the mass adoption of robots is being called the "fourth industrial revolution," involving technologies—such as avatars, mobile sensors, smart agents, and artificial intelligence—that are "blurring the lines between the physical, digital, and biological spheres" (Kharpal, 2016).

But what if real robots became more like R2-D2, Deep Blue, and Data, performing more interactive tasks and holding leadership roles? The idea might not be that far-fetched. According to Melonee Wise of Fetch Robotics, robots have great potential to become more collaborative and social, performing tasks that only humans could do before (Fitzpatrick, 2016). Robots can already teach foreign languages to children, and some have become counselors. The next step in robotic evolution might just be a robot's capacity to demonstrate leadership qualities. It is important to remember that humans are not unique in their leadership skills: insects such as ants and honeybees have long been known for active leadership among their colonies and swarms, and animals including fish (sticklebacks), macaques, and spider monkeys exert notable leadership qualities among their groups (Pugliese, Acerbi, & Marocco, 2015). If insects, animals, and humans develop and demonstrate leadership skills, why not robots? In studies of small groups of similar robots, robots have been found to demonstrate leadership qualities and, over time, some emerge as leaders. The findings suggest that, like strong human leadership, robot leadership increases the "overall fitness of the group" (Pugliese, Acerbi, & Marocco, 2015).

How will humans adapt to robots as they become woven into the normal fabric of life? Initial research indicates that humans are still uncertain about interacting with robots and feel that bots will not deliver the same level of social presence as humans would (Spence, Westerman, Edwards, & Edwards, 2014). A key step going forward appears to be normalizing robot communication in the general population, much in the way other technologies have been normalized, such as smart watches and self-driving cars.

1. How prevalent do you think robots will become in the next five years? What is their potential for communicating meaningfully with humans?

2. How comfortable are you with robots taking on more human qualities such as collaboration, socializing, and leadership?

3. In which types of task do you think robots could effectively demonstrate leadership skills?

4. What are the downsides with robots becoming more integrated into our life?

connect

As you evaluate interpersonal performance, you are essentially determining what type of climate your group has developed. As we discussed in Chapter 9, supportive climates — in which individuals are open to and supportive of one another's ideas — often have an advantage in being effective and achieving goals.

Interpersonal Performance

How would you describe the relationships among the members of your group? If feelings are strained, awkward, or prickly, the group will probably not function effectively. To evaluate interpersonal performance, observe how well your group members: provide *positive reinforcement* (such as showing appreciation for each other's contributions); show *solidarity* (such as sharing responsibility for both successes and failures); *cooperate freely* (such as pitching in when needed); and *demonstrate respect* (such as focusing disagreements on issues rather than personal character).

Individual Performance

One of the most important assessments you can make is about the predispositions you yourself bring to your group. One negative disposition is **group hate**, the extent to which you detest (or otherwise feel negatively about) working in groups (Keyton & Frey, 2002). People with high group hate value their own independent work and dread having to coordinate efforts with other people, compared to those who enjoy working in groups and value the teamwork experience. Group work can at times be frustrating for anyone, but if you are already negatively oriented toward groups, your attitude may be contributing to your group's difficulties.

In addition to considering your own contribution to the group, your group may also benefit from systematic assessments of all team members. One method is to have each team member rate all of the other team members on a variety of qualities. The ratings may include the extent to which group members prepare for meetings, meet their responsibilities and deadlines, treat other members with respect, deal with conflict appropriately, contribute valuable ideas, and so on.

Both self-assessment and peer evaluations can provide information that can benefit the group by identifying areas of concern or deficiency and suggest specific areas for improvement. This information will help improve the group process and decision making. In sum, assessment is healthy for the life and success of a group.

back to ▶ Brooklyn Nine-Nine

© Fox Network/ Photofest

Let's return to the beginning of this chapter, where we look at Captain Ray Holt, the fictional commanding officer at a New York police precinct on the sitcom *Brooklyn Nine-Nine*. Let's take a look at Holt's leadership in light of what we have learned in this chapter.

▶ There is a clear hierarchy of legitimate power in the NYPD. As commanding officer, Captain Holt has authority over all of his detectives, but even a captain must defer to the chiefs who outrank him. For Holt, this means "being a good soldier" and working in the public affairs office for many years. Holt has developed a level of charisma over time that is appreciated by his detectives.

▶ Holt's power is rooted not only in his rank as captain (legitimate power) but also in his experience as a veteran officer who knows how to solve major cases (expert power). As commanding officer, he also has coercive and reward power—he can reward or punish his detectives based on their performance. Over time, Holt has been able to communicate his vision for the department; through his participative leadership qualities, he has gotten buy-in from his detective colleagues.

▶ In a police squad room, there is an expectation of a directive style of leadership—supervisors lay out clear instructions, and officers are expected to follow them. But Holt knows that, despite their hijinks, his detectives are capable and competent. For this reason, he can take a more achievement-oriented approach, setting goals and providing guidance for meeting those goals.

 **Activities**

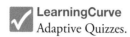

1. LaunchPad for *Real Communication* offers key term videos and encourages self-assessment through adaptive quizzing. Go to **launchpadworks.com** to get access to:

   LearningCurve
   Adaptive Quizzes.

   ▶ Video clips that illustrate key concepts, highlighted in teal in the Real Reference section that follows.

2. Arrange an interview with the chair, president, or director of an organization to determine how the various groups within the organization operate. How closely do these groups conform to the decision-making process discussed in this chapter? Report what you have learned to the class.

3. Create a chart that lists the four leadership styles described in this chapter (directive, participative, supportive, and achievement oriented). Evaluate the leaders of each of the different groups in which you participate—your boss at work, your professors, your resident assistant in the dorm—in terms of their leadership style. Where do they fall on your chart? Do some fit more than one category? Do some fit none of the categories?

4. Select a city, state, or campus problem that is relevant to the members of your class. Form a group to solve the problem using the six-step decision-making process described in this chapter.

real reference ▶ **A Study Tool**

Now that you have finished reading this chapter, you can:

Describe the types of power that leaders employ:
- **Leadership** is the ability to influence others' behaviors and thoughts toward a productive end (p. 266).
- **Legitimate power** comes from an individual's role or title (p. 266).
- **Coercive power** stems from the ability to threaten or harm others (p. 266).
- **Reward power** is derived from the ability to bestow rewards (p. 267).
- **Expert power** comes from the information or knowledge an individual possesses (p. 267).
- **Referent power** stems from the respect and affection that followers have for a leader (p. 267).

Describe how leadership styles should be adapted to the group situation:
- A **directive leader** gives specific instructions (p. 269).
- A **supportive leader** attends to members' emotional and relational needs (p. 269).
- A **participative leader** views members as equals, inviting collaboration (p. 269).
- A delegating leader, whom some call a "hands-off" or **laissez-faire leader**, allows group members to carry out tasks on their own (pp. 269–270).
- An **achievement-oriented leader** sets challenging goals and has high expectations (p. 270).

Identify the qualities that make leaders effective at enacting change:
- **Visionary leaders** envision the long-range future (p. 270).
- **Charismatic leaders** use an engaging personality and dynamic communication style (p. 270).
- **Transformative leaders** energize others and make real changes (p. 272).
- Unethical leadership behaviors include **bullying**; the use of aggressive tactics; and **Machiavellianism**, or leadership by manipulation (pp. 272–274).

Identify how culture affects leadership behavior:
- Leaders from high-context cultures tend to make suggestions rather than dictating orders or imposing solutions (p. 275).
- Masculine leadership values hierarchy and control, and feminine leadership values relationships and nurturing (p. 275).

List the forces that shape a group's decisions:
- **Groupthink** occurs when members avoid challenging the group's ideas or decisions (p. 276).

Explain the six-step group decision process:
- Identify and define the problem (p. 277).
- Analyze the problem (p. 277).
- Generate solutions by **brainstorming**, coming up with as many ideas as possible, and then identifying the criteria that solutions will have to meet (p. 278).
- Evaluate and choose a solution (p. 278).
- Implement the solution (p. 279).
- Assess the results (p. 279).

List behaviors to improve meetings:
- Assess whether the meeting is necessary, ensure that those present are necessary, ask for information in advance, articulate goals, and set an **agenda** (pp. 280–281).
- To manage the meeting, arrive prepared; keep the group focused; keep an eye on the time, perhaps use a **nonbinding straw poll** to manage distractions; manage conflict; summarize periodically; consider making decisions by **consensus**; and follow up (pp. 282–283).

Demonstrate aspects of assessing group performance:
- Informational considerations (p. 285).
- Procedural effectiveness (p. 285).
- Interpersonal performance (p. 286); avoid **group hate**, or negativity toward working in groups (p. 287).

Though Zappos has nearly 1,500 employees, it has managed to keep its warm, welcoming culture with core values such as "Create fun and a little weirdness."

Charley Gallay/Getty Images

 LearningCurve can help you master the material in this chapter.

Go to **launchpadworks.com.**

chapter

12

Communicating in Organizations

Where did you get those shoes? If they arrived on your doorstep just thirty-six hours after you clicked an image of them online, chances are they came from Zappos.com. The company, founded in 1999, has earned a reputation for not only offering customers a huge selection of clothing and accessories, but also for providing a user-friendly at-home shopping experience, complete with free returns. For Zappos, the challenge was maintaining its family-like culture as the company grew from a small start-up into a large, thriving organization with close to fifteen hundred employees.

The company's core business standard, explains Zappos CEO Tony Hsieh, is rooted in what he calls the "three Cs": clothing, customer service, and company culture. It is the last item on the list that Hsieh feels is the most important. By prioritizing positivity, learning, work enjoyment, and employee input within the company's culture, Hsieh says that superb customer service, consistent growth, and brand recognition become a natural by-product. With that sentiment in mind, Zappos recently transitioned to a "holacracy"—an organization characterized by teams who self-organize and self-manage their work rather than working within the traditional hierarchy of boss and employee (Stevens, 2016). Hsieh believes so strongly that the future of Zappos is contingent on the adoption of a holacratic culture that he gave his employees an ultimatum: adapt to the new horizontal power structure and learn how to self-govern, or take a severance package. But in the Zappos spirit, employees would be welcomed back if they changed their mind (Feloni, 2016).

Despite the loss of 18 percent of his workforce Hsieh believes Zappos will see the benefits to the new system once employees recognize the personal empowerment such a system will create. "I want employees to operate in the intersection between what they are passionate about and what's going to help move the company forward. I want them to be able to come up with an idea and then, rather than having to go through a bureaucratic approval process, run with the idea and find people who'd like to join them" (Hsieh, 2016).

After you have finished
reading this chapter, you will
be able to

- Describe and compare
  approaches to managing an
  organization

- Describe ways in which
  organizational culture is
  communicated

- Contrast relational contexts in
  organizations

- Identify the challenges facing
  today's organizations

The management at Zappos takes a particular interest in developing a culture within and around the company that shapes communication. Culture and communication play an important part in all **organizations**, groups with a formal governance and structure. You see this in action every day: your college or university, student groups, sorority or fraternity, religious community, volunteer organizations, and state and local governments are all actively involved in the process of communicating messages about themselves and their members. This is why we stress that **organizational communication**, the interaction necessary to direct an organization toward multiple sets of goals, is about more than meeting agendas and skills or getting along with moody bosses. It is at work in your life *right now* (Eisenberg, Goodall, & Trethewey, 2017). So it is important that we understand these organizations and how we communicate in them. In this chapter, we look at several approaches to managing organizations, issues related to organizational culture, important contexts for communicating in organizations, and common issues facing organizations today.

Approaches to Managing Organizations

For as long as humans have been working together toward shared goals, we have been trying to figure out how to organize ourselves to achieve success. Whether we are talking about effective ways to build a castle; establish a town in the wilderness; or run a factory, preschool, or student government; it is useful to learn the various approaches to managing organizations. Over the centuries, these approaches have changed quite dramatically; the changes have had important implications for how people in organizations work together and communicate. In the following sections, we take a quick trip through time to see how this evolution has played out, beginning with the classical management approach and moving on to the human relations, human resources, and systems approaches.

Classical Management Approach

In the classic children's novel *Charlie and the Chocolate Factory,* Charlie, an impoverished youngster, wins a tour through the most magnificent chocolate factory in the world, run by the highly unusual candy maker Willy Wonka (originally portrayed on film by Gene Wilder and later by Johnny Depp). As Charlie tours the factory with a small group of other children, he sees the Oompa-Loompas, an army of small men. Each Oompa-Loompa is charged with performing a specific task: some do nothing but pour mysterious ingredients into giant, clanking candy-making machines; others focus on guiding the tour boats that ferry the children along rivers of chocolate. Still others work only on packing finished candies into boxes as they come off the assembly lines. You could almost compare the chocolate factory to a car and each worker to a specific part with a specific job—seat belt, brakes, steering wheel, and so on.

To Charlie, the factory might be a novelty or a curiosity, but to organizational communication scholars, it is a pretty clear example of the **classical management approach**, which likens organizations to machines with a focus on maximizing efficiency. Not surprisingly, classical management reached its peak during the Industrial Revolution in the nineteenth century—a time when factories and machinery were proliferating rapidly in various parts of the world, particularly Europe, North America, and Japan.

Classical management depends on two central ideas, both of which have strong implications for communication. The first is a **division of labor**, or the assumption

● **WHETHER YOU ARE** part of a fraternity trying to rush new members or part of Greenpeace's efforts to save the oceans, your organization must communicate its beliefs and goals to the outside world. (top, left) The Washington Post/Getty Images; (top right) JOHN MACDOUGALL/Getty Images; (bottom, left) KAREN BLEIER/Getty Images; (bottom, right) Bob Rowan/Getty Images

that each part of an organization (and each person involved) must carry out a specialized task in order for the organization to run smoothly. This is exactly what you see in *Charlie and the Chocolate Factory:* each worker has a very specific job, and there is little reason for individual workers—or groups of workers on different tasks—to communicate with one another. Classical management approaches also favor **hierarchy**, which refers to the layers of power and authority in an organization. To illustrate, in Willy Wonka's chocolate factory, Willy has the most power to control the working conditions, rewards, and other aspects of life for all the creatures who work in the factory. His team of lower-level "managers" (such as the head of the Oompa-Loompas) has less power. And the assembly-line workers themselves have almost no power at all. Communication in such situations usually flows from the top (management) down to the bottom (the lowest-level workers). It is unlikely that a worker pouring chocolate would contact Willy Wonka to make suggestions for improving the factory.

Human Relations Approach

If reading about the classical management approach makes you want to protest that you are a person, not a cog in a machine, you are not alone. Critics of such organizational practices became more vocal during the Great Depression and World War II, times that were characterized by subpar industrial working conditions and a great separation between employer and employee. These workplace issues sparked the beginning of massive social and economic changes in the United States. For example, Mary Parker Follett (1868–1933) was a Boston social worker who developed new and seemingly radical ideas about leadership, community, and communication. She believed that "only cooperation among people working together in groups under a visionary leadership produced excellence in the workplace, the neighborhood and the community" (Eisenberg, Goodall, & Trethewey, 2017). Follett and others set the stage for the **human relations approach** to management, which considers the human needs of organizational members (enjoying interpersonal relationships, sharing ideas with others, feeling like a member of a group, etc.).

and you?

Are you involved in or familiar with any organizations that favor hierarchy and a division of labor? What are the pros and cons for communication in such organizations?

● **THESE OOMPA-LOOMPAS** from *Charlie and the Chocolate Factory* are responsible for rowing a boat down the chocolate-filled river and not much else! Everett Collection, Inc/ Courtesy Everett Collection

The benefits of this approach came into sharper focus in the 1930s, when an experiment was conducted at Western Electric's Hawthorne plant in Cicero, Illinois, to find out why employees were dissatisfied and unproductive. The researchers separated workers into two different rooms. In one room, the researchers slowly increased the amount of light; in the other, the amount of light was held constant. Much to the researchers' surprise, both groups of workers showed an increase in productivity, regardless of the amount of light they were exposed to. Why? It turns out that the employees were motivated by the increased attention they were receiving from management rather than the increased amount of light (Eisenberg, Goodall, & Trethewey, 2017).

In organizations managed with the human relations approach, managers express more interest in their employees (e.g., asking them how they are doing or giving them praise). They provide incentives for good work and emphasize that "we're all in this together," so employees have a greater sense of belonging to a larger cause or purpose. Organizational members are also encouraged to interact with each other on a more personal level, allowing for greater satisfaction and connectedness with the organization.

Human Resources Approach

The human relations approach was an improvement over the classical approach in both employee satisfaction and organizational productivity. But it fell short of valuing employees' own perspectives and goals regarding the organization. The **human resources approach** takes the basic ideas of human relations and goes one step further: it considers employees as assets to the organization who can be fulfilled by participating and contributing useful ideas (Eisenberg, Goodall, & Trethewey, 2017; Miller, 2009).

In Chapter 16, we examine Abraham Maslow's hierarchy of needs, which asserts that people's basic needs (food and shelter) must be fulfilled before they can achieve higher needs (friendship, love, and enjoyable work). Maslow's work has had a powerful impact on communication in organizations. For instance, we now know that when managers allow the fulfillment of higher-level needs (such as self-worth) in addition to lower-level needs (such as worker safety), workers respond by performing better, remaining motivated, and ultimately increasing their productivity. This benefits both the employees and the organization (Eisenberg, Goodall, & Trethewey, 2017).

The human resources approach can also be applied to other organizational situations. Imagine that you are a new member of a synagogue, and your rabbi notices that you have a knack for working with kids. He or she might motivate you to fulfill your potential by volunteering with the Hebrew school class each week. You feel proud of your accomplishments in helping the kids, and your synagogue's educational mission is also being served.

The Systems Approach

You can see that the human relations and human resources approaches to management have had a huge impact on the view of organizational members. No longer would an employee be considered just a "cog in the machine" as in the classical approach; an employee has become recognized as a person with feelings and ambitions who is a valuable, contributing member of an organization. But there is another approach to management that is less concerned with the uniqueness of individual needs or organizational goals and instead focuses on the interconnectedness of the parts of an organization. The **systems approach** views an organization as a unique whole made up of important members who have interdependent relationships within their particular environment (O'Hair, Friedrich, & Dixon, 2016). Much like an ecosystem in which plants, animals, and weather patterns affect one another, so too do the members of an organization as well as outside forces in the environment: all affect each other and the organization as a whole.

Figure 12.1 shows how a college or university works as a system. Its members include faculty, students, office staff, financial aid staff, and the bursar, all of whom have relationships and interactions with one another. The college exists within an environment, which includes other systems that directly affect it. These other systems might be the city and state where the college is located, the legislature that sets tuition, local employers who offer students full-time or part-time jobs, the families that the students come from or live with, and the high schools that supply many of the students.

Two of the most important components of organizations as systems are openness and adaptability. **Openness** in a system refers to an organization's awareness of its own imbalances and problems. Let's say that our college begins receiving messages from local elementary schools that the university's student teachers seem poorly prepared for the classroom. The university has two choices: it can ignore this feedback about the health of its program, or it can look to correct the problem, perhaps restructuring its elementary education program with feedback from local educators, professors, students, and government and policy representatives. The latter choice clearly helps the organization move forward by allowing for change and

● **THE HUMAN RESOURCES** approach values your assets and contributions. Tim Klein/Photodisc/Getty Images

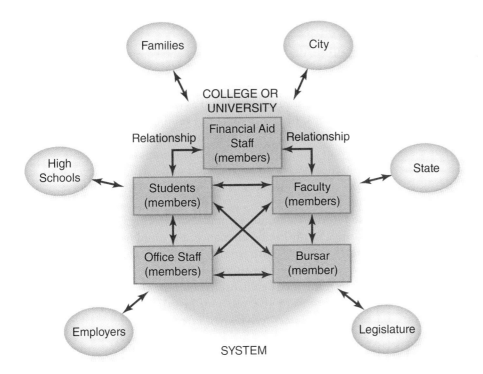

FIGURE 12.1
A COLLEGE OR UNIVERSITY SYSTEM

and you?

Think of a situation when an organization you belonged to was faced with criticism. Was the organization open to suggestions for change, or was it closed off from such discussions? What was the end result?

growth in light of changing times and circumstances. This ability to adjust is known as **adaptability**. And at the heart of it all is communication. If everyone involved in the system, from students to professors to principals, keeps to themselves and never voices concerns or ideas, the system can become closed and collapse under the weight of its own problems.

Communicating Organizational Culture

The management approaches you learned about in the preceding section can cause one organization to feel quite different from another. If you were working in a nineteenth-century factory that valued classical management, you probably would not have team birthday parties or picnics the way you might under the management of the human resources approach, which values individuals. Yet understanding how different organizations come to have such different atmospheres is more complex than simply understanding their management styles. We must come to understand **organizational culture**, an organization's unique set of beliefs, values, norms, and ways of doing things (O'Hair, Friedrich, & Dixon, 2016). Of course, *communication* plays a pivotal role in both the shaping and expression of organizational culture. We explore how by looking at the popular Trader Joe's grocery store chain in the sections that follow.

Organizational Storytelling

Do you enjoy grocery shopping? We often do not. The checkout lines are long, the store lighting is glaring, and there is always someone who leaves a cart in the middle of the aisle so that you cannot get by. But if you are lucky enough to live near a Trader Joe's, you might have a very different experience: employees smile and recommend their favorite salsa, food prices remain reasonable despite nationwide increases, and the colorful South Seas decor gives the place a bold, fun appearance. This is because Trader Joe's has developed an organizational culture that values a friendly, neighborhood feel while offering quality food from all over the world at more affordable prices.

One of the ways that Trader Joe's forms and ensures its cultural values is through **organizational storytelling**, the communication of the company's values through stories and accounts (Gomez, 2015), both externally (to an outside audience) and internally (within the company). An organization telling a story is not so different from a parent telling a story to a young child. Just as fairy tales and children's books teach kids important lessons, like the dangers of talking to strangers, organizational stories help would-be customers and potential members answer the question "What is this company all about?" or "Why should I support or join this organization?" They also help members of an organization understand why they work for a company or embrace the cultural values of a particular organization (Aust, 2004; James & Minnis, 2004).

What Trader Joe's stories communicate and shape its organizational culture? First, consider the store's South Pacific ambiance: the employees wear Hawaiian shirts, and hand-lettered signs feature tropical icons like palm trees and coconuts. Trader Joe's also tells stories of its ability to acquire fine merchandise at low prices — someone with really nice penmanship takes the time to write puns on a giant chalkboard ("Leaf it to us to give you your favorite bagged salads"). Trader Joe's website and newsletter (*Trader Joe's Fearless Flyer*) present fun drawings, facts about the company, and cleverly written highlights of featured products. (Is anyone up for a Lemon Raspberry Zinger Bundt cake?)

and you?

Think about a store that you shop at frequently. What messages do the store layout and decor send customers? Does the store offer any literature or brochures about itself? Does it have a website? If so, what do these media communicate about the organization?

In addition, like many successful organizations, Trader Joe's makes use of metaphors in its storytelling. A *metaphor* is a figure of speech that likens one thing to something else in a literal way, although there is no literal connection between the two (Jacobs & Heracleous, 2006). Trader Joe's metaphor is, essentially, "We are a ship." The employees at Trader Joe's are all crew members, including the captain (store manager) and the first mate (assistant store manager; Lewis, 2005). Each member is essential to keeping the ship running, which makes for friendly employees and happy customers.

Trader Joe's also makes use of stories about **organizational heroes**, individuals who have achieved great things for the organization through persistence and commitment, often in the face of great risk (James & Minnis, 2004; Schulman, 1996). Trader Joe's employees and would-be customers alike all learn about "Trader Joe" himself, a Stanford University M.B.A. graduate named Joe Coulombe who opened a chain of Pronto Market convenience stores in the Los Angeles area during the 1950s.

● **AT TRADER JOE'S,** employees always have bright smiles — and plenty of tasty food recommendations. Andy Kropa/Redux

In the 1960s, 7-Eleven stores invaded southern California, threatening to crush Joe's business. Rather than admit defeat, Coulombe changed his tactics: trusting that the burgeoning airline industry would entice more Americans to travel—and that those Americans would want to find the foods they enjoyed abroad once they were back home—Coulombe began stocking imported foods other convenience stores did not carry. Thus began the first Trader Joe's in 1967 (Hoover, 2006).

Learning About Organizational Culture

Could someone who dislikes people, Hawaiian shirts, and exotic foods find a successful career at Trader Joe's? **Organizational assimilation** is the process by which newcomers learn the nuances of the organization and determine if they fit in (Cohen & Avanzino, 2010). Studies suggest that successful assimilation is often based on a newcomer's ability to figure out and make use of behaviors that will be appropriate and effective in a given organization, especially communicating up the line (Goldman & Myers, 2015). That is, they have the ability to recognize and remain sensitive to what their superiors care about. Typically, new organizational members are quite motivated to get these behaviors figured out because the uncertainty of not knowing what to do or say can be challenging (Cohen & Avanzino, 2010). Organizations understand this as well and generally seek to help. That is why religious organizations often have new-member classes and employers often have an orientation program to acquaint newcomers with the organization.

At Trader Joe's, for example, new employees are subject to the group "huddle," when all staff members at the store come together in a circle to share information and introduce themselves, perhaps noting where they are from or how long they have been with Trader Joe's. The idea is to make each new employee feel like part of the team (or in this case, crew) and to get to know everyone.

Similarly, an additional perk of working for Trader Joe's is the free samples. Employees are always encouraged to try new products and even make up recipes for everyone to try (Lewis, 2005). This is one way that employees become actively

connect

Strategies that help reduce uncertainty in interpersonal relationships (Chapter 8) can also help in new organizational settings. At a new job, you might use *passive strategies* to learn whether joking with peers is acceptable; *interactive strategies*, like asking where to find office supplies; or *active strategies*, like asking a colleague how your new boss reacts to difficult situations. Such strategies help you assimilate faster and more comfortably.

real communicator

NAME: Kibibi Springs
OCCUPATION: Marketing Communication Professional
Courtesy Kibibi Springs

I know a lot about organizations. Not only did I work for major corporations for years as an employee, but I also continue to work with them now as a consultant on programs to improve organizations. Although lots of consultants claim to be able to improve performance and profitability, the work I do focuses on changing the *culture* and overall wellness of the organization. Basically, we teach professionals how to redesign their habits and communication skills to improve their quality of life within the structure of the organization and within the framework of a healthy lifestyle.

As I ascended the corporate ladder, I found that I couldn't be happy if my job was my whole identity. I'd seen so many people lose their health, their families, and even their sanity because they had no work–life balance. I decided to become an entrepreneur and help those people. I had an undergraduate degree in communication and then earned a master's in consumer and organizational psychology. With this combination of strengths, I have been able to work with companies to enact large and small "culture change programs."

Most companies today are concerned about their culture. They want to find and retain good workers. They want to be productive and creative. They want (and need) to adapt to a changing world and new technologies. Younger organizations that come to me are usually in touch with these goals; they ask for help in sustaining the positives and the strong dynamics. Bigger, older organizations often come to me in crisis. Things have gone wrong and they are not sure why. In these cases, I have to analyze the entire organization to find the root(s) of the problem. I often start with management in these situations, interviewing them about goals and culture and looking for the commonality of the core groups. Once I have an understanding of the current culture, I teach them how to be more positive, how to relax, how to ask questions, and how to listen. I help them choose behaviors that advance their personal and professional goals within the framework of a healthy lifestyle — and enable them to pass these on to their workforce.

I encourage everyone to find an organization that employs the whole person — one that is positive about its people as well as its products.

engaged with the products: they feel personally connected to the products and can make heartfelt recommendations to customers, thereby furthering Trader Joe's value of a friendly, interactive shopping experience.

Relational Contexts in Organizations

Popular culture, especially television, portrays how various relationships are played out in work organizations. The classic is *The Office*, but other shows have offered representations of work life, including *Silicon Valley, Good Girls Revolt, Mad Men, 30 Rock,* and *The Americans*. In this section, we explore relationships in businesses and organizations. Three noteworthy relationships are superior–subordinate relationships, mentor–protégé relationships, and peer relationships.

Supervisor–Supervisee Relationships

Few relationships are parodied as often as the relationship between supervisors and the people they manage. Think of Homer Simpson reporting to Mr. Burns, or the gang on *The Office* dealing with the iconic (and awkward) manager Michael Scott.

We often enjoy portrayals of the "bad" boss or the "crazy" boss who causes employees to sit around the lunch table complaining, even though in real life most bosses are fairly reasonable people. Perhaps we find pleasure in these portrayals because supervisors inherently have power over us. Bosses negotiate our salaries and approve our vacation time; they might determine our hours or whether we get promoted. And to achieve anything worthwhile with your supervisor, the two of you must be communicating regularly. The supervisor–supervisee relationship is an important ingredient in maintaining employees' commitment to the job and organization (Jablin, 1987; Teven, 2007a).

If you are involved in a professional, community, or student organization where people are reporting to you, do not be a Mr. Burns! You should know how to get the most out of your conversations with the people you supervise. Often you can improve communication by following just a few simple steps:

▶ Schedule adequate time for important conversations. For example, if you are the president of a student organization and need to speak to the treasurer about his messy bookkeeping, do not do it in the ten minutes you have between classes. Set up an appointment to allow adequate time to discuss the problem and generate solutions.

▶ Ask supervisees for suggestions and ideas. For example, if you are working as a manager in a bank, you might ask the tellers for suggestions to make the work schedule more equitable.

▶ Demonstrate that you are listening when a supervisee is speaking to you by giving appropriate verbal and nonverbal responses, such as paraphrasing what you are hearing and nodding. Those in positions of power need to respect those who report to them by being responsive to their time, ideas, and suggestions. Always keep in mind that you were once in a similar position. Utilize the knowledge you accumulated as a supervisee to be an effective supervisor.

Even if you manage several people, you almost certainly report to a supervisor yourself—and it is important that you be able to communicate competently in this context as well. You can certainly follow the guidelines regarding listening and avoiding distractions that we mentioned earlier, but there are a few additional points to consider when you are the person with less power:

▶ Spend some time thinking about what you would like to say to your boss. What are the main points you want to make? What do you hope to achieve through this discussion? It is embarrassing to start talking with a supervisor only to realize that you forgot what you wanted to say.

▶ Spend some time *rehearsing* what you want to say to your manager. You might even ask a friend or family member to rehearse the conversation with you so that you can hear yourself speak.

▶ When you speak with your manager, try to avoid being emotional or hurling accusations such as "You always . . ." or "You never. . . ." It is more productive to be specific and logical and to ask for clarification: "When you removed me from the Edwards project, I took that to mean that you didn't think I was capable of handling it. Am I misunderstanding something?"

▶ Be sure to make appropriate eye contact, avoid fidgeting, and use an appropriate tone of voice. Shifty eyes, rapid movements, or a sarcastic tone can make you come across as guilty, hostile, or anxious—not desirable when discussing a difficult situation with your manager.

and you?

Have you ever worked for or otherwise come across a "bad" boss? What characteristics made them that way? Do you think those in positions of power are ever judged unfairly? Why?

Mentor–Protégé Relationships

One important relationship in organizations is between mentor and protégé. A **mentor** is a seasoned, respected member of an organization who serves as a role model for a less experienced individual, his or her **protégé** (Jain, Chaudhary, & Jain, 2016). Research shows that mentoring actually provides a number of key benefits for everyone involved (Crossley & Silverman, 2016). For one thing, it accelerates the protégé's assimilation into the organization and its culture, which helps the newcomer become productive faster and thus helps the organization meet its goals (particularly in reducing the number of members leaving an organization; Madlock & Kennedy-Lightsey, 2010). In one study, protégés reported that mentors helped make their careers more successful by providing coaching, sponsorship, protection, counseling, and ensuring they were given challenging work and received adequate exposure and visibility (Dunleavy & Millette, 2007). Protégés experience greater job satisfaction, and the mentors benefit by receiving recognition as their protégés begin to achieve in the organization (Kalbfleisch, 2002; Madlock & Kennedy-Lightsey, 2010). Mentors also benefit from their protégés by seeing a different perspective of the field, through the lens of inexperience. A protégé might question, for example, why the organization continues to rely on older methods of outreach (such as traditional advertising) over newer ones (such as social media) to promote its causes.

Many colleges and universities set up mentorships for incoming students in order to help them adjust to life at the college or perhaps even life away from home. In many cases, second-, third-, or fourth-year students agree to be "big brothers" or "big sisters" to help the newcomers figure out campus parking, where to get a decent sandwich between classes, or which professors to take or avoid. First-year students may then become mentors themselves in future years. As you can imagine, the communication between mentor and protégé changes over time in this example. At first, the protégé may rely quite heavily on the mentor, since everything in the college environment is new and perhaps somewhat frightening. However, as the first-year student adjusts and begins to feel comfortable and self-assured, he or she will rely less and less on the mentor. By the next fall, the protégé may well be on an equal par with the mentor, and the relationship may have turned into a friendship or may have dissolved entirely. Understanding that mentor–protégé relationships go through four distinct stages—initiation, cultivation, separation, and redefinition—can help both parties adjust to these natural changes. See Table 12.1 for more on these stages and the communication that takes place during each.

If you are new to an organization—be it a community college, a house of worship, or a job—and a mentorship interests you, see if the organization has a formal program. If such a program does not exist, you can still find a mentor, albeit in a more informal way. Consider the following tips (Kram, 1983):

▶ Ask your peers (colleagues, members of a congregation, etc.) to recommend individuals who might be interested in serving as a mentor.

▶ Identify people who have progressed in the organization in ways that interest you and determine whether one of them would make a good mentor.

▶ Build rapport with someone you think would be an effective mentor. Ask if he or she would like to sponsor you in a mentor–protégé relationship. Explain why you think he or she would be a good mentor and describe your qualifications as a protégé—such as your ability to learn or to cultivate networks quickly.

● **WITH COLLEGE MENTORING** programs, older students help new arrivals to acclimate, from navigating an unfamiliar campus to completing those first daunting class assignments. Marty Heitner/The Image Works

and you?

Have you ever been involved in a mentoring relationship? If so, did you find that this relationship benefited you in any way? Did it benefit your organization as well? How would you describe the changes in communication that took place over the course of the relationship?

connect

For competent communication in the evolving relationship between mentor and protégé, you need to understand key aspects of the relational context — history, goals, and expectations — discussed in Chapter 1. As a protégé, you might be uncomfortable if your company mentor asked you for professional advice; it might be equally awkward to ask your mentor for advice on searching for a new job when you first meet. Such communication defies expectations.

TABLE 12.1
STAGES IN MENTOR–PROTÉGÉ RELATIONSHIPS

Stage	Communication Goal	Mentor Responsibilities	Protégé Responsibilities
Initiation	Get to know one another	• Show support through counseling and coaching • Help protégé set goals	• Demonstrate openness to suggestions and loyalty to the mentor
Cultivation	Form a mutually beneficial bond	• Promote the protégé throughout the organization (e.g., by introducing him or her to influential people) • Communicate knowledge about how to work best with key people and what the organization's culture is	• Put new learning to use (e.g., by forging relationships with influential people) • Share personal perspective and insights with mentor
Separation	Drift apart as protégé gains skill	• Spend less time with protégé	• Take more initiative in the organization • Strive for development or promotion
Redefinition	Become peers	• Occasionally provide advice or support as needed	• Stay in touch with mentor at times if additional advice is required

Peer Relationships

One of the most fun aspects of watching workplace dramas like *How to Get Away with Murder* is keeping track of the web of relationships among Professor Keating's students and their clients. Friendships, secret crushes, full-fledged romances, and bitter resentments could definitely keep your night interesting! Yet these interactions also interest us as scholars because such **peer relationships** reveal the importance of **peer communication**, communication between individuals at the same level of authority in an organization. Researchers, management coaches, and popular magazines warn that Americans are spending more and more time in the workplace, leaving less time for outside personal relationships. Yet we all need friends and confidants. So where do we find them? You guessed it—in the organizations we devote time to, particularly the organizations we work for. Some current thinking, however, seems to say contradictory things about whether this phenomenon is healthy.

The Gallup Poll has consistently reported that many people have best friends at work. These findings have powerful implications for employers. Studies show that employees with a best friend at work tend to be more focused, more passionate, and more loyal to their organizations. They get sick less often, suffer fewer accidents, and change jobs less frequently. They even have more satisfied customers (Friedman, 2014). Perhaps this is the thinking behind organizational initiatives to help employees get to know one another—office picnics, hospital softball teams, and school Frisbee and golf tournaments.

Relationships with colleagues and other organizational members can be both career enhancing and personally satisfying; many workplace friendships last long after one or

● **ANNALISE KEATING'S STUDENTS** spend so much time at her office (which is also her home) that their work life *is* their social life—and what results is a complex web of peer relationships. © ABC/Photofest

evaluating communication ethics

More Than Friends at Work

You have begun to notice that two colleagues at work, Cheryl and Michael, are spending an inordinate amount of time together. It is clear that they are romantically involved. Because they work together on several projects, it is natural that they spend a lot of time together; however, their conduct during working hours is affecting your department's performance and forcing you and your colleagues to work harder. You have approached Michael about it, noting that "people are beginning to notice" how much time he spends with Cheryl. They cooled it for a few days after that, but gradually returned to their old behavior.

Although the company has a policy requiring employees to disclose any romantic relationships between coworkers, you disagree with it, thinking it is an invasion of privacy. But you also know that Michael and Cheryl's goofing off is starting to affect their work: both have missed deadlines. Making matters worse, their relationship has become a hot topic of gossip, distracting other members of your team from getting their work done. How should you handle this situation?

1. What is the issue here, Cheryl and Michael's relationship or their behavior? If they acted more professionally, would their romantic relationship matter?

2. How does your opinion of the company policy factor into your decision? Does your coworkers' flirtation change your opinion?

3. How could you get Cheryl and Michael to change their behavior? Is going to human resources a reasonable option?

connect

When communicating with peers in organizations, remember *communication privacy management* (Chapter 8), which helps you understand how people perceive and manage personal information. You may decide that certain topics, such as your romantic life, are off-limits at work. You must determine for yourself what is private in different relationships — and it is also wise to consider the cultural expectations of your organization before sharing.

and you?

Who are your three closest friends? Are they members of any organizations that you belong to? If so, how has your joint membership affected the friendship in positive or negative ways?

both friends leave a job. But it is important to be mindful as you cultivate such relationships. The following tips can help (Rosen, 2004):

▶ *Take it slow.* When you meet someone new in your organization (be it your job or your residence hall association), do not blurt out all of your personal details right away. Take time to get to know this potential friend.

▶ *Know your territory.* Organizations have different cultures, as you have learned. Keep that in mind before you post pictures of your romantic partner all over your gym locker for the rest of the soccer team to see.

▶ *Accept an expiration date.* Sometimes friendships simply do not last outside of the context in which they grew. You may have found that you lost a few of your high school friends when you started college; this point is also particularly true for friendships on the job. Accept that life sometimes works out this way and that no one is to blame.

Remember that we are rarely given a choice in who our workmates are, but regardless, we *must* work together to achieve our desired goals. Although it is likely that we will make friends at work, the transient nature of those friendships can lead us to make mistakes by assuming these friendships are the same as those we make outside of work.

Organizational Challenges

Diversity is a word you likely hear a lot nowadays. We use it throughout this book to highlight the importance of understanding and respecting people from various cocultures with experiences different from our own. But you also hear about companies needing to "diversify" and the importance of tailoring messages to a "diverse" audience.

What does it all mean? It means that today's organizations need to branch out and be open to new ideas and experiences. They must make use of new communication technology and address colleagues and other organizations worldwide. Organizational members must find ways to balance the multitude of pressures for their time and must learn to be tolerant of each other's differences and behave competently and respectfully at all times. We examine these important issues in the sections that follow.

Workplace Conflict

Today's diverse workplace requires employees to be able to work with a variety of colleagues who may differ in culture, religion, race, ethnicity, age, gender, and sexual orientation (Mayhew, 2016). In addition, most jobs require employees to work in actual teams, which entails close interaction with others who have different personalities, ideas, interests, and goals. When people work closely together, conflicts may arise, which can have negative effects on performance and productivity (Carton & Tewfik, 2016). Although not all conflict is bad, if it is handled poorly it can foster tension and animosity. Unconstructive reactions include the following (Gottman, 1994):

▶ *Criticism* involves commenting on another's personality or character rather than focusing on his or her bothersome behavior. Because organizations value accountability and can blame individuals for any failures or problems, they can be a magnet for criticism. Although criticism can be positive if it is constructive, it can become a problem when it becomes personal.

▶ *Defensiveness* is a self-protective response to another's actions or accusations. When something goes wrong in an organization, people often deny responsibility, make excuses, and counterattack. Because people have an inherent need to protect themselves, they may even lie (perhaps even to themselves) to avoid facing consequences or to cover up mistakes (Knapp, 2008).

▶ *Contempt* includes communicating with the negative intent of making the person feel rejected from the community. Much like bullying, it may include insults, sarcasm, name-calling, ridicule, hostile humor, and/or body language such as rolling one's eyes.

▶ *Ostracism* involves completely ignoring another individual in the workplace. People tend to view this as more abusive even than bullying (O'Reilly, Robinson, Berdahl, & Banki, 2015). When a coworker ignores and neglects another person, the human thread connecting them is snapped, and the targeted person feels disrespected and alienated.

What should you do if you are witness to these types of negative behaviors in an organization—or, worse, are dealing with them yourself? These tips may help you get past interpersonal conflict in a constructive way.

▶ Stop conflicts before they even start. If you are interacting with another person and feel that he or she is behaving in a way that might lead to conflict (such as sending brusque emails or ignoring your advice), either give this person the benefit of the doubt or gently bring up your concerns.

▶ If you do find yourself in conflict with another, try to talk to the person one-on-one in a nonthreatening manner. Focus on the specific behavior at hand and try to find a solution or compromise to work more smoothly together in the future.

▶ If you cannot get past the conflict, consider bringing in a mediator (such as a supervisor or human resources representative) so that you can both air your concerns in a neutral setting.

connect

Conflict such as criticism, contempt, and stonewalling can arise in other types of interpersonal relationships (Chapter 9) as well. Remember that cooperative strategies (such as focusing on the issue and considering options and alternatives) can help deal with these types of issues.

and you?

In your experience, which communication channel is best suited to workplace conflict? Why has this channel worked better for you? What are advantages of both face-to-face and computer mediated channels with regards to conflict resolution?

Using Technology

Advances in communication technology—including instant social media messaging, professional networking sites, and videoconferencing—enable members of organizations to communicate more easily, particularly with clients and colleagues who work off-site or in home offices. But they have also introduced new challenges for organizations.

First, there is the question of figuring out which channel is most appropriate for a particular message in an organizational setting. We discussed this dilemma in earlier chapters—such as whether you would text or call a friend with an apology. But there are additional ethical and legal considerations when choosing channels in organizations. If you are a manager, you simply cannot fire someone in an email with the entire department copied. Rather, you would most likely need to have a private face-to-face meeting—or perhaps a phone call if the employee works elsewhere in the country or the world. Research shows that most people do make conscious decisions about which communication vehicle to use based on the situational and relational contexts. Table 12.2 offers a look at various organizational goals and people's perceptions about the most competent channel for achieving those goals.

In Chapter 2, we mentioned the use of enterprise social media (ESM) as a means for keeping people digitally connected across an organization. Like a type of Facebook for the workplace, ESM is rapidly becoming recognized as a means for great efficiency and information sharing through more powerful communication channels (Leonardi, Huysman, & Steinfield, 2013). While some experts believe that ESM generates two key effects—establishing networks and accessing content—it is also argued that ESM can fundamentally affect how people interact in organizations (Kane, 2015). At a minimum, organizational members have greater opportunities to develop relationships with a larger number of people.

With such a variety of communication technologies available to organizational members to keep in close contact with one another, it should come as no surprise that people wind up using technology to achieve personal goals as well. Twenty years ago, employees might have gotten in trouble if they spent too much time making personal phone calls on the job. So consider how much more distracting it can be to have the ability to bank online, text your romantic partner, and read your brother's blog during the day. Eighty-nine percent of workers surveyed by Salary.com reported they had wasted time at work, with much of it spent on the internet (39 percent) and social media (38 percent). What's more, organizations are not just concerned about *when* you are using social media, but also about *what* you are posting—particularly whether you are posting comments about the organization or individuals associated with it. Consider, for example, the case of Natalie Munroe, a high school English teacher who was suspended and faced termination over unflattering comments she made about her students on her personal blog. The blog was relatively anonymous—Munroe never used her full name or identified individual students—and was only followed by nine friends and family members. In addition, the vast majority of posts had nothing to do with the school, the students, or

TABLE 12.2

TECHNOLOGY AND THE WORKPLACE

Percentage of working internet users who responded that these technologies were "very important" for their jobs.

Email	61%
Internet	54%
Landline phone	35%
Cell or smartphone	24%
Social networking sites	4%

Information from Pew Research Center. (2014, September). Technology's impact on workers.

wired for communication

Working Here, There, and Everywhere

When Marissa Mayer took over as CEO at the struggling internet company Yahoo, it was not surprising that she would implement organizational techniques used at her wildly successful former employer Google. In a controversial step, she put an end to the company's work-at-home policy. Telecommuting, she explained, was "not what's right for Yahoo right now" (Mayer, quoted in Tkaczyk, 2013).

Reactions to the move were mixed. Mayer, a new mother as well as a new CEO, had a nursery built next to her office at Yahoo so she could take her baby to work. Some thought it hypocritical to deny other parents the option to work at home near their own children. Some worried that employees who used to work well at home would be less productive when faced once again with the distractions of a busy office environment.

But others point out that Mayer was hired to bring the kind of energy and innovation that define Google to its failing competitor, and much of that innovation is spurred by the communication environment at the Googleplex — a sprawling campus designed to keep employees happy while they collaborate and interact face-to-face (Rampell & Miller, 2013).

Mayer herself acknowledged that there were trade-offs in both situations. "People are more productive when they're alone," she explained a few months after the announcement. "But they're more collaborative and innovative when they're together" (Mayer, quoted in Tkaczyk, 2013).

In a turn of events, Mayer announced on her own blog in summer of 2016 that Verizon was acquiring Yahoo's operating system. Many critics took note that this was one more failure of Yahoo under Mayer's leadership, yet Mayer insists that this was an important step to unlock the potential for new work in mobile, video, social media, and native advertising (marissamayer.tumblr.com, 2016).

1. Mayer's assertion suggests that prioritizing innovation over productivity is "right for Yahoo right now." What factors would influence a company's decision to maximize one over the other?

2. Why was a change in human resources policy such big news? Does Mayer's gender play a role?

3. What does your ideal work situation look like? Do you envision a career spent working at home, in a collaborative office, or in another kind of setting? Do you think Yahoo will be a more or less attractive place to work in the future?

the teaching profession (Werner, 2011). But as with many other high-profile social networking suspensions and terminations, organizations have a keen interest in the way employees represent them in the virtual world.

Concerns over employee internet use have led many organizations to an increase in workplace **surveillance**, or monitoring of employees to see how they are using technology (Johnston, 2016). On some levels, monitoring seems to make sense, particularly when employees are spending time on questionable nonwork-related activities. Yet it still raises several important ethical questions: Does monitoring constitute an invasion of employees' privacy? Should workers accept monitoring as a fact of organizational life? These questions are stimulating important research and lively debates in legal circles, but no one seems to have a clear answer. One thing seems obvious, however: in any organization, you will be much more productive if you limit the amount of time you spend using communication technologies for personal matters.

And what happens if work intrudes on your online life — for example, if your supervisor attempts to "friend" you on Facebook? This might be an unprofessional move on the part of your supervisor in certain work situations, so business professionals recommend that you ignore this request (Peluchette, Karl, & Fertig, 2013). However, if you feel that you *must* accept the friend request, you can and should take advantage of your privacy settings to limit what your supervisor can see. On the

and you?

In your workplace experience, has publicizing your Facebook (or other social media) ever been in your best interest? Have you restricted your privacy settings out of fear of being judged and treated differently at work? Should companies be allowed access to your Facebook, or would this be an invasion of your privacy?

other hand, if Facebook privacy is not a huge priority for you in your place of work, it might be beneficial to be more public with your supervisor and colleagues. This allows them to see your interests and personality more candidly and can remove barriers to conversations and possibly help friendships and working partnerships to blossom. On the company's side, being able to see an employee's Facebook page can help to keep track of them while on company time. If an employee is posting status updates on social media while an important project is only hours away from a deadline, a manager will see that the employee may need guidance with time management.

Globalization

We are living in an age where the other side of the world is an instant message away. If you have bought something with a "Made in China" sticker or recently seen a foreign film at your local theater, you have experienced the effects of globalization. **Globalization** is the growing interdependence and connectivity of societies and economies around the world.

Globalization is especially evident in the business world. Increases in communication technology and the convenience of travel have allowed companies to expand their labor force beyond geographical boundaries. More often than not, when you call customer service for help on the Xbox you bought in the United States, the person who picks up the phone is in India. More and more services are being outsourced to developing countries, where wages and operating costs are lower. Take Kenneth Tham, a high school sophomore in California. Most afternoons, he signs on to an online tutoring service, TutorVista. His tutor is Ramya Tadikonda, a twenty-six-year-old mother in Chennai (formerly Madras), India. TutorVista's president, John J. Stuppy, thinks that in this day and age, global tutoring offers the most potential because it makes "high-quality, one-on-one tutoring affordable and accessible to the masses" (Lohr, 2007). This example highlights a few of the benefits of globalization. U.S. companies benefit from the lower costs of operating in other countries, and people in those countries benefit from better-paying jobs and a higher quality of life.

One type of business that has recently burst onto the global scene is social enterprise—organizations that, in addition to seeking financial success, specifically aim to improve the quality of people's lives or the environment. **Global social enterprise (GSE)** is a movement centered on helping underdeveloped economies reach greater potential through improved innovation, entrepreneurship, and regional stability as well as by developing legal structures, stabilizing financial systems, and raising money (Richardson, 2016). GSEs have been experimenting, for example, in the Middle East, North Africa, and Costa Rica. In each case, the local economies want to boost their population's standard of living and are interested in partnering with others to build financial and educational capacity. One company, Educall, sells tutoring services for orphans or other disadvantaged youth (Richardson, 2016), while another, Skills Motion, helps to reduce unemployment by using online platforms to conduct business. Artisans are supported by The Anou, an organization that helps to open up markets for their arts and crafts. GSEs are often start-up companies that want to serve the underprivileged; those that

● **HAVE YOU EVER** bought something in the United States with a "Made in China" label? That is globalization at work! Goran Bogicevic/Shutterstock

are successful in reducing poverty and inequality understand how to effectively leverage organizational communication skills steeped in digital tools.

Globalization is a powerful force, and its impact on organizations is undeniable. It is important to mention, however, that without clear global labor laws, there are unethical practices, such as human trafficking, that are difficult to control and police.

Work–Life Balance

Diane is a single mom with a seven-year-old son. She works forty hours a week as a receptionist in a medical clinic and is currently completing courses to become a dental hygienist. She is also the "room parent" for her son's second-grade class and is frequently called on to help bake for classroom celebrations and to chaperone class trips. Luis is a nineteen-year-old sophomore at a state university. He takes six classes, with the hopes of graduating one semester early, and works two part-time jobs to help meet the cost of tuition.

Diane and Luis have different lives, different goals, and different constraints. Yet they have one thing in common: they are sinking under intense pressures from the organizations in their lives. But their pressures are not just a matter of time management. High intensity and demanding workplaces create harmful and unnecessary risk (Reid & Ramarajan, 2016). Diane must maintain a cheerful demeanor with patients who are often upset about their ailments or frustrated with medical bureaucracy, quickly and competently process mountains of paperwork, and still find the time and energy to be supportive to her son's teacher. Luis's jobs may not be as intense, but his classes are very demanding. He has to exert a great deal of time and intellectual effort to understand all of the concepts and complete his assignments, while also responsibly

● **BURNOUT IS THE HARMFUL** result of prolonged labor and stress as well as a reminder of how vital it is to strike a manageable balance between work and life. Peopleimages/Getty Images

communication across cultures

Work–Life Balance: Around the Globe and Around the Block

If you are like most Americans, chances are that when you consider a job or career, you think not only about salary but also about benefits. Some of the most appealing companies to work for offer enticements like flexible work hours, in-house dining, child care, and even laundry services. These kinds of perks are relatively new and rare. But what about the most basic benefit of any job — time away from the job.

Two weeks of vacation time is standard in most U.S. companies — but it is not guaranteed by law. According to recent studies, the average private sector worker in the United States receives only about sixteen paid vacation days per year, down from twenty days in 2000 (Mohn, 2014). Almost one in four U.S. workers has no paid time off at all. Of course, most successful U.S. companies do offer vacation time to employees, even if they are not required by law to do so. But lower-wage workers typically receive fewer paid days off (seven on average) than higher-wage workers (an average of thirteen; Ray, Sanes, & Schmitt, 2013; Ray & Schmitt, 2007).

In other developed nations, things are quite different. Workers in the United Kingdom are guaranteed twenty-eight vacation days per year; in Austria and Portugal, workers get twenty-two vacation days in addition to thirteen paid holidays. Canadians enjoy a minimum of ten vacation days and nine holidays. In some of these nations, employers are even required to provide a little extra pay to help with vacation expenses (Ray, Sanes, & Schmitt, 2013; Ray & Schmitt, 2007).

think about this

1. Does it surprise you that vacation time is not mandated in the United States but is in other nations? Do you think Americans would be more or less productive if they had more vacation time?

2. Consider cultural variations. How is the individualist culture of the United States reflected in policies on and attitudes toward vacation time?

3. What are your expectations for getting time off from work? Do you expect time off for holidays like the Fourth of July and Thanksgiving? Do you feel differently about religious holidays versus national holidays?

juggling the work hours and duties of both of his jobs. He rarely has time to spend with his friends. What Luis and Diane are struggling to achieve is **work–life balance**, which is success in one's personal *and* professional life. If they do not manage successfully, they may find that something has to give, which could mean poor job performance, neglect of family and friends, or both. Organizations are increasingly recognizing the work–life struggle; in an effort to recruit and retain the best job candidates, many offer flexible work arrangements, stress-management programs, onsite child care, or other creative work–life options. For particularly demanding or high intensity workplaces, recommendations for organizations include rewarding people's work, not just the time they put in; ensuring that people to take time for personal matters, and requiring vacations (Reid & Ramarajan, 2016). The adoption of healthy work–life practices may be a necessity for successful business. Research indicates work–life balance can improve employee performance, which therefore increases organizational productivity and profitability (PMS, 2015).

So if you are feeling burned out or on the verge of collapsing from organizational pressure, what should you do? Here are a few tips that scholars, medical doctors, and other professionals find helpful (Mayo Clinic, 2012):

▶ *Keep a log.* Track everything you do for one week, including school- and work-related activities. Note which activities are nonnegotiable (such as a mandatory math class), and decide which other commitments matter the most to you. Consider cutting obligations that are not fulfilling or necessary.

▶ *Manage your time.* Organizing your life can help you feel more in control of your circumstances. Set up specific times to study, work, and have fun — and try your best to stick to your schedule.

what about you?

Are You Off Balance?

1. Which statement best describes you after you leave work for the day?
   - A. I do not think about work again until I arrive the next morning.
   - B. I usually check my work email before going to bed.
   - C. I check my work email or make calls three or four times during the evening.

2. A big project requires you to stay late to meet a deadline. You think to yourself:
   - A. "This is happening way too much. I'll have to talk to my supervisor about it."
   - B. "Oh, well, I'll take off a little early next week to make up for it."
   - C. "I wonder if Bud, the night watchman, will bring me a sandwich, like he always does."

3. Which statement best describes your typical vacation?
   - A. I kick back, relax, and savor the time off.
   - B. I check in with my organization at least once so that people know I am available.
   - C. I continue to check my email because you never know when an emergency might arise.

4. It is Tuesday, and you arrive home at 5:30 P.M. How do your housemates or family react?
   - A. They say hello and discuss dinner plans.
   - B. They act surprised — they never know if I will be on time or not.
   - C. They wonder if I have been fired because I am home so early.

5. What are you most likely to do to manage your time at home?
   - A. I organize chores and write to-do lists.
   - B. I try to run errands on days off from work or school.
   - C. I tackle chores and errands one at a time as needed.

If your answers are mostly As: You are leading a fairly well-balanced life — congratulations! You may, however, need to give your organization more priority now and then, particularly during time-sensitive projects.

If your answers are mostly Bs: You are striking a great balance! Keep up the good work.

If your answers are mostly Cs: You are likely headed toward burnout. Consider the strategies we discuss to find more balance.

Information from CNN.com/living. (2008).

▶ *Leave work at work.* Be mindful of the boundary between work and home. Even though you might have the technology to connect to anyone at any time from virtually anywhere, make a conscious decision to separate work from personal time. When you are with your family, for instance, keep your laptop in your briefcase or backpack.

▶ *Nurture yourself.* Set aside time each day for an activity that you enjoy, such as watching a particular TV show, working out, or listening to music.

▶ *Get enough sleep.* Enough said!

and you?

Consider the suggestions we have offered to help you balance your life commitments. Do you practice any of these currently? Are they realistic for your life and the organizations you belong to? If not, what impediments prevent you from making such changes?

connect

Cultural differences, like those discussed in Chapter 6, can lead to perceptions of harassment when communicators fail to remember the cultural context. Gestures that are entirely appropriate in one culture might be considered offensive elsewhere. The same can be said for verbal messages such as commenting on an individual's appearance. Companies and communicators should take time to clarify perceptions and adapt messages in order to avoid miscommunication.

Sexual Harassment

There are days when none of us want to be at work or at school, particularly when the weather is nice or there is another fun activity to take part in. Imagine, however, if your main reason for not wanting to head to class or to your job is fear. For many women and men around the world, a fear of being bullied or harassed in the workplace, on campus, or in other settings is far too common.

One particularly offensive type of harassment is **sexual harassment**, which the U.S. Equal Employment Opportunity Commission (EEOC; 2016) defines as "unwelcome or unwanted sexual conduct that is either very serious or occurs frequently. The harasser may be another employee, a supervisor, the company owner or even a customer. The harasser may be male or female. The sexual conduct can be verbal, physical, in writing or in pictures. Illegal sexual harassment creates a hostile or intimidating work place and interferes with an employee's job performance." Specific conduct that can create such an environment may include sexist remarks; embarrassing jokes; taunting; displays of pornographic photographs; and unwanted physical contact such as touching, kissing, or grabbing. Organizations are also observing the use of computer-mediated communication to engage in sexual harassment conduct (Ritter, 2014).

Sexual harassment costs organizations millions of dollars every year and robs individuals of opportunities, dignity, and sense of self-worth. Victims of sexual harassment also suffer adverse psychological and health effects from this aberrant behavior (McDonald, 2012). For this reason, organizations have instituted official codes of conduct and clear definitions and penalties for sexual harassment. Many even require training to educate organizational members. For example, some programs discuss gendered communication, noting that women socialized in feminine nurturing are more likely than men to disclose personal information in the workplace. Men, who tend to be more private about personal information at work, may interpret that behavior as flirting and may respond with a sexual advance. Similarly, men may use smiling, extensive eye contact, and touch as signals that they are sexually attracted to someone, whereas many women use these same nonverbal behaviors to demonstrate their interest in a conversation topic and their support of the person who is speaking (Berryman-Fink, 1993). By understanding and being aware of such communication differences, incidents can be prevented before they happen. Nonetheless, when incidents do occur, victims should recognize that the law is on their side; they should feel empowered to take action against an illegal act. If you are a victim of sexual harassment—or even if you think you might be—consider the following communication strategies:

▶ Clearly and firmly tell the harasser that his or her advances are not welcome.

▶ Immediately report the incident to someone who can assist you: a trusted professor, a counselor, or your boss. If the harasser is your boss, you can contact a representative in your organization's human resources department.

▶ Document each incident in writing. Include a description of the incident, the date, the person or persons involved, and any action you took.

▶ If anyone else in the organization witnessed the harassing behavior, have each person verify the details of the incident and add that information to your documentation.

It is also important to be careful not to inadvertently behave in a harassing manner yourself. For example, if a friend emails a dirty joke or pornographic photo to you at work, *do not forward it to anyone else in the organization.* It is not appropriate under any circumstances. And if your organization is like many, it may well fire you on the spot.

 Zappos

At the beginning of the chapter, we took a look at how Zappos endeavors to create a corporate culture based on core values. Let's revisit the culture at Zappos now that we have learned a bit more about the way organizations shape, and are shaped by, communication.

▶ Hsieh made big changes in Zappo's culture. The company's core values reflect not merely employee-centric ideas like pursuing "weirdness" or building team spirit, but also ideas that are important to the company's financial stability, such as the holacratic culture in which teams self-organize and manage their own work.

▶ The company also places a premium on communication. The new headquarters is designed to foster face-to-face communication, with central entrances and corridors where top corporate officers, including Hsieh, work not in posh corner offices but in an open-plan, common work space in full view of coworkers and anyone taking a tour of the space (Spillman, 2013).

▶ One key issue facing large companies today is the debate over flexible time and work-at-home policies. At Zappos, the goal is clearly on keeping employees in a face-to-face environment and on reducing bureaucracy.

▶ Although Zappos is taking clear and committed steps toward cultivating its organizational culture, the company recognizes that culture does not form overnight. Hsieh feels that the process can take anywhere from five years to a lifetime. In fact, Hsieh wishes he had made cultural changes even sooner to reap the benefits faster (Guzman, 2016).

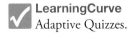 Activities

LaunchPad
macmillan learning

1. LaunchPad for *Real Communication* offers key term videos and encourages self-assessment through adaptive quizzing. Go to **launchpadworks.com** to get access to:

LearningCurve
Adaptive Quizzes.

Video clips that illustrate key concepts, highlighted in teal in the Real Reference section that follows.

2. Compare two organizations that you belong to or have regular contact with (such as a social organization, a volunteer organization, or a company). Describe the type of management approach at these two organizations. Also think about how the two organizations differ in their organizational culture. Be specific about how their values, artifacts, slogans, or assimilation practices vary.

3. Workplace comedies and dramas typically play off situations that actually arise in organizational settings. Watch a few episodes of such workplace sitcoms as *Parks and Recreation* and *Workaholics* or workplace dramas like *Grey's Anatomy* and *How to Get Away with Murder* and reflect on the different organizational contexts shown. What are the supervisor–supervisee relationships like? Are there any mentor–protégé relationships? What about peer relationships? How do these various relationships affect the way the organization functions?

4. In this chapter, we talk about the challenges that today's organizations face, including work–life balance, sexual harassment, and communication technology. Does your organization — be it a college or university, a club or campus organization, or a business — also tussle with these challenges? What challenges are specific to your organization? How might your organization minimize or adapt to these challenges?

real reference ▶ A Study Tool

Now that you have finished reading this chapter, you can:

Describe and compare approaches to managing an organization:

▶ **Organizations** are groups with a formal governance and structure (p. 292).

▶ **Organizational communication** is the interaction necessary to direct an organization toward multiple sets of goals (p. 292).

▶ The **classical management approach** focuses on how to make an organization run efficiently. This approach is dependent on two main ideas: the **division of labor**, the assumption that each part of the organization has a specific function, and **hierarchy**, the layers of power in an organization (pp. 292–293).

▶ The **human relations approach** considers the human needs of organizational members (p. 293).

▶ The **human resources approach** also values employees as assets to the organization who can be fulfilled by participating and contributing useful ideas (p. 294).

▶ The **systems approach** views an organization as a whole in which all members have interdependent relationships. Two key components of this approach are **openness**, an organization's awareness of its problems, and **adaptability**, an organization's allowance for change and growth (pp. 295–296).

Describe ways in which **organizational culture** is communicated:

▶ Through **organizational storytelling**, the communication of the organization's values through stories to the organization's members and to the outside world (p. 296).

▶ Using **organizational heroes**, the people who achieve great things for the organization (p. 297).

▶ Through **organizational assimilation**, the process by which people "learn the ropes" of the organization (p. 297).

Contrast relational contexts in organizations:

▶ In supervisor–supervisee relationships, the supervisor has power over the supervisee (pp. 298–299).

- In mentor–protégé relationships, the **mentor** is a respected member of the organization and serves as a role model for a less experienced individual, the **protégé** (p. 300).
- **Peer relationships** are the friendships that form between colleagues at an organization as a result of **peer communication**, communication between individuals at the same level of authority (p. 301).

Identify the challenges facing today's organizations:

- Given workplace diversity (of background, culture, and personality), conflict can often arise. If it results in behavior such as criticism, defensiveness, contempt, or stonewalling, then it must be dealt with so that colleagues can continue to work together effectively and peacefully (p. 303).
- Although the wealth of new communication technology has enabled easier communication, there is the added challenge of figuring out which channel to use (p. 304).
- The proliferation of communication technology has increased organizations' use of workplace **surveillance**, or the monitoring of employees to see how they are using the internet and social media at work (p. 305).
- **Globalization**, the growing interdependence and connectivity of societies and economies around the world, reduces barriers between countries for business (p. 306). **Global social enterprises (GSE)** attempt to help underdeveloped economies reach greater potential through improved innovation, entrepreneurship, and regional stability as well as by developing legal structures, stabilizing financial systems, and raising money (p. 306).
- Many struggle with **work–life balance** to achieve success in both their work and personal lives (pp. 307–309).
- *Harassment* is any communication that repeatedly hurts, offends, or embarrasses an individual, creating a hostile environment. One common type is **sexual harassment**, unwanted verbal or physical conduct of a sexual nature that affects an individual's employment; interferes with work performance; or creates an intimidating, hostile, or offensive work environment (pp. 310–311).

Apple fans became accustomed to the late Steve Jobs's releasing new devices or services with a dynamic and instructional keynote.

 LearningCurve can help you master the material in this chapter.
Go to **launchpadworks.com.**

chapter
13
Preparing and Researching Presentations

Since the early 1980s, Macintosh users have sung Apple's praises with a level of enthusiasm and devotion usually reserved for favored sports teams. The late Steve Jobs, the company's founder and former CEO, is still considered by many as one of the best corporate presenters ever (Shattuck, 2016). Whenever Apple launched a new product or service, Jobs was there, dressed in his trademark black turtleneck and beat-up sneakers, to introduce it.

Jobs always prepared for and practiced his presentations. He made sure he was intimately familiar with the company's products; in fact, many of the most revolutionary innovations at Apple were created from his own ideas and his frustrations with existing technology. A virtual music store where customers could legally download music for as little as a dollar a song and then carry them around in their pocket on a device smaller than a deck of cards? That was Jobs's idea. A mobile phone with only one button, a touchscreen, and the ability to add on a seemingly infinite number of applications? Jobs again (Sonnenfeld, 2011).

Jobs was well known for his effective and appropriate use of presentation aids. In many cases, his topic—be it the iPhone, iPad, iPod, or Mac—*was* the presentation aid. But because he was always so prepared for his speaking event, he was never entirely dependent on those aids. Communication coach Carmine Gallo notes that when a technological mishap occurred, Jobs was unfazed: "[He] casually laughed off the glitch, told a story, and got back to his presentation when his team resolved the issue. He never missed a beat and certainly didn't get flustered." How was he able to do this? "Jobs was legendary for his preparation. He would rehearse on stage for many hours over many weeks prior to the launch of a major product. He knew every detail of every demo and every font on every slide. As a result the presentation was delivered flawlessly" (Gallo, 2012).

Jobs's presentation style has influenced those following in his footsteps, notably his successor, Tim Cook, whose presentations continue to draw excitement and media attention around the globe.

**After you have finished
reading this chapter, you
will be able to**

- Describe the power of public
  speaking and how preparation
  eases natural nervousness

- Identify the purpose of your
  speech

- Conduct audience analysis

- Choose an appropriate topic
  and develop it

- Support and enliven your
  speech with effective research

- Give proper credit to sources
  and take responsibility for your
  speech

A public figure is expected to speak well, but few public figures — or people in general — are naturally gifted at public speaking. Fortunately, the ability to speak appropriately and effectively in a public environment can be learned, developed, and improved. Steve Jobs may have made the process look easy, but think about how ineffective his speeches would have been had he relied entirely on his cool presentation aids without preparing ahead of time.

As you will learn in this chapter, the initial groundwork of becoming a confident, competent speaker and developing strong presentations lies in preparation — namely, clarifying the purpose of your speech, analyzing your audience, choosing an appropriate topic, conducting research, and taking responsibility for your speech. Yet before we address these issues, we discuss why public speaking is so important in the first place.

The Power of Public Speaking

Jack has what his Irish mother called the gift of blarney. He is an eloquent conversationalist who dominates the discourse in business meetings and at cocktail parties. But put him in front of an audience, and he will panic. Jack's ability to charm friends and colleagues, impress potential dates, and talk his way out of parking tickets disappears completely once the atmosphere changes from informal to formal and his conversational partners are reduced to a more passive audience.

Public speaking always includes a speaker who has a reason for speaking, an audience who gives the speaker attention, and a message that is meant to accomplish a specific purpose (O'Hair, Stewart, & Rubenstein, 2018). It is an incredibly powerful form of communication that has, in fact, changed the world. From the ancient philosophers, who taught debate skills for use in the courts of ancient Greece, to nineteenth-century American abolitionists, who argued to end slavery in the United States, public speakers have charted the course of civilization. In fact, for centuries, oratory was *the* primary mode of public communication, and the most effective orators usually had the most influence in society. Today's influential "orators" may do some of their speaking on television (an official holding a press conference) or on social media (an activist posting a persuasive video), but their ability to speak well is still just as important. Public speaking has a critical role in the democratic process and in shaping society. Just think about what Jack could do if he used his powers of persuasion on a larger and more formal scale. As an informed and conscientious citizen, you too have the opportunity to promote social change by speaking out publicly on topics that matter to you.

Learning how to speak publicly can also play a powerful role in your personal and professional life, giving you an edge over less skilled communicators and putting you in a leadership role (Ahlfeldt, 2009; O'Hair & Stewart, 1998). Companies and personnel managers all over the United States have stated that public speaking is one of the most important skills a potential employee can possess (Bianca, 2013; National Association of Colleges and Employers, 2015).

What if you feel anxious about public speaking? First of all, realize that you are not alone: 75 percent of people experience pounding hearts and sweaty palms when they think about getting up in front of an audience (Richmond & McCroskey, 1998). Second, recognize that through patience and practice, you can counter some of this anxiety, if not conquer it altogether. Completing a course in communication is a great first step (Zabava, Ford, & Wolvin, 1993) as is following the advice we lay out here.

This chapter and the chapters that follow show you how to approach public speaking calmly and pragmatically. The first step lies with preparation, the focus of this chapter. The next step focuses on organization, which we talk about in Chapter 14. In Chapter 15, we discuss the causes of public speaking anxiety and offer techniques to manage any concerns you may have. For now, know that being concerned about giving a speech is natural, but preparation and solid effort can enable you to conquer your nervousness and make you a successful speaker (Bodie, 2010; Schroeder, 2002).

Clarify the General Purpose of Your Speech

In many real-life situations, choosing a topic and purpose for a speech is not a difficult task. You speak because you volunteered — or were forced — to speak on a specific topic for which your expertise is relevant to the situation. For example, you are a public health nurse giving a community presentation on the importance of early screening for breast or prostate cancer. In other cases, the parameters for a speech are quite general: a high school valedictorian or keynote speaker, for example, has to write a speech that both honors and inspires a large group. The possibilities for such speeches are endless. This communication class may provide a similar challenge — finding a speech topic and purpose that fit within your instructor's guidelines, which may range from very specific ("give a five-minute speech defending the constitutional right to free speech") to quite vague ("give a persuasive speech").

Speaking assignments usually fit within one of three general purposes: informative, persuasive, and special occasion.

Informative Speeches

In our information society, managing and communicating information are keys to success (Berrisford, 2006). *Informative speeches* aim to increase your audience's understanding or knowledge by presenting new, relevant, and useful information. Such speeches can take a variety of forms. They might explain a process or plan, describe particular objects or places, or characterize a particular state of affairs. You can expect to give informative speeches in a variety of professional situations, such as presenting reports to supervisors or stakeholders, running training sessions for a company, and teaching in formal education classes.

Consider a TED Talk given by cognitive neuroscientist Sarah-Jayne Blakemore about the social and cognitive development of the adolescent brain. Blakemore highlights the newest brain imaging technology that tracks how the brain develops in this critical life phase. Through her direct, informative, and engaging style, she connects with her audience and introduces a potentially confusing and challenging topic clearly, complete with attention-grabbing anecdotes, statistics, and humor. A brief excerpt from her presentation is offered in Sample Speech 13.1.

Sample Speech 13.1

The Mysterious Workings of the Adolescent Brain

Sarah-Jayne Blakemore

Fifteen years ago, it was widely assumed that the vast majority of brain development takes place in the first few years of life. Back then, 15 years ago, we didn't have the ability to look inside the living human brain and track development across the life span. In the past decade or so, mainly due to advances in brain imaging technology such as magnetic resonance

and you?

Have you ever experienced the power of a speech? Think about a specific presentation that you have seen — be it a watershed national event or a more personal experience such as a eulogy at a loved one's funeral. What about the speech stirred your emotions?

imaging, or MRI, neuroscientists have started to look inside the living human brain of all ages, and to track changes in brain structure and brain function. So we use structural MRI if you'd like to take a snapshot, a photograph, at really high resolution of the inside of the living human brain, and we can ask questions like, how much gray matter does the brain contain, and how does that change with age? And we also use functional MRI, called fMRI, to take a video, a movie, of brain activity when participants are taking part in some kind of task like thinking or feeling or perceiving something. •

> • Blakemore defines structural MRI and functional MRI by relating them to a photograph and a movie — two things her audience members are familiar with.

Many labs around the world are involved in this kind of research, and we now have a really rich and detailed picture of how the living human brain develops. This picture has radically changed the way we think about human brain development by revealing that it's not all over in early childhood, and instead, the brain continues to develop right throughout adolescence and into the 20s and 30s.

Adolescence is defined as the period of life that starts with the biological, hormonal, and physical changes of puberty and ends at the age at which an individual attains a stable, independent role in society. (Laughter) It can go on a long time. (Laughter) • One of the brain regions that changes most dramatically during adolescence is called prefrontal cortex. So this is a model of the human brain, and this is prefrontal cortex, right at the front. • Prefrontal cortex is an interesting brain area. It's proportionally much bigger in humans than in any other species, and it's involved in a whole range of high-level cognitive functions, things like decision making, planning, planning what you're going to do tomorrow or next week or next year, inhibiting inappropriate behavior — so, stopping yourself from saying something really rude or doing something really stupid. It's also involved in social interaction, understanding other people, and self-awareness. MRI studies looking at the development of this region have shown that it really undergoes dramatic development during the period of adolescence.

> • Blakemore uses humor to connect with her audience.

> • Here Blakemore uses a visual aid, a model of the human brain, to explain a difficult concept and to help orient her listeners.

Source: S. J. Blakemore. (2012, June). TED Talks: The Mysterious Workings of the Adolescent Brain. Retrieved from http://www.ted.com/talks/sarah_jayne_blakemore_the_mysterious_workings_of_the_adolescent_brain

● **AS A MUSICIAN,** Ricky Martin uses melody and lyrics to move his audience. As an activist, he harnesses the persuasive power of statistics as a call to action. Matt Jelonek/Getty Images

Persuasive Speeches

Persuasive speeches are very common in daily life and are a major focus of public speaking classes (Mazer & Titsworth, 2012). *Persuasive speeches* are intended to influence the attitudes, beliefs, and behaviors of your audience. Although they often ask for a *change* from your audience, persuasive speeches can also reaffirm existing attitudes, beliefs, and behaviors: a politician speaking at a rally of core constituents probably does not need to change their minds about anything, but she uses persuasive speaking nonetheless to get them excited about her platform or energized for her reelection campaign. In other cases, a persuasive speech is a more straightforward call to action. In Sample Speech 13.2, for example, the entertainer and human rights activist Ricky Martin urges members of the international community to step up efforts to end human trafficking. A United Nations goodwill ambassador, Martin offers both facts and statistics related to this global crime, outlines efforts to combat it, and calls for support.

Sample Speech 13.2

Speech at the Vienna Forum

Rɪᴄᴋʏ Mᴀʀᴛɪɴ

As a musician, activist, and universal citizen, I thank the United Nations Global Initiative to Fight Human Trafficking for allowing the Ricky Martin Foundation to share our commitment to end this horrible crime. Since this modern-day form of slavery has no geographical boundaries, the truly international reach of this unprecedented forum is an essential platform to combat this global nightmare.

My commitment toward this cause was born from a humbling experience. In my 2002 trip to India I witnessed the horrors of human trafficking as we rescued three trembling girls [who were] living on the streets in plastic bags. Saving these girls from falling prey to exploitation was a personal awakening. •

I immediately knew the Foundation had to fiercely battle this scourge. That was six years ago. . . . Since then the Foundation expanded and launched People for Children, an international initiative that condemns child exploitation. The project's goal is to provide awareness, education, and support for worldwide efforts seeking the elimination of human trafficking—with special emphasis on children.

This unscrupulous market generates anywhere from $12 to $32 billion annually, an amount only surpassed by the trafficking of arms and drugs. . . . My hope is to secure every child the right to be a child through a not-for-profit organization conceived as a vehicle to enforce their basic human rights in partnership with other organizations, socially responsible corporations, and individuals. . . . •

I am certain that our voices, together with the power of other organizations that work against this horrible crime, will continue to galvanize efforts to prevent, suppress, and punish human trafficking.

Changing attitudes and human behavior is difficult, but never forget that multiple small triumphs over a long period of time are tantamount to social change.

As a foundation that supports the objectives of this historic forum that aims to put this crime on the global agenda, be certain that:

We will continue to tell the world that human trafficking exists; we will keep educating the masses; and we will keep working on prevention, protection, and prosecution measures in our campaigns to alleviate the factors that make children, women, and men vulnerable to the most vicious violation of human rights.

Human trafficking has no place in our world today. I urge you to join our fight. React. It's time. •

Source: United Nations Global Initiative to Fight Human Trafficking. (2008, February 13). *Speech at the Vienna Forum by Ricky Martin.* Retrieved from www.ungift.org/ungift/en/vf /speeches/martin.html

• Note how Martin effectively uses a real-life personal experience to awaken his audience to the horror of the situation.

• Here, Martin lays out facts about this international crime and clearly describes his persuasive goal for his speech.

• Note how Martin ends his speech with a call to action to join the fight against human trafficking.

Special-Occasion Speeches

Special-occasion speeches use the principles of both informative and persuasive speaking for occasions such as introducing a speaker, accepting an honor or award, presenting a memorial, or celebrating an achievement. Almost certainly at some point in your life you will be called on to deliver a speech at a wedding, a toast at a retirement party, or a eulogy at a funeral. Special-occasion speeches are frequently delivered on the national and world stage as well. For example, while speeches made by politicians usually fall under persuasive speeches, some presidential addresses are made to celebrate or memorialize occasions. In his farewell address to the nation in January 2017, former President Barack Obama celebrated the country he was proud to serve for the past eight years. Despite a tense political climate, he stressed to all Americans—his audience—the need to participate in democracy. We can see in Sample Speech 13.3, an excerpt from Obama's speech, that uplifting ideas can work well at an occasion like the ending of a presidency.

Sample Speech 13.3

Farewell Address (2017)

Barack Obama

My fellow Americans—Michelle and I have been so touched by all the well wishes that we've received over the past few weeks. But tonight, it's my turn to say thanks. Whether we have seen eye-to-eye or rarely agreed at all, my conversations with you, the American people, in living rooms and in schools, at farms, on factory floors, at diners and on distant military outposts—those conversations are what have kept me honest, and kept me inspired, and kept me going. And every day, I have learned from you. You made me a better President, and you made me a better man . . . •

After eight years as your President, I still believe that. And it's not just my belief. It's the beating heart of our American idea—our bold experiment in self-government. It's the conviction that we are all created equal, endowed by our Creator with certain unalienable rights, among them life, liberty, and the pursuit of happiness. It's the insistence that these rights, while self-evident, have never been self-executing; that We, the People, through the instrument of our democracy, can form a more perfect union . . . •

And that's not easy to do. For too many of us, it's become safer to retreat into our own bubbles, whether in our neighborhoods or on college campuses, or places of worship, or especially our social media feeds, surrounded by people who look like us and share the same political outlook and never challenge our assumptions. The rise of naked partisanship, and increasing economic and regional stratification, the splintering of our media into a channel for every taste—all this makes this great sorting seem natural, even inevitable. And increasingly, we become so secure in our bubbles that we start accepting only information, whether it's true or not, that fits our opinions, instead of basing our opinions on the evidence that is out there. It falls to each of us to be those anxious, jealous guardians of our democracy; to embrace the joyous task we've been given to continually try to improve this great nation of ours. Because for all our outward differences, we, in fact, all share the same proud title, the most important office in a democracy: Citizen . . .

So, you see, that's what our democracy demands. It needs you. Not just when there's an election, not just when your own narrow interest is at stake, but over the full span of a lifetime. If you're tired of arguing with strangers on the Internet, try talking with one of them in real life. If something needs fixing, then lace up your shoes and do some organizing. If you're disappointed by your elected officials, grab a clipboard, get some signatures, and run for office yourself. Show up. Dive in. • Stay at it.

My fellow Americans, it has been the honor of my life to serve you. I won't stop. In fact, I will be right there with you, as a citizen, for all my

• Obama reveals humility by expressing his thanks to the American people for inspiring and teaching him, regardless of whether they agreed on issues.

• As is common in presidential speeches, Obama invokes the original ideals that the United States was founded upon, reminding Americans of the nation's values.

• After discussing some of the challenges the country faces, Obama encourages the audience to participate in democracy in order to live up to the country's ideals.

remaining days. But for now, whether you are young or whether you're young at heart, I do have one final ask of you as your President—the same thing I asked when you took a chance on me eight years ago. • I'm asking you to believe. Not in my ability to bring about change—but in yours.

Thank you. God bless you. May God continue to bless the United States of America.

• Obama concludes the speech with a call-to-action.

Analyze Your Audience

As you will quickly discover, **audience analysis**—a highly systematic process of getting to know your listeners relative to the topic and the speech occasion—is a critical step in the speech preparation process (O'Hair, Stewart, & Rubenstein, 2018; Yook, 2004). Because you are asking the audience members to accept your message—to learn new information; to change their attitudes, beliefs, or behaviors; or to recommit themselves to a cause or organization—it is important for you to understand them. You must consider not only their expectations but also the unique situational factors affecting them as well as their demographic and psychographic background and their potential reactions to your speech. Gaining this understanding will be crucial to choosing and shaping a topic that will resonate with them.

Considering Audience Expectations and Situational Factors

People naturally bring different sets of expectations and emotions to a speech event (O'Hair, Stewart, & Rubenstein, 2018). And as with other forms of communication discussed in this book, competent public speaking involves understanding and acknowledging the expectations of your communication partners—in this case, your audience.

Audiences are likely to have expectations about your speech based on the speaking situation, their cultural norms for public speaking, and even their knowledge about you as an individual or as a speaker. For example, think about the types of expectations you bring to a wedding toast. Would you expect a best man to say the bride is untrustworthy because she cheated on her taxes last year? This would clearly defy tradition and cultural expectations. Similarly, as we learned from some Russian colleagues, an American businessperson giving a speech in Moscow might defy audience expectations by coming right to the point when informing them about a particular technology. In Russia, audiences expect speeches to favor storytelling rather than direct fact sharing.

Audiences can also be influenced by a variety of situational factors that you cannot always plan for. Be aware of issues such as the time of day of your speech, events happening in the outside world, or the comfort and attractiveness of the room. These issues do matter when attempting to hold an audience's attention. Even the size of the audience is a relevant situational factor, as large (more than forty members) or small audiences may demand more or less interpersonal interaction, depending on your topic. To be a competent speaker, you should consider all of these factors when preparing your speech.

Considering Audience Demographics and Psychographics

Although understanding audience expectations and situational factors is an important component of audience analysis, it is only one of the important steps. You should also consider your audience's *demographics* and *psychographics*. **Demographics** are

and you?

Have you ever attended a speaking event where the speaker did not behave appropriately for the occasion? How did it make you feel as a listener?

connect

Analyzing expectations in a speaking situation may seem difficult, but you frequently do this work in other communication contexts. As we learn in Chapter 8, relational partners must address each other's expectations in order for the relationship to grow. Similarly, the speaker must remember the audience's expectations for the speaking occasion (e.g., level of formality or appropriate language) in order to be competent and successful.

● **THE BANE** of a school presenter's existence? Fidgety kids who would much rather poke their neighbors than pay attention. Pool/Getty Images

and you?

Have you ever found yourself feeling disconnected from a speaker, be it a course instructor or a politician, because he or she failed to consider your age, gender, interests, or lifestyle? Conversely, have you ever found a speaker particularly effective because he or she did consider such factors?

the quantifiable social categories of groups of people. Your analysis might identify statistics for audience members' gender, socioeconomic status (including income, occupation, and education), religious and political affiliations, family status (married, single, divorced, partnered, with children, without children), age, and ethnic background. Other statistics that might be relevant include student enrollment status (full or part time), student residential status (living on or off campus), major area of study, or the geographical regions your fellow students hail from. In addition to understanding their demographic categories, it can be important to analyze your audience's **psychographics**—their psychological qualities, such as attitudes, values, lifestyles, behaviors, and interests (Kotler & Keller, 2011; Paul, 2001). Market researchers are particularly interested in psychographics, as having such information allows them to more effectively market products to specific targets. To learn about people's psychological profiles, researchers closely monitor internet traffic, discussions, and trends on social media to see what people think about topics ranging from health and fitness to parenting.

Understanding demographics and psychographics can lead speakers to topics that will be of interest and will carry meaning for specific audiences. For example, one of the most easily quantifiable and useful demographic statistics to consider is the age range of your audience. If you have a good sense of how old most of your audience members are, you will be able to choose a topic that is relevant to concerns of their generation and ensure that the examples and anecdotes you use in your speech will resonate with the age groups you are addressing.

As we learned in Chapter 6, some audience characteristics will be more *salient*—or significant—in some speaking situations than in others. For example, if your audience members are mostly Latina women in their fifties who have survived breast cancer, their status as survivors is not likely to be salient if you are informing them about the importance of maximizing their annual contributions to their 401(k) plans before retiring in the next fifteen years. But if you are persuading a group to contribute money to the American Cancer Society in order to support new research campaigns, their experience fighting cancer should be firmly in your mind as you develop and deliver your speech.

Now, you are probably thinking, "How can I possibly know all of the demographics and psychographics of my audience members?" You are right, of course. You cannot necessarily know that the woman who sits three rows back on the left side of the classroom is an engineering major from a Lithuanian, middle-class family with a part-time job who writes for a tech blog and buys organic produce. But you can look for some general traits and trends. For example, most school websites make data available on factors like age, race, gender, and religion and often provide information on the percentage of students receiving financial aid, the number of students living on campus versus those who commute, full-time versus part-time students, and so on. You can also pay attention to general opinion polls on your proposed topic or consider the types of topics your classmates discuss in class or on social media.

There are some limitations of demographic and psychographic information that deserve mention here. Sometimes speakers—including politicians and advertisers—mistakenly apply stereotypes to demographic groups or overgeneralize about common opinions and beliefs of group members. And, in some cases, the results of demographic and psychographic data collection can be flawed or even downright wrong (Sprague, Stuart, & Bodary, 2012). Because of this, it is important to be mindful in the way you use this information. For example, your class may be 75 percent Catholic, but that does not *automatically* mean that they will be

● **ANGELINA JOLIE** often dons stylish all-black outfits in her role as an activist but alters her image based on the audience and context: formal wear for a press conference, casual clothes for field work. (left) ADRIAN DENNIS/Getty Images; (right) KHALIL MAZRAAWI/ Getty Images

interested in a speech related to the Church. Additionally, they may not agree with the official positions of the Church. That's why it is important to anticipate how your particular audience members might respond to your speech—even before you officially choose your topic and conduct your research.

Anticipating Your Audience's Response

As speech instructors, we openly confess that we get tired of hearing speeches on gun control, abortion, euthanasia, and abolishing the electoral college. These topics are surely worthy of thoughtful public discourse, but we have heard the same arguments over and over and are interested in learning about new topics. All audience members feel this way from time to time. You may be required to attend meetings at work that have nothing to do with your projects or your job; you may sit through a sermon at your house of worship that feels unrelated to your life experiences. When you are the speaker, it is always useful to remember these experiences and to do your best to ensure that you do not cause your audience to react the same way. Considering a few practical points, and adapting your speech accordingly, can certainly help:

▶ *Consider audience motivation.* Is your audience choosing to listen to your speech or are they required to attend? Voluntary audiences tend to be motivated to listen because they have *chosen* to hear what you say and are likely interested in your speech topic. The audience members in your class, however, are usually required to listen—and some of them may be entirely unmotivated to do so. Therefore, you must work to choose a relevant, engaging topic that they will care about and to engage them with your delivery skills (a topic we address in Chapter 15).

▶ *Seek common ground.* Do you and your audience members share certain opinions or experiences with one another? If so, you can capitalize on this **homogeny**—or sameness—by delivering a message that will keep their attention. For example, when his university changed its taxation policies for graduate students receiving stipends, Eduardo delivered a presentation informing his fellow students of the steps they would need to take to ensure proper tax withholding. It did not matter that the students hailed from assorted fields and departments because they were all stuck dealing with the same confusing tax questions.

what about you?

Assessing Your Audience Analysis

Before you prepare your presentation, you must be sure you have sufficiently considered your unique audience. Complete the following questionnaire prior to each presentation to make sure that your research and planning address your audience's needs, interests, backgrounds, and so on. Depending on the presentation, some factors may be irrelevant. Do not panic if you cannot discern every single trait, but you should have a sense of many or most.

Mark the number that most closely matches your feelings of preparedness regarding each statement: 5 = extremely confident; 4 = somewhat confident; 3 = unsure; 2 = somewhat unconfident; and 1 = extremely unconfident.

_____ 1. I know the ages of my audience members.

_____ 2. I am aware of the socioeconomic status of my audience members.

_____ 3. I know the family status (marital status, children) of my audience members.

_____ 4. I know the religious affiliations of my audience members.

_____ 5. I know the political affiliations of my audience members.

_____ 6. I know the ethnic background of my audience members.

_____ 7. I know how familiar my audience members are with my presentation topic.

_____ 8. I know the gender of my audience members.

_____ 9. I am aware of the sexual orientation of my audience members.

_____ 10. I am aware of how my audience members view me.

_____ 11. I know that my topic will be interesting to my audience.

_____ 12. I have identified ways to motivate my audience to listen.

_____ 13. I have carefully considered which aspects of my topic will interest my audience.

_____ 14. I have learned about the interests and life situations of my audience members.

_____ 15. I have considered my audience's expectations for my presentation.

_____ 16. I have considered the situational factors surrounding the delivery of my presentation.

Add your numbers together here: _____

Results
64–80: High confidence in audience analysis
33–63: Medium confidence in audience analysis
32–16: Low confidence in audience analysis

Generally, the lower your number, the greater is the need to revisit the audience analysis coverage in this chapter and seek more information about your audience members.

▶ *Determine prior exposure.* Audience members' interest in your speech may differ greatly depending on whether they have previously been exposed to your ideas and arguments. Having a general sense of what they know about the topic—and how they have reacted to it in the past—will help you prepare. For example, if your informative speech on evolution-based approaches to health (such as the popular "Paleo diet") went over well with your classmates, then it is reasonable to think that they might be open to a persuasive speech on why they should engage in a more "primal" lifestyle.

▶ *Consider disposition.* As noted earlier, your audience's preexisting attitudes toward a particular message—or even toward you as a speaker—can have an impact on how they receive your speech. If you are a company executive informing employees that they will not be receiving an annual pay raise, you can anticipate that your audience will be angry with the message (and may well dislike you as a speaker). You would be well advised to focus on areas of agreement, seek common ground, and attempt mutual understanding rather than sweeping changes in attitudes. (We address how to adjust your speech to receptive, hostile, and neutral audiences in Chapter 17.)

As was the case on gathering demographic and psychographic information on your audience members, you may wonder exactly *how* you go about finding information to anticipate your audience's reaction to your speech. Here are a few steps you can take that may yield incredibly helpful information.

▶ *Observe people.* People watching is a hobby for some but a must for speakers! You can learn a lot by casually observing those around you. How do fellow students react to topics discussed in class—particularly if the topics are controversial? What types of speakers do they seem to respond to?

▶ *Get to know people.* This may seem like common sense, but you would be surprised how often students complete a course without making personal connections. Talk to a few people who sit next to you in class or engage with discussion forums in your online course. Ask questions. Learn more about your classmates' hobbies and life situations as well as other factors that might help you develop an effective speech.

▶ *Survey and interview your audience.* You might also want to assess your audience on a more formal level. After receiving approval from your instructor, you might develop and distribute a short questionnaire to determine your classmates' opinions on a topic you are considering for your speech. Or you might talk with several members of a student organization to get feedback on your topic before you deliver your speech at the next group meeting.

▶ *Use the internet.* Do a search for opinion polls on your topic, especially polls that gauge the views of college students or other key demographic groups in your audience. Examine the kind of attention the issue has been getting on campus or in the local media (such as the school's newspaper or website).

All of the information you gain about your audience members—from their expectations and situational constraints to their demographics and possible reactions—sets the stage for you to move forward in developing an effective and appropriate speech. The next step is choosing your topic.

connect

When surveying and interviewing your audience to help anticipate their response to your speech, it is important to develop the most useful questions possible. For example, you want to consider whether to ask *open*, *closed*, or *bipolar questions* to get the information you need. And you want to avoid unethical directed, leading, and loaded questions. See the Interviewing Appendix for more information.

real communicator

NAME: Matt Schermerhorn
OCCUPATION: Sports Manager
Courtesy of Matt Schermerhorn

Imagine spending your day walking around the stadium during a Major League Baseball game talking to fans. That's my job — I get paid to watch baseball! Of course, it's only a small part of what I do in sports management for a Major League Baseball team. As you may know, those of us in this exciting field do everything from managing teams to managing events, sports venues, and recreation. It's a privilege to get to wear so many hats.

Everyone in my field shares a lifelong love of sports. But even if you consider yourself a particular sport's greatest fan, your passion may not be enough to land a sports management position. It's a tough market. I interned in sports management for my college baseball team while I was getting my degree in communication, along with studying the business, legal, and marketing aspects of sports management. My internship and my communication degree got me my position — everyone else in my work group had a previous contact on the team.

I'm on the special events and promotions team, where my communication skills get put to use in the planning and research for our public presentations. I think public speaking is the greatest skill you can have — not just in terms of giving speeches in front of large groups but also giving a "pitch" to the senior executives who are deciding on sponsorship and offering short, "feel-good-about-our-team" messages to community groups or charitable organizations.

Even social media marketing promotions require me to understand my audience and plan my message accordingly. Twitter is huge for us; it's currently our most efficient way to reach the general public in terms of news distribution. We don't just tweet randomly, however; tweets that come from the franchise have to be professionally crafted (though this certainly doesn't imply that they're dull or boring!).

Lots of planning and research go into all the events that support a major league team. We solicit and manage sponsors and help them design the best promotions for their product. Again, audience analysis is key; we can't afford to look bad because someone chose an image or a word (in an attempt to be creative or funny) that offends or annoys a client or the fans. The in-game entertainment that we provide fans is carefully researched and organized, too. As I go around the stadium on game day, I constantly assess whether or not our entertainment is engaging the diverse crowd members. I get feedback from teens and seniors, families and singles, and people of various ethnic backgrounds; I adjust our next presentation or event accordingly, whether it is directed to the sponsors or the fans.

There are so many communication skills I rely on in this job — from public speaking, to interviewing, to project leadership and group team building. I feel fortunate to have such a diverse, interesting, and fun job. I know I'm selling my company every day and I never stop learning.

Choose Your Topic

Choosing a topic can seem like a daunting task, but it does not have to be. As noted, you will want to consider the audience's expectations for the speech and topics that will interest them, taking their demographics and psychographics into account. In this course, you may have some guidance in that your instructor may give you a specific assignment. Be certain of your instructor's expectations for your speech, asking questions if necessary, to ensure that your topic and speech are appropriate. In searching for a good topic, you might try two proven strategies for generating ideas: considering personal interests, and brainstorming and clustering.

Finding a Topic That Intrigues You

It is difficult to give a persuasive speech about something you do not find particularly inspiring or an informative speech on a topic you know nothing about. Finding a topic that is interesting to you will prove useful, making you more motivated to research, refine your ideas, and generate audience enthusiasm.

But when you have a variety of interests, it can be hard to pinpoint one to speak about. One way to get started is to write up a list of topics that interest you. For example, take a look at the variety of interests listed in Table 13.1. Creating a thorough and detailed list of topics that interest you (or even others) can be a great tool for stimulating speech ideas.

● **CHOOSING** a topic from among numerous ideas and interests will call for some thinking and writing. Get creative! Radius Images/Alamy

Brainstorming and Clustering

Once you have determined a very general topic—from your interests or an instructor's assignment—you need to start amassing information, thinking creatively, and considering problems and solutions related to your topic. This is a process known as **brainstorming**.

While you are brainstorming, you might consider using a technique for identifying potential topics called **clustering** (Smith, 1993). It begins with a core idea from which the writer branches out into a web of related thoughts and ideas. Rather than generating a list of ideas, clustering "spills" ideas in a visual way. To begin, simply write a main word or phrase in a circle; then create a web or collection of ideas inspired by the nucleus word or phrase. See Figure 13.1 for a sample of clustering for the nucleus phrase *country music*. As the process continues, you will be struck by some concepts that might be suitable topics for your speech. In a sense, it is like Googling your own brain, starting out with a word or concept and branching to form a web of links to related thoughts.

TABLE 13.1
PERSONAL INTEREST TOPICS

Personal Experiences	Controversial Issues	Current Events	Hobbies	Beliefs and Values
Camping trips	Gun control	The economy and	Rock climbing	Social justice
Life-threatening event	Smoking bans	new job prospects	Hiking	Environmentalism
Education	Sexting	National debt	Cycling	Supernatural events
Organizations	Immigration	Sporting events	Blogging	Humanitarianism
Accomplishments	Prayer in public schools	Musical	Cooking	Spirituality
Military service	Internet privacy	performances	Online gaming	Forgiveness
Volunteer work	National health care	Acts of terrorism	Auto restoration	Retribution
Social media addictions		Global warming		
		Celebrity deaths		

Information from D. O'Hair, R. Stewart, & H. Rubenstein (2018), tab. 7.4, p. 98.

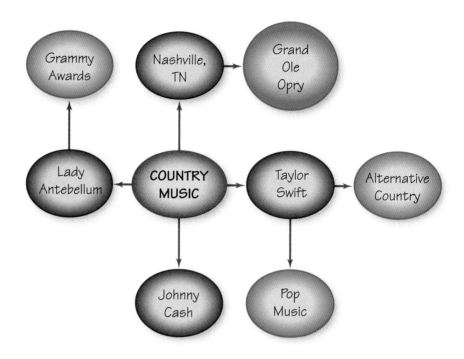

Narrowing Your Topic

Now that you have searched for potential topics, it is time to make a choice. Your goal is to select the topic that best meets the following three criteria:

1. Is it a topic you are interested in and know something about?

2. Does the topic meet the criteria specified in the assignment?

3. Is it a topic that your audience will find worthwhile?

Once you are satisfied that your topic meets these criteria, you can begin to consider how to break down your topic further so that it is more specific and manageable. This will aid you a great deal in your research (a topic we discuss later in this chapter) because it is considerably easier to find information on a specific topic (traditional Jewish foods served for Passover) than an extremely general one (the Jewish faith). One way to narrow down your topic is to break it up into categories. Write your general topic at the top of a list, with each succeeding word a more specific or concrete topic. As illustrated in Figure 13.2, you might begin with the very general topic of volunteering and then narrow the topic down a step at a time until you focus on one particular volunteer program (e.g., Read to a Child) and decide to persuade your listeners about the advantages of offering personal time to read to a local elementary school child.

Determining the Specific Purpose of Your Speech

Once you have narrowed your topic, you need to zero in on a specific purpose for your speech. Ask yourself: "What is it about my topic that I want my audience to learn, do, consider, or agree with?" A **specific purpose statement** expresses both the topic and the general speech purpose in action form and in terms of the specific objectives you hope to achieve with your presentation.

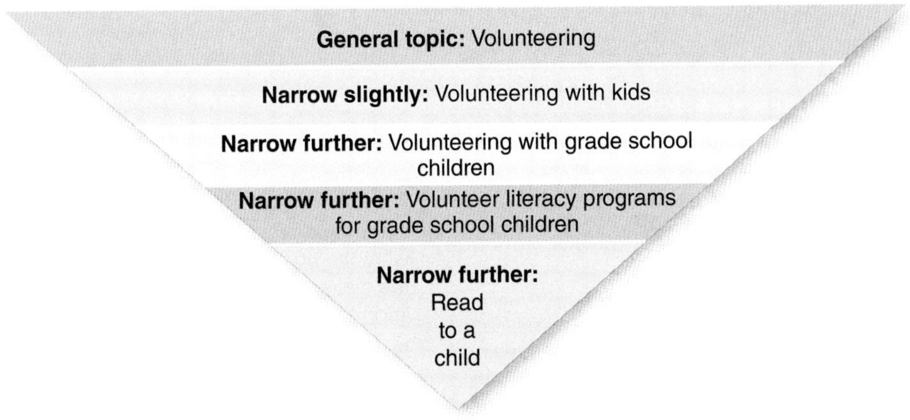

General topic: Volunteering

Narrow slightly: Volunteering with kids

Narrow further: Volunteering with grade school children

Narrow further: Volunteer literacy programs for grade school children

Narrow further: Read to a child

FIGURE 13.2

NARROWING YOUR TOPIC Start with a general idea and become increasingly specific until you have a manageable topic for your speech.

Let's consider an example. Imagine again that you are giving a persuasive speech on volunteering. Your general purpose and specific purpose might look like this:

Topic: Volunteer reading programs

General purpose: To persuade

Specific purpose: To have audience members realize the importance of reading with local elementary school children so that they sign up for a volunteer reading program such as Read to a Child

There is an additional level of specificity to consider when preparing your speech. It is called the *thesis statement*—you are probably familiar with this term from high school or college writing courses. We help you understand and develop your own thesis in the next section.

Developing a Thesis Statement

Once you have identified your topic, general purpose, and specific speech purpose, you encapsulate your speech in the form of a **thesis statement**, a statement that clearly summarizes the specific takeaway points that you want the audience to get out of your speech. For example, a possible thesis statement for the speech about volunteer reading programs might look like this:

Thesis statement: Volunteers who read with local elementary school children through programs such as Read to a Child improve young lives by enhancing children's self-esteem and expanding their possibilities for academic success.

Note how this thesis statement works with the general purpose and specific speech purpose mentioned earlier and how it expresses the core idea that you want your listeners to walk away with. Offering a solid thesis statement your audience will remember long after your visual aids have faded from their minds will help you achieve your general purpose and your specific purpose: to persuade your listeners to get out there and read with local kids. For additional examples of thesis statements, see Table 13.2.

connect

Your thesis statement helps you stay focused on your goals for communicating with others in a public speaking situation. But staying focused on goals also matters in communication contexts such as running a meeting. As we discussed in Chapter 11, clearly stating the purpose of your meeting and organizing your agenda around it helps everyone stay focused and makes you more likely to achieve your goals.

TABLE 13.2

GENERATING A THESIS STATEMENT

Topic	General Purpose	Specific Purpose	Thesis Statement
Low-carbohydrate diets	To inform	To inform listeners about low-carbohydrate diets so that they can make good decisions about their own eating habits	Before choosing to start a low-carbohydrate diet, it is important to have a thorough understanding of how carbohydrates affect your body and what the possible benefits and risks of the diet are so that you can make an informed decision about your health.
Study-abroad programs	To persuade	To have listeners realize that studying abroad is an exciting opportunity and encourage them to consider spending a semester taking classes in another country	Studying abroad is an amazing opportunity to learn about another culture, to enhance your educational experience, and to make yourself more appealing to prospective graduate schools and employers.
My grandparents	To honor an amazing couple on their fiftieth wedding anniversary (special occasion)	To celebrate with my family and my grandparents' friends in light of this happy milestone in their lives	In big and small ways, my grandparents have shared their fifty years of love and commitment with their family, their congregation, and their students, having been dedicated teachers for three decades.

Research the Topic

Any speech can provide information or a point of view. A *good* speech, however, should offer listeners something new, some unique information, insight, perspective, or idea that they did not have before. Such original thoughts are usually the product of both deep reflection and careful research.

In a speech, research is information that helps support the points that you make, strengthening your message and your own credibility. For many students, the prospect of researching for a speech or presentation might seem boring, overwhelming, or both—and it can be. But if you start with a topic that intrigues you and you approach your research in a practical way, the research process can actually get you more deeply involved in and committed to the points you want to make in your speech.

connect

The type of information you choose for your speech should be influenced by its general purpose. If you are persuading your audience (Chapter 17) or giving a speech for a special occasion, try using personal anecdotes to touch your audience emotionally. When informing your audience (Chapter 16), make sure that your use of anecdotes illuminates your topic and does not persuade the audience to think a certain way about it.

Types of Information to Consider

A wealth of material is available to enliven your speech and make it more effective. Listeners respond well to a range of compelling information, so try to include a variety of supporting materials in your speech, including testimony, scholarship and statistics, anecdotes, and quotations.

Testimony

When you need to prove a point about which you are not an authority, incorporating the voice of an expert into your speech can lend it some validity. **Expert testimony** is the opinion or judgment of an expert, a professional in his or her field. Opinions from doctors, coaches, engineers, and other qualified, licensed professionals serve as expert testimony. In a speech about knee surgery, for example, you might cite an orthopedic surgeon when explaining the difference between arthroscopy and knee replacement surgery. **Lay testimony** is the opinion of a nonexpert who has personal experience or witnessed an event related to your topic. In a speech on weather disasters, you could provide the testimony from a witness who survived a tornado.

Scholarship and Statistics

For many topics, it can be helpful to bolster testimonies with hard numbers and facts. **Scientific research findings** carry a lot of weight with audiences, particularly if your speech is related to research-oriented topics such as medicine, health, media, or the environment. For example, in a speech about educational television programs, a speaker might point out that studies have found that children who watched *Sesame Street* as preschoolers were more likely to enjoy elementary school and to achieve higher grades even in high school (Huston & Wright, 1998; Kearney & Levine, 2015).

Statistics—information provided in numerical form—can also provide powerful support for a speech, sometimes more than words. Statistics reveal trends, explain the size of something, or illustrate relationships. They can be made more meaningful when paired with or made part of *factual statements*—truthful, realistic accounts based on actual people, places, events, or dates. For example, when speaking about domestic violence, you might use a combination of statistics and factual statements to back your statement that a person is more likely to be killed by a family member or close acquaintance than a stranger:

> Out of 13,636 murders studied in the United States, 30.2% of the victims were murdered by persons known to them (4,119 victims), 13.6% were murdered by family members (1,855 victims), 12.3% were murdered by strangers (1,676 victims), and 43.9% of the relationships were unknown (investigators were not able to establish any relationship). (U.S. Department of Justice, 2010)

Although accuracy is important, we must note that specific numbers and percentages are cumbersome to speak aloud and can be easily forgotten by your audience. Remember that your visual aids can show the specifics while you round numbers and percentages aloud.

Anecdotes

Although facts and statistics are useful evidence, they can also be boring and easily forgotten. An effective way to breathe life into them, and into your speech in general, is including personal details that give faces to statistics and facts and make them part of a memorable and cohesive story. **Anecdotes** are brief, personal stories that have a point or punch line. The preceding statistics on murder would be greatly enhanced if they were paired with one or two personal stories that bring them down to a more intimate and relatable level. Anecdotes can be pointed or emotionally moving; they can also be humorous or inspiring. When used well, they add a personal and memorable element to your speech.

Quotations

You can also call on the words of others to lend your speech a sense of history, perspective, and timeless eloquence. *Quotations,* repeating the exact words of another person, are usually most effective when they are brief, to the point, and clearly

and you?

What type of supporting information do you find most compelling in speeches? Expert testimony? Statistics? Anecdotes? Why? Do you find that your preference depends on the topic of the speech? Why or why not?

communication across cultures

Human Trafficking: Art, Survival, and Advocacy

Brooke Axtell, singer and poet, made a powerful plea when she introduced Katy Perry during the 2015 Grammy Awards. At thirty-four years old, she gave a speech describing her survival of human trafficking and domestic abuse. She asserted, "Authentic love does not devalue another human being. Authentic love does not silence, shame or abuse." It was the perfect segue into Perry's rendition of "By the Grace of God."

Axtell has been a longtime activist against sexual violence (Dockterman, 2015). Her story began when she was seven years old. Her mother was hospitalized and her father traveled often because of his job, so she was left in the care of many nannies. In one of her poetry pieces, "What I Know of Silence," she describes the abuse she suffered when her nanny took her to the basement of an unknown house and sold her to men who raped her. Sadly, Axtell remained silent and carried her childhood pain into adulthood. She revealed that her childhood trauma led her to become involved in an abusive relationship in her adulthood, in which she experienced sexual violence again, this time by her boyfriend. Once she freed herself from that relationship, she discovered the power of art in helping her to recover from the trauma she had experienced in her childhood and adulthood. Since then, Axtell has released three albums and two collections of poetry and has been published widely online. She is the founder of Survivor Healing and Empowerment, a group that supports survivors of rape, abuse, and sex-trafficking and currently serves as the director of communications and survivor leadership for Allies Against Slavery, a group striving to end human trafficking (Brooke Axtell, 2016).

1. How does personal trauma and adversity inspire public speaking and, indeed, public life? Why might a victim of a crime choose to speak out? Why might he or she choose not to speak publicly?

2. What kind of supporting evidence would you look for if you were researching a speech on human trafficking? Should a victim like Axtell be expected to present the same kinds of evidence as you would? Why or why not?

3. Is Axtell's poetry an important cultural element surrounding this discussion? Why or why not?

related to your topic. You might quote a historical figure, a celebrity, a poet, or a playwright. For example, in a speech about motivation, you could quote Michelangelo: "The greatest danger for most of us is not that our aim is too high and we miss it but that it is too low and we reach it." Your sources do not need to be famous—you may be motivated to quote a friend or family member: "My grandfather always told me, 'An education is never a burden.'" Be sure to point out the source of your quote and, if necessary, explain who the person is or was.

Researching Supporting Material

Of course, the facts, statistics, anecdotes, and other supporting material that you want for your speech will not come out of thin air. Now that you have your list of ingredients for your speech, you will need to do some shopping—that is, you will need to go out and find the material. Here's how.

Talk to People

If you are looking for testimony, narratives, real-world examples, and anecdotes, you will need to start talking to people. You may be looking for experts in a particular field or people who have had firsthand experience with an event or occurrence, which can be a challenge. You can try networking with people you know, as well as searching online resources.

You can also talk to people via **surveys**, which involves soliciting answers to a question or series of questions related to your topic from a broad range of

● SURVEYING LOCAL
FARMERS about the effects of
factory farming and mass-produced
food on their livelihood will likely
give you some interesting insights
and quotations to use in your
speech. wdstock/Getty Images

individuals. Conducting a survey can give you a sense of how a group of people view a particular event, idea, or phenomenon. For example, if you are giving an informative speech on the ways text messages get misinterpreted, you might randomly select students on campus and ask them how often their text messages resulted in misinterpretations or conflicts. Results from surveys can be discussed to back up your points. Just remember to consider the credibility of your survey results. For example, did you make sure that the sample of people you surveyed was representative of the larger population of students?

Search the Literature

Published literature lets you reach beyond your own knowledge and experience and can be a valuable resource for supporting material for your speech. If you are giving a speech on hip-hop music, for example, you are likely to find some great material in the pages of a magazine like *Vibe.* If you are looking for studies on mental health issues affecting emergency personnel after the Boston Marathon bombings, you might search through newspaper articles or scholarly journals such as the *Journal of the American Medical Association.*

Most current publications are available in searchable databases in libraries; some can even be accessed online or via a tablet or smartphone apps (although you may have to pay a fee to download complete articles). Such databases give you access to a wealth of stored information. The Internet Movie Database (www.imdb.com), for instance, is a great example of a commonly used database, and its comprehensive information on film, television, and video games is entirely free.

Another type of secondary resource is a **directory**. Directories are created and maintained by people rather than automatically by computers. Because human editors compile them, directories — like the *American Library Directory Online* — often return fewer links but higher-quality results. Directories guide you to the main page of a website organized within a wider subject category. You can also access useful literature through **library gateways** — collections of databases and information sites arranged by subject, generally reviewed and recommended by experts (usually librarians). These gateway collections assist in your research and reference needs because they identify suitable academic pages on the internet. In addition to scholastic resources, many library gateways include links to specialty search engines for biographies, quotations, atlases, maps, encyclopedias, and trivia.

Make the Most of Online Research

Twenty years ago, the first stop on any research mission would have been the library. Today, the internet puts a massive amount of information at your fingertips. In fact, nearly half of all college students are using their smartphones and tablets to do research for their class assignments (Parker, Lenhart, & Moore, 2012). Navigating the vast sea of information — not to mention misinformation — available on the internet can be daunting and, without wise searching, a waste of time. A solid knowledge of search tools can therefore make your searches more fruitful and efficient.

wired for communication

think about this

The Library in the Sky

Wandering the stacks at the library has a certain romantic feel to it. But is it practical? The digitizing of books, newspapers, and journals has effectively removed the walls between centuries of content and end users. If, for example, you want to write an informative speech on the history of your hometown, you could quickly enter the name of your town into any number of digital archives and access a wealth of news articles and literary references to it in major newspapers dating back several centuries (*The New York Times* digital archive, e.g., goes back to 1851). You might find stunning photos of your town from the Associated Press or Corbis photo archives (you can search them for free). The Library of Congress Archive has an ever-growing online collection, where you might find photos, posters, letters, and artifacts. And you will be able to search through more books than any brick-and-mortar library could possibly hold, thanks to a somewhat controversial project started by Google.

The Google Books Library Project, which aims to "make it easier for people to find relevant books — specifically, books they would not find any other way such as those that are out of print," offers searchable digital scans of millions of books through partnerships with major public and university libraries around the world (https://www.google.com/googlebooks/library/). For books in copyright, Google will provide links to sources you can purchase them from as well as libraries from which you can borrow. Books no longer in copyright (most books more than ninety years old are in the public domain) can be viewed in full; you can even download a pdf of the entire book. So if a writer stumbled through your town on the way to the California gold rush in 1849 and wrote about it in a novel, a poem, or work of nonfiction, you can find out what he or she thought about it.

Google Books remains somewhat controversial: a class-action lawsuit on behalf of copyright holders was filed. However, a judge sided with Google and argued that the book search does not infringe copyright (*The New York Times*, 2013). But for researchers — or anyone who is just a little intellectually curious, really — there is no denying that the ability to access primary sources quickly, from anywhere, and often for free, opens new doors of discovery and allows even the most casual internet surfer to stumble onto texts that were out of reach, or perhaps just languishing unnoticed on library shelves, for decades.

1. Primary sources are of particular importance to historians, who rely on firsthand accounts of events and phenomena to understand a particular period. What primary sources would be helpful when researching your hometown's history? How might they be used in a speech?

2. Some see the digitizing of content as a great way to level the intellectual playing field. But how level is it? Google Books is free, but many archives are not, and many Americans still do not have access to the internet at home. How can access be further democratized? Should it be?

3. With so much information going digital, what is your opinion on brick-and-mortar libraries today? Do you think they are as important as they once were? What kind of help can librarians provide?

An internet **search engine** is a program that indexes website content. Search engines such as Google, Yahoo!, and Bing search the internet for documents containing specific keywords that you have chosen. Search engines have some key advantages — they offer access to a huge portion of publicly available websites and give you the ability to search through large databases. But they frequently return irrelevant links, and they do not index the "invisible web" — databases maintained by universities, businesses, the government, or libraries that cannot always be accessed by standard search engines. Another great resource is a **research search engine**, which will search only for research published in academic books, journals, and other periodicals. One of the best research search engines is Google Scholar (scholar.google.com), as it has a wide variety of resources. For example, if you type, "binge drinking" into Google Scholar, the search engine will identify about 91,900 scholarly results. Note, however, that you might need to be logged in to your campus library's database system in order to get access to the full research articles that Google Scholar shows (without having to pay).

Evaluating Supporting Material

Once you have gathered a variety of sources, you must critically evaluate the material and determine which sources you should use. After all, your credibility as a speaker depends largely on the accuracy and credibility of your sources as well as their appropriateness for your topic and your audience.

Credible Sources

In today's media, anyone can put up a blog or a website, edit a wiki, or post a video to YouTube. (This is why many instructors forbid students to use supporting material from Wikipedia.) What's more, a large and growing number of opinion-based publications, broadcasting networks, and websites provide an outlet for research that is heavily biased. Consequently, it is always worth spending a little time evaluating **credibility** — the quality, authority, and reliability — of each source you use. One simple way to approach this is to evaluate the author's credentials. This means that you should note if the author is a medical doctor, Ph.D., attorney, CPA, or other licensed professional and whether he or she is affiliated with a reputable organization or institution. For example, if you are seeking statistics on the health effects of cigarette smoke, an article written by an M.D. affiliated with the American Lung Association would be more credible than an editorial written by a high school French teacher.

A credible source may show a trail of research by supplying details about where the information came from, such as a thorough list of references. In newswriting, source information is integrated into the text. A newspaper or magazine article, for example, will credit information to named sources ("Baseball Commissioner Rob Manfred said. . . .") or credentialed but unnamed sources ("One high-ranking State Department official said, on condition of anonymity. . . .").

The internet poses special problems when it comes to credibility due to the ease with which material can be posted online. Check for balanced, impartial information that is not biased, and note the background or credentials of the authors. If references are listed, verify them to confirm their authenticity. Websites can be quickly assessed for reliability by looking at the domain, or the suffix of the website address. Credible websites often end with .edu (educational institution), .org (organization), or .gov (government).

connect

The sources you cite in your speech are part of your *self-presentation* to your audience (Chapter 3). If your sources are outdated or from your cousin's blog, you will present a self that says, "I am unprepared and I didn't research my topic thoroughly." Conversely, if you offer statistics, facts, and stories from a variety of current, reliable, and compelling sources, you present yourself as trustworthy, prepared, and competent — and your audience is more likely to consider what you are saying.

Up-to-Date Sources

In most cases, you will want to use the most recent information available to keep your speech timely and relevant. Isaiah, for example, is speaking to a group of potential clients about his company's graphic design services. If he makes reference to testimonials from satisfied clients in 2014 and earlier in his speech, the audience may wonder if the company has gone downhill since then. For this reason, always determine when your source was written or last updated; sources without dates may indicate that the information is not as timely or relevant as it could be.

Naturally, one exception to this rule deals with historical or classic speech or research topics. If you are researching a speech to inform your audience about the achievements of early twentieth-century pilot Amelia Earhart, for example, you should feel free to use quotations and statistics from her heyday.

Accurate Sources

When compiling support for your speech, it is important to find accurate sources — sources that are true, correct, and exact. A speaker who presents inaccurate information may very well lose the respect and attention of the audience. There are several ways to help ensure that you are studying accurate sources. In addition to being credible and up to date, accurate sources are exact, meaning that they offer detailed and precise information. A source that notes that 54 percent of Americans over age sixty-five now have access to the internet (Pew Internet, 2015) is more accurate than a source that states that about half of senior citizens have such access. The more precise your sources, the more credibility you will gain with your audience.

Compelling Sources

Support material that is strong, interesting, and believable is considered to be *compelling* information. This kind of information helps your audience understand, process, and retain your message. A speaker might note that 3,154 people were killed and 424,000 people were injured in motor vehicle crashes involving a distracted driver in 2013 (CDC, 2013). Two of the most significant causes of distracted driving are phone calls and text messaging, with 69 percent of U.S. drivers between the ages of eighteen and sixty-four reporting that they talked on the phone while driving in the month before the survey and another 31 percent of the same demographic noting that they had read or sent messages (text or email) while driving during the same time period (CDC, 2013). Now those are some compelling statistics!

To be compelling, your supporting material should also be *vivid*. Vivid material is clear and vibrant, never vague. For example, in a speech about cyclical cicada invasions in the area of Washington, DC, Ana might reference a source describing these bugs as large insects, about one and a half inches long, with red eyes, black bodies, and fragile wings; she might also use a direct quotation from a resident who notes that "there were so many cicadas that the ground, trees, and streets looked like they were covered by an oil slick." Such vivid (and gross) descriptions of information interest listeners. Look for clear, concrete supporting details that encourage the audience to form visual representations of the object or event you are describing.

Ethical Speaking: Take Responsibility for Your Speech

As a responsible public speaker, you must let ethics guide every phase of planning and researching your speech. Being an ethical speaker means being responsible: responsible for ensuring that proper credit is given to other people's ideas, data, and research that you have incorporated into your presentation as well as being responsible for what you say (and how you say it) to your audience. Let's start with what happens when you fail to cite your sources properly: plagiarism.

Recognizing Plagiarism

Plagiarism is the crime of presenting someone else's words, ideas, or intellectual property as your own, intentionally or unintentionally. It is a growing problem and is not limited to the written word — or to students (Park, 2003). Earlier in his career, *Time* columnist and CNN host, Fareed Zakaria, was suspended over an allegation of plagiarism involving a column he wrote on gun control. Zakaria had not cited his sources correctly and later apologized, acknowledging that he had made a mistake. Despite the fact that he was ultimately reinstated, Zakaria certainly suffered the consequences of his actions, particularly an unforgettable blow to his image as a journalist (Haughney, 2012). It took him time and a great deal of effort to rebuild his image.

Most universities and colleges have clear definitions of plagiarism and enforce strict penalties regarding the issue — your school's plagiarism policy may even be included on your class syllabus. If so, *read this document carefully*. The syllabus is like your contract with your professor; by enrolling in the course, you have agreed to follow it.

evaluating communication ethics

think about this

Didn't I Already Say That?

You met Alex in your speech communication class and formed a fast friendship when you realized that you both were from Orlando. You are listening to Alex deliver a speech about gun control in the aftermath of terrorist attacks in a nightclub, the deadliest mass shooting in U.S. history. His speech is compelling, and you are enthralled by his detailed account of how innocent people's lives were tragically taken away by a gunman. Having similar attitudes toward guns, you find yourself nodding in agreement with much of what he says. But when he closes with a passage about the lessons the event taught him — from appreciating the American value of freedom to counting his blessings — it seems eerily familiar. In fact, it is an almost verbatim copy of something you posted on Facebook the summer before you met Alex. When you get back to your dorm room and pull up your Facebook history, you realize that a mutual friend, Elliot, had been moved by your post and shared it on his own page. Alex must have seen it there, because he used it almost wholesale, changing only minor details, like the names of your family and your elementary school.

    You are angry — on many levels. You poured your heart into that post, and although it was only about a hundred words, it took you a good deal of time to write and rewrite until it captured exactly how you were feeling. Now you feel like someone has stolen not only your work but your feelings as well. Even worse, you saw that the class was moved by Alex's — *your* — conclusion, and you are certain he will get a good grade based at least in part on something you wrote. And because your privacy settings are pretty tight, the passage will not come up on a standard internet search, so you know it is unlikely that he will get caught unless you say something. What do you do?

1. Is what Alex did considered plagiarism? Do you even "own" the content you create and post on Facebook?

2. How is your friend Elliot sharing your post different from what Alex did? Does it matter how the content was shared? Was your name credited in Elliot's post?

3. How will you deal with this instance of plagiarism? Should you alert your instructor? Confront Alex? If you were the instructor, how would you handle the situation?

and you?

How do you feel about the fact that even unintentionally using someone else's words, ideas, or intellectual property is still plagiarism? Does it seem unfair that you might suffer severe consequences (such as being expelled) even if you do something without intent? Why or why not?

Despite the problems associated with plagiarism, many students, writers, and speakers remain unsure of how, when, or why they must credit their sources. In fact, many people are shocked to find that they can be guilty of plagiarism with a seemingly unimportant error, like simply failing to include quotation marks or mistakenly deleting one little footnote when completing a paper or speech. To avoid making the same mistake, keep careful track of where all your material comes from and document it properly. In Chapter 14, we explain how to document your sources in your speech; for now, we will focus on the important role of taking accurate and thorough notes during the research phase.

Taking Accurate Notes

The noted historian Doris Kearns Goodwin was accused of using passages from three other books in her own work without proper attribution. After settling with the wronged authors and making corrections to her book, Goodwin explained that the misrepresentation had been the result of a crucial error she had made during the note-taking phase. "Though my footnotes repeatedly cited [another author's] work, I failed to provide quotation marks for phrases that I had taken verbatim, having assumed that these phrases, drawn from my notes, were my words, not hers" (Goodwin, 2002, para. 3).

As this example shows, keeping track of all your outside material and its sources can be challenging, which is why taking accurate notes is so critical. To keep yourself organized, consider using note cards to keep track of references separately. Or place all of your references and source material into an electronic document, such as a word processing file or a note-taking application on your smartphone or tablet. For example, many of our students use the basic Note feature that comes standard on the iPad and iPhone to stay organized, and they have also had good experiences with free, platform-agnostic apps. Evernote, for example, allows you to create and save notes in organized folders; you can even "clip" full internet pages, annotate them to highlight the information you need, and save them as entries for later use, as shown in Figure 13.3.

Regardless of the format you choose, your entry should contain or highlight the quote or material you want to use, along with pertinent information, such as author name, publication information (title, volume, publisher, location, date), and relevant page or paragraph numbers from the source. In addition, each entry should note whether the material is copied *verbatim* (word for word) or *paraphrased* (put into your own words). When you have completed your research, you will be able to shuffle or copy and paste these individual cards or entries as you develop your speech without losing track of their sources.

You will also need to keep a **running bibliography**—a list of resources you have consulted. There are various styles of organizing these resources (including styles dictated by the Modern Language Association, American Psychological Association [APA], etc.), so make sure to ask your instructor what his or her preference is if you are required to hand in this document. Regardless, all styles generally require you to list the following information:

► The complete name of each author or origin of the source if no author is named ("National Science Foundation website," or "*New York Times* editorial")

► The title and subtitle of the source (article, book chapter) and of the larger work in which it appears (magazine, newspaper, journal, book, website)

ARTICLES

Illinois's Glen Carbon Centennial Library was named Library Journal's 2010 Best Small Library in America.

LITERACY-RICH ENVIRONMENTS:

Reading and Writing at Home

Which will your child learn first: to read or to write? Most children develop these skills at the same time. The following are some things you can do to help your children become readers and writers:

Read aloud every day.
- Set aside a regular time for reading that your children can count on.
- Find other times to read; for example, when you're waiting at the doctor's office.
- Read aloud the items you use in daily life: food labels, directions for baking a cake, and birthday cards.
- Listen to your child pretend to read a book from memory.

Have plenty of children's books around your home.
- Keep books where children can reach them.
- Go to the library regularly.
- Look for secondhand books at yard sales and thrift shops.
- Encourage family and friends to give books as gifts.

Stock up on writing and drawing supplies.
- Store things to write on: paper, pads, and a chalkboard.
- Store things to write with: crayons, markers, pencils, and chalk.
- Store supplies for making books: cardboard, a stapler, a hole punch, and laces.
- Save items to cut and paste: junk mail, catalogs, coupons, and old magazines.
- Keep magnet letters on the refrigerator.
- Store alphabet stamps and a stamp pad.

These are great tips for anyone practicing reading with kids--I should mention this in my speech

Source: "Reading and Writing at Home" (n.d.) Reading is Fundamental, retrieved from http://www.rif.org/us/literacy-resources/articles/reading-and-writing-at-home.htm

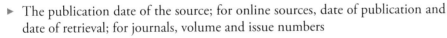
Paraphrased: Plan a regular reading time, keep books around, and visit the library

FIGURE 13.3

IF YOU PREFER to do online research, Evernote can help you to keep a record of your sources and annotate them with notes for your speech.

▶ The publication date of the source; for online sources, date of publication and date of retrieval; for journals, volume and issue numbers

▶ For books, publisher and city of publication; for online resources, the complete URL

▶ Page numbers for the material used and for the entire work being cited

We present an example of a running bibliography in APA style in Figure 13.4.

Speaking Ethically and Responsibly

Your responsibility as a speaker goes beyond simply giving credit to others' work; you need to take responsibility for what *you* say.[1] The First Amendment to the U.S. Constitution guarantees every citizen the right to free speech, but not all speech is ethical. If you use inflammatory, hurtful, or hateful language, even if quoted and cited from another source, you will bear the brunt of the audience's reactions. In addition, it is important to recognize that the right to free speech in the United

● ALTHOUGH THE First Amendment allows anyone to step up on a soapbox and say whatever he or she wants to say, it is still important to refrain from unethical or derogatory speech. NMPFT/DHA/SSPL/The Image Works

---

[1] Much of this discussion was inspired by the work of Michael Josephson, founder and president of the Joseph and Edna Josephson Institute of Ethics in Marina del Rey, California.

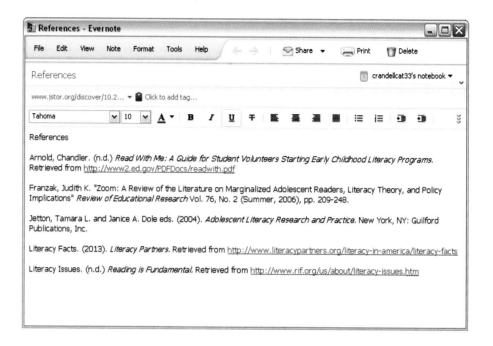

States is not without limits. As Supreme Court Justice Oliver Wendell Holmes wrote, the Constitution "would not protect a man falsely shouting fire in a theater and causing a panic" (*Schenck* v. *United States,* 1919). Speech that endangers people—for example, speech that incites riots, advocates the unlawful overthrowing of the government, or causes unnecessary panic—would not only be ethically questionable but might be illegal as well (*Gitlow* v. *New York*, 1925; *Schenck* v. *United States*, 1919).

Although everyone has different standards for ethical communication, the qualities of dignity and integrity are universally seen as core to the idea of ethics. *Dignity* is feeling worthy, honored, or respected as a person; *integrity* is incorruptibility, the ability to avoid compromise for the sake of personal gain (Gudykunst, Ting-Toomey, Sudweeks, & Stewart, 1995). Basic rules for ethical speaking require that we adhere to four principles: we should strive to be trustworthy, respectful, responsible, and fair in our speeches (Day, 1997).

▶ *Trustworthiness* refers to being honest with your audience about the goal of your message and providing accurate information.

▶ By treating people right, you are showing *respect*. In public speaking, respect is shown by focusing on issues rather than on personalities, allowing the audience the power of choice, and avoiding excluding the audience in discussions.

▶ As a *responsible* public speaker, it is your job to consider the topic and purpose of the speech, evidence and reasoning of the arguments, accuracy of your message, and honest use of emotional appeals.

▶ Ethical public speakers must be *fair* by presenting alternative and opposing views to the audience. A fair speaker will not deny the audience the right to make informed decisions.

and you?

Consider your own personal opinions about ethical speaking. Would you add anything to the four principles noted here? If so, what characteristics would you cite?

 Steve Jobs

At the beginning of this chapter, we talked about how the late Steve Jobs's careful preparation and intimate knowledge of his projects enabled him to be a powerful public speaker on behalf of his company. Let's take a look at his presentation skills in light of what we have learned in this chapter.

▶ Clearly, Steve Jobs enjoyed technology. But he also knew the importance of preparation and practice. If he relied entirely on presentation aids, he would have fallen flat during inevitable technical glitches. His research and preparation shined brighter than his presentation technology.

▶ Jobs also knew his audience. His audience of Apple fans was always eager to hear what he had to say and see what he had to show. He did not bother talking about competing products, because he knew the crowd was more interested in hearing about Apple products.

▶ Prior exposure played a role in the way Jobs presented his products. The original iPod, launched in 2001 along with the iTunes Store, was a revolutionary device, and Jobs's presentation was full of surprises for his audience. When introducing later iterations of the device, Jobs focused only on new features and options.

▶ The company also limits prior exposure by maintaining a high level of secrecy about products in development. When Jobs introduced a *new* product, there was little chance that the crowd had already heard anything more than rumors about it beforehand, which affected how Jobs presented information to the audience.

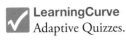 Activities

LaunchPad
macmillan learning

1. LaunchPad for *Real Communication* offers key term videos and encourages self-assessment through adaptive quizzing. Go to **launchpadworks.com** to get access to:

LearningCurve
Adaptive Quizzes.

Video clips that illustrate key concepts, highlighted in teal in the Real Reference section that follows.

2. Think back to a memorable speech you have witnessed, either in person or through the media. What kind of speech was it? Was the speaker trying to inform, persuade, or celebrate? Was he or she successful in that endeavor? Did the speech change the way you felt?

Justin Sullivan/Getty Images

3. Tune in to a few news pundits—for example, Glenn Beck, Rachel Maddow, Tomi Lahren, or Rush Limbaugh—on the radio, on television, or online. Listen carefully to what they say, and consider how they back up their statements. Do they provide source material as they speak? Can you link to their sources from their online blogs? How does the way they back up their points or fail to back them up influence your perceptions of what they say?

4. Take a look at your school's policy on plagiarism. Does your school clearly define what acts constitute plagiarism? How harsh are the punishments? Who is responsible for reporting plagiarism? How is the policy enforced?

5. The next time you read something—a magazine article, a political blog, a work of nonfiction, a chapter in a textbook—take time to think about the research presented in it. What kinds of research did the authors do? How do they back up their statements? What kinds of research materials do they include?

real reference ▶ A Study Tool

Now that you have finished reading this chapter, you can:

Describe the power of **public speaking** and how preparation eases natural nervousness (p. 316).

Identify the purpose of your speech:
- ▶ *Informative speeches* aim to increase the audience's understanding and knowledge of a topic (p. 317).
- ▶ *Persuasive speeches* are intended to influence the beliefs, attitudes, and behaviors of an audience (p. 318).
- ▶ *Special-occasion speeches* are given at common events (like weddings and funerals), and many of us will deliver such a speech at some point in time (p. 319).

Conduct **audience analysis** (p. 321)
- ▶ It is important to understand and appreciate your audience's expectations for the speech as well as key situational factors (p. 321).
- ▶ Knowing **demographics**, the quantifiable characteristics of your audience, and **psychographics**, psychological measures, will help you identify topics that the audience would be interested in learning about (pp. 321–322).
- ▶ You will want to anticipate your audience's response by considering their motivation, seeking common ground (**homogeny**), determining prior exposure, and considering disposition (pp. 323, 325).
- ▶ You can learn about your audience by observing people, getting to know people, conducting interviews and using surveys, and using the internet (p. 325).

Choose an appropriate topic and develop it:
- ▶ Speak about something that inspires you (p. 327).
- ▶ Use **brainstorming** and **clustering** to amass information, think creatively, and consider problems and solutions related to your topic (p. 327).
- ▶ A **specific purpose statement** expresses the topic and the general speech purpose in action form and in terms of the specific objectives you hope to achieve with your presentation (p. 328).

▶ Narrow your topic and write a **thesis statement**, a summary of your central idea (pp. 328–329).

Support and enliven your speech with effective research:

▶ Include **expert testimony**, the opinion of an authority, or **lay testimony**, opinion based on personal experience (pp. 330–331).

▶ **Scientific research findings** carry weight in topics on medicine, health, media, and the environment; **statistics**, information in numerical form, can clarify your presentation (p. 331).

▶ **Anecdotes**, relevant personal stories, bring the human experience to the speech (p. 331).

▶ **Surveys** will add the point of view of larger range of people (p. 332).

▶ Use databases to find material, such as **directories**, **library gateways**, **search engines**, and **research search engines** (pp. 333–335).

Cull from among your sources the material that will be most convincing:

▶ Take time to evaluate the **credibility**— the quality, authority, and reliability—of each source you use (p. 335).

▶ Up-to-date information convinces the audience of its timeliness (p. 336).

▶ Citing accurate and exact sources gains audience respect (p. 336).

▶ Compelling information is influential and interesting (p. 336).

Give proper credit to sources and take responsibility for your speech:

▶ Avoid **plagiarism**, presenting someone else's intellectual property as your own (p. 337).

▶ Keep accurate track of all your references to avoid unintentional errors (pp. 338).

▶ Keeping a **running bibliography**, the list of resources you have consulted, will free you from having to write the same information over and over (p. 338).

▶ Honor the basic rules for ethical speaking (p. 340).

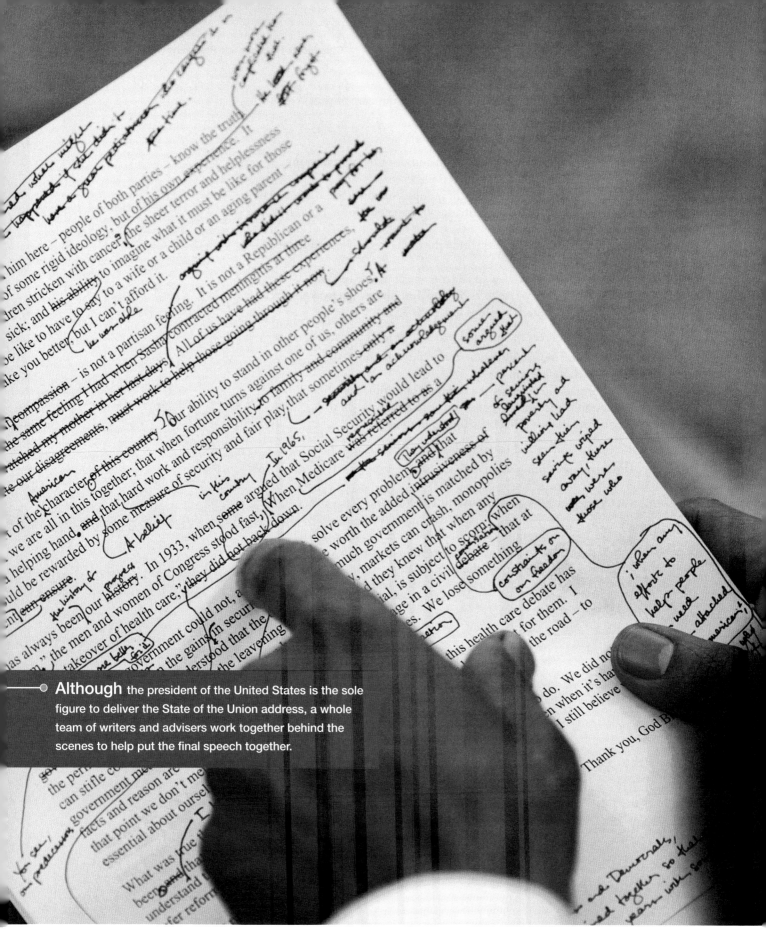

Although the president of the United States is the sole figure to deliver the State of the Union address, a whole team of writers and advisers work together behind the scenes to help put the final speech together.

 LearningCurve can help you master the material in this chapter.
Go to **launchpadworks.com**.

chapter

14

Organizing, Writing, and Outlining Presentations

The Constitution of the United States of America makes a simple demand of the president. "He shall from time to time give to the Congress Information of the State of the Union, and recommend to their Consideration such Measures as he shall judge necessary and expedient" (art. 2, sec. 3).

For much of our nation's history, the State of the Union address was a lengthy letter to Congress read to members of the Senate and House by a congressional clerk. But over time, it has evolved into an elaborate and highly politicized annual affair that allows the president to present major ideas and issues directly to the public: the Monroe Doctrine (James Monroe, 1823), the Four Freedoms (Franklin D. Roosevelt, 1941), the War on Terror (George W. Bush, 2002), and the economic overhaul (Barack Obama, 2013) were all detailed for the American people during State of the Union addresses (Amadeo, 2013; Longley, 2007; Schmidt, 2015).

And so each January, White House speechwriters face the daunting task of addressing both Congress and the nation with a speech that outlines what is going on in foreign and domestic policy in a way that flatters the president and garners support for the following year's agenda. To make the task even more difficult, speechwriters must also navigate a deluge of requests from lobbyists, political consultants, and everyday citizens eager to get their pet project, policy, or idea into the president's speech. "Everybody wants [a] piece of the action," lamented former White House speechwriter Chriss Winston. "The speechwriter's job is to keep [the speech] on broad themes so it doesn't sink of its own weight." President Obama's director of speechwriting, Cody Keenan, took pains to craft just the right language to invoke the daily struggles of ordinary Americans. Keenan, like many before him, was known to pull all-nighters and frequently submit updated drafts of the speech to the president (Schuppe & Alexander, 2016).

**After you have finished
reading this chapter, you will
be able to**

- Organize and support your
  main points

- Choose an appropriate
  organizational pattern for your
  speech

- Move smoothly from point to
  point

- Choose appropriate and
  powerful language

- Develop a strong introduction
  and conclusion, crucial parts of
  all speeches

- Prepare an effective outline

Imagine that you are building a bridge, a skyscraper, or even a house. You might have ambitious blueprints, but before you can build it, you need to form a solid foundation and develop a structurally sound framework. Any architect will tell you that even the most exciting and lofty designs are useless without these two crucial components. Skimp on either one and your structure will crack, shift, or collapse.

Building a speech follows a similar process. Whether you are writing a national address for the president of the United States or a 5-minute class presentation, you will be unable to make your point if your speech is not structurally sound. As we discussed in Chapter 13, you begin with your idea and then build your foundation with research and a clear thesis statement. The next step is to develop your framework—the overall structure of your presentation. In this chapter, we focus on organizing all of your ideas and information into a clear and practical framework and integrating them into a well-written speech. We begin by considering the main points of your speech.

Organizing Your Speech

You have your purpose, your research, and your thesis. But before you begin writing, it is best to organize your ideas—to set out the points you want to make, examples you plan to use to support them, and the basic order in which you want to present them. And you will want to do all of this *before* you write your introduction or conclusion. In this section, we focus on identifying your main points and developing your supporting points, in addition to considering useful ways to arrange those points and connect them in your speech.

Identifying Your Main Points

First and foremost, you must determine the **main points** of your speech, which are the central claims that support your specific speech purpose and your thesis statement (which you learned about in Chapter 13). That is, you need to identify and organize key ideas that will lead the audience members to accept or think about what you are asking them to do, believe, or consider.

Before you begin developing your main points, you may be wondering how many you will need in your speech. In some cases, your instructor may provide guidelines; however, because each speech is unique, there is often no specific number required. The general rule is that audiences have trouble remembering more than three or four main points (Moisala et al., 2015; Penn State, 2016). So it is important to choose them wisely. Some points, although valid, may not serve your thesis as well as others. You may wish to create a hierarchy and rank your ideas according to which ones seem to be the strongest and best suited to the goals of your speech. With this in mind, let's consider how main points work in action. Suppose you are giving a persuasive speech advocating for listeners to resist the temptation of texting while driving. What key points do you think would influence your listeners to see the immediate dangers of this behavior? Perhaps they would be motivated to do so if they knew the scope of the problem:

> **Main Point 1:** Driver distraction, specifically mobile phone use while operating a motor vehicle, is a growing problem in the United States.

You might further your argument by acknowledging the attempts governments and organizations have made to combat the problem:

> **Main Point 2:** Although many states have passed laws that ban mobile phone use while driving, these restrictions have not been particularly effective at solving the problem.

Finally, you might propose that the most promising solution lies with individuals making commitments to drive without distractions:

> **Main Point 3:** The only way to prevent distracted driving is to not drive while distracted! Each of us in this room has an obligation to be part of the solution by silencing our mobile phones in the car or even by making a public pledge not to text and drive.

Note that each main point includes only one major idea. This prevents you from overwhelming your audience with too much information and makes it easier for you to supply the examples, testimonies, statistics, and facts to back up each point. When in doubt about developing your main points, ask yourself, "Does this point prove my thesis? Does it help me achieve my specific purpose?" If you can confidently answer yes, then you are on the right track.

Supporting Your Main Points

Each main point — as well as your speech as a whole — is fully fleshed out with the use of **subpoints** that provide support for the main points. Subpoints use your research to back up your main points in the same way that your main points back up your thesis statement and specific purpose. You can use a similar test to check their usefulness, asking yourself, "Does this bit of information back up my main point?" For example, three subpoints under our first main point about driver mobile phone use as a growing traffic safety threat might be:

▶ The National Safety Council (2016) estimates that at least 1.6 million crashes each year involve drivers texting on cell phones.

▶ The risk of a crash is 23.2 percent greater when texting while driving versus driving when not distracted (Gardner, 2011).

▶ Every year in the United States, 3,179 people are killed in crashes reported to involve a distracted driver (National Highway Traffic Safety Administration, 2014).

Like main points, subpoints may — and often should — be backed up with more information, referred to as sub-subpoints.

Well-chosen supporting points will naturally fall under your main point in a clear hierarchy of ideas, forming the basic outline of your speech. Each main point should be supported by a number of coordinating subpoints, each carrying equal weight, as well as sub-subpoints that carry less weight. The resulting structure reflects a pyramidlike hierarchy of ideas: a foundation of many sub-subpoints supports a structure of fewer but larger subpoints, which in turn supports a few main points, which together support the thesis statement and ultimately your specific purpose. This structural hierarchy of points, depicted in Figure 14.1, ensures that you have presented a coherent and sturdy argument in support of your thesis and specific purpose. Later in the chapter, we show you how to use an outline to detail this hierarchy of points in a text format, but next we consider helpful ways to arrange your points.

Arranging Your Points

Think about creating a Flickr or social media photo album of your recent trip to Europe. How would you arrange your pictures? You could work chronologically, simply uploading individual photos to one album in the order in which they

connect

When deciding which types of material to use to support your speech points, keep the cultural context in mind (Chapters 1 and 6). Cultural variables affect the type of research to which audience members respond. For example, if your audience consists of concerned parents of teenagers, they will likely be responsive to statistics and facts about teen driving distraction.

● **THINK OF YOUR MAIN POINTS** and subpoints as Russian *matryoshka* dolls — each sub-subpoint should nest inside a subpoint, which should nest inside your main point. Comstock Images/Getty Images

FIGURE 14.1

HIERARCHY OF POINTS Note how many sub-subpoints support a smaller number of subpoints. Each subpoint supports the main point. And the main point supports your thesis.

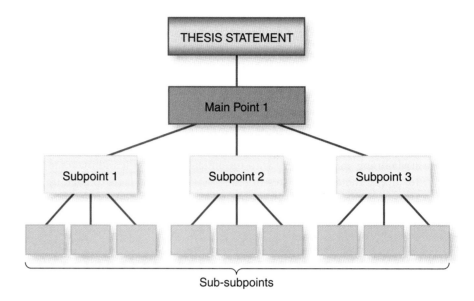

and you?

Organizing your main points and subpoints for a speech may seem overwhelming, but you have likely done this type of work before. Good, clear writing — whether an academic paper or an important letter — requires similar organization. Think of a particular piece of writing you were nervous about — a term paper or a private message to a potential romantic partner. How did you go about organizing your points? How did you decide what to include and what to leave out?

were taken. Alternatively, you might arrange them by topic, with separate albums for specific cities or countries visited or by types of activities (like one album for historical sites visited and another for silly photos with friends).

You have similar options when preparing a speech. During the process of sorting out your main points and subpoints, you are taking the initial step of arranging your ideas in a sequence. Here are common arrangements, or patterns, to consider.

Chronological Pattern

Often it makes sense to organize your points according to time: what happened first, second, and so on. A **chronological pattern** presents the main points of a message forward (or backward) in a systematic, time-related fashion. For example, you might use a chronological presentation when speaking about the development of Picasso's style over the course of his life. A chronological organization can be especially effective when analyzing a step-by-step process, such as a presentation on the stages of grief or how to use a particular smartphone app to add various filters to your photos.

Topical Pattern

Also known as a *categorical pattern,* the **topical pattern** is based on organization into categories, such as persons, places, things, or processes. Thus you might use it to describe the various departments in an organization, the characteristics of a successful employment interview, or the reasons for giving a charitable contribution to a specific organization.

One key concern when selecting this approach is the sequencing of topics, that is, which topic to offer first, second, and so on. Depending on the circumstances, you might choose an ascending or descending order, for example, according to increasing or decreasing importance, familiarity, or topic complexity. The **primacy–recency effect** can offer guidance in that studies show that audiences are most likely to remember points you raise at the very beginning (primacy) or at the very end (recency) of a message (Petty, Tormala, Hawkins, & Wegener, 2001), indicating that you might place your strongest point first or last so that your audience members keep it in mind long after the end of your presentation.

Spatial Pattern

The geographical or **spatial pattern** arranges main points in terms of their physical proximity in relation to each other (north to south, bottom to top, left to right, outside to inside, etc.). As an organizational pattern, it is most useful when describing objects, places, or scenes in terms of their component parts. For example, you might describe the major islands of Hawaii, arranging them from west to east.

Problem–Solution Pattern

If you are trying to call an audience to action to address a particular problem, the **problem–solution pattern** of organization can be especially effective. This pattern involves dramatizing an obstacle and then narrowing alternative remedies down to the one that you recommend. The message is organized to focus on three key points:

● **DECIDING HOW** to organize your speech, like figuring out how to display family photos on a wall or arranging pictures from a recent trip in a social media album, can be tricky because there are so many options to consider: you can do it chronologically, topically, or even spatially. Agencja Fotograficzna Caro/Alamy

1. There is a problem that requires a change in attitude, belief, or behavior.

2. A number of possible solutions might solve this problem.

3. Your solution is the one that will provide the most effective and efficient remedy.

Topics that lend themselves to this pattern include business, social, economic, and political problems for which you can propose a workable solution. For example, the persuasive speech described earlier about convincing listeners not to text while driving follows this pattern. The first main point established the problem, the second point described the ineffectiveness of current government efforts to address the issue, and the third main point proposed a solution — that listeners themselves make the pledge not to text while driving.

Cause–Effect Pattern

With the **cause–effect pattern**, you attempt to organize the message around cause-to-effect or effect-to-cause relationships. That is, you might move from a discussion of the origins or causes of a phenomenon (such as rising transportation costs) to the eventual results or effects (increases in the cost of groceries). You can also work in reverse, starting with a description of present conditions (such as the price of a gallon of a milk) and then examining apparent or possible causes (the cost of getting milk from the dairy to your supermarket). The choice of strategy is often based on which element — cause or effect — is more familiar to the intended audience: if your audience does not know much about transportation costs, for example, it might be best to start with the cost of milk — a very familiar expense — and work backward from there. The cause–effect pattern of organization is especially useful when your purpose is to get your audience to agree with or understand your point rather than to call people to action.

Narrative Pattern

Speakers often tie their points together in a way that presents a vivid story, complete with characters, settings, plot, and imagery. This is called a **narrative pattern**. However, most speeches built largely on a story (or a series of stories) are likely to incorporate elements of other organizational arrangements. For example, you might

evaluating communication ethics

The Ethics of Using Research

Six years ago, you and a group of dog-loving friends and neighbors cleaned up an abandoned lot and created "Central Bark," a public dog run. With the help of a GoFundMe campaign and the city's permission, members of the group installed fences, lighting, benches, and a fountain and organized volunteers to ensure the site is clean and cared for. But a few weeks ago, a child was bitten by a dog while walking near the park. Now local residents are concerned that the park is a danger to public safety; there have been calls to ban all dogs from the space. In hopes of keeping the dog run open, your group has asked you to come up with a few key arguments, backed up with solid research, to present to the local civic association at its next meeting.

Like others in the neighborhood, you want to keep dangerous animals out of the park, but you also know that this is the first incident in or around the park, and the dog involved was unleashed and outside of the dog run when the event occurred. You believe that the dog run is a valuable part of the neighborhood, not only because it provides pet owners with an enclosed place to let their dogs play, but also because your group transformed an unused, derelict lot. Prior to the dog run opening, the lot was a known location for drug transactions and the site of several assaults. Through research, you find there have been no such crimes recorded there since your group took over the lot six years ago. You are delighted by these statistics and believe that they prove that the improvements your group made have actually made the area safer than it was before. But further statistics you find show that, during the same time frame, drug-related crimes have plummeted across your town — not only at the lot location. If you just present the data for the location, you think you may be able to persuade the board to keep the park open, but you also know that your data may be flawed. What do you do?

1. Just how flawed is your data? Is it possible that the improvements to the lot really have had an impact on crime at that specific location? How might you find out?

2. What other ideas might you propose in order to ensure that dog attacks do not happen again? How can you ensure that only responsible dog owners use the park? What kind of evidence would you seek to support your proposals?

3. Bearing in mind that a child has been injured, is it possible that the park really should be closed? What kind of research should you conduct to obtain unbiased information on how dog runs like Central Bark impact public safety?

● **WHEN ORGANIZING** your speech in a narrative pattern, put your feet in a storyboard artist's shoes. Visualize your outline as a storyboard, and think of your speech points as scenes. JOHN THYS/Getty Images

present a story in a cause–effect design, in which you first reveal that something happened (such as a small aircraft crash) and then describe the events that led up to the accident (the causes).

Motivated Sequence Pattern

The **motivated sequence pattern** is a five-step plan for organizing a speech that can be useful in a variety of contexts. Based on the psychological elements of advertising, the motivated sequence pattern includes five phases: attention, need, satisfaction, visualization, and action. These five steps are designed to motivate listeners and may be modified to suit the desired outcome of your speech. Presentations that lend themselves to the motivated sequence include persuasive presentations, inspirational speeches, graduation addresses, speeches advocating social change, and motivational talks. For a more detailed discussion and examples of this approach to sequencing, please see pp. 453–456 in Chapter 17.

Finally, it is important to note that many of the previously mentioned patterns can be used together. In fact, effective speeches usually do have a combination of patterns. For instance, you might use a cause–effect pattern for your first main point, but a spatial pattern for your second.

Connecting Your Points

When you are pulling together, supporting, and arranging your points, you may find yourself falling into what we like to call the "grocery list trap." Essentially, this is where your speech begins to seem like a thorough list of good but seemingly unrelated ideas. So how do you move smoothly from one point to another? The key lies in your use of transitions, signposts, and internal previews and summaries.

Transitions

Transitions are sentences that connect different points, thoughts, and details in a way that allows them to flow naturally from one to the next. Clear transitions show the audience where your speech is heading and how your ideas and supporting

and you?

Transitions help to clarify messages and keep them flowing in oral and written forms of communication. But do transitions function similarly in mediated communication contexts? For example, how do you transition between points and ideas via text message or social media posts?

---

communication across cultures

Evidence, Popular Culture, and the "*CSI* Effect"

"We've got a match." If you have ever watched *CSI* or any of its several spin-offs, you know that those words are usually the clincher in a comparison of evidence from the murder scene to something belonging to a suspect — be it DNA, carpet fibers, or bullets. Inspired by real-life forensics scientists, show creator Anthony Zuiker wanted to "make science cool and fun for America" (Boniello, 2015). American audiences have tuned in to watch the brilliant teams of fictional forensic scientists work tirelessly to find and present evidence that indisputably solves crimes.

The trouble is that most of the evidence presented by the show's crime scene investigators is far from indisputable, and the show's portrayal of forensic science is sometimes closer to science fiction than science fact. Fiber evidence, for example, can be examined for possible connections, but no scientist would be able to testify under oath that a specific fiber came from a specific vehicle. Only DNA evidence really comes close to what most scientists would consider mathematical certainty (Toobin, 2007). The show also misleads juries about the technology available to prosecutors — much of the technology shown is beyond the reach of most departments or simply does not exist — as well as the time frame for obtaining results (Clements, 2015). Mike Murphy, the Las Vegas coroner whose lab was the inspiration for the original *CSI* show, explains that "people expect us to have DNA back in 20 minutes or that we're supposed to solve a crime in 60 minutes with three commercials. It doesn't happen that way" (Rath, 2011).

Some legal scholars and prosecutors worry that the popularity of shows like *CSI* may bias American juries in what they call the "*CSI* effect" (Clements, 2015). Jurors who follow the shows may believe they have developed a level of expertise about forensic evidence, expect the availability of *CSI*-like evidence in every case, and believe that such evidence is the only acceptable kind of proof of a person's guilt (Boniello, 2015).

think about this

1. Do you watch police procedurals like *CSI*? How realistic do you think they are? Does popular culture have an impact on how individuals perceive evidence or detective work? Do you think you would be a more sophisticated juror than someone who does not watch such shows?

2. If you were on a jury in a criminal trial, what would your expectations for evidence be? Would you be unwilling to convict someone unless there were "scientific" evidence rather than eyewitness testimony or circumstantial evidence?

3. Do you think that shows like *CSI* have an ethical responsibility to depict forensic science more realistically? Or is it the audience's responsibility to separate entertainment from reality?

● **DIRECT THE AUDIENCE** from one point in your speech to the next with signpost words or phrases, such as "similarly" or "on the other hand." Sascha Burkard/Shutterstock

material are connected. They also alert your audience that you will be making a point. Consider the following examples of transitions:

► "I've just described some of the amazing activities you can enjoy in our national parks, so let me tell you about two parks that you can visit within a three-hour drive of our campus."

► "In addition to the environmental benefits of riding your bike to school, there are fantastic financial and health benefits that you can enjoy."

Notice how the transitions in both examples also serve to alert your audience that you will be making a point that you want them to remember. Transitions, therefore, are essential to making your points clear and easy to follow.

Signposts

Effective speakers make regular use of **signposts**, key words or phrases within sentences that signify transitions between points. Think of signposts as links or pivot points at which you either connect one point to another ("similarly," "next," "once again,") or move from one point to a related but perhaps opposing or alternative point ("however," "on the other hand").

► "*Another way* you can help to fight puppy mills is to boycott pet stores that sell animals from disreputable sources."

► "*The third problem* with our current emergency room system is that there simply isn't enough money to fund our ERs."

Table 14.1 details various examples of signposts and considers how they function effectively to achieve a specific purpose.

Internal Previews and Internal Summaries

Like a good map that shows travelers points along the way to their destination, **internal previews** prime the audience for the content immediately ahead. They often work best in conjunction with **internal summaries**, which allow the speaker to crystallize the points made in one section of a speech before moving to the next section. For example:

► "So far, I have presented two reasons why you should visit the dentist annually. First, it prevents gum disease. Second, it also helps you avoid tooth decay. Now I will address my third point: regular visits to the dentist will benefit your overall good health."

► "Now that I have explained what asthma is and the two main types of asthma, allergic and nonallergic, I will discuss what you can do to avoid an asthma attack."

By first summarizing and then previewing, the speaker has created a useful transition that gracefully moves the speech forward while offering audiences an opportunity to synthesize the information already received.

TABLE 14.1
USEFUL SIGNPOSTS

Function	Example
To show comparison	Similarly, In the same way, In comparison
To contrast ideas, facts, or data	On the other hand, Alternatively, In spite of
To illustrate cause and effect	It follows, then, that, Consequently, Therefore, Thus
To indicate explanation	For example, In other words, To clarify
To introduce additional examples	Another way in which, Just as, Likewise, In a similar fashion
To emphasize significance	It's important to remember that, Above all, Bear in mind
To indicate sequence of time or events	First, Second, Third, Finally, First and foremost, Once, Now, Then, Until now, Before, After, Earlier, Later, Primarily
To summarize	As we've seen, Altogether, Finally, In conclusion

Information from D. O'Hair, R. Stewart, & H. Rubenstein (2018).

Using Language That Works

Now you know quite a bit about identifying, supporting, arranging, and moving between the main points of your speech. But to describe and explain the points themselves, you must make competent language choices that bring your ideas to life. The words that you choose for your speech are clearly powerful, so it is important to think about them *now,* in the preparation and writing stages, so that you can eventually incorporate them into your actual presentation.

Respect Your Audience

Most audiences are composed of men and women from many different cultures, races, religious backgrounds, lifestyles, and educational levels. Therefore, it is important to use unbiased and appropriate language that makes the entire audience feel included and respected.

connect

Part of using language your audience understands involves a careful consideration of *jargon* — technical language specific to a particular industry, organization, or group (see Chapter 4). Jargon might be useful among a very homogenous group, but it can alienate audience members in other settings. A doctor might use medical jargon when addressing colleagues but needs to use everyday terms when addressing other groups.

and you?

Have you ever been part of an audience that had to sit through a speech when the speaker failed to use language the audience easily understood? Do you remember anything important from this speech — or even its main point? How did you feel during the speech?

Keep It Simple

Albert Einstein once advised, "Make everything as simple as possible, but no simpler." This applies to language: speakers and writers who use unfamiliar or inappropriately complex language are not as effective as those who speak directly and in terms that their audience can readily understand and interpret. You do not need to "dumb down" your points; just make your points in a language that is clear, simple, and unambiguous so that your audience can follow what you are saying. In addition, there is no speaker quite as dreaded as the long-winded one who repeats the same points or uses six examples where one would suffice. (Admit it — we have all sat through speeches like this!) If you keep your speech short and to the point, you have a better chance of reaching your audience with your intended message.

Use Vivid Language

Language paints a picture for an audience. The more vivid your terms, the more audience members can use their imaginations and their senses. For example, if you say you have a car, your listeners get a common, forgettable fact. If you tell them that your father drove a faded orange 1972 Volkswagen Beetle with a dent in the left fender and a broken taillight, you give them a very clear and memorable picture of this vehicle. You may assume your great, eye-catching slides and props will paint the picture for you, but you must not forget that words count — often even more than your PowerPoint presentation.

● AUDIENCE MEMBERS would not conjure up this clear and memorable a picture in their minds unless it was painted with vivid language by the speaker. ilbusca/istockphoto.com

connect

Chapters 5 and 15 cover nonverbal aspects of speech, such as rate, pauses, tone, volume, and pitch. In many cases, these factors can help you use repetition effectively. For example, if you repeat a phrase with an upward inflection of voice followed by a pause, you will help the audience anticipate the next line and enhance their retention of your main points.

Incorporate Repetition, Allusion, and Comparisons

In 1851, American abolitionist and women's rights activist Sojourner Truth delivered an effective and memorable speech at the Women's Convention in Akron, Ohio. The speech known as "Ain't I a Woman?" is effective not only because of its powerful message about the evils of slavery and the mistreatment of women but also because Truth's passionate use of language helped make a lasting impression on her listeners. Consider, for example, her use of repetition, allusion, and comparisons. (See Sample Speech 14.1.)

Repetition

Repetition — saying compelling terms, phrases, or even entire sentences more than once — can help increase the likelihood that the audience will remember what matters most in your speech. In Truth's speech, she repeats "Ain't I a woman?" several times. This repetition highlights each of the injustices she feels and influences audience members to consider Truth deserving of the rights and privileges withheld from her. Repetition can also be used to remind your audience of your thesis statement. If you strategically tie each point back into your overarching theme, the audience is less likely to get lost or be confused with where you may be going with a specific point.

Allusion

An *allusion* is making a vague or indirect reference to people, historical events, or concepts that an audience will recognize in order to give deeper meaning to the message and possibly evoke emotional responses. Allusions can also provide grounded context that goes beyond what you are saying directly. In Truth's "Ain't I a Woman?" speech, for example, she uses allusion with the words "If the first woman God ever made was strong enough to turn the world upside down all alone, these women together ought to be able to turn it back, and get it right side up again." She is alluding to the biblical figure Eve, who ate the forbidden fruit from the tree of the knowledge of good and evil, and upset the harmonious balance between God and humankind. Truth does not take time to explain this story; she knows that her audience will understand her reference and uses allusion to add power and emotion to her message.

● **SOJOURNER TRUTH'S** "Ain't I a Woman?" speech uses vivid and effective language to persuade. Library of Congress, Prints & Photographs Division, Reproduction number LC-DIG-ppmsca-08978

I Sell the Shadow to Support the Substance.
SOJOURNER TRUTH.

Sample Speech 14.1

Ain't I a Woman?

SOJOURNER TRUTH

Well, children, where there is so much racket there must be something out of kilter. I think that 'twixt the negroes of the South and the women at the North, all talking about rights, the white men will be in a fix pretty soon. But what's all this here talking about?

That man over there says the women need to be helped into carriages, and lifted over ditches, and to have the best place everywhere. Nobody ever helps me into carriages, or over mud-puddles, or gives me any best place! And ain't I a woman? Look at me! Look at my arm! I have ploughed and planted, and gathered into barns, and no man could head me! And ain't I a woman? I could work as much and eat as much as a man — when I could get it — and bear the lash as well! And ain't I a woman? I have borne thirteen children, and seen most all sold off to slavery, and when I cried out with my mother's grief, none but Jesus heard me! And ain't I a woman? ●

Then they talk about this thing in the head; what's this they call it? [member of the audience whispers "intellect"] That's it, honey. What's that got to do with women's rights or negroes' rights? If my cup won't hold but a pint, and yours holds a quart, wouldn't you be mean not to let me have my little half measure full?

Then that little man in black there, he says women can't have as much rights as men, 'cause Christ wasn't a woman! Where did your Christ come from? Where did your Christ come from? From God and a woman! Man had nothing to do with Him.

If the first woman God ever made was strong enough to turn the world upside down all alone, these women together ought to be able to turn it back, and get it right side up again. And now they is asking to do it, the men better let them. ●

Obliged to you for hearing me, and now old Sojourner ain't got nothing more to say.

Source: From Sojourner Truth, "Ain't I a Woman?" speech delivered at the Women's Convention in Akron, Ohio, May 1851. Retrieved from http://www.feminist.com/resources/artspeech/genwom/sojour.htm

● Notice how Truth encourages the audience to extend this existing belief about women to her, as she too is a woman.

● Truth invokes religious stories that are familiar to the audience members in her effort to persuade them.

Comparisons: Similes and Metaphors

Comparisons can provide imagery that can help your audience more clearly see your point. A *simile* is a figure of speech that uses *like* or *as* to compare two things ("as sweet as honey"; "clever like a fox"). Truth uses a simile to conjure up the images of her strength and fortitude when she states, "I could work as much and eat as much as a man—when I could get it—and bear the lash as well!"

Like a simile, a *metaphor* likens one thing to another; however, it does not contain the word *like* or *as*—it presents the comparison as though it were a statement of fact ("my house was a pig sty"). If you say, for example, "The fog was a heavy blanket over the city," your audience knows of course that it is not a real blanket; the phrasing helps them envision how completely the fog covered the city.

Although vivid language is important, be on the lookout for clichés that can easily slip into your speech, taking away from your content. Beginning your speech with, "The recipe for success is . . ." only weakens its effect. Similarly, saying "The rest is history" at the end of your speech, for example, is a cliché that can suggest you did not put much thought into the conclusion. The next section provides more effective ways to begin and end your speech.

Crafting a Strong Introduction

Like a lead paragraph of a news story that hooks in readers, the introduction to your speech must accomplish four crucial tasks: grab your audience's attention, introduce your purpose and topic, offer a preview of your main points, and give your listeners a sense of who you are and why they should want to hear what you have to say. Recall the "primacy" part of the *primacy–recency effect* discussed earlier in this chapter. Your introduction is the first thing your audience will hear and therefore sets the tone and the stage for the rest of your speech.

Capture Your Audience's Attention

Finding a creative, attention-grabbing opening can be a struggle. However, in the end it will be well worth the effort, for your first words can and do make a big impression on your audience (Hockenbury & Hockenbury, 2009). If you open with something as boring as, "Hi, my name is . . ." or "Today I'm going to talk about . . . ," your audience may conclude that there is nothing more interesting to follow. In many cases, it is a good idea to finalize your introduction after the bulk of your speech is complete. This can be an advantage because you will approach your introduction armed with your main points and your supporting material—and probably a few ideas on how to make it lively! Consider the following suggestions.

Use Surprise

It is likely that during research on your topic, you came across a fact, statistic, quote, or story that truly surprised you. Chances are that such information will likewise come as a surprise to your audience. A startling statement uses unusual or unexpected information to get an audience's attention. For example, in a speech on sleep deprivation, you might begin your speech as follows:

> Did you know that every semester, university students are legally drunk for one week straight? Yet despite feeling drunk, they never drink a drop of alcohol. During finals week, students at the University of Oklahoma sleep an average of five hours per night. Sleep deprivation—getting five hours or less of sleep per night—can affect reaction time and mental sharpness. After being awake for seventeen hours straight, a sleep-deprived person has the reaction time and mental sharpness of someone with a blood alcohol concentration of 0.05, which is considered legally drunk throughout most of Europe.

connect

Your speech introduction is the first impression you give your audience. But introductions are important in other contexts as well. The Interviewing Appendix shows how your résumé and cover letter give a potential employer an introduction to you and your abilities. If your résumé has typos or other errors, your first impression will be less than stellar — just as a disorganized or inappropriate speech introduction leaves a negative impression with your audience.

and you?

Take a look at your research. Of all the evidence you have gathered for your speech, what jumps out at you? Did you come across any statistics that shocked you? Did you encounter any individuals whose stories touched you — with humor, sadness, or surprise? Think about how any of the statistics, facts, anecdotes, and quotes you have gathered might be worked into an effective introduction.

Tell a Story

Real-world stories can be particularly effective when worked into your opening, where they can make audiences feel invested in a person before they even know what your thesis is. For example, Leah thinks her audience will tune out if she simply informs them that she is going to discuss the secret costs of credit cards. But what if she opens with a story? For example:

> A few months ago, my friend Monica decided that she positively *needed* to own a pair of Jimmy Choo boots. Now, I'll admit, these were some amazing boots: black leather, calf-high, four-inch heels. But they cost — are you sitting down? — $895.00. Like most of us, Monica didn't have that kind of cash lying around, so she bought the boots on credit, figuring that she would pay them off month by month. Despite the fact that she diligently puts $50 toward her payment each and every month, it's going to take Monica 102 months — more than eight years — to pay for those boots. In addition, she'll pay over $750 in interest, which is almost as much as the boots cost in the first place!

By telling a story, Leah puts a familiar face on her subject; she has also caught the attention of anyone who has ever had the experience of really wanting something they could not afford — which is pretty much anyone! Note, however, that stories can take time to tell, so it is important to limit the details only to what matters most. You do not want your audience distracted by unnecessary information or thinking that you are taking forever to get to the point.

Start with a Quote

Leading with a quotation can connect you as a speaker to real people and real situations. For example, Kenneth is preparing an informative speech on Alzheimer's disease. In his opening, he uses a quote from former president Ronald Reagan, who passed away after a ten-year struggle with the disease:

> "I now begin the journey that will lead me to the sunset of my life." That's how Ronald Reagan, upon learning he would be afflicted with Alzheimer's disease, described the illness that would eventually rob him of the eloquence, wit, and intelligence that had defined him as an actor, politician, and president. I'm here today to talk about the tragedy of Alzheimer's disease.

Quotations can come from famous sources, like Reagan, or from everyday people. Table 14.2 offers tips for using quotes wisely.

● **PRESIDENT RONALD REAGAN** earned his reputation as a gifted public speaker by recognizing the interaction between speaker and audience and presenting himself as approachable and self-assured. Wally McNamee/Getty Images

TABLE 14.2
USING QUOTES WISELY

Use quotes worth using.	Do not quote something that you could say or explain more effectively in your own words; paraphrase instead, with an attribution to the original source.
Use relevant quotes.	Even the prettiest bit of prose is useless if it does not support your points.
Include a clear attribution.	Whether you are quoting Shakespeare or your six-year-old nephew, it is important that audiences know who said what.
Is the quote from a notable source?	Cite not only the author in your speech but also the date and the work in which the quote appeared, if relevant.
Double-check for accuracy.	You do not want to misquote anyone in your speech, so it is important that you proofread your copy against the original. If you have used an online quote source, it is wise to double-check the quote against additional sources known to be reliable because many online quotes fail to provide accurate source information.

Ask a Question

Posing a question is a great way to get the audience's attention and to make people think. Rather than simply presenting information, posing a question invites listeners to react, in effect making them participants in the speech (O'Hair, O'Rourke, & O'Hair, 2000). For example, "Would you leave your child in a room full of anonymous strangers? No? Then why would you allow your child to participate in online chats?" Asking something startling can add to the effect: not only have you gotten your listeners' attention by saying something provocative, but you have also asked them to internalize what you have said and to react to it. As a result, your audience is likely to be more interested in and open to what you are about to say.

Make Them Laugh

Humor is another effective way to begin your speech. Usually, humor that is brief, is relevant to your topic, and makes a point is most effective. (And when it is well done, humor helps you and your audience members relax!) For example, consider this opening, which makes the audience laugh but is also clearly tied to the main topic of the speech: "I find that the key to multitasking is to lower your expectations. Sure, I can do two things at once—if I do them poorly! Today, I want to talk about the hazards of multitasking."

Introduce Your Purpose and Thesis

Whether you capture your audience's attention with stories, questions, or quotations, it is *essential* that your introduction also clearly establishes what your speech is about and what you hope to achieve by speaking. You do this by incorporating your thesis statement. Imagine that you just caught your audience's attention with the description of a fun-filled and active day: kayaking on a pristine lake, hiking in a rain forest, rock climbing on a craggy coastline, and so on. You would then introduce your thesis: "All of these activities—and many more—are available to you in one of our nation's most diverse protected spaces: Olympic National Park. I hope to persuade you to visit and to take advantage of all this park has to offer."

● YOU DO NOT HAVE TO TURN YOUR SPEECH into a stand-up comic performance, but a good opening joke will pique the audience's interest. Digital Vision/Getty Images

Preview Your Main Points

Another key goal for your introduction is to provide a preview of the main points that will be covered in the body of the speech, in the order that you will talk about them. For example, if you are giving a speech about why students should enroll in an art course, you might say: "There are two reasons why every college student should enroll in an art course. First, it provides students with a creative outlet; second, it teaches students useful and creative ways of thinking about their own subjects of study." Audiences prefer to listen to speakers who are prepared and have a plan the audience can follow; by previewing, you offer a mental outline that your listeners can follow as they attend to your speech.

Connect with Your Audience

Another goal for your introduction is to establish a relationship with your listeners, providing them with a sense of who you are and why they should listen to what you have to say. Like participants in an interview, the members of your audience will come to your speech with three questions in mind. They will be curious about the nature of your speech—will it be boring, interesting, or inspiring? They will also be wondering what they will get from it—will the speech be worth their time and attention? Finally, they will be curious about you as a speaker—will they like and trust you? Your introduction should provide enough information to allow the audience to develop a favorable impression of you and your speech.

One way that a speaker can establish a relationship with the audience is to demonstrate why listeners should care about the topic. First, make sure that you verbally link the topic to the audience's interests. You should also try to appeal to your listeners' personal needs—let them know what is in it for them. For example, a college recruiter speaking at a high school might talk about what his school offers prospective students. He might also touch on recent local or national events to show the relevance of the school's curriculum.

● **WHETHER IN THE TELEVISION** show *Suits* or a real-world courtroom, one of the most crucial moments in a trial is the closing statement. It's the lawyer's last chance to make his or her case to the jury. Everett Collection, Inc/ Courtesy Everett Collection

Writing a Strong Conclusion

There is a reason why courtroom dramas like television's *Suits* almost always include footage of the hero lawyer's closing statements. When a wealth of evidence, testimony, and facts have been presented, it is easy for juries (and television audiences) to get bogged down in the details and lose track of the bigger, more dramatic picture. For any speaker, it is important to end a presentation with a compelling and pointed conclusion. Once again, the "recency" part of the primacy–recency effect reminds us that the conclusion is the *last* thing the audience will hear in your speech, and it is likely what they will remember most. As such, a speech conclusion must address a number of functions.

Signal the End

Your conclusion should alert the audience that the speech is coming to a close. For example, you might use a transitional phrase or signpost, such as "In conclusion," "Finally," or "Let me close by saying. . . ." Such phrases tell audiences that you are about to conclude and are asking for their full attention one last time. Remember to keep it brief. Audiences do not like to be overwhelmed with a lot of new information at the end.

Reinforce Your Topic, Purpose, and Main Points

The conclusion of your speech is the last opportunity you will have to reinforce the topic and purpose of your speech as well as to remind your audience about the key points you want to live on in their memories. In other words, competent speakers should reiterate this essential information so that listeners are able to mentally check off what they have heard and what they should remember. For example, "Today, I discussed the benefits of seeing your physician for an annual physical, even if you are young and feeling fine. Not only can this simple visit offer peace of mind and help to prevent costly medical conditions in the future, but it may also save your life if you have an underlying medical problem that requires early diagnosis and treatment."

Make an Impact

Your conclusion should be memorable and interesting for your audience members, a culmination of all your efforts to develop your points and share your research. Several techniques used for introductions can also be useful for memorable conclusions.

Quotations

Carefully chosen quotes from historical figures, writers, philosophers, or celebrities can leave the audience with something to think about. For example, if you are concluding a speech that illustrates the importance of friendships, you might quote the writer Edna Buchanan: "Friends are the family you choose for yourself" (www.ednabuchanan.com). A strong quotation helps make an unforgettable impression.

Statements and Questions

In some types of speeches, it can be especially effective to end with a statement or question that drives home your main point. This rhetorical device is important for conclusions because you want to emphasize the points you made during your speech and have the audience feel connected to your ideas. For example, you might end a speech explaining how to change the oil in your car with a simple statement that sums up your thesis: "Remember, the best way to protect your car is to change the oil every three thousand miles—and it's something you can do yourself."

real communicator

NAME: Mark Weinfeld
OCCUPATION: Advertising Strategic Planner and Brand Marketing Researcher
Courtesy Mark Weinfeld

Did you ever wonder how companies discover their brand values? This is what I do. I split my time between strategic planning at a full-service advertising agency and directing research for a marketing consultancy. In my thirty years of experience, I have built some strong brands and given damaged or forgotten brands a second life. I have helped food companies, hotels, baseball teams, restaurants, car companies, and makers of electronics, tires, and personal products.

For our advertising clients, I manage the process of shaping the brand's position, researching and deeply understanding their customers, and developing campaign briefs to produce marketing communications. I also work with clients to help them define their "why" and in turn discover their brand values. We use our research findings to recommend strategic plans that put these values into practice so that they are lived out on a daily basis within an organization.

My role as a strategic planner has changed dramatically in recent years. Planners used to assist in the creative development process simply by bringing the voice of the consumer to the table.

Today, with digital and mobile platforms becoming the dominant advertising media, data and feedback from consumers is available and unlimited. Now that clients expect tangible results from every advertising medium, we, as planners, have become data scientists: we need to be able to present a tremendous amount of technical information and feedback to help our clients and colleagues better understand how consumers react to marketing messages. Yet at the same time, we still need to motivate and inspire our creative partners by communicating insight — not just reporting data.

One important communication skill I have learned over the years is how to write well. Many young people today do not have the discipline to write a persuasive document. We have become a nation of quick emails and texts, and our writing skills have suffered. Writing skills are not something that most employers teach and, therefore, if you have not learned (and practiced) these skills in college, it is hard to succeed in a communications career. My advice to college students is to polish your writing and take a variety of courses.

A Final Story

Stories can be as effective for conclusions as they are for introductions. Stories should always tie in to your speech topic, be relatively short, and make a related point. For example, if you are advocating a college-level foreign-language requirement for your college, you might tell this well-known tale: "Mother Mouse was crossing the street with her three children. She got about halfway across when she saw a cat, ready to pounce upon them. The cat and Mother Mouse eyeballed each other for several minutes. Finally, Mother Mouse let out an enormous 'WOOF!' The cat ran away. Mother Mouse turned to her children and said, 'NOW do you see the advantage of a second language?'"

Reference the Introduction

A final suggestion for creating a strong conclusion is to remind the audience of how you began the speech. If you told a dramatic, powerful story in the introduction, finish it or add a new insight in the conclusion; if you asked a question, answer it. For example, if you began your persuasive speech about cyberbullying with a story about the tragic suicide of Tyler Clemente (who jumped from New York City's George Washington Bridge after being bullied), you might say: "We must never forget Tyler Clemente and the other young lives cut short by senseless bullying. Who knows? Your best friend, your younger brother, or your son could just have easily been on that bridge that fateful September evening."

Challenge the Audience to Respond

Whether you are giving an informative or persuasive speech, as the speaker, you must consider what you want your audience to *do* with the information you are providing. In an informative speech, you can challenge your audience members to make use of the information in a particular way (O'Hair, Stewart, & Rubenstein, 2018). For example, you may extend an invitation to your listeners: "Please log on to the website later tonight for a live podcast for more information and to join the conversation."

In most persuasive speeches, the challenge will come through a **call to action** that asks listeners to act in response to the speech; see the problem in a new way; or change their beliefs, actions, and behavior (O'Hair, Stewart, & Rubenstein, 2018). For example, "Sign this petition. In doing so, you will make a difference in someone's life and make our voices heard" or "Don't forget to vote next Tuesday!"

Outlining Your Speech

At this point, you have all of the building blocks for a successful speech. Now you are ready to pull all of your hard work together in the form of an **outline**—a structured form of your speech content (Fraleigh & Tuman, 2011). An effective outline helps you confirm that your points are arranged clearly and properly, ensures that you have cited your all-important research, and assists you in your speech delivery. (In fact, many instructors require students to turn in a formal outline before the presentation. Be sure to check on your instructor's preferences.)

You may already be familiar with the basics of outlining from your high school courses or from your college composition class. We now refresh you with a discussion of the essentials of outlining before we move to types of outlines and the heart of this section: the preparation and speaking outlines.

and you?

Reflect on a time when you were challenged by a speaker through a *call to action*. What was/was not effective about that speech? Do you think it depends on the gravity and scope of the subject?

wired for communication

Bullets on the Brain

There is something sinister in the world of public speaking. You have undoubtedly been exposed to it, at work or at school. It is probably in your home computer. And according to one of the nation's leading experts, it is making all of us stupid.

Edward Tufte is a professor emeritus of graphic design at Yale University. He maintains a research emphasis in political science, computer science, and statistics and has been academia's most influential voice on the subject of the visual display of information for over three decades. He is an expert on the use of graphs and visual aids to explain all types of information, from train schedules to empirical data. He uses computers to crunch numbers and present quantitative information. But Tufte is no fan of presentation software (such as Microsoft PowerPoint, Apple Keynote, Google Presentations, and Prezi). The problem, Tufte (2003) explains, is that programs like PowerPoint force presentations into an outline format, with little development beyond a series of bulleted lists. Because a typical slide contains a mere forty words — about eight seconds of reading — presentations become a succession of short, boring lists of facts, presented out of context and with little room for evaluation. In short, Power-Point is *presenter*-centered, not *content*- or *audience*-centered (Tufte, 2006).

Of course, current software programs offer you the opportunity to do more than just present bulleted lists. They can add real visual interest to a speech, enabling you to easily share photographs, cartoons, data charts, and graphics with an audience. The problem is when presenters rely on the program to design the content of their speeches rather than to enhance it. Tufte finds that a program's format "routinely disrupts, dominates, and trivializes content" (Tufte, 2003).

The best remedy? Make sure you have good content and only use visual displays that really convey meaning. A solid graph, for example, does not just present numbers: it helps the audience to understand the numbers you are presenting. Most importantly, remember that pictures may be pretty, but content is still king. "If your numbers are boring, then you've got the wrong numbers," Tufte writes. "If your words or images are not on point, making them dance in color won't make them relevant."

1. The use of visuals during lectures and presentations is nothing new — instructors and presenters made use of overhead projectors and slide shows for decades before computers arrived on the academic scene. Why is Tufte being so hard on speakers who use them now?

2. We have spent much of this chapter talking about the importance of outlining and of communicating your final outline clearly to your audience. How is that different from presenting your outline in slide form?

3. Are there some subjects or types of speeches that lend themselves to software presentations? Are there others that do not?

Essentials of Outlining

In every phase of outlining, basic guidelines will help you structure and prepare your speech. A solid outline will clearly reveal the structure of your arguments and the hierarchy of your points.

connect

The ability to outline complex information into manageable steps is useful beyond public speaking. Chapter 10 covered task roles in groups, which involve people organizing the activities that help achieve a group's goals. If you and your siblings want to plan a huge celebration for your parents' twenty-fifth wedding anniversary, you should outline the steps needed to make it happen: creating a guest list, contacting and comparing venues, sending out invitations, and so on.

▶ *Use standard symbols.* What an outline does, essentially, is put the hierarchy of points visualized in Figure 14.1 (p. 348) into a text format. To do this, outlines generally use roman numerals, letters, and standard numbers to indicate different levels of importance in the hierarchy.

I. Main Point

    A. Subpoint

    B. Subpoint

        1. Sub-subpoint

        2. Sub-subpoint

If you need to break down the sub-subpoints even further, you may use lowercase letters (a, b, etc.) to create sub-sub-subpoints.

▶ *Use subdivisions properly.* It is basic logic that a whole of anything—a sandwich, a doughnut, or an outline heading—can never be split into fewer than two pieces. Therefore, as you divide your ideas from main points to subpoints, remember that each numbered or lettered entry must come in a series of at least two points: if you have a I, you must have a II; if you have an A, you must have a B; and so on.

▶ *Separate the parts of your speech.* It is typically helpful to label your introduction, conclusion, and even your transitions to distinguish them from the body of your speech (your main points and supporting subpoints).

▶ *Call out your specific purpose and thesis.* Many instructors want students to include this pertinent information at the top of the outline, so check with your instructor to determine his or her preference. You may feel that you already know this information by heart, but it can be helpful to see it at the top of your outline page, ensuring that all your main points support the purpose and thesis. Also, you may wind up tweaking them a bit as you work your way through the outlining process.

● **ORGANIZATION IS ESSENTIAL** in preparing a speech. Using sticky notes will help you clarify and position your main points and subpoints and provide structure when outlining your speech. Elnur/Shutterstock

▶ *Cite your sources.* As discussed in Chapter 13, it is extremely important to give proper citations in your speech. As you work on the outline, you should always mark where a specific point requires credit. Directly after the point, either insert a footnote or a reference in parentheses; once you complete the outline, arrange the references in order on a separate sheet headed "Works Cited," "Notes," or "References." Citations can be presented in a variety of formats, including styles dictated by such organizations as the Modern Language Association (MLA) and the American Psychological Association (APA). See Figure 14.2 for a sample of how you might handle references in APA format. Your instructor may have his or her own preferences about how to handle citations, so when in doubt, ask.

▶ *Give your speech a title.* Once all of your ideas and points are organized on paper, you can give your speech a catchy title that captures its essence. You might consider using a provocative question or part of a memorable quotation that you have used in the body of the speech.

At every phase of development, you should review your outline for sound organization. When reviewing, you should see a clear hierarchy of points reflected in each tier of your structure. A weak link in the outline—an unsupported argument, an unrelated point—reveals an overall weakness in the way you have presented and defended your thesis. A solid outline shows not only how well you have organized your material but also how each point is supported by two or more subpoints, making a stronger case for your thesis statement. It also shows the scope and validity of your research by detailing your evidence with complete citations.

If sitting in front of a blank document and typing a formal outline feels too overwhelming, you might want to take advantage of free outlining and mind-mapping applications and tools available online. For example, SimpleMind (available on your desktop and for Apple or Android devices) allows you to create a visual mind map, creating and connecting your hierarchy of points in colored circles. Take a look at Figure 14.3 to see how such an application might help you get started on your outline.

FIGURE 14.2

REFERENCES (IN APA STYLE)

References

American Academy of Sleep Medicine. (2010, February 15). Sleep problems and sleepiness increase the risk of motor vehicle accidents in adolescents. *Science Daily*. Retrieved from http://www.sciencedaily.com/releases/2010/02/100215081728.htm

Breus, M. J. (2013). Quality sleep, quality relationship. In *Sleep well with Michael Breus, PhD ABSM*. Retrieved from http://blogs.webmd.com/sleep-disorders/2013/07/quality-sleep-quality-relationship.html

Centers for Disease Control and Prevention. (2015, September 3). Insufficient sleep is a public health problem. Retrieved from http://www.cdc.gov/features/dssleep/

Centers for Disease Control and Prevention. (2008, February 28). CDC study reveals adults may not get enough rest or sleep. Retrieved from http://www.cdc.gov/media/pressrel/2008/r080228.htm

Farberov, Snejana. (2013). Sleep-deprived new mom who killed a nanny and injured a toddler when she ran a red light while driving one day after giving birth is sentenced to just 48 hours in prison. *Daily Mail*. Retrieved from http://www.dailymail.co.uk/news/article-2338271/Christina-Padilla-Sleep-deprived-new-mom-killed-nanny-injured-toddler-ran-red-light-day-giving-birth-sentenced-just-48-HOURS-jail.html

National Sleep Foundation. (2015). 2015 Sleep in America™ Poll. Retrieved from http://www.sleephealthjournal.org/pb/assets/raw/Health%20Advance/journals/sleh/2015SleepinAmericaPollSummaryofFindings.pdf

International Bedroom Poll: Summary of findings. Retrieved from http://www.sleepfoundation.org/sites/default/files/RPT495a.pdf

St. Lawrence University. (2007, December 1). All-nighters equal lower grades. *Science Daily*. Retrieved from www.sciencedaily.com/releases/2007/11/071130162518.htm

Skerritt, P. D. (2011, January 12). Your health at work: Sleep deprivation's true workplace costs. *Harvard Business Review*. Retrieved from http://blogs.hbr.org/your-health-at-work/2011/01/sleep-deprivations-true-workpl.htm

Zamosky, Lisa. (2011). Having trouble sleeping? In *WebMD: Sleep Disorders Health Center*. Retrieved from http://www.webmd.com/sleep-disorders/features/having-trouble-sleeping

Styles of Outlines

There are three basic approaches you can take to outlining your speech, which vary according to the level of detail. All three formats — sentence outlines, phrase outlines, and key-word outlines — can be valuable tools in developing and eventually delivering your speech. In most cases, you move from one format to another as you progress from preparing your speech to actually delivering it.

Sentence Outline

The first type of outline is the **sentence outline**, which offers the full text of what you want to say in your speech. Sentence outlines are generally used as you develop

FIGURE 14.3

MIND MAPPING can be a great way to organize your ideas if you prefer a more visual style of outline.

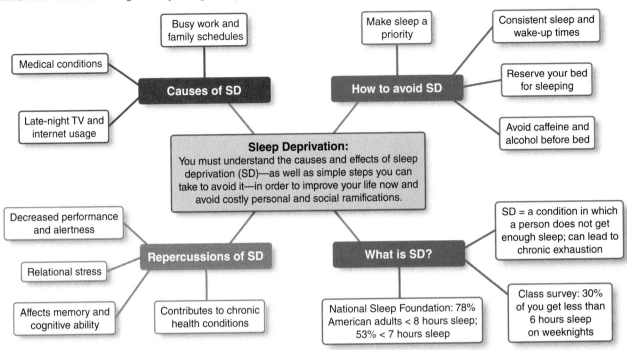

and prepare early drafts of your speech because they help you become more comfortable with all aspects of your speech. They are typically not ideal for your actual presentation because many speakers wind up reading directly from the outline, missing out on valuable eye contact with the audience. Consider the following example from Sample Speech Outline 14.1 (see p. 369) regarding sleep deprivation:

II. There are many causes of sleep deprivation, according to the Centers for Disease Control and Prevention.

    A. Busy work and family schedules contribute to sleep deprivation.

        1. As college students, many of us are trying to handle full-time course work and full- or part-time jobs to help pay for tuition, in addition to maintaining relationships with loved ones.

        2. New parents are often incredibly sleep deprived as they attempt to adjust to life with an infant as well as those infamous nighttime feedings.

        3. Shift workers (including police officers, nurses, pilots, etc.) often have trouble establishing good sleep habits because their schedules change frequently and they are sometimes required to work the night shift.

    B. Late-night television and internet use can interfere with the ability to fall asleep or can prevent individuals from adhering to a bedtime schedule.

    C. The increasing prevalence of electronics (such as cell phones) in teens' bedrooms creates a culture of evening engagement and light exposure that negatively impact sleep time, sleep quality, and daytime alertness.

    D. The use of caffeine and alcohol can also make it difficult to fall asleep and stay asleep.

    E. Some medical conditions — including insomnia and obstructive sleep apnea — also make sleeping incredibly difficult.

● AS YOU DEVELOP YOUR SPEECH, you transition from a more detailed preparation outline to a speaking outline that will equip you for the actual presentation. DWaschnig/ Shutterstock

Phrase Outline

A **phrase outline** takes parts of sentences and uses those phrases as instant reminders of what the point or subpoint means. Consider the following example:

II. Many causes of sleep deprivation (CDC)

    A. Busy work and personal lives

        1. Students struggling with school and work

        2. New parents adjusting to baby schedule

        3. Shift work disrupting sleep

    B. Use of TV or computer late at night

    C. Use of cell phone/social media

    D. Use of caffeine and alcohol

    E. Medical conditions—insomnia and sleep apnea

The phrase outline is often preferred because it offers a clear road map of the presentation, with reminders of key points and phrases, while also allowing speakers to deliver a speech rather than simply read it.

Key-Word Outline

A **key-word outline** is the briefest possible outline, consisting of specific "key words" from the sentence outline to jog the speaker's memory. This type of outline allows the speaker to maintain maximum eye contact with the audience, though the speaker must be *extremely* familiar with the content of the speech. A key-word outline is as follows:

II. SD causes (CDC)

    A. Family and work

        1. College students

        2. New parents

        3. Shift workers

    B. Television and internet

    C. Social media/cell phone

    D. Caffeine and alcohol

    E. Medical conditions—insomnia, apnea

From Preparation Outline to Speaking Outline

In most public speaking situations, you will use the basics you have learned to create two outlines. The first is a **preparation outline** (sometimes called a *working outline*), a draft that you will use, and probably revisit and revise continually, throughout the preparation for your speech. The function of a preparation outline is to firm up your thesis statement, establish and organize your main points, and develop your supporting points. It should also help you "map out" the relationships between your main points and supporting points. From the preparation outline, you will eventually develop a **speaking outline**, or *delivery outline,* which is your final speech plan, complete with details, delivery tips, and important notes about presentational aids (which we will discuss in Chapter 15).

what about you?

Assessing Your Outlining Skills

An important element of speech preparation is the ability to establish your speech topic, thesis, main points, supporting points, and transitions. You can assess your ability to recognize these elements in the following preparation outline for an informative speech on obsessive–compulsive personality disorder (OCPD).

Instructions: Place the numbers of the elements listed here into the following organizational outline.

Topic: _____   Thesis: _____

   I. (main point) _____

      A. (subpoint) _____

      B. (subpoint) _____

      C. (subpoint) _____

      D. (subpoint) _____

      E. (subpoint) _____

(transition) _____

   II. (main point) _____

      A. (subpoint) _____

      B. (subpoint) _____

      C. (subpoint) _____

      D. (subpoint) _____

1. I have presented the five signature symptoms of OCPD and will now examine the condition's suspected causes.

2. Adopting a miserly spending style toward both self and others.

3. Perfectionism that interferes with task completion.

4. There are five primary symptoms of OCPD.

5. OCPD.

6. Faulty parenting.

7. Heredity.

8. OCPD is a treatable mental illness that often goes unrecognized because of a lack of information or confusion about the symptoms and causes.

9. Harsh punishment/meager rewards.

10. Preoccupation with details, rules, lists, order, organization, or schedules to the extent that the major point of the activity is lost.

11. Recognize the symptoms and causes of OCPD to identify proper help.

12. Medical professionals generally agree on four major causes for OCPD.

13. Stubbornness and inflexibility about matters of morality, ethics, or values.

14. Significant event/circumstance that triggers OCPD.

15. Inability to discard worn-out objects even when they have no sentimental value.

Answers: Topic: 5; Thesis: 8, Main Point I: 4, Subpoints I-A-E: 2, 3, 10, 13, and 15; Transition: 1: Main Point II: 12; Subpoints II-A-D: 6, 7, 9, 14.

You may find a sentence outline works well when you are working on your preparation outline; as you move toward a final speaking outline, it is best to switch from a sentence format to a phrase or key-word approach (or a combination of the two). To do this, look at your full sentences and pull out key words, phrases, or headers that will jog your memory and serve as guideposts as you speak. Sample Speech Outline 14.1 shows the full progression from preparation outline to speaking outline.

Your speaking outline should also include **delivery cues**, brief reminders about important information related to the delivery of your speech that are for your eyes alone. You may want to include reminders to show a presentation aid or speak slowly at the beginning of the speech, when you are the most nervous. We discuss more about delivery in Chapter 15. Table 14.3 offers a variety of delivery cues that may be helpful to you.

Another important aspect of your speaking outline is that it should contain notes for your **oral citations**, the references to source materials that you mention in the narrative of your speech. After a sentence or phrase in your outline, you might simply place the source in parentheses so that you remember to give credit. For example, the key words "SD-financial costs (Skerritt, HBR)" should prompt you to say: "Sleep deprivation costs businesses more than $3,000 per employee annually, in terms of lowered productivity, according to a report by Patrick Skerritt in *The Harvard Business Review*." For material quoted word for word from the source, the oral citation must clarify that the material is in fact quoted rather than your own expression ("As Skerritt notes, 'This doesn't include the cost of absenteeism—those with insomnia missed an extra five days a year compared to good sleepers'"). In such instances, you will likely want to use full sentences in your outline, rather than key words or phrases, to ensure that you do not misquote or misrepresent your source.

TABLE 14.3

USEFUL DELIVERY CUES

Delivery Cue	Purpose	Example That May Appear in Your Outline
Transition	A segue from one topic or idea to another; might be a simple reminder that you are changing tone here or a specific example or story that takes the speech from one topic to another	• [TRANSITION] • [TRANSITION: Use dog story!]
Timing and speaking rate	A reminder to use a specific speaking rate, either for emphasis or to quell anxiety	• [Slow down here] • [Speed up here] • [Repeat for emphasis]
Volume and nonverbal behavior	A reminder to raise or lower your voice at particular points in your speech or to use particular gestures or body movements for emphasis	• [Louder] • [Softly] • [Thump on podium] • [Count out on fingers]
Sources	Sources for cited material	• [Dowd, M. (2007, May 23). Pass the clam dip. *The New York Times*.]
Statistics	Statistics for reference, with source	• [U.S. Census Bureau: 64% of voting-age citizens voted in 2004, 60% in 2000]
Quotations	Exact wording of a quotation you plan to use	• [Dwight D. Eisenhower: "I've always found that plans are useless, but planning is indispensable."]
Pronunciations	Phonetic reminders for difficult-to-pronounce names or words	• [Hermione (her-MY-uh-nee)] • [Kiribati (kee-ree-BAHSS)]
Visual aids	Reminder when to incorporate particular visual aids	• [Census chart] • [Show model]

Information from D. O'Hair, R. Stewart, & H. Rubenstein (2018), p. 211.

Finally, you should choose a comfortable format for using your speaking outline in front of your audience. You may transfer the outline to note cards, which will enable you to flip through notes quickly, create virtual note cards on your smartphone or tablet, or just use a standard-size sheet of paper. In many classroom situations, your instructor will indicate the preferred format.

Sample Speech Outline 14.1

From Preparation Outline to Speaking Outline

Title: Sleep It Off: Understanding the Dangers of Sleep Deprivation
General Purpose: To inform
Specific Speech Purpose: To inform my audience about the dangers of sleep deprivation so that they may take appropriate steps to avoid this troubling medical issue.
Thesis Statement: You must understand the causes and effects of sleep deprivation—as well as simple steps you can take to avoid it—in order to improve your life now and avoid costly personal and social ramifications.

Sample Preparation Outline •

> • Note that the speaker uses a sentence outline style throughout the preparation outline.

Introduction

I. Do you ever feel like you're struggling to juggle relationships, work, and classes? Many of us do and, often enough, the first thing we cut out of our busy daily routine is sleep. •

II. For better or worse, the human body needs an adequate amount of sleep to function properly, and my research indicates that we simply aren't getting enough of it.

> • The speaker opens with an attention-getting question and offers a response that the audience will likely relate to.

III. You must understand the causes and effects of sleep deprivation, as well as simple steps to take to avoid it, to improve your life now and avoid costly personal and social ramifications. •

> • Thesis statement

IV. Today I will speak about sleep deprivation. I will begin by explaining what it is, move on to its causes and effects, and then examine simple solutions to the problem. •

> • Preview of main points

Transition: So what exactly is sleep deprivation?
Body

I. In a personal communication with Dr. Arkeenah Jones, a family physician, on March 15, 2013, she noted that sleep deprivation is a condition in which a person does not get enough sleep, which can lead to chronic exhaustion. •

> • Main point 1

A. The National Sleep Foundation's 2013 Bedroom Poll notes that 78 percent of American adults polled sleep less than eight hours per night, with 53 percent getting less than the minimum recommended seven hours sleep per night.

B. The results of the survey I passed out last week reveal that 30 percent of people in this very classroom get less than six hours of sleep on weeknights.

Transition: By a show of hands, how many people in this room *like* to sleep? • I thought so. If we enjoy sleeping so much, why are we not getting enough of it?

> • The speaker keeps her audience involved in the speech by asking questions.

II. There are many causes of sleep deprivation, according to the Centers for Disease Control and Prevention. •

> • Main point 2

> ## and you?
>
> How do you outline? Do you think of an outline as a hard-and-fast map, written before you begin writing and strictly adhered to throughout the process? Or do you start with a rough outline, revising and refining the organization as you move through the writing process?

A. Busy work and family schedules contribute to sleep deprivation.

1. As college students, many of us are trying to handle full-time course work and full- or part-time jobs to help pay for tuition in addition to maintaining relationships with loved ones. •

2. New parents are often incredibly sleep deprived as they attempt to adjust to life with an infant as well as those infamous nighttime feedings.

3. Shift workers (including police officers, nurses, and pilots, etc.) often have trouble establishing good sleep habits because their schedules change frequently and they are sometimes required to work the night shift.

B. Late-night television and internet use can interfere with the ability to fall asleep or can prevent individuals from adhering to a bedtime schedule.

C. The use of caffeine and alcohol can also make it difficult to fall asleep and stay asleep.

D. Some medical conditions — including insomnia and obstructive sleep apnea — also make sleeping incredibly difficult.

Transition: As we've seen, busy schedules, an overuse of media, the intake of alcohol and caffeine, and medical conditions can all cause sleep deprivation. • Now, why does sleep deprivation truly matter so much?

III. Sleep deprivation can have negative effects on the health and safety of individuals and the community at large. •

A. According to Lisa Zamosky, a health columnist for the *Los Angeles Times* and writer for WebMD, sleep deprivation is linked to poor concentration and lack of energy.

1. Sleep deprivation decreases workplace productivity at a cost of more than $3,000 per employee annually, as noted by Patrick Skerritt in the *Harvard Business Review.*

2. Sleep deprivation is a leading cause of automobile accidents, especially among adolescent motorists, according to a 2010 report by the American Academy of Sleep Medicine. •

B. Dr. Michael J. Breus, WebMD's "sleep doctor," also noted that sleep deprivation causes relational stress.

1. In my own life, I certainly find that I argue more with friends and family when I'm exhausted than I do when I'm well rested. •

2. The results of the survey I conducted indicate that 55 percent of the members of this class find that "arguing with a loved one" is a problematic outcome of not getting enough sleep.

C. Dr. Arkeenah Jones noted that sleep deprivation affects memory and cognitive ability.

1. In fact, a Centers for Disease Control and Prevention study noted that 23.2 percent of sleep-deprived individuals report difficulties with concentration. Similarly, 18.2 percent report difficulty remembering information.

2. Dr. Pamela Thatcher, a psychology professor at St. Lawrence University, conducted a study in which she discovered that students who pull all-night study sessions typically have lower GPAs than those who do not.

• The speaker continually makes her topic relevant to the audience.

• The speaker effectively uses an internal summary in her transition to her next main point.

• Main point 3

• The speaker continually uses oral citations to give credit to her sources.

• The speaker builds credibility by noting that she too is prone to the effects of sleep deprivation.

D. Sleep deprivation can contribute to chronic health conditions, including depression, obesity, and diabetes, according to the Centers for Disease Control and Prevention.

Transition: So far, we've discussed the common causes of sleep deprivation as well as their negative—and potentially tragic—effects. At this point, you may be wondering how to avoid sleep deprivation altogether. I will discuss several suggestions now. •

IV. You can avoid sleep deprivation with a few simple changes to your daily routine.

    A. Make sleeping a priority in your life, along with your other commitments.
    B. Have consistent sleep and wake-up times, even on weekends.
    C. Don't watch television, play on your laptop, or even study in bed. Try to reserve your bed for sleeping.
    D. Don't drink alcohol or consume caffeine too close to bedtime.

• The speaker transitions to her final main point with an internal summary and an internal preview.

Transition: Regulating your schedule and developing good habits are essential for preventing sleep deprivation.

Conclusion

I. Sadly, a realization about the dangers of sleep deprivation came too late for Christine Padilla, a new mother who ran a red light while fatigued and driving just thirty-three hours after giving birth. Padilla struck a nanny pushing a toddler in a stroller, killing the forty-one-year-old woman and seriously injuring the little boy, according to a report by Snejana Farberoy in *The Daily Mail*. •

• The speaker signals the end of her speech with a tragic story that drives home her main points.

II. As you've seen today, sleep deprivation is a concerning problem for individuals and communities.

    A. It has many causes, ranging from busy schedules and media use to caffeine and alcohol consumption and medical problems.
    B. Its effects can be devastating, as I've detailed in this speech.
    C. Luckily, many of us can prevent sleep deprivation by making simple changes to our daily routines. •

• The speaker reiterates her main points.

III. Now go get some rest . . . after all of today's speeches are over, that is! •

• The speaker uses a memorable statement and humor to end her speech.

Sample Speaking Outline

Introduction [Speak slowly! Look at audience!]

I. Juggling commitments? Many give up sleeping.
II. We need sleep; research = we don't get enough.
III. Be informed about sleep deprivation (SD) to improve life and prevent negative consequences. •
IV. I will discuss SD: what, causes, effects, prevention. •

• Thesis statement. The speaker is so familiar with her speech purpose and thesis that she only needs a brief reminder.

Transition: What is SD?

Body

I. SD = not enough sleep; can lead to chronic exhaustion (Dr. Arkeenah Jones, personal communication, March 15, 2013). •

• Key-word preview of main points

• Main point 1

    A. A new survey of more than 440,000 Americans finds that about a third of adults do not get enough sleep (Centers for Disease Control and Prevention, 2015).

- Main point 2

65% of American adults sleep <8 hours per night (National Sleep Foundation's 2015 survey). •

B. 30% of people in class sleep <6 hours on weeknights (my survey).

Transition: *Like* to sleep? Then why not sleeping? [**Smile, encourage audience response**]

- The speaker retains a bit more detail in this subpoint in order to keep her statistics straight.

II. SD causes (CDC) •

A. Family and work

1. College students—course work, jobs, relationship
2. New parents—crying, hungry babies
3. Shift workers—trouble with consistent schedules

B. Television and internet
C. Caffeine and alcohol
D. Medical conditions—insomnia and obstructive sleep apnea

Transition: Causes: schedules, media, alcohol/caffeine/medical conditions. Who cares?

- Main point 3

III. SD has negative effects for individuals and community. •

A. Decreases performance and alertness (Lisa Zamosky, health columnist for the *Los Angeles Times* and writer for WebMD)

1. Decreases workplace productivity; costs >$3,000 per employee annually (Patrick D. Skerritt, *Harvard Business Review*)
2. Causes auto accidents, especially teens (American Academy of Sleep Medicine, February 2010) •

- The speaker makes sure that her oral citations are clear throughout the speaking outline.

B. Causes relational stress (Dr. Michael J. Breus, WebMD's "sleep doctor")

1. True for me!
2. 55% of class fights with loved ones from SD (my survey)

C. Affects memory and cognitive ability (Dr. Jones)
1. 23.2% report difficulties with concentration; 18.2% report difficulty remembering info (CDC)
2. All-nighters lead to lower GPA (Dr. Pamela Thatcher, psychology professor at St. Lawrence University)

D. Chronic health conditions—depression, obesity, diabetes (CDC)

Transition: Discussed causes and effects. How to prevent SD?

- In an earlier practice, the speaker noted her tendency to read directly from notes, preventing useful interaction with the audience.

IV. Daily routine changes • [**Don't read as list. Look up!**] •

A. Prioritize sleeping
B. Consistent sleep and wake-up times
C. No TV/internet in bed; just sleep
D. No alcohol/caffeine close to bedtime

Transition: Changes in routine and good habits prevent SD.

- Main point 4

Conclusion

- The speaker uses effective delivery cues throughout her speech. Here she reminds herself to use a visual aid.

I. Christine Padilla, fatigued mother driving 33 hours after birth, kills nanny and severely injures toddler (Snejana Farberoy, *Daily Mail*, 2013). [**Show image of crash**] •

II. SD is a concerning problem for individuals and communities.

    A. Causes: busy schedules, media use, alcohol/caffeine/medical problems

    B. Devastating effects

    C. Mostly preventable with simple changes

III. Get some rest!

 The State of the Union Address

The White House/
Getty Images

As this chapter shows, organizing, writing, and outlining your speech are crucial steps in eventually delivering an effective presentation. Recall our discussion of White House speechwriters preparing the State of the Union address from the beginning of the chapter. What considerations and challenges will affect their organization and outlines? How will their organization influence their audiences' perceptions of the speech?

▶ Ideas will come in from every direction, so planning and organization are key. David Frum, a former White House speechwriter, observed that "the planning for the next State of the Union really begins the day after the last State of the Union" (as cited in Jackson, 2006).

▶ Speechwriters need to bear in mind that they are writing for two different — albeit not mutually exclusive — audiences. Chriss Winston (2002) points out that members of Congress and Washington insiders judge the speech primarily on its policy content, whereas everyday Americans tend to look for leadership qualities and their own values in the president. The challenge lies in choosing content and language that speak to both groups.

▶ The key to avoiding what Cody Keenan (Schuppe & Alexander, 2016) refers to as the speech "sinking on its own weight" lies in skillfully building unifying themes among the many policies under discussion, rather than jumping from point to point. Barack Obama's speechwriters always aimed to invoke the struggle of ordinary Americans by using language that would appeal to them. This would often involve numerous updates of speech drafts and consulting with the president.

▶ Creating unified themes is also crucial to keeping the content (and length) of the speech from spiraling out of control. President Bill Clinton was known for long State of the Union speeches that detailed many policy proposals, while President George W. Bush preferred to stick to big ideas. President Barack Obama chose in his second term to use current events, including major storms and shootings, to advance his agenda items, such as climate change, gun control legislation, and technology and innovation in jobs.

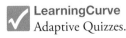 Activities

LaunchPad
macmillan learning

1. LaunchPad for *Real Communication* offers key term videos and encourages self-assessment through adaptive quizzing. Go to **launchpadworks.com** to get access to:

✓ **LearningCurve**
Adaptive Quizzes.

▶ Video clips that illustrate key concepts, highlighted in teal in the Real Reference section that follows.

2. Take a look at the outline of this chapter in the Contents (p. 345). Do you see a clear hierarchy of points and subpoints? Within the chapter, how are transitions used to move from point to point? How might the techniques used in this chapter work in your speech?

3. Read a famous or familiar speech (such as Martin Luther King Jr's "I Have a Dream" speech) or watch one online. (A great site to consider is TED, which offers inspirational speeches about "ideas worth spreading." See ted.com.) Next, create an outline for your chosen speech. Can you follow a clear sequence of points? Do the subpoints support the speaker's main points?

4. When creating the outline for your speech, write each main point on a separate index card. Spread the cards out on a table and then pick them up in the most logical order. Does this order match the order of your outline? How did you choose to arrange the topics—spatially, chronologically, or topically?

5. Establishing a relationship with the audience is important when giving a speech. Make a list of all of the possible members of your audience. How do you plan to connect with all members of the audience? Pretend you are giving a speech at your old high school. Will your introduction affect the seniors the same way it will affect the principal?

6. Pick a general topic and try to come up with several different attention-getters for that topic. Here's an example for the topic "dogs":

   ▶ Tell a funny story about your dog.

   ▶ "Did you know that the human mouth contains more germs than a dog's mouth?"

   ▶ "In my hometown, there is a dog that walks upright like a human because he does not have any front legs."

   ▶ "Did you know that approximately ten million unwanted dogs are euthanized annually in the United States?"

Try this with a topic such as your favorite food, favorite vacation spot, or some other appealing topic.

real reference ▶ A Study Tool

Now that you have finished reading this chapter, you can:

Organize and support your main points:

▶ Identify your **main points**, the central claims that support your specific speech purpose and your thesis statement (p. 346).

▶ **Subpoints** support your main points, using the statistics, stories, and other forms of research you discovered on your topic (p. 347).

Choose an appropriate organizational pattern for your speech:

▶ A **chronological pattern** presents main points in a systematic, time-related fashion (p. 348).

▶ A **topical pattern** is based on categories, such as person, place, thing, or process (p. 348). The **primacy–recency effect** argues that audiences are most likely to remember what comes at the beginning and end of messages (p. 348).

▶ A **spatial pattern** arranges points according to physical proximity or direction from one to the next (p. 349).

▶ The **problem–solution pattern** first presents an obstacle and then suggestions for overcoming it (p. 349).

▶ The **cause–effect pattern** moves from the cause of a phenomenon to the results or vice versa (p. 349).

▶ The **narrative pattern** uses a story line to tie points together (p. 349).

▶ The **motivated sequence pattern** uses a five-step plan to motivate listeners: attention, need, satisfaction, visualization, and action (p. 350).

Move smoothly from point to point:

▶ Build strong **transitions**, sentences that connect the points so that topics flow naturally (p. 351).

▶ Use **signposts**, key words or phrases that signify transitions (p. 352).

▶ **Internal previews** prime the audience for the content immediately ahead (p. 352).

▶ **Internal summaries** crystallize points in one section before moving on (p. 352).

Choose appropriate and powerful language:

▶ Consider your audience when you choose your words (p. 353).

▶ Use simple, unambiguous words (p. 354).

▶ Be concise (p. 354).

▶ Use vivid language (p. 354).

▶ Use repetition, allusion, similes, and metaphors to make a lasting impression (pp. 354–356).

Develop a strong introduction, a crucial part of all speeches:

▶ Grab listeners' attention with surprise, a good story, a quote, a question, or humor (pp. 356–358).

▶ Introduce your purpose and thesis (p. 358).

▶ Preview your main points to provide a mental outline for your audience (p. 358).

▶ Establish a relationship with the audience (p. 358).

Conclude with the same strength as in the introduction:

▶ Signal the end to ask for listeners' full attention, and wrap up quickly (p. 359).

▶ Reiterate your topic, purpose, and main points (p. 359).

▶ Make a final impact with a memorable closing quote, statement, question, or story (pp. 360–361).

▶ Challenge the audience to respond with a **call to action**—what you hope they will do in response to the speech (p. 361).

Prepare an effective outline:

▶ The **outline** puts the hierarchy of points into a text format (p. 361).

▶ The hierarchy of points for a strong outline will show each point supported by two or more subpoints (p. 362).

▶ There are three essential styles of outlines (from most detailed to sparest): **sentence outline**, **phrase outline**, and **key-word outline** (pp. 364–366).

▶ Write a **preparation outline** (or working outline) to organize and develop your speech (p. 366).

▶ The **speaking outline** (or delivery outline) is your final speech plan (p. 366).

▶ Add **delivery cues**, brief reminders about important information, to your speaking outline (p. 368).

▶ **Oral citations**, references to source materials to be included in your narrative, should also be included in your speaking outline (p. 368).

Britain's King George VI overcame a stutter to lead the nation in a time of war — and also inspired a young boy, who grew up to pen *The King's Speech*.

Popperfoto/Getty Images

 LearningCurve can help you master the material in this chapter.

Go to **launchpadworks.com**

15

Delivering Presentations

On September 3, 1939, Britain's King George VI took to the radio waves to inform an anxious Great Britain that the nation was, for the second time in a generation, at war. "In this grave hour," the king began, "perhaps the most fateful in history, I send to every household of my peoples, both at home and overseas, this message, spoken with the same depth of feeling for each one of you as if I were able to cross your threshold and speak to you myself."

Given the opportunity, it is quite possible that he would have preferred to address each of his subjects in that very personal manner rather than via a live radio broadcast. George VI — born Albert Frederick Arthur George, and known to those closest to him as Albert — had suffered since childhood from a crippling nervous stammer (more commonly called a stutter on this side of the Atlantic). Second in line for the throne, he only became king after his elder brother, the dashing Edward, famously abdicated the British throne in order to marry an American divorcée in 1936. Thus Albert was thrust into a position of leadership that he did not want but was bound by duty and honor to fulfill. And less than three years into his unexpected reign, the reluctant king was called upon to address the nation as it plunged once again into war.

Albert managed to address the nation with surprising grace. He was not perfect, but he managed to get through the speech and deliver his message to a frightened and uncertain public. One listener was David Seidler, a young British boy who had evacuated to the United States before the Blitz and who, like the king, suffered from what he describes as a "profound" stutter. "I heard these wonderful, moving speeches, and had heard that he had been a terrible stutterer," Seidler recalls. "If he could cure himself, it gave me hope" (Horn, 2010). Seidler grew up to become a screenwriter and penned the Academy Award–winning film *The King's Speech*. Seidler, who overcame his stutter as a teenager, accepted his Oscar "on behalf of all the stutterers in the world. We have a voice. We have been heard" (Seidler, 2011).

chapter
outcomes

After you have finished reading this chapter, you will be able to

- Manage your speech anxiety
- Deliver your speech in a confident manner
- Employ effective vocal cues
- Employ effective visual cues
- Establish a connection with your audience
- Enhance your words with effective presentation aids
- Make efficient use of your practice time

Many people feel anxious about delivering speeches—and some manage to avoid it. But consider the nervousness and challenges that King George and David Seidler managed to overcome in the process of finding their voices. As their stories illustrate, with the right tools and plenty of practice, even the most nervous or challenged individuals can become accomplished and engaging speakers. In this chapter, you will learn the basics of effective speech delivery that will help you connect with your audience and deliver an effective presentation. We begin by acknowledging the nervousness you may naturally experience before moving on to key methods of delivery, guidelines for effective delivery and presentation aids, and tips for practicing your speech.

Understand and Address Anxiety

Comedian Jerry Seinfeld once joked, "According to most studies, people's number one fear is public speaking. Number two is death. . . . This means to the average person, if you go to a funeral, you're better off in the casket than doing the eulogy" (as cited in Peck, 2007). Although Seinfeld's statistics are overstated (Dwyer & Davidson, 2012; Ledbetter, 2015), it is true that speechmaking can cause **public speaking anxiety (PSA)**, the nervousness we experience when we know we have to communicate publicly to an audience (Behnke & Sawyer, 1999; Bippus & Daly, 1999). Although we might think of PSA as an emotional challenge, it often manifests itself with physical symptoms, including a rapid heartbeat, erratic breathing, increased sweating, and a general feeling of uneasiness.

For some individuals, this nervousness goes far beyond giving a speech and extends to such essential speaking tasks as answering a question in class, meeting new people, interviewing for a job, or voicing an opinion. **Communication apprehension (CA)** is this more general fear or anxiety about having to communicate with other people (McCroskey, 1977). Yet speaking up or speaking out can clearly enhance personal opportunities and career prospects. In fact, your ability to communicate well influences others' perceptions of your competence, confidence, and work ethic.

So what do you do if you still struggle with anxiety? Don't despair! Whether you suffer from PSA or even the more general CA, you can learn to control your nervousness. In more severe cases, you might consider meeting with a trained counselor. Workshops on college campuses have also proven successful in helping students to reduce their speech anxiety, increase their confidence, and enhance their communication skill set (Tillson, 2015). For less disruptive symptoms, you might simply find comfort in the fact that nervousness is a natural part of life—and that it can actually spur you on to do your best (in the case of a speech, this may mean preparing more thoroughly and practicing more diligently). And remember that there is an empowering effect that comes with successful public speaking. It is an accomplishment that has the potential to boost your confidence in many facets of life. We offer here some advice on how to identify your anxiety triggers and build your confidence.

Identify Anxiety Triggers

Before you can conquer your nervousness, you need to identify it. Just what has you so frightened? Research, as well as our personal experiences, points to several key factors, including upsetting experiences, fear of evaluation, and distaste for attention (Ayres, 2005; Bodie, 2010).

Upsetting Experiences

Anna forgot her line in the second grade school play, and the audience laughed. They thought it was adorable, but to Anna, the experience was devastating. It is fairly common for a negative experience in our past to shape our expectations for the future, but it is important to remember that it is never too late to learn or improve personal skills. Anna needs to think about other skills that she has mastered, despite her initial nervousness: she was anxious the first time she drove a car, for example. With practice, she was able to master it — even though she failed her first road test. She needs to approach public speaking with the same "try, try again" attitude.

Fear of Evaluation

Anna's anxiety about public speaking may be not only about speaking but also about being *evaluated* on her speaking abilities. We all feel this way from time to time, but Anna must remember that her instructor will consider other aspects of her speech preparation, including her organization and research. In addition, she should recall that she is not under the intense scrutiny that she imagines. In most public speaking situations, the audience wants the speaker to succeed. In fact, research shows that audiences are usually far less aware of a speaker's nervousness than the speaker is (Sawyer & Behnke, 2002). Keeping the presentation in this perspective will help Anna to feel less anxiety.

● **PUBLIC SPEAKING** anxiety manifests itself both psychologically and physically, but it can be overcome by identifying the triggers of the anxiety and building confidence. Dave & Les Jacobs/Getty Images

Distaste for Attention

Alonzo loves to sing in the car, in the shower, and at concerts. But he refuses to sing a solo in his church choir because being the center of attention makes him feel incredibly uncomfortable. Although he may be able to avoid singing a solo, he will likely have to speak publicly at some point. He can minimize his discomfort with being the center of attention by thinking of his speech as an opportunity to communicate with a group rather than to perform. In other words, if he were to give the best-man speech at his brother's wedding, he would be communicating with a group of family members and close friends rather than putting on a performance. Similarly, when giving a speech for his human communication course, he is part of a group — nervous speakers with similar hopes of succeeding.

Build Your Confidence

Most people can cope effectively with periodic bouts of public speaking anxiety by applying the following advice, which can also be employed for more general cases of communication apprehension.

> ▶ *Embrace your anxiety.* Anxiety can have positive effects, such as driving you to be more prepared and giving you energy. For example, anxiety over forgetting your speech's main points might cause you to prepare with solid notes. By thinking about what might go wrong, you can come up with simple solutions for just about any scenario. In addition, that jolt of adrenaline you feel before starting to speak can also be a source of energy to make your points with enthusiasm — use it!

connect

Since many people are apprehensive about speaking publicly, we might assume that communication apprehension (CA) is limited to this context. However, throughout this book, you learn that anxiety can occur in many contexts. Some people experience high levels of CA in interpersonal relationships (Chapter 8) whereas others get anxious when working in groups (Chapter 10). And still others find that interviews (Appendix A) trigger CA. The techniques in this chapter are useful in all situations where CA occurs.

what about you?

○ Personal Report of Public Speaking Anxiety

Directions: Following are statements that people sometimes make about themselves in the context of delivering a speech. Indicate whether you believe each statement applies to *you* by marking whether you strongly disagree = 1; disagree = 2; neutral = 3; agree = 4; or strongly agree = 5.

_____ 1. While preparing for giving a speech, I feel tense and nervous.

_____ 2. I feel tense when I see the words "speech" and "public speech" on a course outline when studying.

_____ 3. My thoughts become confused and jumbled when I am giving a speech.

_____ 4. I get anxious when I think about a speech coming up.

_____ 5. When the instructor announces a speaking assignment in class, I can feel myself getting tense.

_____ 6. My hands tremble when I am giving a speech.

_____ 7. I am in constant fear of forgetting what I prepared to say.

_____ 8. I get anxious if someone asks me something about my topic that I do not know.

_____ 9. I perspire just before starting a speech.

_____ 10. I notice my heart beating fast when I start my speech.

_____ 11. I experience considerable anxiety while sitting in the room just before my speech starts.

_____ 12. Certain parts of my body feel very tense and rigid while giving a speech.

_____ 13. Realizing that only a little time remains in a speech makes me very tense and anxious.

_____ 14. I do poorly on speeches because I am anxious.

_____ 15. I feel anxious when the teacher announces the date of a speaking assignment.

_____ 16. When I make a mistake giving a speech, I find it hard to concentrate on the parts that follow.

_____ 17. During an important speech, I experience a feeling of helplessness building up inside me.

_____ 18. I have trouble falling asleep the night before a speech.

_____ 19. I feel anxious while waiting to give my speech.

_____ 20. While giving a speech, I get so nervous I forget facts I know.

Scoring: Add your scores together for statements 1–20 to assess your level of public speaking anxiety: high anxiety: 80–100; moderate anxiety: 41–79; low anxiety: 20–40.

Information from J. C. McCroskey (1970).

▶ *Desensitize yourself.* Sometimes the best way to get over something is to "just do it." You address your fear of public speaking by making attempts to get up in front of a crowd in less threatening situations, like asking a question in class or at a community meeting. You might even try singing karaoke with friends — nobody expects you to be any good at it, anyway, and it might be fun!

▶ *Visualize your success.* Research shows that people with high speech anxiety tend to concentrate on negative thoughts before giving their speeches (Ayres & Hopf, 1993). In order to reduce those thoughts (and their accompanying anxiety), it is important to spend time imagining positive scenarios and personal success, a technique known as **performance visualization** (Ayres, 2005; Ayres & Hopf, 1993). Performance visualization allows you to define situations and reduce uncertainty (Honeycutt, Choi, & DeBerry, 2009), so go ahead and imagine yourself standing before your audience with confidence and grace — and it just may happen.

▶ *Take care of yourself.* In order to be productive, remember to take care of yourself in the days leading up to your speech: get enough rest, budget your time effectively to make room for your speech practice sessions, try to eat a light meal before the presentation, and try relaxation techniques (such as deep breathing, yoga, a calming walk, listening to one of your favorite songs, or laughing with friends).

● **PRACTICING DEEP BREATHING** can help you learn to relax your muscles and focus your attention. fizkes/Shutterstock

▶ *Be prepared!* As we have mentioned, adequately preparing for your speech will increase the likelihood of success and lessen your apprehension (Smith & Frymier, 2006). Research demonstrates that confidence does come through preparation and skill building, which means that conducting thorough research, organizing your points, and preparing a useful outline will help you achieve a positive outcome (Schroeder, 2002).

▶ *Rehearse your delivery.* Once you have your speech prepared, practice it out loud by yourself so that you can hear how you sound and build confidence in your timing, phrasing, and gestures. Then ask a few friends or family members to observe your speech so that you gain some experience and comfort with an audience — a friendly one. Ask your friends to critique your delivery and then try again with their feedback in mind. Having your friends there may initially make you nervous, but that's the idea. Practicing in front of others gets you used to facing your anxiety and speaking well in spite of it, so that when the time comes for the real thing, you are ready.

▶ *Challenge yourself.* We ultimately learn and grow as individuals by pushing ourselves to accomplish things that we have not tried or felt confident with before. Instead of viewing your speech event as something to dread, reframe your thoughts and view it as an opportunity to gain a valuable new skill.

With a more realistic understanding of the role of anxiety — and with these tips for addressing it in mind — we now move on to the various methods of delivery that you may confront over the course of your life as a student, professional, and citizen.

and you?

Have you ever had an embarrassing public speaking moment? What did you do? Did it affect your confidence level or your perception of your own competence? Now compare this to how you reacted to someone else's embarrassing speaking moment. Did you think less of a fellow student who flubbed a few words or dropped his or her note cards?

connect

Chapter 3 discusses *self-efficacy*, or your ability to predict your likelihood of success in a given situation. If you believe that you cannot succeed at giving a speech, asking someone for a date, or interviewing for a job, you are more likely to avoid such communication. In any of these examples, performance visualization can help you manage your thoughts so that you can achieve your goals.

wired for communication

Face Your Public Speaking Fears in Virtual Reality

Picture yourself at a podium in front of a huge audience. The people in the audience look bored, even sleepy. As you stand before them, every yawn, cough, and shuffle of their feet echo in the vast auditorium. You struggle to make eye contact with one person or another, but their responses seem far off, their expressions disconnected from everything you are doing and saying.

This may sound like a very real situation — or a very realistic nightmare. In fact, it is a virtual reality simulation designed to help individuals suffering from public speaking anxiety overcome their fear. Companies specializing in virtual reality therapy (VRT) use three-dimensional imaging software, video footage, and sometimes mechanized props that simulate movement to create artificial representations of stress-inducing environments. Clients wear helmets, and motion sensors allow them to interact with the virtual reality environment. "It's a therapist's dream," notes one psychologist who has used the simulations to treat certain social anxieties. "To help people deal with their problems, you must get them exposed to what they fear most" (Lubell, 2004).

The effectiveness of VRT on public speaking anxiety seems promising. One study showed that VRT participation was equally as effective as standard cognitive-behavioral therapy (CBT) but that participants were more likely to continue with VRT treatment than with CBT. And at the one-year follow-up session, VRT participants had maintained their improvement (Safir, Wallach, & Bar-Zvi, 2012). The VRT programs are also currently being employed to help those individuals with speech impairments. When someone has a speech disorder such as stuttering, it is almost always accompanied by public speaking anxiety. One study found that VRTs are significantly effective in training people with a variety of speech disorders (Chen et al., 2016). A virtual speech-language pathologist designs an appropriate therapy program based on the profile of the individual under therapy, the specific disorder, and the short- and long-term goals.

think about this

1. Do you think virtual reality simulations would be helpful aids in preparing for public speaking? Whom might they help more, individuals with moderate speech anxiety or severe speech anxiety?

2. What are the benefits of practicing in front of a virtual audience? How would it compare to a real one?

3. What aspects of the public speaking situation do you think a VRT simulation could effectively simulate? What aspects would be impossible to capture?

Methods of Delivery

You might think of a great speaker as someone who is eloquent yet also sounds as though he or she is speaking without having prepared a written speech. Although that is possible in certain situations, most speakers spend time preparing in the ways we have already discussed in Chapters 13 and 14—writing a speech and preparing an outline of some sort. Deciding just how to prepare for your speech affects, and is affected by, your choice of delivery style. We examine four specific delivery options and the potential benefits and pitfalls of each.

Speaking from Manuscript

If you have watched television anchors deliver the news or candidates give formal campaign speeches, you may have noticed that they read from a teleprompter screen. That is because they are delivering a speech from manuscript. When you speak from manuscript, you write your entire speech out and then read it word for word from the written text because your allegiance is to the exact words that you have prepared. Speaking from manuscript is common for political speeches because they are often long and will likely be quoted and interpreted extensively afterwards.

A mistake in the delivery of such a speech might not merely embarrass the politician but may also affect world events. Manuscript delivery is useful in any situation where accuracy, time constraints, or worries about misinterpretation outweigh the need for a casual and natural delivery style.

However, manuscript delivery also has a number of downsides. First, it is time-consuming, involving tremendous skill and practice and countless rewrites to get the written message exactly right; this makes it a better fit for politicians and news anchors (who have a team of writers at their disposal) than a college student. Second, the static nature of reading from a written speech—whether from a manuscript or a teleprompter—limits your ability to communicate nonverbally with movements, facial expressions, gestures, eye contact, and vocal variety. As you learn later in this chapter, planning and rehearsal are crucial for overcoming these tendencies when delivering a speech from manuscript.

● **SPEAKING FROM** manuscript is a fitting method of delivery for TV news anchors such as Lester Holt, for whom accuracy and time constraints are critical. Ethan Miller/Getty Images

Speaking from Memory

Speaking from memory is an ancient public speaking tradition referred to as **oratory**. In this style of speaking, you prepare the speech in the manuscript form as just described but then commit the words to memory. Examples of oratory today include some religious sermons and most stand-up comedy monologues. However, oratory delivery is fairly uncommon as a form of public speaking, as it is both time-consuming and risky. A speaker who forgets a word or phrase can easily lose his or her place in the speech, panic, and never recover. But even if every line is delivered perfectly, the very nature of memorization can create a barrier between speaker and audience. Having memorized the speech, the speaker may deliver it as if the audience was not there. So, like reading from a manuscript, speaking from memory requires the speaker to make special effort not to seem distant or unconnected with the audience.

Speaking Spontaneously

Impromptu speaking refers to situations where you speak to an audience without any warning or preparation. (Talk about public speaking fears!) When you are unexpectedly called on to speak in class or in a business meeting or are suddenly motivated to give a toast at a party, you must speak impromptu. The secret to excelling at impromptu speaking is to understand that it is never entirely spontaneous; if you are always prepared to give a speech unexpectedly, no speech is entirely unexpected. For example, although seemingly spontaneous, candidates in political debates usually have a prepared rebuttal for any of the accusation combinations their opponents can muster.

One major aspect of preparation is the ability to think on your feet: when called on to speak unexpectedly, begin by first acknowledging the person who introduced or called on you and then repeat or rephrase the question or issue. This will give you a moment to focus on the topic and quickly construct a plan. Usually you want to choose a simple format easily applied to the topic, such as noting advantages and disadvantages or cause and effect.

connect

In an impromptu speaking situation, you should be aware of the relational, situational, and cultural contexts in which you are communicating (Chapter 1). This knowledge will help you tailor your speech to be appropriate and effective, whether you are giving a toast at a friend's wedding, surrounded by her religious family members, or at an international meeting of a professional association, surrounded by colleagues.

● **NO PUBLIC SPEAKERS** must think on their feet as much as debaters. These political candidates must not only present and defend their sides of key issues but must also anticipate and address what their opponents might say. AP Photo /Robert F. Bukaty

Another way to prepare for spontaneous public speaking is to listen to others. Determine if you have some personal application of a point or an example that a speaker has made that either substantiates or refutes another speaker. Most audiences enjoy hearing speakers tell a brief story that illustrates a point that another speaker made or a theme from the event itself.

Speaking Extemporaneously

Have you witnessed those calm, collected speakers who seem to be making it up as they go along in a surprisingly organized manner? They are likely engaging in **extemporaneous speaking**.

When you speak extemporaneously, you plan the content, organization, and delivery well in advance; however, instead of writing the entire speech out word for word, you speak from an outline of key words and phrases or speaking aids, such as PowerPoint or Prezi virtual canvas. Extemporaneous speaking involves delivering your speech in an impromptu style, even though the speech is neither spontaneous nor unrehearsed. Most speakers favor extemporaneous delivery: they can fully prepare and rehearse their presentations while economizing on time because they need not determine in advance the exact words that they want to use.

One downside to extemporaneous speaking is that it is difficult to use precise timing or wording; speakers can easily get off track, become wordy or repetitive, or exceed their allotted time. Even experienced college instructors may find themselves going off on tangents in class, given their passion and enthusiasm for their subject. Student speakers often face the same challenge. If your speech instructor gives precise time length requirements for your speech assignment, you are encouraged to carefully consider the degree of extemporaneousness in your delivery.

So what is the secret to succeeding at extemporaneous speaking? You can achieve success and confidence through practice and preparation. Consider the following suggestions:

▶ *Prepare well in advance.* You can begin preparing for an extemporaneous speech as soon as you decide on a topic. Think about some possible points you want to make and how you might support them.

● **WILL FERRELL** and his costars ad-libbed much in the *Anchorman* movies, not unlike what you will do when speaking extemporaneously. © DreamWorks Pictures/Photofest

▶ *Do not forget the outline!* As mentioned in Chapter 14, your key-word or phrase outline keeps you focused, but gives you lots of flexibility with your word choice.

▶ *Practice truly makes perfect.* Each time you practice your speech, you will give a slightly different performance. When you get really familiar with the points you want to make, you may end up memorizing parts of it; however, a little bit of it will change each and every time, allowing for a more natural delivery.

Guidelines for Effective Delivery

Everything from selecting a topic and researching information to outlining your presentation is a prerequisite to the big moment: actually delivering your speech. In this section, we take a fresh look at a point that we have emphasized throughout this book: how you say something is as important as what you say. That is, audiences receive information not only from the actual words that you speak but also through two channels of nonverbal communication: the vocal and the visual. These channels directly impact your ability to connect with your audience whether you are presenting to a small group, a large audience, or even in an online environment.

● **EFFECTIVE SPEAKING** is a crucial skill. Whether you are a sports star giving a press conference or a climbing instructor giving a safety demonstration, you need to know how to deliver your words in an articulate and expressive manner. (top left) Chris Graythen/Getty Images; (top right) Jim Jordan Photography/Getty Images; (bottom left) Jeff Kravitz/Getty Images; (bottom right) Jeff Morgan 13/Alamy

and you?

Many of us feel awkward when we hear our voices on a recording; however, rather than feel uncomfortable, you should learn to embrace your speaking voice. What aspects of your vocal delivery are unique to you? How might you, like Seth Rogen, utilize these features to create a confident speaking style all your own?

Effective Vocal Delivery

Actor Seth Rogen is the rare comedian who uses a monotone voice to great comic effect—his delivery of zinging punch lines in a flat, unchanging tone adds an extra layer of irony to films like *Neighbors 2: Sorority Rising* (2016), *This Is the End* (2013), *The Interview* (2014), and *Knocked Up* (2007). But listening to Rogen deliver a long speech in the same style would likely lull you to sleep. By using varying aspects of your voice, you can engage your audience as well as convey confidence and trustworthiness. Through practice, you can learn to control the elements of vocal delivery, which include pitch, volume, rate, pauses, pronunciation, and articulation.

Vary Your Pitch

To be an effective public speaker, you must make use of the range of vocal sounds that the human voice is capable of producing. These variations of sound range from high to low—like musical notes—and are known as *pitch*. You are speaking in a **monotone** (like Seth Rogen or Ben Stein) when you do not vary your pitch at all, and a monotonous speaker can be painful for listeners. So how do you ensure that you are using your pitch effectively? One way to practice is to record yourself speaking ahead of time to determine if there are places where you need to use more energy and fluctuate your pitch levels.

Adjust Your Speaking Rate and Volume

Speakers can use vocal cues to signal to the audience what needs their attention. Just as we use boldface and italic type on the pages of this book to emphasize certain words and phrases, as a speaker you can use audible cues to emphasize certain points.

How fast or slow you speak is known as your **speaking rate**, and it can also be a key factor in effective speaking. You want to speak slowly enough that your audience is able to hear and absorb what you say but quickly enough to capture the urgency and importance of what you are saying. Typically, if you speak faster, compared with surrounding material, you signal your enthusiasm for the content, and the audience's interest will follow. When you slow down, your rate signals a degree of seriousness and concern. Your speech rate should also be appropriate for the amount of content you can cover effectively in the time allotted. You do not want to end up speaking too quickly to cram in more information nor too slowly to stretch out a sparse speech. Some professional speakers employ the use of handheld index cards. If used subtly, index cards can be a huge help to a speaker, especially when used to plan rate, volume, and pitch of the vocal delivery.

Changes in *volume*—how loudly or quietly you speak—can also be used to emphasize certain points. What do you want to stand out from your speech for the audience to remember? Is it a statistic, a name, or a product? Think about giving one word or phrase in every few sentences some "punch." This differentiates the word or phrase from its context.

Use Pauses for Effect

Because many speakers believe that their overall goal is to talk, they pause too infrequently. The truth is that good speakers do not fill every second of a speech with words. Taking a moment between statements, words, or phrases adds drama by giving the audience time to reflect on what you have said and anticipate what will follow. For example, in Martin Luther King Jr.'s famous "I Have a Dream" speech, King's use of pauses, combined with rhetorical tools like repetition, helped to build drama and anticipation as he delivered his speech.

Pauses can also be combined with opposing phrases (such as "from" and "to") to emphasize contrasting ideas (Lawrence, 2015). For example, to draw attention to an inventor's moment of discovery, a speaker might say, "from failure [pause] to success."

Speak Clearly and Precisely

One of the quickest ways to lose credibility with your audience is to mispronounce a word—especially one that is specifically related to the subject of your presentation. **Pronunciation** is the correct formation of word sounds. Many words in the English language are frequently mispronounced, to the point that individuals are not even aware that they are saying these words incorrectly! Presidential mispronunciations in particular are fodder for late night talk show hosts. Take, for example, Donald Trump's mispronunciation of the word *Nevada* (ne-VAH-da) or George W. Bush's mispronunciation of the word *strategy* ("strategery").

But even if presidents occasionally err in their pronunciation, they frequently articulate well. **Articulation** is the clarity and fluency with which the words are spoken (regardless of whether they are pronounced correctly). To speak clearly and coherently is to be articulate. One way to strengthen your articulation is to do alliteration drills ahead of the presentation (e.g., *Sally sells seashells*, or *Peter Piper picked . . .*). You could also practice difficult sections of your speech with a pen in your mouth.

Practicing these articulation techniques can also help you avoid the problem of **mumbling**—omitting certain sounds in a word, running words together, and

and you?

How do you react when you hear speakers with an accent that is different from yours? Do you find them difficult to understand or make assumptions about them based on the way they speak? How might your own accent be an advantage or disadvantage in your next speaking situation?

● **AS STEWIE DEMONSTRATES** in *Family Guy*, a proper British accent and certain patterns of pronunciation can make a person sound more intelligent or authoritative. © 20th Century Fox/Everett Collection/Courtesy Everett Collection

speaking so softly that a listener can hardly hear. Most people mumble because they either are in a hurry, suffer from communication apprehension, or are not prepared to speak clearly.

Finally, audience perceptions about a speaker can also be affected by **accents**, patterns of pronunciation that are specific to a certain upbringing, geographical region, or culture. Although the word choices of individuals from different cultures may vary from time to time, the greatest difference you hear is in their emphasis on syllables and rhythm while speaking. In the United States, southern speakers tend to drawl (use a slower pace) and elongate vowel sounds. Speakers from the Northeast tend to omit "r" sounds from the middle of words such as *park* ("pahk"), whereas midwesterners sometimes insert an "r" sound into words such as *wash* ("warsh"). If your audience speaks with a different accent from yours, you may need to enunciate your words more carefully so that they can better understand you.

Effective Visual Delivery

In the same way that a monotone can lull an audience to sleep, so can a stale, dull physical presence. This does not mean that you need to be doing cartwheels throughout your speech, but it does mean that you should look up from your note cards once in a while. Otherwise, you will be little more than a talking head, and your audience will quickly lose interest. What's more, effective visual cues — like dressing appropriately, using effective eye behavior, incorporating facial expressions and gestures, and controlling body movements — can enhance a presentation, helping you clarify and emphasize your points in an interesting and compelling way.

Dress for the Occasion

If you are like most people, you probably hop out of bed in the morning, open your closet, and hope that you have something decent and clean to wear to work or class. However, on the day of your speech — just like the day of a job interview or an important date — you do not want to leave your appearance to chance.

According to image consultants, the way you dress is essentially your visual résumé; it can either help to present you as competent and prepared or as disheveled and unqualified (Parente, 2013). Indeed, research indicates that attractive people are more persuasive (Davies, Goetz, & Shackelford, 2008; Palmer & Peterson, 2016). However, that does not mean that you need to have Hollywood-perfect hair or an expensive wardrobe to be an impressive speaker. Rather, you can signal authority and enhance your credibility by dressing professionally in neat clothing — like a pair of black pants or skirt with a button-down shirt or a simple sweater (Cialdini, 2008; Pratkanis & Aronson, 2001). You should certainly avoid looking overly casual (e.g., wearing flip-flops and a tank top) unless a casual appearance is crucial to your presentation. Indeed, you might look a little silly demonstrating surfing

connect

Recall from Chapter 5 that *artifacts* — accessories carried on the body for decoration or identification — send powerful messages about you. If you are not sure whether to cover up your tattoos or keep your tongue ring in, consider your topic, the occasion, your own comfort level, and what you can glean as the comfort level of the audience. And do not forget that your instructor can offer valuable guidance.

● **DRESSING FOR THE DAY OF YOUR SPEECH** means keeping in mind the message you want to send to your audience. A neat, professional appearance will signal to your listeners that they can trust what you are saying. (left) Lou Cypher/AGE Fotostock; (right) Stockbyte/Getty Images

communication across cultures

think about this

You Sound Like You're From . . . .

English may be a common language, but each of us actually speaks it somewhat differently. A sweet southern drawl, for example, sounds markedly different from the rapid clip of a native New Yorker, and neither accent sounds much like the midwestern voice of the anchor on the nightly news. For better or worse, our dialects carry with them certain baggage. When we open our mouths to speak, we are conveying not only the specific message we intended to share, but often also a wealth of information about who we are.

Whether we recognize it or not, most of us speak with some sort of regional accent that is intrinsically tied to the place where we live. Our speech is also affected by ethnic background and socioeconomic status — what linguists call social dialect (Wolfram & Schilling-Estes, 2006). In any case, we might be judged harshly based on the way that we speak: Americans, for example, tend to perceive midwestern accents as the most "correct," whereas strong southern and New York City accents are perceived as signs of lower intelligence (Preston, 1998). The less fluent you seem to your audience, the less credible they perceive you (Podlipský, Šimá, & Petráž, 2016). Similar judgments are common in almost every culture. In the United Kingdom, BBC business reporter Stephanie McGovern notes that her northern accent, which is perceived in England as being "common" or "working class," elicits a strong reaction from viewers as well as others in the industry. "I've had tweets questioning whether I really did go to university," McGovern says, "because surely I would have lost my accent if I did; a letter suggesting, very politely, that I get correction therapy; and an email saying I should get back to my council estate [the British term for a public housing project] and leave the serious work to the clever folk" (McGovern, quoted in Duell, 2013).

That is why many people whose jobs require public speaking go to great pains to shed their regional accents. Many of them head to speech coaches like the late Sam Chwat, the "speech coach to the stars," whose clients included the actors Robert DeNiro and Julia Roberts as well as a host of corporate executives and public figures who need to unlearn their hometown accent — or learn a new one (Woo, 2011).

1. What type of accent do you have? How do you feel it is perceived by others from different regions in the United States or even abroad?

2. If a speaker has a strong regional accent, should he or she try to lessen it when speaking publicly? Are there any public speaking situations where a strong regional accent might be beneficial?

3. Can you recognize social dialects within your own region? What perceptions do they carry?

---

positions on your surfboard in a tie or dress. The key is to dress appropriately for the image you wish to present, given your topic and your audience.

Use Effective Eye Behavior

You have probably heard some questionable advice about looking at your audience members while giving a speech: "Just look over their heads at the wall," or (worse), "Just pretend your audience is naked and don't stare." Not only are these suggestions awkward, but they are ineffective as well because competent speakers are aware of the power of their eye behavior.

As noted in Chapter 5, eye contact is an important form of nonverbal communication. When communicating with a relational partner, it can be both effective and appropriate, depending on the cultural context. In fact, in the United States and many other Western cultures, a lack of eye contact can make a person seem suspicious or untrustworthy. In public speaking, making direct eye contact can signal respect and interest to the audience (Axtell, 1991). But how can a speaker make and maintain eye contact with a group of individuals?

One way is to move your eyes from one person to another (in a small group) or one section of people to another (in a large group), a technique called **scanning**. To use it, picture yourself standing in front of the audience, and then divide the room into four imaginary sections. As you move from idea to idea in your speech, move your eye contact into a new section. Select a friendly looking person in the quadrant, and focus your eye contact directly on that person while completing the idea (just make sure you do not pick a friend who will try to make you laugh!). Then change quadrants and select a person from the new group. Tips for using the scanning technique are offered in Table 15.1.

Incorporate Facial Expressions and Gestures

Have you ever seen a cartoon in which a character's face contorts with the jaw dropping to the floor or the eyes bugging out? The animator certainly gets the point across—this character is either entirely surprised or seriously confused. Your facial expressions, although not as exaggerated as those of a cartoon character, serve a similar purpose: they let your audience know when your words arouse fear, anger, happiness, joy, frustration, or other emotions. The critical factor is that your expressions must match the verbal message that you are sending in your speech. For example, you are unlikely to smile when delivering a eulogy—unless you are recounting a particularly funny or endearing memory about the deceased.

Like facial expressions, gestures amplify the meaning of your speech. Clenching your fist, counting with your fingers, and spreading your hands far apart to indicate distance or size all reinforce or clarify your message. What is most important is that your gestures are appropriate and natural. So if you want to show emotion but feel awkward putting your hand over your heart, do not do it; your audience will be able to tell that you feel uncomfortable.

Control Body Movements

In addition to eye behavior, facial expressions, and gestures, your audience cannot help but notice your body. In most speaking situations you encounter, the best way to highlight your speech content is to restrict your body movements so that the audience can focus on your words. Consider, for example, your **posture**, or the position of your arms and legs and how you carry your body. Generally, when a speaker slumps forward or leans on a podium or desk, rocks back and forth, or paces forward and backward, the audience perceives the speaker as unpolished and listeners' attention shifts from the message to the speaker's body movements.

TABLE 15.1

TIPS FOR SCANNING YOUR AUDIENCE

Work in sections	Do not scan from left to right or right to left. Always work in sections and move randomly from one section to another.
Avoid the "lighthouse" effect	You will look like a human lighthouse (or a lawn sprinkler) if you simply rotate your upper torso from left to right while you talk, looking at no one person in particular.
Look people in the eye	Avoid looking at people's foreheads or over their heads; look them in the eye, even if they are not looking back at you.
Focus for a moment	Remember to pause long enough on an individual so that the person can recognize that you are looking directly at him or her.
Do not jump away	If someone is not looking at you, stay with the person anyway until you have finished your thought. Then move on to another.
Divide large groups	If the audience is too large for you to get to everyone, look at small groups of two or three people sitting together.

How do you prevent such movements from happening, particularly if you are someone who fidgets when nervous? One useful technique is called **planting**. Stand with your legs apart at a distance that is equal to your shoulders. Bend your knees slightly so that they do not lock. From this position, you are able to gesture freely, and when you are ready to move, you can take a few steps, replant, and continue speaking. The key is to plant following every movement that you make.

Connecting with Your Audience

It is through vocal and visual delivery that speakers are able to interact with their audiences—that is what makes public speaking different from just writing a good presentation. When you compose an essay, you write it and it goes off to the reader. But speaking before an audience is more than just providing information through words; it is an interaction between speaker and audience.

Indeed, gifted speakers like former presidents Ronald Reagan and Bill Clinton were always aware of this and became known for their ability to deliver even the most formal speeches in a style that felt conversational, personal, and connected. That is because both were able to use their words, voices, and gestures to convey the way they felt about a subject. They also spoke directly to their audiences in a way that felt unrehearsed and sincere. We now look at the way our words converge with our vocal and visual delivery to establish such a connection with the audience. We also consider the ways we can adapt our delivery to suit the audience's needs and expectations.

evaluating communication ethics

think about this

Judging Speeches

At the beginning of this chapter, you read about the struggles that people with physical challenges (such as King George VI) face when delivering speeches. But how do culture and ethics collide when it comes time to actually judge or assign a grade to a presentation?

Imagine that your speech class is engaging in peer evaluation. In groups of six, you practice delivering your speech before the final presentation to the entire class.

One woman in your group, Evelyn, has cerebral palsy, a neurological disorder that permanently affects body movements and muscle coordination. It can have a diverse number of symptoms, but Evelyn struggles most with slurred speech, balance, and exaggerated reflexes. Evelyn is quite comfortable talking about her disability and appears to be a confident speaker. Yet as she talks, you find it somewhat difficult to understand her speech. Because many of her words are slurred, you feel like you are missing a few main points. As much as you try not to, you find the fact that she sways when she speaks and that she must grip the back of her chair for balance somewhat distracting.

You feel bad making these comments to Evelyn on her first evaluation, and so you focus your remarks on improvements she can make on the outline. But you are worried about how the rest of the class will react to Evelyn and even what sort of grade she might get from your professor. You are now facing your second round of evaluations for Evelyn.

1. Is it ethical to share your concerns with Evelyn? Or is it more appropriate to keep quiet in this situation?

2. Would you feel differently offering Evelyn critical feedback in an online peer assessment situation? Why or why not?

Expressing Emotion

If you do not feel passion about your topic, you can be sure that your audience will not feel it either. One of your responsibilities is to ensure that, throughout your speech, the audience feels the same emotions that you do for your subject matter. Many Americans, regardless of their political affiliation, felt an intimate connection to President Obama when he addressed the media in the immediate aftermath of the Sandy Hook Elementary School shootings in December 2012. While remaining authoritative and in control, he also expressed his grief in a way that rang true to everyone watching or listening. He was not just speaking as a president that day, but as a parent. When an audience feels that a speaker is simply acting, they may question the sincerity of the message.

Adapting to Your Audience

One common mistake speakers make is to speak to — or even at — the audience, rather than to speak *with* the audience. In addition to making eye contact, this means listening to audience reactions, paying attention to listeners' body movements, and continually gauging their responses to what you say and do so that you can make adjustments to your speech as you go along. For example, if you observe audience members frowning or squinting, it may be a sign of misunderstanding. You can take this as a cue to slow down or emphasize key points more explicitly. Alternatively, if you notice your audience members responding with smiles, focused eye contact, or even laughter, you probably want to maintain the style of speaking that produced such a positive reaction.

Creating Immediacy with Your Audience

As you learned in Chapter 5, immediacy is a feeling of closeness, involvement, and warmth communicated between people through nonverbal behavior (Andersen, Guerrero, & Jones, 2006; Prager, 2000). We often think of immediacy as being an important facet of close interpersonal relationships. This is certainly true — but it is also an important component of building trust in the relationship between the speaker and the audience (Currie, 2015).

Speakers enhance their immediacy with their audience by following many of the guidelines we have already set forth in this chapter: establishing and maintaining eye contact with audience members, smiling, moving toward the audience, using inclusive gestures and posture, speaking in a relaxed or conversational tone or style, and using humor. Research shows that audiences respond favorably to speaker immediacy in a variety of settings (Teven, 2007a, 2007b, 2010; Teven & Hanson, 2004). However, as is the case with interpersonal relationships, immediacy is a two-way street. Audiences, like speakers, help to foster this feeling of closeness and trust by listening actively, responding with eye contact, nodding, and offering nonverbal indications of agreement, surprise, confusion, and so on.

Additional Guidelines for Online Speech Delivery

There are special points to keep in mind when you are delivering a speech for an online course. All of the points we have already made largely still apply (e.g., dressing appropriately and looking up from your notes), but you should also consider the following tips for an effective presentation:

▶ *Be clear about your assignment.* Different instructors have different requirements for online speeches. Some may require you to assemble your own audience and record the speech; others may expect you to stream to a live audience via Skype or a similar program; still others may allow you to record your speech by yourself and submit it. *Always check on your instructor's preferences.*

▶ *Be mindful of speaking rate and volume.* These factors are particularly important when recording presentations for online delivery since you will not be able to adjust as you go based on your audience's nonverbal appearance of comprehension or confusion. Be sure that your volume is sufficient to be picked up clearly by your video recorder or microphone.

▶ *Note the location of your video camera.* Your camera is the "eyes" of the audience; they will see what it sees. Make sure that your background (e.g., a wall in your home or dorm) does not have a lot of distracting elements on display. Also adjust your zoom lens to capture the upper half of your body as well your presentation aids. If you and your aids are too close to the camera, the audience may feel claustrophobic; if the camera is too far away, the audience may strain to comprehend your facial expressions or the writing on your poster.

▶ *Involve your audience.* Even if you do not have an audience that is physically present, you can still create a sense of immediacy by establishing eye contact with the camera, smiling, using inclusive gestures and posture, speaking in a conversational tone, and using humor.

real communicator

NAME: Tonya Graves
OCCUPATION: Singer and Actress
Courtesy Tonya Graves

When I went to college to Study communication in New York state many years ago, I never dreamed that I'd have a career as a singer and actress in Central Europe. But on my first night in Prague, I went to Agharta Jazz Club and met the acclaimed Czech blues guitarist Luboš Andršt. He invited me onstage to sing, and I've been singing and acting ever since.

Singing and acting involve many of the same delivery skills that I used in my communication courses, particularly my introductory public speaking course. I have to overcome anxiety sometimes in addition to building my confidence before a performance. I tend to do that by paying attention to my breathing and by imagining a receptive, engaged audience. As with giving a speech, I have to practice enough to feel confident and prepared, but not so much that my performance becomes mechanical or lifeless.

Blues, jazz, swing, funk, soul, dance, and pop music — I love them all! When I sing this variety in a given performance, I need to adjust my voice and facial expression to both the style and the lyrics so that my passion for the music comes across as appropriate and also conveys the emotional message I'm trying to send.

An effective performance depends on the situation, too. If I'm in front of a live audience, like in a jazz club, I'm very intent on establishing immediacy with the audience by making eye contact with real people (and, no, I don't imagine them naked! That's terrible advice!). This helps me feel more comfortable and also ensures that the patrons feel connected to the performance. On the other hand, when I'm in a recording studio, I imagine my audience and adjust my voice intensity to make up for the lack of personal contact. I imagine this is much like what today's students do when they prepare to give a speech in an online course in which the "audience" is an iPhone camera. My delivery is even more complex when I create a music video, as in the single "39 Reasons" (check it out on YouTube); my orange dress and blue scarf were designed to move and "float," accenting my thirty-nine reasons to sing the blues. Everything about my performance — from how I dress to how I prepare to how I deliver — is all part of delivering Tonya Graves to the world!

● **BILL GATES** was certainly thinking outside of the box — or the jar! — when he released mosquitoes into the auditorium to aid a presentation on malaria.
Fernando Castillo/Getty Images

▶ *Take your presentation seriously.* Just because your audience is remote or self-assembled does not mean that your topic, your audience, and the occasion are not important or worthy of respect.

Effective Presentation Aids

Bill Gates is a technology buff, to be sure. He is the man behind Microsoft, the company that invented the ubiquitous presentation software, PowerPoint. So when he gives speeches on behalf of the Bill and Melinda Gates Foundation, it is not surprising that he uses PowerPoint slides to graphically display information on changing death rates from malaria in poor countries and the impact of mosquito netting, vaccines, and other preventatives. But Gates also thinks outside the technological box when it comes to presentation aids: "Malaria is, of course, spread by mosquitoes," he tells the crowd. "I've brought some here," he adds, as he opens a jar to let a small fleet of (uninfected) insects fly around the auditorium. "There's no reason only poor people should have the experience" (Gates, 2009). This simple presentation aid got the audience's attention and made the fight against malaria familiar to all those who have ever swatted a mosquito off their arm on a summer evening. Of course, there are ethical concerns about such a stunt. What if we are talking about the Zika virus? Releasing mosquitoes might be powerful for Bill Gates as the speaker but could put his audience in danger.

Like Gates, today's speakers online and in person have many tools to create dramatic visual presentations that enhance their words and deepen the audience's understanding of the topic. We now explore how these presentation aids work.

The Function of Presentation Aids

Although presentation aids can be a valuable asset to a speech, heightening an audience's interest and helping you convey technical information, these aids should *supplement* your speech, not substitute for it. Sure, you may have a moving video or shocking image to share with the audience. But if you do not connect it to a thoroughly researched topic, as part of a well-organized speaking outline and effective delivery, then it will fall flat. To be truly useful, presentation aids must enhance your speech, accomplishing three goals:

▶ *Help listeners process and retain information.* Effective presentation aids can increase an audience's ability to retain information by highlighting key points in addition to helping the audience see relationships among concepts, variables, or items. Always make a point, refer to the presentation aid, direct the listeners' attention to where you want them to focus, and then restate, reiterate, or rephrase what you have said.

▶ *Promote interest and motivation.* Properly used presentation aids can engage your audience members or at least get their attention. If you show terms, photographs, statistics, tables, and other items that truly reinforce your spoken message, the audience will be more likely to go along with you.

▶ *Convey information clearly and concisely.* Effective presentation aids can help simplify complex material. There is no comparison between the amount of time it would take you to read a series of figures versus showing them on a table, graph, or chart. A good visual can present a lot of information in a clear, concise, and simple matter, saving the speaker's time for interpretation and elaboration.

Types of Presentation Aids

Students often ask, "What type of visual aid should I use for my speech?" The answer to that question is never entirely straightforward because it depends on your topic, the needs of your individual speech, the constraints of your speaking time and location, the demands of an in-person versus an online presentation, and a myriad of additional factors. What we can share, however, is a look at the dominant types of presentation aids and their general purposes for speakers. We begin by considering props and models before moving on to media clips and images, graphs and charts, posters, flip charts and marker boards, and presentation slideware.

Props and Models

Some things, people, places, or processes are difficult to describe with only words and gestures. An object, or **prop**, removes the burden from the audience of having to imagine what something looks like as you speak. For instance, if you are giving an informative speech on the way to tune a guitar, you might find it difficult to explain the process without demonstrating the procedure on an actual guitar. Adjusting a tuning key to show how it affects the pitch of a given string would be an effective visual (and audio) aid.

If a prop is large and cumbersome or too small to be easily viewed by your audience members (particularly for online speeches), then consider using a **model**, an appropriately scaled object. One of our past students brought in a small-scale model of the Soviet nuclear submarine the *Kursk* to demonstrate how the vessel tragically encountered problems, exploded, and sank.

Be mindful and considerate when selecting and using props and models in your presentation. One of us had a student give a speech on ocean pollution using a live fish in a bowl as a prop. He poured the contaminants he was discussing into the bowl, and his classmates (and instructor) were understandably horrified and distraught when the fish died. The speaker made a powerful point through this prop, but he was entirely inconsiderate of the speaking situation and his audience's expectations in addition to unethically contradicting his premise that we should save ocean wildlife.

Similarly, avoid objects that may be dangerous or even illegal, such as firearms, knives, chemicals, and so on. (You would be surprised to know about some of the scary props we have seen students try to use over the years, ranging from weapons to unfriendly dogs.) Think safety first!

Media Clips and Images

Images, including still photos as well as film, television, and internet video or audio clips, can add another dimension to and stimulate interest in your speech by providing vivid illustrations or clarifications of topics that are difficult to capture with words alone. A speaker informing an audience about reconstructive surgery for cleft palate, for example, might show a photograph of a child born with the condition as well as postsurgical photos, rather than just trying to describe the condition and outcome.

and you?

Think back on a variety of different public presentations you have witnessed — speeches by fellow students, presentations by instructors, political debates, and so on. What is the most effective use of a visual aid that you have encountered? What is the least effective? Why?

● **AN INTERESTING PROP** can be a helpful visual aid. This speaker might have trouble illustrating certain muscles and nerves in the human body without a model. SUSANA GONZALEZ/Getty Images

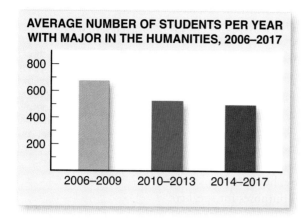

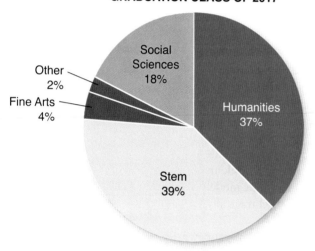

SAMPLES OF EFFECTIVE GRAPHS Bar graphs use bars of varying lengths to make comparisons. Pie charts depict the division of a whole.

When choosing media clips and images, keep a few points in mind:

▶ Make sure that your speaking site is equipped with the equipment you will need to make your selection viewable to your audience.

▶ Keep your video and audio clips short (say, one to two minutes maximum, depending on the length of the speech).

▶ Do not overwhelm your audience with ten illustrations or photographs when two or three would suffice.

▶ Make sure photographs are properly edited and cropped. Your goal is to draw your audience's attention to a specific aspect of the photograph and not overwhelm them with background information.

Graphs and Charts

When you are delivering a speech rich in statistics, data, and facts, visual aids can be indispensable presentation tools (see Figure 15.1). You can actually cut your presentation time drastically and increase your listeners' interest by pointing to some figures on a graph rather than reading them aloud, number by number. Graphs take several different forms. **Bar graphs** show the relationship of two or more sets of figures. A figure comparing trends in college majors over time, for example, is well illustrated with a bar graph. **Pie charts** show percentages of a circle divided proportionately; for example, a university registrar office uses a pie chart to reveal the percentage of college students' selections of particular academic majors on campus. A pie chart should ideally have from two to five segments; under no circumstances should it have more than eight since it will become difficult for the audience to read. If you have too many categories, you can add the smallest ones up and present them in a single segment.

Posters, Flip Charts, and Whiteboards

Posters provide a large, physical display of key words or images that can be a useful way for you to guide your audience's attention (especially if your speaking site is not suitable for computer display). For example, if you are informing your audience about the magnitude of the D-Day invasion of World War II, you could position one poster showing the very young faces of the soldiers alongside another showing the enormous coastline of beaches and cliffs at Normandy. As you ask your audience to look from the soldiers to the beaches, they can better imagine what it must have been like to run toward those cliffs in the midst of gunfire.

Flip charts and whiteboards, which are still common in professional settings, have a distinct advantage for displaying words and ideas over posters: they can invite and organize audience participation. For example, when presenting a new health insurance plan to a group of managers, a human resources representative might open the speech by asking the managers, "What aspects of health insurance matter most to your employees?" The audience members may respond with comments like "flexibility" or "low copays," which the speaker can jot down on the flip chart or board. He can then refer to each priority as he addresses them in his speech.

Whiteboards, collboards, and flip charts are also valuable when you wish to "unfold" an idea, step by step, before an audience, such as a coach using a board to break down a certain defense or offense.

Just remember that your use of flip charts and whiteboards should never be distracting. In other words, your audience may become irritated if you are constantly flipping back and forth between pages or running around to point to multiple diagrams on the board. It is helpful to keep a few key points in mind:

▶ Use large and legible print so that your audience members (particularly online audience members) do not strain to understand your visual aid.

▶ Use vivid colors to make your posters and whiteboard notes more appealing.

▶ Avoid cramming together more than one main idea or point unless it has a very specific purpose to enhance your meaning (e.g., a collage of photos of missing and exploited children in your area).

▶ If possible, use a pointer and stand near the poster to limit excessive movement.

▶ Make sure that all the words you use on the poster and whiteboard are spelled correctly.

● **BEWARE THE TERRIBLE**
PowerPoint slide! A long bulleted list of all your speaking points against a distracting background is a surefire way to detract from your speech. A clean slide with a few key points will keep the attention on you and your message. Bloomicon/Shutterstock

Handouts

Handouts are particularly useful when your audience can benefit from having specific information from your presentation at a future point. For example, if you are seeking to persuade your classmates to utilize your campus career services office, you might have a single-page handout with pertinent information, such as the website, office hours, contact information, services, upcoming events, and so on.

In a face-to-face class, be sure to distribute your handouts at an appropriate time. You do not want to create any unnecessary distractions with noise from shuffling papers! Unless you want your audience to follow along during some part of your speech, it is often best to distribute your handouts at the end of your speech, but check to see if your instructor has any preferences.

Presentation Slideware

Sitting through hours of slides from your Aunt Sonja's vacation is boring. Sitting through a slide show that essentially repeats your speech outline can be positively unbearable.

Presentation slideware (such as Microsoft PowerPoint, Apple Keynote, Google Slides, and Prezi), when used appropriately, allows you to have a one-stop home for lots of different presentation aids without having to awkwardly move back and forth between media. However, presentation slideware is frequently

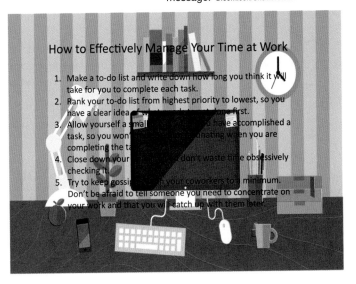

HOW TO EFFECTIVELY MANAGE YOUR TIME AT WORK

• Make to-do lists

• Take short breaks after each task

• Hide your email window

• Keep socializing to a minimum

misused by speakers who plug meaningless text or pointless visuals into slides without considering how to keep the audience's attention. You may, in fact, be familiar with the phrase "death by PowerPoint" (DuFrene & Lehman, 2004).

Too often speakers allow their slides to dominate their presentations, attempting to wow the audience with their technical proficiency rather than focusing on interesting points or well-researched evidence. We often warn our students that the fancier and more detailed the digital presentation, the more suspicious we are of the information being presented.

If you decide to use presentation software in your speech, here are some tips for developing effective slides:

▶ Become familiar with all of the features and options of your specific software before you begin to plug in your presentation information.

▶ Use as few slides as possible. More is not always better! In fact, research suggests that audience members remember an average of four slides from a twenty-slide, stand-alone, text-only PowerPoint presentation (Simon, 2016).

▶ Ensure that each slide addresses only one topic or idea for simplicity and clarity. Use only a minimal amount of text and avoid irrelevant information.

▶ Make sure the font is large enough for easy viewing (we suggest forty-point type for titles and twenty-point type and above for all other text) and be sure to spell-check those visible words.

▶ Use only design elements that truly enhance meaning. (No cheesy graphics, please.)

▶ Be prepared to give the same speech without slides in case of a technology glitch. Having backup handouts or transparencies is one idea; in any case, make sure your presentation is effective even without your slides.

▶ Prepare and practice in advance! As we discuss in the next section, you need to give yourself enough time to organize, reorganize, edit, and feel comfortable moving between slides.

Practicing Your Speech

If there is one key to developing skill as a public speaker, it is practice. Practice transforms nervous public speakers into confident ones and good public speakers into great ones, particularly when speakers pay attention to four important points: remembering the speaking outline, practicing with presentation aids, simulating the speaking situation, and practicing the actual delivery.

Remember Your Speaking Outline

By now you know the benefits of creating a speaking outline consisting of key words and phrases. Now it is time to practice from it. Review your speaking outline to make sure that all of your key words and phrases work as prompts—if you cannot remember that the letters "SD" stand for "sleep deprivation," for example, you might need to write that term out.

Practice Using Presentation Aids

Recall our discussion in Chapter 13 of the annual keynote presentations of the late Steve Jobs. Clearly, Jobs rehearsed his presentations, including his use of presentation software and other technological aids—in fact, he knew it all well enough to

connect

The words in your speaking outline must prompt you to remember your ideas. During your rehearsal, you will discover whether you have chosen key words that are at an appropriate level of *abstraction*, or vagueness versus concreteness (Chapter 4). If the word is too vague, it may not jog your memory under pressure. But if it is too concrete, you may be tempted to read directly from your notes. You will need to practice under realistic conditions to discover the right level of abstraction.

work around it when inevitable technological glitches arose. When practicing with your presentation aids, consider the following tips:

▶ *Eliminate surprises.* If you are using any kind of technology, practice with it long before you deliver your speech. A video or audio clip that did not download properly may stall or disrupt your presentation.

▶ *Test the facilities in advance.* Be proactive. Will your speaking site's wireless connection be fast enough to stream a clip from Netflix or YouTube? You will rest easier if you test it out beforehand. Likewise, you should do sound checks for video and audio clips to make sure that the entire audience can see and/or hear them.

▶ *Write notes to yourself.* In your outline, make sure that you provide delivery cues to let yourself know when to move to the next item or when to show an image or play a clip. This will help you avoid rushing ahead to get to a particular aid as well as ensure that you do not forget any.

▶ *Rehearse any demonstrations with a partner.* When your presentation aid is actually a live prop (e.g., a student in your own class), you need to practice with this person in advance of the presentation.

▶ *Have a backup plan.* What will you do if something malfunctions during your speech? If a video clip will not play, can you tell it as a story? You might have a handout prepared for your audience members in case your software does not work.

Simulate the Situation

You already know that few people can simply walk up to a podium for the first time and deliver a perfect speech. Seasoned public speakers often look and sound great in large part because they have done it before and done it often. Exposing yourself to some of the more unnerving aspects of public speaking—for example, an audience or a self-recording—through simulation can help you become more comfortable. For example:

▶ *Create similar conditions.* Think about the room in which you will deliver your speech: what is its size, space, and layout? Keep these things in mind as you rehearse—or even better, arrange to rehearse in the room where you will be speaking. Awareness of these conditions will help you practice eye contact, movement, gestures, and your use of notes.

▶ *Practice in front of someone.* As discussed earlier, one method for getting over anxiety is to practice speaking in front of other people. You can even "practice upward": practice first in front of one friend, then two, then three, and so on, until you are comfortable speaking before a fairly large group.

▶ *Keep an eye on your time.* Use the timer on your phone to stay on target with your allotted speech time. You might even keep track of how much time you spend on each point, particularly if you have a tendency to go into a lot of detail early on or to rush at the end.

Practice Your Delivery

In any speech, your objective should be to communicate a message to an audience. If your message is clear, the audience will connect with it; if it is buried in a sea of mumbling or forced to compete with distracting body movements, the audience

will miss your point. As you practice, you can improve the aspects of delivery you studied in this chapter and concentrate on your message.

▶ *Focus on your message.* Concentrate on the way that you express an argument, paraphrase a quotation, or explain a statistic. If you focus on your message, the right delivery will usually follow naturally.

▶ *Use mirrors cautiously.* Conventional wisdom has advocated rehearsing in front of a mirror in order to practice eye contact, maximize facial expressions, and assess gestures and movement. But you will not have mirrors when you deliver the speech; they can also make you feel self-conscious, distracting you from your message.

▶ *Record a practice session.* Recording your performance will allow you to get a sense of how well you project your voice, articulate your points, and use non-verbal cues.

▶ *Ask for feedback.* See if you can find a person or two to listen to your speech who will give you an honest and constructive critique of your performance. Ask what they remember most about your presentation. Did they focus mostly on your content, or were they distracted by your postures, gestures, or stammering? Were your presentation aids helpful, or were they distracting or confusing?

and you?

After you have practiced in front of one or more friends, family members, or classmates, consider their feedback. Was anything about the feedback surprising? Did they note the strengths and weaknesses that you expected them to pick up on, based on your own self-assessment? If not, how might you incorporate their feedback into your next practice session?

back to ▶ *The King's Speech*

Popperfoto/Getty Images

At the beginning of the chapter, we talked about Britain's King George VI (also known as Albert), who was thrust into a position that demanded public speaking skills even though he struggled with a challenging stutter. Let's think about Albert's journey—as well as that of David Seidler, who was inspired by Albert's story and eventually brought it to the screen with *The King's Speech*—in light of what we've learned in this chapter.

▶ Albert struggled with his stammer for years and was only able to get it under control after prolonged, and somewhat experimental, speech therapy. Fortunately, by the time he was unexpectedly crowned king, he had made great progress. Had his position as a royal prince not required him to speak publicly, he might have avoided speech therapy. He was prepared to speak—even though he did not wish to do so and never expected to have to do so, at least not as king.

▶ As a king in the early twentieth century, Albert had to contend with emerging media—particularly radio—when giving speeches. Although he still had to contend with the transactional nature of public speeches (in which he had to interact with and adjust to the audience), radio gave him the opportunity to gain confidence and practice: the audience's feedback is limited in radio's linear model of communication.

▶ The audience plays a role in the success of any speech, and it is likely that British citizens, facing the uncertainty of world war, *wanted* the king to succeed. As actor Colin Firth (who portrayed the king in David Seidler's *The King's Speech*) noted, "People knew this man was facing his demons just by speaking to them. I think there was a sense that it cost him something. They found it valiant" (CBS News, 2010).

things to try ▶ Activities

1. LaunchPad for *Real Communication* offers key term videos and encourages self-assessment through adaptive quizzing. Go to **launchpadworks.com** to get access to:

LearningCurve
Adaptive Quizzes.

Video clips that illustrate key concepts, highlighted in teal in the Real Reference section that follows.

2. *The King's Speech* centers on Albert's address to the British people on September 3, 1939, at the outbreak of World War II, audio recordings of which are available online. Listen to them, and consider how you would have received the king's message if you were a British citizen at that time. What do you think of his delivery? Do you think your knowledge of his struggles with stammering affect the way you rate his delivery?

3. While in class, select a partner and give a one- to two-minute impromptu speech on a topic of your choice. Your partner will write down both negative and positive feedback to share with you, and you will do the same in return. Then team up with another pair of partners. You and your original partner will take turns giving the same speeches again, incorporating improvements suggested by your partner the first time around. The new partners in your group will likely give both negative and positive feedback. Listen carefully and apply their advice. Now add another pair of partners to your group, for a total of six people, and give your speech one last time. Think of the feedback from all three sessions. If you received the same negative feedback more than once, you know where further improvement is needed. Did you feel more confident giving your speech the third time than you did the first time?

4. Pay attention to how you meet people and the general first impression you receive from someone. Ask yourself what makes you feel the way you do about the person. Does the person make you feel comfortable by smiling at you, looking you in the

eye, or coming across as sincere? If you can pinpoint the reasons for your own first impressions, you can better understand what an audience expects from a speaker and adjust your own behaviors in order to make a good impression.

5. When practicing a speech, pay attention to your gestures and body movements. Practice once using movements that you feel are appropriate and comfortable; then practice in front of a friend. Ask how appropriate your movements actually look. Are you using too many gestures? Too few?

6. Search YouTube for a segment with a speaker giving a speech or visit TED talks (the topic does not matter). Turn off the volume so you can only see (not hear) the speech. Analyze the physical speech delivery of the speaker. Make two lists, one with the problems with his or her speech delivery, and another with things the speaker does well (e.g., maintains eye contact). Then watch the speech again, this time with the volume on. Listen carefully to the speaker's vocal delivery (such as pitch, rate, and volume). What do you notice about the speaker's voice? Compare your lists and note all of your observations as you prepare for your own speech.

real reference ▶ A Study Tool

Now that you have finished reading this chapter, you can:

Identify and control your anxieties:

▶ **Public speaking anxiety (PSA)** is the nervousness we experience when we know we have to communicate publicly to an audience (p. 378).

▶ **Communication apprehension (CA)**, the general fear or anxiety surrounding communication with others, is a common barrier to effective delivery (p. 378).

▶ Common anxiety triggers include upsetting past experiences, fear of evaluation, and distaste for attention (p. 379).

▶ Confidence comes from being prepared, desensitizing yourself, visualizing success (particularly through **performance visualization**), taking care of yourself, and lots of practice (pp. 379–381).

Choose a delivery style best suited to you and your speaking situation:

▶ Speaking from manuscript is helpful when you need to get the details 100 percent correct but can be static and dull (pp. 382–383).

▶ Speaking from memory, referred to as **oratory**, doesn't invite rapport with the audience and is rare today (p. 383).

▶ Speaking spontaneously—when you're asked to speak with no warning beforehand—is known as **impromptu speaking** (pp. 383–384).

▶ **Extemporaneous speaking** makes the speech look easy and spontaneous, but it's actually based on an outline of key points and practice, practice, practice (pp. 384–385).

Employ effective vocal cues:

▶ Use *pitch* to vary your sound range and avoid a **monotone** (p. 386).

▶ Cue the audience as to what's important by adjusting your **speaking rate** and *volume* (p. 386).

▶ Add drama to the speech by pausing for effect (p. 386).

▶ Speak clearly and precisely: use proper **pronunciation**, practice careful **articulation**, and avoid **mumbling** (pp. 387–388).

▶ If you have an **accent**, be aware of how it might influence your audience (p. 388).

Employ effective visual cues:

▶ Dress appropriately for the speaking occasion (p. 388).

▶ Make brief eye contact with almost everyone, using the technique known as **scanning** (p. 390).

▶ Facial expressions and gestures must match the verbal message of your speech (p. 390).

▶ Maintain a steady, confident **posture** by positioning your legs at a distance equal to your shoulders, with slightly bent knees, in the stance known as **planting** (pp. 390–391).

Connect with your audience:

▶ Share your passion for the topic with your audience through effective use of emotion (p. 392).

▶ Gauge the audience response and adapt to it (p. 392).

▶ Generate immediacy with your audience (p. 392).

Enhance your words with effective presentation aids:

▶ Effective presentation aids help listeners process and retain information, promote interest and motivation, and convey information clearly and concisely (p. 394).

▶ Based on the needs of your presentation, you can choose among helpful presentation aid types, including **props** and **models**, media clips and images, graphs and charts (including **bar graphs** and **pie charts**), posters and transparencies, flip charts and whiteboards, handouts, and presentation slideware (pp. 395–398).

Make efficient use of your practice time:

▶ Make sure the key words in your speaking outline are meaningful prompts (p. 398).

▶ Do a run-through with your presentation aids (particularly the electronic ones), and try to simulate the actual speaking conditions (p. 399).

▶ Focus on the message (p. 400).

Dr. Neil deGrasse Tyson shoulders a hefty load: educating the public about astrophysics. His flair for informative speaking has earned him widespread praise.

Bryan Bedder/Getty Images

 LearningCurve can help you master the material in this chapter.

Go to **launchpadworks.com**.

chapter 16

Informative Speaking

"What happens if you get sucked into a black hole?" "Why was Pluto demoted to 'dwarf planet' status?" It is not surprising that people enjoy asking questions of Dr. Neil deGrasse Tyson, noted astrophysicist and the director of the Hayden Planetarium at the American Museum of Natural History. What is surprising, however, is that people recognize Tyson at all. After all, scientists—even noted scientists—are not often celebrities, and unless you are a fan of the television show *The Big Bang Theory*, astrophysics is a field that seems far removed from everyday life. Yet Tyson has, in many ways, become the face of science today, having written several best-selling books and given lectures around the country. He also hosts the PBS series *NOVA Science-NOW* and has made appearances on *The Daily Show*, *The Colbert Report*, and *Jeopardy!* Tyson recently began hosting the late-night talk show *Star Talk* on the National Geographic Channel, where he interviews pop culture celebrities and asks them about their life experiences with science (Berenson, 2015). *Time* magazine voted him one of the one hundred most influential people in the world, and *Discover Magazine* selected him as one of the "10 Most Influential People in Science," (Kruglinski, 2008). He has more than 3.5 million Facebook fans and over seven million followers on Twitter.

Tyson's popularity is rooted in both his cosmic expertise and his communication skills, which have been recognized by NASA, the Rotary International, and the science advocacy group EarthSky. He has a particular knack for presenting the vast mysteries of the universe in ways that laypeople can understand. During a presentation at the University of Texas, for example, Tyson noted, "We have no evidence to show whether the universe is infinite or finite," before explaining that astrophysicists can only go so far to calculate a horizon—similar to the horizon line viewed from a ship at sea. He then continued that comparison: "Yet a ship is pretty sure that the ocean goes beyond the horizon of the ship, just as we are pretty sure the universe extends beyond our particular horizon. We just don't know how far" (Tyson, 2009).

Tyson recognizes the challenge of informing the general public about complex scientific and cosmic issues that researchers devote decades to understanding: "It was not a priority of mine to communicate science to the public," Tyson says. "What I found was that enough members of the public wanted to know what was going on in the universe that I decided . . . to get a little better at it so I could satisfy this cosmic curiosity" (cited in Byrd, 2010).

After you have finished reading this chapter, you will be able to

- Identify the goals of informative speaking

- Distinguish the eight categories of informative speeches

- Outline the four major approaches to informative speeches

- Employ strategies to make your audience hungry for information

- Structure your speech to make it easy to listen to

ike Neil deGrasse Tyson, the best informative speakers share information, teach us something new, or help us understand an idea. Clearly, Tyson has a talent for informative presentations. He knows how to analyze his audience members and tailor his presentations to engage them quickly. He organizes his information clearly and efficiently so that listeners can learn it with ease and presents information in an honest and ethical manner. In this chapter, we take a look at how you can use these same techniques to deliver competent informative speeches in any situation.

The Goals of Informative Speaking

As you recall from Chapter 13, the purpose of **informative speaking** is to increase the audience's understanding or knowledge; put more simply, the objective is for your audience to learn something. But to be a truly effective informative speaker, your presentation must not only fill your listeners' informational needs but also do so with respect for their opinions, backgrounds, and experiences. You need to be objective by focusing on informing your audience, not persuading them. You also need to be ethical by presenting relevant and reliable information. In this section, we examine these goals and investigate ways that you can ensure that your speech remains true to them at every phase of development and delivery.

Meeting the Audience's Informational Needs

Effective speakers engage their listeners because they have made the effort to understand the needs of their audience members. In informative speaking, the object is for your audience to learn something *new*, so you want to avoid delivering a long list of facts that are already common knowledge. Understanding your listeners' needs also involves choosing an appropriate topic and making that topic relevant to your listeners. Suppose you want to inform your audience about malicious computer programs, commonly known as "malware." Let's take a look at these points, using malware as an example.

▶ *Gauge what the audience already knows.* Estimating the knowledge level of the audience helps determine where to begin, how much information to share, and at what level of difficulty the audience can understand and still maintain interest. If your goal is to inform an audience of fellow students about malware, for instance, you might assume that they have some experience with annoying computer viruses, but that they may not be familiar with other types of malicious software or how to detect or remove malware from their computers. In that case, your tasks would involve describing the types of malware (like Trojan horse viruses, adware, spyware, etc.), the functions of malware (for hackers), steps to prevent malware from disrupting their lives, and what to do if their computers are affected.

▶ *Decide on an appropriate approach to the topic.* Involving your listeners through the appropriate use of language and presentation aids gives them the impression that you have fine-tuned the speech just for them. You might present the story of the 2013 security breach at Target, the biggest retail hack in U.S. history, in which malware illegally transmitted personal data from over 40 million credit cards to hackers. Seventy million customers had information such as their name, address, phone number, and email addresses hacked in the breach. Be sure to consider the different types of sources at your disposal: visual images, personal accounts, statistics, and expert testimony. These sorts of things will captivate your audience and help them remember the new information you are teaching them.

▶ *Make the topic relevant to each member of the audience.* Always specifically connect the subject to the audience by pointing out how it is pertinent and useful to your listeners' lives. For example, you might appeal to your audience members' sense of injustice when you share stories of fellow students who have lost term papers — or worse — finances or personal identity information to malware. You can offer them peace of mind by offering suggestions to prevent hackers from accessing their personal information in the first place and on what to do should their private information be compromised.

Informing, Not Persuading

Informative speaking often serves as the base for persuasive speaking: indeed, persuasive speakers typically use information as part of their attempt to influence audiences to behave in a certain way. But although informative speaking and persuasive speaking are naturally related, it is important to recognize that they differ in one very important way: an informative speech is intended to be **objective** — to present facts and information in a straightforward and evenhanded way, free of influence from the speaker's personal thoughts or opinions. A persuasive speech, by contrast, is expected to be **subjective** — to present facts and information in order to convince the audience of the speaker's point of view. Of course, it is difficult to be completely objective, because in any speech you must make choices about your language and supporting materials that have subtle differences in meaning and interpretation. Indeed, even in professional news, reports of "just the facts" can be infused with bias. However, you can maintain as much objectivity as possible by continually challenging yourself about whether you are being fair to different points of view. Ask yourself, "Could someone disagree with me about this point?" If the answer is yes, then you probably need to reframe your point or openly acknowledge that there are different approaches to understanding the information you are presenting. It is important to examine your process at every step in the development of the speech to ensure that you are being truly objective. Some of the issues you need to evaluate are examined in Table 16.1.

Speaking Appropriately and Ethically

Objectivity is not the only consideration you must bear in mind when delivering an informative speech. You must also consider the ethical implications for your audience members of the information you provide (Sides, 2000).

First, ethical speakers must choose appropriate topics for discussion. A fellow communication instructor told us that one of her students gave an informative presentation on how to grow marijuana. No matter what your opinion is on the legalization of marijuana, its use is still illegal in most states, so informing your audience about how to grow it is simply unethical. It is similarly unethical to explain how to cheat in poker, cut in line at a movie theater, or avoid getting a speeding ticket when driving too fast on the highway.

connect

Meeting your audience's informational needs is important in various contexts. When you are running a group meeting (Chapter 11), gauge what your audience already knows and make the content of the meeting relevant. No one wants to sit through a two-hour meeting on details of a situation that the group members already understand. And do not make your topic — the reason you have gathered — seem confusing or irrelevant.

● **WHEN YOU ARE** speaking to an audience that is knowledgeable about your topic, you do not want to bore them with a long list of facts they already know. Tell them something new! Sam Edwards/Getty Images

TABLE 16.1

INFORMATIVE VERSUS
PERSUASIVE SPEAKING

	Informative Speeches	Persuasive Speeches
Approach	From a perspective of inquiry or discovery; the speaker researches a topic to find out what information exists and shares it with an audience.	From a perspective of advocating a position or desired outcome; the speaker researches a topic to find information that supports a particular point of view and then tries to convince an audience to change an attitude or take some action based on that point of view.
Objectivity	The speaker reports information objectively, in the role of a messenger.	The speaker argues a case subjectively and speaks from a particular point of view.
Use of facts and information	The speaker sets out the current facts or state of affairs concerning the topic.	The speaker builds a case that he or she is passionate about and includes information that supports his or her favored position.
Expression of opinions	The speaker may provide others' opinions but refrains from giving his or her own.	The speaker provides others' opinions that support his or her own position or viewpoint; the speaker may mention differing opinions only to rebut or discredit them.

and you?

Have you ever had a sense that a speaker was intentionally leaving some information out or that the information was somehow unreliable? How did it make you feel about the speaker? Did it change the way you thought about the information he or she provided? What was the audience's response?

An ethical speaker has a responsibility to provide an audience with information that is relevant and reliable in a way that is respectful of both the audience and the subject. If your speech misinforms your audience or ridicules their beliefs, you are not being respectful of them. If your speech reveals highly personal or embarrassing information about someone (especially without permission), you are not being respectful of your subject. In addition, ethical speakers must avoid plagiarism by orally citing sources and providing a complete list of references at the end of a speech outline.

Topics for Informative Presentations

When it comes to choosing a topic for an informative speech, there are countless options. You can speak about something very concrete, such as a person, place, thing, process, or event; or about something more abstract, such as a concept or phenomenon. In many cases, your topic will fit into more than one category: for example, a speech on the phenomenon of hip-hop music might include descriptions of the genre (thing) as well as of particular bands (people) and performances (events). You might also talk about the way the music developed over time (process). We now explore eight categories for informative speech topics (Allen & McKerrow, 1985).

People

If there is one subject that fascinates most people, it is other people. That is why we might sneak a peek at *In Touch Weekly* or *the National Enquirer* when we are stuck in line at the grocery store (even if we are not that interested in the latest gossip

about the Kardashian sisters). The life of another person can certainly make for an interesting informative speech topic. You might give a speech about someone who is famous (or infamous)—indeed, audiences are usually receptive to learning about someone who is famous simply because they revere or worship celebrity (Lee & Yang, 2013; Spitzberg & Cupach, 2008). On the other hand, an obscure but interesting person, such as Dr. Catherine Hamlin (who provided free medical care to young women in Ethiopia), can also be a great speech topic.

The key to giving a successful speech about another person is to focus on the person's human qualities as well as his or her achievements. In addition, you should show not merely what these people did but also *why* and *how* they did it. In other words, give your audience a real sense of who they are or were. To meet this goal, your speech should include anecdotes, quotes, and stories that show the motivations behind their actions. Chapter 13 offers help in adding these speech supports.

Places

Like people, places can be interesting and compelling topics for an informative speech. You might focus on an inspired description of a real but perhaps unfamiliar place (the surface of Mars, the Arctic tundra) or even a fictional one (the Wall from *Game of Thrones* or the desert of Jakku in *Star Wars*). Even a very familiar place offers opportunities to provide audiences with some new information. For example, you might investigate the oldest building on your campus or in your town and detail some of its history. This will allow you not only to describe the place but also to talk about the people who designed and built it and how the building has been changed over the years.

Objects and Phenomena

Why do dogs howl? What is the astronomical importance of Stonehenge? An important source of ideas for informative speeches comes from exploring things that are not human. Objects and phenomena may include living things (like

connect

Your audience is an important variable to consider as you choose your topic. Your goal in an informative presentation is to meet the audience's informational needs, so you must understand their knowledge and interests. Before you decide to inform your audience about backyard gardening, solicit information about your listeners by using the strategies in Chapter 13. If you learn that most of your audience members live in apartments, they probably will not care about gardening in a backyard they do not have.

communication across cultures

Let's Talk About Sex

Few subjects can make an audience as uncomfortable as sex. Religious beliefs, age, experience, and even politics inform not only people's views about sex but also the degree to which they are willing to discuss sexual matters publicly. In many cases, for example, it is unthinkable for Muslims to discuss sexual practices, especially with strangers (El Ahl & Steinvorth, 2006). In many Muslim communities, state support or religious principles impact attitudes towards same-sex relationships (Bonthuys & Erlank, 2012; Helbling & Traunmüller, 2016). In many villages in South Africa, sex is a taboo many women do not — or are told they should not — discuss (le Roux, 2006). And even in cultures without such restrictions, talking about sex is often considered impolite and can make listeners feel embarrassed or uneasy. In diverse populations like the United States, speakers — including health care providers, educators, social workers, and policymakers — must be responsive to the sensitive nature of sexual openness when they speak to audiences.

Some people are already learning how. One of these individuals is Heba Kotb (Jayyusi & Roald, 2016; Raman, 2007), whose weekly television program offers information on sex to women throughout the Middle East. Kotb, who has a doctorate in human sexuality, clinical sexology, and pastoral counseling and is a devout Muslim, remains respectful of her audience's — and her own — religious beliefs by framing her discussion in a religious context, accompanying scientific information about the body with explanations of how Islamic texts address the subject at hand. Indeed, both medical experts and Islamic clerics participate in her show. She also pays careful attention to nonverbal communication: she wears the traditional Muslim headscarf and speaks in a serious tone and uses serious facial expressions. Kotb's sensitive approach, taking cultural taboos, norms, and beliefs into account, seems to allow her to talk more freely about this once forbidden topic.

1. Kotb's approach to informing women about sex is far from the often lighthearted and humorous approaches used by talk show hosts in the United States. How might her approach to informative speaking be perceived in the United States?

2. Imagine that you have to give an informative speech about a sexual topic in front of your nursing class. How would you approach the subject? Would you handle it differently if you were speaking in front of your parents or religious community?

3. Does gender play a role in public speaking? Would Kotb's message be as well received by her audience if she were a man?

---

animals, plants, even entire ecosystems), as well as inanimate objects, such as the Egyptian pyramids, smartphone-connected contact lenses, pre-Columbian artifacts, or the *Mona Lisa*. Objects can also be imaginary (lightsabers), hypothetical (homes on Mars), or even entire phenomena (the El Niño wind patterns in the western United States). Audiences usually find these types of speeches interesting because they captivate the imagination or stress a topic that the audience had not previously considered as having an impact on their lives.

Events

Noteworthy occurrences (past and present) are good topics for informative speeches. Our understanding of the world is shaped by significant historical events — the U.S. Civil War, the assassination of John F. Kennedy, the Apollo 11 moon landing, and the terrorist attacks on September 11. Current or recent events may also be compelling, such as the Rio Olympic Games or the 2016 U.S. presidential election. At a more intimate level, events of local significance can also make interesting topics for speeches, such as the upcoming student film festival at your campus.

evaluating communication ethics

Ulterior Motives

As captain of the swim team, you have been asked to deliver an informative speech to your school's alumni during homecoming week detailing the team's past three seasons and hopes for the future. You have outlined a short, simple speech that notes individual members' personal bests, team achievements, and the coach's laudable efforts to recruit promising high school athletes. When your coach reviews your speech outline, she asks you to include more about the many scholarships that the school makes available to athletes.

You know that the coach has many motives for asking you to include more information about scholarship money. She is hoping, first and foremost, to convince alumni to support the team financially in order to entice more financially strapped but talented swimmers to choose your school. But you are torn: you know that most of the money that goes to your school's sports programs is devoted to the larger and more popular basketball program. You are also annoyed because four years ago, the coach recruited you as a high school scholar-athlete with a partial scholarship that she promised would grow to a full scholarship the following year. The full scholarship never materialized; you are now about to graduate with huge student loans that you had thought you would be able to avoid when you chose to attend this school over others that had courted you.

As team captain, you are proud of your team's record and eager to inform the alumni about it. But you also do not want to give them information that you feel is somewhat misleading. What should you do?

1. What are the ethical obligations of a speaker in preparing informative presentations? Can you ignore the coach's request and just say what you want to say?

2. Is the coach's request really an attempt to inform alumni of what the swim program needs in order to persuade them to donate money?

3. Are *your* motivations ethical? Do you want to avoid talking about scholarship money because you think it will never materialize or because you are angry that the coach misled you?

You can also build an informative speech around important, tragic, funny, or instructive events in your personal life—the day you went skydiving, the day you witnessed a flash mob, the death of a close friend, or the birth of your first child. Just remember that these stories of personal events must be truthful. Exaggeration and fabrication are never ethical!

In addition to helping an audience to understand the meaning of personal, local, and historical single events, a speaker can also explore the social significance of *collections* of events. You might, for example, talk about the significance of dances for Native American tribes; high school football games in your hometown; or the role of weddings, reunions, and funerals in your family.

● YOUR SPEECH does not necessarily have to be about a historical event. The first time you went skydiving can be just as compelling a topic as the first time man walked on the moon. (left) Digital Vision/Getty Images; (right) NASA

Processes

A process is a series of actions, changes, or functions that brings about a particular result. Process speeches help an audience understand the stages or steps through which a particular outcome is produced and usually fall into one of two categories. The first type is a speech that explains how something works or develops. For example, you might give a speech detailing how a hybrid car works, how the human brain system processes sound, or how lightning forms. The second type of process speech teaches how to do something: how to knit, for example, or how to sync your data on your mobile devices. For this type of speech, it is often helpful to incorporate props, visuals, or hands-on demonstrations into your presentation.

Concepts

Although people, places, objects, events, and processes are concrete things that we can readily visualize, concepts are abstract or complex ideas, like "art," "patriotism," "artificial intelligence," or "loyalty," which are much more difficult for us to understand. Concepts also include theories (Einstein's relativity), value systems (a particular religion), or beliefs (the possibility of extraterrestrial life). Remember that when you make a speech about value systems or beliefs, you are attempting to educate your audience about them, not persuading your audience to adopt them. The challenge of a concept speech, then, is to take a general idea, theory, or thought and make it clear and meaningful for your audience.

Despite the challenge, many worthwhile informative speeches focus on the explanation of a concept. The idea of *ethnocentrism,* the belief that one's cultural ways are superior to those of other cultures, would be an informative speech about a concept (Armstrong & Kaplowitz, 2001). Ethnocentrism can impact the way information is disseminated and taught within a culture (Samovar, Porter, & McDaniel, 2016). You could make reference to important historical events that were influenced by ethnocentrism: the Holocaust, ethnic cleansing in Bosnia and Rwanda, or the September 11 terrorist attacks.

Issues

An issue is a problem or matter of dispute that people hope to resolve. Informative speeches about issues provide an overview or a report of problems in order to increase understanding and awareness. Issues include social and personal problems (such as racial profiling, post-traumatic stress disorder, or unemployment) as well as

● **DO YOU THINK** you could be objective about abortion? If not, it is probably a good idea to stay away from this topic for your informative speech. (left) AP Photo/Nati Harnik; (right) AP Photo/Bill Haber

ideas, activities, and circumstances over which opinions vary widely (such as birth control or affirmative action).

Because of the controversial nature of many issues, giving an informative presentation on one can be a challenge, as it can be difficult to keep your own opinions from influencing the speech. But if you keep your focus on delivering a speech that is truly one of discovery, inquiry, and objectivity, then even controversial topics often break down into more manageable components that you can look at objectively. For example, if you were to give an informative speech on stem cell research, you could break all of your information down into groups of basic facts: what the current laws say, where the stem cells come from, how the research is done, and why such research is being conducted. You could also address the controversy over the issue itself by presenting differing opinions from both within and outside the scientific community. If, however, you take a look at the research and plot your speech points but still doubt your ability to describe an issue objectively, you probably should save the topic for a persuasive speech.

Plans and Policies

Your community has a proposal for a new recycling program; your college has installed a network of bike paths. In an informative speech about plans and policies, you try to help an audience understand the important dimensions of potential courses of action. Such speeches do not argue for or against a particular plan or policy; they simply lay out the facts of what is planned or what policy has been implemented. However, like issue speeches, plan and policy speeches can easily evolve into persuasive addresses, so you must be very careful to focus on unbiased facts; if you find yourself unable to keep your opinion from influencing your speech, consider a different topic.

Approaches to Conveying Information

Once you have selected a topic for an informative speech, you can develop it in a variety of ways. Here we briefly describe four major approaches to informative speeches: description, demonstration, definition, and explanation. These approaches will help you develop the most effective way to share information with your audience.

Description

Description is a way of verbally expressing things you have experienced with your senses. Although most speeches use some type of description, some focus on this task more closely than others. The primary task of a **descriptive presentation** is to paint a mental picture for your audience to portray places, events, persons, objects, or processes clearly and vividly. An effective descriptive speech begins with a well-structured idea of what you want to describe and why. As you move through the development process, you emphasize important details and eliminate unimportant ones, all the while considering ways to make the details more vivid for your audience.

Descriptive speeches are most effective when the topic is personally connected to the speaker. Consider the following excerpt from President Barack Obama's "They Picked the Wrong City" speech to honor those killed and wounded in the Boston Marathon bombings.

and you?

Would you find it hard to speak in a purely informative manner on certain subjects? Would you be able to speak, for example, in a nonpersuasive way about your religious beliefs? Your favorite film? Or a musical act that you just cannot stand?

connect

At this point, you may have many good topics for an informative speech. But if you need more ideas, remember the advice we offered in Chapter 13 on searching for topics. Try *brainstorming* or *clustering*, soliciting ideas from others, or using the internet to identify possible topics. Always ask yourself: Is this topic interesting to me? Do I know enough about it? Is it a good topic for an informative speech?

● **RACHAEL RAY** demonstrates her resourceful culinary abilities.
Brad Barket/Getty Images

Many people found Obama's description of the youngest victim, Martin Richard, to be particularly moving:

> And our hearts are broken for 8-year-old Martin, with his big smile and bright eyes. His last hours were as perfect as an 8-year-old boy could hope for, with his family, eating ice cream at a sporting event. And we're left with two enduring images of this little boy, forever smiling for his beloved Bruins and forever expressing a wish he made on a blue poster board: No more hurting people. Peace. No more hurting people. Peace.[1]

From these few vivid lines, audience members learn who Martin was and are moved by this young boy's advocacy of peace; they can imagine who he might have become had his life not been cut so short.

Demonstration

"Would you believe you can make impressive and delectable meals at home in less time than it takes to get takeout?" (foodnetwork.com). Television cook Rachael Ray shows her audiences how in *30-Minute Meals*. Doing almost all of the preparation and cooking in real time as the show is taped, Ray reveals an important truth: often the best way to explain how something works is to demonstrate it. **Demonstration speeches** answer "how to" questions—how to use a Roku, how to bake a pie crust, how to salsa dance—by showing an audience the way something works. In this case, Ray uses a combination of explanatory narration and physical demonstration to show how she whips up Tuscan pesto-dressed penne or coconut-ginger rice with chickpeas and chilies, while making use of props, models, and other visual aids. YouTube personalities also frequently use demonstration techniques to teach people how to do things such as change a flat tire. Although these videos may not be "speeches" per se, they often follow the same principles of informative speaking that we discuss in this chapter and can be excellent source material.

The key to delivering an effective demonstration speech is to begin with a clear statement of purpose and to follow a very straightforward organizational pattern. In most cases, a chronological pattern works best for a demonstration, with the process broken down into a number of steps that are presented in order of completion. The following steps in the process of decorative painting techniques illustrate a demonstration speech in chronological order. You can imagine the speaker showing each of the three methods.

> To demonstrate how to liven up a room with faux paint, you can use three popular types of decorative wall painting: color washing, sponging on, and ragging off.
>
> Color washing hides flaws in the wall and gives it a textured look. First, paint your wall a base color. Next, with short strokes, brush one or more glaze colors loosely over the contrasting base color (show photographs).
>
> The sponging-on technique gives the wall depth and texture with a variable pattern. Apply two or more coats of paint—satin, flat, semigloss, or gloss—on your wall. After the base coat dries, apply a glaze coat using a sea sponge (show sea sponge and photograph).
>
> Ragging off gives the wall a delicate, evenly textured appearance. Apply two base coats of two colors. While the second color is still wet, use a clean dry rag wrapped around a paint roller, and roll it across the wall (demonstrate technique).[2]

---

[1] The full text of President Obama's speech on April 18, 2013, can be found at www.ajc.com/news/news/national/transcript-obamas-speech-boston-marathon-bombings/nXQRz

[2] We thank Daniel Bernard and Cory Cunningham and their students for contributing the examples featured in this discussion.

wired for communication

Talk Among Yourselves

There is little doubt that technology is changing the nature of classroom lectures. Many instructors embrace new technologies to enhance their lectures — they might incorporate slideware presentations, offer audio or video clips, or use a computer to run a statistical analysis during class. But some professors suggest that the best use of technology might be to eliminate classroom lectures altogether.

Eric Mazur, a Harvard physics professor, believes that the traditional lecture format, in which teachers speak and students listen and take notes, is not the most effective method for teaching or the most efficient use of classroom time. Mazur was astounded after a colleague's research showed that thousands of students who had completed the introductory physics course at universities around the country still did not have an accurate understanding of the nature of force (a fundamental concept for the discipline). He administered the test to his own students and found that they were no different. He began to try different methods for teaching the concept. Then, "I did something I had never done in my teaching career. . . . I said, 'Why don't you discuss it with each other?'" (Mazur, quoted in Lambert, 2012). He was shocked when students had figured it out after a scant three minutes of classroom chaos. Those who understood the concept were quickly able to defend their explanations of the concept, while those who had it wrong could not and, thus, students taught each other.

In what is now known as the "flipped classroom," Mazur and other instructional pioneers require students to watch short prerecorded lectures online or find their own learning resources. That frees up in-person class time so students can work with each other and the professor on homework problems and collaborative activities. The idea is for students to "own" their education rather than just being passive recipients (Pathak, 2015).

1. Why might instructors be hesitant to present lectures online? How might students be resistant to having to watch lectures or find their own resources outside of class?

2. Does Mazur's approach make class time more or less valuable? What happens if students come to class unprepared?

3. If students are engaged in peer learning during class, what is the instructor's role? Is he or she considered a facilitator or still engaged in public speaking?

Definition

Most informative speeches require that the speaker define a term or clarify an idea at some point (see "Clarifying Concepts" in the next section for more discussion). For some topics, however, the *entire speech* is focused on definitions. The main goal of **definitional speeches** is to provide answers to "what" questions. Such questions as "What is torture?" and "What is marriage?" have prompted heated political and cultural debates in recent years, making it clear that an entire speech could easily be devoted to defining such complex ideas. When you define something, you identify its essential qualities and meaning. Following are various ways to do this, and a definitional speech often incorporates more than one of these techniques.

▶ An **operational definition** defines something by explaining what it is or what it does. For example, a salsa can be defined by what it is: "A salsa is a condiment, usually made of tomatoes, onions, and peppers, common in Latin American cuisine." Alternatively, it can be defined by what it does: "Salsas are most commonly used as dipping sauces for fried tortilla chips, but they also work well alongside grilled fish."

▶ **Definition by negation** defines something by telling what it is not. For example, "A salsa is not the same as taco or picante sauce."

connect

When offering definitions, competent speakers remember that words have *connotative meanings* — emotional meanings — for people (Chapter 4). Consider the words *marriage* and *torture*. Even if you offer clear dictionary definitions of these terms, your audience may have strong attitudes about them that are influenced by their cultural backgrounds. As an informative speaker, you should be aware of the power of connotative meanings while not trying to persuade people to feel differently about terms.

● **DOCTORS ESSENTIALLY** give explanatory speeches to their patients, describing the causes of a medical condition and how it may be treated. Image Source/Getty Images

▶ **Definition by example** defines something by offering concrete examples of what it is. For example, "Salsas include the basic tomato version you get at your local Mexican restaurant as well as variants made from mangoes, pineapples, or tomatillos."

▶ **Definition by synonym** defines something by using words that closely mean the same thing. For example, "A salsa is basically just a chunky sauce, similar to a chutney in Indian cuisine."

▶ **Definition by etymology** defines something by using the origin of a word or phrase. For example, "Salsa is the Spanish and Italian word for sauce, derived from the Latin word for 'salty.'"

Explanation

Explanatory presentations delve into more complexity than the other approaches to conveying information or creating awareness. **Explanatory speeches** answer such questions as "Why?" or "What does that mean?" To make your points in an explanatory speech, you must provide reasons or causes and show relationships among things; you must use interpretation and analysis. To this end, you should keep three main goals in mind: clarifying concepts, explaining the "big picture," and challenging intuition.

Clarifying Concepts

When providing complex explanations, an audience may have difficulty even understanding the meaning and use of certain terms. So it is important to clarify your concepts. You may find it useful to use one of the definition techniques discussed earlier. One particularly effective strategy is to provide **elucidating explanations**—details that illuminate the concept's meaning and use. Good elucidating explanations do three things. First, they define a concept by listing each of its critical features. For example, notice in the following sentence how the speaker provides succinct illustrations for the concept of rhetoric: "Aristotle described the canons of rhetoric as consisting of *pathos* (appeal to emotions), *logos* (appeal to logic), and *ethos* (appeal to character)." Second, elucidating explanations contrast examples of the concept. For instance, the speaker may use an example of a gun control argument to show how the "canons of rhetoric" contrast: "You may hear someone using pathos to make an emotional, well-intentioned argument for more gun control to prevent violence, citing that guns have led to mass murders and made it much easier to kill using assault weapons. You may also hear someone else using logos to describe the need for only partial gun control, stating that laws against murder and violence do not apply to those who have given up on life and intend to die while killing as many people as they can." In this case, the speaker's illustration of pathos and logos deepen the audience's understanding of the concept of rhetoric.

Explaining the Big Picture

Sometimes an idea is difficult for an audience because its complexity makes its main points—the "big picture"—hard to grasp. In this case, speakers might use a quasi-scientific explanation. Just as scientists develop models of the world, **quasi-scientific explanations** provide a model or picture of the key dimensions of some phenomenon for a particular audience. These explanations work particularly well for speakers presenting complex topics to laypeople, such as how microchips work, the similarities and differences between levees and dams, or how DNA molecules pass along genetic information.

what about you?

Informative or Persuasive?

Speakers sometimes have a hard time clarifying the general purpose of their presentation topic. Does the speech intend to impart information (informative speech) or to suggest a change in attitudes, belief, or behavior (persuasive speech)? Consider the speech topics that follow, marking "I" for those that seem informative and "P" for those that could be persuasive.

_____ 1. How therapy dogs are trained

_____ 2. Why you should add omega fatty acids to your diet

_____ 3. How omega fatty acids modulate inflammatory responses

_____ 4. Title IX harms male athletes and eliminates important programs

_____ 5. Why you should become an organ donor

_____ 6. The importance of restricting handguns

_____ 7. How fracking works

_____ 8. The benefits of volunteer reading programs for at-risk children

_____ 9. Fracking should be banned

_____ 10. Why college athletes should be paid

Answers: 1. I; 2. P; 3. I; 4. P; 5. P; 6. P; 7. I; 8. I; 9. P; 10. P

Effective quasi-scientific explanations highlight the main points with such features as titles, organizing analogies, presentation aids, and signposts ("The first key point is . . ."). Good quasi-scientific explanations also connect key points by using transitional phrases (such as "for example"), connectives ("because"), and diagrams depicting relationships among parts.

Challenging Intuition

Some ideas in explanatory speeches may run contrary to what intuition tells us. Consider the polio vaccine, which was tested in 1952 and used an injected dose of an inactive (essentially, dead) polio virus. The notion of using something that makes people sick to prevent people from getting sick is counterintuitive. Imagine how difficult this must have been to explain to patients and worried parents at the time.

If you are giving an informative speech on how vaccines work or another counterintuitive idea, you might want to design your talk around transformative explanations. **Transformative explanations** are designed to help speakers transform "theories" about phenomena into more accepted notions. For your speech on vaccines, you might describe how exposing the body to a weak version of the virus essentially teaches the body to develop its defenses itself against the real disease. Similarly, suppose you are giving a speech about "Brexit," Great Britain's recent vote to exit the European Union. Although many commentators were astounded at a vote that seemed to be against Britain's own economic interests, you could explain how the people of Great Britain who voted yes to the Brexit may have felt that they were being governed by a distant and intrusive European system.

● **KIMONOS** are beautiful, but you will still need to make them relevant to your audience if you really want to draw them in. Christian Kober/Robert Harding/Newscom

Guidelines for Informative Speeches

In Chapters 13 through 15, we provided the basics for developing, preparing, writing, and delivering effective presentations. In this section, we look at how you can tailor those basic strategies to the needs of an informative speech. Your first goal as a speaker is to get your audience interested in your topic. But you also want to make sure that your speech is easy to listen to. It is hard to inform people who are struggling to keep up with you—or wishing they were somewhere else!

Create Information Hunger

Can you recall a teacher who had the ability to get you interested in a certain subject area? The same techniques work when it comes to public speaking. You want to make your audience hungry for the information you are going to present—get them excited about, or at least interested in, your topic. Ask yourself, "How will my audience benefit from this information?" If you cannot come up with a compelling reason for each person to pay attention to what you say, you need to rethink your topic. Several strategies help you create information hunger, including arousing curiosity and working your topic.

Arouse People's Curiosity

A few years ago, we watched a student inform the audience about kimonos. A kimono is a long, loose Japanese robe with wide sleeves traditionally worn with a broad sash as an outer garment. The speaker defined a kimono, contrasted different types of kimonos, and then demonstrated how to get into one and wear it properly. Although her speech was interesting and her demonstration was effective, in the end we had no idea why we had listened to it! The problem was that although she competently explained the historical and cultural significance of the kimono and gave a detailed demonstration of the process of designing and wearing one, she did little to make the audience interested in the subject as a whole. She might have fared better had she offered some sort of connection between the kimono and the daily lives of the audience. For example:

> Think of your favorite article or ensemble of clothing—that one perfect item or outfit that you just hope you have the occasion to wear. Would you have worn it ten years ago? Will it still be stylish ten years from now? Magazine editors and clothing designers like to throw the word *timeless* around, claiming that some things—the Armani suit, the little black dress—will never go out of fashion. But the truth is that style is a fickle thing, and lapels, hemlines, colors, and waistbands change with the tides. Today, I'm going to talk about an article of clothing that truly is timeless, one that is worn by both men and women and has remained largely unchanged in shape and form for over one thousand years. I'm speaking, of course, about the traditional garment of Japan, the kimono.

Here we pique people's interest by asking them first to think about their own experience—about something they own or wish to own. We then draw them into our subject, the kimono, by contrasting it with what Westerners tend to consider "classic" fashion. Such comparisons and personalization of the subject can help keep the audience interested.

Work Your Topic

In many real-world situations, you may be asked to explain, define, describe, or demonstrate something that strikes you as boring or irrelevant. A CEO will frequently need to address shareholders with reports of profits and losses, for example, and spokespersons for government agencies are often required to make statements about public policies or current events.

In such cases, the speaker must find the relevance of the subject and establish it for the audience quickly and assertively. If your topic seems somehow disconnected from your audience, it is your job to find the relevance. Can you save the audience money or time? Can you help people do something better or improve quality? Even if the benefit is not for the short term, could listening to your speech help them in some way in the future, once they become parents or graduate students or homeowners? Unless you present a clear benefit that people can derive from listening to you, you will not get or keep their attention.

For example, imagine that you are an office manager and need to deliver a presentation to explain how to fill out the company's new expense reports. One way to get your colleagues interested is to show them why learning to do this task is important for them personally:

> I know it's hard to get excited about something as mundane as filing expense reports. But the good news is that our new electronic transmittal system will get your reimbursements to you faster and more reliably. As you know, it typically takes four to six weeks for an expense report to be routed, approved, and transmitted to accounts payable and another two weeks for accounts payable to cut the check. With this new system, we'll be able to have funds deposited directly to your bank account in as little as ten business days. So with that in mind, let's take a look at how the new system works.

By clearly connecting the subject with the lives and needs of your listeners, you are more likely to have their attention as you demonstrate the less interesting aspects of the process.

● **PEOPLE USUALLY** groan at the thought of sitting through a boring software presentation, but if the speaker makes it relevant to their needs, they might change their minds. PeopleImages/Getty Images

and you?

What techniques can you use to look at a subject and find its relevance to you or your audience? How can these tactics help you create more interesting informative speeches?

Make It Easy

Creating a good informative speech is hard work; listening to one should not be. Your job as speaker is to find and distill a lot of information in a way that is easy for your audience to listen to, absorb, and learn. In short, you need to do your listeners' work for them. There are a number of objectives to bear in mind as you prepare.

Choose a Clear Organization and Structure

When people are presented with new information, they need to organize it in their minds in a way that makes sense to them. You can help them in this endeavor by organizing your speech around a clear and logical structure (McCroskey & Mehrley, 1969). Recall from Chapter 14 that there are a number of arrangements for presentations. Your choice of organizational pattern depends on your topic, and every speech has several organizational options.

For example, if you are planning to deliver a speech on the history of punk rock, you might choose a chronological organization, beginning with garage bands from the mid-1960s, following through the peak of the 1970s with bands like the Sex Pistols and the Ramones, continuing through the postpunk era, and ending with more modern punk-influenced bands like Green Day, Sheer Mag, and Fall Out Boy. But you also might find it interesting to approach the topic spatially, noting differences between American and British punk, or even causally, demonstrating how the form arose as a reaction to the popular music that preceded it as well as

● **IF YOUR SPEECH** is on punk rock, you might organize it chronologically, moving from the Ramones to Fall Out Boy. (left) Sire Records/Getty Images; (right) Andrew Benge/Getty Images

to the economic and political climate of the times. Table 16.2 offers some ideas for using organizational approaches to different informative topics in addition to considering the approaches we discussed earlier (definition, description, demonstration, and explanation).

Emphasize Important Points

Another way to make it easy for your audience to follow your speech is to draw their attention to your important points. As you learned in Chapter 14, one of the best means to achieve this is by using a preview device and a concluding summary. The preview device tells the audience what you are going to cover ("First, I will discuss X, second, Y, and third, Z"). A concluding summary reviews what the audience heard during the speech ("Today, I talked about X, then showed you Y, and, finally, discussed Z").

Careful and deliberate use of phrases like "The key issue here is . . ." and "I have three main points regarding this piece of legislation" can also signal to your audience that you are about to say something important. In some cases, you might actually highlight what is important by saying so, even telling the audience directly when you are discussing something you want them to remember. This not only supports the organization of your speech but also gives people useful tools for organizing the information as they listen. It is important to make certain, however, that you do not contradict yourself. If you say, "I have one key point to make," and you then list four points of equal importance, you will likely confuse (and annoy) your audience.

Do Not Overwhelm Your Audience

Have you ever sat through a lecture in which the speaker crammed in so much information that you could hardly follow it? Ironically, too many points can make a speech seem pointless. Research shows that receivers' attention and interest levels drop significantly due to information overload. Simply put, too much information overwhelms the audience (Van Zandt, 2004; Wecker, 2012).

Your goal, then, is to keep your presentation as simple as possible. As you review and rehearse your speech, critically evaluate each and every fact, point, and example—indeed, every word—to make certain that it makes a meaningful contribution to your speech. Eliminate anything that is redundant or tangential. However, aiming for simplicity does not meaning "dumbing down" your speech. You want to strike a balance—make it effortless for your listeners to understand

TABLE 16.2

TYPES OF INFORMATIVE SPEECHES, SAMPLE TOPICS, INFORMATIONAL STRATEGIES, AND ORGANIZATIONAL PATTERNS

Subject Matter	Sample Topics	Informational Strategy (definition, description, etc.)	Suggested Organizational Patterns
Speeches about objects or phenomena	• Egyptian pyramids • Pre-Columbian artifacts • *Mona Lisa* • El Niño wind patterns	*Define* and *describe* the object or phenomenon in question. Depending on your specific speech purpose, either conclude at that point or continue with an in-depth *explanation* or a *demonstration* of the object or phenomenon.	You might use a *topical* pattern if you are explaining the categories for Pre-Columbian artifacts. Conversely, you might use a *chronological* pattern if your speech focuses on a historical timeline of the artifacts.
Speeches about people	• Celebrities • Inventors • Athletes • Politicians • British royalty	Paint a vivid picture of your subject using a *description*. Use *explanation* to address the person's or group's significance.	*Narrative* patterns could be useful for speeches about people since stories can include rich details about a person's life. The *chronological* pattern can also be useful to describe someone's life events or achievements.
Speeches about events	• The terrorist attacks on September 11 • The 2011 earthquake and tsunami in Japan • The 2013 Boston Marathon bombings	Use *description* to paint a vivid picture. Use *explanation* to analyze the meaning of the event.	You might use a *chronological* pattern for a topic focusing on events if time or sequence is relevant to your purpose.
Speeches about processes	• How a hybrid car works • How lightning forms • How to sew or knit • How to sync your data on your mobile devices	If physically showing a process, rely on *demonstration*. If explaining a process, vary strategies as needed.	*Cause–effect* patterns of speech organization are helpful in explaining processes of various kinds. Additional patterns of organization could include *spatial* or *chronological*.
Speeches about issues	• Racial profiling • Post-traumatic stress disorder • Anxiety or phobias • Police brutality	Focus on *description* and *explanation*.	*Topical* and *spatial* patterns can be particularly useful for speeches about issues (which can easily become persuasive).
Speeches about concepts	• Art • Patriotism • Extraterrestrial life • Ethnocentrism • Time travel	Focus on clear *definitions* and *explanations*; the more difficult a concept is, the more ways you will want to define and explain it. Vivid *description* can also be useful.	Consider *topical* organizational patterns for speeches about concepts, as well as the *narrative* pattern. The *spatial* pattern may also work well for your purposes.

Information from D. O'Hair, R. Stewart, & H. Rubenstein (2018).

by providing just the right amount of substantive information — nothing more, nothing less.

Build on Prior Knowledge

People are more open to new ideas when they understand how the new information relates to things they already know about. For example, in a speech about online fashion businesses, you may wish to introduce your audience to the concept of the "virtual model image." You could remind your listeners about the tradition of trying on clothes in a store to see how certain garments look on their particular body types (a familiar idea). You can then point out that by supplying your measurements online, you can use the virtual model image to achieve a similar visual picture of what you would look like in outfits, but without ever having to go to a store (new idea).

real communicator

NAME: K. C. Ellis

OCCUPATION: Group Vice President of Client Services, Financial Services Industry

Courtesy K.C. Ellis

I never dreamed I'd work in financial services when I graduated with my communication degree. I had taken one economics class (accounting) in college and decided finance didn't hold a lot of appeal for me. Then I went to a campus information session where a representative from the company that eventually hired me said they often brought on people who didn't know the difference between a bull and a bear market. They were instead looking for smart, motivated people who could communicate well and had the desire to learn.

My firm manages assets for high-net-worth clients, providing proactive, customized service over the phone and in person. One of my first roles at the firm was to act as a liaison between our clients and our portfolio team. I was tasked with effectively communicating our investment strategy to clients while answering their questions, which could range from complicated investment theory to simple operational requests. Given that each client has a completely different background (in terms of his or her occupation, age, gender, investment experience, etc.), I had to learn how to be flexible in my communication. Through listening to clients, I could find out their depth of knowledge, likes and dislikes, and past experience — and then use this information to provide them with the most helpful, customized answers.

Over my ten years at the company, I've served in a number of roles around the firm: operations, customer service, management, and event planning. I've enjoyed all of them, even the less traditional finance roles. For example, in event planning, I learned valuable skills such as public speaking, negotiation, and managing vendors and onsite staff. Large-scale events require the work of many people — and good communication between them is essential.

Over the past few years, I've moved into a management capacity, and about 25 percent of my time is now spent interviewing potential hires. Despite their different backgrounds, the candidates need to be able to communicate clearly and directly and explain complex concepts in a simple, understandable way. They also must have empathy — they need to be able to relay information in a way that best suits the client. Successful portfolio management requires investors to be patient and disciplined. Much of what we do is aimed at helping clients stay committed to appropriate, long-term plans. Whether we're interacting with clients through in-person events, written communication or phone calls, we're focusing on helping them achieve their goals.

Define Your Terms

Defining your terms is not just for definitional speeches. In any speech, your audience will follow you better if you help them to understand the words or ideas that they do not know. If audience members find themselves wondering what or who you are talking about, you will lose their attention. When a term comes up that requires definition, you should explain it clearly and succinctly before moving on. If you think an audience is familiar with a word but you just want to be sure, you can simply allude to a more common synonym: "People tend to think of rhinoplasties—commonly referred to as 'nose jobs'—as cosmetic in nature, but in fact many are performed to help improve nasal functioning."

Definitions often provide necessary clarity for proper nouns as well. Audiences may not have a strong background in geography, politics, or world events, so it can be useful to identify organizations and individuals in the same way that you would define a term: "People for the Ethical Treatment of Animals, or PETA, is the largest animal rights organization in the world," or "Colin Powell, a former U.S. Army general and secretary of state under President George W. Bush, noted that. . . ." Seamlessly inserting such identifying information enables unfamiliar audience members to continue to participate in your presentation, while giving you some credibility among audience members who do know the terms.

Use Interesting and Appropriate Examples

Examples not only support your key points but also provide interesting and exciting ways for your audience to visualize what you are talking about. If you are giving a speech about the career of Clint Eastwood and your goal is to inform your audience about his films as both actor and director, you would provide examples of some of his most popular movies (*Dirty Harry, In the Line of Fire*), his early western films (*Fistful of Dollars, For a Few Dollars More, Hang 'Em High*), his lesser-known films (*The First Traveling Saleslady, Honkytonk Man*), and his directorial efforts (*Gran Torino, Million Dollar Baby, American Sniper, Sully*). You might also provide quotes from reviews of his films to show the way Eastwood has been perceived at different points in his career.

When you are offering examples to explain a concept, it is important to choose examples that your audience will understand. Some examples may be familiar enough that you can make quick references to them with little explanation. If you are giving a speech today on community planning and rebuilding after disasters, you could probably mention the flooding and damage after Hurricane Matthew hit the southeastern United States in 2016, or Haiti after the 2010 earthquake, and almost any adult member of your audience will get it. Other examples or audiences might require more detail and explanation. For example, in a speech about conformity, you might wish to use as an example the 1978 incident in Jonestown, Guyana, when more than nine hundred members of a religious cult committed mass suicide by drinking cyanide-laced punch. Your audience analysis here is crucial: if you are speaking to college students, you probably need to offer a good deal of explanation to make this example work. However, an audience consisting mainly of baby boomers, historians, or social psychologists would require little more than a brief reference to "Jonestown" to get the point of the example.

and you?

Consider your specific speech purpose. What are your objectives for your informative speech? Now consider what types of presentation aids might help you achieve your purpose. How might you use aids to drive home the point you are trying to make or the central idea that you wish to convey to your audience?

Use Appropriate Presentation Aids

As you recall from Chapter 15, presentation aids can add value to your speech by guiding audiences through the information you present. For example, in a speech about the meaning of a person's credit score, the speaker might show (via slides or handouts) sample credit reports. Seeing actual reports with real numbers underscores the importance of your message: that credit scores change depending on how people manage their financial accounts.

● **PRESENTATION AIDS** are especially appropriate in informative speaking because they enable the audience to not only hear about but also to visualize a new topic. Hero Images/Getty Images

Informative speeches also benefit greatly from the use of graphic presentation aids. In a speech describing a process, for example, a flowchart outlining the steps you describe can help audiences visualize how the process works. Graphs can also be helpful in conveying numerical or statistical information. The combination of hearing your message (the speech content) and seeing your message (through presentation aids) helps the audience better retain the content.

Let's take a look at an informative speech by Anna Davis, a student in a college-level communication course. She chose to inform her audience about how and why social media is being harnessed as a tool to advance social causes and motivate people to act on them.

Anna organizes the speech in a topical pattern: each of her main points is a subtopic or category of the overall speech topic of social

media movements. This is one of the most frequently used patterns for informative speeches. Anna's speaking outline and references are included here as well.

Sample Student Informative Speech 16.1

Social Media, Social Identity, and Social Causes

By Anna Davis

Anna starts her speech by enthusiastically telling a personal story.

Just before my first year of college, I was excited and nervous about meeting other new students on campus. As soon as dorm assignments were announced, we all began "friending" each other on Facebook and following each other on Twitter. • This is how I found out that my roommate was an obsessive soccer fan and had seen all of Quentin Tarantino's movies. The school also sponsored online forums, allowing me to learn about different student groups and to find like-minded people across campus. For example, I connected immediately with students who share my interest in animal rescue and adoption. These online connections and groups helped my college friendships develop quickly and meaningfully, and gave me a sense of belonging on campus before I even arrived. •

• Anna makes her attention getter *relevant* to the audience by referencing the social media tools that nearly everyone in her class will be familiar with.

Today I'd like to share with you how social media is being used, not only to help students connect but also as a powerful tool to advance social causes and motivate us to act on their behalf. We'll start by looking at a compelling theory of why social media is so uniquely suited to forging connections. Next, I'll review some data on social media's meteoric rise. Finally, we'll see how today's activists are harnessing social media to support an array of social causes to make life better for us all. •

• Anna's personal example helps establish her *ethos*, or credibility. It also relates to her speech thesis, which explains how social media helps everyone answer the question, "Who am I?"

Let's begin our conversation about these intriguing developments in communication by considering the underlying reasons why we want to use social media in the first place. What is it that drives us to connect through social media with like-minded people and groups?

• Anna's preview statement organizes her speech. Each section is previewed so listeners can anticipate what is coming.

Anna keeps the audience engaged with animated facial expressions.

Social identity theory offers a compelling answer to this question. First, let me define the concept of social identity. Social identity refers to how you understand yourself in relation to your group memberships. • Michael Hogg, a professor of social psychology at Claremont University, focuses on social identity research. In his 2006 book on contemporary social psychological theories, Hogg explains that group affiliations provide us with an important source of identity, and we therefore want our groups to be valued positively in relation to other groups. • By "affiliations" I simply mean the groups that we join and perhaps link to online.

• By defining technical terms here, Anna can use them later in the speech with the assurance that the audience will understand precisely what she means.

Social psychologist Henry Tajfel—one of the founders of social identity theory—spent years considering how we form our social identities. Tajfel believes that the groups to which we attach ourselves, both online and off, help answer the very important question, "Who am I?" According to Tajfel's 1979 book *The Social Psychology of Intergroup Relations*, we associate

• By paraphrasing an expert in the field, Anna helps establish credibility for her speech.

with certain groups to help resolve the anxiety brought about by this fundamental question of identity. By selecting certain groups and not others, we define who we are and develop a sense of belonging in the social world. •

Social media sites such as Facebook provide a platform for this type of social identity formation by offering participants certain tools, such as the ability to "friend" people, groups, and even brands, and to "like" certain posts. The simple act of friending, for example, promotes social affiliation between two individuals, and our Facebook friends are collectively a source of social identity. Because we are proclaiming something important to our groups, announcing that we are in a serious relationship takes on great social significance. As we all know, it's not official until it's "Facebook official."

As you can see, social identity theory gives us insight into the reasons behind the popularity of social media sites: They let us proclaim to ourselves and the world, "This is who I am." Even so, the near miraculous rate of growth of these sites over the past decade is surprising.

Anna explains the graph while gesturing at the slides.

According to Marcia Clemmit's 2010 *CQ Researcher* article on social networking, Facebook had over one million members in 2005 — just one year after its launch. This growth from zero to a million in one year was quite an impressive feat. Today, according to a May 2013 article on the number of active Facebook users published by the Associated Press, Facebook harbors over 1.16 billion members. • That's almost four times the population of the United States.

Like Facebook, Twitter's growth has also been astronomical. Shea Bennett, editor of the Mediabistro-sponsored blog *AllTwitter*, reports in an October 2013 article that Twitter had 218 million active users at the end of June 2013. Like Facebook, its success can be largely attributed to the demand for virtual communities that enable users to connect with one another.

While making her point, Anna uses strong eye contact.

As the data clearly show, people around the world are defining themselves socially and answering the question, "Who am I?" through the use of social media sites. • And social movement organizations have taken note. Organizations of all kinds are using social media to get their messages across to global consumers and spur their members into action.

Social movements, defined by Princeton.edu as "a group of people with a common ideology who try together to achieve certain general goals," range across the political and social spectrum. Consider Occupy Wall Street and the Tea Party. Both of these organizations communicate their messages and build support through social media sites. • For example, they use Facebook to announce events and link to petitions. In fact, a non-

When stating facts, Anna refers to her note cards.

profit organization called Social Movement Technologies created a Facebook page to help individual social movement organizations get out their message.

But social media is not just being used as a platform for informing the public of a group's mission and activities or even merely to get people to

• This transition helps listeners prepare for the next main point of Anna's speech.

• To help her audience understand the large numbers she quotes, Anna relates the number of Facebook users to the population of the United States, so the audience can get a sense of just how big 1.16 billion people really is.

• The subtle repetition of the question "Who am I?" relates this main point back to the speech thesis.

• Anna uses examples that are well balanced and that do not express a bias.

sign petitions. Increasingly, activists are deploying social media to motivate like-minded people to get into the fight.

To get a sense of what this means, consider the recent efforts of a seventeen-year-old skateboarder from St. Cloud, Minnesota. •

• Using real examples, such as Austin's, helps Anna's audience imagine and relate to her claims more directly.

Anna connects to the audience with a real-life story.

For three years, Austin Lee found himself struggling to get support for a skate park in his local community. But when he decided to use Facebook for his cause, things changed nearly overnight. Lee's posting attracted 1,085 members, and even drew a portion of those members to city council meetings on behalf of his cause. David Unze of *USA Today* reported that Lee won the approval—and $500,000—for his skate park (2010). And it all happened within one day of Lee's original posting on Facebook.

So as you can see, if you can use social media to convince people to identify with what you want to accomplish, success is possible. Lee's accomplishment shows us that we not only identify and affiliate ourselves with groups but also are willing to actively work toward accomplishing their goals.

Today I hope I've shown that the skyrocketing use of social media sites over the past decade is no accident. The human desire to develop a positive sense of social identity through group affiliation is one reason for this phenomenon. Capitalizing on this universal psychological drive, social movement organizations are harnessing these technologies to accomplish their goals. Social media sites allow us to communicate, express, and identify with one another in ways that encourage affiliation as well as action.

Anna concludes her speech on a warm, personal note.

Whether it's a major political movement or a teenager's desire for a local skate park, social media technologies are powerful.

So as you tweet about new groups or see the next "Facebook official" status update, think about what groups you like, whom you have friended, and what those affiliations may be able to do for you. •

• To make her final words count, Anna's concluding statement is memorable and succinct and summarizes her thesis.

References

Associated Press. (2013, May 1). Number of active users at Facebook over the years. *Yahoo! News.* Retrieved from news.yahoo.com/number-active-users-facebook-over-230449748.html

Bennett, S. (2013, October 4). How many active users does Twitter have, and how fast is it growing? [Web log post]. Retrieved October 16, 2013, from www.mediabistro.com/alltwitter/tag/twitter-active-users

Brenner, J., & Smith, A. (2013, August 5). 72% of online adults are social networking site users. *Pew Internet and American Life Project.* Retrieved from www.pewinternet.org/~/media//Files/Reports/2013/PIP_Social_networking_sites_update.pdf

Clemmitt, M. (2010, September 17). Social networking. *CQ Researcher,* 20(32). Retrieved August 17, 2013, from www.cqpress.com/product/Researcher-Social-Networking-v20-32.html

Constine, J. (2012, February 12). Pinterest hits 10 million U.S. monthly uniques faster than any standalone site ever. [Web log post]. Retrieved August 17, 2013, from techcrunch.com/2012/02/07/pinterest-monthly-uniques

Hogg, M. (2006). Social identity theory. In P. J. Burke (Ed.), *Contemporary social psychological theories* (pp. 111–136). Palo Alto, CA: Stanford University Press.

Lipsman, A. (2011, August 30). Tumblr defies its name as user growth accelerates. [Web log post]. Retrieved August 17, 2013, from www.comscore.com /Insights/Blog/Tumblr_Defies_its_Name_as_User_Growth_Accelerates

Madden, M., Lenhart, A., Cortesi, S., Gasser, U., Duggan, M., Smith, A., & Beaton, M. (2013, May 21). Teens, social media, and privacy. *Pew Internet and American Life Project.* Retrieved from www.pewinternet.org /Reports/2013/Teens-Social-Media-And-Privacy.aspx

Occupy Wall Street. (n.d.). In Facebook [Group page]. Retrieved August 17, 2013, from www.facebook.com/OccupyWallSt

Social movement. (n.d.). *Wordnetweb.Princeton.edu.* Retrieved from wordnetweb.princeton.edu/perl/webwn?s=social%20movement

Social Movement Technologies. (n.d.). In Facebook [Group page]. Retrieved August 17, 2013, from www.facebook.com/SocialMovementTechnologies

Tajfel, H., & Turner, J. C. (1979). An integrative theory of intergroup conflict. In W. G. Austin & S. Worchel (Eds.), *The social psychology of intergroup relations* (pp. 33–47). Monterey, CA: Brooks/Cole.

The Tea Party. (n.d.). In *Facebook* [Group page]. Retrieved August 17, 2013, from www.facebook.com/TheTeaParty.net

Twitter. (2011, March 14). #numbers. [Web log post]. Retrieved from blog .twitter.com/2011/numbers

Unze, D. (2010, March 26). Facebook helps spark movements. *USA Today.* Retrieved from usatoday30.usatoday.com/news/nation/2010-03-25 -facebook_N.htm

Speaking Outline

Anna Davis

Social Media, Social Identity, and Social Causes

General Purpose: To inform
Specific Purpose: To inform my audience members about how social media sites help shape their sense of identity.
Thesis Statement: Today I'd like to share with you how social media is being used, not only to help students connect, but also as a powerful tool to advance social causes and motivate us to act on their behalf.

Introduction

I. **Attention Getter:** How I learned about my roommate via Facebook /Twitter

II. School-sponsored online forums helped me connect with like-minded others.

III. "These online connections and groups helped my college friendships develop quickly and meaningfully, and gave me a sense of belonging on campus before I even arrived."

IV. **Speech Thesis:** Today I'd like to share with you how social media is being used, not only to help students connect, but also as a powerful tool to advance social causes and motivate us to act on their behalf.

    A. Preview main points
    B. Social identity theory
    C. Popularity of social media
    D. How activists harness social media

Body

I. Social identity theory drives us to connect with others.
    A. **Definition:** Social identity refers to how you understand yourself in relation to your group memberships.
        1. Michael Hogg, a professor of social psychology at Claremont University
        2. Group affiliations provide us with an important source of identity, and we therefore want our groups to be valued positively in relation to other groups.
    B. Social psychologist Henry Tajfel. Group affiliations help answer the question, Who am I?
        1. Tajfel's 1979 book *The Social Psychology of Intergroup Relations*. We associate with certain groups to help resolve the anxiety brought about by the question of identity.
    C. Social media sites provide a platform for social identity formation.
        1. "Friending" people, groups, and even brands and "liking" certain posts
        2. It's not official until it's "Facebook official."
    D. Social media sites let us proclaim to the world, "This is who I am."

Transition: Even so, rate of growth surprising

II. Growth rate of social media sites is astronomical.
    A. **[Show slides]** Marcia Clemmit's 2010 *CQ Researcher* article on social networking, Facebook had over one million members in 2005—just one year after its launch.
        1. Associated Press May 2013 article put the number of active Facebook users at over 1.16 billion members. Four times the population of the United States.
    B. Shea Bennett, editor of the Mediabistro blog *AllTwitter*, in an October 2013 article, listed Twitter at 218 million active users in June 2013.
    C. People around the world define themselves socially and answer the question, "Who am I?" on social media sites.

Transition: Social movement organizations have taken note.

III. Organizations of all kinds use social media to get their messages across to global consumers and spur their members into action.
    A. Princeton.edu defines social movements as "a group of people with a common ideology who try together to achieve certain general goals."
    B. Consider Occupy Wall Street and the Tea Party.
        1. Both communicate their messages and build support through social media sites; for example, link to petitions.
        2. Nonprofit organization Social Movement Technologies helps individual social movement organizations get out their message.

    C.   Activists use social media to motivate like-minded people to get into the fight.

    D.   Example: Austin Lee, seventeen-year-old skateboarder from St. Cloud, Minnesota, wanted a skate park.

        1.   Facebook posting gathered 1,085 members to group, some even went to city council meetings.

        2.   David Unze of *USA Today* reported that Lee won the approval—and $500,000—for his skate park (2010).

Transition/Internal Summary: Today I hope I've shown you skyrocketing use is no accident.

Conclusion

    I.   Positive sense of social identity through group affiliation drives popularity of social media sites.

    II.   Social media sites allow us to communicate, express, and identify with one another in ways that encourage affiliation as well as action.

    III.   Remember the impact of group affiliations when you post online.

back to ▶ Neil deGrasse Tyson

Bryan Bedder/Getty Images

At the beginning of this chapter, we read about astrophysicist Neil deGrasse Tyson, who is widely respected not only as one of the foremost researchers on space but also as one of science's most competent and enthusiastic communicators. Let's consider how his informative presentations measure up to the concepts outlined in this chapter:

▶ Tyson knows his listeners. He understands that while they are not well versed in astrophysics, they are curious about it. He makes abstract topics tangible by using familiar metaphors and examples. When speaking to an audience of fellow astrophysicists, he would not have to take such measures.

▶ Tyson uses effective nonverbal communication in his presentations. He uses appropriate gestures, laughs heartily at his own jokes, moves around the stage rather than gluing himself to a podium, and uses a tone of voice that generates a casual atmosphere. His trademark vests—embroidered with images of the cosmos—indicate his enthusiasm for the subject.

▶ Like everyone, Tyson has personal opinions and beliefs. But when he is speaking informatively, he limits his discussions to facts. In his discussion of the universe noted at the beginning of this chapter, for example, Tyson explains, "None of this is about 'belief.' It's about 'what does the evidence show'?" (Tyson, 2009).

things to try ▶ Activities

LaunchPad
macmillan learning

1. LaunchPad for *Real Communication* offers key term videos and encourages self-assessment through adaptive quizzing. Go to **launchpadworks.com** to get access to:

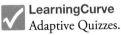
LearningCurve
Adaptive Quizzes.

Video clips that illustrate key concepts, highlighted in teal in the Real Reference section that follows.

2. Review Anna's speech on social media movements in this chapter. Into what category does the topic of this speech fall? Which approach or approaches (description, demonstration, definition, or explanation) did the speaker use, and was she successful in using those approaches? Did the speaker prove herself to be reliable and well informed? In what ways did she attempt to create information hunger and make the speech easy to listen to? Was she successful?

3. Informative speeches are everywhere—in your classroom, on the news, and in your community. Watch an informative speech (or read a transcript, available at the websites of many government agencies and officials). Apply the concepts you have learned in this chapter to these informative presentations. For example, is the presentation well organized and well delivered? Does the speaker or author present information objectively? At any point in the speech, do you feel as though the speaker is trying to persuade you to do or believe something? It is important to be a critical listener in order to catch the often subtle differences between informing and persuading.

4. Locate a persuasive speech that you found particularly compelling. Print it out and edit it, removing any and all of the material that you feel is persuasive in nature (e.g., the speaker's opinions, any notably biased statements, any evidence that you feel is subjective rather than objective). Does the remainder of the speech hold up as an informative speech? How could you change it to make it a purely informative presentation?

5. Think of a topic that you find excruciatingly dull (e.g., balancing your checkbook, studying for a required course you do not like, or taking a summer or part-time job doing something utterly mind-numbing). What would you do if you had to give an informative presentation on such a subject? Based on the information presented in this chapter, can you think of ways to build a presentation on the topic that is informative and interesting? As strange as this task may sound, it is likely that you will have to do something like this at times in your career. (Recall the example from this chapter on informing employees about a new electronic reimbursement system.)

6. Imagine a process you do every day, such as driving a car. Think about how you would explain the process to someone who has never done it or even seen it done before. Consider different ways you could make the level of the presentation appropriate for different audiences. Talking to a child, for example, you might simply say that pressing on the gas pedal makes the car go; you might offer more detail when speaking to adults, explaining how the car works.

real reference ▶ A Study Tool

Now that you have finished reading this chapter, you can:

Describe the goals of informative speaking:

▶ Use **informative speaking** to teach the audience something new (p. 406).
▶ Gauge what the audience already knows to determine where to begin (p. 406).
▶ Find an approach that will engage the audience (p. 406).
▶ Explain the subject's relevance to the audience (p. 407).
▶ Present facts and information in an **objective**, evenhanded way, unlike in a persuasive speech, which is **subjective** and presents a point of view (p. 407).
▶ Speak ethically (pp. 407–408).

List and describe each of the eight categories of informative speeches:

▶ People: focus on human qualities as well as achievements (pp. 408–409).
▶ Places: find new aspects of known places or describe the unfamiliar (p. 409).

- ▶ Objects and phenomena: focus on any nonhuman topic (pp. 409–410).
- ▶ Events: describe noteworthy events in history or relate a personal experience (pp. 410–411).
- ▶ Processes: show how something works or teach how to do something (p. 412).
- ▶ Concepts: explain an abstract idea (p. 412).
- ▶ Issues: remain objective to report on a social or personal problem (pp. 412–413).
- ▶ Plans and policies: describe the important dimensions of potential courses of action (p. 413).

Outline the four major approaches to informative speeches:

- ▶ The **descriptive presentation** paints a mental picture, portraying places, events, persons, objects, or processes (p. 413).
- ▶ **Demonstration speeches** combine explanatory narration and physical demonstration (p. 414).
- ▶ There are five categories of **definitional speeches**: an **operational definition** defines something by explaining what it is or what it does; **definition by negation** defines something by telling what it is not; **definition by example** offers concrete examples; **definition by synonym** defines something with closely related words; **definition by etymology** explains the origin of a word or phrase (pp. 415–416).
- ▶ **Explanatory speeches** answer the question "Why?" with **elucidating explanations**, with **quasi-scientific explanations** or models, or with **transformative explanations** that change preconceptions (pp. 416–417).

Employ strategies to make your audience hungry for information:

- ▶ Make listeners curious by personalizing the topic and contrasting it to what they know (p. 418).
- ▶ Present a clear benefit to learning about the topic (p. 419).
- ▶ Stress the topic's relevance (p. 419).

Structure your speech to make it easy to listen to:

- ▶ Devise a clear, logical structure (pp. 419–420).
- ▶ Signal your audience when you are about to say something important (p. 420).
- ▶ Keep it simple (pp. 420–421).
- ▶ Relate new ideas to familiar ideas (p. 421).
- ▶ Define terms your audience may not know (p. 422).
- ▶ Select interesting examples (p. 423).
- ▶ Use strong presentation aids (p. 423).

Jamie Oliver accepted his TED prize with a persuasive address on obesity and food education, in which he explained causes, identified solutions, and ended on a personal appeal.

Gustavo Caballero/Getty Images

 LearningCurve can help you master the material in this chapter.

Go to **launchpadworks.com**.

chapter

17

Persuasive Speaking

Suppose you have found a magic lamp with a genie inside. The genie will grant you one wish, but there is a catch: you need to convince him that your wish is worthwhile and will have a positive impact on the world. Each year, TED (short for Technology, Entertainment, and Design), an organization devoted to "ideas worth spreading," plays the role of this magic genie. Winners receive $1,000,000 to turn a beneficial and world-changing idea into reality. After months of preparation, TED Prize winners then unveil their wishes and plans at the annual TED conference (TED Prize, 2016).

TED Prize winner and celebrity chef Jamie Oliver presented his wish: "To teach every child about food." He opened his speech with a simple statement identifying an important social and medical problem: "In the next 18 minutes when I do our chat, four Americans that are alive will be dead from the food that they eat" (Oliver, 2010). Oliver went on to discuss the realities of obesity in the United States and elsewhere, noting the personal health costs as well as the financial costs of caring for people suffering from preventable, diet-related diseases. He then discussed his experiences educating Americans in West Virginia as part of his *Food Revolution* television program.

Oliver openly considered the causes of the problem he was addressing: a lack of education about healthy food choices at home and in schools; school lunch programs focused on economics rather than on nutrition; a food industry that promotes highly processed, unhealthy foods rather than more costly, healthier options; and confusing or misleading labeling on the foods we buy. He proposed solutions, pointing to successful school lunch programs that could be easily rolled out on a larger scale for a relatively small influx of cash. He also explained how food businesses can—and indeed must—be an integral part of the solution.

Oliver ended his speech by reminding his listeners of his personal wish and his goal for speaking that day: to form "a strong sustainable movement to educate every child about food, to inspire families to cook again, and to empower people everywhere to fight obesity" (Oliver, 2010). Oliver's message appears to have been effective, as his Food Revolution movement has grown into multiple global campaigns and continues to gain support (Jamie's Food Revolution, 2016).

After you have finished
reading this chapter, you
will be able to

- Define the goals of persuasive
  speaking

- Develop a persuasive topic
  and thesis

- Build persuasive arguments
  specifically tailored for your
  intended audience

- Explain three forms of
  rhetorical proof: ethos, logos,
  and pathos

- Avoid using logical fallacies,
  deceptive forms of reasoning

- Organize a persuasive speech
  for your audience

What do you think of when you hear the word *persuasion*? When we ask students this question, they often mistakenly think of sneaky used-car salespeople and dishonest politicians. They also point to manipulative leaders, like an unscrupulous supervisor at work or a bully at school, who use communication to achieve their own selfish goals while exploiting or harming others in the process. The first two examples might involve people at least *attempting* to be persuasive in selling cars or policies, but their dishonesty certainly involves unethical communication. Examples of exploitative leaders or bullies are a clear-cut description of **coercion**, the act of using manipulation, threats, intimidation, or violence to gain compliance.

Persuasion, far different from coercion, is the process of influencing (often changing or reinforcing) others' attitudes, beliefs, and behaviors on a given topic. When done properly and respectfully, it is also a highly ethical practice. Think of all of the important accomplishments that can come from a competent use of persuasion, such as raising money to support victims of natural disasters. Persuasion is also a tool that you use every day, whether you are persuading your roommates to take a speech class with you or convincing your four-year-old to eat his peas. In this chapter, we examine the nature and goals of persuasive speaking while helping you consider your audience, the support for your speech, and helpful organizational patterns.

The Goals of Persuasive Speaking

Persuasive speaking is speech that is intended to influence the attitudes, beliefs, and behavior of your audience. So as you develop goals for your speech, it is important to know what your audience members' existing attitudes, beliefs, and behaviors actually are.

▶ **Attitudes** are our general evaluations of people, ideas, objects, or events (Stiff & Mongeau, 2003). They are our *feelings* about something, our judgments of good or bad, important or unimportant, boring or interesting, and so on. Your audience, for example, might have a positive attitude toward sports ("Playing sports is fun") or exercise ("Exercising regularly is good"). One persuasive goal may then be simply to reinforce these attitudes and get them to feel even better about engaging in sports or exercising on a daily/weekly basis.

▶ **Beliefs** are the ways in which we perceive reality (Stiff & Mongeau, 2003). They are our thoughts about what is true and real and refer to how confident we are about the existence or validity of something. Your audience probably has a few general beliefs about the effects of exercise ("Exercising results in a healthy body"). In this case, your persuasive goal might be to change their beliefs about specific *kinds* of exercise, such as arguing that short, high-intensity interval training has more beneficial health effects than longer "chronic cardio" workouts.

▶ **Behavior** is the manner in which we act or function. It refers to what we *do*, often in response to our attitudes and beliefs (Homer, 2006). For example, if your attitude about exercise is really positive and you believe that it contributes to a healthy body, you will probably be more likely to get out there and walk or jog or lift weights. But attitudes do not always go with behavior. You may find that your audience would like to be more active, but they are so busy with work and school that they just cannot find the time. Your persuasive goal in this case (in addition to reinforcing their desire) may be to convince them to take action by showing them how easy it is to squeeze in a very short, intense daily workout.

Speaking to persuade your listeners involves some informative speaking. In order to convince your audience to exercise more, you would probably need to explain the scientific evidence of health benefits. In a presidential campaign, for example, the candidates inform you about their plans and goals for the nation; however, their primary goal is to influence your attitudes and beliefs about their (or their opponents') suitability for the presidency. They want to influence your behavior by getting you to vote for them.

Influencing your audience, therefore, often involves multiple goals. This can sometimes mean attempting to radically change the attitudes, beliefs, and behavior of a hostile audience. But often it means reinforcing existing attitudes and motivating behavior change. For example, when a political party attempts to rally its base, its goal is not to change its faithful listeners' minds but to strengthen their support and get them more actively involved. Of course, to do this effectively, the party would benefit from doing audience analysis (discussed in Chapter 13) to first correctly identify its listeners' existing attitudes and beliefs.

Developing a Persuasive Topic and Thesis

An effective topic for a persuasive speech shares characteristics with an informative one: it should be something that you are interested in, that you know something about, and that is specific enough that you can find a variety of appropriate sources on the topic but not so specific that you cannot possibly develop it. When your purpose is to persuade, however, you must also keep a few other points in mind.

First, your topic should be one that people could have reasonable disagreement about or resistance to. Issues such as human cloning, immigration reform, and government wiretapping lend themselves to a persuasive purpose because people hold strongly differing opinions about them. Second, the topic must allow the speaker to develop a message intended to cause a degree of change in the audience. For example, the topic of mandatory smoking bans could seek changes from different audiences who hold very different views: encouraging action (a change in behavior) from people who already agree that smoking should be banned in public or seeking a change in the attitudes of smokers who currently see no problem with smoking in public places.

Once you have determined that a particular topic interests you and can be persuasive, it is time to think about developing your thesis statement. In a persuasive speech, thesis statements are often given as a proposition, or a statement about

connect

As you consider your audience's attitudes, beliefs, and behavior, don't forget the cultural context (Chapter 1) and their group affiliations (Chapter 6). Your listeners' gender, religious beliefs, socioeconomic status, and ethnicity— as well as their personal experiences—inform their attitudes, beliefs, and behavior. If you fail to respect these factors, you may fail to persuade your audience.

● **IN THE TV SERIES** *House of Cards*, U.S. Rep. Francis Underwood of South Carolina is a ruthless politician who takes coercion to the next level by manipulating, lying to, and backstabbing his targets to infiltrate the presidency. © Netflix/ Photofest

your viewpoint or position on an issue. We examine three types of propositions: propositions of fact, propositions of value, and propositions of policy.

Propositions of Fact

If you have ever argued on behalf of something you believed to be true, you have made a **proposition of fact**—a claim of what is or what is not. Persuasive speeches built on propositions of fact commonly involve issues that are open to interpretation and on which there are conflicting beliefs or evidence. The truth of the statement may be debatable, but the goal of the speech is clear: you want to align the audience's perception or opinion of the fact with your own. Although it may seem simple to state your belief and back up your points with research that persuades your audience, it can actually be quite challenging. Propositions of fact get at the heart of how you view the world, and your viewpoints may be quite different from how members of your audience perceive reality. Consider the following proposition-of-fact thesis statements:

▶ "Single people are as capable of raising happy, healthy, well-adjusted children as are married couples."

▶ "Extending unemployment benefits actually hurts, rather than helps, people's ability to survive in a shaky economy."

▶ "Eating wheat, even whole wheat, can be dangerous for your health."

Each statement is presented as a fact, but audiences understand that they are the beliefs of the speaker, presented for the listeners' consideration.

● **FROM PROPOSING** to improve the quality of campus dining to championing for more money for student events, propositions of policy are common in student government elections. Image Source Plus/Alamy

Propositions of Value

Some speeches go beyond discussing what is or what is not and make claims about something's worth. Such evaluative claims are called **propositions of value**. In speeches of this type, you seek to convince an audience that something meets or does not meet a specific standard of goodness or quality of right or wrong. For example:

▶ "Torturing prisoners of war is immoral."

▶ "The newly implemented playoff system has greatly improved college football."

▶ "Organized religion has done a great deal of good for the world."

Each statement offers a judgment about the overall value of the person, event, object, way of life, condition, or action discussed. Like propositions of fact, it is clear to the audience that these statements of value are not absolute truths but rather the opinion of the speaker.

Propositions of Policy

The third type of proposition is concerned with what *should* happen. In **propositions of policy**, the speaker makes claims about what goal, policy, or course of action should be pursued. For example:

▶ "Bathrooms should no longer be separated by gender."

what about you?

Persuasion Resistance

As you listen to other speakers (professors, parents, bosses, friends, classmates), you often—consciously or unconsciously—assess their attempts to persuade you. The extent to which you feel that your behavioral freedom is threatened or that your choices are limited by their persuasive efforts is called your "resistance." To determine your level of resistance, read each statement that follows and indicate how much you agree or disagree: 5 = strongly agree; 4 = agree; 3 = unsure; 2 = disagree, and 1 = strongly disagree.

_____ 1. I resist the attempts of others to influence me.

_____ 2. Being urged to change my views triggers a sense of resistance in me.

_____ 3. I find contradicting others stimulating.

_____ 4. When someone tries to persuade me, I usually think, "I'm going to do the exact opposite."

_____ 5. The thought of being dependent on others aggravates me.

_____ 6. I consider advice from others to be pushy.

_____ 7. I become frustrated when I am unable to make my own decision.

_____ 8. It irritates me when someone points out things that are obvious to me.

_____ 9. I become angry when others try to make choices for me.

_____ 10. Advice and recommendations usually induce me to do just the opposite.

_____ 11. I am content only when I make my own choices.

_____ 12. It makes me angry when another person is held up as a role model for me to follow.

_____ 13. When someone tries to get me to do something, I resist.

_____ 14. It disappoints me to see others easily persuaded.

Add your numbers here: _____

14–28: Low resistance   29–55: Medium resistance   56–70: High resistance

The higher your resistance, the less likely you are to be persuaded. You may even strengthen an attitude that is contrary to the position of the person attempting to persuade you, because you react so strongly to your choices and freedom being limited. Lower resistance is associated with less perceived threat to your free will and more willingness to change your point of view.

Information from S. M. Hong & S. Faedda (1996).

▶ "Colleges and universities should not consider race when making admissions decisions."

▶ "Driving a vehicle that gets great gas mileage (say, more than twenty-five miles per gallon) should be a tax deduction in the United States."

In advocating for any of these statements, your task as the speaker would be to persuade the audience that a current policy or practice is not working or needs

and you?

During a campaign season, pay attention to the candidates' speeches and debates, or visit presidentialrhetoric.com to view recent and past presidential speeches. How often does the speaker put forth propositions of fact? Of value? Of policy? Does one type of proposition affect you more than others?

improvement. Propositions of policy are common during election campaigns as candidates—especially challengers—offer their ideas and plans for what a government should do and how they would do it.

No matter what your topic, and no matter which type of proposition you are advocating, you need to know as much as possible about your listeners in order to persuade them effectively. This is the topic of the next section.

Understanding Your Audience

A student once told us an interesting story about audience analysis. At a church service the Sunday after Thanksgiving, her pastor gave a sermon on the religious meaning of Christmas (likely in response to the shopping binges of Black Friday and Cyber Monday). He was hoping to persuade his audience to avoid getting caught up in commercialism, present swapping, and credit card debt. "He was passionate about the topic, and his points were right on," the student said, "but the congregation already agreed with him. It almost felt like he was angry with us or something. It was uncomfortable."

Knowing your audience before developing your speech will help you determine your specific purpose—whether to try to change or to reaffirm the audience's attitudes, beliefs, and behavior. Had our student's pastor considered that his audience may already agree with him, he could have focused on bolstering their commitment rather than making them feel scolded. Knowing your audience will also help you tailor the content of the speech—your organization, research, and supporting points.

Your Audience's Existing Attitudes

According to **social judgment theory** (Sherif, Sherif, & Nebergall, 1965), your ability to successfully persuade your audience depends on the audience's current attitudes or disposition toward your topic, as well as how strongly they feel about their current position. When your audience members hear new information, they consider whether that information or proposed change supports or contradicts their current beliefs. They also consider whether to accept that new information or reject it and maintain their current position.

Let's consider this theory in light of the following example: you are the student government president at a regional college where it is easy for students to visit their hometowns on the weekends. As such, your school has gained a reputation of being a "suitcase" school, making for dull weekends for those students who remain on campus. To address this problem, you propose that the school ban first- and second-year students from having cars on campus so that they stick around and invest more in their life at school.

When you speak about this topic, you should think about portions of your audience each having a different possible **anchor position**—their position on the topic at the outset of the speech (Sherif & Sherif, 1967). If students in your audience are highly involved in the issue—it is part of their personal identity or value system—their anchor positions will be particularly strong (Stiff, 1994). But others may not have thought much about it and have a weaker initial position. How strongly the audience members feel about their anchor position will also affect their different **latitudes**—ranges of acceptable and unacceptable viewpoints—about your topic. These varying anchor positions and latitudes might result in three different kinds of audiences for your speech:

▶ A **receptive audience** already leans toward your viewpoints and your message. These audience members might be residential students who are around on the weekends and wish there were more to do. They probably have a large **latitude of acceptance**; that is, they would be open to a wide range of proposals you could make regarding keeping first- and second-year students on campus. Persuasive messages that fall into this acceptable range are judged to be fairly close to the audience's own position and will likely be effective at moving an audience (Smith, Atkin, Martell, Allen, & Hembroff, 2006).

▶ A **hostile audience** opposes your message (and perhaps you personally). This is the hardest type of audience to persuade, particularly if you are trying to change people's behavior. In this audience, you will certainly find first- and second-year students who live on campus but want to spend their weekends away. This audience would likely have a very strong anchor position, which means they would also have a large **latitude of rejection**: they would find unacceptable most proposals that aim to keep them from leaving campus.

▶ A **neutral audience** falls between the receptive audience and the hostile audience: its members neither support nor oppose you. Nonresidential commuting students (who are off campus on weekends anyway) might fall into this category. This audience would probably have a large **latitude of noncommitment**; that is, a range of positions on which they could go either way. If your persuasive message fits into this range of noncommital positions, you have a good chance at convincing them to go your way.

● **LEONARDO DICAPRIO** found a receptive audience when he spoke at the United Nations and educated the public about environmental issues. He is a strong advocate for combatting climate change and global warming through persuasive campaigns. Jemal Countess/Getty Images

So how do you persuade these distinct groups of individuals? Your receptive audience already basically agrees with your goal of keeping more students on campus on the weekends, so that allows you simply to reaffirm their attitudes and then try to get them to accept your proposals for how to achieve the goal. Your neutral audience may need more information about the issue: for example, how *exactly* does the student weekend flight impact campus life? Most important, they will need to know why they should care. Perhaps, for example, if there were more fun events on campus on the weekends, commuting students would be more interested in getting involved and becoming more attached to the campus community. Your hostile audience will, of course, require special consideration. You want these audience members to find you trustworthy and full of goodwill so that they do not reject you out of hand. You want to avoid making them feel as though you are trying to force them to accept your views, as research shows that such behavior will backfire and cause your audience to be less likely to engage with you (Brehm, 1966; Brehm & Brehm, 1981; Rains, 2013) and less likely to accept your message (Ball & Goodboy, 2014; Olison & Roloff, 2012). Instead, acknowledge their points of view and look for ways to bridge the gap between your beliefs and their beliefs.

Your Audience's Readiness to Change

Another approach to understanding your audience is to apply the **stages of change model** (Prochaska, 1994; Prochaska & Norcross, 2001). Often applied in health campaigns (such as trying to persuade people to stop smoking or to use condoms), this model helps predict the level of your audience's motivational readiness toward modifying behavior. The five stages are precontemplation, contemplation, preparation, action, and maintenance.

▶ In the first stage, *precontemplation*, individuals are not ready to change their behavior; they may not be even aware that the behavior is problematic. For example, a heavy smoker may not see anything wrong with smoking. She may selectively filter information about the negative health effects of smoking because this information causes anxiety. Hence, a persuasive speaker (e.g., a doctor, nurse, or concerned friend) must be able to convince the individual that there is a problem.

▶ In the second stage, *contemplation*, individuals begin to recognize the consequences of their behavior. The smoker might seek information about smoking cessation or smoking-induced health hazards. Individuals usually experience uncertainty and conflict at this stage, so persuasive speakers might help them identify barriers to change.

▶ In the third stage, *preparation*, individuals move to planning and preparing for the changes they have been contemplating. Our heavy smoker might be willing to experiment with changes but cannot quite get the nerve to do it, so persuasive speakers might suggest planning a specific day to go "cold turkey" or asking friends to be on hand to provide emotional support.

▶ By the fourth stage, *action*, an individual has made a change and enacted new behaviors, which require a great deal of willpower. The former smoker may be very tempted to pick up a cigarette but must stay focused on her new, healthy behavior. A persuasive speaker might acknowledge and reward such success and continue to provide emotional support.

▶ In the final stage, *maintenance*, the behavior change is fully integrated into the individual's life, and she works to prevent a relapse. The former smoker finds that social reinforcements (such as feeling better and receiving compliments) help her maintain her new, healthy lifestyle. Persuasive speakers should continue to offer support, help to resist temptation, and reinforce messages. Should the former smoker relapse, she goes back to the beginning of the cycle and earlier stages as she attempts to quit smoking again.

If you can determine the stage of change your audience is experiencing, you are in the best position to be able to persuade them to enact or strengthen those changes.

Your Audience's Needs

If you feel that a local school is not giving your child sufficient opportunity to learn art or music, you probably will not be very receptive to a speech about the importance of fund-raising for the school's new football uniforms. New uniforms do not address your personal *needs*, or deficits that create tension (the lack of funding for your child's artistic education). According to foundational research on human needs (Maslow, 1954), an individual's motivations, priorities, and behavior are influenced primarily by that person's needs. Known as the **hierarchy of needs**, the theory argues that needs are arranged in a hierarchical structure of five categories (see Figure 17.1), from low

FIGURE 17.1

MASLOW'S HIERARCHY OF NEEDS

| 5 |
| Self-Actualizing Needs |
| 4 |
| Esteem/Ego-Status Needs |
| 3 |
| Belongingness/Social Needs |
| 2 |
| Safety Needs |
| 1 |
| Physiological/Survival Needs |

(immature) to high (mature). The most basic needs must be met before an individual can become concerned with needs further up in the hierarchy.

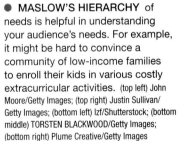
connect

1. *Physiological/survival needs:* These are basic survival needs, such as air, water, food, shelter, sleep, clothing, and so on.

2. *Safety needs:* These are needs for security, orderliness, protective rules, and avoidance of risk. They include not only actual physical safety but also safety from emotional injury.

3. *Belongingness/social needs:* These needs are centered around interactions with others. They include the desire to be accepted and liked by other people and the need for love, affection, and affiliation. These needs are normally met by family ties, friendships, and membership in work and social groups.

4. *Esteem/ego-status needs:* These needs involve validation—being accepted by a group and being recognized for achievement, mastery, competence, and so on. They can be satisfied by special recognition, promotions, power, and achievement. Unlike the previous three categories, esteem needs are not satisfied internally; they require praise and acknowledgment from others.

5. *Self-actualizing needs:* Needs at the highest level focus on personal development and self-fulfillment—becoming what you can become. Instead of looking for recognition of your worth from others, you seek to measure up to your own criteria for personal success.

Maslow's famous *hierarchy of needs* matters in organizations as well. As you learned in Chapter 12, the *human resources approach* to management helps managers to better understand the higher-level needs of their employees, such as self-esteem and personal development, which helps employees to feel more *self-actualized* in their communication (Chapter 3) and motivated to achieve on the job.

The implications of Maslow's hierarchy for persuasive speaking are straightforward: understanding your audience's needs will help you determine your strategy for persuading your listeners. The message must target the unfulfilled need of the audience: a need that is already met will not move them, nor will one that seems too far out of reach in the hierarchy. For example, if people are worried about whether they can provide adequate daily food and clothing for their children, you are probably going to have a hard time convincing them of the importance of raising money for new sports uniforms. However, for an audience whose survival and safety needs are already met, new uniforms may satisfy for them a social need to feel connected to the school community or a status need to show off to other schools.

● **MASLOW'S HIERARCHY** of needs is helpful in understanding your audience's needs. For example, it might be hard to convince a community of low-income families to enroll their kids in various costly extracurricular activities. (top left) John Moore/Getty Images; (top right) Justin Sullivan/Getty Images; (bottom left) Izf/Shutterstock; (bottom middle) TORSTEN BLACKWOOD/Getty Images; (bottom right) Plume Creative/Getty Images

connect

It will be hard to get your audience to engage in *central processing* if you cannot get them to listen to your speech. As you learned in Chapter 7, you need to encourage thoughtful *active listening*. Although your audience certainly bears some of the responsibility, you can help by making sure that you offer relevant, effective supporting material (Chapter 13) and ensuring that your delivery is easy to listen to (Chapter 15).

Your Audience's Motivation and Interest

Along with appealing to audience needs, you can also persuade listeners—especially neutral listeners—by anticipating their question, "How is this relevant to me?" The **Elaboration Likelihood Model (ELM)** is based on the belief that listeners process persuasive messages by one of two routes, depending on how important—how relevant—the message is to them (Petty & Cacioppo, 1986; see also Kruglanski et al., 2006). When they are motivated and personally involved in the content of a message, they engage in **central processing**—they think critically about the speaker's message, question it, and seriously consider the strengths of the arguments being presented. When listeners lack motivation to listen critically or are unable to do so, they engage in **peripheral processing** of information, paying attention to things other than the central message, such as the speaker's reputation, the emotional manipulation used in the speech, or superficial factors, such as the length of the speech or the attractiveness of the speaker.

Whenever possible, you want your audience to engage in central processing, as it produces deeper, more long-lasting changes in audience perspective than peripheral processing does. Audience members who process peripherally can certainly be influenced; however, they are less likely to experience meaningful long-term changes in attitudes or behavior.

wired for communication

think about this

Interactive Advertising: Persuasion for a Millennial Audience

If you were born between 1980 and 2000, advertisers want you, even if they are not quite sure what to do with you. They call you the millennials, or Generation Y (because you follow Generation X). Some say that if you were born in the late 1990s to beyond 2000, you are part of an even newer group, Generation Z. Your Generation X predecessors (born between 1964 and 1979) were challenging enough, with their tendency to videotape television programs and speed through commercials. But you are even trickier, with your TV and video streaming and customized, commercial-free programming. This presents a challenge for advertisers, as well as a wealth of opportunities. They want to reach you, they want to persuade you, and they are just starting to figure out how.

One strategy they are employing is viral marketing—marketing that takes advantage of preexisting social networks. While viral marketing exists offline (where it is better known as a word-of-mouth campaign), it blossoms online. Advertisers can produce an advertisement and get it in front of millions of potential customers, provided that you find it funny or compelling enough to forward a link to your friends (Elliott, 2010).

Marketers have also tapped into your generation's unprecedented technological know-how to get you involved in the advertising process. User-generated content is persuasive on several levels. Contests for user-generated advertisements can boost interest in a product or service, and the ads themselves can potentially go viral. They also lend an edgy, young image to the product being advertised. Converse sneakers, for example, posted user-generated videos on its website, which became an online hit; Mastercard solicits users to create copy for its ongoing "Priceless" campaign (Bosman, 2006). More recently, advertisers have started trolling through public feeds on Facebook and Twitter, looking for posts related to their products or services. A mobile team responds to such posts, delivering palettes of crunchy goodness to cracker-loving Tweeters (Elliott, 2010). Whether these new tricks of the advertising trade will lure in your millennial or Generation Z dollars is yet to be determined.

1. How many advertisements do you think you encounter in a day? How persuasive do you think they are?

2. Do you think user-generated content is more persuasive to people in their twenties than traditional advertisements? Do you think it is as persuasive to people in other age groups?

3. When advertisements appear on an internet page, are you annoyed? What kind of internet ad would prompt you to click it?

To put the principles of the ELM model of persuasion into practice, consider the following points:

▶ *Make certain that your message is relevant.* Use language and examples to connect your message to your listeners' lives.

▶ *Be sure to present your message at an appropriate level of understanding.* You cannot persuade your audience members if they do not understand the message.

▶ *Establish credibility with the audience.* Show your research, cite experts, and (if relevant) clearly explain your own credentials and experience.

▶ *Establish a common bond with your listeners.* Ensure that they see you as trustworthy. Clearly explain why you support this specific message; if you have a specific interest in it, let them know.

These steps will increase the odds that your persuasive appeal will produce lasting, rather than fleeting, changes in the audience's attitudes and behavior (O'Hair, Stewart, & Rubenstein, 2018).

Strategies for Persuasive Speaking

> When the conduct of men is designed to be influenced, persuasion, kind unassuming persuasion, should ever be adopted. It is an old and true maxim that "a drop of honey catches more flies than a gallon of gall." So with men, if you would win a man to your cause, first convince him that you are his sincere friend. Therein is a drop of honey that catches his heart, which, say what he will, is the great highroad to his reason, and which, once gained, you will find but little trouble in convincing him of the justice of your cause. . . . (Lincoln, 1842, para. 6)

This quote from President Abraham Lincoln truly touches on the important strategies to keep in mind as you persuade your audience. However, it was actually the Greek philosopher Aristotle who first named the three means of persuasion or **forms of rhetorical proof** that comprise major persuasive speaking strategies. The first, appeal to ethos, concerns the qualifications and personality of the speaker; the second, appeal to logos, concerns the nature of the message in a speech; the third, appeal to pathos, concerns the nature of the audience's feelings. According to Aristotle—and generations of theorists and practitioners that followed him—you can build an effective persuasive speech by incorporating a combination of these factors. We examine each of these appeals in turn, in addition to considering examples of problematic reasoning that undermine your effective use of ethos, logos, and pathos.

Ethos

If audience members have little or no regard for the speaker, they will not respond positively to persuasive appeals; attitude change in your audience is related to the audience's positive perception of *you*, the speaker, on a personal level (Teven & Katt, 2016; McCroskey & Teven, 1999). Aristotle believed that speechmaking should emphasize the quality and impact of ideas but recognized that issues like a speaker's competence, character/trustworthiness, and goodwill also play an important role in how well the audience listens to and accepts the message. He referred to this effect of the speaker as **ethos**, the speaker's credibility.

evaluating communication ethics

Sensitivity or Free Speech?

Persuasive speeches can often involve controversial topics. For your persuasive speech, you have selected the topic of preventing rape on college campuses because you think it is an important issue in today's culture. Your instructor has approved your topic, you have conducted your library research, and you are scheduled to give your speech one week from today. You have just heard a rumor, however, that someone in your class has been a victim of sexual assault on your campus, and you are anxious about how this classmate may react to your speech.

You bring your concern to your professor, who tells you that you have the option to provide a trigger warning to the class prior to your speech. *Trigger warnings* are statements before a lecture, reading or other activity that inform the audience of potentially sensitive material, such as depictions of violence (Barnes, 2016). Professors are expected to issue trigger warnings if something in a course might cause a strong emotional response. For example, psychology instructors regularly warn students to avoid four behaviors: stigmatizing mental illness, diagnosing oneself, diagnosing others, and sharing too much personal information (Boysen, Wells, & Dawson, 2016).

According to a recent study, most students support trigger warnings: 61 percent of students surveyed said universities should provide them, and 55 percent said students who "don't maintain a safe space" should be disciplined (Barnes, 2016). Students have increasingly demanded trigger warnings in regard to course topics they believe will elicit strong, negative emotions (Wilson, 2015). They have expressed a desire for their campuses to be free from words, ideas, and subjects that might offend them or cause emotional discomfort. Trigger warnings can protect students from psychological harm.

At this point, issuing a trigger warning seems like the right thing to do, but then your professor goes on to tell you that faculty on campus have strong opinions about trigger warnings. Many faculty argue that trigger warnings go too far in accommodating students: they reduce academic freedom and have a chilling effect on the content that can and should be discussed in classrooms (American Association of University Professors, 2014). According to one study, most instructors had neutral or negative opinions about trigger warnings (Boysen et al., 2016). Rather than trying to protect students from words and ideas that they will inevitably encounter in life, campuses should prepare students to thrive in a world full of words and ideas that they cannot control (Lukiandff & Haidt, 2015).

After your instructor tells you about the faculty's perspective, you remember how much you wanted to speak about rape prevention because you felt it was critical for your peers to hear. You believe you have the right to speak about what you want. And yet, you are still sensitive to your classmate's potential reaction.

1. How can you communicate your emotional sensitivity to your classmate about your topic? Does your classmate's emotional state trump the audience's need to hear this information?

2. What kind of controversial material constitutes the mention of a trigger warning in a speech? What is your responsibility as the speaker to use trigger warnings?

3. Do you think instructor warnings may increase students' comfort in class, encourage interest, and allow them to learn more about a topic, or might they sensitize students and engender negative reactions to course materials that might have otherwise been harmless?

Exactly how does a speaker convey ethos or credibility? One key element is the speaker's competence, or knowledge and experience with the subject matter. You can show this quality by demonstrating your excellent preparation, personal acquaintance with the topic, familiarity with the work of experts, and superb organization. A second key element of credibility is *character* or *trustworthiness*, or the degree to which a speaker seems unbiased and fair. You may demonstrate a great deal of knowledge; however, if your audience thinks that you are lying or have a biased agenda (such as trying to persuade them to invest in your business), they may still not find you credible. A third element of credibility is *goodwill*, the degree to which an audience perceives the speaker caring for them and having their best interests at heart (Teven & McCroskey, 1997). Remember that one of your responsibilities in giving a speech is to help your audience make informed choices. To show goodwill, you should provide listeners with all the information they need to make a decision, as well as respect their values and address their needs.

Other qualities can enhance the ethos of a speaker in addition to the three elements of credibility. For example, audiences tend to be more easily persuaded by speakers who they perceive as being similar to them in background, attitudes, interests, and goals, a concept known as *homophily* (Wrench, McCroskey, & Richmond, 2008). Research also reveals that we trust (and are more easily persuaded by) speakers we like (Teven, 2008). However, if a speaker is similar to us and very likable but unprepared, uninformed, or disorganized (i.e., not competent), we probably will not find him or her to be particularly credible. In other words, when liking and credibility come into conflict (e.g., when we like a source with low credibility), credibility outweighs liking and we are unlikely to be moved by the speaker's message (Frymier & Nadler, 2013).

Finally, audiences tend to respond to a speaker's physical attractiveness, which, if evaluated positively, helps a speaker seem more likable and more credible (Cialdini, 2016; Yoon, Kim, & Kim, 1998) and can positively impact attitude and behavior change (Chaiken, 1979; O'Keefe, 2002). For example, studies in advertising and marketing find that physically attractive models are more effective at selling products than their less attractive counterparts, and the positive effect of attractiveness on persuasion seems to be greater when models are female and the audience is male (Teven & Winters, 2007). Attractiveness does not always lead to persuasion, but it does seem to matter more if receivers have low involvement or rely on peripheral processing (Petty & Cacioppo, 1986).

Logos

Many persuasive speeches focus on issues that require considerable thought. Should the United States adopt a national health care plan? Are certain television programs too violent for children? When an audience needs to make an important decision or reach a conclusion regarding a complicated issue, appeals to reason and logic are necessary. Aristotle used the term **logos** to refer to persuasive appeals directed at the audience's reasoning on a topic.

Reasoning is the line of thought we use to make judgments based on facts and inferences from the world around us. This basic human capability lies at the heart of logical proof: when we offer our evidence to our audience in hopes that our listeners will reach the same logical conclusions as we have, we are appealing to their reason. There are two types of reasoning: inductive and deductive.

Inductive reasoning occurs when you draw general conclusions based on specific evidence. When you reason inductively, you essentially start by gathering the specific examples, incidents, cases, or statistics and draw them into a conclusion that ties them all together. For example, if you work at an animal shelter and have been bitten or snapped at several times by small dogs but never by a large dog, then you might conclude inductively that small dogs are more vicious than large dogs.

Deductive reasoning, by contrast, proceeds from the general principle to the specific examples. You begin with a general argument or hypothesis and then see how it applies to specific cases, incidents, and locations. The most popular way to argue deductively is with a **syllogism**, a three-line deductive argument that draws a specific conclusion from two general premises (a major and a minor premise). Consider this syllogism:

Major premise: All cats are mammals.

Minor premise: Fluffy is a cat.

Conclusion: Therefore, Fluffy is a mammal.

● **DEREK JETER** needs to display ethos when he speaks at events for the Turn 2 Foundation, an organization he founded in 1996 that empowers young people to make healthy choices and strive to become leaders. Matthew Eisman/Getty Images

connect

Part of revealing *ethos* to your audience is offering an accurate, ethical presentation of yourself. As you learned in Chapter 3, *self-presentation* is often strategic—you reveal or hide particular things about yourself to achieve a goal. But if you are giving a speech on the importance of safe driving and you fail to mention that you have been issued five tickets for speeding, you are not being ethical. Your ethos would be increased if you shared your story and the lesson you have learned from it.

The speaker starts with a proposed conclusion or argument and then tests that argument by gathering facts and observations and evidence. Applied to a speech, you might use a syllogism in the following ways:

Major premise: Regular cleanings and visits to the dentist will help keep your teeth in excellent condition and reduce your chances of developing costly medical complications.

Minor premise: The proposed student dental insurance plan is affordable and provides for two free cleanings per year.

Conclusion: Therefore, adopting the proposed student dental insurance plan will keep your teeth in excellent condition and help you avoid costly medical complications.

The extent to which your syllogism is persuasive depends on how well the audience accepts the major premise of your case. If the people in your audience do accept your major premise that regular cleanings and visits to the dentist will help keep their teeth in excellent condition and prevent medical complications, then they may believe that the student dental insurance plan that you are advocating is worthwhile and may be inclined to sign up.

and you?

Think about the last major purchase you made. Now consider the information you had prior to the purchase (advertisements, reviews in the media, advice from others). Did you rely primarily on emotional appeals, ethical appeals, or logical appeals?

communication across cultures

Persuading Across Borders

Actress and activist Angelina Jolie, a goodwill ambassador for the United Nations Refugee Agency, speaks frequently with the desire to raise awareness of and influence policies related to the plight of refugees worldwide. This can be a particular challenge culturally, as some groups in wealthy and stable nations are rather removed from the experiences of refugees and cannot fathom what it would be like to be robbed not merely of one's home but also of one's sense of security, even one's country, by political turmoil or natural disaster.

In one such speech marking World Refugee Day, Jolie explained:

I'm here today to say that refugees are not numbers. They are not even just refugees. They are mothers, and daughters, and fathers, and sons. They are farmers, teachers, doctors, engineers. They're individuals, all. And most of all they are survivors, each one with a remarkable story that tells of resilience in the face of great loss. They are the most impressive people I have ever met. And they are also some of the world's most vulnerable. Stripped of home and country, refugees are buffeted from every ill wind that blows across this planet (Jolie, 2009).

By evoking American values like family, individualism, and hard work in her appeal for assistance for refugees worldwide, Jolie establishes that helping refugees is an ethical goal that her American audience should commit to. She engages her audience members emotions by noting that refugees are *just like the rest of us* — people with families, professions, and lives that matter.

Jolie follows up by detailing the kindness, generosity, and character she has seen in the refugees she has met during her charitable work. In this way, she puts a human face on the plight of refugees while also establishing her own credibility, showing she is not merely a movie star lending her face to a cause: she is on the ground working for the change she is advocating.

think about this

1. Many celebrities work with the United Nations as goodwill ambassadors for a variety of causes. Why would a famous actor or singer be more persuasive than, say, a journalist or a medical doctor?

2. What kinds of cultural values speak to you in a persuasive speech? Do you think that Jolie's focus on resilience and individuals would be as crucial in a more collectivist culture?

3. Does putting a human face on displaced people make them seem more real or deserving of help? How else might Jolie make an audience feel more connected to refugees?

Pathos

Another means of persuasion is appealing to the listeners' emotions. The term Aristotle used for this is **pathos**. It requires creating a certain feeling in the audience, often through emotionally charged language and description. For example, consider this statement: "The sight of fishermen slashing and slicing baby seals should send chills through even the numbest and most stoic fur-wearers on Earth." Makes your skin crawl, doesn't it?

Although emotion can be a powerful means of moving an audience, emotional appeals may not be effective if used in isolation—particularly if the emotion you arouse is fear (Nabi, 1999; Rothman, Salovey, Turvey, & Fishkin, 1993). In fact, fear appeals are typically only effective if the speaker can get the audience to see that the threat is serious, that it is likely to happen to them, and that there is a specific action they can take to avoid the threat (Boster & Mongeau, 1984; Maddux & Rogers, 1983).

Pathos is typically most effective when used alongside logos and ethos, which offer ways of dealing with and addressing the emotions. For example, consider the Montana Meth Project (2013), "a large-scale prevention program aimed at reducing meth use through public service messaging, public policy, and community outreach" in the state of Montana. The ads of this organization, as well as those of similar organizations in other states in the U.S., are indeed emotional, graphic, and frightening. They play into viewers' love of family and friends, fear of poor health and degenerating appearance, and sense of shame and horror. A particularly moving print ad depicts an unconscious young woman in an emergency room. It reads, "No one ever thinks they'll wake up here. Meth will change that" (Montana Meth Project, 2013). But the logical appeal is also sound—teenagers who become addicted to methamphetamine will destroy themselves and their loved ones—and the credibility of the source enhances the persuasiveness of the emotional appeal. The project's follow-up research showed that the campaign had overwhelmingly positive results: teen meth use in Montana declined by 63 percent, adult meth use declined by 72 percent, and meth-related crime decreased by 62 percent (Montana Meth Project, 2013). Engagement with the Montana Meth Campaign was also found to have potential health benefits, as people got into conversations about meth use and about the campaign (Richards, 2014).

Avoiding Logical Fallacies

In a predictable scene from any number of movies, TV shows, or actual lives, a teenager argues with her parents that she should be allowed to go to a party because all her friends are going. The exasperated parents roll their eyes and counter, "If your friends

connect

Your word choices have a powerful impact on your audience, as words have different meanings for different people (as we discussed in Chapter 4). Let's say you are persuading your audience to adopt a healthy diet. Some people define healthy as animal proteins, good fats, and high fiber, whereas others perceive healthy as a purely plant-based vegan diet. To make sure your audience is on the same page, define how *you* are using the term.

were all jumping off a bridge, would you jump, too?" In their attempts to persuade the other, both the parents and the child fail miserably. In the eyes of the parents, "All of my friends are going" is not a valid reason why their kid should go to the party, whereas comparing a party to jumping off a bridge makes no sense to the teenager either.

Logical fallacies are invalid or deceptive forms of reasoning. Although they may, at times, be effective in persuading uncritical listeners, active audience members will reject you as a speaker as well as your argument when they hear a fallacy creep into your speech (Hansen, 2002). So be on guard against using these fallacies yourself and be on the lookout for these fallacies as you listen to other speakers' arguments.

Bandwagoning

When a teenager says, "All of my friends are going" as an argument, she is guilty of using the **bandwagon fallacy**—claiming a statement is true or an action is reasonable because it is popular. Unfortunately, bandwagoning can sometimes persuade passive audience members who assume that an argument must be correct if others accept it (Bardone & Magnani, 2010). But credible speakers and critical audience members must be careful not to confuse consensus with fact. A large number of people believing in ghosts is not proof that ghosts exist.

Reduction to the Absurd

When parents counter their daughter's request to go to a party with her friends by comparing it to following them off a bridge, they are extending their argument to the level of absurdity. A fallacy known as **reduction to the absurd** means that pushing an argument beyond its logical limits can cause it to unravel. The teenager sees no connection between going to a party (which may have minor negative outcomes but is otherwise fun) and jumping off a bridge (which is certain death).

Red Herring

When a speaker relies on irrelevant information for his or her argument, thereby diverting the direction of the argument, he or she is guilty of the **red herring fallacy** (so named for a popular myth about a fish's scent throwing hounds off track of a pursuit). You would be using a red herring if you said, for example, "A police officer gave me a ticket for going 70, but yesterday, I saw a driver cut across three lanes of traffic without signaling while going 80—at least! Why aren't cops chasing down these dangerous drivers instead?" There may well be worse drivers than you, but that does not change the fact that you broke the law.

Personal Attack

A speaker who criticizes a person rather than the issue at hand is guilty of the *ad hominem* **fallacy**—an attack on a person instead of on the person's arguments. From the Latin meaning "to the man," the *ad hominem* fallacy is a common feature of political campaigns. For example, if a speaker says, "Terry Malone is the better candidate for district court judge because she is happily married, whereas her opponent just kicked his wife out of their house," the argument is focused on the individual and not the person's particular qualifications for the job.

Hasty Generalization

A **hasty generalization** is a reasoning flaw in which a speaker makes a broad generalization based on isolated examples or insufficient evidence. For example, suppose

Jeff notes in his speech that actor and comedian George Burns smoked for decades and lived to be a hundred years old and then concludes that smoking cannot really be that bad. Jeff's claim would be unreasonable (and dangerous) if it were to draw a universal conclusion about the health risks of smoking from the case study of one person.

Begging the Question

Speakers who use the fallacy of **begging the question** present arguments that no one can verify because they are not accompanied by valid evidence. For example, if Amanda notes, "People only watch *True Blood* because *The Walking Dead* is so awesome," she is basing her argument on an unprovable premise (the notion that *The Walking Dead* is awesome—which is a subjective opinion rather than a verifiable fact). If you accept Amanda's premise, you must accept her conclusion. For this reason, this fallacy is often referred to as a *circular argument*.

● **POLITICAL RACES** take a turn for the worse and run on logical fallacies when candidates campaign against their opponents with personal attacks. Mark Makela/Getty Images

Either–or Fallacy

Speakers might try to persuade by using the **either–or fallacy** (sometimes called the *false dilemma fallacy*), presenting only two alternatives on a subject and failing to acknowledge other alternatives. For example, in a speech about local sports teams, Charlie states, "In this town, you're either a Bears fan or a Packers fan." He fails to acknowledge that there might be fans of other football teams living in the city or individuals who do not care about football at all.

Appeal to Tradition

A local community board informs a merchant group that existing "blue laws" preventing them from doing business on Sundays will continue because those laws have been on the books since the town's founding. This kind of argument is a fallacy known as an **appeal to tradition**—an argument that uses tradition as proof. When speakers appeal to tradition, they are suggesting that listeners should agree with their point because "that's the way it has always been."

The Slippery Slope

A speaker who uses the **slippery slope fallacy** attests that an event must clearly occur as a result of another event without showing any proof that the second event is caused by the first. For example, "Video surveillance cameras should not be installed in major metropolitan areas. The next thing you know, the government will be reading our text messages."

The Naturalistic Fallacy

The **naturalistic fallacy** originates from British philosopher G. E. Moore, who argued that it is illogical to appeal to (or have an inherent bias for) nature; that is, saying that what is natural is right or good and that anything unnatural (e.g., synthetic or human-made) is wrong or bad (*Principia Ethica*, 1903). For example, advocating that vaccines are unnecessary on the basis that the human immune system can conquer disease naturally (without medical assistance) fails to regard the fact that vaccines have saved innumerable lives from diseases like polio.

real communicator

NAME: Katie McGill

OCCUPATION: Director of Development for Higher Education, Fund-Raiser, Spokesperson

Courtesy Katie McGill

Fund-raising has always been at the heart of my career. I've worked in public radio fund-raising and health care development, but I found my passion for higher education when I served as associate director for marketing and communications for alumni relations at the university where I work. I developed newsletters, web articles, and events to engage alumni and continued my fund-raising efforts by running the alumni membership program. Now, I'm the director of development for the College of Communications. In all of these jobs, being able to write an effective email or funding proposal or carefully script talking points can be the deciding factor when making the case for financial support.

Our students are amazingly talented. Our goal is to help provide education, training, and opportunities for them to succeed. Development can make a tremendous impact in funding these opportunities. Persuasion is a hugely important component of my job. In order to get people to talk with me in the first place, I have to persuade them! When I have the opportunity to talk to

someone one-on-one, I want to learn about the person or organization more fully. Once I hear what an individual or organization's needs are, then I can communicate the opportunities at the college that most closely align with their passions. Whether I'm talking on the phone, writing an email, or drafting a proposal or grant application, communicating the need and the benefit of support for our students is paramount. Development at my university can be a joyful experience, filled with challenges and rewards. It is exciting to see a company, organization, or individual enthusiastic to provide life-changing opportunities for our students. There is no better feeling than matching a program need with a donor who is passionate about supporting the program. And, after all our development efforts for the year are complete, there is nothing more important than communicating the results to our donors and supporters — letting them know how their support has made a difference, and whom we were able to impact with their donation.

and you?

What kinds of logical fallacies do you regularly see used in the media? What is your reaction when advertisers, political campaigns, or pundits try to persuade you using faulty logic?

Avoiding these logical fallacies goes a long way toward building ethos with your audience — particularly if the audience is hostile toward your speech topic. You want to rely on facts, research, honest emotion, and your own well-rehearsed presentation to persuade your audience. If you are finding yourself slipping into any logical fallacy to persuade your listeners, you are lacking solid, compelling evidence in that area of your speech.

Organizing Patterns in Persuasive Speaking

Once you have a topic, audience research, and thoughts about how to deal with logic, emotion, and competence in your presentation, it is time to organize this information. As you recall from Chapter 14, there are a number of organizational strategies available for your speech; your choice depends on your objective, your audience, and your available time. When it comes to persuasive speeches, certain organizational strategies can be particularly helpful, including the problem–solution pattern, the refutational organizational pattern, the comparative advantage pattern, and Monroe's motivated sequence.

Problem–Solution Pattern

As discussed in Chapter 14, when you use a *problem–solution pattern* for your speech, you establish and prove the existence of a problem and then present a solution. When your objective is to persuade, you also need to add a set of arguments for your proposed solution. This format is valuable because it allows you to establish common ground with your audience about the existence of a problem before moving to more delicate matters (your solution). Although audience members may disagree with the evidence and reasoning you use to build your case, your presentation allows for the possibility that they will find the information interesting and plausible. In some cases, an audience may reject a solution that you present but at least leave convinced that "something has to be done."

For example, note in the following outline that the first two main points consider the problem and the third main point offers a solution:

Thesis: Current methods for recycling in our county are inadequate.

Main point 1: Each local community in our area county has its own unique recycling plan and system.

Main point 2: The current system for recycling generates low participation by citizens.

Main point 3: Recycling should be a county-wide, not a local community, responsibility.

A variation on this layout is to use a problem–cause–solution format, making the second point the cause of the problem. This format is often useful because getting your listeners to understand the cause helps them reflect on the problem, and it makes your solution seem plausible or even inevitable. In the following example, the first main point proves the problem, the second main point proves the cause, and the third main point offers a solution:

Thesis: U.S. presidents should be able to serve more than two terms.

Main point 1: Acceptance of foreign and domestic politics is harmed by changes in administrations.

Main point 2: Historically, our country's greatest periods of weakness have occurred with changes in the presidency.

Main point 3: The American people should choose whether a president is worthy of serving up to four consecutive terms.

This type of format tends to work particularly well when you are presenting a proposition of policy because it often proposes a course of action or a series of steps to achieve resolution.

● **WHEN SPEAKING ABOUT** recycling, you might use the problem–solution pattern to clearly establish the problem before persuading your audience with a solution. RL Productions/ Getty Images

Refutational Organizational Pattern

If people in your audience have strong objections to a position you are promoting or are familiar with the competing views about your issue, you will be wise to present, and then refute, the arguments against your main point. This strategy can be an effective way to engage, if not fully persuade, an informed audience (Allen, 1991; Pizzutti, Basso, & Albornoz, 2016; O'Keefe, 1999). In the **refutational organizational pattern**, speakers begin by presenting main points that are opposed to their own position and then follow them with main points that support their own position. Though you can use this pattern when the opposing side has weak arguments that you can easily attack, it is to your advantage to select—and then disprove—the strongest points that support the opposing position (DiSanza & Legge, 2002). This may win over hostile audience members who might otherwise be using those opposing arguments in their minds to reject your stance.

In your first main point, you should present the opposing position. Describe that claim and identify at least one key piece of evidence that supports it. In the second main point, you should present the possible effects or implications of that claim. Your third main point should present arguments and evidence for your own position. The final main point should contrast your position with the one that you started with and leave no doubt in the listeners' minds of the superiority of your viewpoint. For example:

> *Thesis:* Universities are justified in distributing condoms to students free of charge or at reduced prices.
>
> *Main point 1:* Some parents claim that providing condoms is immoral and encourages casual sex among students.
>
> *Main point 2:* Sexual relations, regardless of moral values, will occur among students in a college atmosphere.
>
> *Main point 3:* If condoms are difficult to obtain, sexual activity will result in unwanted pregnancies and sexually transmitted infections.
>
> *Main point 4:* Students will engage in sexual relations regardless of whether condoms are available, so it is to everyone's advantage that students have easy access to safe sex methods.

The use of this format with a hostile audience can actually help you build credibility. Having established a sense of respect and goodwill between speaker and audience by acknowledging opposing viewpoints, you can then move on to explain the reasons why you believe, nonetheless, that your thesis is true.

Comparative Advantage Pattern

Another way to organize speech points is to show that your proposed solution is superior to other possible alternatives for resolving a problem. This arrangement, called the **comparative advantage pattern**, is most effective when your audience is already aware of the issue or problem and agrees that a solution is needed. Because listeners are aware of the issue, you can skip over establishing its existence and can move directly to favorably comparing your position with the alternatives. With this strategy, you are assuming that your audience is open to various alternative solutions.

To maintain your credibility, it is important that you identify alternatives that your audience is familiar with as well as those that are supported by opposing interests. If you omit familiar alternatives, your listeners will wonder if you are fully informed on the topic and become skeptical of your comparative alternative as well as your credibility. The final step in a comparative advantage speech is to drive home the unique advantages of your option relative to competing options with brief but compelling evidence.

> *Thesis:* New members of our hospital's board of directors must be conflict-free.
>
> *Main point 1:* Justin Davis is an officer in two other organizations.
>
> *Main point 2:* Vivian Alvarez will spend six months next year in London.

and you?

Have you ever sat through a lecture where the instructor offered a point of view different from your own? Did the instructor acknowledge differing viewpoints? If so, what was your reaction to hearing the instructor's argument against your belief? Did you respect the speaker more or less for addressing your counterpoints?

Main point 3: Lillian Rosenthal's husband served as our director two years ago.

Main point 4: Sam Dhatri has no potential conflicts for service.

Monroe's Motivated Sequence

In Chapter 14, we gave you a brief introduction to Monroe's *motivated sequence pattern* for organizing your speech. It is a variant of the problem–solution pattern and has proved quite effective for persuasive speaking, particularly when you want your audience to do something (such as buy a product or donate time or money to a cause). We elaborate on Monroe's five-step sequence here:

Step 1: Attention. The attention step gets the audience interested in listening to your speech. It often highlights how the speech will be relevant to them.

> It's two in the morning and you're staring at a blank screen on your computer. You've got a term paper for your history class and a lab report to finish, but these aren't what have you worried right now. It's figuring out your résumé—how to take your work, personal, and educational experiences and cram them all onto one page.

Step 2: Need. This step allows you to identify a need or problem that matters to your audience. You want to show that this issue should be addressed.

> Each person in this room will be applying for internships and jobs; such positions are highly competitive. Your résumé, for better or worse, will make a first impression on your potential employer.

Step 3: Satisfaction. The satisfaction step allows you to show your audience the solution that you have identified to meet the problem or need addressed in step 2. This step is crucial, as you are offering the audience members a proposal to reinforce or change their attitudes, beliefs, or behavior regarding the problem or need at hand.

> Visiting our college's Office of Career Services is a great way to get help and direction for your résumé. The professionals employed there will be able to help make your job application materials stand out while making the process seem less overwhelming.

Step 4: Visualization. As its name implies, the visualization step helps your audience see how your proposed solution might play out and how they might benefit.

> Instead of sitting up at your computer at 2 A.M., you could be sitting with Tamela, a career counselor, at 2 P.M. as she makes suggestions for formatting your résumé or asks you questions about your past work experiences in order to highlight achievements that you had never even thought to mention.

Step 5: Action. This final step clarifies what you want your audience members to do. This may involve reconsidering their attitudes, beliefs, or behavior.

> Make an appointment with a career counselor today. Don't wait—you need those early morning hours for that history term paper, not your résumé!

Now that you have considered organizational patterns and have a solid grasp on how to handle persuasive speaking, let's take a look at a sample speech by Elijah Lui. In this speech, Elijah is persuading his audience to recognize the problem of

● **WHEN PERSUADING STUDENTS** to utilize their college's career center, use the visualization step in Monroe's motivated sequence to help your audience members picture themselves discussing how to improve their résumés with a college counselor. *Hill Street Studios/Getty Images*

cyberbullying and explaining how listeners can address and prevent it. Organizationally, the speech is arranged along the lines of the problem–solution pattern. Note that Elijah uses a variety of sources to support his arguments. Be sure to check out Elijah's reference list as well as his speaking outline, both of which follow the speech sample.

LaunchPad
macmillan learning

▶ **Watch It Now**
To see Elijah deliver his speech, go to **launchpadworks.com** and watch the sample speech video for Chapter 17. You should critique his topic, preparation, and delivery—so watch carefully!

• Elijah begins his speech with a dramatic example that captures the audience's attention.

Sample Student Persuasive Speech 17.1

Preventing Cyberbullying

ELIJAH LUI

Elijah cleans before recording his online speech so that the background is not distracting.

On the evening of September 22, 2010, • Rutgers University freshman Tyler Clementi updated his Facebook status: "Jumping off the gw [George Washington] bridge sorry." According to Lisa Foderaro's report in *The New York Times*, a few hours later Clementi did just that. But what would cause a bright student and talented musician with a promising future to take his own life? A bully with a webcam.

According to a May 21, 2012, report on CNN, Clementi's roommate was sentenced to thirty days in jail, three years of probation, three hundred hours of community service, and $10,000 in restitution for using a webcam to view and transmit images of Clementi in an intimate encounter with another young man. Tyler Clementi's story is tragic, but it's not an isolated event. On September 9, 2013, 12-year-old Rebecca Sedwick jumped to her death after allegedly being tormented by two girls on Facebook. A few months earlier, Rehtaeh Parsons, a 17-year-old Canadian high school student, hanged herself after cell phone pictures of her being sexually assaulted were distributed by the alleged attackers. What is going on here? In a word—it's *cyberbullying*. •

• Elijah introduces his topic with a rhetorical question.

Elijah sits far enough from the camera so that his body movements and gestures can be seen.

My name is Elijah, and I'm here today to confront the growing problem of electronic harassment experienced by Tyler Clementi and so many others. I'll start with a look at the various forms cyberbullying takes and describe the scope of the problem. But I'm not here just to talk about one more social ill; I want to show you how you and your loved ones can stay safe — both by scrupulously guarding your personal information and by actively thwarting cyberbullies. Finally, should you or someone you know become a victim, I want you to be able to respond constructively. •

• Elijah sets up the organizational pattern of the speech, indicating that he will describe a problem and offer solutions.

• Elijah qualifies his source and demonstrates its credibility.

• Elijah begins the body of his speech by ensuring that his audience knows what cyberbullying means.

As you can imagine from the heartbreaking story I've shared about Tyler Clementi, cyberbullying poses serious mental health risks to the nation's children, teens, and young adults. The Cyberbullying Research Center, a leading resource on the topic, defines *cyberbullying* as "willful and repeated harm inflicted through the use of computers, cell phones, and other electronic devices." • Cyberbullying can take many forms, including posting or sending harassing messages via websites, blogs, or text messages; posting embarrassing or private photos of someone without their permission; recording or videotaping someone and sharing it without permission; and creating fake websites or social networking profiles in someone else's name to humiliate them. Often these acts are done anonymously.

Recent research paints a chilling picture of the frequency and harm of electronic harassment. According to Hani Morgan, an education professor at the University of Southern Mississippi, the statistics vary widely, but a 2011 report by the National Crime Prevention Council found that 43 percent of teens had been the victims of cyberbullying in the last year. Although most of the research to date has focused on cyberbullying among middle school and high school students, a 2012 study published in the *Journal of School Violence* confirmed that the problem of electronic harassment continues into college. Psychologists Allison Schenk and William Fremouw found that nearly 9 percent of university students had experienced cyberbullying; that means that at least two or three people listening to this speech know what I'm describing because they've felt it. As we have seen with Tyler, Rebecca, Rehtaeh, and too many others, cyberbullying has tragically cut short promising lives. But consequences less dramatic than suicide take a serious toll on cyberbullying's victims. The same study by Schenk and Fremouw reported more symptoms of depression and anxiety, as well as difficulty concentrating, among bullied college students. •

• Elijah effectively puts his research to work throughout this section, making sure to give credit to his reputable sources.

As Professor Morgan explains, the anonymity of unsigned messages and fake user names marks cyberbullying as a dangerous evolution of a long-standing face-to-face bullying problem, but you can take steps to protect yourself. • For one, you can be vigilant about safeguarding your personal information. Our school's information technology office lists the following advice on its website. First, never, ever leave your laptops unattended. Second, keep your account passwords and Social Security numbers completely private. Third, use the most secure privacy settings on your social networking sites. Finally, think carefully about the types of pictures of yourself and your friends that you post online and restrict views of them to "friends only." Each of these steps can minimize opportunities for bullies to harm or embarrass you in some way.

Elijah uses strong eye contact to project confidence.

• Elijah effectively transitions to offering solutions and practical steps to avoid cyberbullying.

In addition to zealously guarding your personal information, you can help combat cyberbullying by being a voice against it whenever you see it happening. • Several organizations have websites that provide information you can use to be part of the solution. The Facebook group Don't Stand By, Stand Up! is a student-led organization formed soon after the suicide of Tyler Clementi. The group urges internet users to take a stand against cyberbullying by recognizing that bullies — in all forms — rarely succeed in their harassment without the support and attention of bystanders. The National Crime Prevention Council website gives specific tips on how to thwart a bully's attempts. The first is to refuse to pass bullying messages along to others — whether via text or photo messaging, social networking, or email — and to let the original sender know that you find the message offensive or stupid. Despite your best efforts to keep your personal information private and speak out against cyberbullying, you may still become a victim.

• This transition summarizes the previous point and previews the next one.

Online safety expert Parry Aftab's website, Stopcyberbullying.org, advises victims to use the "Stop, Block, and Tell" method to respond to bullying behaviors directed against them. Though often taught to younger children, this response makes sense in any case of cyberbullying. After receiving a bullying message, you should first stop. In other words, do nothing. Take five minutes to cool down, take a walk, breathe deeply, or do whatever will help to calm down the understandable anger you are feeling. Then, block: prevent the cyberbully from having any future communication with you. This may mean anything from removing him or her from your social networking site's "friends" list to having your cell phone service provider block the bully from being able to call or text you. The third step is to tell someone about the abuse without embarrassment or shame. For example, you might call campus security or confide in a counselor at the health and counseling center — particularly if the abuse has been going on for a long time and you feel that your self-esteem or relationships have been affected. Similarly, parents of younger children should encourage their children to report any bullying to a trusted adult.

Today we've ventured into the very real — and very dangerous — world of cyberbullying. We've seen cyberbullying's negative impact on people of all ages. We've also seen how you can counter this potentially deadly problem by being vigilant about protecting your personal information and speaking out against cyberbullying. And if you or someone you know experiences cyberbullying, you can react constructively with the Stop, Block, and Tell method. •

• Elijah signals the conclusion of his speech with a summary of his main points.

Elijah uses appropriate facial expressions to convey the seriousness of his topic.

Cyberbullying isn't just someone else's problem. It's very likely something you need to guard against now or in the future — as a student today or as a parent tomorrow. I urge each of you to make a personal commitment to do your part to combat the problem. Refuse to stay silent in the face of cyberbullying. • Resolve that you will never send or pass along cyberbullying messages of any kind, no matter how harmless doing so might seem. This act alone can make a world of difference in the life of the intended victim. And wouldn't you want someone to take this simple step for you?

• Elijah issues a call to action.

We must never forget Tyler Clementi and the other young lives cut short by unnecessary bullying. Who knows? Your best friend, your younger brother, or your son could just have easily been on that bridge that fateful September evening. •

• By stressing the personal relevance of his topic to his audience, Elijah leaves his listeners with something to think about.

References

Foderaro, L. W. (2010, September 30). Private moment made public, then a fatal jump. *The New York Times.* Retrieved from query.nytimes.com/gst/fullpage.html?res=9B07E6D91638F933A0575AC0A9669D8B63

Hayes, A. (2012, May 21). Prosecutors to appeal 30-day sentence in Rutgers gay bullying case. Retrieved from www.cnn.com/2012/05/21/justice/new-jersey-rutgers-sentencing/index.html

Hinduja, S., & Patchin, J. W. (2010). *Cyberbullying: Identification, prevention, and response* [Fact Sheet]. Retrieved from www.cyberbullying.us/Cyberbullying_Identification_Prevention_Response_Fact_Sheet.pdf

Martinez, M. (2013, October 28). Charges in Rebecca Sedwick's suicide suggest "tipping point" in bullying cases. Retrieved from www.cnn.com/2013/10/25/us/rebecca-sedwick-bullying-suicide-case/index.html

Morgan, H. (2013, May/June). Malicious use of technology: What schools, parents, and teachers can do to prevent cyberbullying. *Childhood Education*, 89(3), 146–151.

Newton, P. (2013, April 10). Canadian teen commits suicide after alleged rape, bullying. Retrieved from www.cnn.com/2013/04/10/justice/canada-teen-suicide/index.html

Schenk, A. M., & Fremouw, W. J. (2012, January). Prevalence, psychological impact, and coping of cyberbully victims among college students. *The Journal of School Violence*, 11(1), 21–37.

Stop, block and tell! (n.d.). Retrieved November 1, 2013, from www. stopcyberbullying.org/take_action/stop_block_and_tell.html

Stop cyberbullying before it starts. (n.d.). Retrieved on February 9, 2011, from www.ncpc.org/resources/files/pdf/bullying/cyberbullying.pdf

Speaking Outline

Elijah Lui

Preventing Cyberbullying

General Purpose: To persuade
Specific Purpose: To persuade my audience to understand and confront the growing problem of cyberbullying.
Thesis Statement: I'm here today to confront the growing problem of cyberbullying experienced by Tyler Clementi and so many others.

Introduction

I. **Attention Getter:** Relate tragic stories of cyberbullying.
  A. 9/22/10: Rutgers U freshman Tyler Clementi (TC) updates Facebook (FB) "Jumping off gw [George Washington] Bridge sorry." He does. (Foderaro, NYT, Sept. 29, 2010)
  B. TC's roommate convicted of invasion of privacy. Used webcam to transmit private images. Clementi's roommate sentenced to 30 days in jail, 3 years of probation, 300 hours community service, and $10,000 in restitution. (Hayes, CNN, May 21, 2012)
  C. 12-year-old Rebecca Sedwick (RS) commits suicide after Facebook tormenting. (Martinez, CNN, Oct. 28, 2013)
  D. 17-year-old Canadian high school student Rehtaeh Parsons (RP) hangs herself after photos of her sexual assault distributed by alleged attackers.

II. What is going on here? Cyberbullying (CB)

III. Introduce self.

IV. Will discuss forms and scope of CB; staying safe from and responding to CB.

Body

I. Forms of CB
  A. "Willful and repeated harm inflicted through the use of computers, cell phones, and other electronic devices" (CB Research Center)
  B. Posting/sending harassing messages via websites, blogs, texts
  C. Posting embarrassing photos w/o permission

D. Recording/videotaping someone and sharing w/o permission
E. Creating fake websites/profiles to humiliate

Transition: Recent CB research paints a chilling picture.

II. Scope of CB
   A. 2011 study by Hani Morgan, University of Southern Mississippi: 42% of teens experienced CB.
   B. 2012 study by Allison Schenk and William Fremouw (*Journal of School Violence*)
      1. Nearly 9% of college students experience CB.
      2. Probably 2 or 3 of you have too.
   C. Consequences of CB
      1. As in the cases of Tyler, Rebecca, and Rehtaeh, CB can lead to suicide.
      2. In others, symptoms include depression, anxiety, and difficulty concentrating.

Transition: CB is a dangerous evolution of face-to-face bullying. You can protect yourself, though.

III. Steps for staying safe from CB
   A. Safeguard personal information (school IT office).
      1. Never leave laptop unattended.
      2. Keep passwords and SSN private.
      3. Use privacy settings.
      4. Post photos with caution.
   B. Be a voice against CB.
      1. Don't Stand By, Stand Up! (formed in honor of TC on FB): bullies don't succeed without help.
      2. Don't pass on CB messages, and inform the senders that their messages are offensive/stupid. (National Crime Prevention Council)

Transition: You may still become a CB victim.

IV. Responding to CB: use "stop, block, tell." (Parry Aftab, July 28, 2009, Frontline interview)
   A. Stop: take 5, cool down, walk, breathe deeply.
   B. Block: prevent communication—remove bully from social networking lists and block cell #.
   C. Tell: campus security, counselor, etc. Children tell parent, teacher, principal.

Transition/Internal Summary: We've seen CB's negative impact and discussed countering CB (privacy, speak out, "stop, block, tell").

Conclusion

I. CB is not someone else's problem.
II. Call to action: make a personal commitment to combat CB.
   A. Refuse to be silent.
   B. Never pass along CB messages.
   C. Voice your concerns at the campus and community levels.
III. Don't forget TC and other CB victims. Your loved one could be next.

back to   Jamie Oliver's TED Prize–Winning Wish

Gustavo Caballero/Getty Images

At the beginning of this chapter, we discussed celebrity chef Jamie Oliver's TED speech, in which he presented his wish to educate children about food (Oliver, 2010). Let's consider his speech in light of what we have learned in this chapter.

▶ Oliver has done his share of informative speaking: as a celebrity chef and former star of *Food Revolution*, he gives regular cooking demonstrations that are designed to teach techniques and provide information about food. But this speech, and much of the speaking he does as an activist, is persuasive in nature—he wants to teach people to use the information he provides to change their lives and improve their health, as well as the health of the public at large.

▶ Oliver organizes his TED speech with a problem–cause–solution pattern. First, he identifies the problem, offering startling statistics and compelling personal stories. He then details the causes behind the problem before moving on to solutions, such as giving people the proper information and tools to change their eating behavior and take charge of their lives. He ends with his "wish," his purpose for speaking, hoping to motivate his audience to make it a reality.

▶ Oliver successfully uses presentation aids during his speech: photos of people who are dying from obesity-related diseases, a graphic detailing deaths from diet-related illnesses like type 2 diabetes and heart disease, and, for maximum impact, a wheelbarrow filled with sugar cubes to demonstrate the amount of sugar an average child consumes in five years by drinking just two containers of chocolate milk per day.

▶ Oliver considers his audience when he speaks. He knows that the crowd at his TED speech is receptive to his message; they gave him the award, after all. His message is therefore directed at broad solutions at the institutional level—changes he knows the TED audience can help enact. When speaking to individuals who are less educated about or interested in food and nutrition, he would likely focus on change at the personal level.

things to try   Activities

 LaunchPad
macmillan learning

1. LaunchPad for *Real Communication* offers key term videos and encourages self-assessment through adaptive quizzing. Go to **launchpadworks.com** to get access to:

 LearningCurve
Adaptive Quizzes.

▶ Video clips that illustrate key concepts, highlighted in teal in the Real Reference section that follows.

2. Check out a persuasive speech video. You can view one of the persuasive speech videos that accompany this textbook or check one out on YouTube. Listen to and watch the speech critically in light of what you have learned about persuasion. Does the speaker use a clear proposition of fact, value, or policy as a thesis statement? What do you feel the speaker is aiming at—influencing your beliefs, attitudes, or behavior? Maybe all three? Is the speaker's use of rhetorical proofs effective? Consider the elements we have discussed: ethos (character), logos (reasoning), and pathos (emotion).

3. On your next grocery store trip or while waiting in a doctor's office, look through magazine advertisements (bridal magazines are particularly interesting to search). As you look for examples of appeals to ethos, logos, and pathos, consider the following questions:

   ▶ What magazine and ads did you choose to examine?
   ▶ Which form of proof do you find most persuasive? Why?
   ▶ Which form of proof do you find least persuasive? Why?
   ▶ Is there a form of proof used consistently in the ads of the particular magazine you looked at? Why do you think that is?

4. At one point in this chapter, we asked you to think of a time when an instructor presented a viewpoint that went against one of your deeply held beliefs. Now it's time for you to be the speaker.

   ▶ Choose a topic that you feel very passionate about (a controversial topic would work best here).
   ▶ Now imagine that you are presenting the topic to a receptive audience, a neutral audience, and a hostile audience. What do you as a speaker need to do in order to prepare to present your topic to each type of audience? What do you know about your listeners' dispositions? What do you know about their needs? What is most relevant to them?
   ▶ Particularly when dealing with neutral and hostile audiences, what are ways that you can bridge the gap between your beliefs and those of your audience members? How can you generate goodwill and understanding?
   ▶ Is there a particular organizational pattern that would best suit you, your topic, or your audience? For example, are you sufficiently comfortable with and knowledgeable enough about your hostile audience's counterpoints to be able to refute them using the refutational organizational pattern?

real reference ▶ A Study Tool

Now that you have finished reading this chapter, you can:

Define the goals of persuasive speaking:
▶ **Coercion** involves manipulation, threats, intimidation, or violence (p. 434).
▶ **Persuasive speaking** uses the process of **persuasion** to influence **attitudes, beliefs**, and **behavior** (p. 434).

Develop a persuasive topic and thesis:
▶ Choose a topic that is controversial and aim to create change in the audience (p. 435).
▶ Thesis statements are often given as a proposition, a statement of your viewpoint on an issue (p. 435).
▶ A **proposition of fact** is a claim of what is or what is not and addresses how people perceive reality (p. 436).
▶ A **proposition of value** makes claims about something's worth (p. 436).
▶ A **proposition of policy** concerns what should happen and makes claims about what goal, policy, or course of action should be pursued (pp. 436–438).

Evaluate your listeners and tailor your speech to them:
▶ **Social judgment theory** holds that your ability to persuade depends on audience members' attitudes toward your topic (p. 438).
▶ A **receptive audience** agrees with you (p. 438).
▶ **Latitude of acceptance and rejection (or noncommitment)** refers to the range of positions on a topic that are acceptable or unacceptable to your audience, influenced by their original or **anchor position** (pp. 438–439).

▶ A **neutral audience** neither supports nor opposes you. A **hostile audience** opposes your message (p. 439).

▶ The **stages of change model** helps predict your audience members' motivational readiness and progress toward modifying behavior. The five stages are precontemplation, contemplation, preparation, action, and maintenance (pp. 439–440).

▶ Maslow's **hierarchy of needs** holds that our most basic needs must be met before we can worry about needs farther up the hierarchy (pp. 440–441).

▶ The **Elaboration Likelihood Model (ELM)** highlights the importance of relevance to persuasion and holds that listeners will process persuasive messages by one of two routes: **central processing** (deep, motivated thinking) or **peripheral processing** (unmotivated, less critical thought; p. 442).

Explain three **forms of rhetorical proof** (or classical appeal): ethos, logos, and pathos:

▶ The speaker's moral character, or **ethos**, influences the audience's reaction to the message (p. 443).

▶ **Logos** refers to appeals to the audience's **reasoning**, judgments based on facts and inferences (p. 445).

▶ **Inductive reasoning** involves drawing general conclusions from specific evidence; **deductive reasoning** applies general arguments to specific cases (p. 445).

▶ A **syllogism** is a three-line deductive argument, drawing a conclusion from two general premises (p. 445).

▶ **Pathos** appeals to the listeners' emotions (p. 447).

Identify the **logical fallacies**, deceptive forms of reasoning:

▶ The **bandwagon fallacy**: a statement is considered true because it is popular (p. 448).

▶ **Reduction to the absurd**: an argument is pushed beyond its logical limits (p. 448).

▶ The **red herring fallacy**: irrelevant information is used to divert the direction of the argument (p. 448).

▶ The *ad hominem* **fallacy**: a personal attack; the focus is on a person rather than on the issue (p. 448).

▶ A **hasty generalization** is a reasoning flaw in which a speaker makes a broad generalization based on isolated examples (p. 448).

▶ **Begging the question**: advancing an argument that cannot be proved because there is no valid evidence (p. 449).

▶ **Either–or fallacy**: only two alternatives are presented, omitting other alternatives (p. 449).

▶ **Appeal to tradition**: "that's the way it has always been" is the only reason given (p. 449).

▶ The **slippery slope fallacy**: one event is presented as the result of another, without showing proof (p. 449).

▶ The **naturalistic fallacy**: anything natural is right or good; anything humanmade is wrong or bad (p. 449).

Choose an appropriate organizational strategy (or **organizing patterns**) for your speech:

▶ The *problem–solution pattern* proves the existence of a problem and then presents a solution (p. 450).

▶ The **refutational organizational pattern** presents the main points of the opposition to an argument and then refutes them (p. 451).

▶ The **comparative advantage pattern** tells why your viewpoint is superior to other viewpoints on the issue (p. 452).

▶ Monroe's *motivated sequence pattern* is a five-step process (p. 453).

INTERVIEWEES are often caught off guard by man-on-the-street interviews.

Marco Brivio/AGE Fotostock

 LearningCurve can help you master the material in this chapter.

Go to **launchpadworks.com**.

appendix

A

Competent Interviewing

Vicente was visiting New York City. One afternoon, a man with a microphone (and a film crew) approached him in Rockefeller Plaza and asked if he had heard of the new *Star Wars* movie, *Star Wars: The Pork Invasion*. Vicente was conflicted. Should he correct the pleasant interviewer? "You mean, *Star Wars: The Force Awakens*?" Or should he play along, politely ignoring the man's ludicrous alternate title for the famous movie? Vicente, like many passersby, became the subject of a comedic man-on-the-street (MOS) interview, in which a short video is used to make something funny out of the response from a (possibly very uninformed) person. Such interviews are random, unscientific samplings of opinion, gathered by stopping people in public places. MOS interviewers ask people to point to France on a map, and they confidently point to Ireland as its location. MOS interviewers ask what interviewees think of California's plan to schedule earthquakes at more convenient times for the population, and they offer their opinions on a plan that does not exist (earthquakes cannot be scheduled!).

While MOS interviews have recently become a staple of comedy shows, serious MOS interviews have been used for years as brief sampling tools in areas such as market testing, public relations, and social marketing. They can be quite effective when they illustrate findings that are documented by scientific polling. Other MOS interviews document impressions and emotions; for example, in the months following the Japanese attack on Pearl Harbor in 1941, MOS interviews conducted across the United States captured the opinions and fears of citizens and remain a powerful historical document today.

At their best and worst, MOS interviews are only one type of interview; however, they illustrate the complexity of this form of communication.

After you have finished
reading this Appendix, you
will be able to

- Define the nature of interviews

- Outline the different types of
interviews

- Describe the three parts of an
interview: opening, questions,
and conclusion

- Devise an interview strategy
from the interviewer's point of
view

- Prepare for the role of
interviewee

- Secure job interviews and
manage them with confidence

How would you have responded to the MOS interviewer? Would you have taken him seriously? Would you risk looking like a fool if you "took the bait" of a bogus question? And how does a MOS interview relate to other interviews—from serious news features to job interviews? Here, we look at interviews from a communication standpoint—how they relate to other forms of communication, what kinds of factors are at work in an interview situation, and how anyone—from recent college graduates to marketing experts, to real and fake news pundits—can improve their interviewing skills.

The Nature of Interviews

Although interviewing is not exactly like grabbing lunch with a friend, the same principles that apply to competent communication in other contexts are also at work in an interview (O'Hair, Friedrich, & Dixon, 2016). There are some differences, however. An **interview** is a transaction that is more structured and goal-driven than other forms of communication (Huffcutt, Culbertson, & Riforgiate, 2015). The communication is deliberate and purposeful for at least one of the parties involved and often involves attempts to influence others.

▶ *Interviews are planned.* At least one of the participants has a predetermined reason for initiating the interview (e.g., to gather information).

▶ *Interviews are goal-driven.* Because a goal exists in advance of the interaction, at least one of the participants plans a strategy for initiating, conducting, and concluding the interview.

▶ *Interviews are structured.* The primary goal of an interview is almost always defined at the beginning of the meeting, unlike most conversations with friends. Interview relationships are more formally structured, and clear status differences often exist. One party usually expects to exert more control than the other.

▶ *Interviews are dyadic.* Like many forms of interpersonal communication, the interview is dyadic, meaning that it involves two parties. In some instances, a "party" consists of more than one person, as when survey researchers conduct group interviews or when job applicants appear before a panel of interviewers. In such situations, even though many individuals are involved, there are only two parties (interviewers and interviewees), each with a role to play.

▶ *Interviews are transactional.* Interviews involve two-way communication in which both parties take turns in speaking and listening roles with a heavy dependence on questions and answers. Even in the listening role, they provide valuable nonverbal feedback.

▶ *Interviews are context-dependent.* Interviews may occur online, on the telephone, via a videoconference, in person, or in the virtual world of avatars (Davis, 2014). These different contexts affect the length, style, and tone of messages that interview participants can send as well as the type of relationship that participants can establish in their exchange (McGuigan, 2011).

Think back to the MOS interviews. They are not only dyadic and transactional but also planned. Questions are written ahead of time and the interviews are structured in a way that helps achieve a goal: a hilarious spoof on selected topics

● **ALL INTERVIEWS,** whether a question-and-answer session on the red carpet or a serious job interview, are goal-driven as well as dyadic and interactive in nature. (left) Kevork Djansezian/Getty Images; (middle top) © The CW/Courtesy Everett Collection; (middle bottom) Creatas/Getty Images; (right) Thomas Barwick/Getty Images

or a chronicle of key responses to an important event. One difference is that the interviewee responses are often distorted or cut off—something you might not expect in other interviews.

Types of Interviews

What type of scene plays out in your mind when you think of the word *interview*? Maybe you think about an upcoming job interview for a position you really want or maybe you remember entrance interviews for college. But interviewing encompasses much more than just getting a job or getting into the right school. In this section, we look at the different types of interviews that play a role in our lives (Stewart & Cash, 2014).

Information-Gathering Interviews

If you watch crime shows like *CSI* or binge-watch past episodes of *True Detective*, you have heard people peppered with questions about where they have been, who they have seen, or what they know. The interviewers are trying to obtain *information* from witnesses and suspects (Jundi, Vrij, Hope, Mann, & Hillman, 2013) by collecting attitudes, opinions, facts, data, and experiences through an **information-gathering interview**. We are exposed to the results of such interviews every day; perhaps you have compiled a survey about experiences with campus parking, listened to recent poll results on a community issue, or interviewed your communication professor about career possibilities. In all these instances, the interview serves to transfer knowledge from one party to the other.

 Service-oriented interviews (also known as helping interviews) are one type of information-gathering interview. Representatives at help desks or customer service lines conduct interviews designed to cull information and provide advice, service, or support based on the information you give them when you think your laptop has water damage or you find unauthorized charges on your credit card bill.

connect

Ethical considerations are important when planning a persuasive interview. As you learned in Chapter 17, there is a difference between persuading people and coercing them with threats. If you are going door to door to support a political candidate, remember that your job is to give people information — not to intimidate or belittle them into supporting your candidate. That is clearly unethical communication.

Many television and radio shows involve interviews dealing with politics, crime, governments, the military, international events, weather, and sports. These **media interviews** seek to get information about people and events and sometimes analyze the information or express opinions and emotions. Through interviewing famous people, TV personality Barbara Walters became famous herself; however, some argue that the big TV interviews she conducted became a thing of the past with her retirement (Mahlermay, 2014). In fact, modern-day journalistic interviews have been criticized for asking "invasive and insensitive questions" designed to confirm the preexisting biases of the interviewer (Kessler, 2014) and for not questioning some of the biases of their interviewees (Jaco, 2014).

Media interviews vary, of course. Some sports interviews with coaches and athletes on the field or court capture a snapshot of their emotions in the heat of a win or defeat, whereas official postgame interviews provide more predictable, controlled answers. Often media interviews occur in the talk-show format. On the Golf Channel's *Feherty,* retired professional golfer David Feherty interviews famous golfers as if they are on *The View, Dr. Phil,* or the *Ellen DeGeneres Show.*

Although all types of interviews involve information gathering to some extent, we look next at other distinct types of interviews.

Persuasive Interviews

If you have ever been confronted by your parents about where you were and why you are late, you know they were after information. However, the pressure and intensity might have made it seem like an **interrogation**. Designed to force information (or confession), interrogation interviews are persuasive; they are designed to pressure the interviewee to give information they are hesitant to share. While interrogations may occur in schools or businesses (e.g., designed to find out who stole something or defaced property), interrogations by the military or police often suffer bad press. Fortunately, interrogations that once were brutal, humiliating, and largely ineffective have been fine-tuned in recent years to secure much more reliable information from suspected terrorists by developing rapport, flattering the detainee, and asking direct questions (Stone, 2015). Similarly, police training in pre-interrogation strategies that focus on building rapport rather than psychologically coercive ones like blaming have had positive results with both adults and juvenile suspects (Cleary & Warner, 2016).

While interrogations involve intense pressure, the goal of most **persuasive interviews** is simply to elicit some change in the interviewee's behavior or opinions. They involve questions aimed at securing support for or against a candidate (political), convincing others to give blood during a campus campaign (volunteer), or requesting money for an organization or cause (philanthropic).

Problem-solving interviews are persuasive in that they influence participants to deal with problems, tensions, or conflicts. In the movie *The Edge of Seventeen* (2016), high school junior Nadine turns to her history teacher for help addressing problems with her older brother, Darian, who is dating her best friend, Krista. By asking questions, giving information, and helping Nadine formulate solutions, her teacher helps her deal with her problems, tensions, and conflicts. Problem-solving interviews can also occur in the workplace, such as when you and your supervisor meet to figure out how you can most effectively work from home during snow days. They may occur in medical situations, when medical professionals meet with families to decide end-of-life care (Johnstone, Hutchinson, Redley, & Rawson, 2016) or when your doctor interviews you about difficulties in your life that may affect your

● **WHEN NADINE STRUGGLES** with Relationships in *The Edge of Seventeen*, her history teacher helps her by taking her through problem-solving interviews. Everett Collection, Inc/Courtesy Everett Collection

physical well-being. Remember that you have a role to play in these interviews, too; preparing problem-solving questions before meeting with your supervisor or your doctor will help you get answers during the interview (Dwamena, Mavis, Holmes-Rovner, Walsh, & Loyson, 2009).

Another type of persuasive interview is the **motivational interview**, which elicits change collaboratively. Here interviewers use questioning that is designed to inspire and strengthen personal motivation (Miller & Rollnick, 2013). Showing acceptance and compassion, interviewers can help interviewees become more confident in their ability to make behavioral changes, for example, to lose weight (Wong & Cheng, 2013), deal with pain (Tse, Vong, & Tang, 2013), avoid high-risk drinking and illicit drug use (Kazemi, Levine, Dmochowski, Nies, & Sun, 2013), quit smoking (Myhre & Adelman, 2013), or develop new strategies for dealing with anger (Murphy, 2013).

Appraisal Interviews

In just about every career — including your academic career — **performance appraisals** are a regular part of reviewing your accomplishments and developing goals for the future. In most corporate environments, performance appraisals are highly structured routines dictated by company policies, involving a written appraisal accompanied by an interview between supervisor and employee. In other less structured performance appraisals, you might meet with your professor to discuss a project or paper or lobby for a change in your grade. Formal appraisals that give only critical, negative feedback do little to improve employee behavior (Asmuß, 2008) and can be very stressful. Effective appraisals will offer insight into strengths as well as weaknesses and help both parties focus on the development of mutual goals for the future (Asmuß, 2013). In other words, if the appraisal interview offers reassurance about what you are doing well and focuses on collaborative goal-setting and continuous improvement, it is less threatening and more useful (Culbert, 2010, 2011).

Exit Interviews

Recruiting and training new people is an expensive process in terms of both time and money, so most organizations want to keep good employees. By conducting **exit interviews** with employees who opt to leave the organization, employers can identify organizational problems — such as poor management style, noncompetitive salary, or weak employee benefits — that might affect employee retention. Your college might conduct an exit interview with you as you graduate to identify the highs and lows of your college experience (and perhaps recruit you for the alumni association).

Exit interviews should be carefully evaluated, as people leaving an organization may hide their true reasons for departing, trying to put a "positive face" on the situation. Also, interviewers may take that information at face value, reporting more confidence back to the organization than is warranted (Gordon, 2011). In fact, leaving an organization requires people to not only physically disengage but also to deal with feelings of ambivalence and an adjustment in identity as they start to focus on their future (Davis & Myers, 2012). These complexities may not be revealed by a standard exit interview.

and you?

Do you think of a problem-solving interview as a reprimand or as an opportunity to create needed changes? How can you change the nature of an interview with a negative tone into a more positive experience?

● **AN EXIT INTERVIEW** provides the chance to voice some of the frustrations you experienced as an employee while letting the employer learn about ways to improve the organization in the future. Eric Audras/ Getty Images

● **ENGAGED COUPLES** might meet with a variety of people and hold selection interviews if they want to hire a wedding planner. Radius Images/Getty Images

connect

The opening of an interview is much like the introduction to a speech. As we discussed in Chapter 14, speech introductions help you achieve four goals: capturing your audience's attention, introducing your purpose, previewing your main points, and connecting with your audience. Openings in both contexts establish the interaction that follows, so your success in engaging your listeners depends on your competency from the start.

Selection Interviews

If you are like most college students, the **selection interview** is probably most relevant to you. The primary goal of a selection interview is to secure or fill a position within an organization and usually involves recruiting, screening, hiring, and placing new candidates (Joyce, 2008; O'Hair, Friedrich, & Dixon, 2016). Additionally, members of an organization (such as a university, company, sorority, fraternity, volunteer agency) and candidates evaluate one another by exchanging information to determine if they would make a good match. Similar exchanges occur between parties choosing a wedding planner, a real estate agent, or a contractor. Usually both parties want to make a good impression: the interviewer wants to persuade the interviewee about the value of the position, the business, or the organization, while the interviewee wants to sell his or her unique qualities and abilities.

The **job interview** is the most common type of selection interview in business, government, military, and other professional organizations, with the end goal of filling a position of employment. Since job interviewing is usually very important to college students, we devote much of this chapter to helping you become more competent in job interviews.

Interview Format

Whether you are interviewing for a job, answering questions for a news reporter, or even watching guests on *The Ellen DeGeneres Show,* you will note the same basic pattern: an opening, the questions, and a conclusion.

The Opening

Talk- or variety-show hosts interview a lot of famous people, who are welcomed with audience clapping and cheering. But if you are not a movie star plugging your latest project, you probably do not have to worry about a big audience response. Whether you are the interviewer or interviewee, your interview will likely begin in a calm manner, setting the tone for the discourse to follow. In fact, many of the interviews on television today are more like conversations, which give the interview a relational quality. As you begin an interview, you should think about three inter-related issues:

▶ The *task:* the nature of this interview and how it will proceed

▶ The *relationship:* whether you like or trust the other party

▶ *Motivation:* what you hope to gain by participating in the interview

For example, Eva is interviewing sales associates for her company. The associates will want to know about the topic of the interview and how long it will take (the task). They want to know something about her and how much she knows about them and their work (the relationship). They want to know how they (or someone else) will benefit from participating in the interview (the motivation). Eva needs to plan what she can say or do at the *start* of the interview to be responsive to these needs (see Table A.1 for examples of opening techniques).

Goal	Description	Example
Clarify the *task*	Orient the interviewee, who may not be well informed about the reason for the interview.	"As you may know, we're looking for ways to increase productivity among our sales associates. I'm hoping you will help me jump-start this initiative."
Define the *relationship*	Make a connection to a respected third party to put the interviewee at ease.	"I was referred to you by Liam Fitzpatrick, who told me that you've done great work for him in the past."
Determine the *motivation*	Request the interviewee's advice or assistance with an issue.	"Perhaps you can give me insight into how the company might help you and other associates do your job even better than you already do."

evaluating communication ethics

Surveys: Interviewing at Large

Imagine that you are an officer in your college's alumni association. You have been asked to interview other alumni to contribute to marketing materials that will help increase the number and quality of students applying to your school. Your association wants to show how much graduates enjoyed their school experience and how well they have succeeded in their careers.

You produce a simple one-page survey that asks alumni to rate their school and their postgraduate experience from poor to excellent. You plan to mail the survey to everyone listed in the alumni register. You are hoping to produce marketing materials noting the high percentage of graduates who rate their experience as "excellent." But when you submit your plan and survey draft to the alumni association, you are shot down. "We don't want to hear from everyone," says the alumni president. "We only want to hear from successful graduates who are working at *Fortune* 500 companies or who have made big names for themselves in the sciences."

You are asked instead to create an in-depth survey and conduct it by phone with graduates who have donated $1,000 or more to the school in the past five years. You know that this will skew the results of your survey toward alumni who love the school and who have been financially successful since graduating. The association is asking you to present this information as though these alumni are representative of all graduates when they only represent a minority. You know that many graduates have gone on to successful and fulfilling, if less lucrative, careers in education and the arts. You are hesitant to conduct a survey that will paint an inaccurate picture of the school for prospective students. What should you do?

think about this

1. Does your plan for a survey of all graduates present a more accurate picture of the school than a telephone survey with only the wealthiest graduates?

2. What about students who attended the school but did not graduate or who are not in the alumni rolls? Should they be part of your survey as well?

3. Does it really matter? Remember, this survey is for material to be used in marketing. Will prospective students automatically infer that every student at the school goes on to a high-profile, six- or seven-figure salary career?

The Questions

Once you have set the stage with an appropriate opening by identifying the purpose of the interview and how it will proceed, you need to develop the questions that structure the interview. A response is solicited from the interviewee, which then prompts reactions from the interviewer. To have the most effective and most successful interview possible, whether you are the interviewer or interviewee, you need to understand question type, impact, and sequence.

● **PROSPECTIVE STUDENTS** on a campus tour should ask their student guides open questions ("What's the social scene like?") and closed questions ("Is the dining hall open on the weekends?") to figure out what student life is *really* like. AP Photo/The News-Gazette, Robin Scholz

Types of Questions

Questions structure the interview and vary in two distinct ways: the amount of freedom the respondent has and how the questions relate to what has happened in the course of the interview.

First, questions vary in terms of how much leeway the interviewee has in generating responses. An **open question** gives the interviewee great freedom in terms of how to respond. Questions like "What's it like being a student here?" and "What issues will influence your vote in this election?" allow the interviewee to determine the amount and depth of information provided. Interviewers often ask open questions when the interviewee knows more about a topic than the interviewer does or to help the interviewee relax (there is no "correct" answer, so no answer is wrong).

Closed questions, on the other hand, give less freedom to the interviewee by being direct and limiting answers to specific choices. For example, an interviewer conducting a survey of student attitudes toward parking on campus might ask, "Do you usually arrive on campus in the morning, afternoon, or evening?" or "Do you use the parking structure or nearby lots?" The simplest form of a closed question is the **bipolar question**, for which there are only two possible responses, "yes" and "no" ("Do you normally eat breakfast?" "Do you own a car?" "Did you vote in the last election?"). To allow for more variation in their answers, interviewees can be asked to respond to a scale, as with the question, "How would you rate parking availability on campus?"

1	2	3	4	5
Very poor	Poor	Adequate	Good	Excellent

Questions also vary in terms of how they relate to what has happened so far in the interview. **Primary questions** introduce new topics; **secondary questions** seek clarification or elaboration of primary question responses. For example, if you are interviewing an older family member, you might open by asking "What can you tell me about my family history?" This primary question might be followed by a number of secondary questions, such as "How did my grandparents meet?" and "How did they deal with their parents' disapproval of their marriage?" Some of the more common forms of secondary questions are illustrated in Table A.2.

Question Impact

In addition to considering question type, interviewers must also consider the potential impact that the question structure might have on the interviewee's response. A good question is clear, relevant, and civil. To create clear questions that generate productive responses, consider the following criteria:

▶ Make questions understandable. Ask the classic and simple news reporter's questions of who, what, when, where, why, and how before you proceed to more complex ones.

▶ Ensure that the wording is direct and simple, so that interviewees know exactly what you are asking. For example, asking, "For whom did you vote in the last mayoral election?" will get you a more precise answer than asking, "How do you vote?"

▶ Keep the questions short and to the point.

TABLE A.2

SECONDARY QUESTIONS

Behavior	Definition	Example
Clarification	Directly requests more information	"Could you tell me more about the reasons you chose to join the military after high school?"
Elaboration	Extends the request for a response	"Can you remember any specific difficult moments with customers when you worked as a sales clerk?"
Paraphrasing	Rephrases the questioner's response to establish understanding	"So you're saying that the type of people you work with is more important to you than location?"
Encouragement	Uses brief sounds and phrases to indicate attentiveness and interest	"Uh-huh," "I see," "That's interesting," "Good," "Yes, I understand."
Summarizing	Pulls together major points and seeks confirmation of correctness	"Let's see if I've got it: your ideal job involves working in a metropolitan area with an appreciative boss, supportive colleagues, and interesting work?"
Clearinghouse	Asks if you have elicited all the important or available information	"Have you had a chance to tell me all you wanted?"

Information from D. O'Hair, G. W. Friedrich, & L. D. Dixon (2016).

▶ Phrase questions positively and remain civil (Ben-Porath, 2010). For example, asking, "Have you voted in campus student government elections?" is objective and nonjudgmental; "You haven't ever voted in the campus student government elections, have you?" uses negative phrasing and, in addition to being confusing, sounds accusatory and biased.

Competent interviewers not only use questions that are clear, relevant, and positive, but they *avoid* questions that aim to advance hidden agendas. **Directed questions** suggest or imply an answer. If the direction is subtle ("Wouldn't it be fun if we all got together to paint my apartment this weekend?"), it is termed a **leading question**. Other directed questions are bolder in their biasing effect and are called **loaded questions** ("When was the last time you cheated on an exam?" assumes, of course, that you *have* cheated). **Neutral questions**, on the other hand, avoid directing interviewees by providing no hint concerning the expected response ("What is your opinion of the administration on this campus?"). (See Table A-3 for more examples of directed versus neutral questions.)

Question Sequence

The order in which the questions are asked can affect both the accomplishment of the interviewer's goals and the comfort level of the interviewee. There are three main "shapes" that guide the ordering of questions: the funnel, inverted funnel, and tunnel sequences (Figure A.1).

In the **funnel sequence**, the interviewer starts with broad, open-ended questions (picture the big end of a funnel) to maximize the person's response and moves to narrower, more specific questions to clarify the answer and fill in missing information. The funnel sequence works best with respondents who feel at ease with the topic and the interviewer.

▶ "What do you think about children playing physical contact sports?" (general)

connect

Even neutral questions can become leading questions if you fail to consider nonverbal communication (Chapter 5). If you grimace, roll your eyes, or change your tone of voice when you ask the neutral question, "What, if anything, is your attitude toward fraternities and sororities on this campus?" you are actually asking a leading question (and letting others know your attitude toward the Greek system on campus).

real communicator

NAME: Cynthia Guadalupe Inda
OCCUPATION: Trial Attorney
Courtesy Cynthia Inda

When I mention that I'm a lawyer, many people are surprised to learn that I spend a great deal of time interviewing people. In fact, I like to think of my job as asking questions and culling information in ways similar to talk-show hosts, counselors, and reporters.

When I was with a district attorney's office, my biggest challenge was interviewing many witnesses for the dozens of cases I was assigned in a limited amount of time. In order to do my job effectively, I needed to interview all the witnesses quickly and efficiently — but not make them feel rushed.

The talk-show host aspect of my job is putting people at ease during an interview. People are often intimidated by lawyers, so I look people in the eye, smile, and try to be as down-to-earth as possible (like I do in my personal life). When dealing with Spanish-speaking witnesses, I always conduct interviews in Spanish. I find that this typically helps to put them at ease because the courtroom doesn't seem as foreign and intimidating when you are introduced to it by someone who also speaks your native language.

The counselor aspect of my job is having empathy for people's situations. I often tell people who are afraid to bring charges or get involved in any way that I understand their fear and reticence and encourage them to just tell the judge exactly what they are telling me. If an interviewee is very upset, I'll often switch the subject away from the task at hand; I get them talking about themselves instead of the law. They usually relax and it makes it easier to get back to the interview questions.

The reporter aspect of my job is in culling information from my interviewees to focus on what is essential to the case. Preparation really matters here. When I have witnesses on the stand, my questions are targeted toward the achievement of a goal. I ask open-ended questions, but I also have a series of background and clarifying questions to help make my point. When I'm cross-examining a witness, however, my questions are much more closed: I try to ask only questions that call for "yes" or "no" responses. The facts established by the "yes" or "no" answers I'm searching for give less credibility to the opposition's case.

Effective interviewing skills are crucial to my professional success and the well-being of my clients. Interviewing is not all work — I have fun getting to know people and helping them achieve justice.

▶ "What particular dangers are you concerned about?" (specific)

▶ "Have you witnessed any children getting concussions or breaking bones?" (very specific)

The **inverted funnel sequence** starts with narrow, closed questions and moves to more open-ended questions. The inverted funnel works best with interviewees who are emotional or reticent and need help "warming up."

TABLE A.3

LEADING, LOADED, AND NEUTRAL QUESTIONS

Question Behavior	Definition	Example
Leading	Questions that subtly direct interviewees to the correct or desired answer	"Do you take home office supplies, like most employees?"
Loaded	Extremely leading questions that almost dictate a "guilty" answer	"When was the last time you took home supplies from the office?"
Neutral	Questions that allow respondents to answer without pressure from the interviewer's wording	"Do you think the office should provide you with supplies to work at home?"

- ▸ "Did you perform a Mozart piece for your high school piano recital?" (very specific)

- ▸ "What other classical compositions are you comfortable playing?" (specific)

- ▸ "What was your experience taking classical piano lessons as a child?" (general)

In the **tunnel sequence**, all the questions are at one level. The tunnel sequence works particularly well in polls and surveys. A large tunnel would involve a series of broad, open-ended questions. A small tunnel (the more common form) would ask a series of narrow, closed questions, as in the following example:

- ▸ "Have you attended any multicultural events on campus?" (specific)

- ▸ "Have you attended any sporting events?" (specific)

- ▸ "Have you attended any guest lectures?" (specific)

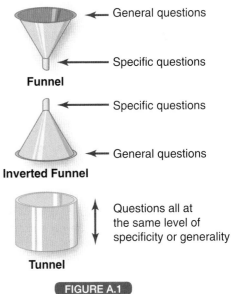

FIGURE A.1

FUNNEL, INVERTED FUNNEL, AND TUNNEL SEQUENCES

The Conclusion

Once the purpose of the interview has been achieved, the interaction should come to a comfortable and satisfying close. This phase of the interview is especially important because it often determines the impression the interviewee retains of the entire interview.

There are important norms involved when individuals take leave of each other, so in closing the interview, the interviewer needs to employ both verbal and nonverbal strategies to serve three important functions (Von Raffler-Engel, 1983):

- ▸ To *conclude,* or signal the end of the interview

- ▸ To *summarize,* or review the substantive conclusions produced by the interview

- ▸ To *support*, or express satisfaction with the interaction and project what will happen next

Table A.4 illustrates closing strategies to help you conclude, summarize, and support. As these sample statements indicate, bringing the interview to a close is largely the responsibility of the interviewer. In the next section, we look at how this and other responsibilities fall to the interviewer and interviewee.

Roles and Responsibilities in Interviews

Jan, a thirty-year-old high school biology teacher, is seeking a new career. She can approach this job hunt in two ways. First, she could simply answer advertisements for open positions and hope to be called in for an interview. Alternatively, she could identify people or organizations that she thinks she would like to work for and arrange for information-gathering interviews with them. In the first approach, Jan, the job hunter, fills the role of *interviewee*—she answers questions posed by the interviewer. In the second example, Jan acts as the *interviewer*, asking people in various positions for information about potential career paths in their industry.

TABLE A.4

CLOSING STRATEGIES

Behavior	Definition	Example
Declare the completion of the purpose or task.	The word *well* signals a close; people assume the end is near and prepare to take their leave.	"Well, we've covered a lot of territory today."
Signal that time for the meeting is up.	Remind interviewees of the time limit announced in the opening of the interview. Avoid abruptness so they don't feel pushed along an assembly line.	"We have just a few minutes left, so. . . ."
Explain the reason for the closing.	Explain real reasons to avoid strain in future interactions.	"Unfortunately, I've got another meeting in fifteen minutes, so we'll have to start wrapping things up."
Express appreciation or satisfaction.	Thank the interviewee for information, help, a sale, a story, employment, and so on.	"Thank you for your interest in our cause."
Plan for the next meeting.	Reveal what will happen next (date, time, place, topic, content, purpose) or arranges for the next interview.	"We should follow up on this next week; my assistant will call you to arrange a time."
Summarize the interview.	Repeat important information, solidify agreements, or verify accuracy.	"We've come to three major agreements here today." (List them briefly.)

Information from C. J. Stewart & W. B. Cash, Jr. (2014).

So how are these roles different? How are they similar? Let's find out (Stewart & Cash, 2014).

Interviewer Responsibilities

In any interview situation, competent interviewers have at least four responsibilities: they must (1) identify potential barriers, (2) make the interviewee comfortable, (3) ask ethical and appropriate questions, and (4) effectively listen and respond to the interviewee.

Identify Potential Barriers

Before heading into an interview situation, interviewers should take time to eliminate barriers that might disrupt the interview. For example, is the location quiet, private and tidy? Is lighting adequate, is the room appropriate to the interview purpose, and is enough time allotted to complete the interview satisfactorily? If not, make those adjustments before the interview begins.

Make the Interviewee Comfortable

Interviewees, particularly job applicants and medical patients, are often very nervous in interview situations — and understandably so. A good interviewer should adapt to the situational and relational contexts to help the interviewee feel at ease (Ralston, Kirkwood, & Burant, 2003). It would be effective and appropriate, for example, for an interviewer to smile, make eye contact, and offer a handshake. But be sure to keep these behaviors appropriate to the context; imagine how inappropriate it would be if your doctor entered the examining room and gave you a big hug or if a job interviewer told you about his problems with his partner's parents.

Ask Ethical and Appropriate Questions

Although questions and question sequences can result in productive interviews, it is important to remember that good questions are also ethical and appropriate

and you?

Have you ever been asked unethical, biased, or uncivil questions? Did you ever, knowingly or unknowingly, use these types of questions yourself? How can you deal with questions like these if you find yourself in that uncomfortable position?

(and avoid the leading and loaded questions discussed earlier). For example, if Erik is a representative from his school newspaper interviewing a biology professor about her recent grant from the National Institutes of Health (NIH), his questions should stick to her research and her plans to implement a new lab on campus. It would be inappropriate for him to ask how much money she personally will be receiving from the NIH or whether she expects to receive a promotion and salary increase from the university after receiving the award.

On a job interview, certain unethical and inappropriate questions are also unlawful. We cover these later in this chapter.

● **MANY INTERVIEWS** use standing up or a handshake to indicate the completion of the interview. Your interview should also have a simple, comfortable conclusion. sturti/Getty Images

Listen and Respond Effectively

The role of the interviewer is not limited to structuring an interview and asking questions. After all, an effective interviewer needs to listen, respond, and evaluate the information that those questions reveal. Throughout the interview, the interviewer should keep both immediate and future goals in mind by making notes (written or mental) during the interview.

Interviewee Responsibilities

The interviewer is responsible for quite a bit of work in an interview situation, but the interviewee should also take on three major responsibilities: (1) clarifying personal goals, (2) being prepared, and (3) listening and responding effectively.

Clarify and Fulfill Personal Goals

One of the most important things that an interviewee can bring to the interview is a clear sense of personal goals. If you have a clear idea of what *you* want to achieve in the interview, you will feel less anxious; you can then look for opportunities to advance your goals by noticing specific openings in the conversation where you might give personal examples that advance your cause. Be assertive, don't exaggerate, and show interest and warmth in the other person (Feiler & Powell, 2016).

Prepare Yourself Responsibly

Your school's career services office and your previous employment situations have likely prepared you for the fact that you will need to draft a résumé and a cover letter in advance of a job interview, but all interviews benefit from some preparation.

For one thing, you want to be well rested and alert. From personal experience, we urge you not to skip meals — more than a few of our students have had growling stomachs during interviews. You also want to consider the context and be dressed appropriately for the occasion; this is especially important for official job interviews, where you should match or exceed the dress policy at that place of business. Also remember to plan what you should bring with you to the interview: copies of your résumé to a job interview, for example, or your medical history to an interview with a new doctor.

and you?

Have you ever been in an interview where you felt that the interviewer neglected his or her responsibilities? In what ways did the interviewer fail? How would you have handled things differently?

● **THE KIND OF JOB** you are interviewing for dictates how to dress. For an interview with the typically more conservative finance industry, you will need a suit. For an interview at an art gallery, you *might* wear a more casual outfit. (top) Simon Watson/Getty Images; (bottom) Garo / Phanie / Superstock

connect

Consider the relational context in competent communication (Chapter 1). It is effective and appropriate to respond differently to the same question posed by your doctor, your mother, your boss, and your romantic partner. How intimate you are with the person, your relational history, what you know about him or her, and status differences between you have a profound effect on the interview situation.

Listen and Respond Effectively

Just as interviewers must listen and respond effectively, so must the interviewee. For example, in a performance appraisal, be ready to ethically highlight your individual achievements or contributions when your boss asks you to assess your own performance.

Shared Responsibilities

Both interviewer and interviewee share in the responsibility to adapt to each other and the interview situation appropriately—both verbally and nonverbally. If a professor in your department is interviewing you to see if you would be a good fit for the honors program, you would typically treat the interview quite formally by using a professional, formal address when speaking to the professor ("Dr. Edmunds"). But if you have known this professor for three years, you babysit her children, and she insists that you call her Emilia, you can adapt, feeling free to use her first name and a less strict, more personal style of conversation.

If the interview takes place in a conference room with multiple interviewers, the interviewee can adapt by making appropriate eye contact with each of the interviewers and behaving more formally. But this also depends on the situation. If you are applying to become a barista, and are interviewing on a bench outside the coffee shop, you can consider the situation less formal. In this case, you also need to avoid distractions from the people and noise around you. Additionally, many interviews today are computer-mediated; online data collection has the potential to both strengthen and complement other datasets with its speed and reach, but the relational aspects of a face-to-face interview are missing (Curasi, 2001; James & Busher, 2009; Josselson, 2013),

Culture also plays a role in job interview situations (Gardner, Reithel, Foley, Cogliser, & Walumbwa, 2009), affecting both judgments and evaluations (Manroop, Boekhorst, & Harrison, 2013). Non-native accents, for example, may be difficult to understand and may negatively impact the interview situation unless the parties spend initial time establishing rapport to increase attraction and understandability (Deprez-Sims & Morris, 2010, 2013). Another cultural factor influencing job interviews is the willingness to talk directly about accomplishments. People from some ethnic and religious backgrounds may consider such talk to be inappropriately boastful. For example, research shows that rather than clearly state a strength ("I have extremely strong organizational skills"), African-American interviewees often tell stories about themselves to illustrate their strengths. However, because European-American interviewers often judge storytelling candidates to be "unfocused," African Americans who adapt by directly listing their strengths for a job are perceived more positively in interviews (Hecht, Jackson, & Ribeau, 2003). Conversely, a European-American interviewer who looks for the message behind the interviewee's story has competently adapted as well. In fact, many job interviewers now recognize the advantages of behavioral questions ("Tell me about a time when you handled a problem successfully") rather than a trait-type question ("Are you a problem solver?") because they offer more insight into the person and their potential ("Identify soft skills when hiring," 2016).

The Job Interview

While job interviews involve many of the competent behaviors you have already learned in this text, from audience adaptation to language choice to nonverbal communication (Bloch, 2011), reminding yourself of these behaviors before you go into the interview will greatly increase your confidence and performance. In the

communication across cultures

think about this

Cultural Competence in Social Work

If you ever find yourself struggling — economically, emotionally, or physically — there is someone who can help. In hospitals, schools, government agencies, and nonprofits, social workers are often the point people for individuals in need of health care, mental health services, social support, or simply assistance in navigating large bureaucratic systems such as immigration or the legal system.

Social workers first assess client needs by asking questions and listening to answers. Just about every aspect of the social worker's responsibilities depends on skillful interviewing (Kadushin & Kadushin, 2013). A mother who does not wish to leave the hospital after delivering her baby, for example, might say that she does not feel well. But a skilled social worker will explore further to consider other factors that might be impacting the mother's decision, such as postpartum depression, family violence, physical condition of the home, fear of parenting, lack of social support to care for the child, or economic uncertainty. Only if social workers can identify these concerns will they be able to link the mother with resources and services to ensure a healthy and safe situation for the family.

In this role, cultural competence is essential. A social worker seeking to help an undocumented immigrant who is the victim of a crime, for example, will often face language barriers that can make communication difficult. Fear of deportation may make the accused client reluctant to seek assistance. The client may worry that testifying in court will put his or her job in jeopardy; in cases of sexual assault, culturally bound gender expectations can make it difficult for some clients to speak frankly about what happened (Clarke, 2014).

1. If you were admitted into a hospital for extended care, would you be able to have a frank discussion with a social worker about your own medical history? What about your sexual history? Is your ability to speak openly culturally bound?

2. How can social workers pay attention to salient cultural factors without resorting to stereotyping their clients based on culture or gender?

3. For social workers, which is more important: Asking the right questions or listening to and interpreting answers? How important are follow-up questions?

remaining pages of this chapter, we describe how job interviews usually occur and offer solid advice on how to prepare for, engage in, and follow up on the process (Muir, 2008).

Get the Interview

The first step involves actually getting the interview. This important phase involves three interrelated tasks: locating jobs and doing homework on the organizations, preparing materials to be used in the process (the résumé and cover letter), and building realistic expectations about the interviewing process.

Search for a Position

The first element of preinterview preparation involves identifying potential jobs and then researching the field and the organizations. Although there are many strategies for locating jobs, your three best sources are likely to be people you know or manage to meet, placement centers, and discipline-specific job sites.

A great place to start is with family, friends, professors, former employers, and individuals working in your field of interest. You should also plan to network (Brazeel, 2009). **Networking** is the process of using interconnected groups or associations of persons you know to develop relationships with their connections that you do not know. Contact the people you know who work in your field or who might know someone who does, let these individuals know the kind of job you are looking for, and ask for suggestions. You can also make

● **PREPARING YOUR MATERIALS,** practicing sample answers, and dressing for the interview will help maximize your confidence and performance. (left) Kevin Dodge/Getty Images; (right) claudiobaba/Getty Images

● **THERE ARE** many different avenues that you can explore when you begin your job hunt. Industry-specific magazines like *Variety*, job placement centers, and employment websites are all good places to start. (left) Variety Media, LLC; (top right) Courtesy of careeronestop.org; (bottom right) Bloomberg/Getty Images

connect

Preparing for a job interview is similar to preparing for a speech. In Chapter 13, we suggested studying your audience to know how to present information they will find useful and interesting; in a job interview, you must do the same. Your goal is to learn about the organization's culture (Chapter 12): Is it a formal or informal place? What does the organization value? This information helps you adapt your communication competently and impress a hiring manager.

new contacts via social networking services (Fieseler, Meckel, & Müller, 2014). Use social media like Facebook for more informal networking and professional sites like LinkedIn for more formal connections. You also can network efficiently through an organization for professionals in your chosen field (many offer student memberships). Whichever connections you make, be sure to remind your contacts of how you met or why you are getting in touch.

Placement centers are another source of jobs. Most college campuses have a centralized placement center where recruiters from major companies come to interview potential employees. And don't forget print media and internet-based publications; search for career-specific publications that will help you better focus on your chosen career path, such as *Media Career Guide: Preparing for Jobs in the 21st Century* (Culver & Seguin, 2013).

Finally, start looking for specific job openings. Although general employment websites (like Monster.com) can be starting places, they may not yield significant results simply because they attract a large number of applicants (O'Loughlin, 2016); you have less chance of being noticed in a pool of a thousand (or more) than in one of a hundred. A more productive search uses sites that cater to specific industries or even a particular organization's site. For example, mediabistro.com and entertainmentcareers.net focus on jobs in the media and entertainment industries, respectively. You can also find job postings on the websites of most major companies and organizations (look for links to "Careers" or "Employment"). Consider using job information and posting aggregators (such as LexisNexis) that will let you set criteria or parameters for the types or even geographic locations of positions you want. Doing so will put you in touch with sites that have less traffic and give you a better chance of being noticed.

Prepare Your Materials

Once you have identified potential jobs, you need to contact the people who are in a position to hire you. As a job applicant, the crucial first impression you make on a potential employer will likely be via your written materials—a formal cover letter and résumé. In this section, we show you how to prepare these materials so that they communicate the right message about you (Ding & Ding, 2013).

But first, a cautionary note: *before* you send off these written materials, make sure you have cleaned up any searchable information that does not portray you in a favorable light (Brandenburg, 2008; Holson, 2010). If you use social networking sites, adjust your privacy settings to ensure that you have not been, and cannot be, tagged in any photographs that you would not want a potential employer to see and that the details of your profile are not visible to anyone other than your approved friends. Perform searches for your name and email address to make sure that any comments you have left on public forums or chat rooms do not come back to haunt you. Consider also asking your friends to search and review your sites for negative information.

The résumé. Begin by pulling together a **résumé**—a printed summary of your education, work experience, and accomplishments (see Figure A.2). It is a vehicle for making a positive first impression on potential employers. An effective résumé

---

wired for communication

Pre-Presenting Yourself: Your Online Persona

Savvy job applicants prepare for a job interview by doing an internet search to learn about potential employers, from benefits to corporate culture. But inexperienced job hunters often fail to realize that those searches go both ways. As easily as you Google a company name, a potential employer does a search on you. You might have a fantastic résumé and the most professional suit for your first interview, but what you have posted on social media, discussion board blogs, or internet pages might very well be the most important factor in shaping the first impression you make on a potential employer. Research suggests that more than three-quarters of employers Google candidates' names when seeking to fill positions (Levit, 2010).

Consider one president of a small company looking to hire a summer intern. When he came across a promising candidate, he did a quick online check that included his Facebook page. There, the candidate described his interests in marijuana use, shooting people, and obsessive sex. That the student was clearly exaggerating did not matter: his lack of judgment regarding what to say about himself publicly took him out of the running for the position (Finder, 2006). Prevent potential employer access to negative information by Googling yourself. One man doing this found an essay he had posted on a student website a few years prior, called "Lying Your Way to the Top." Only after he had it removed did he begin getting calls (Finder, 2006).

In addition to cleaning up whatever indiscretions may exist online, savvy candidates will take advantage of the internet to cultivate an impression that is professional and impressive. Create a profile on professional sites like LinkedIn and CareerRocket and post relevant comments on highly-read blogs with links back to your own professional sites. As you develop your online presence more thoroughly, it can be helpful to make use of search engine optimization tools that will improve your Google ranking (Levit, 2010). By eliminating content you do not want employers to see, and creating content that you do want them to see, you can ensure your online presence is as impressive as your résumé.

think about this

1. Take a moment to Google yourself. Search not only for your name but also your email address. What comes up?

2. Do you have a Facebook page or Twitter feed? Think objectively about the impression that your posts to these sites convey. Would you hire you?

3. Have you been known to comment on news items or blogs in ways that might reveal your personal opinions? Do you think it is ethical for employers to be looking at your postings?

4. How can you create a better online image for yourself?

tells just enough about you to make employers believe they need your skills and experience, so it does not need to include everything about you since age ten (Herman, 2016). Your résumé should be one page, formatted clearly, and presented in a clean font like Helvetica (Kitroeff, 2015).

No two résumés look exactly alike, but most should contain the following general information:

▶ *Contact information.* Include a permanent address, phone number, and both your email and LinkedIn contacts. Make sure that your voice mail greets callers with a clear, professional message, and check it often. If you have an odd or cute address for your regular email (partygirl@provider.com, numberonedad@ provider.net), consider opening another account with a more serious name for your professional communication.

▶ *Employment objective.* Be concise and specific about what you are looking for in a position and what your career goals are. If you are applying for several types of jobs, you should create multiple résumés tailored to specific positions. Often a software program will be applied to your résumé before any human sees it, so use concrete descriptions of the relevant professional skills and competencies

FIGURE A.2
SAMPLE RÉSUMÉ

Valerie Roses
111 A Street, Apt. 2C, Lafayette, IN 47901
(765) 375-7111

val.roses@serviceprovider.com • LinkedIn.com: Valerie Z. Roses

OBJECTIVE
To obtain an entry-level marketing/advertising position where I can use my strong research and writing skills while expanding my knowledge of marketing and advertising processes.

EDUCATION
Purdue University, *West Lafayette, IN*   2013–2017
    Bachelor of Arts, Communication, May 2017   GPA: 3.7/4.0
    Honors: Recipient, Lamb Scholar (2016); Member, Lambda Pi Eta honor society.

RELATED WORK EXPERIENCE
Intern, Bohlsen Gp, PR, *Indianapolis, IN*   *Fall 2016–present*
    Researched and compiled media distribution lists to retail locations. Drafted e-marketing messages for social media. Assisted staff in writing press releases and strategy documents.
Marketing assistant, A Marketing, Indianapolis, *IN*   *Summer 2016*
    Analyzed consumer data from company databases. Helped evaluate marketing data for campaign design and feasibility. Drafted client cost comparisons and accountability documents.
Tutor, Communication Lab, *Purdue University*   *Fall 2014–Spring 2016*
    Assisted students in preparing speeches, outlines, and visual aids. Counseled students regarding sources for speeches and papers. Reviewed speech delivery.

SKILLS AND INTERESTS
Languages: Fluent in English; proficient in written and conversational Spanish

Computer: Word, Excel, PowerPoint, FileMaker Pro, internet research

you possess (Fertik & Thompson, 2015). When your résumé gets to a live person, he or she will usually infer your professional knowledge, interpersonal skills, and general mental ability from your résumé (Chen, Huang, & Lee, 2011). Choose your words carefully.

▶ *Education.* List the institutions you have attended, their locations, and the dates of attendance. List degrees received (or expected), academic majors, and areas of concentration. Awards and GPA can be listed *if* they enhance your marketability.

▶ *Work experience.* If your work experiences are all in the same area, list them in reverse chronological order (most recent ones first), focusing on concrete examples of achievement or skills that you have mastered. Explain job functions as well as titles. Remember that prospective employers read this section carefully to discover how your experience, abilities, and achievements relate to their organization's needs. You can make this easier for them with a clear and organized presentation of yourself—so there is usually no need to include long-past jobs that have no relevance to your current job search.

▶ *Activities.* For some employers, participation in a variety of academic, extracurricular, or social activities indicates that you are motivated and get involved. Include only activities that you can link clearly to your career objective, emphasizing accomplishments and leadership roles.

▶ *Special skills.* Do you speak fluent Spanish? Are you skilled in a particular programming language? Have you managed a charity race in your community? Don't be shy—let potential employers know this information if your accomplishments show dedication and determination that may be useful to the organization.

▶ *References.* Your references are typically professors, previous supervisors, or anyone else who can confirm your employment history and attest to your work ethic and character. Some organizations want you to include your references (with current contact information) with your résumé; others will ask for those once you get your first interview (Joyce, 2008). Be sure your references have agreed to vouch for you, and note the availability of references in your cover letter or résumé.

Once your résumé is complete, take some time to prepare it for electronic submission. Make sure it is readable on all platforms by saving it as a pdf document. This will mean that employers can read it regardless of what type of computer they have. You should also name the file carefully, so that employers will be able to identify it easily. Include your name (or just your last name) in the file title, along with the word *résumé* and perhaps a date (e.g., *RosesRésumé Jan2017.pdf*).

The cover letter. Whenever you send your résumé to a potential employer, it should be accompanied by a formal **cover letter** (see Figure A.3), a one-page letter indicating your interest in a specific position. The cover letter gives you the opportunity to express how you learned of the position and the organization, how your skills and interests can benefit the organization, and why you are interested in applying for this particular job. Because a cover letter also serves as a means by which you can demonstrate your written communication skills, make sure that you use correct grammar, punctuation, and spelling and a clean font. Proofread carefully!

Some prospective employers accept emails as cover letters. When you email a hiring manager or a human resources representative at an organization, include the same information as you would in a cover letter. If you are unsure of the protocol, it is always best to be more formal and include/attach an official cover letter along

and you?

Is your résumé up to date, in preparation for any unexpected opportunities? How might pulling together a solid résumé be beneficial even when you are not on the job hunt?

111 A Street, Apt. 2C
Lafayette, IN 47901

June 7, 2017
Joaquin Bennet
V.P. of Digital Strategy
Next Decade Marketing
8888 Keystone Crossing
Indianapolis, IN 46240

Dear Mr. Bennet:

   I was excited to see the posting for a junior marketing assistant position with Next Decade Marketing. I admire your organization's dedication to your clients and your vow to manage their marketing dollars effectively. I would be honored to interview for the position that would allow me to use my creative and analytical skills to further your mission.

   My experience with two different marketing companies has strengthened my knowledge of marketing practices and given me insight into the campaign options that meet the client's goals and budget; I have demonstrated my teamwork and collaboration skills in both companies. I bring solid writing and editing skills to this position as well as strong presentation skills.

   In addition, the many research classes I took at Purdue prepared me to design and analyze consumer data and apply the results to marketing campaigns. By critically observing the client and the situation, I have leveraged my intern experiences to give me hands-on experience with our data-driven world.

   I have included my résumé as requested in the job posting and can provide references as required. I look forward to discussing my experiences and perspectives with you in person. I can be contacted at val.roses@serviceprovider.com; at LinkedIn.com: Valerie Z. Roses; or by phone at (765) 375-7111. Thank you for your kind consideration.

Sincerely,

Val Roses

Val Roses

with your email. Be sure to include a subject line (e.g., Roses marketing position application) and proofread your email carefully before you press "Send."

Build Realistic Expectations

The final component of job hunting involves developing realistic expectations about the process. Because only a few résumés will make it through the screening process, and you will not be the only candidate called for an interview, you will likely face rejection at least once during the course of a job search—either because there was a better-qualified applicant or because an equally qualified candidate had some advantage (such as a personal contact in the company). Remember that rejection is common—the inevitable result of a tight job market and a less-than-perfect selection process. Perseverance pays. If you approach the job search intelligently and persistently, you will eventually get a job (Rampell, 2013).

Conduct the Interview

After a diligent job search, you have finally been called for an interview. Now what? Well, now you impress the socks off your interviewer by making your best first impression, preparing for and anticipating different types of questions, preparing questions of your own, and following up after your interview.

Make a Good First Impression

Salina, who works in a nonprofit organization, interviewed a candidate who came forty-five minutes late to the interview. To make matters worse, he explained his tardiness by noting that he had to "run home" to get his mom to help him with his tie. Later, Salina had a phone interview with a young woman who did not bother to ensure that she had adequate cell phone reception, meaning that the question "What did you say?" dominated the conversation. What these candidates did not realize is that the interview is a communication transaction that begins with impressions that can set the stage for the rest of the interview.

In any interview, both verbal and nonverbal behaviors contribute to a good first impression. As you prepare for the interview, review your impression-management skills to help your actual performance (Kleinmann & Klehe, 2011). Practice expansive and open "power poses" beforehand to remind yourself of the power of your nonverbal behaviors to communicate enthusiasm and confidence (Cuddy, Wilmuth, Yap, & Carney, 2015). You can also prepare mentally—for example, remembering a personal experience in which you were powerful or took control will result in stronger impressions in the interview (Lammers, Dubois, Rucker, & Galinsky, 2013). Choose words that will communicate how you are flexible and adaptable—the two criteria employers consider most important in a job candidate (followed by willingness to learn, loyalty, and self-reliance; Iva & Eliška, 2016).

In a more practical sense, try to control the things you can at the outset. Give yourself plenty of extra time to get there so that if something comes up (traffic, a stalled train) you will still make it on time. Have your clothing ready ahead of time. If it is a phone (or Skype) interview, make sure your equipment

connect

In Chapter 15, you learned that communication apprehension is a general fear of real or anticipated communication with a person or persons. Speaking before an audience causes anxiety for many people — and so does speaking with a hiring manager. To make sure anxiety doesn't adversely affect your communication, try some of our suggestions for building confidence (Chapter 14), such as performance visualization and preparing for the unexpected.

● **COMEDIAN DANA CARVEY** uses nonverbal behaviors and vocal impressions to make impressions of people in the public eye — not usually flattering! Ethan Miller/Getty Images

(e.g., computer, cell phone) are charged and have a strong connection (Kennedy, McGeeney, & Keeter, 2016). Find a quiet place where you can talk undisturbed and where there are no visual or auditory distractions (Dizik, 2011). The possible pitfalls with electronic interviews were painfully—and hilariously—obvious during a live BBC interview when political expert Professor Robert Kelly was being interviewed at home, and his young children wandered into his office while he was on camera. They provided a great distraction for the television audience until their mother realized what was happening and removed them. The video quickly went viral (ABC News, 2017).

During the interview, do your best to control your nervousness so that you don't appear hesitant, halting, unsure, or jittery (Tsa, Chen, & Chiu, 2005). Respond in a timely manner to each question (responding too quickly or slowly decreases hireability ratings; Brosy, Bangerter, & Mayor, 2016). Specifically, sit or stand as the other person directs; lower or raise your vocal tone, rate, and pitch to fit in with the tone and pacing of the other person (DeGroot & Gooty, 2009). Limit gestures so that you don't distract the interviewer from your words—and relax enough to express genuine smiles (Krumhuber, Manstead, Cosker, Marshall, & Rosin, 2009; Woodzicka, 2008). Adjust the amount of smiling to the seriousness of the job, usually by smiling more in the middle of the interview than at the beginning or end (Ruben, Hall, & Schmid Mast, 2015). If you practice with an understanding friend (or even record yourself), you can identify your positive behaviors and minimize any distracting behavior before you go into the interview situation. Remember that it is normal to be nervous during a job interview. But if you have prepared yourself adequately—you have researched the organization and anticipated the kinds of questions you might be asked—you are in the best position to be yourself and show the interviewer what you have to offer.

Anticipate Common Questions

To discover whether there is a potential match between an applicant and a position, an interviewer typically explores five areas of information as they relate to the specific job:

▶ *Ability.* First, based on the résumé and the interview, questions will assess your experience, education, training, intelligence, and ability to do what the job requires.

▶ *Desire.* Second, questions will focus on your desire or motivation to use your abilities to do a good job by exploring such things as your record of changes in jobs, schools, and majors; reasons for wanting this job; knowledge of the company; and concrete examples of prior success that indicate your drive to achieve.

▶ *Personality.* The third area involves an assessment of your personality and how well you are likely to fit into the position and the organization. Questions are designed to discover your personal goals, degree of independence and self-reliance, imagination and creativity, and ability to manage or lead.

▶ *Character.* A fourth area of judgment is that of character, learning about your personal behavior, honesty, responsibility, and accuracy and objectivity in reports.

▶ *Health.* This is a sensitive topic in interviews; certain questions about your health and medical background are unlawful. But if a health issue directly affects your ability to do the job in question, the interviewer may ask. For example, if you are applying for a position at a candy factory, the interviewer

TABLE A.5

COMMON INTERVIEW
QUESTIONS

- Tell me about what led you to choose your particular field/academic major. How satisfied have you been with your choice?

- What positive things would your previous boss say about you?

- Why do you want to/did you leave your current employer?

- What do you know about our organization that caused you to become interested in us?

- Describe a time you exercised leadership.

- Describe a time when you demonstrated initiative in your position.

- Describe a project that did not turn out the way you wanted. How would you make it work if you had another chance at it?

- Describe a time when you worked through a difficult coworker situation. How would that coworker describe you today?

- If I gave you this job, what would you accomplish in the first three months?

- Are there any questions that you want to ask?

may ask if you have a peanut allergy; you would be unable to work in a plant where peanuts are processed.

Research finds that you are more likely to be hired if you pay careful attention to the questions asked (or problems posed) and try to assess (silently) the criteria that the interviewer is using. You will then be better able to adapt your behavior to enhance your competence in the interview (Ingold, Kleinmann, König, Melchers, & Iddekinge, 2015).

Some examples of frequently asked interview questions are offered in Table A.5.

Deal with Difficult or Unethical Questions

"What fictional character most clearly reflects your outlook on life?" This is an actual question that an interviewer asked a colleague of ours some years ago when she was applying to college. To this day, she remembers the question because she panicked — not because she lacked an answer, but because she was not expecting the question. An interviewer might use such unexpected questions to seek insights into the way candidates view themselves or to judge how well they think on their feet. Some questions are simply tricky — they offer a challenge to the interviewee but also a great opportunity to show flexibility and strength.

Other questions are more than just difficult: they are unethical and sometimes even unlawful. Questions that have no direct bearing on job performance and have the potential to lead to discrimination based on race, color, religion, national origin, sex, age, disability, and marital or family status are illegal in the United States (O'Hair, Friedrich, & Dixon, 2016). Although an organization whose employees ask illegal questions during employment interviews can be subject to a variety of penalties imposed by the federal government's Equal Employment Opportunity Commission (EEOC), such questions continue to be asked, and applicants must consider how to answer them. There are at least five tactics you can use to respond to illegal questions (Stewart & Cash, 2014). By answering briefly but directly, tactfully refusing to answer, or neutralizing the question, you respond without giving too much information or inviting further inquiry. You can also consider posing a tactful inquiry — that is, asking another question in response — or using the question as an opportunity to present some positive information about yourself. These five strategies are outlined with examples in Table A.6.

connect

Much as you would practice a speech out loud before officially giving it to a group (Chapter 15), practicing common interview questions aloud (either to yourself or to a willing friend) is a surefire way to increase your confidence in the moment. You may even consider taping yourself to get a sense of both your verbal and nonverbal behavior when answering interview questions.

what about you?

• How Well Do You Interview?

Reviewing your past interviewing behaviors can help you identify where you have excelled and where you need to improve. Use the following five-point scale to rate your behavior in one or more past job interviews: 5 = always; 4 = most of the time; 3 = sometimes; 2 = almost never; and 1 = didn't know how to do this. Then total your score after completing the questionnaire to see where you fit in.

_____ 1. I dress appropriately for the interview.

_____ 2. I bring a copy of my résumé and a list of references or other relevant material.

_____ 3. I prepare sample answers to questions I am likely to be asked.

_____ 4. I bring a notepad and pen and turn off (and put away) electronic devices.

_____ 5. I greet and make eye contact with the receptionist.

_____ 6. If I need to wait, I sit quietly and patiently (without taking or making phone calls).

_____ 7. I do not chew gum or candy, nor (if I smoke) do I have cigarettes visible.

_____ 8. I make eye contact with the interviewer initially and for a few seconds at a time thereafter.

_____ 9. I shake the interviewer's hand firmly.

_____ 10. I smile and nod appropriately when the interviewer is talking.

_____ 11. I speak loudly enough to be heard and keep an even tone to my speech.

_____ 12. I sit upright (not stiffly) and lean slightly forward without crossing my legs.

_____ 13. I listen carefully to the interviewer and do not interrupt.

_____ 14. I avoid frowning and other negative facial expressions.

_____ 15. I answer questions thoroughly.

_____ 16. I speak clearly, avoiding slang.

_____ 17. I check to be sure the interviewer has understood my answer.

_____ 18. I illustrate my answers with specific examples of how I accomplished tasks or managed situations.

_____ 19. If asked, I provide specific examples of the work environment that make me most productive and happy.

_____ 20. When leaving the interview, I smile, shake hands, and thank the interviewer for meeting with me.

74–100: You are likely to make favorable impressions in job interviews by adapting to the situation, preparing yourself and your materials, and monitoring your verbal and nonverbal behavior appropriately throughout the interview.

47–73: You have some strengths in job interviewing but could improve if you spent more time preparing by researching the organization and adapting your verbal and nonverbal behaviors to the situation.

20–46: You probably feel a lot of anxiety as you approach an interview. Work to reduce that anxiety by researching the organization, getting help with your résumé, asking for advice from reputable sources, and conducting mock interviews in which you practice answering behavioral questions with confidence and ease.

TABLE A.6

TACTICS FOR RESPONDING
TO UNLAWFUL QUESTIONS

Tactic	Sample Unlawful Question	Sample Answer
Answer directly but briefly.	"Do you attend church regularly?"	"Yes, I do."
Pose a tactful inquiry.	"What does your husband do?"	"Why do you ask?" (in a nondefensive tone of voice)
Tactfully refuse to answer.	"Do you have children?"	"My family plans will not interfere with my ability to perform this position."
Neutralize.	"What happens if your partner needs to relocate?"	"My partner and I would discuss moves that either of us might have to consider in the future."
Take advantage of the question.	"Where were you born?"	"I am quite proud that my background is Egyptian because it has helped me deal effectively with people of various ethnic backgrounds."

Information from C. J. Stewart & W. B. Cash (2014).

Ask Questions of Your Own

Of course, the interviewer should not be the only person asking questions in a job interview. A candidate for any job should arrive at an interview prepared to ask thoughtful questions about the position and related career paths within the organization as well as about the organization itself; these questions should help you meet your own goals for the interview (Huffcutt, Culbertson, & Riforgiate, 2015). These questions should indicate that the applicant has done solid homework (your preinterview research and preparation can shine here) and is able and willing to do a good job for the company.

Not having any questions of your own often implies disinterest. But avoid focusing on questions about your own compensation and benefits, such as, "How much vacation will I get?"—at least not at the first interview. Instead, try to pose thoughtful questions that show your interest while enhancing your understanding of the position and the potential for your future, such as, "I noticed in your annual report that you are developing a new training program. If I were hired, would I be in it?" A "final" question that can be very helpful (since it gives you a chance to deal with any hesitations the hiring manager might have) is, "Do you have any questions about my qualifications and abilities to do the job?" And when the interview is wrapping up, be sure to ask what to expect next, such as, "What is your time frame for filling this position?"

Follow Up After the Interview

You should continue to demonstrate good manners once the interview is over. Thank the interviewer, as well as anyone else you have met within the organization, as you leave. Follow up immediately with a written or emailed (or both) note of appreciation. Thank the interviewer not only for the interview but also for the chance to expand your knowledge of the organization and the industry. Put in writing how excited you are about the chance to work with such a dynamic organization. Send along any support materials that you discussed

and you?

Have you ever gone through an interview process to secure a job or admission to college? How prepared did you feel for your first interview? If you could do it again, what would you do differently?

during the interview (perhaps a writing sample). Because few interviewees remember to send additional materials and a note of thanks, you will certainly stand out.

back to ▶ MOS Interviews

At the beginning of this Appendix, we talked about man-on-the-street (MOS) interviews. Let's examine the nature of those interviews in the context of what we have learned here.

▸ Like all interviews, MOS interviews are planned and dyadic. However, the "sound-bite" edits of the comedic ones focus on the most embarrassing or uninformed responses for media appeal—something you do not usually have to be worried about in the traditional types of interviews we covered in this chapter. The MOS interviewer exerts an unusual amount of control at the expense of the interviewee.

▸ MOS interviews in the wake of Pearl Harbor were followed by two more series of MOS interviews titled "Dear Mr. President." They revealed a portrait of everyday life in America that included differing opinions concerning World War II, racial prejudice, and labor disputes. These MOS interviews were serious journalistic records of a cross section of U.S. life and attitudes in the 1940s; as such, these records can give historians and social scientists comparative insights into life then versus today.

▸ Public opinion polls on the telephone, in person, or on the internet are more extensive than the quicker MOS interviews. One study found that interviewees feel a certain need to present themselves in a positive light when being interviewed by another real person rather than answering the same survey questions online. Thus, while interviewees may stay more focused with a live interviewer who can provide clarification during the interview, they may overstate socially desirable behaviors and attitudes, attempting to avoid any disapproval (Pew Research Center, 2015).

 Activities

LaunchPad
macmillan learning

1. LaunchPad for *Real Communication* offers key term videos and encourages self-assessment through adaptive quizzing. Go to **launchpadworks.com** to get access to:

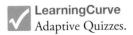
LearningCurve
Adaptive Quizzes.

2. Observe a press conference on television. Who is being interviewed? Who is conducting the interview? What is the goal of the press conference? How is control distributed? List five questions that are asked and then label them according to the types listed in this chapter (open, closed, bipolar, primary, and secondary). Did the questioning involve a particular sequence (funnel, inverted funnel, or tunnel)? What did you learn about this interview format by answering these questions?

3. Go online to research illegal job interview questions and the subtle differences between legal and illegal ones. Organize a discussion with your classmates about how you would respond to illegal questions in a job interview. Practice and compare your responses.

4. Assess your goals for employment and then design (or revise) a résumé for the job that interests you the most. Use the guidelines in this chapter to make it clear and action-oriented. Prepare additional résumés for other positions, keeping in mind that it should highlight the aspects of your training and experience most relevant to each particular position. Discuss your résumé with other students in the class; ask them if your goals are clear. Can they tell what job you are seeking based on the different résumés you show them? Compare your résumé to theirs; although the format may be similar, the content should be unique to you.

5. Create a questionnaire that you will use the next time you visit a physician. Focus your questions on what is already known about your condition and what you want to know about possible treatment. You may also want to ask questions about the training and experience of the physician in a way that will give you the information you want without you seeming contentious. If you have no medical issues, perhaps your questionnaire can be designed for someone else (a child, a friend, or a relative who could benefit from your help).

6. Conduct an in-depth information-gathering interview and then write a four- to five-page report in which you summarize the information you received. Comment on what you learned about the interview process. The interview must last at least one hour, and the interviewee must be a close acquaintance who is older than you and has children (consider interviewing one of your parents). The interview must cover at least two of the following topics related to the person:

   a. Philosophy of raising children (discipline, finances, making friends, respect for authority, character formation)

   b. Political beliefs (political affiliation and commitment, involvement in civic affairs, involvement in government)

   c. Religious beliefs (their effect on the person's life and how these beliefs relate to family life)

   d. Goals in life and how the person is working to achieve these goals

   e. Philosophy of leisure time (ideally how one should spend leisure time versus how this person actually spends it)

 A Study Tool

Now that you have finished reading this Appendix, you can:

Define the nature of interviews:

▶ An **interview** is a deliberate and purposeful transaction between two parties (p. 464).

▶ Interviews are planned, goal-driven, structured, dyadic, transactional, and context-dependent (p. 464).

Outline the different types of interviews:

▶ The **information-gathering interview** serves to transfer knowledge from one party to the other (p. 465). **Service-oriented interviews** provide advice or support after getting necessary information (p. 465). **Media interviews** question and analyze people, politics, media, and events (p. 466).

▶ **Persuasive interview** questions are designed to change the interviewee's behavior or opinions (p. 466). An **interrogation** persuasively pressures the interviewee for information. A **problem-solving interview** deals with problems, tensions, or conflicts (p. 466). **Motivational interviews** use goal-oriented questions designed to strengthen personal motivation to change (p. 467).

▶ **Performance appraisals** allow you to review accomplishments and plan future goals (p. 467).

▶ In **exit interviews**, employers seek to identify organizational problems that might affect employee retention (p. 467).

▶ In a **selection interview**, the primary goal is to fill a position in an organization (p. 468). Selection interviews designed to gain employment are **job interviews** (p. 468).

Describe the three parts of an interview: opening, questions, and conclusion:

▶ An interview should open with the topic and length (the task), something about the interviewer and how information will be used (the relationship), and who will benefit (the motivation; p. 468).

▶ Questions and answers accomplish the goals of the interview (p. 470).

▶ An **open question** gives the interviewee freedom to respond (p. 470).

▶ **Closed questions** limit answers to specific choices; **bipolar questions** can be answered with only "yes" or "no" (p. 470).

▶ **Primary questions** introduce new topics; **secondary questions** seek clarification (p. 470).

▶ **Directed questions**, **leading questions**, or **loaded questions** may subtly or even blatantly influence the answer, whereas **neutral questions** do not hint at a preferred answer (p. 472).

▶ There are three main structures for ordering interview questions: the **funnel sequence**, **inverted funnel sequence**, or **tunnel sequence** (p. 473).

▶ Interviewers use verbal and nonverbal strategies to conclude and summarize the interview (p. 473).

Devise an interview strategy from the interviewer's point of view:

▶ Consider potential barriers that might be disruptive (p. 474).

▶ Find ways to put the interviewee at ease (p. 474).

▶ Make sure the questions are ethical and appropriate (p. 474).

▶ Remember to listen well and take notes (p. 475).

Prepare for the role of interviewee:

- ▶ Have a clear idea of what you want to achieve in the interview (p. 475).
- ▶ Do not arrive tired or hungry. Dress appropriately, and bring needed documents (p. 475).
- ▶ Listen and respond effectively (p. 476).
- ▶ Share the responsibility of adapting to the situation and the person, being particularly sensitive to cultural differences (p. 476).

Secure job interviews and manage them with confidence:

- ▶ Locate jobs through networking connections, placement centers, and job-specific sites (p. 477).
- ▶ **Networking** involves meeting new people through people you already know (p. 477).
- ▶ Write an effective **résumé** and **cover letter** (pp. 479, 481).
- ▶ Remember that rejection is not uncommon (p. 482).
- ▶ Impression management involves both verbal and nonverbal behaviors (p. 483).
- ▶ Come prepared to answer standard questions about your abilities, desire, personality, character, and health (p. 484).
- ▶ Answer difficult questions honestly but be brief; decline to answer or defuse questions that are unlawful (p. 485).
- ▶ Ask thoughtful questions about the position and the organization (p. 487).
- ▶ Follow up with a note of thanks (p. 487).

TODAY'S TEENS experience more media on a daily basis than their parents did in an entire week.

 LearningCurve can help you master the material in this chapter.

Go to **launchpadworks.com.**

Mass and Mediated Communication

Sandie and Chris fell in love during the 1980s, while spending late evenings together watching *Late Night with David Letterman*. Twenty or so years later, their teenage daughter Abigail sits in front of a laptop on a Saturday morning, streaming a video of Jimmy Fallon sitting behind Letterman's old desk at NBC. Her older sister Alice, while Skyping from college a few minutes earlier, had told her about a funny sketch, so she sends Alice a Snapchat of herself laughing at the video. There are dog-eared copies of her favorite *Hunger Games* books on her bed, and she checks the comments on her latest blog post about how *Divergent* doesn't come close. She also keeps an eye on Instagram on her phone, as she likes to keep up with her friends and favorite celebrities (she follows author/vlogger John Green). Later, she texts her friends to make plans to go to the movies, but not before checking out a few trailers on YouTube.

That afternoon, while babysitting her ten-year-old brother, Harry, Abigail spends an hour playing the latest *Lego Star Wars* game with him on their Xbox. Abigail also lets Harry play Minecraft on her phone while she watches *Nerdy Nummies* on her laptop (she wants to bake him Pokémon cookies for his birthday). After dinner, she is off to the movies and conscientiously turns off her phone—it is the first time she has been disconnected all day.

By the time Abigail goes to sleep, she has experienced more media than her parents did in a week when they were her age. Meanwhile, Chris and Sandie pull up last night's *Tonight Show with Jimmy Fallon* on DVR, grateful that they no longer have to stay up to watch late night television.

After you have finished reading this Appendix, you will be
able to

- Distinguish different types of
  mass communication

- Explain how the business of
  media and the principle of
  free speech shape the kinds
  of media messages you
  encounter

- Identify the ways in which
  mass media may influence
  your attitudes and behaviors

- Describe how digital media
  technologies can affect your
  participation in the social and
  political process

- Practice skills for becoming
  a more mindful and media
  literate consumer

Most of us, like Abigail and her family, spend a great deal of time with these interconnecting media technologies, often using many of them simultaneously (eMarketer, 2016). In this appendix, we look at mass and mediated communication and discuss the blurred lines between the two. We explore the forces that shape how mass media messages are made, such as the economics of the media industries and the attempts at government influence, and we discuss the potential effects that media have on us as audience members. Finally, we examine the uniquely personal and interactive nature of digital mass media, as well as what we can do to become competent media users.

The Nature of Mass Media

We often find ourselves talking about "the media" ("What are the media saying about that scandal?"), but the media are not actually one unified entity. They take many different forms and have many different uses and effects, as we see with Abigail and her family.

As we learned in Chapter 2, **mediated communication** occurs when there is some technology, such as a print or electronic channel, that is used to deliver messages between sources and receivers. We use many forms of media (phone, email, social networking sites) to communicate in interpersonal, small group, organizational, public, and intercultural contexts. When mediated communication occurs on a very broad scale, we refer to it as **mass communication**. There are many kinds of media that deliver large-scale communication messages, ranging from broadcast television to YouTube channels to online news blogs. They have some qualities in common, as well as some key distinctions. Together they play an important part in our daily lives.

Types of Mass Communication

Before the advent of the internet and digital communication devices, mass communication only included types of media that have the following characteristics:

▶ *Large audiences*: Media messages target (and reach) enormous audiences, typically described in millions (of viewers, readers, listeners, etc.).

▶ *Professional communicators*: The sources of messages tend to be people whose livelihoods depend on the success of communication—publishers, actors, writers, reporters, advertising executives, or even the guard at the studio gate.

▶ *Limited feedback*: Mass media messages are delivered with less interactivity and opportunity for feedback than other forms of communication, which makes it more difficult for sources to know their audience.

These qualities still apply to many traditional mass media rooted in the entertainment and news industries. These mass media include print media, feature films, broadcast television and radio, and cable and satellite television and radio. See Table B.1 for the key differences between these types.

From an audience member's perspective, it is difficult to distinguish broadcast from cable TV or other video programming. After all, a TV comedy from NBC (whether watched live, on DVR, or streamed online) looks and sounds just like a show from Comedy Central or a comedian's YouTube video. And most audiences no longer receive live network channels directly from the airwaves anyway: broadcast signals are now included with cable subscriptions or can be streamed on the internet. But it is important to remember that broadcast programming is still economically and legally treated as distinct—broadcast's technical differences are what led to different business models for generating revenue as well as different forms of regulation.

In addition to the traditional mass media are, of course, the digital communication technologies we use on our computers, smartphones, and tablets, as we discussed in Chapter 2. Although digital media are used for many non-mass kinds of communication, such as texting a friend or sharing a video to a group, they too facilitate communication on a broad scale. Mass communication via digital media has challenged the qualities of traditional mass media previously mentioned.

► *Larger audiences* are still sought after, but the sizes vary widely, depending whether you are talking about YouTube views, Instagram followers, or subscribers to Netflix.

► *Professional communicators*, such as those previously mentioned, use digital media to promote and stream their movies and TV shows. However, nonprofessional users can also use digital media to create and promote their own video channels or news blogs.

► *Interactive feedback* is increasingly commonplace. Users can comment on blogs and videos as well as share content and opinions via social media.

Indeed, the digital media environment has blurred the difference between many types of communication. If you are watching a video clip from the Jimmy Fallon show on your phone that your friend shared with you on Facebook, are you watching TV? Sort of, but not in the traditional way. Are you creating interpersonal intimacy with your friend? Probably, but the clip was also shared with millions of other people. This merging of traditional mass communication with digital computing and telecommunication technologies is called **media convergence**. Convergence is a critical part of living in a digital media environment, and it affects how mass media content is shaped as well as how mass media messages can influence audiences (Pavlik & McIntosh, 2016).

The Pervasiveness of Media

With broadband internet access, global satellite technology, and 24/7 news and entertainment content, many of us have mass media content available to us at all times. The average adult spends over ten hours per day consuming media, including about

● **LOOK FAMILIAR?** Streaming videos on digital devices blurs the line between the formerly distinct media of television and telephone. martin-dm/ Getty Images

connect

Traditional mass media tended to operate along the lines of the linear model of communication presented in Chapter 1. Messages were sent out and there was not much feedback, if any. But emerging technologies provide audiences with increased opportunity for interaction — in fact, many messages depend on audience interaction to become "mass media" messages. Every time you forward a link — or choose not to — you are playing a role in that transaction.

TABLE B.1

TYPES OF TRADITIONAL MASS MEDIA

Print media	Books, magazines, or newspapers purchased in hard copy versions.
Feature films	Movies seen in theaters or purchased on DVD (later available to stream on digital devices).
Broadcast television and radio	Signals transmitted from local stations through the free airwaves to receivers (such as an AM/FM car radio or a TV set). Broadcast TV is often called "network" television, because TV broadcasters typically air programming from one of the major networks — ABC, NBC, CBS, Fox, and The CW. "Prime-time" TV refers to shows aired on these channels from 8 P.M. until 11 P.M., targeting the largest audiences.
Cable and satellite television and radio	Signals beamed to and from a satellite and then transmitted to audiences from a local cable company (such as Comcast or Time Warner) or a satellite service (such as DirecTV). Audiences pay for a subscription to get access to various packages of channels that their cable or satellite service provides. "Basic" services include a wide variety of fairly specialized channels, such as ESPN, AMC, FX, Disney, Fox News, CNN, Comedy Central, Food Network, and so on. "Premium" channels, such as HBO and Showtime, usually cost extra.

● **IN-FLIGHT BOREDOM** is a thing of the past, as increasingly more airlines allow passengers to customize their entertainment experience with access to personal in-flight television, movies, and music. Saha Entertainment/Getty Images

five hours of live or recorded TV; two hours of AM/FM radio; and over three hours on digital media via computers, smartphones, or tablets (Nielsen, 2016). Children and teens also spend about nine hours on a typical day devoted to media, including TV, movies, computers, smartphone entertainment, video games, music/audio, and print (Common Sense Media, 2015). Of course, much of this time is spent **media multitasking**—using more than one media type at the same time—and that overlapping usage allows kids and adults to pack nearly eleven hours of content into their daily lives. In fact, in today's digital media environment, it is almost impossible to *escape* media (Pavlik & McIntosh, 2016).

Understanding Mass Media Messages

There are several important factors that help shape the kinds of mass media messages that are made and delivered. In this section, we discuss these key influences, including the economics of a high-risk media industry, the principle of free speech and government regulation, and the role of media bias.

The Business of Media

For the professionals, media organizations range from tiny production companies to huge international conglomerates (such as Sony) that are parent companies to a number of other large organizations (such as Sony Pictures Entertainment, which itself is the parent company of Columbia Pictures and Screen Gems, among others). Some companies form just for the purpose of making one movie or television show, whereas others, such as Universal and Netflix, oversee, purchase, or distribute thousands of movies and TV programs each year. There are also media companies (such as Defy Media) that now focus exclusively on creating and promoting digital video content, such as YouTube shows and channels. But all of these companies are businesses—they need to make money to stay in business.

Sources of Revenue

There are two main sources of revenue for the mass media: consumer purchases and advertising. Consumers pay directly for media messages, such as going to the movies; subscribing to cable, satellite, or on-demand online streaming services; and buying magazines, e-books, or DVDs. Advertising dollars also support many of the same media that consumers purchase (magazines, newspapers, cable TV) because purchases alone are not enough to keep these industries afloat. Advertising is also the *sole* support for several other media, including broadcast TV and radio and much of the internet (such as blogs and YouTube videos). Advertising rates are determined mainly by how many people are in the audience (and for how long). For print media, this means circulation size (the number of people who buy or subscribe to newspapers and magazines); for broadcast and cable TV and radio, this primarily means ratings—the number of households that are in the viewing/listening audience for a given time slot, including those who record and watch several days later. For websites and streamed TV content on computers or mobile devices, usage data can get more complicated, but everything gets measured—from unique hits or views (i.e., individual visitors to a site or a video) and the amount of time people spend browsing to people's patterns of click-through behavior with links. The total numbers of subscribers (such as to a YouTube channel) or followers (such as for an Instagram personality) are also important. Your "second screen" time matters as well—advertisers want to know, for example, how often while you are watching AMC's *The Walking Dead* you also participate on your mobile device with the AMC Story Sync app.

Big box-office and high ratings are keys to mass media success because mass communication messages are expensive to make and deliver. For example, the production and promotion costs of a half-hour network TV sitcom can range from several hundred thousand dollars per episode to several million. Such high investment costs mean that profit can be elusive. In fact, most new TV shows are canceled, few movies become blockbusters, most novels do not become bestsellers, and few albums have strong sales (Vogel, 2015). How, then, do they ever make money? The few blockbuster movies, bestselling books, and hit television shows or albums must make up for all the rest. In economics, this is called **exponentiality**: relatively few items bring most of the income, while the rest add only a little (Vogel, 2015). Across the media industries, about 80 to 90 percent of mass media revenue comes from only 10 to 20 percent of the products made.

Part of the challenge in achieving financial success is due to **audience fragmentation**, the spread of audience members across a wide spectrum of entertainment choices. Before the abundance of cable TV channels and internet media content, the hit TV shows of network television could regularly command audience sizes of fifteen- to twenty-million viewers (*Happy Days* averaged 22 million in 1977). Today, even shows in the top twenty-five are fortunate to find themselves with five to ten million viewers. The traditional media are competing for your attention with many alternative avenues of entertainment, including popular YouTubers and Instagram stars. Even *you* might be competing with the media giants yourself as you build a following for your blog and earn advertising to support your efforts.

Broad Versus Narrow Appeal

For the traditional mass media, particularly broadcast television, messages must have very broad appeal to attract the millions of viewers that the networks need in order to sell profitable advertising time. The Super Bowl is such a widely popular event (over one hundred million viewers) that the cost of advertising is extremely expensive: in 2017, a thirty-second commercial during the Super Bowl cost about $5 million. Live presidential debates (over eighty million viewers) and sports playoff games (over twenty million) are also reliably large audiences for broadcast TV networks (ABC, CBS, NBC, Fox) as well as cable news (Fox News, CNN) and sports

● **FOLLOWING THE** economic principle of exponentiality, blockbusters such as *Finding Dory* bring in most of the film industry's profits and pick up the slack of box office bombs such as *Alice Through the Looking Glass.* (left) Everett Collection, Inc/Courtesy Everett Collection; (right) Everett Collection, Inc/Courtesy Everett Collection

channels (ESPN, NFL Network). But prime-time TV requires programming that attracts several million viewers on a *regular* basis. The conventional way for television to capture broad audiences has been to rely on content that is often described as **low culture** — entertainment that appeals to most people's baser instincts, typified by lurid, sensational images and news stories charged with sex, violence, scandal, and abuse (Berger, 2007). In addition, the broadcast networks have relied on programming that does not require a great deal of thought or cultural sophistication, leading critics to echo the sentiments of former Federal Communications Commission (FCC) Chairman Newton Minow when, in 1961, he first called commercial television a "vast wasteland" (Minow, 1961; Minow & Cate, 2003).

But, wait, you say: Aren't there a lot of popular shows on television right now that are intellectually stimulating, well written, and impressively produced? Scholars agree and have made the case that the landscape of television during the last twenty years has actually gotten "smarter" (Mittel, 2015). Although there is much popular content on TV that remains highly conventional, the past two decades have seen a huge increase in critically acclaimed and popular TV shows with **narrative complexity** — complicated plots and connections between characters, a blurring of reality and fantasy, and time that is not always linear or chronological. Beginning with innovative shows like *The X-Files* (1993–2002) and *Buffy the Vampire Slayer* (1997–2003) and continuing with programs like *Doctor Who* (since 2005), *Game of Thrones* (since 2011), and *Better Call Saul* (since 2015), intricate plots, subplots, and "story arcs" weave between stand-alone episodes and continuous serial storytelling (Mittel, 2015). Many of these shows give you a cognitive "workout" because you must think carefully to make sense of what is happening (Johnson, 2005).

What spurred this trend? The explosion of media choices — originally through cable channels and DVDs, and now through online streaming — has allowed audiences to become more demanding, and there is money to be made in meeting that demand (Johnson, 2005). Many of these are *hit* shows, after all. But even without major hits, uniquely appealing shows are possible because of another major industry trend. **Narrowcasting** (also called *niche marketing*) is the process of targeting narrower, more specific audiences. Although we are still talking about large numbers (hundreds of thousands up to the low millions), with the diverse array of specialty media outlets, media industries can tap into multiple groups of viewers that, although smaller, are loyal and often passionate audiences (Mittel, 2015). For example, video on demand (VOD) streaming services like Netflix enable shows to generate and maintain a loyal fan base. Viewers can watch their favorites repeatedly or "binge" watch — meaning to view episode after episode in one sitting. Fans can also provide reviews or discuss show content online with others. It takes a unique show to withstand this level of viewer scrutiny (Gay, 2014).

Niche programming is also increasingly possible because of sources of revenue besides traditional advertising. Broadcast and cable programmers can feature advertisers' products within the shows themselves, of course, but even more income is being raised in deals made with international broadcasters and with VOD services like Hulu (Adalian, 2013). Thus, although it is not surprising that a megahit like Fox's *Empire* (with an average of sixteen million viewers each week) pulls in solid advertising revenue, shows with smaller, dedicated audiences (like FX's *It's Always Sunny in Philadelphia,* with just over a million viewers each episode) can still be profitable (Patten, 2016).

● NARROWCAST TV program *It's Always Sunny in Philadelphia* has amassed a unique and loyal audience to enable it to compete with more mainstream TV fare. Everett Collection, Inc/ Courtesy Everett Collection

evaluating communication ethics

Music Piracy

You and your friend Zach are really into a local band called Spikefish. You have attended their concerts and bought their T-shirts. Spikefish has begun to gather a larger following as well; their songs are now available to purchase through online music sites such as iTunes and Amazon. Zach tells you that you don't have to buy the songs — he has found a website that allows you to download them for free. Of course, it is illegal not to buy the songs, but Zach says that everybody does it, and as long as you don't download too much too often, you're probably not going to get caught. He gets a lot of his music this way, from struggling new bands like Spikefish to mega-successful established artists like U2.

Zach's argument is that you're not really hurting the band by illegally downloading music because it's the corporations — the record labels — that make the real money, and he doesn't care about them. He also says that in some ways, illegal downloading helps the bands — by making people more interested in their music, more likely to attend their concerts, and perhaps more likely to buy some of their music legally in the future. You think that bands deserve to earn the fruit of their labors and talents, and you know that it is wrong to engage in what is clearly illegal conduct. But you also really want your music and it seems so easy to get away with illegal downloading. What should you do? What do you say to Zach?

1. Does the likelihood of getting caught matter in your decision whether or not to download? Why or why not? Does it matter that illegal downloading is widespread?

2. What do you think about Zach's argument that stealing from a "corporation" is more defensible than stealing from an individual artist or band? What adverse impacts might there also be for the artists themselves?

3. Does it make a difference that some bands are struggling artists, while others are millionaires? Why or why not?

Of course, narrowcasting does not necessarily result in more intellectually demanding or sophisticated content. Many specialty cable channels (such as the youth-oriented MTV) have plenty of low-culture programming (*Teen Mom OG* perhaps?). But digital technologies also present opportunities for media professionals to capitalize on the passionate special audiences that are an important part of an increasingly fragmented media landscape.

Minimizing Risk

The desire for an audience often means minimizing risk wherever possible. Most media professionals do this in part by promoting content that they believe reflects the cultural and moral values of their audiences. They do extensive audience research, attempting to understand the passions, commitments, values, and relational bonds of viewers and listeners. They also engage in **self-censorship**, carefully monitoring their own content and eliminating messages that they believe might offend their viewers or sponsors. For example, if TV network executives believe a show's script is too explicit or its message is too politically risky, they may insist on rewrites or prevent the show from airing altogether.

The fear of offending viewers or advertisers does not mean that media avoid controversy. Indeed, controversy can be used to increase ratings. We discussed earlier that lurid, sensational coverage is common across news media outlets, whether about celebrity sex scandals and drug overdoses or political corruption and gruesome murder cases. Entertainment programming can also benefit from controversy — two weeks after singer Miley Cyrus gave a sexually provocative performance at the MTV

and you?

Are you more likely to spend your moviegoing dollars on a known entity — a sequel to a film you love, a retelling of a favorite story, or a movie adaptation of a television show you loved as a child — than you are on an original concept? Of the movies you saw in the theater over the past year, how many were truly original?

● **RATHER THAN** diminishing her fame, Miley Cyrus's behavior brought her more notoriety. Jeff Kravitz/Getty Images

Music Awards, the "Wrecking Ball" video she released on YouTube received more than ten million hits in a matter of hours ("Back to Twerk," 2013). And her subsequent appearance hosting *Saturday Night Live* boosted that show's ratings to its highest in months (Alter, 2013). Controversy does not always translate into high ratings or long-term success, but it can often generate short-term spikes in public attention, especially on social media.

Perhaps the most prominent way media industries try to minimize risk is to repeat what has already proven to work. Although they do aim to discover a fresh new idea that will lead to the next big blockbuster or hit TV show, that kind of success is difficult to predict in advance. Media professionals often count on the sure thing: the products or ideas that have *already been* successful. Thus, profitable films — from *Finding Nemo* to *The Fast and the Furious* — are usually followed by a sequel (or seven, or eight . . .). Popular films are also frequently derived from successful novels (*Hunger Games*), graphic novels and comic book franchises (*The Avengers*), or previously made films (*Carrie, RoboCop*). For television, this means spin-offs (*Family Guy* begat *The Cleveland Show*) and copycat shows (the hugely successful *American Idol* was an Americanized version of the British hit *Pop Idol* and has been succeeded by another singing competition show, *The Voice*). Although some such outings are failures, studios continue to mine familiar stories and characters that they know audiences already know and enjoy.

Free Speech and Media Bias

A now infamous Super Bowl halftime show featured a moment in 2004 that permanently entered the cultural lexicon as a "wardrobe malfunction" — performer Justin Timberlake pulled off part of Janet Jackson's bustier, exposing her breast. CBS stations around the country faced major fines for indecency. After years of legal battling, CBS eventually prevailed and did not have to pay the fines, mainly because the courts found ambiguity in how indecency rules were being enforced at that time (Denniston, 2012). The debate continues today over how much *right* the government has to fine networks or censor objectionable messages, a controversy rooted in competing interpretations of constitutional law.

The First Amendment

The First Amendment to the U.S. Constitution states, "Congress shall make no law . . . abridging the freedom of speech, or of the press." The principle here is that news media and individual citizens of a well-functioning republic need to be free to criticize their government and speak their views. The U.S. Supreme Court has argued that although the quality of speech may vary greatly, the resulting **marketplace of ideas** — the open forum in which ideas compete — is beneficial for society as a whole (*Abrams* v. *United States*, 1919). This means that, even when speech is offensive, the government cannot ban it, punish it, or restrict it, except under very rare circumstances. Interestingly, this does not mean that the U.S. government has not *tried* to exercise control over media content. But its attempts at regulation are often struck down by the courts as unconstitutional (such as bans on pornography and heavy regulation of political campaign speech). The regulations that U.S. courts allow mostly involve rules about technical issues, such as broadcast signals or ownership of stations and copyright laws. In effect, the U.S. government actually has little direct influence on media *content* compared to the governments of other countries.

Do all of the U.S. media benefit from this protection? The courts have generally held that creative expression *is* protected speech, whether in print, on TV, in movies, or on the internet. However, the courts have also upheld some content regulations for some kinds of media, particularly broadcasting, as we see in the next section.

Electronic Media Regulation

As we discussed earlier, there are technical differences between broadcast signals and cable, satellite, or internet channels. Recall that broadcast signals are carried over the airwaves from a station transmitter to a receiver. For radio, these are the AM/FM stations you might listen to in your car. For television, they are the major networks (ABC, CBS, NBC, FOX, and The CW) and other independent local stations. Although broadcast TV channels today may look just like cable TV channels or any show you might watch online, there is an important legal distinction.

Broadcast frequencies are limited, and the airwaves are essentially considered a public resource, so the government—through the FCC—can regulate which private companies may broadcast over them. In order to keep their broadcasting licenses, broadcasters must agree to serve the public interest. Cable and satellite providers, on the other hand, as well as internet content generators, have not been subject to the same kinds of regulations.

Although the First Amendment right to free speech and press does apply to broadcasters, broadcast television networks and radio stations are subject to some speech restrictions. The courts have held that the government can impose restrictions that serve a "compelling government interest" (i.e., the government has a really good reason for doing it, such as to protect children), and only when the regulation is the "least restrictive" way to serve that interest (i.e., the government cannot ban all adult TV content just to be able to protect kids from seeing it; *Action for Children's Television* v. *FCC*, 1991).

In the Janet Jackson Super Bowl incident discussed earlier, CBS stations were originally fined because the FCC said that the dance number violated a ban on broadcast **indecency**. *Indecency* legally means "patently offensive . . . sexual or excretory activities or organs" (*Federal Communications Commission* v. *Pacifica Foundation*, 1978); however, in practice, it means talking about or showing sexual or other bodily functions in a very lewd or vulgar way. This is a very subjective evaluation, of course, which is why broadcasters frequently end up fighting over their fines in court.

The U.S. Supreme Court has upheld the government's expressed interest in protecting children from indecent content (*Federal Communications Commission* v. *Pacifica Foundation*, 1978). However, the courts have also said that the ban must be limited only to specific times of day (such as 6 A.M. to 10 P.M.), when children are likely to be in the audience (*Action for Children's Television* v. *FCC*, 1995). Remember that this ban does not apply to cable and satellite channels or to the internet—so MTV, Comedy Central, and YouTube, for example, could choose to air nudity or use bad language at any time (depending, of course, on whether they think their advertisers or audiences would approve).

Although indecency rules are what you may hear most about, there are also other important areas of media regulation. Much FCC action is directed at how the media corporations conduct their business, such as approving or denying mergers. The FCC has also recently expanded its influence over the internet, including controversial attempts to limit the control that internet service providers have over the online traffic that flows through their services.

● WHEN *SATURDAY NIGHT LIVE* premiered on broadcast network NBC in 1975, the original cast of the "Not Ready for Prime Time Players" was relegated to a late-night airtime to allow for its often boundary-pushing sketch comedy. ©NBC/Photofest

communication across cultures

The Sesame Effect

Grover, Big Bird, and Cookie Monster have helped many generations of American pre-schoolers learn their letters and numbers. Designed to help disadvantaged children get quality educational experiences, the Muppet characters of TV's *Sesame Street* have also taught children about social issues and coping with life's challenges — everything from making new friends to going to the dentist to working hard to achieve a goal. But American children are not the only beneficiaries. Over thirty international versions of *Sesame Street* aim to address the needs of children in low- and middle-income countries (Cole & Lee, 2016).

Many American media companies send their productions abroad, but what makes international adaptations of *Sesame Street* different is that the content is locally created and culturally specific. Co-productions between the Sesame Workshop (the non-profit group behind *Sesame Street*) and local organizations, charities, and government programs generate their own curriculum and even their own Muppet characters (Cole, 2016). Tuktuki is a six-year-old girl Muppet in Bangladesh who goes to school and loves to learn. Raya prides herself on her personal hygiene and takes the embarrassment out of discussing sanitation practices in Nigeria. And in Afghanistan, Kajkoal loves to ask questions and encourages curiosity about occupations that might otherwise seem out of reach.

Like the original *Sesame Street*, the aim is to be "fun, furry, informative, and flexible" (Cole, 2016). And also like the original, extensive research goes into the planning, development, and production of every episode. Studies across multiple countries have shown a significant positive impact on many learning outcomes, including academic skills, health and safety habits, and respect and appreciation for others (Mares & Pan, 2013). By building up young children around the world, *Sesame Street* strives to build a brighter global future (Cole & Lee, 2016).

1. Why do you think the Sesame Workshop creates special programs for each country? Wouldn't it be a lot easier just to dub American episodes into other languages?

2. Although *Sesame Street* was designed to help disadvantaged children catch up with children who can attend preschool, it has had a positive impact on advantaged children as well. Is this a problem? Why or why not?

3. What is the benefit of putting so much research into the creation of the show as well as into the evaluation of its effectiveness on learning? Why not just look at the show's popularity?

connect

Although traditional news media strive for objectivity, it is unlikely that any media message can be presented entirely without bias. As noted in Chapter 1, every communication transaction is influenced by the relational, situational, and cultural contexts in which communication occurs. As audience members, we should be aware of the way these contexts might bias not only the media but also our own perceptions of media messages.

Media Bias

As we have discussed throughout this book, our own thoughts, opinions, and experiences influence the messages we send as well as the way we interpret the messages we receive. These communication biases are also at work when it comes to mass media. Most scholars agree that media sources — both news and entertainment — express some degree of bias in their viewpoints and in their content. News coverage of a presidential campaign, for example, can be quite different, depending on the political leanings of the network or news organization doing the reporting as well as the personal ideologies of individual reporters, editors, and producers.

In the latter half of the twentieth century, news organizations across the mass media generally expressed commitment to the goal of objectivity — that is, they were primarily concerned with facts and attempted to keep in check personal or political bias, prejudice, or interpretation. Although embraced as a laudable goal, both consumers and journalists over the years have questioned whether this goal has been (or even can be) met (Duffy, Thorson, & Vultee, 2009; Figdor, 2010). In any case, today's media are increasingly embracing more partisan news in order to compete in a crowded marketplace (Groeling, 2013; Stroud, 2011). Cable news networks tend to narrowcast to one viewpoint or another in search of higher ratings, and online news sources represent a wide range of ideologically partial reporting—from the *Breitbart* series of websites on the right to the *Huffington Post* on the left. Thus the variety of ideologies represented by media today makes it difficult to pin any particular bias on "mainstream" media as a whole.

That does not mean, however, that bias is unimportant. Studies suggest that partisans of both parties find news coverage credible only when it presents information either in a "balanced" way or in a way favorable to their own views (Metzger, Hartsell, & Flanagin, 2015). In other words, we tend to see those with whom we agree as less biased sources than those with whom we disagree. Our perception of bias also influences our online behavior—posting critical comments on unfavorable news stories and promoting the favorable ones on social media (Chung, Munno, & Moritz, 2015). And when we perceive the news media in general as biased against us, we tend to decrease our news exposure altogether (Ardèvol-Abreu & de Zúñiga, 2016).

Critics on the right *and* the left agree that bias in the media is often a function of the economics and constraints of the news-gathering process (Farnsworth & Lichter, 2010). The 24/7 news cycle with multiple technological outlets to fill may lead to overreliance on easy sources—particularly spokespersons for government or interest groups. In fact, cozy relationships are often courted between journalists and campaign managers or government officials, which can lead to coverage spun in a way favorable toward the official providing access (Shafer, 2016). Journalists must also simplify complex issues and put them into a context that audiences understand (Scheufele & Tewksbury, 2007). **Framing** refers to the *way* issues in the news get presented in order to relate to audiences' existing schemas (Cacciatore, Scheufele, & Iyengar, 2016). For example, during election campaigns, the news often frames each candidate's actions as though they were maneuvers in a "horse race" (e.g., "Will this new revelation pull the candidate ahead? What will the opposition do to try to stay in the lead?"). Such framing is important because public impressions of candidates and campaign events may become a function of who is ahead or behind in the "race," rather than an evaluation of each candidate's detailed positions on issues.

Effects of Mass Media

James gets in trouble at school for trying to kickbox his classmates like they do in video games. Olivia watches a lot of YouTube videos about putting on makeup and worries that she is not pretty enough for her classmates to like her. Are media messages influencing the attitudes and behaviors of these students? We have already

LIBERAL COMMENTATOR Rachel Maddow and conservative Sean Hannity hail from opposite ends of the spectrum of politicized news coverage, and they are not subtle in their partisanship. (left) Brendan Hoffman/ Getty Images (right) Rob Kim/Getty Images

seen how audiences and other factors shape media messages. In this section, we explore the research and theories about how mass media messages might actually shape *us*.

Selectivity and the Active Audience

connect

As we learned in Chapter 6, the listening process involves a series of decisions about which messages we will select and attend to. This process is especially important in how we process mass media messages — the sheer volume of messages means that media must present appealing, clever, and memorable messages in order to compete for our attention.

Do you remember any TV commercials you saw last night? Did you read every post of every friend on Facebook? Probably not. We make specific choices about which messages we select and pay attention to. This selectivity means that audiences are not passive sponges that absorb everything media throw at them. Rather, many communication scholars argue that audiences, even children, are instead active cognitive processors of information (Huston, Bickham, Lee, & Wright, 2007). Being active does not mean, however, that we critically evaluate the messages we see (although we can certainly do that): it means that we look for cues that tell us whether something on TV (or in other media) is interesting, relevant, or otherwise worth noticing (Valkenburg & Peter, 2013). It also refers to the idea that different people have different reactions and interpretations of the same media messages. The concepts of selectivity and an active audience suggest that media effects are much more limited than we might otherwise believe.

Uses and Gratifications

Rather than looking at what media do *to us*, the **uses and gratifications perspective** focuses on what *we do* with media — that is, the way we make media choices (uses) in order to satisfy our needs and goals (gratifications; Blumler & Katz, 1974). We might watch comedies or fantasy to escape our troubles at work or search the internet for updated information on local tornado warnings. In fact, media are competing with the many ways we can meet our needs — when we are feeling lonely, we can get together with friends or phone a family member. Media are also competing with each other — we can check Instagram, watch a beloved TV character, or tune in to our favorite sports commentator (Knoblock-Westerwick, 2015).

Of course, what solves loneliness for *you* might just be escape or entertainment to *me*. It is all in the individual's perceptions of the media choices available. For example, you may enjoy the physical sensation of excitement that comes from violent action or horror movies, whereas your roommate may find those movies upsetting and prefer instead to wallow in an emotional "tearjerker" (Valkenburg, Peter, & Walther, 2016). Even watching and sharing internet cat videos can be a "guilty pleasure" for a cat lover who wishes to improve her mood at work (Myrick, 2015).

When we come to *expect* that media serve our needs, it can lead to **media dependence** (Ball-Rokeach, 1998). Certainly in times of crisis, such as during emergencies like earthquakes, tornadoes, and blizzards, most of us become dependent on media for information and connection to the world. But even without crisis, many people find that they depend on media for specific needs. Adolescents and young adults, for example, may compulsively use social media to feed a poor ego (Andreassen, Pallesen, & Griffiths, 2017). The utility of microblogs (like Twitter) for obtaining and spreading information in real time may make it difficult for habitual users to disengage (Wang, Lee, & Hua, 2015). Some people have become so obsessed with playing online video games that the American Psychiatric Association has included internet gaming disorder as a condition that warrants further research (Internet Gaming Disorder, 2013). This research suggests that what the viewer or listener *brings* to the media experience is important.

Reinforcing Existing Attitudes

One important way in which selectivity limits the effects of media is our tendency to select and evaluate media in a way that confirms our existing views. For example, we often choose our news sources based on whether we trust the source or anticipate that they will agree with us (Yeo, Xenos, Brossard, & Scheufele, 2015). Democrats and liberals more often prefer CNN and NPR and avoid Fox News; Republicans and conservatives do the opposite (Iyengar & Hahn, 2009). Similarly, when we watch political debates, we tend to interpret our preferred candidate as the winner and to remember the information that confirms our previous opinions about the candidates.

Increasingly, diverse media outlets and digital channels make it easier than ever to engage in **preference-based reinforcement**—attending to an increasingly narrow range of entertainment and news messages that support our existing opinions (Cacciatore, Scheufele, & Iyengar, 2016). Some critics lament the fact that we can so easily insulate ourselves from opposing views, arguing that it polarizes us as citizens and is unhealthy for democracy (Sunstein, 2007). But the case can also be made that the ability of audiences to self-filter messages is empowering and is at least better than having others (such as professional media editors or the government) do all the filtering *for* us. In fact, research shows that exposing ourselves to coverage that supports our views encourages us to become more politically engaged and active (Wojcieszak, Bimber, Feldman, & Stroud, 2016). And our diverse social networks (such as different generational family members, work acquaintances, and close friends all together on Facebook) may actually force us to endure greater exposure to opposing opinions than would interpersonal communication or traditional mass media (Messing & Westwood, 2012). Such unwelcome exposure may explain why, after the 2016 presidential election, there was a frenzy of "unfriending" and "unfollowing" of political adversaries on Facebook, even close relations (see e.g., Selyukh, 2016).

The Third-Person Effect

Another way that selectivity may limit media effects is the fact that we tend to overestimate how much influence media actually have on people. The **third-person effect** is a well-documented tendency we have to assume that negative media messages and bias have a much greater influence on *other people* than on ourselves or people we think are like us (Davison, 1983; Sun, Pan, & Shen, 2008). The third-person effect can lead to censorship when we believe it will protect "other" people who we (or our government or religious community) do not think are able to handle certain media messages. Studies also find that the effect is particularly strong for social networking—we think others are more influenced by Facebook than we ourselves are (Lev-On, 2017) and for online news—we assume people's comments (if polite), will persuade others more than ourselves (Chen & Ng, 2016). With all media, you need to be aware that you may be overestimating the effect on others or underestimating the effect on yourself (or both).

Influences on Attitudes and Behaviors

Although selectivity may give audiences some power and make them resistant to being affected by media, there are several areas where media *do* have more substantial influences on audiences. These include encouraging people to imitate behavior, cultivating cultural attitudes, and setting the political issue agenda.

connect

In addition to our news choices, we tend to choose entertainment media that show positive portrayals of our in-group members (as discussed in Chapter 6). We like to see ourselves presented in media, and narrowcasting is an attempt by entertainment media to capitalize on this tendency by reaching out to different cocultures.

● SEEING ACTION FIGURES LIKE THE POWER RANGERS GET REWARDS FOR FIGHTING may lead children to try to imitate this aggressive behavior. Everett Collection, Inc/ Courtesy Everett Collection

and you?

Do you think that your communication behavior is influenced by media messages? What about the clothes you wear? Your use of slang? Might you be modeling behaviors based on media messages without even realizing it?

and you?

In what ways have mediated messages shaped your perceptions of the world? Do you think your views of different people (and places) may have been shaped by what you have seen in entertainment or news media?

Social Cognitive Theory

According to **social cognitive theory**, we learn behavior by watching the behaviors of those whom we have identified as models (Bandura, 2001, 2009). We must first attend to the modeled behavior, remember it, and then have the ability and motivation to imitate it. We are particularly likely to imitate modeled behaviors when we see that the models are rewarded for what they do—when your big brother gets lots of praise for playing the guitar, you then try to play the guitar! How does this apply to media effects? Media provide many modeled behaviors for children and adults to learn from and imitate, both positive (sharing, giving to charity) and negative (violence). Decades of studies looking at the effects of television violence on children's behavior have found that children are more likely to be aggressive after viewing rewarded rather than punished TV violence (see Strasburger & Wilson, 2014, for a review). Most studies are limited to examining short-term effects (behavior right after viewing), so it is unclear whether children would make long-term behavior changes after a one-time viewing experience, especially if they later get in trouble at home or school for being aggressive.

There are several factors besides rewards and punishments that can increase the likelihood of imitating behaviors we witness on television (violent or otherwise). Children are more likely to imitate behavior that is realistic (as opposed to fantasy), justified (the character has a good reason for doing it), and committed by characters the children identify with (the hero or villain; Wilson et al., 2002). For adolescents, the behavior of their peers is also important. TV violence tends to increase aggression among teens who also see their peers as more aggressive (Fikkers, Piotrowski, Lugtig, & Valkenburg, 2016). The good news is that providing strong, likable, and realistic *positive* role models for children and teens can promote good behavior. But remember that children are not "sponges" of media behavior—like adults, their own unique interests and motivations also affect their interpretations of media models and their likelihood of imitation (Ferguson & Dyck, 2012).

Cultivation Theory

If you watch a lot of reality TV about cosmetic surgery, are you more likely to believe that plastic surgery is normal and acceptable? **Cultivation theory** argues that a steady, long-term diet of heavy television viewing results in perceptions of reality that match the (distorted) view of reality presented on television (Gerbner, Gross, Morgan, & Signorielli, 1994). Originally developed in the 1970s, the theory did not distinguish between different kinds of programs; it treated the entire TV world as basically the same—dominated by messages about crime and violence. The theory proposed that the more TV you watch, the more you will develop a perception of the world as a scary, violent place. Studies showed that individuals who watch a lot of television were indeed more likely to be afraid of crime or of walking alone at night, to estimate greater police activity, and to mistrust other people (Gerbner, Gross, Morgan, & Signorielli, 1994).

However, the explosion of television channels, genres, and new media has led to criticism of the idea that all television messages are the same; research during the past two decades has largely shifted toward looking at correlations between attitudes and heavy viewing of certain *types* of media messages—young girls who consume a lot of "thin media" messages having poorer body image, for example (Harrison & Cantor, 1997; Tiggemann, 2005). But critics of cultivation theory argue not only that the effects are pretty small but also that it is impossible to determine whether *any* of the correlations that cultivation studies find are actually media effects (Nabi, 2009). This is because the causal direction could arguably be going the other way:

girls who have poor body image or low self-esteem are likely to seek out messages that confirm their views (i.e., by finding thin models to compare themselves to). Similarly, people who are already accepting of plastic surgery are the very people most likely to want to watch shows about it. Still, it is important to be aware of our media "diet," as this may well be connected to the kinds of stereotypes, attitudes, and perceptions we are developing or reinforcing.

Agenda Setting

Whether or not media have the ability to cultivate our attitudes about issues, there is evidence that media *do* have an impact on what issues we think about in the first place. **Agenda setting** is the idea that extensive media coverage of a particular issue or event, such as health care reform in Washington or a major storm on the Eastern Seaboard, will "set the agenda" for what issues people are thinking and talking about (see McCombs, 2005). Issues that do not get much coverage will not seem very important.

Agenda setting is important because we use the issues we are thinking about to evaluate political leaders and potential policy decisions (Scheufele & Iyengar, 2012). For example, if an incident of gun violence gets nonstop news coverage and social media chatter, then we may be more likely to evaluate current political leaders in terms of their stance on gun control (as opposed to their position on other issues). Politicians may even be more successful at pushing policy decisions about guns during this time. This is why presidents, congressional leaders, and political activist groups all take such pains to try to control the press and social media agenda (Farnsworth, 2015).

Control of the news and social media agenda is not easy. With a diverse range of media news outlets available online, people can select their own news agendas and promote particular stories among their own social networks. But there is evidence that traditional media do still have an agenda-setting effect, although it is weakened for people who use multiple online news sources (Shehata & Strömbäck, 2013). In addition, agenda-setting effects may be a two-way process online, in which news stories encourage people to search for those issues online, while people's own online searches or Facebook or Twitter posts also influence the coverage in the news media (Ragas, Tran, & Martin, 2014).

Mass Communication in a Digital Age

Earlier in this chapter, we argued that media convergence means a blurring of the lines between traditional mass communication and digital computing and telecommunication technologies (Pavlik & McIntosh, 2016). Indeed, our discussion of the shape and influence of mass communication messages throughout this chapter has involved both traditional media and their digital counterparts. However, other aspects of the digital mass media environment warrant special attention. In this section, we explore the uniquely personal and interactive world of mass communication online.

Mass Self-Communication

With traditional media, only the professionals (news organizations, television networks, studios, etc.), acting as **gatekeepers**, control the creation and distribution of information and entertainment. Those outlets require enormous capital

● **DUE IN GREAT** part to vanity-focused TV programs and reality stars, plastic surgery — even in extreme forms — is perceived as almost routine, particularly among females, like Kylie Jenner. Robert Kamau/Getty Images

connect

If you consider your mass media experience as part of your overall culture and relational history — as explained in Chapter 6 — it is easy to see how your perceptions of cocultures that are different from your own might be shaped by media messages. But the mass media can challenge stereotypes as easily as they can reinforce them. Modern television shows, in particular, feature diverse casts and story lines and may help to broaden some individuals' cultural horizons.

and you?

How do you access media? Do you read printed material? Do you have a broadband connection? Do you have cable/satellite television? A smartphone? All of the above? How typical do you think you are compared to others your age in terms of the number of ways you can access media?

investment as well as highly technical production skills and capability. Digital media use, on the other hand, does not require the same degree of skill, money, or access. In fact, anyone with an internet connection has the opportunity to discover and provide competing voices to those of traditional media. As a result, rather than just being receivers of mass communication messages, we are now engaging in **mass self-communication**, each of us creating, sending, and relaying the messages that interest us personally, but with the potential to reach enormous audiences (Valkenburg, Peter, & Walther, 2016).

Individual Contributions to Culture

Even artist Andy Warhol, who once predicted that everyone would eventually have the opportunity to be famous for fifteen minutes, might have been surprised by the ease with which anyone can put themselves into media today. Mass self-communication offers opportunities for individuals and groups to participate more actively in the political process and contribute more directly to the culture. For example, in the news media, **citizen journalists** are nonprofessionals who report and comment on events in their communities. They may connect directly with the public by blogging, tweeting, or uploading their smartphone videos or share content with the professional news organizations. Many see themselves as alternative sources of information that provide resistance to the biases of the "mainstream" news (Wall, 2015).

wired for communication

think about this

New Life Through Digital Media?

Imagine that a friend shares a link to an online fan site devoted to a television program. There are forums where fans review episodes, discuss the actors, or explain the themes. The site also notes upcoming events or conferences in cities across the United States; it even has a section where fans submit their own creative works related to the show (fiction, poetry, artwork). This is not surprising, of course, as the internet is littered with such venues. But what might surprise you is that all of this fan activity is for a show that ended over a decade ago. *Buffy the Vampire Slayer* ran on American television from 1997 to 2003. Despite achieving only modest ratings across its broadcast career, it has remained a pop culture juggernaut through its online fandom afterlife. There is even a commitment to the show among some media scholars, who hold regular conferences and publish journals devoted to academic analyses of *Buffy* and creator Joss Whedon's other productions (such as *Firefly*; Whedon Studies Association, 2016).

Digital technology certainly did not create the fandom experience — *Star Trek* and *Star Wars* fans have been stapling together "fanzines" and attending science fiction conventions for decades — but the internet and social media have facilitated the formation and maintenance of such fan groups. Online fandom allows fans to more easily connect with one another to develop personal relationships as well as to rewatch and reanalyze episodes of their favorite shows (one blogger recently coordinated a year-long "*Buffy* rewatch," complete with podcasts, blog entries, and fan-scholar comments for every episode). Digital media can also facilitate the "rebooting" of canceled, cult-favorite shows with new episodes. Netflix, for example, fulfilled the wishes of millions of *Arrested Development* fans by producing a long-awaited fifth season and making it available all at once for immediate binge-watching. And of course fans themselves often post their own videos and animated shorts in an effort to generate new love for their old favorites.

1. Have you ever contributed fan fiction or comments to a fan blog or forum for one of your favorite shows? Why or why not? Why do some fans get involved online and others do not?

2. Not all popular or critically acclaimed shows end up with a strong internet afterlife. What do you think it is about a TV show or movie that might cause it to be singled out for the kind of devotional attention lavished on a show like *Buffy*?

3. To what extent do you think that writers or producers of TV shows care about the commentary in online fan groups? How might this influence the creative development of the shows?

Individuals can also contribute their creative voices or interesting experiences to the entertainment media. **User-generated content** ranges from simple home videos or Snapchat stories, to elaborate mash-ups of popular songs, to ongoing YouTube channels that are not unlike professional television shows (Pavlik & McIntosh, 2016). People's real lives or personalities, at least as represented online, can be as entertaining and interesting as professionally produced content. One college community even enjoyed a "real-life" day-long romantic comedy that played out on its school's Snapchat story. Two students became interested in each other via videos but kept missing each other's posts — the campus community became obsessed ("help Vikings Fan find Memorial Library Girl!") until the couple were finally able to meet later that night in person (Geller, 2016).

Of course, not all self-contributions result in messages going "viral" (spreading throughout the internet or social media) or achieving personal fame. Teen idol Justin Bieber and YouTuber PewDiePie may have risen to sustained fame online; however, many others' online lives are much more short-lived. Fame online is click-driven; it is based on spreading through social networks rather than promotion through massive public relations budgets. YouTubers, for example, tend to be more successful when they establish a personal connection with their viewers (Jarvey, 2015). To gain this connection, according to some popular YouTubers, you must be authentic and relatable (rather than focusing on glossy productions), listen to your fans and adapt your content accordingly, and encourage engagement through interactive participation (such as promoting hashtags, holding live streaming events, soliciting viewer videos; "Stars of YouTube . . .", 2015).

Effects of Personal Expression

One simple Tumblr post about the colors of a dress became, for a time, the talk of the internet (Ahuja, 2015). Across multiple social media platforms, people hotly debated whether the dress was blue and black or white and gold. The originator of the post had thought that her Tumblr buddies might respond, but she was overwhelmed that so many other people, including celebrities, became so interested and involved (Walker, 2015). Media scholars have traditionally focused on explaining how media might affect people as audience members, such as in the theories discussed in this chapter. But with mass self-communication, there are also potential effects on people as *creators* of content. An **expression effect** is the influence on the self that comes from seeing that our messages have an influence on others (Pingree, 2007). For example, from our posts on social media (and the responses to them) we may gain or lose self-esteem. By participating in viral cultural conversations, we may feel more important in our social communities. Studies also show that creating political messages on the internet can enhance the sender's own civic involvement,

connect

In an age when anyone has access to mass media, public speaking becomes an even more important skill. Social media give voice to those whom traditional, more linear forms of mass media tended to ignore. And the opportunity for instant audience feedback — in the form of responses, retweets, and replies — makes social media an especially interactive forum for those who seek public access.

and that the persona we use to present ourselves online can influence our offline personalities (see Valkenburg, Peter, & Walther, 2016).

Media Personalization

As we create, share, and consume digital media content as mass self-communicators, we are creating a customized news and entertainment experience. Remember that with all types of mass media we selectively choose messages to fulfill our needs and reinforce our attitudes. In the digital world, we also actively *interact* with these choices (we click, comment, like, view, subscribe). These actions send masses of data to social media platforms, advertisers, news outlets, and political operatives. The result is a highly personalized set of media messages arranged just for *you*. You have probably noticed, for example, that Facebook, YouTube, and Netflix all direct you to content that is similar to what you have already clicked on or liked.

The presidential races of 2012 and 2016 both capitalized on media personalization through **tailored persuasion** — carefully targeting customized ads toward people's unique characteristics and concerns (Cacciatore, Scheufele, & Iyengar, 2016). Barack Obama's campaign used teams of statisticians and social media strategists to mine large amounts of online user data to adapt campaign messages toward individual voters (Isenberg, 2012). Donald Trump's campaign analyzed social media traffic to sense real-time shifts in support — this allowed staffers to kill ineffective ads immediately and upscale better ones as well as organize spur-of-the-moment live rallies in key geographic locations. Rather than spending money on broadly-targeted TV advertising, "the campaign was sending more than 100,000 uniquely tweaked ads to targeted voters each day" (Bertoni, 2016).

Some scholars worry that the trend toward personalized targeting, particularly from marketers, may produce troubling cultural changes (Couldry & Turow, 2014). Research shows that most of us have no idea how much personal data about us is being collected as we click nor how the data is being used to categorize us; and although we may be unhappy about the loss of control over what marketers

FIGURE B.1

PERSONALIZED TARGETING
AND DIGITAL REALITIES

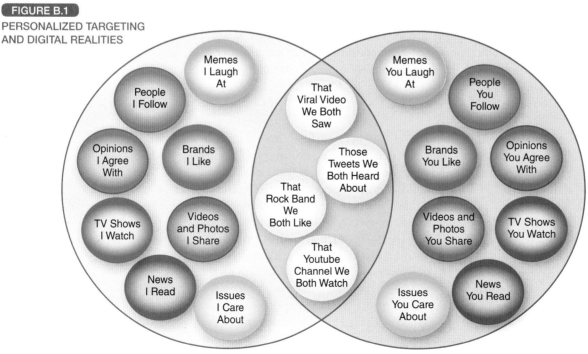

MY DIGITAL REALITY   **YOUR DIGITAL REALITY**

can learn about us, most of us are also largely resigned to having to give up our information if we wish to participate in a digital economy (Turow, Hennessy, & Draper, 2015). The problem is that if our data is used to customize everything from the ads we see to the prices we get offered, it becomes difficult for us to gauge how fairly (or unfairly) we are being treated relative to other consumers.

An additional concern is that our usage data will continue to separate us into such unique consumer and audience segments that we may lose some of the social connection that comes from widely shared cultural experiences (Couldry & Turow, 2014). We each may even be getting a very different picture of the basic "facts" of events or the social issues that matter—in short, a different social reality, as we can see in Figure B.1. On the other hand, the same tools that we use to separate ourselves also provide far greater avenues than other forms of communication for us to reach out and listen to others; that is, if we learn to use these channels effectively.

Ineffective Participation

When Amy's twin girls were born almost three months prematurely, her husband Vern got online right away to find out everything he could about "preemies." But his search quickly became overwhelming: for every opinion in one direction, there seemed to be someone else giving the opposite advice. The sheer volume of messages made available by converging media can lead to **information overload**, the difficulty in sorting through and making sense of vast amounts of information. Apart from the difficulty for individuals, information overload can also hinder the ability of government agencies to act on shared information and make it difficult for employees to share information effectively within their companies (Pavlik & McIntosh, 2016). Media multitasking can exacerbate the problem, as studies show that multitasking hinders our ability to attend to and focus on the information we most need (Chen & Yan, 2016; Wang, Irwin, Cooper, & Srivastava, 2015).

It can also be difficult to evaluate the quality of information in digital media. Some information is edited by professional journalists; some is user contributed and edited (such as Wikipedia); and some is unedited information posted on forums, blogs, or social media. Rumors, hoaxes, and conspiracy theories abound (cataloged and investigated at Snopes.com, among others). Even messages that look like "news" may really be comedic parodies or outright falsely distributed reports. The potential for effective citizen participation is limited when users create or distribute false or other dangerous kinds of information online.

Participation is also ineffective when users fail to think critically about the information they find on the internet. Much like with the traditional media, a site that *looks* credible, with professional design and impressive depth of content, may be given higher credence even if it might otherwise be suspect given its origins or sponsorship (Flanagin & Metzger, 2007). To make good on the promises of digital media for social and political participation, we need to devote our attention to the *quality* of our own and others' mediated communication.

Competent Media Consumers

Media scholars argue that the way to avoid or counteract negative media effects is by becoming **media literate** (Potter, 2008; Potter & Byrne, 2009). This means developing an understanding of your own media habits and critically evaluating and analyzing media sources and messages. To become media literate, you should practice the following skills.

● **THIS ERA MAY** well be considered the "Too Much Information Age," as digital media deliver more content than we can process. Francisco Diez Photography/Getty Images

and you?

Are you media literate? Do you critique what you read, hear, and watch — or is most of it just background noise to you? Do you think that the media you choose *not* to attend to might have an effect on you?

Monitor Your Media Use and Exposure

Like counting calories or carbohydrates, being aware of what you consume can end up making you consume less or at least make wiser choices about your media diet. Parents often find that if they limit the hours per day or week of their children's "screen time" (TV, video games, internet use), children tend to be much more selective in their media choices. Monitoring your own media use — including what you read or watch intentionally as well as the peripheral messages you are exposed to along the way — encourages you to take more responsibility for your exposure to media messages.

Consider the Source of Media Messages

Remember that every message you receive has a source, and it is your job to question its credibility. If you understand the biases and goals of media sources — from advertisers and journalists to filmmakers and bloggers — you will be in a better position to know whether to resist or accept their messages. Bear in mind the economics of media, and think about how the business of mass communication might affect the messages you receive. Compare the messages you get with those of others in your circle of friends, so that you can see how marketers may be tailoring their messages differently to different people. And remember to be just as critical with material that supports your views as you are with material that does not.

Be Aware of Media Effects

Bear in mind how the media effects we discussed earlier in the chapter influence the way you receive, interpret, and react to media messages. They can reinforce your opinions on specific issues, or encourage you to participate in certain behaviors. Which media messages do you choose to attend to, and which do you tend to ignore? How do media messages make you feel? Do you think that you are more immune to media effects than others?

Understand the Grammar of Media

Media each have a **grammar** — a set of rules and conventions that dictates how they operate. When you grow up with a medium, you often take for granted some of this grammar: you learned pretty early that a movie screen going wavy is a sign of a flashback or dream sequence. But it is also useful to pay attention to other forms of television and internet grammar, such as how video clips can be edited and arranged to maximize emotional impact. Understanding media conventions helps you recognize the limitations of media, so that you can better separate, for example, TV sitcom logic from real-life situations. You can also better appreciate the genres you love, distinguish the good from poor versions of these forms, and recognize the value of parodies of these conventions (such as the *Daily Show* on Comedy Central or *The Onion* website).

With digital media technology, there are many more grammars that you have to learn: Twitter and Facebook, for example, have their own vernacular, privacy settings, and ways of sharing information. You need to understand where your messages are going and to whom as well as what it may mean in different online contexts to, for example, *subscribe*, *like*, or *retweet*. Identifying and supporting the companies or online retail outlets that tell you openly how they use your online data may also

real communicator

NAME: Molly Ludwig
OCCUPATION: Senior Vice President of a Market Research Company
Courtesy Molly Ludwig

A television producer wants to improve the Nielsen ratings for his show: "We're doing great with kids 11 to 12, but not with the 7 to 8s. Let's find out why not." That's my job — to research how to improve my client's show. I specialize in focus groups, guided discussions among media consumers to find out what they really think and feel. There are two key parts to my job. The first is the focus group itself, where you have to listen attentively to the discussion and guide the conversation in order to touch on all of your objectives. The second part is client management: translating what a client wants to know into familiar language for consumers, then analyzing the focus group discussion and retranslating to the client.

Focus groups involve multiple responsibilities. First we figure out who should participate, such as hard-core fans versus kids who only watch a show occasionally. Then we develop a discussion guide with thoughtful questions. The discussion itself, however, has to be organic. During the focus group, it is important to make sure everyone feels comfortable and to let them know that if they disagree, they should speak up. Reacting to their nonverbal communication is also important. If I see someone raise an eyebrow while others are talking, I'll say, "You seem skeptical. What do you think?" A quiet person may have something important to say.

For our report to the client, we aim to tell the story honestly about people's reactions. We might have found that the sarcasm and innuendo in their show is hitting with the 12-year-olds but goes over the heads of the 7-year-olds. We also provide specific recommendations, such as, "They really want to see more of this character, but she doesn't have a strong enough future arc" or "They want these characters to be better friends."

I apply many of the concepts and skills I learned in my communication classes every day. I rely on small-group communication and interviewing skills, and understanding entertainment media and persuasion helps me speak to different audiences. It's also important to be a good listener. For an audience researcher, it's up to *you* to listen to the clients and then to the consumers, and be able to put that all together to help your clients reach their goal.

● ON *THE DAILY SHOW,* TREVOR NOAH explores current events with satirical news segments and humorous interviews. Brad Barket/Getty Images

help you have more control over the way marketers might be targeting you. If public advocacy groups can encourage this openness through "naming, praising, or shaming" companies based on their level of transparency, this may also help us more broadly as a society become digitally literate (Turow, Hennessy, & Draper, 2015).

Actively Evaluate Media Messages

By putting together all of the previously mentioned skills, you can critically evaluate media messages and become a more competent participant in mass communication. Ask yourself what was great about a television episode (was it insightful, clever, funny, or moving?) and what was poor (was it unbelievable, unrealistic, or clichéd?). Consider carefully what underlying themes or values are being presented in your entertainment and news content. Are these consistent with your own values? *Should* they be?

what about you?

How Engaged Are You with Digital Mass Media?

To see how often you consume and contribute to digital mass communication, respond to each item below using the following scale: 1 = never; 2 = rarely; 3 = sometimes; 4 = often; and 5 = very often.

How often do you:

_____ 1. Read the comments people have posted on someone's blog.

_____ 2. Provide comments on someone else's blog.

_____ 3. Write or update your own blog.

_____ 4. Read messages on microblogs (such as tweets on Twitter or posts on Tumblr).

_____ 5. Write or post messages on microblogs (such as tweets on Twitter or posts on Tumblr).

_____ 6. Read or look up information on a Wikipedia or other "Wiki" page.

_____ 7. Write or change some information on Wikipedia or other "Wiki" page.

_____ 8. Provide answers to social question and answer sites (like Yahoo! Answers).

_____ 9. Look up answers on social question and answer sites (like Yahoo! Answers).

_____ 10. Read ratings, written reviews, or testimonials on a website.

_____ 11. Contribute your own ratings, reviews, or testimonials on a website.

_____ 12. Watch videos on video-sharing sites (such as YouTube).

_____ 13. Upload your own videos to video-sharing sites (such as YouTube).

_____ 14. Follow links to articles or videos people have shared on social media.

_____ 15. Post or share your own links to articles or videos on social media.

_____ Add your scores for items 1, 4, 6, 9, 10, 12, and 14. Higher scores on these items mean that you are a more active digital media *consumer*. You take advantage of the content available to you to learn from and enjoy media messages.

_____ Add your scores for items 2, 3, 5, 7, 8, 11, 13, and 15. Higher scores on these items mean that you are a more active digital media *contributor*. You participate in media, adding your thoughts to online discussions or providing your own entertainment content for others.

If you score highly on both sets of items, you are maximizing your engagement with media.

Information from K. P. Hocevar, A. J. Flanagin, & M. J. Metzger (2014).

Might these images be suggesting that you compromise your morals or engage in unhealthy behavior?

Take time to think critically about the messages you send as well as those you receive. Be mindful when posting on Facebook or Twitter: Are you sharing articles from trustworthy sources? Can you attest to the accuracy of the information you are relaying? Are you respecting the values of others in your social network? Remember, as both a consumer and a producer of media messages, it is up to you to communicate competently and *ethically*.

 Abigail's Multimedia Family

At the beginning of this chapter, we talked about teenager Abigail and the many types of mass and mediated communication that she and her family use in a single day, much of it at the same time. Consider Abigail's media experiences in light of what you have learned in this chapter.

▶ Abigail is experiencing media convergence. She combines traditional forms of mass media—television and books—with more interactive computer technology as she streams her favorite shows on the internet and comments on blogs. Traditional media are still prominent, but these media interact with her use of texting and social networking. Even her "family time" with her brother is connected to media (video games and YouTube).

▶ Because of all of the different forms of media that Abigail has access to, she can be very selective about what she uses and why. She is not likely to bother with content that she does not like or want. Thus, media content creators (filmmakers, television producers, etc.) must be sure to include messages that appeal to her and others in her demographic group.

▶ Abigail uses social media not only to make connections with her peers but also to contribute her own comments and feelings about cultural phenomena, such as the *Hunger Games* trilogy and author John Green. As a mass self-communicator, she is herself an important part of the cultural conversation.

 Activities

 LaunchPad
macmillan learning

1. LaunchPad for *Real Communication* offers key term videos and encourages self-assessment through adaptive quizzing. Go to **launchpadworks.com** to get access to:

✓ **LearningCurve**
Adaptive Quizzes.

▶ Video clips that illustrate key concepts, highlighted in teal in the Real Reference section that follows.

2. Take notes as you watch one of your usual TV programs. What are some underlying messages of the story or the events? What are the values and traits of the

characters you like the most and the least? Are they stereotypical? If so, what would a nonstereotypical character actually look like?

3. Compare the news coverage for a political controversy on the websites of Fox News, CNN, MSNBC, NPR, and the wire services (AP and Reuters). What are the similarities? What are the differences? Then check the websites for both Media Matters for America and Media Research Center (or its offshoot, News-Busters) and see how each of these media watchdogs criticizes the coverage. What biases do the watchdogs themselves seem to spout?

4. Think of a controversial issue about which you have very strong opinions. Write one paragraph describing the key problem and its main causes, taking care to present your information as objectively as possible. Send it to a few friends. Can they detect where you stand on the issue based on the way you have presented your message? Have you really remained objective? Is it possible to inform without some bias when it comes to divisive issues?

5. List your five favorite YouTubers or YouTube channels. What do they have in common? Are these the same top five that your friends would list? Why or why not? What is it specifically that you like about these people or their shows? What needs are being met by watching them? How do you think they affect you?

 **real reference** A Study Tool

Now that you have finished reading this Appendix, you can:

Distinguish different types of mass communication:

▶ **Mediated communication** occurs when there is some technology that is used to deliver messages; when it occurs on a very broad scale, we refer to it as **mass communication** (p. 494).

▶ **Media convergence** means the blurred distinctions between traditional and digital media forms; we often engage in **media multitasking**, using more than one media type at the same time (pp. 495–496).

Explain how the business of media and the principle of free speech shape the kinds of media messages you encounter:

▶ Most media are businesses that must attract audiences and advertising dollars to remain profitable. **Exponentiality** means that relatively few items bring in most of the income; **audience fragmentation** makes it difficult to reach a large audience for any one media source (p. 497).

▶ Media often cater to **low culture** in order to attract broad audiences, but they have also found success in programs with **narrative complexity**. They target niche audiences through **narrowcasting** (p. 498).

▶ Media producers minimize risk by conducting extensive audience research and engaging in **self-censorship** as well as by relying on proven formulas for success (p. 499).

▶ The principle of free speech fosters a **marketplace of ideas**; **however**, the courts have allowed a few restrictions on First Amendment freedoms (such as limitations on broadcast **indecency**; pp. 500–501).

▶ Like all forms of communication, mass communication can be biased. **Framing** refers to the particular ways that issues are presented in the news (p. 503).

Identify the ways in which mass media may influence your attitudes and behaviors:

▶ The **uses and gratifications perspective** argues that we make media choices in order to satisfy our needs and goals. The expectation that media can satisfy all these needs can lead to **media dependence** (p. 504).

▸ We often select media that provide **preference-based reinforcement** of our existing attitudes; we tend to think that media messages have more of an effect on others than they do on us, a phenomena known as the **third-person effect** (p. 505).

▸ **Social cognitive theory** argues that we learn behavior by watching how media models behave (p. 506).

▸ In **cultivation theory**, a steady, long-term diet of TV viewing can distort our perceptions of the world (p. 506).

▸ News coverage can have an **agenda-setting** effect — we tend to judge the importance of issues by the amount of new coverage they get (p. 507).

Describe how digital media technologies can affect your participation in the social and political process:

▸ Traditional media no longer serve as the sole **gatekeeper** for information and creative content (p. 507). The internet allows everyone to create, send, and relay their messages through **mass self-communication** (p. 508).

▸ Digital media allow individuals to contribute to culture as **citizen journalists** and to create other kinds of **user-generated content**, which can result in **expression effects** on the self (pp. 508–509).

▸ Data gathered about us online can be used for **tailored persuasion** — targeting each of us with personally customized political and product advertising (p. 510).

▸ Ineffective participation in the digital world can be the result of **information overload**. A failure to think critically about media also hinders participation (p. 511).

Practice skills for becoming a more mindful and **media literate** consumer (pp. 511–514):

▸ Monitor your media use and exposure.

▸ Consider the source of media messages.

▸ Be aware of media effects.

▸ Understand the **grammar** of media.

▸ Actively evaluate media messages.

glossary

abstraction ladder: A model that ranks communication from specific, which ensures clarity, to general and vague.

accent: A pattern of pronunciation that is specific to a certain upbringing, geographical region, or culture.

accenting: Nonverbal behavior that clarifies and emphasizes specific information in a verbal message.

accommodation: Adapting and adjusting one's language and nonverbal behaviors for other people or cultures.

achievement-oriented leader: A leader who sets challenging goals and communicates high expectations and standards to members.

active listeners: Active participants in making choices about selecting, attending, understanding, and responding.

active strategies: In relationship management, strategies that allow one to obtain information about a person more directly, by seeking information from a third party.

adaptability: An organization's ability to adjust to changing times and circumstances.

adaptors: Body movements that satisfy some physical or psychological need, such as rubbing your eyes when you are tired or twisting your hair when you are nervous or bored.

***ad hominem* fallacy:** A logical fallacy that entails attacking a person instead of the person's arguments.

adjourning: The stage of group development in which members reflect on their accomplishments and failures as well as determine whether the group will disassemble or take on another project.

affect displays: Body movements that convey feelings, moods, and reactions; they are often unintentional, reflecting the sender's emotions.

affective listening: The component of listening that refers to your attitude toward listening to a person or message.

affiliation: The affect, or feelings, we have for others.

agenda: A plan for a meeting that details the subject and goal, logistics, and a schedule.

agenda setting: The idea that extensive media coverage of a particular issue will "set the agenda" for what issues people are thinking and talking about.

all-channel network: A network in which all members are an equal distance from one another and all members interact with each other.

analytical listening: Listening to explore all ideas before making judgments.

anchor position: An audience's position on a topic at the outset of the speech.

anecdotes: Brief, personal stories that have a point or punch line.

antigroup roles: Roles that create problems because they serve individual members' priorities at the expense of overall group needs.

apologize: To openly take responsibility for your own misbehavior in a miscommunication.

appeal to tradition: A logical fallacy in which the speaker uses tradition as proof, suggesting that listeners should agree with his or her point because "that's the way it has always been."

argumentativeness: A particular form of assertiveness, in which a person tends to express positions on controversial issues and verbally attack the positions that other people take.

articulation: The clarity and forcefulness with which sounds are made, regardless of whether they are pronounced correctly.

artifacts: Accessories carried or used on the body for decoration or identification.

assertiveness: The use of communication messages that demonstrate confidence, dominance, and forcefulness to achieve personal goals.

attending: The step in the listening process of focusing attention on both the presence and communication of someone else.

attitudes: Our general evaluations of people, ideas, objects, or events.

attributions: Personal characteristics that are used to explain other people's behavior.

audience analysis: A highly systematic process of getting to know one's listeners relative to the topic and speech occasion.

audience fragmentation: The spreading of audience members across a wide spectrum of entertainment choices, causing media sources to have difficulty reaching large audiences.

avoiding: An escapist tactic used to stay away from direct conflict, for example, walking away, changing the subject, or postponing conflict.

back-channel cues: Vocalizations that signal when we want to talk versus when we are just encouraging others to continue their talking.

bandwagon fallacy: Accepting a statement as true because it is popular.

bar graph: A presentation aid that shows the relationship of two or more sets of figures.

begging the question: A logical fallacy in which the speaker presents arguments that no one can verify because they are not accompanied by valid evidence.

behavior: Observable communication, including both verbal and nonverbal messages; the manner in which we act or function in response to our attitudes and beliefs.

behavioral component of listening: The component of listening that involves giving feedback to show that you understand and remember the information given.

behavioral confirmation: Acting in a way that makes one's expectations about a group come true.

behavioral flexibility: The ability to have a number of communication behaviors at one's disposal and the willingness to use different behaviors in different situations.

beliefs: The ways in which people perceive reality; our feelings about what is true and real and how confident we are about the existence or validity of something.

biased language: Words that are infused with subtle meanings that influence our perceptions about the subject.

biased listening: Listening that involves zeroing in only on bits of information that interest the listener, disregarding other messages or parts of messages, confirming an existing point of view.

bipolar question: The most closed form of a question, for which there are only two possible responses, "yes" and "no."

bonding: The process of relational partners sharing formal symbolic messages with the world that their relationship is important and cherished.

boundary turbulence: Readjusting the need for privacy against the need for self-disclosure and connection when there is a threat to one's privacy boundaries.

brainstorming: A process that entails focusing on a general area of interest, amassing information, thinking creatively, and considering problems and solutions related to the topic.

bullying: Behaviors such as harsh criticism, name-calling, gossip, slander, personal attacks, or threats to safety or job security, used to try to acquire and keep control over an entire group or individual members within a group.

call to action: In a persuasive speech, a challenge to listeners to act in response to the speech, see the problem in a new way, or change their beliefs, actions, and behavior.

cause–effect pattern: A pattern of speech arrangement that organizes the message around cause-to-effect or effect-to-cause relationships.

central processing: Thinking critically about the speaker's message, questioning it, and seriously considering acting on it; occurs when listeners are motivated and personally involved in the content of a message.

chain network: A network in which information is passed from one member to the next rather than shared among members.

channel: The method through which communication occurs.

channel discrepancy: When one set of communication behaviors says one thing, and another set says something different.

charismatic leaders: Vibrant, likable communicators who generate a positive image among their followers.

chronemics: The study of how people perceive the use of time.

chronological pattern: A pattern of speech arrangement that presents the main points of a message forward (or backward) in a systematic, time-related fashion.

civility: The social norm for appropriate behavior.

classical management approach: An approach to organizational communication that likens organizations to machines, with a focus on maximizing efficiency.

clique: A small subgroup of individuals who have bonded together within a group; also called *coalitions*.

closed question: A type of interview question that gives less freedom to the interviewee by restricting answer choices.

clustering: A technique for identifying potential speech topics whereby the writer begins with a core idea and branches out into a web of related thoughts and ideas.

coculture: A smaller group of people within a culture who are distinguished by features such as race, religion, age, generation, political affiliation, gender, sexual orientation, economic status, educational level, occupation, and a host of other factors.

code: A set of symbols that are joined to create a meaningful message.

code switching: A type of accommodation in which communicators change from one language repertoire to another to fit into a particular group.

coercion: The act of using manipulation, threats, intimidation, or violence to gain compliance.

coercive power: Power that stems from a person's ability to threaten or harm others.

cognitions: Thoughts that communicators have about themselves and others.

cognitive complexity: Ability to consider multiple scenarios, formulate multiple theories, and make multiple interpretations when encoding and decoding messages.

cognitive listening: The component of listening that involves the mental processes of selecting messages to focus on, giving them attention, and then trying to understand them.

cognitive language: The specific system of symbols that one uses to describe people, things, and situations in one's mind.

cohesion: The degree to which group members have bonded, like each other, and consider themselves to be one entity.

collaborating: Conflict style that involves finding a win-win solution that satisfies all parties.

collectivist culture: A culture in which individuals perceive themselves first and foremost as members of a group and communicate from that perspective.

communication: The process by which individuals use symbols, signs, and behaviors to exchange information.

communication accommodation theory: Theory that explains how language and identity shape communication in various contexts.

communication acquisition: The process of learning individual words in a language and learning to use that language appropriately and effectively in the context of the situation.

communication apprehension (CA): Fear or anxiety associated with communication, which is often a common barrier to effective delivery.

communication climate: The dominant temper, attitudes, and outlook of relational partners.

communication privacy management (CPM) theory: An explanation of how people perceive the information they hold about themselves and whether they will disclose or protect it.

communication processing: The means by which we gather, organize, and evaluate the information we receive.

communication skills: Behaviors based on social understandings that help communicators achieve their goals.

comparative advantage pattern: An organizing pattern for persuasive speaking in which the speaker shows that his or her viewpoint is superior to other viewpoints on the topic.

competent communication: Communication that is effective and appropriate for a given situation, in which the communicators continually evaluate and reassess their own communication process.

competent communication model: A transactional model of communication in which communicators send and receive messages simultaneously within relational, situational, and cultural contexts.

competitive strategies: Conflict styles that promote the interests of individuals who see conflict as "win–lose" battles.

complementing: Nonverbal behavior that matches (without actually mirroring) the verbal message it accompanies.

compromising: A way to resolve conflict in which both parties must give up something to gain something.

confabulation: The phenomenon in which passive listeners fabricate and defend distorted memories, unaware that the information is false.

conflict: A negative interaction between two or more interdependent people, rooted in some actual or perceived disagreement.

conflict management: The way we engage in conflict and address disagreements with relational partners.

connotative meaning: The emotional or attitudinal response people have to a word.

consensus: Group solidarity in sentiment, belief, or decision.

contact cultures: Cultures that depend on touch as an important form of communication.

context collapse: The blurring of social boundaries on social media and combining of formerly separate audiences.

contradicting: Nonverbal behavior that conveys meaning opposite of the verbal message.

control: The ability of one person, group, or organization to influence situations, and the manner in which their relationships with others are conducted.

convergence: When speakers shift their language or nonverbal behaviors toward each other's way of communicating.

cooperative strategies: Strategies that benefit a relationship, serve mutual rather than individual goals, and strive to produce solutions that benefit both parties.

costs: The negative elements of a relationship.

countercoalitions: Subgroups that are positioned against other subgroups.

cover letter: A one-page letter indicating interest in a specific position.

credibility: The quality, authority, and reliability of a source of information.

critical listening: Listening to find inconsistencies or errors in the speaker.

crowdfunding: Raising public support and financial backing for charity and social causes using websites and social media campaigns.

crowdsourcing: Gathering information or help solving a problem from large internet audiences.

cultivation theory: The argument that a steady, long-term diet of heavy television viewing results in perceptions of reality that match the (distorted) view of reality presented on television.

culture: A learned system of thought and behavior that belongs to and typifies a relatively large group of people; the composite of their shared beliefs, values, and practices.

cyberbullying: Multiple abusive attacks on individual targets conducted through electronic channels.

deception: The attempt to convince others of something that is false.

declining stage: The stage at which a relationship begins to come apart.

decoding: The process of receiving a message by interpreting and assigning meaning to it.

deductive reasoning: The line of thought that occurs when one draws specific conclusions from a general argument.

defensive climate: A communication climate in which the people involved feel threatened or controlled.

defensive listening: Responding with aggression and arguing with the speaker without fully listening to the message.

definitional speech: A presentation whose main goal is to provide answers to "what" questions by explaining to an audience what something is.

definition by etymology: Defining something by using the origin of a word or phrase.

definition by example: Defining something by offering concrete examples of what it is.

definition by negation: Defining something by telling what it is not.

definition by synonym: Defining something by using words that mean almost the same thing.

delivery cues: In a speech outline, brief reminders about important information related to the delivery of the speech.

demographics: The systematic study of the quantifiable characteristics of a large group.

demonstration speech: A speech that answers "how" questions by showing an audience the way something works.

denotative meaning: The basic, consistently accepted definition of a word.

descriptive presentation: An approach to conveying information that involves painting a mental picture for the audience.

dialectical tensions: Tensions that arise when opposing or conflicting goals exist in a relationship; can be external or internal.

digital communication: The transmission of digitally encoded data (text, images, video, voice) over electronic networks.

digital disparity: The gap between the haves and have-nots in terms of regular access to modern technology, especially broadband connections, and the ability to use it effectively.

directed question: A type of interview question that suggests or implies the answer that is expected.

direct fighting: Conflict style in which people use assertiveness to argue openly to get their way, which can sometimes lead to verbal aggressiveness.

directive leader: A leader who controls the group's communication by conveying specific instructions to members.

directory: A type of secondary resource that is created and maintained by people rather than automatically by computers; guides visitors to the main page of a website organized within a wider subject category.

discrimination: Behavior toward a person or group based solely on their membership in a particular group, class, or category.

distorted perception: Inaccurate, unbalanced, or inappropriate schemas.

division of labor: An aspect of the classical management approach that assumes each part of an organization (and each person involved) must carry out a specialized task for the organization to run smoothly.

dyad: A pair of people.

either–or fallacy: A fallacy in which the speaker presents only two alternatives on a subject and fails to acknowledge other alternatives; also known as the *false dilemma fallacy*.

Elaboration Likelihood Model (ELM): A model that highlights the importance of relevance to persuasion and holds that listeners process persuasive messages by one of two routes, depending on how important the message is to them.

elucidating explanation: An explanation that illuminates a concept's meaning and use.

emblems: Movements and gestures that have a direct verbal translation in a particular group or culture.

encoding: The process of mentally constructing a message for production.

enterprise social media: Platforms that enable organizations to allow workers to post and view organizational messages and engage with work teams on idea-sharing.

equivocation: Use of words that have unclear or misleading definitions.

escapist strategies: Strategies that people use to try to prevent or avoid direct conflict.

ethical communication: Interactions in which individuals consider the moral choices they make in their relationships with others.

ethnocentrism: A belief in the superiority of one's own culture or group and a tendency to view other cultures through the lens of one's own.

ethos: A form of rhetorical proof that appeals to ethics and concerns the qualifications and personality of the speaker.

euphemism: An inoffensive word or phrase that substitutes for terms that might be perceived as upsetting.

evasion: Intentionally failing to provide specific details.

exit interview: An interview that employers hold with employees who opt to leave the company to identify organizational problems that might affect future employee retention.

expert power: Power that comes from the information or knowledge that a leader possesses.

expert testimony: The opinion or judgment of an expert, a professional in his or her field.

explanatory speech: A speech that answers the question "Why" or "What does that mean?" by offering thorough explanations of meaning.

exploratory stage: The stage of a relationship in which one seeks relatively superficial information from one's partner.

exponentiality: The economic principle that relatively few items bring most of the income to a particular industry, while the rest add only a little.

expression effect: The influence on the self that comes from seeing one's message have an influence on others.

extemporaneous speaking: A style of public speaking that involves delivery with few or no notes, but for which the speaker carefully prepares in advance.

family: A small social group bound by ties of blood, civil contract (such as marriage, civil union, or adoption), and a commitment to care for and be responsible for one another, usually in a shared household.

feedback: A message from the receiver to the sender that illustrates responses that naturally occur when two or more people communicate.

feeling: The use of language to express emotion; one of the five functional communication competencies.

feminine culture: A culture that places value on relationships and quality of life; sometimes referred to as a *nurturing culture*.

forgive: A conflict reconciliation strategy in which people emotionally move past the conflict and let go of the bitterness and resentment.

forming: The stage of group development in which group members try to negotiate who will be in charge and what the group's goals will be.

forms of rhetorical proof: Means of persuasion that include *ethos*, *logos*, and *pathos*; first named by Aristotle.

framing: The way particular issues in the news are presented in order to relate to audiences' existing schemas.

friendship: A close and caring relationship between two people that is perceived as mutually satisfying and beneficial.

function: An explanation of how communication behaviors work to accomplish goals in personal, group, organizational, or public situations.

fundamental attribution error: The tendency to overemphasize the internal and underestimate the external causes of behaviors we observe in others.

funnel sequence: A pattern of questioning that progresses from broad, open-ended questions to narrower, more closed questions.

gatekeepers: Those organizations and individuals who control the creation and distribution of information and entertainment.

gender: The behavioral and cultural traits assigned to one's sex; determined by the way members of a particular culture define notions of masculinity and femininity.

generation: A group of people who were born into a specific time frame, along with its events and social changes that shape attitudes and behavior.

global social enterprises (GSE): organizations which attempt to help underdeveloped economies reach greater potential through improved innovation, entrepreneurship, and regional stability as well as by developing legal structures, stabilizing financial systems, and raising money.

globalization: The growing interdependence and connectivity of societies and economies around the world.

gossip: Talk or rumors about personal affairs of others, sometimes serving to solidify group membership.

grammar: The system of rules for creating words, phrases, and sentences in a particular language.

grammar of media: For each form of media, a set of rules and conventions that dictate how it operates.

group: A collection of more than two people who share some kind of relationship, communicate in an interdependent fashion, and collaborate toward some shared purpose.

grouphate: The extent to which a person detests (or otherwise feels negatively about) working in groups.

groupthink: A situation in which group members strive to maintain cohesiveness and minimize conflict by refusing to critically examine ideas, analyze proposals, or test solutions.

haptics: The study of touch as a form of communication.

hasty generalization: A reasoning flaw in which a speaker makes a broad generalization based on isolated examples or insufficient evidence.

hatespeech: Language that employs offensive words to deride a person or group.

hearing: The physiological process of perceiving sound; the process through which sound waves are picked up by the ears and transmitted to the brain.

hierarchy: The layers of power and authority in an organization.

hierarchy of needs: A hierarchical structure that identifies needs in five categories, from low (immature) to high (mature).

high-context culture: A culture that relies on contextual cues—such as time, place, relationship, and situation—to both interpret meaning and send subtle messages.

high language: A more formal, polite, or "mainstream" language, used in business contexts, in the classroom, and at formal social gatherings.

homogeny: Sameness, as applied to a public speaker and his or her audience.

hostile audience: An audience that opposes the speaker's message and perhaps the speaker personally—the hardest type of audience to persuade.

human relations approach: Management approach that considers the human needs of organizational members.

human resources approach: An approach to management that considers organizational productivity from workers' perspectives and considers them assets who can contribute their useful ideas to improve the organization.

hurtful language: Inappropriate, damaging, mean, sarcastic, or offensive statements that affect others in negative ways.

hyperbole: Vivid, colorful language with great emotional intensity and often exaggeration.

hyperpersonal communication: A phenomenon surrounding online communication in which a lack of proximity, visual contact, or nonverbal cues results in enhanced intimacy.

illustrators: Body movements that reinforce verbal messages and visually help explain what is being said.

imagining: The ability to think, play, and be creative in communication—one of the five functional communication competencies.

immediacy: The feeling of closeness, involvement, and warmth between people as communicated by nonverbal behavior.

impersonal communication: Messages that are role-based, with little relational development or expressed emotion.

impromptu speaking: A style of public speaking that is spontaneous, without any warning or preparation.

inclusion: To involve others in our lives and to be involved in the lives of others.

indecency: Discussing or showing sexual or other bodily functions in a very lewd or vulgar way.

indirect fighting: Conflict style that involves using passive-aggressive tactics to express conflict without engaging in it openly.

individualist culture: A culture whose members place value on autonomy and privacy, with relatively little attention to status and hierarchy based on age or family connections.

inductive reasoning: The line of thought that occurs when one draws general conclusions based on specific evidence.

informal–formal dimension: A psychological aspect of the situational context of communication, dealing with our perceptions of personal versus impersonal situations.

information-gathering interview: An interview that serves to transfer knowledge from one party to another by collecting attitudes, opinions, facts, data, and experiences.

information overload: The difficulty in sorting through and making sense of vast amounts of information, created by the volume of messages made available by converging media.

informative speaking: A form of public speaking intended to increase the audience's understanding or knowledge.

informing: The use of language to both give and receive information; one of the five functional communication competencies.

in-group: The group with which one identifies and to which one feels one belongs.

initiating stage: The stage of a relationship in which one makes contact with another person.

insensitive listening: Listening that occurs when we fail to pay attention to the emotional content of someone's message, instead taking it at face value.

integrating: The process of relational partners "becoming one."

intensification stage: The stage of a relationship in which relational partners become increasingly intimate and move their communication toward more personal self-disclosures.

interaction appearance theory: The argument that people change their opinion about the attributions of someone, particularly physical attractiveness, the more they interact with that person.

interaction management: Nonverbal cues used to manage the impressions and regulate interactions of communicators in a variety of relationships and situations.

interaction model: Communication between a sender and a receiver that incorporates feedback.

interactive strategies: In relationship management, strategies that allow one to obtain information by speaking directly with a person rather than observing or asking others for information about the person.

intercultural communication: The communication between people from different cultures who have different worldviews.

intercultural sensitivity: Mindfulness of behaviors that may offend others.

interdependence: Mutual dependence, where the actions of each partner affect the other(s).

intergroup communication: A branch of the communication discipline that focuses on how communication within and between groups affects relationships.

intergroup contact theory: The argument that interaction between members of different social groups generates a possibility for more positive attitudes to emerge.

internal preview: In public speaking, an extended transition that primes the audience for the content immediately ahead.

internal summary: An extended transition that allows the speaker to crystallize the points made in one section of a speech before moving to the next section.

internet of things: A new stage of web-based technology in which digital technologies will be embedded in all aspects of daily life.

interpersonal communication: The exchange of verbal and nonverbal messages between two people who have a relationship and are influenced by the partner's messages.

interrogation: A type of interview in which the interviewer persuasively pressures the interviewee for information.

interview: An interaction between two parties that is deliberate and purposeful for at least one of the parties involved.

intimacy: Closeness and understanding of a relational partner.

inverted funnel sequence: A pattern of questioning that progresses from narrow, closed questions to more open-ended questions.

jargon: Technical language that is specific to members of a particular profession, interest group, or hobby.

job interview: A type of selection interview, with the end goal of filling a position of employment.

key-word outline: The briefest type of outline, consisting of specific "key words" from the sentence outline to jog the speaker's memory.

kinesics: The way gestures and body movements communicate meaning.

laissez-faire leader: The leader who trusts others to handle their own responsibilities, does not take part in the group's discussions or work efforts, and provides feedback only when asked.

labeling: Using terms that stereotype people according to their group membership and ignoring their individual differences.

language: The system of symbols (words) that we use to think about and communicate experiences and feelings.

latitude of acceptance: The range of positions on a topic that are acceptable to an audience based on their *anchor position*.

latitude of noncommitment: A range of positions on a topic the audience is not sure about.

latitude of rejection: The range of positions on a topic that are unacceptable to an audience based on their *anchor position*.

latitudes: Ranges of acceptable and unacceptable viewpoints about a topic.

lay testimony: The opinion of a nonexpert who has personal experience of or has witnessed an event related to the speaker's topic.

leadership: The ability to direct or influence others' behaviors and thoughts toward a productive end.

leading question: A type of directed question that subtly suggests or implies the answer that is expected.

leakage cues: Uncontrolled, nonverbal messages that can reveal one's feelings, but can also be ambiguous.

legitimate power: Power that comes from an individual's role or title.

library gateway: A collection of databases and information sites arranged by subject, generally reviewed and recommended by experts (usually librarians).

linear model (of communication): Communication in which a sender originates a message, which is carried through a channel—perhaps interfered with by noise—to the receiver.

listening: The process of recognizing, understanding, accurately interpreting, and responding effectively to the messages communicated by others.

listening apprehension: A state of uneasiness, anxiety, fear, or dread associated with a listening opportunity; also known as *receiver apprehension*.

listening barrier: A factor that interferes with the ability to accurately comprehend information and respond appropriately.

listening fidelity: The degree to which the thoughts of the listener and the thoughts and intentions of the message producer match following their communication.

loaded question: A type of directed question that boldly suggests the answer that is expected.

logical fallacy: An invalid or deceptive form of reasoning.

logos: A form of rhetorical proof that appeals to logic and is directed at the audience's reasoning on a topic.

love: A deep affection for and attachment to another person involving emotional ties, with varying degrees of passion, commitment, and intimacy.

low-context culture: A culture that uses very direct language and relies less on situational factors to communicate.

low culture: Entertainment that appeals to most people's baser instincts, typified by lurid, sensational images and stories charged with sex, violence, scandal, and abuse.

low language: A more informal, easygoing language, used in informal and comfortable environments.

Machiavellianism: Unethical leadership style named for sixteenth-century philosopher Niccolò Machiavelli, who advised rulers to use deceit, flattery, and other exploitative measures strategically to achieve their desired ends.

main points: In public speaking, the central claims that support the specific speech purpose and thesis statement.

marketplace of ideas: The open forum in which ideas compete.

masculine culture: A culture that places value on assertiveness, achievement, ambition, and competitiveness; sometimes referred to as an *achievement culture*.

masking: A facial management technique in which an expression that shows true feeling is replaced with an expression that shows appropriate feeling for a given interaction.

mass communication: The occurrence of mediated communication on a very broad scale.

mass self-communication: Messages created, sent or relayed by an individual over the internet on a very broad scale.

media convergence: The merging of traditional mass communication with digital computing and telecommunication technologies.

media dependence: The expectation that media will serve certain needs.

media interviews: Information-gathering interviews that question and analyze people, politics, media, and events.

media literate: Having an understanding of one's own media habits and critically evaluating and analyzing media sources and messages.

media multitasking: Using more than one media type at the same time.

media synchronicity theory: The theory stating that some channels enable greater ability to communicate back-and-forth rapidly in a coordinated exchange of messages.

mediated communication: The use of technology to deliver messages between sources and receivers.

mentor: A seasoned, respected member of an organization who serves as a role model for a less experienced individual.

message: The words or actions originated by a sender.

mindfulness: The process of being focused on the task at hand—necessary for competent communication.

mindlessness: A passive state in which the communicator is a less critical processor of information, characterized by reduced cognitive activity, inaccurate recall, and uncritical evaluation.

model: A presentation aid—an appropriately scaled object.

moderators (mods): Individuals present on online discussion boards to uphold the rules of the site and give members a sense of organization. Also known as *mods*.

monochronic culture: A culture that treats time as a limited resource, as a commodity that can be saved or wasted.

monopolistic listening: Listening in order to control the communication interaction.

monotone: A way of speaking in which the speaker does not vary his or her vocal pitch.

motivated sequence pattern: A pattern of speech arrangement that entails five phases based on the psychological elements of advertising: attention, need, satisfaction, visualization, and action.

motivational interview: A type of persuasive interview that attempts to elicit change collaboratively through goal-oriented questioning designed to inspire and strengthen personal motivation.

multitasking: Attending to several things at once.

mumbling: Omitting certain sounds in a word, running words together, or speaking so softly that listeners can hardly hear.

narratives: Stories about oneself or one's experiences to aid in self-presentation.

narrative complexity: In mass media, complicated plots and connections between characters, a blurring of reality and fantasy, and time that is not always linear or chronological.

narrative pattern: A pattern of speech arrangement that ties points together in a way that presents a vivid story, complete with characters, settings, plot, and imagery.

narrowcasting: In mass media, the process of targeting smaller, specific audiences; also known as *niche marketing*.

naturalness: The degrees to which a channel is communicative by stimulating more biologically natural communication usually experienced in real-life interactions.

naturalistic fallacy: An appeal to nature saying that what is natural is right or good and that anything unnatural is wrong or bad.

negativity bias: Inaccurate perception occuring when an individual focuses on the negative over positive or neutral attributes of another.

network: A pattern of interaction that governs who speaks with whom in a group and about what.

networking: The process of using interconnected groups or associations of persons one knows to develop relationships with their connections whom one does not know.

neutral audience: An audience that falls between the receptive audience and the hostile audience; neither supports nor opposes the speaker.

neutral question: A type of interview question that provides no hint to the interviewee concerning the expected response.

noise: Interference with a message that makes its final form different from the original.

nonbinding straw poll: An informal vote on a decision that can help a group move forward when time is an issue.

noncontact culture: A culture that is less touch sensitive or even tends to avoid touch.

nonverbal codes: Symbols we use to send messages without, or in addition to, words.

nonverbal communication: The process of intentionally or unintentionally signaling meaning through behavior other than words.

norming: The stage of group development in which members establish agreed-upon norms that govern expected behavior.

norms: Recurring patterns of behavior or thinking that come to be accepted in a group as the "usual" way of doing things.

objective: Expressing or presenting facts and information in a straightforward and evenhanded way, free of influence from the speaker's personal thoughts or opinions.

obliging: An escapist tactic used to stay away from direct conflict, for example, giving in to the other person's wishes.

oculesics: The study of the use of eyes to communicate.

online peer-to-peer support: The engagement with and reliance on internet social connections to help with personal, physical, and mental health problems.

openness: An organization's awareness of its own imbalances and problems.

open question: A type of interview question that gives the interviewee great freedom in terms of how to respond.

operational definition: Defining something by explaining what it is or what it does.

oral citation: A reference to source materials that the speaker mentions in the narrative of a speech.

oratory: A form of public speaking in which a speech is committed to memory.

organization: A group with a formal governance and structure.

organizational assimilation: The process by which newcomers learn the nuances of the organization and determine if they fit in.

organizational communication: The interaction necessary to direct a group toward multiple sets of goals.

organizational culture: An organization's unique set of beliefs, values, norms, and ways of doing things.

organizational hero: An individual who achieves great things for an organization through persistence and commitment, often in the face of great risk.

organizational storytelling: The communication of the company's values through stories and accounts, both externally (to an outside audience) and internally (within the company).

outcome: The product of an interchange.

out-groups: Those groups one defines as "others."

outline: A structured form of a speech's content.

overaccommodate: Going too far in changing one's language or nonverbal behavior, based on an incorrect or stereotypical notion of another group.

paralanguage: The vocalized sounds that accompany words.

paraphrasing: A part of listening empathetically that involves guessing at feelings and rephrasing what one thinks the speaker has said.

parasocial interactions: One-sided relationships in which individuals extend emotional energy, interest, and time with celebrities or other media images who are completely unaware of their existence.

participative leader: A leader who views group members as equals, welcomes their opinions, summarizes points that have been raised, and identifies problems that need discussion rather than dictating solutions.

passive listeners: Those who fail to make active choices in the listening process.

passive strategies: Observing others in communication situations without actually interacting with them.

pathos: A form of rhetorical proof that concerns the nature of the audience's feelings and appeals to their emotions.

peer communication: Communication between individuals at the same level of authority in an organization.

peer relationships: The friendships that form between colleagues at an organization as a result of *peer communication.*

perception: A cognitive process through which one interprets one's experiences and comes to one's own unique understandings.

performance appraisal: An interview designed to review an individual or party's accomplishments and develop goals for the future; used in corporate and academic environments.

performance visualization: Spending time imagining positive scenarios and personal success in order to reduce negative thoughts and their accompanying anxiety.

performing: The stage of group development in which members combine their skills and knowledge to work toward the group's goals and overcome hurdles.

peripheral processing: Giving little thought to a message or even dismissing it as irrelevant, too complex to follow, or simply unimportant; occurs when listeners lack motivation to listen critically or are unable to do so.

persuasion: The process of influencing others' attitudes, beliefs, and behaviors on a given topic.

persuasive interview: An interview in which questions are designed to elicit some change in the interviewee's behavior or opinions.

persuasive speaking: Speech that is intended to influence the attitudes, beliefs, and behaviors of an audience.

phishing: The attempt by cyber criminals to obtain the personal information of others by sending messages that encourage them to reply or open an attachment.

phrase outline: A type of outline that takes parts of sentences and uses those phrases as instant reminders of what the point or subpoint means.

pie chart: A presentation aid that shows percentages of a circle divided proportionately.

pitch: Variations in the voice that give prominence to certain words or syllables.

plagiarism: The crime of presenting someone else's words, ideas, or intellectual property as one's own, intentionally or unintentionally.

planting: A technique for limiting and controlling body movements during speech delivery by keeping the legs firmly set apart at a shoulder-width distance.

politically correct language: Language that replaces exclusive or negative words with more neutral terms.

polychronic culture: A culture whose members are comfortable dealing with multiple people and tasks at the same time.

posture: The position of one's arms and legs and how one carries the body.

power distance: The way in which a culture accepts and expects the division of power among individuals.

pragmatics: The ability to use the symbol systems of a culture appropriately.

preference-based reinforcement: The selection of media that supports the media consumer's preexisting beliefs and values.

prejudice: A deep-seated feeling of unkindness and ill will toward particular groups, usually based on negative stereotypes and feelings of superiority over those groups.

preparation outline: A draft outline the speaker will use, and probably revisit and revise continually, throughout the preparation for a speech; also known as a *working outline*.

primacy–recency effect: In public speaking, the tendency for audiences to remember points the speaker raises at the very beginning, or at the very end, of a message.

primary group: A long-lasting group that forms around the relationships that mean the most to its members.

primary question: A type of interview question that introduces new topics.

problem–solution pattern: A pattern of speech arrangement that involves dramatizing an obstacle and then narrowing alternative remedies down to the one the speaker wants to recommend.

problem-solving group: A group with a specific mission.

problem-solving interview: An interview that is used to deal with problems, tensions, or conflicts.

process: The methods by which an outcome is accomplished.

productive conflict: Conflict that is managed effectively.

profanity: Words or expressions considered insulting, rude, vulgar, or disrespectful.

pronunciation: The correct formation of word sounds.

prop: A presentation aid—an object that removes the burden from the audience of having to imagine what something looks like as the speaker is presenting.

proposition of fact: A claim of what is or what is not.

proposition of policy: A claim about what goal, policy, or course of action should be pursued.

proposition of value: A claim about something's worth.

protégé: A new or inexperienced member of an organization who is trained or mentored by a more seasoned member.

provocation: The intentional instigation of conflict.

proxemics: The study of the way we use and communicate with space.

proximity: A state of physical nearness.

pseudolistening: Pretending to listen when one is actually not paying attention at all.

psychographics: Psychological qualities of an audience, such as attitudes, values, lifestyles, behaviors, and interests.

public–private dimension: An aspect of the situational context of communication dealing with the physical space that affects our nonverbal communication.

public speaking: A powerful form of communication that includes a speaker who has a reason for speaking, an audience that gives the speaker attention, and a message that is meant to accomplish a specific purpose.

public speaking anxiety (PSA): The nervousness one experiences when one knows one has to communicate publicly to an audience.

punctuated equilibrium: A stage of group development in which groups experience a period of inertia or inactivity until they become aware of time, pressure, and looming deadlines, which then compel group members to take action.

quasi-scientific explanation: An explanation that models or pictures the key dimensions of some phenomenon for a typical audience.

reasoning: The line of thought we use to make judgments based on facts and inferences from the world around us.

receiver: The target of a message.

receptive audience: An audience that already agrees with the speaker's viewpoints and message and is likely to respond favorably to the speech.

reconciliation: A repair strategy for rekindling a terminated relationship.

red herring fallacy: A fallacy in which the speaker relies on irrelevant information for his or her argument, thereby diverting the direction of the argument.

reduction to the absurd: A logical fallacy that entails extending an argument beyond its logical limits to the level of absurdity; also known as *reductio ad absurdum*.

referent power: Power that stems from the admiration, respect, or affection that followers have for a leader.

refutational organizational pattern: An organizing pattern for persuasive speaking in which the speaker begins by presenting main points that are opposed to his or her own position and then follows them with main points that support his or her own position.

regulating: Using nonverbal cues to aid in the coordination of verbal interaction.

regulators: Body movements that help us manage our interactions.

relational dialectics theory: The theory that *dialectical tensions* are contradictory feelings that tug at us in every relationship.

relational listening: Listening to establish and maintain relationships.

relational network: A web of relationships that connects individuals to one another.

relationships: The interconnection or interdependence between two or more people required to achieve goals.

remember: recall information as a listener by providing feedback or paraphrasing.

repair tactics: Ways to save or repair a relationship.

repeating: Nonverbal behavior that offers a clear nonverbal cue that repeats and mirrors the verbal message.

replicability: The ability of digital messages to be shared with larger audiences.

research search engine: A search engine that searches only for research published in academic books, journals, and other periodicals.

résumé: A printed summary of one's education, work experiences, and accomplishments.

reward power: Power that derives from an individual's capacity to provide rewards.

rewards: The beneficial elements of a relationship.

rhetoric: The art of speaking well.

richness: The degree to which a particular channel is communicative by allowing more visual, vocal, and personality cues.

ritualizing: Learning the rules for managing conversations and relationships; one of the five functional communication competencies.

role conflict: A situation that arises in a group whenever expectations for members' behavior are incompatible.

running bibliography: A list of resources the speaker has consulted, to which he or she can refer on note cards.

salient: Brought to mind in the moment; one's social identity and communication shift depending on which of one's multiple group memberships is salient in a given moment.

Sapir-Whorf hypothesis: The claim that the words a culture uses or does not use influence its members' thinking.

scanning: A technique for making brief eye contact with almost everyone in an audience by moving one's eyes from one person or section of people to another.

schema: A mental structure that puts together individual but related bits of information.

scientific research findings: Hard numbers and facts that are particularly useful for public speeches on medicine, health, media, or the environment.

search engine: A program that indexes web content and searches all over the internet for documents containing specific keywords that the researcher has chosen.

secondary questions: Types of interview questions that seeks clarification or an elaboration of responses to primary questions.

selecting: The step in the listening process of choosing one sound over another when faced with competing stimuli.

selection interview: An interview whose primary goal is to secure or fill a position within an organization.

selective perception: Active, critical thought resulting in a communicator succumbing to the biased nature of perception.

self-actualization: The feelings and thoughts one experiences when one knows that one has negotiated a communication situation as well as possible.

self-adequacy: The feelings one experiences when one assesses one's own communication competence as sufficient or acceptable—less positive than *self-actualization*.

self-censorship: In mass media, carefully monitoring content and eliminating messages that might offend viewers or sponsors.

self-concept: One's awareness and understanding of who one is, as interpreted and influenced by one's thoughts, actions, abilities, values, goals, and ideals.

self-denigration: A negative assessment about a communication experience that involves criticizing or attacking oneself.

self-directed work team (SDWT): A group of skilled workers who take responsibility for producing high-quality finished work.

self-disclosure: Revealing oneself to others by sharing information about oneself.

self-efficacy: The ability to predict, based on self-concept and self-esteem, one's effectiveness in a communication situation.

self-esteem: How one feels about oneself, usually in a particular situation.

self-fulfilling prophecy: A prediction that causes an individual to alter his or her behavior in a way that makes the prediction more likely to occur.

self-monitoring: The ability to watch one's environment and others in it for cues as to how to present oneself in particular situations.

self-presentation: Intentional communication designed to show elements of self for strategic purposes; how one lets others know about oneself.

self-serving bias: The idea that we usually attribute our own successes to internal factors while explaining our failures by attributing them to situational or external effects.

semantics: The study of the relationship among symbols, objects, people, and concepts—refers to the meaning that words have for people, either because of their definitions or because of their placement in a sentence's structure (syntax).

sender: The individual who originates communication, with words or action.

sentence outline: A type of outline that offers the full text of a speech, often the exact words that the speaker wants to say to the audience.

service-oriented interview: An interview that is designed to cull information and provide advice, service, or support based on that information; used, for example, by customer service representatives.

sexual harassment: "Unwelcome sexual advances, requests for sexual favors, and other verbal or physical harassment of a sexual nature . . . when it is so frequent or severe that it creates a hostile or offensive work environment or when it results in an adverse employment decision (such as the victim being fired or demoted)" (from the U.S. Equal Employment Opportunity Commission, 2011).

signposts: Key words or phrases within sentences that signify transitions between main points.

situational context: The social environment, physical place, and specific events that affect a situation.

slang: Language that is informal, nonstandard, and usually particular to a specific group.

slippery slope fallacy: A logical fallacy that is employed when a speaker attests that some event must clearly occur as a result of another event without showing any proof that the second event is caused by the first.

social capital: The valuable resources, such as information and support, that come from having connections and relationships among people.

social cognitive theory: The theory that we learn behavior by watching the behaviors of those whom we have identified as models.

social comparison theory: A theory that explains our tendency to compare ourselves to others, such as friends and acquaintances or popular figures in the media, as we develop our ideas about ourselves.

social constructivism: The idea that schemas are socially constructed perceptions of reality.

social exchange theory: A theory that explains the process of balancing the advantages and disadvantages of a relationship.

social group: A group in which membership offers opportunities to form relationships with others.

social identity theory: The theory that we each have a *personal identity*, which is our sense of our unique individual personality, and a *social identity*, the part of our self-concept that comes from group memberships.

social information processing (SIP) theory: The theory that communicators use unique language and stylistic cues in their online messages to develop relationships that are as close as those that grow from face-to-face contact; because using text takes time, the process may take longer to become intimate.

social judgment theory: The theory that a speaker's ability to successfully persuade an audience depends on the audience's current attitudes or disposition toward the topic.

social loafing: Failure to invest the same level of effort in the group that people would put in if they were working alone or with one other person.

social ostracism: The exclusion of a particular group member (or members).

social penetration theory (SPT): The theory that partners move from superficial levels to greater intimacy through self-disclosure.

social relationships: Relationships that are functional within a specific context but are less intimate than friendships.

social roles: Group roles that evolve to reflect individual members' personality traits and interests.

spatial pattern: A pattern of speech arrangement that arranges main points in terms of their physical proximity or position in relation to each other (north to south, east to west, bottom to top, left to right, outside to inside, and so on).

speaking outline: The final speech plan, complete with details, delivery tips, and important notes about presentation aids; also known as the *delivery outline*.

speaking rate: How fast or slowly one speaks.

specific purpose statement: A statement that expresses both the topic and the general speech purpose in action form and in terms of the specific objectives the speaker hopes to achieve with his or her presentation.

speech repertoire: A set of complex language behaviors or language possibilities that one calls on to most effectively and appropriately meet the demands of a given relationship, situation, or cultural environment.

stable stage: The stage of a relationship in which it is no longer volatile or temporary; both partners have a great deal of knowledge about one another, their expectations are accurate and realistic, and they feel comfortable with their motives for being in the relationship.

stages of change model: Approach to understanding your audience's disposition that helps predict audience members' motivational readiness toward modifying behavior and includes five stages: precontemplation, contemplation, preparation, action, and maintenance.

statistics: Information provided in numerical form.

stereotyping: The act of organizing information about groups of people into categories so that we can generalize about their attitudes, behaviors, skills, morals, and habits.

storming: The stage of group development in which members inevitably begin experiencing conflicts over issues such as who will lead the group and what roles members will play.

strategic topic avoidance: When one or both relational partners maneuver the conversation away from undesirable topics because of the potential for embarrassment, vulnerability, or relational decline.

study groups: Groups that are formed for the specific purpose of helping students prepare for exams.

subjective: Presenting facts and information from a particular point of view.

subpoints: In public speaking, points that provide support for the main points.

substituting: Replacing words with nonverbal cues.

support group: A set of individuals who come together to address personal problems while benefiting from the support of others with similar issues.

supportive climate: A communication climate that offers communicators a chance to practice empathy and honestly explore the issues involved in the conflict situation.

supportive leader: A leader who attends to group members' emotional needs.

surveillance: Monitoring of employees to see how they are using technology at work, particularly the internet and social media.

survey: To solicit answers to a question or series of questions related to one's speech topic from a broad range of individuals.

syllogism: A three-line deductive argument that draws a specific conclusion from two general premises (a major and a minor premise).

symbols: Arbitrary constructions (usually in the form of language or behaviors) that refer to people, things, and concepts.

synchronicity: The ability to communicate back-and-forth rapidly in a coordinated exchange of messages.

systems approach: An approach to management that views an organization as a unique whole consisting of important members who have interdependent relationships in their particular environment.

tailored persuasion: The careful, targeted customization of ads for individuals, based on their unique interests, characteristics and concerns.

taking conflict personally (TCP): Feeling so threatened by conflict that most disagreements are taken as personal insults or assaults.

task-oriented listening: Listening that is used to focus on clear and pertinent information quickly.

task roles: Roles that are concerned with the accomplishment of the group's goals.

team: A group that works together to carry out a project or specific endeavor or to compete against other teams.

termination ritual: A final get-together to celebrate a group's achievements.

termination stage: The end of a relationship; may come about by a gradual decline in the relationship or by sudden death.

territoriality: The claiming of an area, with or without legal basis, through continuous occupation of that area.

thesis statement: A statement that conveys the central idea or core assumption about the speaker's topic.

third-person effect: The tendency to assume that negative media messages and bias have a much greater influence on other people than on oneself or people one thinks are like oneself.

time orientation: The way cultures communicate about and with time.

tone: A modulation of the voice, usually expressing a particular feeling or mood.

topical pattern: A pattern of speech arrangement that is based on organization into categories, such as persons, places, things, or processes.

transactional: Involving two or more people acting in both sender and receiver roles whose messages are dependent on and influenced by those of their communication partner.

transformative explanation: An explanation that helps people understand ideas that are counterintuitive and is designed to help speakers transform "theories" about phenomena into more accepted notions.

transformative leaders: Leaders who spark change not only by having a new vision but also by conveying that vision clearly to others and energizing the group toward meeting the goals set forth in the vision.

transitions: Sentences that connect different points, thoughts, and details in a way that allows them to flow naturally from one to the next.

trolling: The posting of provocative or offensive messages to whole forums or discussion boards to elicit some type of general reaction.

truth-default theory (TDT): A theory that describes the tendency of people to believe others without suspecting deception.

sequence: A pattern of questioning in which all questions are at the same level, either broad and open-ended or narrow and closed; commonly used in polls and surveys.

turning points: Positive or negative events or changes that stand out in people's minds as important to defining their relationships.

uncertainty avoidance: The process of adapting behaviors to reduce uncertainty and risk.

uncertainty event: An event or behavioral pattern that causes uncertainty in a relationship.

uncertainty reduction theory: The theory that when two people meet, their main focus is on decreasing the uncertainty about each other.

understanding: The step in the listening process of interpreting and making sense of messages.

understatement: Language that downplays the emotional intensity or importance of events, often with euphemisms.

unproductive conflict: Conflict that is managed poorly and has a negative impact on the individuals and relationships involved.

user-generated content: Songs, videos, and other content that individuals create and share publicly through mass media.

uses and gratifications perspective: A perspective that focuses not on what media does to us, but on what we do with media—that is, the way we make media choices (uses) to satisfy our needs and goals (gratifications).

verbal aggressiveness: Attacks on individuals, rather than on issues.

visionary leaders: Leaders who are able to picture a new or different reality from what currently exists and consider the bigger, long-range picture of the future of the group or organization.

vocalizations: Paralinguistic cues that give information about the speaker's emotional or physical state, for example, laughing, crying, or sighing.

volume: How loud or soft the voice is.

wheel network: A network in which all group members share their information with one central individual, who then shares the information with the rest of the group.

work–life balance: Achieving success in one's personal and professional life.

worldview: The framework through which one interprets the world and the people in it.

references

Aakhus, M., & Rumsey, E. (2010). Crafting supportive communication online: A communication design analysis of conflict in an online support group. *Journal of Applied Communication Research, 38*(1), 65–84.

ABC News. (2013, April 23). Worst first day ever. Retrieved from http://newsfeed.time.com/2013/04/23/worst-first-day-ever-rookie-tv-anchor-fired-for-profanity-in-first-newscast

Abrams v. *United States,* 250 U.S. 616 (1919).

Abudi, G. (2011). The 5 types of power. *Quickbase.* Retrieved on July 1, 2016, from http://quickbase.intuit.com/blog/the-5-types-of-power-in-leadership

Action for Children's Television v. *Federal Communications Commission,* 58 F.3d 654 (ACT III) (D.C. Cir. 1995).

Action for Children's Television v. *Federal Communications Commission,* 932 F.2d 1504 (ACT II) (D.C. Cir. 1991).

Adalian, J. (2013, June). *Under the Dome* and TV's new ad-less ways to make cash. Vulture.com. Retrieved from http://www.vulture.com/2013/06/under-the-dome-tv-revenue-when-ads-fail.html

Adkins, M., & Brashers, D. E. (1995). The power of language in computer-mediated groups. *Management Communication Quarterly, 8,* 289–322.

Adkins, R. PhD. (2006). Elemental truths. Retrieved from http://elementaltruths.blogspot.com/2006/11/conflict-management-quiz.html

Afifi, T., Afifi, W., Merrill, A. F., Denes, A. & Davis, S. (2013). "You need to stop talking about this!": Verbal rumination and the costs of social support. *Human Communication Research, 39*(4), 395–421.

Afifi, T. D., & Coveleski, S. (2015). Relational competence. In A. F. Hannawa & B. H. Spitzberg (Eds.), *Communication competence.* Berlin, Boston: De Gruyter Mouton.

Afifi, T. D., McManus, T., Hutchinson, S., & Baker, B. (2007). Parental divorce disclosures, the factors that prompt them, and their impact on parents' and adolescents' well-being. *Communication Monographs, 74,* 78–103.

Afifi, T. D., McManus, T., Steuber, K., & Coho, A. (2009). Verbal avoidance and dissatisfaction in intimate conflict situations. *Human Communication Research, 35*(3), 357–383.

Ahlfeldt, S. L. (2009). Serving our communities with public speaking skills. *Communication Teacher, 23*(4), 158–161.

Ahuja, M. (2015, December 11). The dress that broke the internet . . . is gone. CNN. Retrieved from http://www.cnn.com/2015/12/11/us/the-dress-that-broke-the-internet-is-gone/

Albada, K. F., Knapp, M. L., & Theune, K. E. (2002). Interaction appearance theory: Changing perceptions of physical attractiveness through social interaction. *Communication Theory, 12,* 8–40.

Albert, N. M., Wocial, L., Meyer, K. H., Na, J., & Trochelman, K. (2008, November). Impact of nurses' uniforms on patient and family perceptions of nurse professionalism. *Applied Nursing Research, 21*(4), 181–190. Retrieved from http://dx.doi.org/10.1016/j.apnr.2007.04.008

Aldeis, D., & Afifi, T. D. (2015). Putative secrets and conflict in romantic relationships over time. *Communication Monographs, 82*(2), 224–251. doi:10.1080/03637751.2014.986747

Alexander, A. L. (2008). Relationship resources for coping with unfulfilled standards in dating relationships: Commitment, satisfaction, and closeness. *Journal of Social and Personal Relationships, 25*(5), 725–747.

Alfano, S. (2006, February 11) Tiger Woods Center Opens for Business. *CBS News.* Retrieved on February 11, 2017, from http://www.cbsnews.com/news/tiger-woods-center-open-for-business/

Alge, B. J., Wiethoff, C., & Klein, H. J. (2003). When does the medium matter? Knowledge-building experiences and opportunities in decision-making teams. *Organizational Behavior and Human Decision Processes, 91,* 26–37.

Allan, T. (2004). *The troubles in Northern Ireland.* Chicago: Heinemann Library/Reed Elsevier Inc.

Allen, J. A., Lehmann-Willenbrock, N., & Sands, S. J. (2016, October). Meetings as a positive boost? How and when meeting satisfaction impacts employee empowerment. *Journal of Business Research, 69*(10), 4340–4347. ISSN 0148-2963. doi:10.1016/j.jbusres.2016.04.011

Allen, L. F., Babin, E. A., & McEwan, B. (2012). Emotional investment: An exploration of young adult friends' emotional experience and expression using an investment model framework. *Journal of Social and Personal Relationships, 29*(2), 206–227.

Allen, M. (1991). Comparing the persuasiveness of one-sided and two-sided messages using meta-analysis. *Western Journal of Speech Communication, 55,* 390–404.

Allen, R. R., & McKerrow, R. E. (1985). *The pragmatics of public communication* (3rd ed.). Dubuque, IA: Kendall/Hunt.

Alon, I., Boulanger, M., Elston, J. A., Galanaki, E., Martínez de Ibarreta, C., Meyers, J., Muñiz-Ferrer, M., & Velez-Calle, A. (2016). Business cultural intelligence quotient: A five-country study. *Thunderbird International Business Review.* doi:10.1002/tie.21826

Alter, C. (2013, October 10). Miley Cyrus reels in best Saturday Night Live ratings since March. *Time.* Retrieved from http://entertainment.time.com/2013/10/10/miley-cyrus-reels-in-best-saturday-night-live-ratings-since-march

Almerico, K. (2014, June 17). Crowdfunding can be really effective—if you know what you're doing. Entrepreneur.com. Retrieved from https://www.entrepreneur.com/article/234516

Altman, I., & Taylor, D. A. (1973). *Social penetration: The development of interpersonal relationships.* New York: Holt, Rinehart and Winston.

Amadeo, K. (2013). Obama State of the Union 2013 Address: Summary and economic impact. Retrieved on May 9, 2014, from http://useconomy.about.com/od/Politics/p/2013-State-of-the-Union-Address.htm

Ambrosius, J. D., & Valenzano III, J. M. (2016). "People in hell want Slurpees": The redefinition of the zombie genre through the salvific portrayal of family on AMC's *The Walking Dead. Communication Monographs, 83*(1), 69–93. doi:10.1080/03637751.2015.1030683

American Association of University Professors. (2014). On trigger warnings. Retrieved from http://www.aaup.org/report/triggerwarnings

Andersen, P. A. (1998). The cognitive valence theory of intimate communication. In M. Palmer & G. A. Barnett (Eds.), *Progress in communication sciences*: Vol. 14. Mutual influence in interpersonal communication theory and research in cognition, affect, and behavior (pp. 39–72). Norwood, NJ: Ablex.

Andersen, P. A., Guerrero, L. K., Buller, D. B., & Jorgensen, P. F. (1998). An empirical comparison of three theories of nonverbal immediacy exchange. *Human Communication Research, 24,* 501–535.

Andersen, P. A., Guerrero, L. K., & Jones, S. M. (2006). Nonverbal behavior in intimate interactions and intimate relationships. In V. Manusov & M. L. Patterson (Eds.), *The SAGE handbook of nonverbal communication* (pp. 259–278). Thousand Oaks, CA: Sage.

Anderson, C. M., & Martin, M. M. (1999). The relationship of argumentativeness and verbal aggressiveness to cohesion, consensus, and satisfaction in small groups. *Communication Reports, 12,* 21–31.

Anderson, C. M., Riddle, B. L., & Martin, M. M. (1999). Socialization in groups. In L. Frey, D. Gouran, & M. Poole (Eds.), *Handbook of group communication theory and research* (pp. 139–163). Thousand Oaks, CA: Sage.

Andreassen, C. S., Pallesen, S., & Griffiths, M. D. (2017). The relationship between addictive use of social media, narcissism, and self-esteem: Findings from a large national survey. *Addictive Behaviors, 64,* 287–293.

Ardèvol-Abreu, A., & de Zúñiga, H. G. (2016). Effects of editorial media bias perception and media trust on the use of traditional, citizen, and social media news. *Journalism & Mass Communication Quarterly, 1*–22.

Andrew, F. T., & Dudley, C. H. (2016, January 20). Gossip is a social skill—not a character flaw. *The Conversation.* Retrieved from https://theconversation.com/gossip-is-a-social-skill-not-a-character-flaw-51629

Antaki, C., Barnes, R., & Leudar, I. (2005). Self-disclosure as a situated interactional practice. *British Journal of Social Psychology, 44*(2), 181–199.

Antheunis, M. L., Valkenburg, P. M., & Peter, J. (2010). Getting acquainted through social network sites: Testing a model of online uncertainty reduction and social attraction. *Computers in Human Behavior, 26*(1), 100–109.

Antonijevic, S. (2008). From text to gesture online: A microethnographic analysis of nonverbal communication in the *Second Life* virtual environment. *Information, Communication & Society, 11*(2), 221–238.

Arasaratnam, L. (2007). Research in intercultural communication competence. *Journal of International Communication, 13,* 66–73.

Armstrong, B., & Kaplowitz, S. A. (2001). Sociolinguistic interference and intercultural coordination: A Bayesian model of communication competence in intercultural communication. *Human Communication Research, 27,* 350–381.

Arnal, L. H., Flinker, A., Kleinschmidt, A., Giraud, A., & Poeppel, D. (2015). Human screams occupy a privileged niche in the communication soundscape. *Current Biology, 25*(15), 2051–2056. doi:10.1016/j.cub.2015.06.043

Ashraf, B. N., Zheng, C., & Arshad, S. (2016). Effects of national culture on bank risk-taking behavior. *Research in International Business and Finance, 37,* 309–326.

Asmuß, B. (2013). The emergence of symmetries and asymmetries in performance appraisal interviews: An interactional perspective. *Economic & Industrial Democracy, 34*(3), 553–570.

Asmuß, B. (2008). Performance appraisal interviews. *Journal of Business Communication, 45*(4), 408–429.

Assilaméhou, Y., & Testé, B. (2013). How you describe a group shows how biased you are: Language abstraction and inferences about a speaker's communicative intentions and attitudes toward a group. *Journal of Language & Social Psychology, 32*(2), 202–211.

Associated Press. (2012, March 15). MLB tries to ease language barrier with new rule. *Tribune-Review.* Retrieved from http://triblive.com/sports/mlb/3670340-74/players-rule-baseball#axzz2qg4exWAI

Associated Press. (2016). North Carolina prisons moving away from solitary confinement. *AP Regional State Report - North Carolina.*

Associated Press. (2010, February 20). Tiger Woods returns to Buddhism. *ISKCON News.* Retrieved from http://news.iskcon.org:80/node/2559/2010-02 23/tiger_woods_returns_to_buddhism

Atwood, J. D. (2012). Couples and money: The last taboo. *American Journal of Family Therapy, 40*(1), 1–19. doi: 10.1080/01926187.2011.600674

Avtgis, T. A., & Rancer, A. S. (2003). Comparing touch apprehension and affective orientation between Asian-American and European-American siblings. *Journal of Intercultural Communication Research, 32*(2), 67–74.

Aust, P. J. (2004). Communicated values as indicators of organizational identity: A method for organizational assessment and its application in a case study. *Communication Studies, 55,* 515–535.

Axtell, B. (2016). Retrieved from http://brookeaxtell.com

Axtell, R. E. (1991). *Gestures: The do's and taboos of body language around the world.* Hoboken, NJ: Wiley.

Ayres, J. (2005). Performance visualization and behavioral disruption: A clarification. *Communication Reports, 18,* 55–63.

Ayres, J., & Hopf, T. (1993). *Coping with speech anxiety.* Norwood, NJ: Ablex.

Ayres, J., Wilcox, A. K., & Ayres, D. M. (1995). Receiver apprehension: An explanatory model and accompanying research. *Communication Education, 44,* 223–235.

Baab, L. M. (2014). *The power of listening: Building skills for mission and ministry.* London: Rowman & Littlefield.

Bachman, G. F., & Guerrero, L. K. (2006). Forgiveness, apology, and communicative responses to hurtful events. *Communication Reports, 19,* 45–56.

Back to twerk. (2013, September 10). *Sydney Morning Herald.* Retrieved from http://www.smh.com.au/entertainment/music/back-to-twerk-miley-cyrus-wrecking-ball-video-goes-ballistic-on-youtube-20130910-2tht6.html

Bailey, J., Steeves, V., Burkell, J., & Regan, P. (2013, April). Negotiating with gender stereotypes on social networking sites: From "Bicycle Face" to Facebook. *Journal of Communication Inquiry, 37*(2), 91–112.

Bailey, S. (2013, August 8). Just say no: How your meeting habit is harming you. *Forbes.* Retrieved on August 23, 2016, from http://blogs.forbes.com/sebastianbailey/?p=1554

Baldwin, M. W., & Keelan, J. P. R. (1999). Interpersonal expectations as a function of self-esteem and sex. *Journal of Social and Personal Relationships, 16,* 822–833.

Balk, D. E. (2011). *Helping the bereaved college student*. New York: Springer Publishing Company.

Ball, H., & Goodboy, A. K. (2014). An experimental investigation of the antecedents and consequences of psychological reactance in the college classroom. *Communication Education, 63*(3), 192–209. doi:10.1080/03634523.2014.918634.

Ball, K. (2010). Workplace surveillance: An overview. *Labor History, 51*(1), 87–106.

Ball-Rokeach, S. J. (1998). A theory of media power and a theory of media use: Different stories, questions, and ways of thinking. *Mass Communication and Society, 1*, 5–40.

Bandura, A. (1982). Self-efficacy mechanism in human agency. *American Psychologist, 37*, 122.

Bandura, A. (2009). Social cognitive theory of mass communication. In J. Bryant & M. B. Oliver (Eds.), *Media effects: Advances in theory and research* (pp. 94–123). New York: Routledge.

Bandura, A. (2001). Social cognitive theory of mass communication. *Media Psychology, 3*, 265–299.

Bardone, E., & Magnani, L. (2010). The appeal of gossiping fallacies and its eco-logical roots. *Pragmatics & Cognition, 18*(2), 365–396.

Barnes, S. (2016). Survey: College students support trigger warnings, but some fear speaking up. NBC. Retrieved on September 23, 2016, from http://www.nbcwashington.com/news/local/Survey-College-Students-Support-Trigger-Warnings-Some-Fear-Speaking-Up-377613641.html

Baron, N. (2008). *Always on: Language in an online and mobile world*. New York: Oxford University Press.

Bates, B. (1988). *Communication and the sexes*. New York: Harper & Row.

Bates, C. (2013). A cultural history of the nurse's uniform. Canadian Museum of Civilization. Gatineau, Quebec, Canada.

Bates, C. (2010). The nurse's cap and its rituals. *Dress, 36*, 21–40. Retrieved from http://www.ingentaconnect.com/content/maney/dre/2010/00000036/00000001/art00003

Bauman, C. W., Trawalter, S., & Unzueta, M. M. (2014). Diverse according to whom? Racial group membership and concerns about discrimination shape diversity judgments. *Personality & Social Psychology Bulletin, 40*(10), 1354–1372. doi:10.1177/0146167214543881

Bavelas, A. (1950). Communication patterns in task-oriented groups. *Journal of the Acoustical Society of America, 22*, 725–730.

Bavelas, J. B., & Chovil, N. (2006). Nonverbal and verbal communication: Hand gestures and facial displays as part of language use in face-to-face dialogue. In V. Manusov & M. L. Patterson (Eds.), *The SAGE handbook of nonverbal communication* (pp. 97–117). Thousand Oaks, CA: Sage.

Baxter, L. A. (1990). Dialectical contradictions in relationship development. *Journal of Social and Personal Relationships, 7*, 69–88.

Baxter, L. A., Braithwaite, D. O., Bryant, L., & Wagner, A. (2004). Stepchildren's perceptions of the contradictions in communication with stepparents. *Journal of Social and Personal Relationships, 21*, 447–467.

Baxter, L. A,. & Bullis, C. (1986). Turning points in developing romantic relationships. *Human Communication Research, 12*, 469–493.

Baxter, L. A., & Montgomery, B. M. (1996). *Relating: Dialogues and dialectics*. New York: Guilford.

Baxter, L. A., & Simon, E. P. (1993). Relationship maintenance strategies and dialectical contradictions in personal relationships. *Journal of Social and Personal Relationships, 10*, 225–242.

Baxter, L. A., & Wilmot, W. W. (1985). Taboo topics in close relationships. *Journal of Social and Personal Relationships, 2*, 253–269.

Bayly, S. (1999). *Caste, society and politics in India from the eighteenth century to the modern age*. Cambridge: Cambridge University Press.

Baym, N. K. (2015). *Personal connections in the digital age*. Cambridge, England: Polity Press.

Baym, N. K., & Boyd, D. (2012). Socially mediated publicness: An introduction. *Journal of Broadcasting & Electronic Media, 56*(3), 320–329.

Bearak, B. (2010, September 6). Dead join the living in a family celebration. *The New York Times*, p. A7.

Becker, J. A., & O'Hair, D. (2007). Machiavellians' motives in organizational citizenship behavior. *Journal of Applied Communication Research, 35*(3), 246–267.

Behnke, R. R., & Sawyer, C. R. (1999). Milestones of anticipatory public speaking anxiety. *Communication Education, 48*, 164–172.

Beiser, V. (2013, May 21). Alone with everyone else. *Pacific Standard*. Retrieved from http://www.psmag.com/culture/pluralistic-ignorance-55562

Bélisle, J-F., & Onur Bodur, H. (August 2010). Avatars as information: Perception of consumers based on their avatars in virtual worlds. *Psychology & Marketing, 27*(8): 741–765. Published online in Wiley InterScience (www.interscience.wiley.com). Retrieved from http://jfbelisle.com/wp-content/uploads/2009/06/Belisle-and-Bodur-2010.pdf

Bellezza, S., Gino, F., & Keinan, A. (2014). The red sneakers effect: Inferring status and competence from signals of nonconformity. *Journal of Consumer Research, 41*(1), 35–54. doi:10.1086/674870

Bellis, T. J., & Wilber, L. A. (2001). Effects of aging and gender on interhemispheric function. *Journal of Speech, Language, and Hearing Research, 44*, 246–264.

Benne, K. D., & Sheats, P. (1948). Functional roles in group members. *Journal of Social Issues, 4*, 41–49.

Bennett, J. M., & Bennett, M. J. (2004). Developing intercultural sensitivity: An integrative approach to global and domestic diversity. In D. Landis, J. M. Bennett, & M. J. Bennett (Eds.), *Handbook of intercultural training*, 3rd ed. (pp. 147–165). Thousand Oaks, CA: Sage.

Bennis, W., & Nanus, B. (1985). *Leaders*. New York: Harper & Row.

Benoit, W. L. (2013). Tiger Woods's image repair: Could he hit one out of the rough? In J. R. Blaney, L. R. Lippert, & J. S. Smith (Eds.), *Repairing the athlete's image: Studies in sports image restoration* (pp. 89–96). Lanham, MD: Lexington Books.

Ben-Porath, E. (2010). Interview effects: Theory and evidence for the impact of televised political interviews on viewer attitudes. *Communication Theory, 20*(3), 323–347.

Bentley, S. C. (2000). Listening in the twenty-first century. *International Journal of Listening, 14*, 129–142.

Berenson, T. (2015). Neil deGrasse Tyson is getting his own talk show. *Time*. Retrieved on September 2, 2016, from http://time.com/3659253/neil-degrasse-tyson-show/

Bergen, K. M. (2010). Accounting for difference: Commuter wives and the master narrative of marriage. *Journal of Applied Communication Research, 38*(1), 47–64.

Berger, A. (2007). *Media and society: A critical perspective*. Lanham, MD: Rowman & Littlefield.

Berger, C. R., & Bradac, J. J. (1982). *Language and social knowledge: Uncertainty in interpersonal relations*. London: Edward Arnold.

Berger, C. R., Roloff, M. E., & Roskos-Ewoldsen, D. R. (Eds.). (2010). *The handbook of communication science* (2nd ed.). Thousand Oaks, CA: Sage.

Berger, J., Wagner, D. G., & Zelditch, M., Jr. (1985). Introduction: Expectation states theory: Review and assessment. In J. Berger & M. Zelditch Jr. (Eds.), *Theoretical research programs: Studies in the growth of theory* (pp. 1–72). Stanford, CA: Stanford University Press.

Berliet, M. (2013, July 3). The importance of kissing beyond the beginning. *Pacific Standard*. Retrieved from http://www.psmag.com/culture/the-importance-of-kissing-beyond-the-beginning-61780

Berrisford, S. (2006). How will you respond to the information crisis? *Strategic Communication Management, 10,* 26–29.

Berryman-Fink, C. (1993). Preventing sexual harassment through male–female communication training. In G. Kreps (Ed.), *Sexual harassment: Communication implications* (pp. 267–280). Cresskill, NJ: Hampton Press.

Bertoni, S. (2016, November 22). Exclusive interview: How Jared Kushner won Trump the White House. *Forbes*. Retrieved from http://www.forbes.com/sites/stevenbertoni/2016/11/22/exclusive-interview-how-jared-kushner-won-trump-the-white-house/#1a0c02e32f50

Bianca, A. (2013). The importance of public speaking skills within organizations. Retrieved on April 29, 2014, from http://mallbusiness.chron.com/importance-public-speaking-skills-within-organizations-12075.html

The big picture: Today's hot photos. (2016, June 19). *E!News*. Retrieved from http://www.eonline.com/photos/6/the-big-picture-today-s-hot-pics/705859

Biever, C. (2004, August). Language may shape human thought. *New Scientist*. Retrieved from https://www.newscientist.com/article/dn6303-language-may-shape-human-thought/

Bippus, A. M., & Daly, J. A. (1999). What do people think causes stage fright? Native attributions about the reasons for public speaking anxiety. *Communication Education, 48,* 63–72.

Birditt, K. S. (2013). Age differences in emotional reactions to daily negative social encounters. *The Journals of Gerontology Series B: Psychological Sciences and Social Sciences*. doi:10.1093/geronb/gbt045

Bishop, G. (2010, February 20). On and off the ice, Ohno is positioned for success. *The New York Times*, p. D3.

Bishop, R. (2000). More than meets the eye: An explanation of literature related to the mass media's role in encouraging changes in body image. In M. E. Roloff (Ed.), *Communication yearbook* (Vol. 23, pp. 271–304). Thousand Oaks, CA: Sage.

Blanchard-Fields, F., Mienaltowski, A., & Seay, R. B. (2007). Age differences in everyday problem-solving effectiveness: Older adults select more effective strategies for interpersonal problems. *Journals of Gerontology, Series B: Psychological Sciences and Social Sciences, 62,* 61–64.

Blaney, J. R. (2013). Introduction: Why sports image restoration and how shall we proceed? In J. R. Blaney, L. R. Lippert, & J. S. Smith (Eds.), *Repairing the athlete's image: Studies in sports image restoration* (pp. 1–5). Lanham, MD: Lexington Books.

Blatter, L. C. (2016, January 22). Oscars red carpet preview: Modesty is the new sexy. *Jewish Telegraphic Agency*. Retrieved from http://www.jta.org/2016/01/22/arts-entertainment/oscars-red-carpet-preview-is-modesty-the-new-sexy

Bloch, J. (2011). Teaching job interviewing skills with the help of television shows. *Business Communication Quarterly, 74*(1), 7–21.

Blumler, J., & Katz, E. (1974). *The uses of mass communications.* Beverly Hills, CA: Sage.

Blumstein, P., & Schwartz, P. (1983). *American couples: Money, work, sex.* New York: Morrow.

Bochner, A. P., & Ellis, C. (1992). Social approaches: Personal narrative as a social approach to interpersonal communication. *Communication Theory* 2, 165–172.

Bodie, G. D. (2010). A racing heart, rattling knees, and ruminative thoughts: Defining, explaining, and treating public speaking anxiety. *Communication Education, 59*(1), 70–105.

Bodie, G. D. (2013). Issues in the measurement of listening. *Communication Research Reports*, 30(1), 76–84.

Bodie, G. D., & Fitch-Hauser, M. (2010). Quantitative research in listening: Explication and overview. In A. D. Wolvin (Ed.), *Listening and human communication in the 21st century* (pp. 46–93). Oxford, England: Blackwell.

Bodie, G. D., & Jones, S. M. (2012). The nature of supportive listening II: The role of verbal person centeredness and nonverbal immediacy. *Western Journal of Communication* 76(3), 250–269.

Bodie, G. D., St. Cyr, K., Pence, M., Rold, M., & Honeycutt, J. (2012). Listening competence in initial interactions I: Distinguishing between what listening is and what listeners do. *International Journal of Listening, 26*(1), 1–28.

Bodie, G. D., Vickery, A. J., & Gearhart, C. C. (2013). The nature of supportive listening, I: Exploring the relation between supportive listeners and supportive people. *International Journal of Listening, 27*(1), 39–49.

Bodie, G. D., Worthing, D., Imhof, M., & Cooper, L. O. (2008). What would a unified field of listening look like? A proposal linking past perspectives and future endeavors. *International Journal of Listening, 22,* 103–122.

Bodie, G. D., Worthington, D. L., & Gearhart, C. C. (2013, January). The listening styles profile-revised (LSP-R): A scale revision and evidence for validity. *Communication Quarterly, 61*(1), 72–90.

Bommelje, R., Houston, J. M., & Smither, R. (2003). Personality characteristics of effective listeners: A five factor perspective. *International Journal of Listening, 17,* 32–46.

Bond, M. (2007). How to spot a fibber. *New Scientist, 195*(2621), 54–56.

Boniello, K. (2015, September 27). "CSI" has ruined the American justice system. *New York Post*. Retrieved from http://nypost.com/2015/09/27/how-csi-twisted-our-jury-system/

Bono, J. E. & Ilies, R. (2006). Charisma, positive emotions and mood contagion. *The Leadership Quarterly, 17,* 317–334.

Bonthuys, E., & Erlank, N. (2012). Modes of (in)tolerance: South African Muslims and same-sex relationships. *Culture, Health & Sexuality, 14*(3), 269–282. doi:10.1080/13691058.2011.621450

Bormann, E. G. (1990). *Small group communication* (3rd ed.). New York: Harper & Row.

Bornstein, D. (2016, May 10). Using tweets and posts to speed up organ donation. *The New York Times*. Retrieved from http://www.nytimes.com/2016/05/10/opinion/using-tweets-and-posts-to-speed-up-organ-donation.html?_r=0

Bosman, J. (2006, August 15). Agencies are watching as ads go online. *The New York Times*. Retrieved from http://www.nytimes.com/2006/08/15/business/media/15adco.html?_r=0

Bosman, J. (2011, January 4). Publisher tinkers with Twain. *The New York Times*. Retrieved from http://www.nytimes.com/2011/01/05/books/05huck.html

Boster, F. J., & Mongeau, P. (1984). Fear-arousing persuasive messages. In R. N. Bostrom (Ed.), *Communication yearbook 8* (pp. 330–375). Beverly Hills, CA: Sage.

Boucher, E. M. (2015). Doubt begets doubt: Causal uncertainty as a predictor of relational uncertainty in romantic relationships.

Communication Reports, 28(1), 12–23. doi:10.1080/08934215.2014.902487

Boyd, D. (2010). Social network sites as networked publics: Affordances, dynamics, and implications. In Z. Papacharissi (Ed.), *A networked self: Identity, community, and culture on social network sites* (pp. 39–58). New York: Routledge.

Boysen, G. A., Wells, A., M., & Dawson, K. J. (2016). Instructors' use of trigger warnings and behavior warnings in abnormal psychology. *Teaching of Psychology, 43*(4), 334–339.

Bradac, J. J. (1983). The language of lovers, flovers, and friends: Communicating in social and personal relationships. *Journal of Language and Social Psychology, 2,* 234.

Bradac, J. J., & Giles, H. (2005). Language and social psychology: Conceptual niceties, complexities, curiosities, monstrosities, and how it all works. In K. L. Fitch & R. E. Sanders (Eds.), *The new handbook of language and social psychology* (pp. 201–230). Mahwah, NJ: Erlbaum.

Bradley, B. H., Anderson, H. J., Baur, J. E., & Klotz, A. C. (2015, September 28). When conflict helps: Integrating evidence for beneficial conflict in groups and teams under three perspectives. *Group Dynamics: Theory, Research, and Practice.* Advance online publication. Retrieved from http://dx.doi.org/10.1037/gdn0000033.

Brandau-Brown, F. E., & Ragsdale, J. D.(2008). Personal, moral, and structural commitment and the repair of marital relationships. *Southern Communication Journal, 73*(1), 68–83.

Brandenburg, C. (2008). The newest way to screen job applicants: A social networker's nightmare. *Federal Communications Law Journal, 60*(3), 597–626.

Brazeel, S. (2009). Networking to top talent or networking your way to top talent. *POWERGRID International, 14*(10), 2.

Brees, D., & Fabry, C. (2011). *Coming back stronger: Unleashing the hidden power of adversity.* Carol Stream, IL: Tyndale House Publishers.

Brehm, J. W. (1966). *A theory of psychological reactance.* New York: Academic Press.

Brehm, J. W., & Brehm, S. S. (1981). *Psychological reactance: A theory of freedom and control.* San Diego, CA: Academic Press.

Breitsohl, J., Wilcox-Jones, J. P., & Harris, I. (2015). Groupthink 2.0: An empirical analysis of customers' conformity-seeking in online communities. *Journal of Customer Behaviour, 14*(2), 87–106. doi:10.1362/147539215X14373846805662

Breslau, J., Setodji, C. M., & Vaughan, C. A. (2016). Is cohesion within military units associated with post-deployment behavioral and mental health outcomes? *Journal of Affective Disorders, 198,* 102–107. doi:10.1016/j.jad.2016.03.053

Brilhart, J. K., & Galanes, G. J. (1992). *Effective group discussion* (7th ed.). Dubuque, IA: Brown.

Brock, C. (2010, March 17). Padres breaking down language barrier. Retrieved from http://m.mlb.com/news/article/8818412/

Brody, L. R. (2000). The socialization of gender differences in emotional expression: Display rules, infant temperament, and differentiation. In A. H. Fischer (Ed.), *Gender and emotion: Social psychological perspectives* (pp. 24–47). Cambridge: Cambridge University Press.

Brooklyn Nine-Nine (2016). Retrieved from http://www.fox.com/brooklyn-nine-nine/full-episodes

Brooklyn Nine-Nine (2013). Pilot. Retrieved from http://www.baltimoresun.com/entertainment/tv/z-on-tv-blog/bal-andre-braugher-wendell-pierce-fall-tv-20130913,0,2233205.story#ixzz2qmOapNNm

Brooks, D. (2015, March 3). Leaving and cleaving. *The New York Times,* p. A29.

Brosy, J., Bangerter, A., & Mayor, E. (2016). Disfluent responses to job interview questions and what they entail. *Discourse Processes, 53*(5/6), 371–391. doi:10.1080/0163853X.2016.1150769

Brouwer, D. C., & Horwitz, L. D. (2015). The cultural politics of progenic Auschwitz tattoos: 157622, A-15510, 4559, . . . *Quarterly Journal of Speech, 101*(3), 534–558. doi:10.1080/00335630.2015.1056748

Bryant, A. (2012, April 7). The phones are out, but the robot is in. *The New York Times.* Retrieved from http://www.nytimes.com/2012/04/08/business/phil-libin-of-evernote-on-its-unusual-corporate-culture.html?pagewanted=all&_r=0

Bryant, G. A., Fessler, D. T., Fusaroli, R., Clint, E., Aarøe, L., Apicella, C. L., . . . Luberti, F. R. (2016). Detecting affiliation in colaughter across 24 societies. *Proceedings of the National Academy of Sciences of the United States of America, 113*(17), 4682–4687. doi:10.1073/pnas.1524993113

Bryant, J., & Pribanic-Smith, E. J. (2010). A historical overview of research in communication science. In C. R. Berger, M. E. Roloff, & D. R. Roskos-Ewoldsen (Eds.), *The handbook of communication science* (2nd ed., pp. 21–36). Thousand Oaks, CA: Sage.

Buck, R. (1988). Emotional education and mass media: A new view of the global village. In R. P. Hawkins, J. M. Wiemann, & S. Pingree (Eds.), *Advancing communication science: Merging mass and interpersonal processes* (pp. 44–76). Beverly Hills, CA: Sage.

Buckels, E. E., Trapnell, P. D., & Paulhus, D. L. (2014). Trolls just want to have fun. *Personality and Individual Differences, 67,* 97–102.

Bui, N. H. (2017). Exploring similarity characteristics, identification, and parasocial interactions in choice of celebrities. *Psychology of Popular Media Culture, 6*(1), 21–31. doi:10.1037/ppm0000082

Burgers, C., Beukeboom, M. K., & Peeters, M. M. E. (2015). How sports fans forge intergroup competition through language: The case of verbal irony. *Human Communication Research, 41*(3), 435–457.

Burgoon, J. K. (1978). A communication model of personal space violations: Explication and an initial test. *Human Communication Research, 4,* 129–142.

Burgoon, J. K., & Bacue, A. E. (2003). Nonverbal communication skills. In J. O. Greene & B. R. Burleson (Eds.), *Handbook of communication and social interaction skills* (pp. 179–219). Mahwah, NJ: Erlbaum.

Burgoon, J. K., Blair, J., & Strom, R. E. (2008). Cognitive biases and nonverbal cue availability in detecting deception. *Human Communication Research, 34*(4), 572–599.

Burgoon, J. K., Buller, D. B., & Woodall, W. G. (1989). *Nonverbal communication: The unspoken dialogue.* New York: Harper & Row.

Burgoon, J. K., & Dunbar, N. E. (2006). Nonverbal expressions of dominance and power in human relationships. In V. Manusov & M. L. Patterson (Eds.), *The SAGE handbook of nonverbal communication* (pp. 279–298). Thousand Oaks, CA: Sage.

Burgoon, J. K., Floyd, K., & Guerrero, L. K. (2010). Nonverbal communication theories of interaction adaptation. In C. R. Berger, M. E. Roloff, & D. R. Roskos-Ewoldsen (Eds.), *The handbook of communication science* (pp. 93–108). Thousand Oaks, CA: Sage.

Burgoon, J. K., & Hoobler, G. D. (2002). Nonverbal signals. In M. L. Knapp & J. A. Daly (Eds.), *Handbook of interpersonal communication* (pp. 240–299). Thousand Oaks, CA: Sage.

Burleson, B. R. (2010). The nature of interpersonal communication: A message-centered approach. In C. R. Berger, M. E. Roloff, & D. R. Roskos-Ewoldsen, *The handbook of communication science* (pp. 145–163). Thousand Oaks, CA: Sage.

Burleson, B. R., Hanasono, L. K., Bodie, G. D., Holmstrom, A. J., Rack, J. J., Gill-Rosier, J., & McCullough, J. D. (2011). Are gender differences in responses to supportive communication a matter of ability, motivation, or both? Reading patterns of situational responses through the lens of a dual-process theory. *Communication Quarterly, 59,* 37–60.

Burleson, B. R., Holmstrom, A. J., & Gilstrap, C. M. (2005). "Guys can't say that to guys": Four experiments assessing the normative motivation account for deficiencies in the emotional support provided by men. *Communication Monographs, 72*(4), 468–501.

Business Week (2005). Why most meetings stink. Retrieved from http://www.businessweek.com/stories/2005-10-30/why-most-meetings-stink

Butler, C. W., & Fitzgerald, R. (2011). "My f***ing personality": Swearing as slips and gaffes in live television broadcasts. *Text & Talk, 31*(5), 525–551.

Byrd, D. (2010, January 16). Neil deGrasse Tyson: "Learning how to think is empowerment." EarthSky.org. Retrieved from http://earthsky.org/human-world/neil-degrasse-tyson

Cacciatore, M. A., Scheufele, D. A., & Iyengar, S. (2016) The end of framing as we know it . . . and the future of media effects. *Mass Communication and Society, 19*(1), 7–23. doi:10.1080/15205436.2015.1068811

Cacioppo, J. T., Cacioppo, S., Gonzaga, G. C., Ogburn, E. L. & VanderWeele, T. J. (2013). Marital satisfaction and break-ups differ across on-line and off-line meeting venues. *Psychological and Cognitive Sciences,* www.pnas.org/cgi/doi/10.1073/pnas.1222447110

Cacioppo, J. T., & Petty, R. E. (1984). The need for cognition: Relationships to attitudinal processes. In R. P. McGlynn, J. E. Maddux, C. Stoltenberg, & J. H. Harvey (Eds.), *Social perception in clinical and counseling psychology.* Lubbock, TX: Texas Tech University Press.

Campos, B., Schoebi, D., Gonzaga, G. C., Gable, S. L. & Keltner, D. (2015). Attuned to the positive? Awareness and responsiveness to others' positive emotion experience and display. *Motivation and Emotion, 39,* 780–794. doi:10.1007/x11-31-015-9494-x

Canary, D. J. (2003). Managing interpersonal conflict: A model of events related to strategic choices. In J. O. Greene & B. R. Burleson (Eds.), *Handbook of communication and social interaction skills* (pp. 515–550). Mahwah, NJ: Erlbaum.

Canary, D. J., & Cody, M. J. (1993). *Interpersonal communication: A goals-based approach.* New York: Bedford/St. Martin's Press.

Canary, D. J., Cody, M. J., & Manusov, V. (2008). *Interpersonal communication: A goals-based approach* (4th ed.). New York: Bedford/St. Martin's.

Canary, D. J., Cody, M. J., & Smith, S. (1994). Compliance-gaining goals: An inductive analysis of actors' goal types, strategies, and successes. In J. A. Daly & J. M. Wiemann (Eds.), *Strategic interpersonal communication* (pp. 33–90). Hillsdale, NJ: Erlbaum.

Canary, D. J., Cunningham, E. M., & Cody, M. J. (1988). Goal types, gender, and locus of control in managing interpersonal conflict. *Communication Research, 15,* 426–446.

Canary, D. J., & Lakey, S. (2012). *Strategic conflict.* London: Routledge.

Canary, D. J., & Spitzberg, B. H. (1993). Loneliness and media gratifications. *Communication Research, 20,* 800–821.

Cann, R., Kempson, R., & Gregormichelaki, E. (2009). *Semantics: An introduction to meaning in language.* Cambridge: Cambridge University Press.

Capella, J. K., & Greene, J. O. (1982). A discrepancy-arousal explanation of mutual influence in expressive behavior for adult and infant–adult interaction. *Communication Monographs, 49,* 89–114.

Caplan, S. (2001). Challenging the mass-interpersonal communication dichotomy: Are we witnessing the emergence of an entirely new communication system? *Electronic Journal of Communication, 11.* Retrieved on March 24, 2003, from http://www.cios.org/getfile/CAPLAN_v11n101

Capozzoli, T. (2002). How to succeed with self-directed work teams. *SuperVision, 63,* 25–26.

Cappella, J. N., & Schreiber, D. M. (2006). The interaction management function of nonverbal cues: Theory and research about mutual behavioral influence in face-to-face settings. In V. Manusov & M. L. Patterson (Eds.), *The SAGE handbook of nonverbal communication* (pp. 361–380). Thousand Oaks, CA: Sage.

Cargile, A. C., & Giles, H. (1996). Intercultural communication training: Review, critique, and a new theoretical framework. In B. R. Burleson (Ed.), *Communication yearbook 19* (pp. 3835–3423). Newbury Park, CA: Sage.

Caridizahavi, O., Carmeli, A., & Arazy, O. (2016). The influence of CEOs' visionary innovation leadership on the performance of high technology ventures: The mediating roles of connectivity and knowledge integration. *Journal of Product Innovation Management, 33*(3), 356–376. doi:10.1111/jpim.12275

Carless, S. A., & DePaola, C. (2000). The measurement of cohesion in work teams. *Small Group Research, 31,* 71–88.

Carli, L. L. (1999). Gender, interpersonal power, and social influence. *Journal of Social Issues, 55,* 81–99.

Carmon, A. F., Western, K. J., Miller, A. N., Pearson, J. C., & Fowler, M. R. (2010). Grieving those we've lost: An examination of family communication patterns and grief reactions. *Communication Research Reports, 27*(3), 253–262. doi:10.1080/08824096.2010.496329

Carpinella, C. M., Hehman, E., Freeman, J. B., & Johnson, K. L. (2016). The gendered face of partisan politics: Consequences of facial sex typicality for vote choice. *Political Communication, 33*(1), 21–38. doi:10.1080/10584609.2014.958260

Carr, D., Freedman, V. A., Cornman, J. C., & Schwarz, N. (2014). Happy marriage, happy life? Marital quality and subjective well-being in later life. *Journal of Marriage & Family, 76*(5), 930–948. doi:10.1111/jomf.12133

Carr-Ruffino, N. (2016). Leadership opportunities for managing diversity. In J. Prescott (Ed.), *Handbook of research on race, gender, and the fight for equality.* Hershey, PA: IGI Global.

Carton, A. M., & Tewfik, B. A. (2016). Perspective—A new look at conflict management in work groups. *Organization Science.* Retrieved on October 10, 2016, from http://pubsonline.informs.org.ezproxy.uky.edu/doi/10.1287/orsc.2016.1085.

Casmir, F. L. (Ed.). (1997). *Ethics in intercultural and international communication.* Mahwah, NJ: Erlbaum.

Cassell, J., Huffaker, D., Tversky, D., & Ferriman, K. (2006). The language of online leadership: Gender and youth engagement on the Internet. *Developmental Psychology, 42*(3), 436–449.

Caughlin, J. (2003). Family communication standards: What counts as excellent family communication, and how are such standards associated with family satisfaction? *Human Communication Research, 29,* 5–40.

CBS News. (2010, November 28). Colin Firth on playing King George VI: Katie Couric talks with *The King's Speech* star about the monarch's battle against a debilitating stutter. Retrieved from http://www.cbsnews.com/stories/2010/11/28/sunday/main7096682.shtml

Cegala, D. (1981). Interaction involvement: A cognitive dimension of communicative competence. *Communication Education, 30,* 109–121.

Census seen lax on diversity. (2010, February 25). *The Washington Times*. Retrieved from http://www.washingtontimes.com /news/2010/feb/25/census-seen-lax-on-diversity

Centers for Disease Control and Prevention (2013). Distracted driving. Retrieved on May 2, 2014, from http://www.cdc.gov /motorvehiclesafety/distracted_driving

Chai, J., Qu, W., Sun, X., Zhang, K., & Ge, Y. (2016). Negativity bias in dangerous drivers. *PLoS ONE, 11*(1), 1–15. doi:10.1371 /journal.pone.0147083

Champion, D. A., Lewis, T. F., & Myers, J. E. (2015). College student alcohol use and abuse: Social norms, health beliefs, and selected socio-demographic variables as explanatory factors. *Journal of Alcohol & Drug Education, 59*(1), 57–82.

Charles, S. T., Piazza, J. R., Luong, G., & Almeida, D. M. (2009). Now you see it, now you don't: Age differences in affective reactivity to social tensions. *Psychology and Aging, 24*(3), 645.

Charlier, S. D., Stewart, G. L., Greco, L. M., & Reeves, C. J. (2016). Emergent leadership in virtual teams: A multilevel investigation of individual communication and team dispersion antecedents. *The Leadership Quarterly, 27*(5), 745–764.

Chaykowski, K. (2016, February 24). Facebook no longer just has a "like" button, thanks to global launch of emoji "reactions." Forbes. com. Retrieved from http://www.forbes.com/sites/kathleenchaykowski/2016/02/24/facebook-no-longer-just-has-a-like-button-thanks-to-global-launch-of-emoji-reactions/#61669d774994

Chen, C. (2016). Forming digital self and parasocial relationships on YouTube. *Journal of Consumer Culture, 16*(1), 232–254. doi:10.1177/1469540514521081

Chen, C., Huang, Y., & Lee, M. (2011). Test of a model linking applicant résumé information and hiring recommendations. *International Journal of Selection & Assessment, 19*(4), 374–387. doi:10.1111/j.1468-2389.2011.00566.x

Chen, G. M., & Ng, Y. M. M. (2016). Third-person perception of online comments: Civil ones persuade you more than me. *Computers and Human Behavior, 55,* 736–742.

Chen, G-M., & Starosta, W. J. (2008). Intercultural communication competence: A synthesis. In M. K. Asante, Y. Miike, & J. Yin (Eds.), *The global intercultural communication reader* (pp. 215–238). New York: Taylor and Francis Group.

Chen, Q., & Yan, Z. (2016). Does multitasking with mobile phones affect learning? A review. *Computers in Human Behavior, 54,* 34–42.

Chen, Y., & Nakazawa, M. (2009). Influences of culture on self-disclosure as relationally situated in intercultural and interracial friendships from a social penetration perspective. *Journal of Intercultural Communication Research, 38*(2), 77–98.

Chen, Y. P., Johnson, C., Lalbakhsh, P., Caellic, T., Deng, G., Tay, D., Erickson, S., Broadbridge, P., Refaie, A. E., Doube, W., & Morris, M. E. (2016). Systematic review of virtual speech therapists for speech disorders. *Computer Speech & Language, 37,* 98–128.

Cheng, J., Danescu-Niculescu-Mizil, C., & Leskovec, J. (2015). Antisocial behavior in online discussion communities. In *Proceedings of the 9th International Conference on Weblogs and Social Media* (ICWSM). Menlo Park, CA: AAAI Press.

Chernow, R. (2004). *Alexander Hamilton.* New York: Penguin Books.

Cheung, E. O., & Gardner, W. L. (2015). The way I make you feel: Social exclusion enhances the ability to manage others' emotions. *Journal of Experimental Social Psychology, 60,* 59–75. doi:10.1016/j.jesp.2015.05.003

Chidambaram, L., & Bostrom, R. P. (1996). Group development: A review and synthesis of the development models (I). *Group Decision and Negotiation, 16*(2), 159–187.

Child, J. T., & Westermann, D. A. (2013). Let's be Facebook friends: Exploring parental Facebook friend requests from a communication privacy management (CPM) perspective. *Journal of Family Communication, 13*(1), 46–59.

Childs, C. (2009). Perfect quiet. *Miller-McCune, 2*(4), 58–67.

Choi, M., & Toma, C. L. (2014). Social sharing through interpersonal media: Patterns and effects on emotional well-being. *Computers in Human Behavior, 36,* 530–541. doi:10.1016/j.chb.2014.04.026

Chou, G., & Edge, N. (2012, February). They are happier and having better lives than I am: The impact of using Facebook on perceptions of others' lives. *Cyberpsychology, Behavior, and Social Networking, 15*(2), 117–121.

Chozick, A. (2011, December 12). Athhilezar? Watch your fantasy world language. *The New York Times*, p. A1.

Christians, C., & Traber, C. (Eds.). (1997). *Communication ethics and universal values.* Thousand Oaks, CA: Sage.

Christie, R., & Geis, F. L. (1970). *Studies in Machiavellianism.* New York: Academic Press.

Chung, J. E. (2014). Medical dramas and viewer perception of health: Testing cultivation effects. *Human Communication Research, 40*(3), 333–349. doi:10.1111/hcre.12026

Chung, M., Munno, G. J., & Moritz, B. (2015). Triggering participation: Exploring the effects of third-person and hostile media perceptions on online participation. *Computers in Human Behavior, 53,* 452–461.

Cialdini, R. B. (2016). *Pre-suasion: A revolutionary way to influence and persuade.* New York: Simon & Schuster.

Cialdini, R. (2008). *Influence: Science and practice* (5th ed.). Englewood Cliffs, NJ: Prentice Hall.

Cirelli, L. K., Einarson, K. M., & Trainor, L. J. (2014). Interpersonal synchrony increases prosocial behavior in infants. *Developmental Science, 17*(6), 1003–1011. doi:10.1111/desc.12193

Clark, A. J. (1989). Communication confidence and listening competence: An investigation of the relationships of willingness to communicate, communication apprehension, and receiver apprehension to comprehension of content and emotional meaning in spoken messages. *Communication Education, 38,* 237–248.

Clarke, I., Flaherty, T. B., Wright, N. D., & McMillen, R. M. (2009). Student intercultural proficiency from study abroad programs. *Journal of Marketing Education, 31*(2), 173–181.

Clarke, J. (2014, February 23). Personal communication.

Clausell, E., & Roisman, G. I. (2009). Outness, Big Five personality traits, and same-sex relationship quality. *Journal of Social and Personal Relationships, 26*(2–3), 211–226.

Cleary, H. D., & Warner, T. C. (2016). Police training in interviewing and interrogation methods: A comparison of techniques used with adult and juvenile suspects. *Law & Human Behavior (American Psychological Association), 40*(3), 270–284. doi:10.1037/ lhb0000175

Clements, P. (2015, August 27). The "CSI" effect: The impact of "television-educated" jurors. *New York Post*. Retrieved from http://drexel.edu/cnhp/news/current/archive/2015 /August/2015-08-27-the-csi-effect/

CNN.com/living. (2008). Retrieved from www.cnn.com/2007 /LIVING/personal/07/30/wlb.quiz.balance/index.html

Cohen, M., & Avanzino, S. (2010). We are people first: Framing organizational assimilation experiences of the physically disabled using co-cultural theory. *Communication Studies, 61*(3), 272–303.

The Colbert Report. (2013, September 12). Better know a district: Washington's 7th-Jim McDermott. Retrieved from http:// www.colbertnation.com/better-know-a-district/429042

/september-12-2013/better-know-a-district-washington-s
-7th-jim-mcdermott, 3:00

The Colbert Report. (2011, March 9). Video clip "Benchpress." Retrieved from http://www.colbertnation.com/the-colbert -report-videos/376920/march-09-2011/bench-press, 3:40

Cohen, R. (2016, April 1). Inside Mick Jagger and Keith Richards's five-decade bromance. *Vanity Fair.* Retrieved from http://www .vanityfair.com/culture/2016/03/mick-jagger-keith-richards -rich-cohen

Cole, C. F. (2016). 29: The global Sesame effect. In C. F. Cole & J. H. Lee (Eds.), *The Sesame Effect: The global impact of the longest street in the world.* New York: Routledge.

Cole, C. F., & Lee. J. H. (2016). Introduction. In C. F. Cole & J. H. Lee (Eds.), *The Sesame Effect: The global impact of the longest street in the world.* New York: Routledge.

Coles, B. A., & West, M. (2016). Trolling the trolls: Online forum users constructions of the nature and properties of trolling. *Computers in Human Behavior, 60,* 233–244.

Collins, K. (2016, February 11). Lena Dunham doesn't want to see herself naked anymore. *The DailyCaller.* Retrieved from http: //dailycaller.com/2016/02/11/lena-dunham-doesnt-want-to-see -herself-naked-anymore/#ixzz4C4YhVWuF

Collins, N. L., Kane, H. S., Metz, M. A., Cleveland, C., Khan, C., Winczewski, L., Bowen, J., & Prok, T. (2014). Psychological, physiological, and behavioral responses to a partner in need: The role of compassionate love. *Journal of Social & Personal Relationships, 31*(5), 601–629.

Colvin, G. (2012, December 3). The art of the self-managing team. *Fortune, 166*(9), 22.

Comadena, M. E. (1984). Brainstorming groups. *Small Group Research, 15,* 251–264.

Comer, D. R. (1998). A model of social loafing in real work groups. *Human Relations, 48,* 647–667.

Common Sense Media (2015, November 3). Landmark report: U.S. teens use an average of nine hours of media per day, tweens use six hours. Retrieved from https://www.commonsensemedia.org /about-us/news/press-releases/landmark-report-us-teens-use-an -average-of-nine-hours-of-media-per-day#

Conley, T. D. (2011). Perceived proposer personality characteristics and gender differences in acceptance of casual sex offers. *Journal of Personality & Social Psychology, 100*(2), 309–329.

Conlin, M. (2006, December 11). Online extra: How to kill meetings. *Business Week.* https://www.bloomberg.com/news/ articles/2006-12-10/smashing-the-clock

Conover, M. D., Ferrara, E., Menczer, F., & Flammini, A. (2013). The digital evolution of Occupy Wall Street. *PLoS ONE 8*(5). doi:10.1371/journal.pone.0064679

Constine, J. (2016, Aug 8). Instagram castrated Snapchat like Facebook neutered Twitter. TechCrunch. Retrieved from https: //techcrunch.com/2016/08/09/the-good-enough-strategy/

Costa, M. (2010). Interpersonal distances in group walking. *Journal of Nonverbal Behavior, 34*(1), 15–26.

Couldry, N., & Turow, J. (2014). Advertising, big data, and the clearance of the public realm: Marketers' new approaches to the content subsidy. *International Journal of Communication, 8,* 1710–1726.

Coviello, L., Sohn, Y., Kramer, A. D., Marlow, C., Franceschetti, M., Christakis, N. A., & Fowler, J. H. (2014). Detecting emotional contagion in massive social networks. *PloS ONE, 9*(3), e90315.

Cox, P. L., & Brobrowski, P. E. (2000). The team charter assignment: Improving the effectiveness of classroom teams. *Journal of Behavioral and Applied Management, 1*(1), 92.

Cox, S. S., Bennett, R. J., Tripp, T. M., & Aquino, K. (2012). An empirical test of forgiveness motives' effects on employees' health and well-being. *Journal of Occupational Health Psychology, 17*(3), 330.

Cragan, J. F., Wright, D. W., & Kasch, C. R. (2008). *Communication in small groups: Theory, process, and skills* (7th ed.). Boston: Cengage.

Cramton, C. D. (1997). Information problems in dispersed teams. *Academy of Management Best Paper Proceedings,* 298–302.

Crane, D. (2000). *Fashion and its social agendas: Class, gender, and identity in clothing.* Chicago: University of Chicago Press.

Crose, B. (2011). Internationalization of the higher education classroom: Strategies to facilitate intercultural learning and academic success. *International Journal of Teaching and Learning in Higher Education, 23*(3), 388–395.

Cross, R., Rebele, R, & Grant, A. (2016, January–February). Collaboration overload. *Harvard Business Review,* 117.

Crossley, M., & Silverman, R. D. (2016). Reflections on mentoring. *Journal of Law, Medicine & Ethics, 44,* 76–80. doi:10.1177/1073110516644233

Croucher, S. M., Bruno, A., McGrath, P., Adams, C., McGahan, C., Suits, A., & Huckins, A. (2012). Conflict styles and high–low context cultures: A cross-cultural extension. *Communication Research Reports, 29*(1), 64–73.

Crouse, K. (May 31, 2017). After Woods's stumble, a chance to stand up. *New York Times,* p. B9.

Crum, C. (2015, November 20). New data shows importance of Facebook shares over likes and comments. WebProNews.com. Retrieved from http://www.webpronews.com/new-data-shows -importance-of-facebook-shares-over-likes-and-comments-2015-11/

Cuddy, A. C., Wilmuth, C. A., Yap, A. J., & Carney, D. R. (2015). Preparatory power posing affects nonverbal presence and job interview performance. *Journal of Applied Psychology, 100*(4), 1286–1295. doi:10.1037/a0038543

Culbert, S. A. (2010). *Get rid of the performance review! How companies can stop intimidating, start managing—and focus on what really matters.* New York: Business Plus/Hachette Book Group.

Culbert, S. A. (2011, March 2). Why your boss is wrong about you. *The New York Times,* p. A25.

Culver, S. H., & Seguin, J. (2013). *Media career guide: Preparing for jobs in the 21st century.* New York: Bedford/St. Martin's.

Cupach, W. R. (2015). Communication competence in the management of conflict. In A. F. Hannawa & B. H. Spitzberg (Eds.), *Communication competence.* Berlin, Boston: De Gruyter Mouton.

Cupach, W. R., & Carson, C. L. (2012). Interpersonal criticism through the lens of communication competence. In R. M. Sutton, M. J. Hornsey, & K. M. Douglas (Eds.), *Feedback: The communication of praise, criticism, and advice* (pp. 139–152). New York: Peter Lang.

Cupach, W. R., & Spitzberg, B. H. (Eds.) (2011). *The dark side of close relationships II.* New York: Routledge.

Curasi, C. F. (2001). A critical exploration of face-to-face interviewing vs. computer-mediated interviewing. *International Journal of Market Research, 43*(4), 361–375.

Curtis, P. (1997). Mudding: Social phenomena in text-based virtual realities. In S. Kiesler (Ed.), *Culture of the Internet* (pp. 121–142). Mahwah, NJ: Erlbaum.

Cutica, I., & Bucciarelli, M. (2011). "The more you gesture, the less I gesture": Co-speech gestures as a measure of mental model quality. *Journal of Nonverbal Behavior, 35*(3), 173–187.

Cvitanic, O. (2013, February 26). From gangnam style to the Harlem shake, why we just can't resist a dance craze. *Pacific Standard.* Retrieved from http://www.psmag.com/blogs/the-101/from

-gangnam-style-to-the-harlem-shake-why-we-just-cant-resist-a
-dance-craze-53266

Dabke, D. (2016). Impact of leader's emotional intelligence and transformational behavior on perceived leadership effectiveness. *Business Perspectives and Research, 4,* 27–40.

Daft, R. L., & Lengel, R. H. (1984). Informational richness: A new approach to managerial behavior and organizational design. In B. M. Staw & L. L. Cummings (Eds.), *Research in organizational behavior* (Vol. 6, pp. 191–233). Greenwich, CT: JAI.

Daft, R. L., & Lengel, R. H. (1986). Organizational information requirements, media richness, and structural design. *Management Science, 32,* 554–571.

Daft, R. L., Lengel, R. H., & Trevino, L. K. (1987). Message equivocality, media selection, and manager performance: Implications for information systems. *MIS Quarterly, 11,* 355–366.

Dailey, R. M., & Palomares, N. A. (2004). Strategic topic avoidance: An investigation of topic avoidance frequency, strategies used, and relational correlates. *Communication Monographs, 71,* 471–496.

Dainton, M., & Gross, J. (2008). The use of negative behaviors to maintain relationships. *Communication Research Reports, 25,* 179–191.

Danet, B., & Herring, S. C. (Eds.). (2007). *The multilingual Internet: Language, culture, and communication online.* New York: Oxford University Press.

Darbonne, A., Uchino, B. N., & Ong, A. D. (2013). What mediates links between age and well-being? A test of social support and interpersonal conflict as potential interpersonal pathways. *Journal of Happiness Studies, 14*(3), 951–963.

Daswani, K. (2012, January 9). More men coloring their hair. *The Los Angeles Times.* Retrieved from http://articles.latimes.com/2012 /jan/29/image/la-ig-mens-hair-color-20120129

Daubenmier, J., Hayden, D., Chang, V., & Epel, E. (2014, October). It's not what you think, it's how you relate to it: Dispositional mindfulness moderates the relationship between psychological distress and the cortisol awakening response. *Psychoneuroendocrinology, 48,* 11–18. doi:10.1016/j.psyneuen.2014.05.012

Davies A., Goetz, A. T., & Shackelford, T. K. (2008). Exploiting the beauty in the eye of the beholder: The use of physical attractiveness as a persuasive tactic. *Personality and Individual Differences, 45,* 302–306.

Davies, M. (2009). The 385+ million word Corpus of Contemporary American English (1990–2008+): Design, architecture, and linguistic insights. *International Journal of Corpus Linguistics, 14*(2), 159–190. doi:10.1075/ijcl.14.2.02dav

Davis, C., & Myers, K. (2012). Communication and member disengagement in planned organizational exit. *Western Journal of Communication, 76*(2), 194–216.

Davis, D. Z. (2014). Interviews with avatars: Navigating the nuances of communicating in virtual worlds. In P. Laufer (Ed.), *Interviewing: The Oregon method* (pp. 209–220). Portland, OR: Center for Journalism Innovation and Civic Engagement.

Davis, J., Foley, A., Crigger, N., & Brannigan, M. C. (2008). Healthcare and listening: A relationship for caring. *International Journal of Listening, 22*(2), 168–175.

Davis, J. L., & Jurgenson, N. (2014). Context collapse: Theorizing context collusions and collisions. *Information, Communication & Society, 17*(4), 476–485.

Davis, M. S. (1973). *Intimate relations.* New York: Free Press.

Davison, W. P. (1983). The third-person effect in communication. *Public Opinion Quarterly, 40,* 1–15.

Day, L. A. (1997). *Ethics in media communications: Cases and controversies.* Belmont, CA: Wadsworth.

Day, M. V. (2016). Why people defend relationship ideology. *Journal of Social and Personal Relationships, 33*(3), 348–360. doi:10.1177/0265407515613164

DeAndrea, D. C., & Walther, J. B. (2011). Attributions for inconsistencies between online and offline self-presentations. *Communication Research, 38*(6), 805–825.

Definition of "feminist." Dictionary.com. Retrieved from http://www .dictionary.com/browse/feminist

Degani, T., & Tokowicz, N. (2010). Semantic ambiguity within and across languages: An integrative review. *The Quarterly Journal of Experimental Psychology, 63*(7), 1266–1303.

DeGroot, T., & Gooty, J. (2009). Can nonverbal cues be used to make meaningful personality attributions in employment interviews? *Journal of Business and Psychology, 24*(2), 179–192.

Dehue, F. (2013). Cyberbullying research: New perspectives and alternative methodologies. Introduction to the special issue. *Journal of Community & Applied Social Psychology, 23*(1), 1–6.

DeKay, S. H. (2009). The communication functions of business attire. *Business Communication Quarterly, 72*(3), 349–350.

DeKay, S. H. (2012). Interpersonal communication in the workplace: A largely unexplored region. *Business Communication Quarterly, 75*(4), 449–452.

Dempsey, A. G., Sulkowski, M. L., Dempsey, J., & Storch, E. A. (2011). Has cyber technology produced a new group of peer aggressors? *Cyberpsychology, Behavior and Social Networking, 1*(5), 297–302.

Dennis, A. R., Fuller, R. M., & Valacich, J. S. (2008). Media, tasks, and communication processes: A theory of media synchronicity. *MIS Quarterly, 32*(3), 575–600.

Denniston, L. (2012, June 29). "Wardrobe malfunction" case finally ends. SCOTUSblog. Retrieved from http://www.scotusblog .com/2012/06/wardrobe-malfunction-case-finally-ends

DePaulo, B. (2015). *How we live now: Redefining home and family in the 21st century.* New York: Simon & Schuster.

Deprez-Sims, A., & Morris, S. B. (2010). Accents in the workplace: Their effects during a job interview. *International Journal of Psychology, 45*(6), 417–426. doi:10.1080/00207594.2010.499 950

Deprez-Sims, A., & Morris, S. B. (2013). The effect of non-native accents on the evaluation of applicants during an employment interview: The development of a path model. *International Journal of Selection & Assessment, 21*(4), 355–367. doi:10.1111/ijsa.12045

Derks, D., Bos, A. E. R., & von Grumbkow, J. (2008). Emoticons and online message interpretation. *Social Science Computer Review, 26*(3), 379–388.

Derlega, V. J., Winstead, B. A., Mathews, A., & Braitman, A. L. (2008). Why does someone reveal highly personal information? Attributions for and against self-disclosure in close relationships. *Communication Research Reports, 25*(2), 115–130.

Dewey, J. (1933). *How we think.* Lexington, MA: Heath.

DiBiase, R., & Gunnoe, J. (2004). Gender and culture differences in touching behavior. *Journal of Social Psychology, 144*(1), 49–62.

Ding, H., & Ding, X. (2013). 360-degree rhetorical analysis of job hunting: A four-part, multimodal project. *Business Communication Quarterly, 76*(2), 239–248.

Distracted Driving 2013. U.S. Department of Transportation, National Highway Traffic Safety Administration. Retrieved from http://www.distraction.gov/downloads/pdfs/Distracted_Driving _2013_Research_note.pdf

Dizik, A. (2011, July 11). 8 important tips for Skype interviews. CNN. Retrieved from http://www.cnn.com/2011/LIVING/07/11/skype.interview.tips.cb

Dockterman, E. (2015). Meet Brooke Axtell, the domestic violence survivor who performed with Katy Perry at the Grammys. *Time.* Retrieved from http://time.com/3700400/grammys-2015-brooke-axtell-katy-perry/

Docter, P., & Del Carmen, R. (Directors). (2015). *Inside out* [Motion picture]. United States: Pixar Animation Studios.

Dominus, S. (2013, October 6). Daniel Radcliffe's next trick is to make Harry Potter disappear. *The New York Times Magazine,* p. 26.

Dominus, S. (2006, September 28). *Extras,* season 2, epsiode 3, Daniel Radcliffe.

Dominus, S. (2012, January 14). *Saturday Night Live,* season 37, episode 12, Daniel Radcliffe and Lana Del Rey.

Donnoli, M., & Wertheim, E. H. (2012). Do offender and victim typical conflict styles affect forgiveness? *International Journal of Conflict Management, 23*(1), 57–76.

Dooling, R. (2011, March 1). Curbing that pesky rude tone. *The New York Times,* p. A27.

Döring, N., & Pöschl, P. (2009). Nonverbal cues in mobile phone text messages: The effects of chronemics and proxemics. In R. Ling & S. W. Campbell (Eds.), *The reconstruction of space and time: Mobile phone practices.* New Brunswick, NJ: Transaction Publishers.

D'Orio, W. (2016, June 11). Hamilton 101. *Scholastic: Education pulse* [Blog post]. Retrieved from http://blogs.scholastic.com/education_pulse/2016/06/hamilton-101.html#.V2ry16JCCpr

Doris, J. (Ed.). (1991). *The suggestibility of children's recollections.* Washington, DC: American Psychological Association.

Doucé, L., & Janssens, W. (2013). The presence of a pleasant ambient scent in a fashion store: The moderating role of shopping motivation and affect intensity. *Environment & Behavior, 45*(2), 215–238.

Doughty, E. A. (2009). Investigating adaptive grieving styles: A Delphi study. *Death Studies, 33*(5), 462–480.

Douglas, C. (2002). The effects of managerial influence behavior on the transition to self-directed work teams. *Journal of Managerial Psychology, 17,* 628–635.

Douglas, C., Martin, J. S., & Krapels, R. H. (2006). Communication in the transition to self-directed work teams. *Journal of Business Communication, 43*(4), 295–321.

Dowd, M. (2012, July 1). The wearing of the green. *The New York Times,* p. SR11.

Dragojevic, M., & Giles, H. (2016). I don't like you because you're hard to understand: The role of processing fluency in the language attitudes process. *Human Communication Research, 42*(3), 396–420.

Dragojevic, M., Giles, H., & Watson, B. M. (2013). Language ideologies and language attitudes: A foundational framework. In H. Giles & B. Watson (Eds.), *The social meanings of language, dialect and accent: International perspectives on speech styles* (pp. 1–25). New York: Peter Lang.

Drescher, G., & Garbers, Y. (2016). Shared leadership and commonality: A policy capturing study. *Leadership Quarterly, 27*(2), 200–217. doi:10.1016/j.leaqua.2016.02.002

Drummond, K. (2010, February 26). New Pentagon sim teaches troops to play nice. *Wired* Danger Room blog. Retrieved from http://www.wired.com/dangerroom/2010/02/newpentagon-sim-teaches-troops-to-play-nice

Ducharme, J., Doyle, A., & Markiewicz, D. (2002). Attachment security with mother and father: Associations with adolescents' reports of interpersonal behavior with parents and peers. *Journal of Social and Personal Relationships, 19,* 203–231.

Duck, S. W. (1984). A perspective on the repair of personal relationships: Repair of what, when? In S. W. Duck (Ed.), *Personal relationships: Vol. 5. Repairing personal relationships.* New York: Macmillan.

Duell, M. (2013). BBC presenter from Middlesbrough claims she gets abuse from viewers because of her northern accent. *Mail Online,* July 16, 2003. Retrieved from http://www.dailymail.co.uk/news/article-2364998/BBC-presenter-Steph-McGovern-claims-gets-abuse-viewers-northern-accent.html#ixzz2cyTVG5I1 (paragraph 8)

Dues, M., & Brown, M. (2004). *Boxing Plato's shadow: An introduction to the study of human communication.* New York: McGraw-Hill.

Duffy, M., Thorson, E., & Vultee, F. (2009). Advocating advocacy: Acknowledging and teaching journalism as persuasion. Paper presented at the annual meeting of the Association for Education in Journalism and Mass Communication, Sheraton Boston, Boston, MA. Retrieved from http://www.allacademic.com/meta/p375952_index.html

DuFrene, D., & Lehman, C. (2004). Concept, content, construction and contingencies: Getting the horse before the PowerPoint cart. *Business Communication Quarterly, 67*(1), 84–88.

Duke, A. (2013, April 16). Justin Bieber hopes Anne Frank "would have been a belieber." Retrieved from http://www.cnn.com/2013/04/14/showbiz/bieber-anne-frank

Dunbar N. E. (2004). Dyadic power theory: Constructing a communication-based theory of relational power. *Journal of Family Communication, 4,* 235–248. doi:10.1207/s15327698jfc0403&4_8

Dunbar, N. E., & Abra, G. (2010). Observations of dyadic power in interpersonal interaction. *Communication Monographs, 77*(4), 657–684.

Dunbar, N. E., & Burgoon, J. K. (2005). Perceptions of power and interactional dominance in interpersonal relationships. *Journal of Social and Personal Relationships, 22*(2), 207–233.

Dunbar, N., Jensen, M., Tower, D., & Burgoon, J. (2014). Synchronization of nonverbal behaviors in detecting mediated and non-mediated deception. *Journal of Nonverbal Behavior, 38*(3), 355–376. doi:10.1007/s10919-014-0179-z

Duncan, S., & Fiske, D. (1977). *Face-to-face interaction.* Hillsdale, NJ: Erlbaum.

Dunleavy, V., & Millette, D. (2007). Measuring mentor roles and protégé initiation strategies: Validating instruments in academic mentoring. *Conference Papers—National Communication Association,* 1. Retrieved from http://www.allacademic.com/meta/p194103_index.html

Dunning, D. (2014, October 27). We are all confident idiots. *Pacific Standard.* Retrieved from https://psmag.com/we-are-all-confident-idiots-56a60eb7febc#.pm575t3pt

Dwamena, F., Mavis, B., Holmes-Rovner, M., Walsh, K., & Loyson, A. (2009). Teaching medical interviewing to patients: The other side of the encounter. *Patient Education and Counseling, 76*(3), 380–384.

Dwyer, K. K., & Davidson, M. M. (2012). Is public speaking really more feared than death? *Communication Research Reports, 29,* 99–107.

Dwyer, K. M., Fredstrom, B. K., Rubin, K. H., Booth-LaForce, C., Rose-Krasnor, L., & Burgess, K. B. (2010). Attachment, social information processing, and friendship quality of early adolescent girls and boys. *Journal of Social and Personal Relationships, 27*(1), 91–116.

Eagly, A., Karau, S., & Makhijani, M. (1995). Gender and the effectiveness of leaders: A meta-analysis. *Psychological Bulletin, 111*, 3–32.

Eck, K. (2016, April 3). The lesson A. J. Clemente taught Van Tieu about small markets. TVSpy. Retrieved from http://www.adweek.com/tvspy/the-lesson-a-j-clemente-taught-van-tieu-about-small-markets/166936

Eckholm, E. (2010, May 10). What's in a name? A lot, as it turns out. *The New York Times*, p. A12.

Editorial. (2016, May 7). Labels like "felon" are an unfair life sentence. *The New York Times*. Retrieved from http://www.nytimes.com/2016/05/08/opinion/sunday/labels-like-felon-are-an-unfair-life-sentence.html

Editorial. (2011, April 5). OMG!!! OED!!! LOL!!!. *The New York Times*, p. A22.

Edwards, B. (2013, November 2). Personal communication.

Edwards, R. (1990). Sensitivity to feedback and the development of self. *Communication Quarterly, 28*, 101–111.

Edwards, S. R., Bradshaw, K. A., & Hinsz, V. B. (2014). Denying rape but endorsing forceful intercourse: Exploring differences among responders. *Violence and Gender, 1*(4), 188–193.

Efran, M. G. (1974). The effect of physical appearance on the judgment of guilt, interpersonal attraction, and severity of recommended punishment in a simulated jury task. *Journal of Research in Personality, 8*, 45–54.

Ehrlinger, J., Johnson, K., Banner, M., Dunning, D., & Kruger, J. (2008). Why the unskilled are unaware: Further explorations of (absent) self-insight among the incompetent. *Organizational Behavior and Human Decision Processes, 105*(1), 98–121.

Eibl-Eibesfeldt, I. (1973). The expressive behavior of the deaf-and-blind-born. In M. von Cranach & I. Vine (Eds.), *Social communication and movement: Studies of interaction and expression in man and chimpanzee* (pp. 163–194). New York: Academic Press.

Eisenberg, E., Trethewey, A. LeGreco, M. & Goodall, H. L., Jr., & (2017). *Organizational communication: Balancing creativity and constraint* (8th ed.). Boston: Bedford/St. Martin's.

Ekman, P., & Friesen, W. V. (1971). Constants across cultures in the face and emotion. *Journal of Personality and Social Psychology, 17*, 124–129.

Ekman, P., & Friesen, W. V. (1969). The repertoire of nonverbal behavior: Categories, origins, usage, and coding. *Semiotica, 1*, 49–98.

Ekman, P., Friesen, W. V., & Ellsworth, P. (1972). *Emotion in the human face: Guidelines for research and an integration of findings.* New York: Pergamon Press.

Ekman, P., Friesen, W. V., O'Sullivan, M., Anthony, C., Diacoyanni-Tariatzis, I., Heider, K., . . . Tzavaras, A. (1987). Universals and cultural differences in the judgments of facial expressions of emotion. *Journal of Personality & Social Psychology, 53*(4), 712–717.

El Ahl, A., & Steinvorth, D. (2006, October 20). Sex and taboos in the Islamic world. *Spiegel Online International*. Retrieved on March 12, 2008, from http://www.spiegel.de/international/spiegel/0,1518,443678,00.html

Elliott, S. (2010, June 30). Food brands get sociable on Facebook and Twitter. *The New York Times*. Retrieved from http://mediadecoder.blogs.nytimes.com/2010/06/30/food-brands-get-sociable-on-facebook-and-twitter

Ellyson, S. L., Dovidio, J. F., & Brown, C. E. (1992). The look of power: Gender differences and similarities in visual dominance behavior. In C. L. Ridgeway (Ed.), *Gender, interaction, and inequality* (pp. 50–80). New York: Springer-Verlag.

eMarketer. (2013, March). Digital set to surpass TV in time spent with US media. Emarketer.com. Retrieved from http://www.emarketer.com/Article/Digital-Set-Surpass-TV-Time-Spent-with-US-Media/1010096

eMarketer. (2016, May 24). Even during TV time, digital devices play prominent role. Emarketer.com. Retrieved from https://www.emarketer.com/Article/Even-During-TV-Time-Digital-Devices-Play-Prominent-Role/1013997

Endo, Y., Heine, S. J., & Lehman, D. R. (2000). Culture and positive illusions in close relationships: How my relationships are better than yours. *Personality and Social Psychology Bulletin, 26,* 1571–1586.

Entertainment Software Association. (2016). Essential facts about the computer and video game industry. Retrieved from http://www.theesa.com/wp-content/uploads/2016/04/Essential-Facts-2016.pdf

Erdur-Baker, O. (2010). Cyberbullying and its correlation to traditional bullying, gender and frequent and risky usage of Internet-mediated communication tools. *New Media and Society, 12*, 109–125.

Evans, A. D., Bender, J., & Lee, K. (2016). Can parents detect 8- to 16-year-olds' lies? Parental biases, confidence, and accuracy. *Journal of Experimental Child Psychology, 147,* 152–158. doi:10.1016/j.jecp.2016.02.011

Ewald, J. (2010). "Do you know where X is?": Direction-giving and male/female direction-givers. *Journal of Pragmatics, 42*(9), 2549–2561.

Ewalt, D. (2005, September 17). Jane Goodall on why words hurt. *Forbes.* Retrieved from https://www.forbes.com/2005/10/19/goodall-jane-chimpanzee-aggression-comm05-cx_de_1024goodallhurt.html

Eyssel, F., & Kuchenbrandt, D. (2012). Social categorization of social robots: Anthropomorphism as a function of robot group membership. *British Journal of Social Psychology, 51*(4), 724–731.

Faiola, A. (2005, September 22). Men in land of samurai find their feminine side. *Washington Post Foreign Service.* Retrieved from http://www.washingtonpost.com/wp-dyn/content/article/2005/09/21/AR2005092102434.html

Farley, S. D. (2008). Attaining status at the expense of likeability: Pilfering power through conversational interruption. *Journal of Nonverbal Behavior, 32*(4), 241–260.

Farnsworth, S. J. (2015). *Spinner in chief: How presidents sell their policies and themselves.* New York: Routledge.

Farnsworth, S. J., & Lichter, S. R. (2010). *The nightly news nightmare: Media coverage of U.S. presidential elections, 1988–2008* (3rd ed.). Lanham, MD: Rowman & Littlefield.

Farroni, T., Csibra, G., Simion, F., & Johnson, M. (2002, July 9). Eye contact detection in humans from birth. *Proceedings of the National Academy of Sciences of the United States of America, 99*, 9602–9605. Retrieved from http://www.pnas.org/cgi/doi/10.1073/pnas.152159999

Federal Communications Commission. (2008, January 8). *Understanding workplace harassment.* Retrieved on September 3, 2008, from http://www.fcc.gov/owd/understandingharassment.html

Federal Communications Commission v. *Pacifica Foundation*, 438 U.S. 726 (1978).

Feiler, A., & Powell, D. (2016). Behavioral expression of job interview anxiety. *Journal of Business & Psychology, 31*(1), 155–171. doi:10.1007/s10869-015-9403-z

Feinberg, M., Willer, R., & Schultz, M. (2014). Gossip and ostracism promote cooperation in groups. *Psychological Science, 25*(3), 656–664. doi:10.1177/0956797613510184

Feloni. R. (2016, January 28). The *Business Insider* interview: Tony Hsieh. *Business Insider*. Retrieved from http://www.businessinsider.com/tony-hsieh-explains-how-zappos-rebounded-from-employee-exodus-2016-1

Feloni, R. (2016, January 14). Zappos CEO Tony Hsieh explains why 18% of employees quit during the company's radical management experiment. *Business Insider*. Retrieved from http://www.businessinsider.com/zappos-ceo-tony-hsieh-on-holacracy-transition-2016-1

Feloni, R. (2016, January 28). Zappos CEO Tony Hsieh reveals what it was like losing 18% of his employees in a radical management experiment — and why it was worth it. *Business Insider*. Retrieved from http://www.businessinsider.com/tony-hsieh-explains-how-zappos-rebounded-from-employee-exodus-2016-1

Fent, B., & MacGeorge, E. L. (2006). Predicting receptiveness to advice: Characteristics of the problem, the advice-giver, and the recipient. *Southern Communication Journal, 71,* 67–85.

Ferguson, C. J., & Dyck, D. (2012). Paradigm change in aggression research: The time has come to retire the General Aggression Model. *Aggression and Violent Behavior, 17*(3), 220–228. doi:10.1016/j.avb.2012.02.007

Fertik, M., & Thompson, D. C. (2015). *The reputation economy: How to optimize your digital footprint in a world where your reputation is your most valuable asset.* New York: Crown Business/Random House.

Festinger, L. (1954). A theory of social comparison processes. *Human Relations, 7,* 117–140.

Fieseler, C., Meckel, M., & Müller, S. (2014). With a little help of my peers. The supportive role of online contacts for the unemployed. *Computers in Human Behavior, 41,* 164–176. doi:10.1016/j.chb.2014.09.01

Figdor, C. (2010). Objectivity in the news: Finding a way forward. *Journal of Mass Media Ethics, 25,* 19–33.

Fikkers, K. M., Piotrowski, J. T., Lugtig, P., & Valkenburg, P. M. (2016). The role of perceived peer norms in the relationship between media violence exposure and adolescents' aggression. *Media Psychology, 19*(1), 4–26.

Filik, R., Țurcan, A., Thompson, D., Harvey, N., Davies, H., & Turner, A. (2015). Sarcasm and emoticons: Comprehension and emotional impact. *The Quarterly Journal of Experimental Psychology,* 1–17.

Finder, A. (2006, June 11). For some, online persona undermines a résumé. *The New York Times*. Retrieved from http://www.nytimes.com/2006/06/11/us/11recruit.html

Fiske, S. T., & Taylor, S. E. (1991). *Social cognition.* New York: McGraw-Hill.

Fitch-Hauser, M., Powers, W. G., O'Brien, K., & Hanson, S. (2007). Extending the conceptualization of listening fidelity. *International Journal of Listening, 21*(2), 81–91.

Fitzpatrick, A. (2016, April 11). Will robots in the workplace destroy our future? *Time*. Retrieved from http://time.com/4277517/grappling-with-the-right-role-for-robots-at-work/

Flanagin, A. J., & Metzger, M. J. (2007). The role of site features, user attributes, and information verification behaviors on the perceived credibility of Web-based information. *New Media & Society, 9,* 319–342.

Flecha-García, M. (2010). Eyebrow raises in dialogue and their relation to discourse structure, utterance function and pitch accents in English. *Speech Communication, 52*(6), 542–554.

Fletcher, C. (1999). Listening to narratives: The dynamics of capturing police experience. *International Journal of Listening, 13,* 46–61.

Floyd, K. (2015). *The loneliness cure: Six strategies for finding real connections in your life.* Avon, MA: Adams Media.

Floyd, K., Boren, J. P., Hannawa, A. F., Hesse, C., McEwan, B., & Veksler, A. E. (2009). Kissing in marital and cohabiting relationships: Effects on blood lipids, stress, and relationship satisfaction. *Western Journal of Communication, 73*(2), 113–133. doi:10.1080/10570310902856071

Flynn, J., Valikoski, T., & Grau, J. (2008). Listening in the business context: Reviewing the state of research. *International Journal of Listening, 22*(2), 141–151.

Foley, J. (May 16, 2014). How social "listening" enables real-time marketing. *Forbes*. Retrieved from http://www.forbes.com/sites/oracle/2014/05/16/how-social-listening-enables-real-time-marketing/#44c0f70343e2

Folger, J. P., Poole, M. S., & Stutman, R. K. (2001). *Working through conflict: Strategies for relationships, groups, and organizations* (4th ed.). New York: Longman.

Foodnetwork.com (n.d.). Retrieved from www.foodnetwork.com/shows/30-minute-meals.html

Forward, G. L., Czech, K., & Lee, C. M. (2011). Assessing Gibb's supportive and defensive communication climate: An examination of measurement and construct validity. *Communication Research Reports, 28*(1), 1–15.

Fotis, A. (2015, April 27). Yik Yak's potential for social good. UMSocial blog. Retrieved from http://socialmedia.umich.edu/blog/yik-yak-social-good/

Fox, J., & Warber, K. M. (2013). Romantic relationship development in the age of Facebook: An exploratory study of emerging adults' perceptions, motives, and behaviors. *Cyberpsychology, Behavior, and Social Networking, 16*(1), 3–7.

Fox, L. (2013). Poll: Voters ready for a woman president. Retrieved from http://www.usnews.com/news/articles/2013/05/02/poll-voters-ready-for-a-woman-president

Fraleigh, D. M., & Tuman, J. S. (2011). *Speak up! An illustrated guide to public speaking* (2nd ed.). New York: Bedford/St. Martin's.

Francioli, L., Conway, P. M., Hansen, Å. M., Holten, A., Grynderup, M. B., Persson, R., Mikkelsen, E. G., Costa, G., & Høgh, A. (2015). Quality of leadership and workplace bullying: The mediating role of social community at work in a two-year follow-up study. *Journal of Business Ethics, 132,* 1–11. doi:10.1007/s1055101529963

Franz, B., Leicht, R., Molenaar, K., & Messner, J. (2016). Impact of team integration and group cohesion on project delivery performance. *Journal of Construction Engineering and Management, 143*(1), 04016088.

Freeman, J. B., & Johnson, K. L. (2016). More than meets the eye: Split-second social perception. *Trends in Cognitive Sciences, 20*(5), 362–374. doi:10.1016/j.tics.2016.03.003

French, J. R. P., & Raven, B. (1959). The bases for power. In D. Cartwright (Ed.), *Studies in social power* (pp. 150–167). Ann Arbor, MI: Institute for Social Research.

Fridlund, A. J., & Russell, J. A. (2006). The functions of facial expressions: What's in a face? In V. Manusov & M. L. Patterson (Eds.), *The SAGE handbook of nonverbal communication* (pp. 299–320). Thousand Oaks, CA: Sage.

Friedman, R. (2014). You need a work best friend. *New York Magazine*. Retrieved from http://nymag.com/scienceofus/2014/12/you-need-a-work-best-friend.html

Friedman, T. L. (2007). *The world is flat: A brief history of the twenty-first century.* New York: Farrar, Straus & Giroux.

Frisbie, A. (2013). Mobile phone text messaging: Implications of response time within an asynchronous medium. Presentation at the Annual Convention of the Organization for the Study of Communication, Language, and Gender, Houghton, MI.

Frisby, B. N., & Sidelinger, R. J. (2013). Violating student expectations: Student disclosures and student reactions in the college classroom. *Communication Studies, 64*(3), 241–258.

Frosch, D. (2013, March 18). Dispute on transgender rights unfolds at a Colorado school. *The New York Times*, p. A10.

Frost, D. M., & Forrester, C. (2013). Closeness discrepancies in romantic relationships: implications for relational well-being, stability, and mental health. *Personality & Social Psychology Bulletin, 39*(4), 456–469. doi:10.1177/0146167213476896

Frum, D. (2000). *How we got here: The '70s.* New York: Basic Books.

Frymier, A. B. (1994). A model of immediacy in the classroom. *Communication Quarterly, 42,* 133–144.

Frymier, A. B., & Nadler, M. K. (2013). *Persuasion: Integrating theory, research, and practice* (3rd ed.). Dubuque, IA: Kendall Hunt.

The Fug Girls. (2016, February 29). 18 best and worst dressed celebrities at the 2016 Oscars. *Cosmopolitan*. Retrieved from http://www.cosmopolitan.com/entertainment/celebs/g5472/oscars-best-worst-dressed-fug-girls-oscars-2016/

Gabriel, T. (2010, November 4). Learning in dorm, because class is on the Web. *The New York Times*. Retrieved from http://www.nytimes.com/2010/11/05/us/05college.html

Gagnon, M., Gosselin, P., Hudon-ven der Buhs, I., Larocque, K., & Milliard, K. (2010). Children's recognition and discrimination of fear and disgust facial expressions. *Journal of Nonverbal Behavior, 34*(1), 27–42.

Galak, J., Gray, K., Elbert, I., & Strohminger, N. (2016). Trickle-down preferences: Preferential conformity to high status peers in fashion choices. *PLoS ONE, 11*(5), 1–11. doi:10.1371/journal.pone.0153448

Gallo, C. (2012). 11 Presentation lessons you can still learn from Steve Jobs. *Forbes*. Retrieved from http://www.forbes.com/sites/carminegallo/2012/10/04/11-presentation-lessons-you-can-still-learn-from-steve-jobs/#3b5041eb1516

Gallois, C., Franklyn-Stokes, A., Giles, H., & Coupland, N. (1988). Communication accommodation in intercultural encounters. In Y. Y. Kim & W. B. Gudykunst (Eds.), *Theories in intercultural communication* (pp. 157–85). Newbury Park, CA: Sage.

Gardner, E. (2015, August 6). "Hamilton" will win hearts and minds. *USA Today*. Retrieved from http://www.usatoday.com/story/life/theater/2015/08/06/hamilton-win-hearts-and-minds/31104087/

Gardner, L. A. (2011). Wat 2 Do Abt Txt'n & Drv'n (aka: What to do about the problem of texting while driving?). *CPCU Journal, 63,* 1–13.

Gardner, W. L., Reithel, B. J., Foley, R. T., Cogliser, C. C., & Walumbwa, F. O. (2009). Attraction to organizational culture profiles: Effects of realistic recruitment and vertical and horizontal individualism–collectivism. *Management Communication Quarterly, 22*(3), 437–472.

Garner, J. T., & Poole, M. S. (2009). Opposites attract: Leadership endorsement as a function of interaction between a leader and a foil. *Western Journal of Communication, 73*(3), 227–247.

Garretson, J., & Suhay, E. (2016). Scientific communication about biological influences on homosexuality and the politics of gay rights. *Political Research Quarterly, 69*(1), 17–29. doi:10.1177/1065912915620050

Gates, B. (2009, February). TED Talks: Bill Gates on Mosquitoes, Malaria, and Education. Retrieved from http://www.ted.com/talks/lang/eng/bill_gates_unplugged.html

Gawande, A. (2009). *The checklist manifesto: How to get things right.* New York: Metropolitan Books.

Gay, V. (2014, January). 45 best TV shows to binge-watch. Newsday.com. Retrieved from http://www.newsday.com/entertainment/tv/45-best-tv-shows-to-binge-watch-1.5631924#46

Gayomali, C. (2013, June 14). How typeface influences the way we read and think: And why everyone hates Comic Sans MS. *The Week*. Retrieved from http://theweek.com/article/index/245632/how-typeface-influences-the-way-we-read-and-think

Gearhart, C. C., & Bodie, G. D. (2011). Active-empathic listening as a general social skill: Evidence from bivariate and canonical correlations. *Communication Reports, 24,* 86–98.

Gearhart, C. C. (2014). Sensory-processing sensitivity and nonverbal decoding: The effect on listening ability and accuracy. *International Journal of Listening, 28*(2), 98–111. doi:10.1080/10904018.2014.880867

Gearhart, C. C., & Bodie, G. D. (2012). Sensory-processing sensitivity and communication apprehension: Dual influences on self-reported stress in a college student sample. *Communication Reports, 25*(1), 27–39. doi:10.1080/08934215.2012.672216

Gearhart, C. C., Denham, J. P., & Bodie, G. D. (2014). Listening as a goal-directed activity. *Western Journal of Communication, 78*(5), 668–684. doi:10.1080/10570314.2014.910888

Geller, L. (2016, May 3). Two college students lived out all your rom-com fantasies through their school's Snapstory. *Aplus.com*. Retrieved from http://aplus.com/a/snapchat-love-story-college?c=11275&utm_campaign=i102&utm_source=a96233

Generous, M. A., Frei, S. S., & Houser, M. L. (2015). When an instructor swears in class: Functions and targets of instructor swearing from college students' retrospective accounts. *Communication Reports, 28*(2), 128–140. doi:10.1080/08934215.2014.927518

Gerbner, G., Gross, L., Morgan, M., & Signorielli, N. (1994). Growing up with television: The cultivation perspective. In J. Bryant & D. Zillmann (Eds.), *Media effects: Advances in theory and research* (pp. 17–41). Hillsdale, NJ: Erlbaum.

Gersick, C. J. G. (1988). Time and transition in work teams: Toward a new model of group development. *The Academy of Management Journal, 31*(1), 9–41.

Gersick, C. J. G., & Hackman, J. R. (1990). Habitual routines in task-performing groups. *Organizational Behavior and Human Decision Processes, 47,* 65–97.

Gibb, J. (1961). Defensive communication. *Journal of Communication, 2,* 141–148.

Giles, D. C. (2002). Parasocial interaction: A review of the literature and a model for future research. *Media Psychology, 4,* 279–305.

Giles, H., Coupland, J., & Coupland, N. (1991). *Contexts of accommodation: Developments in applied sociolinguistics.* Cambridge, England: Cambridge University Press.

Giles, H., Coupland, N., & Wiemann, J. M. (1992). "Talk is cheap . . ." but "My word is my bond": Beliefs about talk. In K. Bolton & H. Kwok (Eds.), *Sociolinguistics today: Eastern and Western perspectives* (pp. 218–243). London: Routledge and Kegan Paul.

Giles, H., Fortman, J., Dailey, R. M., Barker, V., Hajek, C., Anderson, M. C., & Rule, N. O. (2006). Communication accommodation: Law enforcement and the public. In R. M. Dailey & B. A. LePoire (Eds.), *Applied interpersonal communication matters: Family, health, and community relations* (pp. 241–269). New York: Peter Lang.

Giles, H., & LePoire, B. A. (2006). Introduction: The ubiquity and social meaningfulness of nonverbal communication. In V. Manusov & M. L. Patterson (Eds.), *The SAGE handbook of nonverbal communication* (pp. xv–xxvii). Thousand Oaks, CA: Sage.

Giles, H., & Maass, A. (2016). *Advances in intergroup communication.* New York: Peter Lang.

Giles, H., Reid, S., & Harwood, J. (Eds.) (2010). *The dynamics of intergroup communication.* New York: Peter Lang.

Giles, H., & Watson, B. (Eds.). (2013). *The social meanings of language, dialect, and accent: International perspectives on speech styles.* New York: Peter Lang.

Giles, H., & Wiemann, J. M. (1987). Language, social comparison, and power. In C. R. Berger & S. H. Chaffee (Eds.), *Handbook of communication science* (pp. 350–384). Newbury Park, CA: Sage.

Gillath, O., McCall, C., Shaver, P. R., & Blascovich, J. (2008). What can virtual reality teach us about prosocial tendencies in real and virtual environments? *Media Psychology, 11*(2), 259–282.

Gilmore, M. (2013, May 7). Love and war inside the Rolling Stones. *Rolling Stone.* Retrieved from http://www.rollingstone.com /music/news/the-rolling-stones-soul-survivors-20130507

Gitlow v. *New York,* 268 U.S. 652 (1925).

Givhan, R. (2013, April 8). The language of Margaret Thatcher's handbags. *The Daily Beast.* Retrieved from http://www.thedailybeast. com/articles/2011/12/19/the-language-of-margaret-thatcher-s -handbags.html

Giving hope by highlighting the presence of LGBT youth and their allies. (2016). It Gets Better Project. Retrieved on June 21, 2016, from http://www.itgetsbetter.org/content/media

Goffman, E. (1974). *Frame analyses: An essay on organization of experience.* Cambridge, MA: Harvard University Press.

Goffman, E. (1967). *Interaction ritual: Essays on face-to-face behavior.* Garden City, NY: Doubleday.

Goldman, Z. W., & Myers, S. A. (2015). The relationship between organizational assimilation and employees' upward, lateral, and displaced dissent. *Communication Reports, 28*(1), 24–35. doi:10 .1080/08934215.2014.902488

Goleman, D. (1995). *Emotional intelligence: Why it can matter more than IQ.* New York: Bantam Books.

Gomez, L. (2015). Just paying attention: Communication for organizational attention. *International Journal of Business Communication.* doi:10.1177/2329488415600862

Gomez, P. (2016). *Dancing with the Stars*'s Nyle DiMarco: "I've never wanted to hear." *People, 85*(22), 58–63.

Gong, Z. H., & Bucy, E. P. (2016). When nonverbal behaviors overshadow substance in presidential debates. *Communication Currents, 11*(1), 1–3.

Gonzaga, G. C., Campos, B., & Bradbury, T. (2007). Similarity, convergence, and relationship satisfaction in dating and married couples. *Journal of Personality & Social Psychology, 93*(1), 34–48.

Gonzales, A. L., & Hancock, J. T. (2011, January/February). Mirror, mirror on my Facebook wall: Effects of exposure to Facebook on self-esteem. *Cyberpsychology, Behavior, and Social Networking, 14*(1–2), 79–83.

Goodman, J. (2013, March 24). Obsessed? You're not alone. *The New York Times,* p. ST9.

Goodnight, G. T. (2015). Rhetoric and communication: Alternative worlds of inquiry. *Quarterly Journal of Speech, 101*(1), 145–150. doi:10.1080/00335630.2015.9999

Goodrich, A. (2007, March 28). Anxiety about study abroad. *The Georgetown Independent.* Retrieved from http://travel .georgetown.edu/51469.html

Goodwin, D. K. (2002, January 27). How I caused that story. *Time.* Retrieved from http://www.time.com/time/nation /article/0,8599,197614,00.html#ixzz1FMvG5yK9

Gordon, M. E. (2011). The dialectics of the exit interview: A fresh look at conversations about organizational disengagement. *Management Communication Quarterly, 25*(1), 59–86. doi:10.1177/0893318910376914

Gore, J. (2009). The interaction of sex, verbal, and nonverbal cues in same-sex first encounters. *Journal of Nonverbal Behavior, 33*(4), 279–299.

Goss, B., & O'Hair, D. (1988). *Communicating in interpersonal relationships.* New York: Macmillan.

Gottman, J. M. (1994). *What predicts divorce? The relationship between marital processes and marital outcomes.* Hillsdale, NJ: Erlbaum.

Gottman, J. M., & Silver, N. (1999). *The seven principles for making marriages work: A practical guide from the country's foremost relationship expert.* New York: Three Rivers Press.

Gouran, D. S. (2003). Communication skills for group decision making. In J. O. Greene & B. R. Burleson (Eds.), *Handbook of communication and social interaction skills* (pp. 835–870). Mahwah, NJ: Erlbaum.

Granot, Y., Balcetis, E., Schneider, K. E., & Tyler, T. R. (2014). Justice is not blind: Visual attention exaggerates effects of group identification on legal punishment. *Journal of Experimental Psychology: General, 143*(6), 2196–2208. doi:10.1037/a0037893

Gray, F. E. (2010). Specific oral communication skills desired in new accountancy graduates. *Business Communication Quarterly, 73*(1), 40–67.

Greco, B. (1977). Recruiting and retaining high achievers. *Journal of College Placement, 37*(2), 34–40.

Green, T., Wilhelmsen, T., Wilmots, E., Dodd, B., & Quinn, S. (2016). Social anxiety, attributes of online communication and self-disclosure across private and public Facebook communication. *Computers in Human Behavior, 58,* 206–213.

Greenwalk, A. G., Bellezza, F. S., & Banaji, M. R. (1988). Is self-esteem a central ingredient of self-concept? *Personality and Social Psychology Bulletin, 14,* 34–45.

Grenny, J., & Maxfield, D. (2015). Society's new addiction: Getting a "like" over having a life. Vitalsmarts.com. Retrieved from https://www.vitalsmarts.com/press/2015/03/societys-new -addiction-getting-a-like-over-having-a-life/

Griffin, R. (2015, July 22). Social media is changing how college students deal with mental health, for better or worse. Huffpost College. Huffingtonpost.com. Retrieved from http: //www.huffingtonpost.com/entry/social-media-college-mental -health_us_55ae6649e4b08f57d5d28845

Groeling, T. (2013). Media bias by the numbers: Challenges and opportunities in the empirical study of partisan news. *Political Science, 16*(1), 129.

Groot-Alberts, L. (2012). The lament of a broken heart: mourning and grieving in different cultures. How acceptance of difference creates a bridge for healing and hope. *Progress in Palliative Care, 20*(3), 158–162. doi:10.1179/1743291X12Y.0000000024

Grossman, R. B., & Kegl, J. (2007). Moving faces: Categorization of dynamic facial expressions in American Sign Language by deaf and hearing participants. *Journal of Nonverbal Behavior, 31,* 23–28.

Grossman, S. (2013, April 23). Worst first day ever: Rookie TV anchor fired for profanity in first newscast. *Time.* Retrieved from http:

//newsfeed.time.com/2013/04/23/worst-first-day-ever-rookie-tv-anchor-fired-for-profanity-in-first-newscast

Gudykunst, W. B. (2004). *Bridging differences: Effective intergroup communication* (4th ed.). Thousand Oaks, CA: Sage.

Gudykunst, W. B., Ting-Toomey, S., Sudweeks, S., & Stewart, L. P. (1995). *Building bridges: Interpersonal skills for a changing world*. Boston: Houghton Mifflin Company.

Guéguen, N. (2012). Tattoos, piercings, and sexual activity. *Social Behavior & Personality: An International Journal, 40*(9), 1543–1547.

Guerrero, L. K., & Afifi, W. A. (1995). Some things are better left unsaid: Topic avoidance in family relationships. *Communication Quarterly, 43,* 276–296.

Guerrero, L. K., Andersen, P. A., & Afifi, W. A. (2013). *Close encounters: Communication in relationships.* Los Angeles, CA: Sage.

Guerrero, L. K., Farinelli, L., & McEwan, B. (2009). Attachment and relational satisfaction: The mediating effect of emotional communication. *Communication Monographs, 76*(4), 487–514.

Guerrero, L. K., & Floyd, K. (2006). *Nonverbal communication in close relationships.* Mahwah, NJ: Erlbaum.

Guerrero, L. K., La Valley, A. G., & Farinelli, L. (2008). The experience and expression of anger, guilt, and sadness in marriage: An equity theory explanation. *Journal of Social and Personal Relationships, 25*(5), 699–724.

Gunraj, D. N., Drumm-Hewitt, A. M., Dashow, E. M., Upadhyay, S. N., & Klin, C. M. (2016). Texting insincerely: The role of the period in text messaging. *Computers in Human Behavior, 55,* 1067–1075. doi:10.1016/j.chb.2015.11.003

Guzman, Z. (2016, September 13). Zappos CEO Tony Hsieh on getting rid of managers: What I wish I'd done differently. CNBC. Retrieved on October 10, 2016, from http://www.cnbc.com/2016/09/13/zappos-ceo-tony-hsieh-the-thing-i-regret-about-getting-rid-of-managers.html

Haas, J. (2012). Hate speech and stereotypic talk. In H. Giles (Ed.), *The handbook of intergroup communication* (pp. 128–140). New York: Routledge/Taylor and Francis Group.

Hagen, M. H. (2015). Combating social loafing performance reductions in virtual groups with increased cohesion, reduced deindividuation, and heightened evaluation potential through self-disclosure. (Master's thesis). Harvard Extension School, Cambridge, MA.

Haigh, T., Russell, A. L., & Dutton, W. H. (2015). Histories of the internet: Introducing a special issue of information & culture. *Information & Culture, 50*(2), 143–159. doi:10.7560/IC50201

Haines, S. (2014). Interfaith America: "Being both" is a rising trend in the US. *Christian Science Monitor.* Retrieved from http://www.csmonitor.com/The-Culture/Family/2014/1123/Interfaith-America-Being-both-is-a-rising-trend-in-the-US

Hall, E. T. (1959). *The silent language.* New York: Doubleday.

Hall, E. T., & Hall, M. R. (1990). *Understanding cultural differences: Germans, French, and Americans.* Yarmouth, ME: Intercultural Press, Inc.

Hall, J. A. (1998). How big are nonverbal sex differences? The case of smiling and sensitivity to nonverbal cues. In D. J. Canary & K. Dindia (Eds.), *Sex differences and similarities in communication: Critical essays and empirical investigations of sex and gender in interaction* (pp. 155–178). Mahwah, NJ: Erlbaum.

Hall, J. A. (2013). Humor in long-term romantic relationships: The association of general humor styles and relationship-specific functions with relationship satisfaction. *Western Journal of Communication, 77*(3), 272–292.

Hall, J. A., Carter, J. D., & Hogan, T. G. (2000). Gender differences in nonverbal communication of emotion. In A. H. Fischer (Ed.), *Gender and emotion: Social psychological perspectives* (pp. 97–117). Cambridge: Cambridge University Press.

Halone, K., Cunconan, T. M., Coakley, C. G., and Wolvin, A. D. Toward the establishment of general dimensions underlying the listening process. *International Journal of Listening, 12,* 12–28. (1998).

Hameed, M. (2012, December 20). Team Rubicon: Rebuilding the Rockaways. Thirteen.org, MetroFocus. Retrieved from http://www.thirteen.org/metrofocus/2012/12/team-rubicon-rebuilding-the-rockaways (2:30)

Hamlin, J. K., & Baron, A. S. (2014). Agency attribution in infancy: Evidence for a negativity bias. *PLoS ONE, 9*(5), 1–8. doi:10.1371/journal.pone.0096112

Hammick, J. K., & Lee, M. J. (2014). Do shy people feel less communication apprehension online? The effects of virtual reality on the relationship between personality characteristics and communication outcomes. *Computers in Human Behavior, 33,* 302–310.

Hample, D., & Dallinger, J. M. (1995). A Lewinian perspective on taking conflict personally: Revision, refinement, and validation of the instrument. *Communication Quarterly, 43*(3), 297–319.

Han, B., & Cai, D. (2010). Face goals in apology: A cross-cultural comparison of Chinese and U.S. Americans. *Journal of Asian Pacific Communication, 20*(1), 101–123.

Hancock, A. B., Stutts, H. W., & Bass, A. (2015). Perceptions of gender and femininity based on language: Implications for transgender communication therapy. *Language & Speech, 58*(3), 315–333. doi:10.1177/0023830914549084

Hannawa, A. F. & Spitzberg, B. H. (2015). Welcome to the *Handbook of communication competence.* In A. F. Hannawa & B. H. Spitzberg (Eds.), *Communication competence* (pp. 3–8). Berlin, Boston: De Gruyter Mouton.

Hansen-Bundy, B. (2016). Initiate: Ghosting protocol. *Gentlemen's Quarterly, 86*(3), 124.

Hardaker, C. (2010). Trolling in asynchronous computer-mediated communication: From user discussions to academic definitions. *Journal of Politeness Research: Language, Behaviour, Culture, 6*(2), 215–242. doi:10.1515/jplr.2010.011

Harmon, A. (2011, March 19). On Twitter, "What a party!" brings an envious "Enough, already!" *The New York Times,* p. A1.

Harmon, A. H., & Metaxas, P. T. (2010). *How to create a smart mob: Understanding a social network capital.* Unpublished manuscript, Wellesley College. Retrieved from http://cs.wellesley.edu/~pmetaxas/How-to-create-Smart-Mobs%20eDem2010.pdf

Harrigan, J. A., & Taing, K. T. (1997). Fooled by a smile: Detecting anxiety in others. *Journal of Nonverbal Behavior, 21,* 203–221.

Harris, A. L., & Hahn, U. (2011). Unrealistic optimism about future life events: A cautionary note. *Psychological Review, 118*(1), 135–154.

Harris, G. (2011, July 11). New for aspiring doctors, the people skills test. *The New York Times,* p. A1.

Harris, G. (2013, February 14). In India, kisses are on rise, even in public. *The New York Times,* p. A4.

Harris, T. E. (2002). *Applied organizational communication: Principles and pragmatics for future practice* (2nd ed.). Mahwah, NJ: Erlbaum.

Harrison, K., & Cantor, J. (1997). The relationship between media consumption and eating disorders. *Journal of Communication, 47,* 40–66.

Hartnett, S. J. (2010). Communication, social justice, and joyful commitment. *Western Journal of Communication, 74*(1), 68–93.

Harwood, J. (2000). Communication media use in the grandparent-grandchild relationship. *Journal of Communication, 50*(4), 56–78.

Harwood, J., & Giles, H. (Eds.) (2005). *Intergroup communication: Multiple perspectives.* New York: Peter Lang.

Haughney, C. (2012). Time and CNN reinstate journalist after review. *The New York Times.* Retrieved on May 2, 2014, from http://query.nytimes.com/gst/fullpage.html?res=9C00E7DE103BF934A2575BC0A9649D8B63&ref=fareedzakaria

Hauser, C. (2016, April 21). "Buddy check on 22!" Veterans use social media to fight suicide. *The New York Times.* Retrieved from http://www.nytimes.com/2016/04/22/us/veterans-suicide-22-social.html?_r=0

Hawkins, K., & Stewart, R. A. (1991). Effects of communication apprehension on perceptions of leadership and intragroup attraction in small task-oriented groups. *Southern Communication Journal, 57*, 1–10.

Hawkley, L. C., & Cacioppo, J. T. (2010). Loneliness matters: A theoretical and empirical review of consequences and mechanisms. *Annals of Behavioral Medicine, 40*(2), 218–227.

Hayakawa, S. I. (1964). *Language in thought and action.* New York: Harcourt Brace Jovanovich.

Hazel, M., Wongprasert, T. K., & Ayres, J. (2006). Twins: How similar are fraternal and identical twins across four communication variables? *Journal of the Northwest Communication Association, 35*, 46–59.

Heathfield, S. (2016, February 29). 11 tips for managing millennials. *About Money.* Retrieved from http://humanresources.about.com/od/managementtips/a/millenials.htm

Heffernan, E., Coulson, N. S., Henshaw, H., Barry, J. G., & Ferguson, M. A. (2016). Understanding the psychosocial experiences of adults with mild-moderate hearing loss: An application of Leventhal's self-regulatory model. *International Journal of Audiology,* 1–10.

Helbling, M. M., & Traunmüller, R. (2016). How state support of religion shapes attitudes toward Muslim immigrants. *Comparative Political Studies, 49*(3), 391–424.

Henderson, T. (2016, January 8). Americans are moving south, west again. *Stateline.* The Pew Charitable Trusts. Retrieved from http://www.pewtrusts.org/en/research-and-analysis/blogs/stateline/2016/01/08/americans-are-moving-south-west-again

Hendrick, S. S., & Hendrick, C. (1992). *Liking, loving, and relating.* Pacific Grove, CA: Brooks/Cole.

Hendriks, A. (2002). Examining the effects of hegemonic depictions of female bodies on television: A call for theory and programmatic research. *Critical Studies in Media Communication, 19,* 106–123.

Hendrix, H., LaKelly Hunt, H., Luquet, W., & Carlson, J. (2015). Using the Imago dialogue to deepen couples therapy. *Journal of Individual Psychology, 71*(3), 253–272.

Herberman Mash, H. B., Fullerton, C. S., & Ursano, R. J. (2013). Complicated grief and bereavement in young adults following close friend and sibling loss. *Depression & Anxiety (1091–4269), 30*(12), 1202–1210.

Herman, L. (2016, February 25). 22 things you can leave off your resume. *Skillcrush.* Retrieved from http://motto.time.com/4173214/resume-mistakes/

Herman, M. (2013, June 13). Crisis-wracked town bets on Smurf-based economy. *Pacific Standard.* Retrieved from http://www.psmag.com/business-economics/crisis-wracked-town-bets-on-smurf-based-economy-60158

Heslin, R. (1974). *Steps toward a taxonomy of touching.* Paper presented at the Western Psychological Association Convention, Chicago.

Hesse, C., & Rauscher, E. A. (2013). Privacy tendencies and revealing/concealing: The moderating role of emotional competence. *Communication Quarterly, 61*(1), 91–112.

Hicks, A. M., & Diamond, L. M. (2011). Don't go to bed angry: Attachment, conflict, and affective and physiological reactivity. *Personal Relationships, 18*(2), 266–284. doi:http://dx.doi.org/10.1111/j.1475-6811.2011.01355.x

Hill, E. M., Griffiths, F. E., & House, T. (2015, August 19). Spreading of healthy mood in adolescent social networks. *Proceedings. Biological Sciences/The Royal Society, 282*(1813), 1180. doi:10.1098/rspb.2015.1180

Hinkle, L. L. (1999). Nonverbal immediacy communication behaviors and liking in marital relationships. *Communication Research Reports, 16,* 81–90.

Hirsh-Pasek, K., Adamson, L. B., Bakeman, R., Tresch Owen, M., Michnick Golinkoff, R., Pace, A., & Suma, K. (2015). The contribution of early communication quality to low-income children's language success. *Psychological Science, 26*(7), 1071–1083. doi:10.1177/0956797615581493

Hocevar, K. P., Flanagin, A. J., & Metzger, M. J. (2014). Social media self-efficacy and information evaluation online. *Computers in Human Behavior, 39,* 254–262.

Hockenbury, D. H., & Hockenbury, S. E. (2009). *Psychology* (5th ed). New York: Worth.

Hof, R. D. (2016, March 7). Marketers let emojis say it with pictures. *The New York Times,* pp. B1–B5.

Hofmann, W., Finkel, E. J., & Fitzsimons, G. M. (2015). Close relationships and self-regulation: How relationship satisfaction facilitates momentary goal pursuit. *Journal of Personality and Social Psychology, 109*(3), 434-452. doi:10.1037/pspi0000020

Hofstede, G. (1984). *Culture's consequences: International differences in work-related values.* Beverly Hills, CA: Sage.

Hofstede, G. (2001). *Culture's consequences: Comparing values, behaviors, institutions, and organizations across nations.* Thousand Oaks, CA: Sage.

Hofstede, G., Hofstede, G. J., & Minkov, M. (2010). *Cultures and organizations: Software of the mind* (3rd ed.). New York: McGraw-Hill.

Hogg, M., & Giles, H. (2012). Norm talk and identity in intergroup communication. In H. Giles (Ed.), *The handbook of intergroup communication* (pp. 373–387). New York: Routledge/Taylor and Francis Group.

Hoggard, R. (2017, February 10). Tiger faces familiar foe: Uncertainty. Golfchannel.com. Retrieved on February 11, 2017, from http://www.golfchannel.com/news/rex-hoggard/tiger-faces-familiar-foe-uncertainty/

Holson, L. M. (2010, May 8). Tell-all generation learns to keep things offline. *The New York Times,* p. A1.

Holson, L. M. (2008, March 9). Text generation gap: U r 2 old (jk). *The New York Times.* Retrieved from http://www.nytimes.com/2008/03/09/business/09cell.html

Homer, P. M. (2006). Relationships among ad-induced affect, beliefs, and attitudes: Another look. *Journal of Advertising, 35,* 35–51.

Honeycutt, J. M., Choi, C. W., & DeBerry, J. R. (2009). Communication apprehension and imagined interactions. *Communication Research Reports, 26*(3), 228–236.

Honeycutt, J. M., & Wiemann, J. M. (1999). Analysis of functions of talk and reports of imagined interactions (IIs) during engagement and marriage. *Human Communication, 25*, 399–419.

Hong, S. M., & Faedda, S. (1996). Refinement of the Hong psychological reactance scale. *Educational and Psychological Measurement, 56*, 173–182.

Hoover, K. (2006, February). Alumni to know: He brought Trader Joe's to Main Street. *Stanford Business Magazine.* Retrieved from http://www.gsb.stanford/edu

Horn, J. (2010, October 31). The production: How *The King's Speech* found its voice. *Los Angeles Times.* Retrieved from http://articles.latimes.com/2010/oct/31/entertainment/laca-sneaks-kings-speech-20101031

Horovitz, B. (2012, May 3). After Gen X, Millennials, what should the next generation be? *USA Today.* Retrieved from http://usatoday30.usatoday.com/money/advertising/story/2012-05-03/naming-the-next-generation/54737518/1

Horrigan, J. B., & Duggan, M. (2015, December 21). Home broadband 2015: The share of Americans with broadband at home has plateaued, and more rely only on their smartphones for online access. Pew Research Center. Retrieved from http://www.pewinternet.org/2015/12/21/home-broadband-2015/

Houston, J. B., Pfefferbaum, B., Sherman, M. D., Melson, A. G., & Brand, M. W. (2013). Family communication across the military deployment experience: Child and spouse report of communication frequency and quality and associated emotions, behaviors, and reactions. *Journal of Loss & Trauma, 18*(2), 103–119. doi:10.1080/15325024.2012.684576

Howard, D. L. (2004, August 2). Silencing Huck Finn. *The Chronicle of Higher Education.* Retrieved from http://chronicle.com/jobs/2004/08/2004080201c.htm

Howe, J. (2006). The rise of crowdsourcing. *Wired, 14*(6), 1–4.

Howe, N. & Strauss, W. (1992). *Generations: The history of America's future, 1584 to 2069.* New York: Quill.

Howe, W. (2016, March 28–updated). A brief history of the internet. Retrieved from http://www.walthowe.com/navnet/history.html

Hubble, K., Bowen, K. L., Moore, S. C., & van Goozen, S. H. M. (2015). Improving negative emotion recognition in young offenders reduced subsequent crime. *PLoS ONE, 10*(6): e0132035. doi:10.1371/journal.pone.0132035

Huffcutt, A. I., Culbertson, S. S., & Riforgiate, S. E. (2015). Functional forms of competence: Interviewing. In A. F. Hannawa and B. H. Spitzberg (Eds.), *Communication competence* (pp. 431–448). Berlin, Boston: De Gruyter Mouton.

Hui, C. M., Finkel, E. J., Fitzsimons, G. M., Kumashiro, M., & Hofmann, W. (2014). The Manhattan effect: When relationship commitment fails to promote support for partners' interests. *Journal of Personality and Social Psychology, 106*(4), 546–570. doi:10.1037/a0035493

Hullman, G. A., Goodnight, A., & Mougeotte, J. (2012). An examination of perceived relational messages that accompany interpersonal communication motivations. *Open Communication Journal, 6*, 1–7.

Husband, C. (2009). Between listening and understanding. *Continuum: Journal of Media & Cultural Studies, 23*(4), 441–443.

Huston, A. C., Bickham, D. S., Lee, J. H., & Wright, J. C. (2007). From attention to comprehension: How children watch and learn from television. In N. Pecora, J. P. Murray, & E. A. Wartella (Eds.), *Children and television: Fifty years of research* (pp. 41–63). Mahwah, NJ: Erlbaum.

Huston, A., & Wright, J. C. (1998). Television and the informational and educational needs of children. *The Annals of the American Academy of Political and Social Science, 557*(1), 9–23.

Huston, D. (2010). Waking up to ourselves: The use of mindfulness meditation and emotional intelligence in the teaching of communications. *New Directions for Community Colleges, 2010*(151), 39–50.

Hwang, S. J., Quast, L. N., Center, B. A., Chung, C. N., Hahn, H., & Wohkittel, J. (2015). The impact of leadership behaviours on leaders' perceived job performance across cultures: Comparing the role of charismatic, directive, participative, and supportive leadership behaviours in the U.S. and four Confucian Asian countries. *Human Resource Development International, 18*(3), 259–277. doi:10.1080/13678868.2015.1036226

Identify soft skills when hiring: 200 sample questions. (2016). *HR Specialist, 14*(7), 3.

Iedema, R., Jorm, C., Wakefield, J., Ryan, C., & Sorensen, R. (2009). A new structure of attention? Open disclosure of adverse events to patients and their families. *Journal of Language & Social Psychology, 28*(2), 139–157.

Improv Everywhere. (2014, January 12). No pants subway ride 2014 New York report. Retrieved from http://improveverywhere.com/2014/01/12/no-pants-subway-ride-2014-new-york-reports

Infante, D. A. (1988). *Arguing constructively.* Prospect Heights, IL: Waveland Press.

Infante, D. A., & Rancer, A. S. (1982). A conceptualization and measure of argumentativeness. *Journal of Personality Assessment, 45*, 72–80.

Internet Gaming Disorder. (2013). DSM5.org. Retrieved from http://www.dsm5.org/Documents/Internet%20Gaming%20Disorder%20Fact%20Sheet.pdf

Ireland, M. E., Slatcher, R. B., Eastwick, P. W., Scissors, L. E., Finkel, E. J., & Pennebaker, J. W. (2011). Language style matching predicts relationship initiation and stability. *Psychological Science, 22*(1), 39–44. doi:10.1177/0956797610392928

Isenberg, S. (2012). A more perfect union: How President Obama's campaign used big data to rally individual voters. *MIT Technology Review.* Retrieved from http://www.technologyreview.com/featuredstory/509026/how-obamas-team-used-big-data-to-rally-voters/

Iva, V., & Eliška, K. (2016). Flexible graduate is successful graduate. Key factors of successful job interview, results of a comparative analysis. *Journal of Competitiveness, 8*(2), 87–102. doi:10.7441/joc.2016.02.07

Ivic, R. K., & Green, R. J. (2012). Developing charismatic delivery through transformational presentations: Modeling the persona of Steve Jobs. *Communication Teacher, 26*(2), 65–68. doi:10.1080/17404622.2011.643808

Ivy, D., & Backlund, P. (2004). *Gender speak: Personal effectiveness in gender communication* (3rd ed.). New York: McGraw-Hill.

Jablin, F. M. (1987). Organizational entry, assimilation, and exit. In F. M. Jablin, L. L. Putnam, K. H. Roberts, & L. W. Porter (Eds.), *Handbook of organizational communication* (pp. 679–740). Newbury Park, CA: Sage.

Jackl, J. A. (2016). "Love doesn't just happen . . .": Parent-child communication about marriage. *Communication Quarterly, 64*(2), 193–209. doi:10.1080/01463373.2015.1103284

Jackson, D. (2006, January 29). State of the Union address: A meshing of many ideas. *USA Today.* Retrieved from http://www.usatoday.com/news/washington/2006-01-29-sotu-speech_x.htm?POE=click-refer

Jaco, C. (2014). The political interview. In P. Laufer (Ed.), *Interviewing: The Oregon method* (pp. 40–248). Portland, OR: Center for Journalism Innovation and Civic Engagement.

Jacobs, C. D., & Heracleous, L. (2006). Constructing shared understanding: The role of embodied metaphors in organization development. *Journal of Applied Behavioral Science, 42,* 207–227.

Jacobs, T. (2012, December 3). "Slut" label refuses to die. *Pacific Standard.* Retrieved from http://www.alternet.org/gender/why-slut-label-refuses-die

Jacobs, T. (2013, January 16). Chick lit may be hazardous to your self-esteem. *Pacific Standard.* Retrieved from http://www.psmag.com/blogs/news-blog/chick-lit-may-be-hazardous-to-your-self-esteem-51671

Jacobs, T. (2016). The link between selfies and self-delusion: New research finds selfie-takers believe—inaccurately—they look especially appealing in their photographic self-portraits. *Pacific Standard.* Retrieved from https://psmag.com/the-link-between-selfies-and-self-delusion-6bcf9e5f9765

Jacobs, T. (2013, March 27). Mindfulness training boosts test scores. *Pacific Standard.* Retrieved from http://www.psmag.com/blogs/news-blog/mindfulness-training-boosts-test-scores-54431

Jagosh, J., Donald Boudreau, J., Steinert, Y., MacDonald, M. E., & Ingram, L. (2011). The importance of physician listening from the patients' perspective: Enhancing diagnosis, healing, and the doctor–patient relationship. *Patient Education & Counseling, 85*(3), 369–374. doi:10.1016/j.pec.2011.01.028

Jain, R., Chaudhary, B., & Jain, N. (2016). Impact of mentoring on academic performance & career self-efficacy of business students. *Indian Journal of Industrial Relations, 51*(4), 684–693.

James, C. H., & Minnis, W. C. (2004, July–August). Organizational storytelling: It makes sense. *Business Horizons,* pp. 23–32.

James, N., & Busher, H. (2009). *Online interviewing.* Thousand Oaks, CA: Sage.

Jamie's Food Revolution. (2016). What we do. Retrieved from http://www.jamiesfoodrevolution.org/what-we-do

Janis, I. L. (1982). *Groupthink: Psychological studies of policy decisions and fiascoes* (2nd ed.). Boston: Houghton Mifflin.

Janusik, L. (2005). Conversational listening span: A proposed measure of conversational listening. *International Journal of Listening, 19,* 12–28.

Jarvey, N. (2015, November 11). Next gen 2015: YouTube's top 30 influencers. *The Hollywood Reporter.* Retrieved from http://www.hollywoodreporter.com/lists/next-gen-2015-youtubes-top-836437/item/adriene-mishler-youtube-next-gen-836480

Jayyusi, L., & Roald, A. S. (2016). *Media and political contestation in the contemporary Arab world: A decade of change.* New York: Palgrave Macmillan.

Jesudason, S., & Weitz, T. (2015). Eggs and abortion: "Women-protective" language used by opponents in legislative debates over reproductive health. *Journal of Law, Medicine & Ethics, 43*(2), 259–269. doi:10.1111/jlme.12241

Jin, B., & Oh, S. (2010). Cultural differences of social network influence on romantic relationships: A comparison of the United States and South Korea. *Communication Studies, 61*(2), 156–171.

Johansson, C., & Stohl, C. (2012). Cultural competence and institutional contradictions: The hydropower referendum. *Journal of Applied Communication Research, 40*(4), 329–349.

Johnston, C. (2016, March 17). The pickup line gets a makeover. *The New York Times,* p. D9.

Johnson, D. I. (2012). Swearing by peers in the work setting: Expectancy violation valence, perceptions of message, and perceptions of speaker. *Communication Studies, 63*(2), 136–151.

Johnson, D. I., & Lewis, N. (2010). Perceptions of swearing in the work setting: An expectancy violations theory perspective. *Communication Reports, 23,* 106–118.

Johnson, S. D., Suriya, C., Yoon, S. W., Berrett, J. V., & Fleur, J. L. (2002). Team development and group processes of virtual learning teams. *Computers & Education, 39,* 379–393.

Johnson, T. (2010, April 19). Land that job: What interviewers really want you to ask them. *Good Morning America.* Retrieved from http://abcnews.go.com/GMA/JobClub/questions-job-interview/story?id=10409243

Johnston, K. (2016, February 19). Firms step up employee monitoring at work. *Boston Globe.* Retrieved on October 10, 2016, from https://www.bostonglobe.com/business/2016/02/18/firms-step-monitoring-employee-activities-work/2l5hoCjsEZWA0bp10BzPrN/story.html

Johnston, M. K., Weaver, J. B., Watson, K. W., & Barker, L. B. (2000). Listening styles: Biological or psychological differences? *International Journal of Listening, 14,* 32–46.

Johnstone, M., Hutchinson, A. M., Redley, B., & Rawson, H. (2016). Nursing roles and strategies in end-of-life decision making concerning elderly immigrants admitted to acute care hospitals. *Journal of Transcultural Nursing, 27*(5), 471–479.

Joiner, R., Gavin, J., Brosnan, M., Cromby, J., Gregory, H., Guiller, J., . . . & Moon, A. (2013). Comparing first and second generation digital natives' Internet use, Internet anxiety, and Internet identification. *Cyberpsychology, Behavior, and Social Networking, 16*(7), 549–552.

Jolie, A. (2009, June 18). Angelina Jolie speaks on World Refugee Day. Video retrieved from http://www.youtube.com/user/AngelinaJolieUNHCR#p/u/87/qtt1Vs9Lcp0. Quote begins at 0:20 and ends at 1:00.

Jones, E. (2013). Internationalization and employability: The role of intercultural experiences in the development of transferable skills. *Public Money & Management, 33*(2), 95–104.

Jones, C. (2005, May 16). Gay marriage debate still fierce one year later. *USA Today.* Retrieved from http://www.usatoday.com/news/nation/2005-05-16-gay-marriage_x.htm

Jones, D. E., Greenberg, M., & Crowley, M. (2015). Early social-emotional functioning and public health: The relationship between kindergarten social competence and future wellness. *American Journal of Public Health, 105*(11), 2283–2290. doi:10.2105/AJPH.2015.302630

Jones, E. E. (1990). *Interpersonal perception.* New York: Freeman.

Jordet, G., Hartman, E., & Jelle Vuijk, P. (2012). Team history and choking under pressure in major soccer penalty shootouts. *British Journal of Psychology, 103*(2), 268–283.

Josselson, R. (2013). *Interviewing for qualitative inquiry: A relational approach.* New York: Guilford Press.

Joyce, M. P. (2008). Interviewing techniques used in selected organizations today. *Business Communication Quarterly, 71*(3), 376–380.

Judd, J. W. (2015, July 8). A conversation with the psychologist behind "Inside Out." *Pacific Standard.* Retrieved from https://psmag.com/a-conversation-with-the-psychologist-behind-inside-out-417cc145abdd#.jw0qxx2h3

Junco, R. (2015, March 17). Yik Yak and online anonymity are *good* for college students. Wired.com. Retrieved from http://www.wired.com/2015/03/yik-yak-online-anonymity-good-college-students/

Jundi, S., Vrij, A., Hope, L., Mann, S., & Hillman, J. (2013). Establishing evidence through undercover and collective intelligence interviewing. *Psychology, Public Policy, and Law, 19*(3), 297–306. doi:10.1037/a0033571

Kadushin, A., & Kadushin, G. (2013). *The social work interview* (5th ed.). New York: Columbia University Press.

Kahn, A. S., Ratan, R. A., & Williams, D. (2014). Why we distort in self-report: Predictors of self-report errors in video game play. *Journal of Computer-Mediated Communication, 19*(4), 1010–1023. doi:10.1111/jcc4.12056

Kalbfleisch, P. J. (2002). Communicating in mentoring relationships: A theory for enactment. *Communication Theory, 12,* 63–69.

Kalman, Y. M., & Gergle, D. (2014). Letter repetitions in computer-mediated communication: A unique link between spoken and online language. *Computers in Human Behavior, 34,* 187–193.

Kalman, Y. M., & Rafaeli, S. (2011). Online pauses and silence: Chronemic expectancy violations in written computer-mediated communication. *Communication Research, 38*(1), 54–69. doi:10.1177/0093650210378229

Kalman, Y. M., Ravid, G., Raban, D. R., & Rafaeli, S. (2006). Pauses and response latencies: A chronemic analysis of asynchronous CMC. *Journal of Computer-Mediated Communication, 12*(1), 1–23.

Kalman, Y. M., Scissors, L. E., Gill, A. J., & Gergle, D. (2013). Online chronemics convey social information. *Computers in Human Behavior, 29*(3), 1260–1269. doi:10.1016/j.chb.2012.12.036

Kameda, T., Ohtsubo, Y., & Takezawa, M. (1997). Centrality in socio-cognitive networks and social influence: An illustration in a group decision-making context. *Journal of Personality and Social Psychology, 73,* 296–309.

Kane, G. C. (2015). Enterprise social media: Current capabilities and future possibilities. *MIS Quarterly Executive, 14,* 1–17.

Kanter, R. M. (2009). *Supercorp: How vanguard companies create innovation, profits, growth, and social good.* New York: Crown Business.

Karau, S. J., & Williams, K. D. (2001). Understanding individual motivation in groups: The collective effort model. In M. E. Turner (Ed.), *Groups at work: Theory and research. Applied social research* (pp. 113–141). Mahwah, NJ: Erlbaum.

Kasoff, M. (2015, Feb 22). 2 dozen millennials explain why they're obsessed with Snapchat and how they use it. Businessinsider.com. Retrieved from http://www.businessinsider.com/why-millennials-use-snapchat-2015-2

Kato, S., Kato, Y., & Scott, D. (2009). Relationships between emotional states and emoticons in mobile phone email communication in Japan. *International Journal on E-Learning, 8*(3), 385–401.

Kato, T. (2016). Effects of partner forgiveness on romantic break-ups in dating relationships: A longitudinal study. *Personality & Individual Differences, 95,* 185–189. doi:10.1016/j.paid.2016.02.050

Katz, J. E., & Crocker, E. T. (2015). Selfies and photo messaging as visual conversation: Reports from the United States, United Kingdom, and China. *International Journal of Communication, 9,* 1861–1872.

Katzenbach, J. R., & Smith, D. K. (1993). *The wisdom of teams.* Boston: Harvard Business School Press.

Kaufmann, J. (2016, May 15). A tip, a dip, a kiss or a curtsy? *The New York Times,* p. AR12.

Kazemi, D. M., Levine, M. J., Dmochowski, J., Nies, M. A., & Sun, L. (2013). Effects of motivational interviewing intervention on blackouts among college freshmen. *Journal of Nursing Scholarship, 45*(3), 221–229. doi:10.1111/jnu.12022

Kearney, M. S., & Levine, P. B. (2015). *Early childhood education by MOOC: Lessons from Sesame Street.* Cambridge, MA: National Bureau of Economic Research. Retrieved from http://www.nber.org/papers/w21229

Keaten, J. A., & Kelly, L. (2008). "Re: We really need to talk": Affect for communication channels, competence, and fear of negative evaluation. *Communication Quarterly, 56*(4), 407–426.

Keating, C. F. (2006). Why and how the silent self speaks volumes: Functional approaches to nonverbal impression management. In V. Manusov & M. L. Patterson (Eds.), *The SAGE handbook of nonverbal communication* (pp. 321–340). Thousand Oaks, CA: Sage.

Keaton, S. A., & Bodie, G. D. (2011). Explaining social constructivism. *Communication Teacher, 25*(4), 192–196. doi:10.1080/17404622.2011.601725

Keaton, S. A., Bodie, G. D., & Keteyian, R. V. (2015). Relational listening goals influence how people report talking about problems. *Communication Quarterly, 63*(4), 480–494. doi:10.1080/01463373.2015.1062407

Kelly, L., & Keaten, J. A. (2015). The transformation of everyday talk: The impact of communication technology on notions of communication competence. In A. F. Hannawa & B. H. Spitzberg (Eds.), *Communication competence* (pp. 153–189). Berlin, Boston: De Gruyter Mouton.

Keltner, D., & Ekman, P. (2015, July 5). The science of "Inside Out." *The New York Times,* p. 10.

Kemp, J. & Bossarte, R. (2012). Suicide data report 2012. Department of Veterans Affairs, Mental Health Services Suicide Prevention Program. Retrieved from http://www.va.gov/opa/docs/suicide-data-report-2012-final.pdf

Kennedy, C., McGeeney, K., & Keeter, S. (2016, August 1). The twilight of landline interviewing. Pew Research Center. Retrieved from http://www.pewresearch.org/2016/08/01/the-twilight-of-landline-interviewing/

Kennedy, R. (2003). *Nigger: The strange career of a troublesome word.* New York: Vintage Books.

Kessler, L. (2014). Re-thinking the interview. In P. Laufer (Ed.), *Interviewing: The Oregon method* (pp. 281–285). Portland, OR: Center for Journalism Innovation and Civic Engagement.

Kesting, P., Ulhoi, J. P., Song, L. J., & Niu, H. (2015). The impact of leadership styles on innovation management—a review and a synthesis. *Journal of Innovation Management, 3,* 22–41.

Keyton, J. (1993). Group termination: Completing the study of group development. *Small Group Research, 24,* 84–100.

Keyton, J., & Frey, L. R. (2002). The state of traits: Predispositions and group communication. In L. R. Frey (Ed.), *New directions in group communication* (pp. 99–120). Thousand Oaks, CA: Sage.

Kharpal, A. (2016). 3 ways robots and AI will change the way you work. CNBC. Retrieved from http://www.cnbc.com/2016/01/19/davos-3-ways-robots-and-artificial-intelligence-will-change-the-way-you-work.html

Kiesling, S. F. (1998). Men's identities and sociolinguistic variation: The case of fraternity men. *Journal of Sociolinguistics, 2*(1), 69–99.

Kilmann, P. R. (2012). Personality and interpersonal characteristics within distressed marriages. *The Family Journal, 20*(2), 131–139.

Kids' interruption of father's live TV interview goes viral. ABC News. Retrieved from http://abcnews.go.com/GMA/video/kids-interruption-fathers-live-tv-interview-viral-46066197

Kim, H. S., & Sasaki, J. Y. (2014). Cultural neuroscience: Biology of the mind in cultural contexts. *Annual Review of Psychology, 65*(1), 487–514. doi:10.1146/annurev-psych-010213-115040

Kimmelman, M. (2014, September 7). Refugees reshape their camp, at the risk of feeling at home. *The New York Times,* p. A1.

Kircher, M. M. (2016, February 16). Teens reveal what Instagram "likes" mean to them—and why some are better than others. Techinsider.io. Retrieved from http://www.techinsider.io/what-instagram-likes-mean-to-teens-2016-2

Kirchner, L. (2013, June 10). Brain-scan lie detectors just don't work. *Pacific Standard*. Retrieved from http://www.psmag.com/science/brain-scan-lie-detectors-just-dont-work-59584/#.UbZXyOabDMY

Kitroeff, N. (2015, April 27). The best and worst fonts to use on your résumé. Retrieved from http://www.bloomberg.com/news/articles/2015-04-27/the-best-and-worst-fonts-to-use-on-your-r-sum-

Kleinmann, M., & Klehe, U. (2011). Selling oneself: Construct and criterion-related validity of impression management in structured interviews. *Human Performance, 24*(1), 29–46. doi:10.1080/08959285.2010.530634

Kline, S., Horton, B., & Zhang, S. (2005). *How we think, feel, and express love: A cross-cultural comparison between American and East Asian cultures.* Paper presented at the annual meeting of the International Communication Association, New York.

Klocke, U. (2007). How to improve decision making in small groups: Effects of dissent and training interventions. *Small Group Research, 38,* 437–468.

Knapp, M. L. (2008). *Lying and deception in human interaction.* Boston: Pearson.

Knapp, M. L., & Hall, J. A. (2010). *Nonverbal communication in human interaction.* Boston, MA: Wadsworth, Cengage Learning.

Knapp, M. L., & Vangelisti, A. L. (2008). *Interpersonal communication and human relationships.* Boston: Allyn and Bacon.

Knobloch, L. K., Basinger, E. D., Wehrman, E. C., Ebata, A. T., & McGlaughlin, P. C. (2016). Communication of military couples during deployment and reunion: Changes, challenges, benefits, and advice. *Journal of Family Communication, 16*(2), 160–179. doi:10.1080/15267431.2016.1146723

Knobloch, L. K., & Solomon, D. H. (2002). Information seeking beyond initial interaction: Negotiating relational uncertainty within close relationships. *Human Communication Research, 28,* 243–257.

Knobloch-Westerwick, S. (2015). *Choice and preference in media use.* New York: Routledge.

Kobayshi, J., & Viswat, L. (2010). Cultural expectations in expressing disagreement: Differences between Japan and the United States. *Asian EFL Journal, 48.*

Koepfer, C. (2015, May 15). Moving forward with self-directed work teams. *Production Machining.* Retrieved from http://www.productionmachining.com/articles/moving-forward-with-self-directed-work-teams

Koerner, B. I. (2013, September 26). Forget foreign languages and music. Teach our kids to code. *Wired.* Retrieved from http://www.wired.com/opinion/2013/09/ap_code

Kois, D. (2012, April 1). The payoff. *The New York Times Sunday Magazine*, p. MM18.

Kolb, D. M., & Putnam, L. L. (1992). Introduction: The dialectics of disputing. In D. M. Kolb & J. M. Bartunek (Eds.), *Hidden conflict in organizations: Uncovering behind the scenes disputes.* Newbury Park, CA: Sage.

Kotler, P., & Keller, K. (2011). *Marketing management* (14th ed.). Upper Saddle River, NJ: Prentice Hall.

Kowitz, A. C., & Knutson, T. J. (1980). *Decision making in small groups: The search for alternatives.* Needham Heights, MA: Allyn & Bacon.

Kralj Novak, P., Smailović, J., Sluban, B., & Mozetič, I. (2015). Sentiment of emojis. *PLoS ONE, 10*(12), 1–22. doi:10.1371/journal.pone.0144296

Kram, K. E. (1983). Phases of the mentor relationship. *Academy of Management Journal, 12,* 608–625.

Kramer, A. D., Guillory, J. E., & Hancock, J. T. (2014). Experimental evidence of massive-scale emotional contagion through social networks. *Proceedings of the National Academy of Sciences, 111*(24), 8788–8790.

Kramer, M. W., & Pier, P. M. (1999). Students' perceptions of effective and ineffective communication by college teachers. *Southern Communication Journal, 65,* 16–33.

Krayer, K. (2016, August 25). Creative Communication Group. Personal communication.

Krayer, K. (2010). *Influencing skills for effective leadership.* Dallas: University of Dallas College of Business.

Krcmar, M., & Greene, K. (1999). Predicting exposure to and uses of television violence. *Journal of Communication, 49,* 24–46.

Kreamer, A. (2006, June). Back to my roots: A diary of going gray. *More Magazine.* Retrieved from http://www.more.com/beauty/hair/back-my-roots-diary-going-gray (paragraph 1)

Kreamer, A. (2007, September). Sex and the gray haired woman. *More Magazine.* Retrieved from http://www.more.com/relationships/dating-sex-love/sex-and-gray-haired-woman

Kross, E., Verduyn, P., Demiralp, E., Park, J., Lee, D. S., Lin, N., Shablack, H., Jonides, J., & Ybarra, O. (2013). Facebook use predicts declines in subjective well-being in young adults. *PLoS ONE 8*(8): e69841. doi:10.1371/journal.pone.006984

Kruger, J., & Dunning, D. (1999). Unskilled and unaware of it: How difficulties in recognizing one's own incompetence lead to inflated self-assessments. *Journal of Personality and Social Psychology, 77*(6), 1121–1134.

Kruglanski, A. W., Chen, X., Pierro, A., Mannetti, L., Erb, H.-P., & Spiegel, S. (2006). Persuasion according to the unimodel: Implications for cancer communication. *Journal of Communication, 56,* 105–122.

Kruglinski, S. (2008, November 26). The 10 most influential people in science. *Discover.* Retrieved on September, 2, 2016, from http://discovermagazine.com/2008/dec/26-the-10-most-influential-people-in-science

Krumhuber, E., Manstead, A., Cosker, D., Marshall, D., & Rosin, P. (2009). Effects of dynamic attributes of smiles in human and synthetic faces: A simulated job interview setting. *Journal of Nonverbal Behavior, 33*(1), 1–15.

Kuhn, T., & Poole, M. S. (2000). Do conflict management styles affect group decision making? Evidence from a longitudinal field study. *Human Communication Research, 26,* 558–590.

Lagesse, D. (2016, April 3). Baseball is a field of dreams — and dashed hopes — for Dominicans. NPR. Retrieved from http://www.npr.org/sections/goatsandsoda/2016/04/03/472699693/baseball-is-a-field-of-dreams-and-dashed-hopes-for-dominicans

Lam, C. (2016). Improving technical communication group projects: An experimental study of media synchronicity theory training on communication outcomes. *Journal of Business and Technical Communication, 30*(1), 85–112.

Lambert, C. (2012, March–April). Twilight of the lecture: The trend toward "active learning" may overthrow the style of teaching that has ruled universities for 600 years. *Harvard Magazine.* Retrieved from http://harvardmagazine.com/2012/03/twilight-of-the-lecture

Lammers, J., Dubois, D., Rucker, D. D., & Galinsky, A. D. (2013). Power gets the job: Priming power improves interview outcomes. *Journal of Experimental Social Psychology, 49*(4), 776–779. doi:10.1016/j.jesp.2013.02.008.

Landsford, J. E., Antonucci, T. C., Akiyama, H., & Takahashi, K. (2005). A quantitative and qualitative approach to social relationships and well-being in the United States and Japan. *Journal of Comparative Family Studies, 36,* 1–22.

Laserna, C. M., Seih, Y., & Pennebaker, J. W. (2014). Um . . . Who like says you know: Filler word use as a function of age, gender, and personality. *Journal of Language & Social Psychology, 33*(3), 328–338. doi:10.1177/0261927X14526993

Latane, B., Williams, K., & Harkins, S. (1979). Many hands make light the work: The causes and consequences of social loafing. *Journal of Personality and Social Psychology, 37*(6), 822–832.

Launay, J., & Dunbar, R. M. (2015). Playing with strangers: Which shared traits attract us most to new people? *PLoS ONE, 10*(6), 1–17. doi:10.1371/journal.pone.0129688

Launspach, S. (2016). Exemplar narratives: Resources for maintaining solidarity and upholding group standards in an American quilting guild. *Text & Talk, 36,* 179–197.

Lawler, K. (2016, March 30). What it's really like to see "Hamilton." *USA Today.* Retrieved from http://www.usatoday.com/story /life/entertainthis/2016/03/29/hamilton-musical-broadway-lin -manuel-miranda-jonathan-groff-what-its-really-like/82354008/

Lawler, K. A., Younger, J. W., Piferi, R. L., Billington, E., Jobe, R., Edmondson, K., & Jones, W. H. (2003). A change of heart: Cardiovascular correlates of forgiveness in response to interpersonal conflict. *Journal of Behavioral Medicine, 26*(5), 373–393.

Le, V. (2011, March 15). Ask an academic: The secret of boys. *The New Yorker* (blog). Retrieved from http://www.newyorker.com /online/blogs/books/2011/03/ask-an-academic-the-deep-secrets -of-boys-friendships.html?printable=true&currentPage=all

Leathers, D. G. (1997). *Successful nonverbal communication: Principles and applications.* Boston: Allyn & Bacon.

Leal, S., & Vrij, A. (2008). Blinking during and after lying. *Journal of Nonverbal Behavior, 32*(4), 187–194.

Leavitt, H. J. (1951). Some effects of certain communication patterns on group performance. *Journal of Abnormal and Social Psychology, 46,* 38–50.

Ledbetter, A. M. (2008). Chronemic cues and sex differences in relational e-mail: Perceiving immediacy and supportive message quality. *Social Science Computer Review, 26*(4), 486–482.

Ledbetter, S. (2015). America's top fears 2015. *The Chapman University survey on American fears.* Retrieved from https://blogs .chapman.edu/wilkinson/2015/10/13/americas-top-fears-2015/

Lee, E. J. (2007). Effects of gendered language on gender stereotyping in computer-mediated communication: The moderating role of depersonalization and gender-role orientation. *Human Communication Research, 33*(4), 515–535.

Lee, E., & Jang, J. (2013). Not so imaginary interpersonal contact with public figures on social network sites: How affiliative tendency moderates its effects. *Communication Research, 40*(1), 27–51.

Lee, E. H., & Schnall, S. (2014, August). The influence of social power on weight perception. *Journal of Experimental Psychology: General, 143*(4), 1719–1725. doi:10.1037/a0035699.

Lee, J. A. (1973). *The colors of love: An exploration of the ways of loving.* Don Mills, Ontario, Canada: New Press.

Leland, J. (2008, October 7). In "sweetie" and "dear," a hurt for the elderly. *The New York Times,* p. A1.

Lenz, L. (2016, March 21). Learning to talk with Noah. *Pacific Standard.* Retrieved from https://psmag.com/learning-to-talk-with -noah-5737b98fea3a#.ax9j20h1p

Leonardi, P., Huysman, M., & Steinfield, C. (2013). Enterprise social media: Definition, history, and prospects for the study of social technologies in organizations. *Journal of Computer-Mediated Communication, 19,* 1–19. doi:10.1111/jcc4.12029

le Roux, M. (2006, November 27). Let's talk about sex: Cult South African director shatters taboos. *Namibian.* Retrieved from http://www.namibian.com.na/2006/November/africa/065 E8B0EB5.html

Leslie, C. (2016). The secret life of feelings. *Screen Education, 80,* 8–15.

Levi, D. (2017). *Group dynamics for teams.* Los Angeles, CA: Sage.

Levin, D. (2012, August 4). Beach essentials in China: Flip-flops, a towel and a ski mask. *The New York Times,* p. A1.

Levine, T. R., Serota, K. B., Shulman, H., Clare, D. D., Park, H. S., Shaw, A. S., & Lee J. H. (2011). Sender demeanor: Individual differences in sender believability have a powerful impact on deception detection judgments. *Human Communication Research, 37,* 377–403.

Levit, A. (2010, March 14). Master online searches. *The Wall Street Journal.* Retrieved from http://online.wsj.com/news/articles/ SB126852207486461893

Lev-On, A. (2017). The third-person effect on Facebook: The significance of perceived proficiency. *Telematics and Informatics, 34*(4), 252–260.

Lewis, L. (2005). Foster a loyal workforce. In *Trader Joe's adventure: Turning a unique approach to business into a retail and cultural phenomenon* (pp. 137–152). New York: Dearborn/Kaplan.

Lewis, T., & Manusov, V. (2009). Listening to another's distress in everyday relationships. *Communication Quarterly, 57*(3), 282–301.

Li, L., & Pitts, J. (2009). Does it really matter? Using virtual office hours to enhance student–faculty interaction. *Journal of Information Systems Education, 20*(2).

Lian, H., Ferris, D. L., & Brown, D. J. (2012). Does power distance exacerbate or mitigate the effects of abusive supervision: It depends on the outcome. *Journal of Applied Psychology, 97,* 107–123.

Limon, M. S., & La France, B. H. (2005). Communication traits and leadership emergence: Examining the impact of argumentativeness, communication apprehension, and verbal aggressiveness in work groups. *Southern Communication Journal, 70*(2), 123–133.

Lin, R., & Utz, S. (2015). The emotional responses of browsing Facebook: Happiness, envy, and the role of tie strength. *Computers in Human Behavior, 52,* 29–38.

Lincoln, A. (1842, February 22). Temperance address. *Repeat After Us.* Retrieved August 14, 2007, from http://www.repeatafterus.com /title.php?i=9700

Lindlof, T. R. (2008). Constructivism. In W. Donsbach (Ed.), *The international encyclopedia of communication* (Vol. 3, pp. 944–950). Carlton, Victoria, Australia: Blackwell.

Lindsley, S. L. (1999). Communication and "the Mexican way": Stability and trust as core symbols in *maquiladoras. Western Journal of Communication, 63,* 1–31.

Lipinski-Harten, M., & Tafarodi, R. W. (2012). A comparison of conversational quality in online and face-to-face first encounters. *Journal of Language & Social Psychology, 31*(3), 331–341.

Lippman, J. R., & Campbell, S. W. (2014). Damned if you do, damned if you don't . . . if you're a girl: Relational and normative contexts of adolescent sexting in the United States. *Journal of Children and Media 8*(4), 371–386.

Liu, T. (2015). Minority youth, mobile phones and language use: Wa migrant workers' engagements with networked sociality and mobile communication in urban China. *Asian Ethnicity, 16*(3), 334–352. doi:10.1080/14631369.2015.1015255

Locker, M. (2015, January 7). Watch Jimmy Fallon realize he once had a shot at dating Nicole Kidman. Time.com. Retrieved from http://time.com/3657371/jimmy-fallon-nicole-kidman-dating/

Lohr, S. (2007, October 31). Hello, India? I need help with my math. *The New York Times*. Retrieved from http://www.nytimes.com/2007/10/31/business/worldbusiness/31butler.html

Longley, R. (2007, December 31). From time to time: The State of the Union. *About.com: U.S. government info*. Retrieved from http://usgovinfo.about.com/od/thepresidentandcabinet/a/souhistory.htm

Louthan, M. (2009). Listening. *Journal of Failure Analysis & Prevention, 9*(3), 183–184. doi:10.1007/s11668-009-9239-9

Lubell, S. (2004, February 19). On the therapist's couch, a jolt of virtual reality. *The New York Times*. Retrieved from http://www.nytimes.com/2004/02/19/technology/on-the-therapist-s-couch-a-jolt-of-virtual-reality.html

Lucero, M. A., Allen, R. E., & Elzweig, B. (2013). Managing employee social networking: Evolving views from the National Labor Relations Board. *Employee Responsibilities and Rights Journal, 25*(3), 143–158.

Lukacs, V., & Quan-Haase, A. (2015). Romantic breakups on Facebook: New scales for studying post-breakup behaviors, digital distress, and surveillance. *Information, Communication & Society, 18*(5), 492–508. doi:10.1080/1369118X.2015.1008540

Lukiandff, G. & Haidt, J. (2015, September). The coddling of the American mind. *The Atlantic*. Retrieved on September 26, 2016, from http://www.theatlantic.com/magazine/archive/2015/09/the-coddling-of-the-mind.html

Lustig, M. W., & Koester, J. (2006). *Intercultural competence: Interpersonal communication across cultures* (5th ed.). Boston: Allyn & Bacon.

Lutz, C. A. (1996). Engendered emotion: Gender, power, and the rhetoric of emotional control in American discourse. In R. Harre & W. G. Parrott (Eds.), *The emotions: Social, cultural and biological dimensions* (pp. 132–150). Thousand Oaks, CA: Sage.

Machkovech, S. (2016, March 10). Yik Yak's "handles" are just lipstick on an ugly, anonymous yak: New, optional usernames rekindle the debate on location-specific social networks. Arstechnica.com. Retrieved from http://arstechnica.com/business/2016/03/yik-yaks-handles-are-just-lipstick-on-an-ugly-anonymous-yak/

Mackie, D. (2015). Jimmy Fallon and Amy Poehler learned a surprising secret about Tina Fey on The Tonight Show. People.com. Retrieved from http://people.com/tv/jimmy-fallon-and-amy-poehler-learned-a-surprising-secret-about-tina-fey-on-the-tonight-show/

Madden, M. (2012, February 24). Privacy management on social media sites. Pew Research Center. Retrieve from http://www.pewinternet.org/Reports/2012/Privacy-management-on-social-media/Main-findings.aspx?view=all

Madden, M., & Smith, A. (2010, May 26). Reputation management and social media. Pew Research Center. Retrieved from http://www.pewinternet.org/Reports/2010/Reputation-Management.aspx

Maddux, J. E., & Rogers, R. W. (1983). Protection motivation theory and self-efficacy: A revised theory of fear appeals and attitude change. *Journal of Experimental Social Psychology, 19*, 469–479.

Madlock, P. E., & Kennedy-Lightsey, C. (2010). The effects of supervisors' verbal aggressiveness and mentoring on their subordinates. *Journal of Business Communication, 47*(1), 42–62.

Maguire, K. C., & Kinney, T. A. (2010). When distance is problematic: Communication, coping, and relational satisfaction in female college students' long-distance dating relationships. *Journal of Applied Communication Research, 38*(1), 27–46.

Mahlermay, J. (2014, May 16). As Barbara Walters retires, the big TV interview signs off, too. *The New York Times*, p. A1.

Maiden, B., & Perry, B. (2011). Dealing with free-riders in assessed group work: Results from a study at a UK university. *Assessment & Evaluation in Higher Education, 36*(4), 451–464.

Malara, M. (2015). New *Star Wars* BB-8 droid voiced by Bill Hader, Ben Schwartz. UPI Entertainment. Retrieved from http://www.upi.com/Entertainment_News/2015/12/17/New-Star-Wars-BB-8-droid-voiced-by-Bill-Hader-Ben-Schwartz/5301450355917/

Males, M. A., & Brown, E. A. (2014). Teenagers' high arrest rates: Features of young age or youth poverty? *Journal of Adolescent Research, 29*(1), 3–24.

Manning, J. (2014). A constitutive approach to interpersonal communication studies. *Communication Studies, 65*(4), 432–440. doi:10.1080/10510974.2014.927294

Manroop, L., Boekhorst, J. A., & Harrison, J. A. (2013). The influence of cross-cultural differences on job interview selection decisions. *International Journal of Human Resource Management, 24*(18), 3512–3533. doi:10.1080/09585192.2013.777675.

Mansson, D. H., Myers, S. A., & Turner, L. H. (2010). Relational maintenance behaviors in the grandchild-grandparent relationship. *Communication Research Reports, 27*(1), 68–79.

Marcus, L. (2013, October 4). How *Project Runway* is getting deafness right. *New York Magazine*. Retrieved from http://www.vulture.com/2013/10/how-project-runway-is-getting-deafness-right.html

Mares, M., & Pan, Z. (2013). Effects of Sesame Street: A meta-analysis of children's learning in 15 countries. *Journal of Applied Developmental Psychology, 34*, 140–151.

Margolis, J. A., & Ziegert, J. C. (2016). Vertical flow of collectivistic leadership: An examination of the cascade of visionary leadership across levels. *Leadership Quarterly, 27*(2), 334–348. doi:10.1016/j.leaqua.2016.01.005

Markham, (2016, January 21). Should you intervene in a sibling fight? *Aha! Parenting*. Retrieved from http://www.ahaparenting.com/blog/What_To_Do_Sibling_Fight

Markoff, J. (2016, February 15). An artificial, likable voice. *The New York Times*, p. B4.

Markoff, J. & Sengupta, S. (November 22, 2011). Separating you and me? 4.74 degrees. *New York Times*, p. B1.

Maslow, A. (1954). *Motivation and personality*. New York: Harper & Row.

Mast, M. S. (2002). Dominance as expressed and inferred through speaking time. *Human Communication Research, 28*, 420–450.

Matsumoto, D. (1989). Cultural influences on the perception of emotion. *Journal of Cross-Cultural Psychology, 20*(1), 92–105.

Matsumoto, D., & Hwang, H. (2013). Cultural similarities and differences in emblematic gestures. *Journal of Nonverbal Behavior, 37*(1), 1–27. doi:10.1007/s10919-012-0143-8

Maycotte, H. O. (2015, September 22). Forbes.com. Retrieved from http://www.forbes.com/sites/homaycotte/2015/09/22/why-steve-jobs-was-the-exception-and-not-the-rule/#23e10b984ed0

Mayhew, R. (2016). How to handle diversity conflicts in the workplace. *Houston Chronicle*. Retrieved on October 10, 2016, from http://work.chron.com/handle-diversity-conflicts-workplace-13495.html

Mazer, J. P., & Titsworth, S. (2012). Passion and preparation in the basic course: The influence of students' ego-involvement with speech topics and preparation time on public-speaking grades. *Communication Teacher, 26*(4), 236–251. doi:10.1080/17404622.2012.668203

McClanahan, A. (2006, March 9). What does a feminist "look" like? *Pocono Record*. Retrieved April 8, 2008, from http://www.poconorecord.com/article/20060309/news/603090303

McCombs, M. (2005). The agenda-setting function of the press. In G. Overholser & K. H. Jamieson (Eds.), *The press* (pp. 156–168). New York: Oxford University Press.

McConnell, M. (1987). *Challenger: A major malfunction.* Garden City, NY: Doubleday.

McCroskey, J. C. (1997). The communication apprehension perspective. In J. A. Daly & J. C. McCroskey (Eds.), *Avoiding communication: Shyness, reticence, and communication apprehension* (pp. 13–38). Cresskill, NJ: Hampton Press.

McCroskey, J. C. (1970). Measures of communication-bound anxiety. *Speech Monographs, 37*, 269–277.

McCroskey, J. C. (1977). Oral communication apprehension: A summary of recent theory and research. *Human Communication Research, 4*, 78–96.

McCroskey, J. C., & Mehrley, R. S. (1969). The effects of disorganization and nonfluency on attitude change and source credibility. *Speech Monographs, 36*, 13–21.

McCroskey, J. C., & Teven, J. J. (1999). Goodwill: A reexamination of the construct and its measurement. *Communication Monographs, 66*, 90–103.

McDaniel, E., & Andersen, P. A. (1998). International patterns of interpersonal tactile communication: A field study. *Journal of Nonverbal Behavior, 22*, 59–75.

McDaniel, E. R., & Samovar, L. A. (2015). Understanding and applying intercultural communication in the global community: The fundamentals. In L. A. Samovar, R. E. Porter, E. R. McDaniel, & C. S. Roy (Eds.), *Intercultural communication: A reader* (14th ed.). Boston: Cengage Learning.

McDonald, M. (2012, September 10). Making Mandarin mandatory—in kindergartens. *The New York Times*. Retrieved from http://rendezvous.blogs.nytimes.com/2012/09/10/making-mandarin-mandatory-in-u-s-kindergartens

McDonald, P. (2012). Workplace sexual harassment 30 years on: A review of the literature. *International Journal of Management Reviews, 14*, 1–17.

McElwee, J. J. (2016). Pope signals opening on contraception. *National Catholic Reporter, 52*(11), 6.

McLeod, D. N., Detenber, B. H., & Eveland, W. P., Jr. (2001). Behind the third-person effect: Differentiating perceptual processes for self and other. *Journal of Communication, 51*, 678–695.

McWhorter, J. (2013, April). Txtng is killing language. JK!!! TED.com. Retrieved from http://www.ted.com/talks/john_mcwhorter_txtng_is_killing_language_jk.html?utm_campaign=&utm_content=ted-androidapp&awesm=on.ted.com_rBl4&utm_source=getpocket.com&utm_medium=on.ted.com-android-share

McWhorter, J. H. (2014). *The language hoax: Why the world looks the same in any language.* New York: Oxford University Press.

Meagher, B. R., & Marsh, K. L. (2017). Seeking the safety of sociofugal space: Environmental design preferences following social ostracism. *Journal of Experimental Social Psychology, 68*, 192–199.

Mease, J., & Terry, D. (2012). (Organizational [performance] of race): The co-constitutive performance of race and school board in Durham, NC. *Text & Performance Quarterly, 32*, 121–140.

Mello, B. (2009). For K-12 educators: Speaking, listening, and media literacy standards. *Spectra, 45*(3), 11.

Merolla, A. J. (2010). Relational maintenance and noncopresence reconsidered: Conceptualizing geographic separation in close relationships. *Communication Theory, 20*(2), 169–193.

Merolla, A. J., & Harman, J. J. (2016). Relationship-specific hope and constructive conflict management in adult romantic relationships testing an accommodation framework. *Communication Research.* Online First. doi:10.1177/0093650215627484

Merrill, A. F., & Afifi, T. D. (2012). Examining the bidirectional nature of topic avoidance and relationship dissatisfaction: The moderating role of communication skills. *Communication Monographs, 79*(4), 499–521.

Metzger, M. J., Hartsell, E. H., & Flanagin, A. J. (2015). Cognitive dissonance or credibility? A comparison of two theoretical explanations for selective exposure to partisan news. *Communication Research.* Online First. doi:0.1177/0093650215613136

Microsoft, Inc. (2005, March 15). Survey finds workers average only three productive days per week [Press release]. Retrieved April 30, 2008, from http://www.microsoft.com

Miczo, N. (2008). Dependence and independence power, conflict tactics and appraisals in romantic relationships. *Journal of Communication Studies, 1*(1), 56–82.

Milevsky, A. (2016). Direct ways parents impact sibling bonds. *Sibling issues in therapy: Research and practice with children, adolescents, and adults.* New York: Palgrave Macmillan.

Miller, C. C., & Bosman, J. (2013, November 14). Siding with Google, judge says book search does not infringe copyright. *The New York Times*. Retrieved from http://www.nytimes.com/2013/11/15/business/media/judge-sides-with-google-on-book-scanning-suit.html?_r=0

Miller, C. W., & Roloff, M. E. (2007). The effect of face loss on willingness to confront hurtful messages from romantic partners. *Southern Communication Journal, 72*(3), 247–263.

Miller, C. W., & Roloff, M. E. (2014). When hurt continues: Taking conflict personally leads to rumination, residual hurt and negative motivations toward someone who hurt us. *Communication Quarterly, 62*, 193–213. doi:10.1080/01463373.2014.890118

Miller, C. W., Roloff, M. E., & Reznik, R. M. (2014). Hopelessness and interpersonal conflict: Antecedents and consequences of losing hope. *Western Journal of Communication, 78*, 563–585. doi:10.1080/10570314.2014.896026

Miller, D. T., & Morrison, K. R. (2009). Expressing deviant opinions: Believing you are in the majority helps. *Journal of Experimental Social Psychology, 45*(4), 740–747.

Miller, J. (2016, June 9). Finding common ground in interfaith marriage. *The New York Times*. Retrieved from http://www.nytimes.com/2016/06/12/fashion/weddings/interfaith-marriage.html

Miller, K. (2009). *Organizational communication: Approaches and processes* (5th ed.). Boston: Wadsworth.

Miller, L. C., Cooke, K. K., Tsang, J., & Morgan, F. (1992). Should I brag? Nature and impact of positive boastful disclosures for women and men. *Human Communication Research, 18*, 364–399.

Miller, R. (1991, January 31). Personnel execs reveal the truth about job applicants. *Dallas Morning News*, p. 2D.

Miller, W. R., & Rollnick, S. (2013). *Motivational interviewing: Helping people change.* New York: Guilford Press.

Minkov, M., & Hofstede, G. (2014). A replication of Hofstede's uncertainty avoidance dimension across nationally representative samples from Europe. *International Journal of Cross Cultural Management, 14*(2), 161–171.

Minow, N. N. (1961, May 9). Television and the public interest. Speech presented at the meeting of the National Association of Broadcasters, Washington, DC.

Minow, N. N., & Cate, F. H. (2003). Revisiting the vast wasteland. *Federal Communications Law Journal, 55*, 407–434.

Mittel, J. (2015). *Complex TV: The poetics of contemporary television storytelling.* New York: NYU Press.

Mittel, J. (2015). Narrative complexity in contemporary American television. *The Velvet Light Trap, 58*, 29–40.

Mock, B. (2016, April 27). Beyonce's simple but radical porch-front politics. *CityLab.* Retrieved from http://www.citylab.com/housing/2016/04/beyonces-simple-but-radical-porch-front-politics/480006/?utm_source=psmag

Mohn, T. (2014). America's disappearing vacation days. *Forbes.* Retrieved on October 10, 2016, from http://www.forbes.com/sites/tanyamohn/2014/10/22/americas-disappearing-vacation-days/#7c98b169581c

Moisala, M., Salmela, V., Salo, E., Carlson, S., Vuontela, V., Salonen, O., & Alho, K. (2015). Brain activity during divided and selective attention to auditory and visual sentence comprehension tasks. *Frontiers in Human Neuroscience, 9*, 1–15. doi:10.3389/fnhum.2015.00086

Molloy, J. T. (1983). *Molloy's live for success.* New York: Bantam Books.

Money is the top subject for marital spats. (2006, March 20). Webindia123.com. Retrieved May 1, 2006, from http://news.webindia123.com/news/ar_showdetails.asp?id=603200038&cat=&n_date=20060320

Montana Meth Project (2013). Retrieved June 3, 2013, from http://montana.methproject.org

Montoya, M., Massey, A., Hung, Y., & Crisp, C. (2009). Can you hear me now? Communication in virtual product development teams. *Journal of Product Innovation Management, 26*(2), 139–155.

Moore, G. E. (1903). *Principia ethica.* Cambridge, UK: Cambridge University Press.

Mor Barak, M. E., Lizano, E. L., Kim, A., Duan, L., Rhee, M. K., Hsiao, H. Y., & Brimhall, K. C. (2016). The promise of diversity management for climate of inclusion: A state-of-the-art review and meta-analysis. *Human Service Organizations: Management, Leadership & Governance, 40*(4), 305–333.

Moreland, R. L., & Levine, J. M., (1994). *Understanding small groups.* Boston: Allyn & Bacon.

Morreale, S., Staley, S., Stavrositu, C., & Krakowiak, M. (2015). First-year college students' use of communication technologies and their perceptions of communication competence in the 21st century. Communication Education, *64*(1), 107–131.

Morris, D. (1977). *Manwatching.* New York: Abrams.

Morris, R. G., & Worrall, J. L. (2014). Prison architecture and inmate misconduct: A multilevel assessment. *Crime & Delinquency, 60*(7), 1083–1109.

Morrissey, L. (2010). Trolling is *a* art: Towards a schematic classification of intention in Internet trolling. *Griffith Working Papers in Pragmatics and Intercultural Communications, 3*(2), 75–82.

Morse, C. R., & Metts, S. (2011). Situational and communicative predictors of forgiveness following a relational transgression. *Western Journal of Communication, 75*(3), 239–258.

Motley, M. T. (1990). On whether one can(not) communicate: An examination via traditional communication postulates. *Western Journal of Speech Communication, 56,* 1–20.

Muehlenhard, C. L., Humphreys, T. P., Jozkowski, K. N., & Peterson, Z. D. (2016). The complexities of sexual consent among college students: A conceptual and empirical review. *Journal of Sex Research, 53*(4/5), 457–487.

Mueller, P. A., & Oppenheimer, D. M. (2014). The pen is mightier than the keyboard: Advantages of longhand over laptop note taking. *Psychological Science, 25*(6), 1159–1168. doi:10.1177/0956797614524581

Muir, C. (2008). Job interviewing. *Business Communication Quarterly, 71*(3), 374–376.

Mulac, A. J., Wiemann, J. M., Widenmann, S. J., & Gibson, T. W. (1988). Male-female language differences and effects in same-sex and mixed-sex dyads: The gender-linked language effect. *Communication Monographs, 55*, 315–335.

Mulgrew, K. E., & Volcevski-Kostas, D. (2012). Short term exposure to attractive and muscular singers in music video clips negatively affects men's body image and mood. *Body Image, 9*(4), 543–546.

Mullen, C., & Fox Hamilton, N. (2016). Adolescents' response to parental Facebook friend requests: The comparative influence of privacy management, parent-child relational quality, attitude and peer influence. *Computers in Human Behavior, 60,* 165–172. doi:10.1016/j.chb.2016.02.026

Muntigl, P., & Choi, K. T. (2010). Not remembering as a practical epistemic resource in couples therapy. *Discourse Studies, 12*(3), 331–356.

Murphy, C. (2015, June 2). Interfaith marriage is common in U.S., particularly among the recently wed. Pew Research Center. Retrieved from http://www.pewresearch.org/fact-tank/2015/06/02/interfaith-marriage/

Murphy, D. R., Daneman, M., & Schneider, B. A. (2006). Do older adults have difficulty following conversations? *Psychology and Aging, 21,* 49–61.

Murphy, J. J. (2013). *Conducting student-driven interviews: Practical strategies for increasing student involvement and addressing behavior problems.* New York: Routledge.

Murthy, D., Bowman, S., Gross, A. J., & McGarry, M. (2015). Do we tweet differently from our mobile devices? A study of language differences on mobile and web-based Twitter platforms. *Journal of Communication 65*(5), 816–837.

Musicus, A., Tal, A., & Wansink, B. (2015). Eyes in the aisles: Why is Cap'n Crunch looking down at my child? *Environment & Behavior, 47*(7), 715–733. doi:10.1177/0013916514528793

Myhre, K. E., & Adelman, W. (2013). Motivational interviewing: Helping teenaged smokers to quit. *Contemporary Pediatrics, 30*(10), 18–23.

Myrick, J. G. (2015). Emotion regulation, procrastination, and watching cat videos online: Who watches Internet cats, why, and to what effect? *Computers in Human Behavior, 52*, 168–176.

Nabi, R. L. (1999). A cognitive-functional model for the effects of discrete negative emotions on information processing, attitude change, and recall. *Communication Theory, 9*, 292–320.

Nabi, R. L. (2009). Cosmetic surgery makeover programs and intentions to undergo cosmetic enhancements: A consideration of three models of media effects. *Human Communication Research, 35*, 1–27.

Narin, J. (2015, May 3). No labels, no drama, right? *The New York Times*, p. ST1.

Naslund, J. A., Aschbrenner, K. A., Marsch, L. A., & Bartels, S. J. (2016). The future of mental health care: Peer-to-peer support and social media. *Epidemiology and Psychiatric Sciences, 25*, 113–122. doi:10.1017/S2045796015001067

National Association of Colleges and Employers (NACE). (2015). Retrieved from http://www2.binghamton.edu/career-development-center/parents/help-your-student/skills-employers-want.html

National Center for Education Statistics (2012). *The condition of education 2012* (NCES 2012-045).

National Highway Traffic Safety Administration. (2014). Traffic fatalities fall in 2014, but early estimates show 2015 trending higher. Retrieved on August 8, 2016, from http://www.nhtsa.gov/About+NHTSA/Press+Releases/2015/2014-traffic-deaths-drop-but-2015-trending-higher

National Highway Traffic Safety Administration. (2014). What is distracted driving? Retrieved on May 9, 2014, from http://www.distraction.gov/content/get-the-facts/facts-and-statistics.html

The National Safety Council (2016). Cell phone distracted driving. Retrieved on August 8, 2016, from http://www.nsc.org/learn/NSC-Initiatives/Pages/distracted-driving-problem-of-cell-phone-distracted-driving.aspx

Nelson, B. (2002). Making teamwork work. *ABA Bank Marketing, 34,* 10.

Nelson, J. (2011, January 5). Do word changes alter "Huckleberry Finn"? *The New York Times.* Retrieved from http://www.nytimes.com/roomfordebate/2011/01/05/does-one-word-change-huckleberry-finn

Neubaum, G., & Krämer, N. C. (2016). What do we fear? Expected sanctions for expressing minority opinions in offline and online communication. *Communication Research.* doi:10.1177/0093650215623837

Neuliep, J. W. (2012). The relationship among intercultural communication apprehension, ethnocentrism, uncertainty reduction, and communication satisfaction during initial intercultural interaction: An extension of anxiety and uncertainty management (AUM) theory. *Journal of Intercultural Communication Research, 41*(1), 1–16. doi:10.1080/17475759.2011.62323

Neuliep, J. W., & Johnson, M. (2016). A cross-cultural comparison of Ecuadorian and United States face, facework, and conflict styles during interpersonal conflict: An application of face-negotiation theory. *Journal of International and Intercultural Communication, 9*(1), 1–19.

Newman, M. L., Groom, C. J., Handelman, L. D., & Pennebaker, J. W. (2008). Gender differences in language use: An analysis of 14,000 text samples. *Discourse Processes, 45*(3), 211–236.

Newton, C. (2016, April 25). Amid slowing growth, Yik Yak adds a chat function. TheVerge.com. Retrieved from http://www.theverge.com/2016/4/25/11503796/yik-yak-chat-private-messaging

Ng, S. H., & Ng, T. K. (2012). Power of messages through speech and silence. In H. Giles (Ed.), *The handbook of intergroup communication* (pp. 116–127). New York: Routledge/Taylor and Francis.

Nicholas, S. (2009). "I live Hopi, I just don't speak it"—The critical intersection of language, culture, and identity in the lives of contemporary Hopi youth. *Journal of Language, Identity & Education, 8*(5), 321–334.

Nichols, R. G. (2006). The struggle to be human: Keynote address to first International Listening Association convention, February 17, 1980. *International Journal of Listening, 20,* 4–12.

Nichols, R. G., Brown, J. I., & Keller, R. J. (2006). Measurement of communication skills. *International Journal of Listening, 20,* 13–17.

Nicotera, A. M. (1997). Managing conflict communication groups. In L. R. Frey & J. K. Barge (Eds.), *Managing group life: Communicating in decision-making groups* (pp. 104–130). Boston: Houghton Mifflin.

Nielsen (2016, June 27). The total audience report: Q1: 2016. The Nielsen Company. Retrieved from http://www.nielsen.com/us/en/insights/reports/2016/the-total-audience-report-q1-2016.html

Nierenberg, R. (2009). *Maestro: A surprising story about leadership by listening.* New York: Portfolio.

Nomani, A. Q. (2005, December 14). Tapping Islam's feminist roots. *The Seattle Times.* Retrieved March 7, 2008, from http://www.seattletimes.com/opinion/tapping-islams-feminist-roots/

Northhouse, P. G. (2012). *Leadership: Theory and practice* (6th ed.). Thousand Oaks, CA: Sage.

O'Connor, J., Mumford, M., Clifton, T., Gessner, T., & Connelly, M. (1995). Charismatic leaders and destructiveness: An historiometric study. *Leadership Quarterly, 6,* 529–555.

O'Connor, M. (2014, February 20). Addicted to likes: How social media feeds our neediness. NYmag.com. Retrieved from http://nymag.com/thecut/2014/02/addicted-to-likes-social-media-makes-us-needier.html

O'Hair, D., & Cody, M. (1994). Deception. In W. R. Cupach & B. H. Spitzberg (Eds.), *The dark side of interpersonal communication* (pp. 181–213). Hillsdale, NJ: Erlbaum.

O'Hair, D., Friedrich, G., & Dixon, L. (2016). *Strategic communication in business and the professions* (8th ed.). New York: Pearson.

O'Hair, D., & Krayer, K. (1987). *A conversational analysis of reconciliation strategies.* Paper presented at the Western Speech Communication Association, Salt Lake City.

O'Hair, D., O'Rourke, J., & O'Hair, M. J. (2000). *Business communication: A framework for success.* Cincinnati, OH: South-Western.

O'Hair, D., & Stewart, R. (1998). *Public speaking: Challenges and choices.* New York: Bedford/St. Martin's.

O'Hair, D., Stewart, R., & Rubenstein, H. (2018). *A Speaker's Guidebook: Text and Reference* (7th ed.). New York: Bedford/St. Martin's.

O'Keefe, D. J. (1999). How to handle opposing arguments in persuasive messages: A meta-analytic review of the effects of one-sided and two-sided messages. In M. E. Roloff (Ed.), *Communication yearbook 22* (pp. 209–249). Thousand Oaks, CA: Sage.

O'Keefe, D. J. (2002). *Persuasion: Theory and research* (2nd ed.). Thousand Oaks, CA: Sage.

Okhuysen, G., & Waller, M. J. (2002). Focusing on midpoint transitions: An analysis of boundary conditions. *Academy of Management Journal, 45,* 1056–1065.

Olison, W. O., & Roloff, M. E. (2012). Responses to organizational mandates: How voice attenuates psychological reactance and dissent. *Communication Research Reports, 29*(3), 204–216. doi:10.1080/08824096.2012.684984

Oliver, J. (2010, February). Jamie Oliver's TED Prize wish: Teach every child about food. TEDcom. Video retrieved from http://www.ted.com/talks/jamie_oliver.html

O'Loughlin, J. P. (2016, September 10). Senior HR executive, HR Capital Partners. Personal interview.

Ormerod, T. C., & Dando, C. J. (2015). Finding a needle in a haystack: Toward a psychologically informed method for aviation security screening. *Journal of Experimental Psychology: General, 144*(1), 76–84. doi:10.1037/xge0000030

O'Neill, B. (2011). A critique of politically correct language. *Independent Review, 16*(2), 279–291.

O'Neill, T.A., Hancock, S.E., Zivkov, K. Larson, N. L., & Law, S. J. (2016). Team decision making in virtual and face-to-face environments. *Group Decision and Negotiation, 25,* 995. doi:10.1007/s10726-015-9465-3

Opam, K. (2016, March 23). Facebook is building a way to let pages offer temporary profile pics. TheVerge.com. Retrieved from http://www.theverge.com/2016/3/23/11294226/facebook-profile-picture-overlay-pages

Ophir, E, Nass, C., & Wagner, A. D. (2009). Cognitive control in media multitaskers. *Proceedings of the National Academy of Sciences, 106*(37), 15583–15587. Retrieved from http://www.pnas.org/content/106/37/15583.short

Orbe, M. P., Johnson, A. L., Kauffman, L. D., & Cooke-Jackson, A. F. (2014). Memorable first-time sexual experiences: Gendered patterns and nuances. *Communication Quarterly, 62*(3), 285–307. doi:10.1080/01463373.2014.911764

O'Reilly, J., Robinson, S. L., Berdahl, J. L., & Banki, S. (2015). Is negative attention better than no attention? The comparative effects of ostracism and harassment at work. *Organization Science, 26*(3), 774–793. doi:10.1287/orsc.2014.0900

O'Sullivan, P. B. (2000). What you don't know won't hurt me: Impression management functions of communication channels in relationships. *Human Communication Research, 26,* 403–431.

Our mission. (2013, December 18). Facebook newsroom. Retrieved from http://newsroom.fb.com/Key-Facts

Palacios Martínez, I. M., & Núñez Pertejo, P. (2012). He's absolutely massive. It's a super day. Madonna, she is a wicked singer. Youth language and intensification: A corpus-based study. *Text & Talk, 32*(6), 773–796.

Palmer, C. L., & Peterson, R. D. (2016). Halo effects and the attractiveness premium in perceptions of political expertise. *American Politics Research, 44*(2), 353–382. doi:10.1177/1532673X15600517

Palomares, N. A. (2012). Gender and intergroup communication. In H. Giles (Ed.), *The handbook of intergroup communication* (pp. 197–210). New York: Routledge/Taylor and Francis Group.

Palomares, N. A. (2009). Women are sort of more tentative than men, aren't they? How men and women use tentative language differently, similarly, and counterstereotypically as a function of gender salience. *Communication Research, 36*(4), 538–560.

Palomares, N. A., & Lee, E. J. (2010). Virtual gender identity: The linguistic assimilation to gendered avatars in computer-mediated communication. *Journal of Language & Social Psychology, 29*(1), 5–23.

Paolini, S., Harwood, J., & Rubin, M. (2010). Negative intergroup contact makes group members salient: Explaining why intergroup conflict endures. *Personality and Social Psychology Bulletin, 36,* 1723–1738.

Parente, D. (2013). *Visual presence.* The Leadership Style Center. Retrieved on May 12, 2014, from http://theleadershipstylecenter.com/visual-presence

Park, C. (2003). In other (people's) words: Plagiarism by university students—literature and lessons. *Assessment and Evaluation in Higher Education, 28,* 471–488.

Park, G., Yaden, D. B., Schwartz, H. A., Kern, M. L., Eichstaedt, J. C., Kosinski, M., Stillwell, D., Unger, L., & Seligman, M. P. (2016). Women are warmer but no less assertive than men: Gender and language on Facebook. *PLoS ONE, 11*(5), 1–26. doi:10.1371/journal.pone.0155885

Park, W. (2000). A comprehensive empirical investigation of the relationships among variables of the groupthink model. *Journal of Organizational Behavior, 21,* 874–887.

Parker, K., Lenhart, A., & Moore, K. (2012). The digital revolution and higher education. Pew Research Center. Retrieved on April 29, 2014, from http://www.pewinternet.org/2011/08/28/the-digital-revolution-and-higher-education/4

Parker-Pope, T. (2010, April 18). Is marriage good for your health? *The New York Times,* p. MM46.

Partnoy, F. (2012, July 6). Beyond the blink. *The New York Times,* p. SR5.

Patchin, J., & Hinduja, S. (2011). Traditional and nontraditional bullying among youth: A test of general strain theory. *Youth & Society, 43*(2), 727–75.

Pathak, Y. (2015, July 15). The benefits of flipped classrooms. Noodle.com. Retrieved from https://www.noodle.com/articles/the-pros-and-cons-of-flipped-classrooms

Patten, D. (2016). "It's Always Sunny in Philadelphia" ratings hits FXX viewership high in live + 3 results with season 11 debut. Deadline Hollywood. Retrieved from http://deadline.com/2016/01/its-always-sunny-in-philadelphia-ratings-fxx-man-seeking-woman-live-3-1201680656/

Patry, M. W. (2008). Attractive but guilty: Deliberation and the physical attractiveness bias. *Psychological Reports, 102*(3), 727–733.

Patterson, B. R., & O'Hair, D. (1992). Relational reconciliation: Toward a more comprehensive model of relational development. *Communication Research Reports, 9,* 119–127.

Patterson, T. (2006, November). The Colbert Report: How to beat the host at his own game. *Slate.* Retrieved from http://www.slate.com/articles/arts/television/2006/11/the_colbert_retort.html

Paul, P. (2001). Getting inside Gen Y. *American Demographics, 23*(9), 42.

Paulson, M. (2016, May 12). A "Hamilton" star's story: How Leslie Odom Jr. became Aaron Burr, sir. *The New York Times.* Retrieved from http://www.nytimes.com/2016/05/15/theater/a-hamilton-stars-story-how-leslie-odom-jr-became-aaron-burr-sir.html?partner=rss&emc=rss

Paulson, M. (2015, July 12). "Hamilton" heads to Broadway in a hip-hop retelling. *The New York Times.* Retrieved from http://www.nytimes.com/2015/07/13/theater/hamilton-heads-to-broadway-in-a-hip-hop-retelling.html?_r=0

Pavitt, C. (1999). Theorizing about the group communication-leadership relationship. In L. R. Frey, D. S. Gouran, & M. Poole (Eds.), *Handbook of group communication theory and research* (pp. 313–334). Thousand Oaks, CA: Sage.

Pavley, J. (2013, May 26). Technological literacy: Can everyone learn to code? Huffingtonpost.com. Retrieved from http://www.huffingtonpost.com/john-pavley/learning-to-code_b_3337098.html

Pavlik, J. V., & McIntosh, S. (2016). *Converging media: A new introduction to mass communication* (5th ed.). New York: Oxford University Press.

Payne, S. L. (1951). *The art of asking questions.* Princeton, NJ: Princeton University Press.

Pearson, J. C., & Spitzberg, B. H. (1990). *Interpersonal communication: Concepts, components, and contexts* (2nd ed.). Dubuque, IA: Brown.

Pearson, J. C., Turner, L. H., & Todd-Mancillas, W. R. (1991). *Gender and communication* (2nd ed.). Dubuque, IA: Brown.

Peck, J. (2007, December 29). *Top 7 tips for conquering public speaking fear.* Retrieved January 9, 2008, from http://ezinearticles.com/?expert=Jason_Peck

Peluchette, J., Karl, K., & Fertig, J. (2013). A Facebook "friend" request from the boss: Too close for comfort? *Business Horizons, 56,* 291–300.

Peng, D., Han, X., Wei, Z., & Wang, B. (2015). Punctuated equilibrium dynamics in human communications. *Physica A, Statistical Mechanics and Its Applications, 436,* 36–44. doi:10.1016/j.physa.2015.05.007

Penn State. (2016, March 28). Expectation may be essential to memory formation. *Science Daily.* Retrieved on December 23, 2016, from www.sciencedaily.com/releases/2016/03/160328191855.htm

Pennic, F. (2015, May 22). Physician save patient's life through medical crowdsourcing. Hitconsultant.net. Retrieved from http://hitconsultant.net/2015/05/22/physician-save-patients-life-through-medical-crowdsourcing/

Pennington, N. (2013). You don't de-friend the dead: An analysis of grief communication by college students through Facebook profiles. *Death Studies, 37*(7), 617–635, 19. doi:10.1080/07481187.2012.673536

Perez, S. (2014, March 13). Amid bullying & threats of violence, anonymous social app Yik Yak shuts off access to U.S. middle & high school students. Techcrunch.com. Retrieved from http://techcrunch.com/2014/03/13/amid-vicious-bullying-threats-of-violence-anonymous-social-app-yik-yak-shuts-off-access-to-u-s-middle-high-school-students/

Perrin, A. (2015). Social media usage: 2005–2015: 65% of adults now use social networking sites—a nearly tenfold jump in the past decade. Pew Research Center. Retrieved from http://www.pewinternet.org/2015/10/08/social-networking-usage-2005-2015/

Perrin. A., & Duggan M. (2015, June 26). Americans' Internet access: 2000–2015. Pew Research Center Retrieved from http://www.pewinternet.org/2015/06/26/americans-internet-access-2000-2015/

Perry, M. J. (2013, May 13). Stunning college degree gap: Women have earned almost ten million more college degrees than men since 1982. American Enterprise Institute AEIdeas blog. Retrieved from http://www.aei-ideas.org/2013/05/stunning-college-degree-gap-women-have-earned-almost-10-million-more-college-degrees-than-men-since-1982

Petronio, S. (2004). Road to developing communication privacy management theory: Narrative in progress, please stand by. *Journal of Family Communication, 4*, 193–207.

Pettigrew, T. F., & Tropp, L. R. (2006). A meta-analytical test of the intergroup contact theory. *Journal of Personality and Social Psychology, 90*, 751–783.

Petty, R. E., Tormala, Z. L., Hawkins, C., & Wegener, D. T. (2001). Motivation to think and order effects in persuasion: The moderating role of chunking. *Personality and Social Psychology Bulletin, 27*(3), 332–344.

Pew Research Center. (2015, September 28). Modern immigration wave brings 59 million to U.S., driving population growth and change through 2065. Retrieved from http://www.pewhispanic.org/2015/09/28/modern-immigration-wave-brings-59-million-to-u-s-driving-population-growth-and-change-through-2065/

Pew Research Center. (2015, September 3). Most millennials resist the "millennial" label. Retrieved from http://www.people-press.org/2015/09/03/most-millennials-resist-the-millennial-label/

Pew Research Center (2015, May 13). From telephone to the Web: The challenge of mode of interview effects in public opinion polls. Retrieved from http://www.pewresearch.org/2015/05/13/from-telephone-to-the-web-the-challenge-of-mode-of-interview-effects-in-public-opinion-polls/

Phanor-Faury, A. (2010, June 24). "Nude" doesn't translate in fashion. *Essence.* Retrieved from http://www.essence.com/fashion_beauty/fashion/nude_dresses_racial_bias_fashion_world.php

Pickering, J. A., & Sanders, M. R. (2015). Integrating parents' views on sibling relationships to tailor an evidence-based parenting intervention for sibling conflict. *Family Process, 56*(1), 105–125.

Piepenburg, E. (2016, June 12). Why "Hamilton" has heat. *The New York Times.* Retrieved from http://www.nytimes.com/interactive/2015/08/06/theater/20150806-hamilton-broadway.html

Pierce, D. (2015, August 6). Screw texting. It's time to pick a universal messaging app. Wired.com. Retrieved from http://www.wired.com/2015/08/time-to-ditch-texting/

Pingree, R. J. (2007). How messages affect their senders: A more general model of message effects and implications for deliberation. *Communication Theory, 17,* 439–61.

Pines, M. (1997). The civilizing of Genie. In L. F. Kasper (Ed.), *Teaching English through the disciplines: Psychology* (2nd ed.). New York: Whittier.

Pizzutti, C., Basso, K., & Albornoz, M. (2016). The effect of the discounted attribute importance in two-sided messages. *European Journal of Marketing, 50*(9/10), 1703–1725. doi:10.1108/EJM-05-2015-0304

Planalp, S., & Honeycutt, J. (1985). Events that increase uncertainty in personal relationships. *Human Communication Research, 11,* 593–604.

Plus Media Solutions (PMS). (2015). Work-life-balance polices a win-win for businesses and employees, CAP report finds. Washington: Center for American Progress.

Podlipský, V. J., Šimá, S., & Petráž, D. (2016). Is there an interlanguage speech credibility benefit? *Topics in Linguistics, 17*(1), 30–44. doi:10.1515/topling-2016-0003

Pogensky, R. R. (2016, February 2). In defense of ghosting out of relationships. Huffingtonpost.com. Retrieved from http://www.huffingtonpost.com/ryley-rubin-pogensky/ghosting-_b_7855646.html

Pomeroy, R. (2013, April 26). Driving is much deadlier than terrorism—Why isn't it scarier? Retrieved from http://www.realclearscience.com/blog/2013/03/why-we-fear-terrorism-more-than-driving.html

Poole, M. S., & Hollingshead, A. B. (Eds.). (2005). *Theories of small groups: Interdisciplinary perspectives.* Thousand Oaks, CA: Sage.

Potter, W. J. (2008). *Media literacy* (4th ed.). Thousand Oaks, CA: Sage.

Potter, W. J., & Byrne, S. (2009). Media literacy. In R. L. Nabi & M. B. Oliver (Eds.), *The SAGE Handbook of Media Processes and Effects* (pp. 345–360). Thousand Oaks, CA: Sage.

Powers, W. G., & Bodie, G.D. (2003). Listening fidelity: Seeking congruence between cognitions of the receiver and the sender. *International Journal of Listening, 17,* 19–31.

Prager, K. J. (2000). Intimacy in personal relationships. In C. Hendrick & S. S. Hendrick (Eds.), *Close relationships: A sourcebook* (pp. 229–242). Thousand Oaks, CA: Sage.

Pratkanis, A. R., & Aronson, E. (2001). *Age of propaganda: The everyday use and abuse of persuasion.* New York: W. H. Freeman.

Preimesberger, C. (2016, February 23). Facebook gives users five more choices than "like" to emote. *Eweek,* 1.

Prensky, M. (2012). *From digital natives to digital wisdom: Hopeful essays for 21st century learning.* Thousand Oaks, CA: Corwin.

Preston, D. R. (1998). Language myth #17: They speak really bad English down South and in New York City. In L. Bauer & P. Trudgill (Eds.), *Language myths* (pp. 139–149). New York: Penguin Putnam.

Priem, J. S., McLaren, R. M., & Solomon, D. H. (2010). Relational messages, perceptions of hurt, and biological stress reactions to a disconfirming interaction. *Communication Research, 37*(1), 48–72.

Prochaska, J. (1994). Strong and weak principles for progressing from precontemplation to action on the basis of twelve problem behaviors. *Health Psychology, 13,* 47–51.

Prochaska, J. O., & Norcross, J. C. (2001). Stages of change. *Psychotherapy: Theory, Research, Practice, Training, 38,* 443–448.

Proakis, J., & Salehi, M. (2007). *Digital communications* (5th ed.). New York: McGraw-Hill.

Proulx, C. M., & Snyder-Rivas, L. A. (2013). The longitudinal associations between marital happiness, problems, and self-rated health. *Journal of Family Psychology, 27*(2), 194–202. doi:10.1037/a0031877

Pugliese F., Acerbi A., & Marocco, D. (2015). Emergence of leadership in a group of autonomous robots. *PLoS ONE, 10*(9), e0137234. doi:10.1371/journal.pone.0137234

Punyanunt-Carter, N. M. (2005). Father and daughter motives and satisfaction. *Communication Research Reports, 22,* 293–301.

Quenqua, D. (2015, April 12). Press send to meet 140 characters. *The New York Times*, p. ST2.

Quenqua, D. (2012, February 28). They're, like, way ahead of the linguistic currrrve. *The New York Times*, p. D1.

Qvist, B. (2013, May 16). When I mention my "partner," what do you assume? *The Guardian*. Retrieved from http://www.theguardian.com/commentisfree/2013/may/16/partner-girlfriend-sexuality/

Rabinowitz, J. (1995, July 25). Huckleberry Finn without fear: Teachers gather to learn how to teach an American classic, in context. *The New York Times*. Retrieved from http://www.nytimes.com/1995/07/25/nyregion/huckleberry-finn-without-fear-teachers-gather-learn-teach-american-classic.html

Ragas, M. W., Tran, H. L., & Martin, J. A. (2014). Media-induced or search-driven? A study of online agenda-setting effects during the BP oil disaster. *Journalism Studies, 15*(1), 48–63.

Rahim, M. A. (1983). A measure of styles of handling interpersonal conflict. *Academy of Management Journal, 26*(2), 368–376.

Rainie, L. (2012). The new normal in the digital age. Pew Research Center. Retrieved from http://www.pewinternet.org/2012/02/26/the-new-normal-in-the-digital-age/

Rainie, L. (2015a, September 22). Digital divides 2015. Pew Research Center. Retrieved from http://www.pewinternet.org/2015/09/22/digital-divides-2015/

Rainie, L. (2015b, November 20). The changing digital landscape: Where things are heading. Pew Research Center. Retrieved from http://www.pewinternet.org/2015/11/20/the-changing-digital-landscape-where-things-are-heading/

Rainie, L. (2016, March 29). How will the internet of things look by 2025? Pew Research Center. Retrieved from http://www.pewinternet.org/2016/03/29/how-will-the-internet-of-things-look-by-2025/

Rainie, L., Smith, A., & Duggan, M. (2013, February 5). Coming and going on Facebook. Pew Research Center. Retrieved from http://pewinternet.org/Reports/2013/Coming-and-going-on-facebook/Key-Findings.aspx

Rains, S. A. (2013). The nature of psychological reactance revisited: A meta-analytic review. *Human Communication Research, 39*(1), 47–73. doi:10.1111/j.1468-2958.2012.01443

Raising Children Network (2015, May 25). Teenage sibling fighting. Raisingchildren.net. Retrieved from http://raisingchildren.net.au/articles/sibling_fighting_teenagers.html

Ralston, S. M., Kirkwood, W. G., & Burant, P. A. (2003). Helping interviewees tell their stories. *Business Communication Quarterly, 66,* 8–22.

Raman, A. (2007, April 26). Egypt's "Dr. Ruth": Let's talk sex in the Arab world. CNN. Retrieved from http://www.cnn.com/2007/WORLD/meast/04/25/muslim.sextalk/index.html

Rampell, C. (2013, May 4). College graduates fare well in jobs market, even through recession. *The New York Times*, p. B1.

Rampell, C., & Miller, C. C. (2013, February 25). Yahoo orders home workers back to the office. *The New York Times*. Retrieved from http://www.nytimes.com/2013/02/26/technology/yahoo-orders-home-workers-back-to-the-office.html?ref=business&_r=0

Ranjan, P., Kumari, A., & Chakrawarty, A. (2015). How can doctors improve their communication skills? *Journal of Clinical & Diagnostic Research, 9*(3), 1–4. doi:10.7860/JCDR/2015/12072.5712

Rao, M. S. (2015). Spot your leadership style—build your leadership brand. *The Journal of Values-Based Leadership, 8*(1), article 11. Retrieved from http://scholar.valpo.edu/jvbl/vol8/iss1/11

Rappaport, S. D. (2010). Putting listening to work: The essentials of listening. *Journal of Advertising Research, 50*(1), 30–41.

Rawlins, W. K. (1994). Being there and growing apart: Sustaining friendships during adulthood. In D. J. Canary & L. Stafford (Eds.), *Communication and relational maintenance* (pp. 275–294). New York: Academic Press.

Rawlins, W. K. (2008). *The compass of friendship: Narratives, identities, and dialogues.* Thousand Oaks, CA: Sage.

Rawlins, W. K. (1992). *Friendship matters: Communication, dialectics, and the life course.* Piscataway, NJ: Aldine Transaction.

Ray, R., Sanes, M., & Schmitt, J. (2013, May). No-vacation nation revisited. Center for Economic and Policy Research. Retrieved from http://www.cepr.net/index.php/publications/reports/no-vacation-nation-2013

Ray, R., & Schmitt, J. (2007, May). No-vacation nation. Center for Economic and Policy Research. Retrieved from http://cepr.net/publications/reports/no-vacation-nation-2013

Re, D. E., Wang, S. A., He, J. C., & Rule, N. O. (2016). Selfie indulgence: Self-favoring biases in perceptions of selfies. *Social Psychological and Personality Science, 7*(6). doi:10.1177/1948550616644299

Regier, T., Carstensen, A., & Kemp, C. (2016). Languages support efficient communication about the environment: Words for snow revisited. *PLoS ONE, 11*(4), 1–17. doi:10.1371/journal.pone.0151138

Rehling, D. L. (2008). Compassionate listening: A framework for listening to the seriously ill. *International Journal of Listening, 22*(1), 83–89.

Reiber, C., & Garcia, J. R. (2010). Hooking up: Gender differences, evolution, and pluralistic ignorance. *Evolutionary Psychology, 8*(3), 390–404.

Reid, E., & Ramarajan, L. (2016, June). Managing the high-intensity workplace. *Harvard Business Review*, 84–90.

Reis, H. T. (1998). Gender differences in intimacy and related behaviors: Context and process. In D. J. Canary & K. Dindia (Eds.), *Sex differences and similarities in communication: Critical essays and empirical investigations of sex and gender in interaction* (pp. 203–231). Hillsdale, NJ: Erlbaum.

Rentzsch, K., Schröder-Abé, M., & Schütz, A. (2015). Envy mediates the relation between low academic self-esteem and hostile tendencies. *Journal of Research in Personality, 58,* 143–153. doi:10.1016/j.jrp.2015.08.001

Reshwan, R. (2015, March 5). 4 tips for managing millennials: How to create a plan that motivates and educates young employees. *U.S. News & World Report*. Retrieved from http://money.usnews.com/money/blogs/outside-voices-careers/2015/03/05/4-tips-for-managing-millennials

Rettner, R. (2016, February 8). Here's how many Americans actually sleep 7 hours. Livescience.com. Retrieved from http://www.livescience.com/53770-americans-sleep.html

Rheingold, H. (2002). Smart mobs: *The next social revolution.* Cambridge, MA: Perseus Publishing.

Rice, R. E. (1993). Media appropriateness: Using social presence theory to compare traditional and new organizational media. *Human Communication Research, 19*(4), 451–484.

Richards, A. S. (2014). Predicting attitude toward methamphetamine use: The role of antidrug campaign exposure and conversations about meth in Montana. *Health Communication, 29*(2), 124–136.

Richards, K., & Fox, J. (2010). *Life*. New York: Little, Brown, and Company.

Richardson, M. (2016). Can global social enterprise go truly global? *The Guardian*. Retrieved from https://www.theguardian.com/british-council-partner-zone/2016/apr/01/can-social-enterprise-go-truly-global?CMP=share_btn_tw

Richmond, V., & McCroskey, J. C. (1998). *Communication apprehension, avoidance, and effectiveness* (5th ed.). Boston: Allyn & Bacon.

Richmond, V. P., McCroskey, J. C., & Johnson, A. D. (2003). Development of the Nonverbal Immediacy Scale (NIS): Measures of self- and other-perceived nonverbal immediacy. *Communication Quarterly, 51*, 502–515.

Richmond, V. P., McCroskey, J. C., & Payne, S. K. (1991). *Nonverbal behavior in interpersonal relations*. Englewood Cliffs, NJ: Prentice Hall.

Richmond, V. P., Smith, R. S., Jr., Heisel, A. D., & McCroskey, J. C. (2001). Nonverbal immediacy in the physician-patient relationship. *Communication Research Reports, 18*, 211–216.

Rill, L., Balocchi, E., Hopper, M., Denker, K., & Olson, L. N. (2009). Exploration of the relationship between self-esteem, commitment, and verbal aggressiveness in romantic dating relationships. *Communication Reports, 22*(2), 102–113.

Riordan, M. A., & Kreuz, R. J. (2010). Cues in computer-mediated communication: A corpus analysis. *Computers in Human Behavior, 26*, 1806–1817.

Ritter, B. A. (2014). Deviant behavior in computer-mediated communication: Development and validation of a measure of cybersexual harassment. *Journal of Computer-Mediated Communication, 19*(2), 197–214.

Roa, M. (2016). Zika virus outbreak: Reproductive health and rights in Latin America. *Lancet, 387*(10021), 843. doi:10.1016/S0140-6736(16)00331-7

Roberto, A., Carlyle, K. E., Goodall, C. E., & Castle, J. D. (2009). The relationship between parents' verbal aggressiveness and responsiveness and young adult children's attachment style and relational satisfaction with parents. *Journal of Family Communication, 9*(2), 90–106.

Roberts, J. A., & David, M. E. (2016). My life has become a major distraction from my cell phone: Partner phubbing and relationship satisfaction among romantic partners. *Computers in Human Behavior, 54*, 134–141.

Rochman, B. (2011, December 2). Baby name game: How a name can affect your child's future. *Time*. Retrieved from http://healthland.time.com/2011/12/02/how-baby-names-affect-your-childs-future

Rogers Commission. (1986, June 6). *Report of the presidential commission on the space shuttle* Challenger *accident*. Retrieved from http://science.ksc.nasa.gov/shuttle/missions/51-l/docs/rogers-commission/Chapter-5.txt

Roloff, M. E. (1980). Self-awareness and the persuasion process: Do we really know what we are doing? In M. E. Roloff & G. Miller (Eds.), *Persuasion: New directions in theory and research* (pp. 29–66). Beverly Hills, CA: Sage.

Romans, B. (2011, October 14). The joy of going to the library, from the *Wired* science blog *Clastic Detritis*. Retrieved from http://www.wired.com/wiredscience/2011/10/the-joy-of-going-to-the-library (paragraph 2).

Rosener, J. (1990). Ways women lead. *Harvard Business Review, 68,* 119–125.

Rosenthal, M. J. (2001). High-performance teams. *Executive Excellence, 18,* 6.

Ross, C. (2007, March 11). Hare interviewed for "Colbert Report." *The Register-Mail*.

Ross, L., & Nisbett, R. E. (1991). *The person and the situation: Perspectives of social psychology*. Philadelphia: Temple University Press.

Roth, A. (2013, February 1). Russia revives the namesake of "Uncle Joe." *The New York Times*, p. A4.

Roth, Y., Brabham, D. C., & Lemoine, J. F. (2015). Recruiting individuals to a crowdsourcing community: Applying motivational categories to an ad copy test. In F. J. Garrigos-Simon, I. Gil-Pechúan, & S. Estelles-Miguel, (Eds.), *Advances in crowdsourcing* (pp. 15–31). Switzerland: Springer International Publishing.

Rothman, A. J., Salovey, P., Turvey, C., & Fishkin, S. A. (1993). Attributions or responsibility and persuasion: Increasing mammography utilization among women over 40 with an internally oriented message. *Health Psychology, 12*, 39–47.

Roup, C. M., & Chiasson, K. E. (2010). Effect of dichotic listening on self-reported state anxiety. *International Journal of Audiology, 49*(2), 88–94.

Rowbotham, S., Holler, J., Lloyd, D., & Wearden, A. (2012). How do we communicate about pain? A systematic analysis of the semantic contribution of co-speech gestures in pain-focused conversations. *Journal of Nonverbal Behavior, 36*(1), 1–21.

Ruben, B. D. (2005). Linking communication scholarship and professional practice in colleges and universities. *Journal of Applied Communication Research, 33*, 294–304.

Rubin, A. M., Perse, E. M., & Powell, R. A. (1985). Loneliness, parasocial interaction, and local television news viewing. *Human Communication Research, 12*, 155–180.

Rubin, D. L., Hafer, T., & Arata, K. (2000). Reading and listening to oral-based versus literate-based discourse. *Communication Education, 49*, 121–133.

Rubin, J. (2013, February 5). The Internet can offer additional intercultural experiences. *The Chronicle of Higher Education*. Retrieved from http://chronicle.com/blogs/letters/the-internet-can-offer-additional-intercultural-experiences

Rudoren, J. (2012, October 1). Proudly bearing elders' scars, their skin says "never forget." *The New York Times*, p. A1.

Ruscher, J. B. (2001). *Prejudiced communication: A social psychological perspective*. New York: Guilford Press.

Russ. T. L. (2013). The influence of communication apprehension on superiors' propensity for and practice of participative decision making. *Communication Quarterly, 61*, 335–348.

Russ, T. L. (2012). The relationship between communication apprehension and learning preferences in an organizational setting. *Journal of Business Communication, 49*(4), 312–331.

Rutherford, S. (2001). Any difference? An analysis of gender and divisional management styles in a large airline. *Gender, Work and Organization, 8*(3), 326–345.

Safir, M. P., Wallach, H. S., & Bar-Zvi, M. (2012). Virtual reality cognitive-behavior therapy for public speaking anxiety: One-year follow-up. *Behavioral Modification, 36*(2), 235–246. doi:10.1177/0145445511429999

Sahlstein, E., & Dun, T. (2008). "I wanted time to myself and he wanted to be together all the time": Constructing breakups as managing autonomy-connection. *Qualitative Research Reports in Communication, 9*(1), 37–45. doi:10.1080/17459430802400340

Sahlstein, E., Maguire, K. C., & Timmerman, L. (2009). Contradictions and praxis contextualized by wartime deployment: Wives' perspectives revealed through relational dialectics. *Communication Monographs, 76*(4), 421–442.

Salkever, A. (2003, April 24). Home truths about meetings. *Business Week*. Retrieved from https://www.bloomberg.com/news/articles/2003-04-23/home-truths-about-meetings

Samovar, L. A., Porter, R. E., McDaniel, E. R., & Roy, C. S. (2017). *Communication between cultures* (9th ed.). Boston: Cengage Learning.

Samter, W. (2003). Friendship interaction skills across the life span. In J. O. Greene & B. R. Burleson (Eds.), *Handbook of communication and social interaction skills* (pp. 637–684). Mahwah, NJ: Erlbaum.

Sanderson, J. (2013). From loving the hero to despising the villain: Sports fans, Facebook, and social identity threats. *Mass Communication and Society, 16*(4), 487–509.

SANS Institute. (2016). Securing the human: Advanced cybersecurity learning platform. Retrieved from https://securingthehuman.sans.org/security-awareness-training/enduser/

Sapir, E., & Whorf, B. L. (1956). The relation of habitual thought and behavior to language. In J. B. Carroll (Ed.), *Language, thought, and reality: Selected writings of Benjamin Lee Whorf* (pp. 134–159). Cambridge, MA: MIT Press.

Sapru, A., & Bourlard, H. (2015). Automatic recognition of emergent social roles in small group interactions. *IEEE transactions on multimedia.* doi:10.1109/TMM.2015.2408437

Sarich, V., & Miele, F. (2004). *Race: The reality of human differences.* Boulder, CO: Westview Press.

Sashkin, M., & Burke, W. W. (1990). Understanding and assessing organizational leadership. In K. E. Clark & M. B. Clark (Eds.), *Measures of leadership* (pp. 297–326). West Orange, NJ: Leadership Library of America.

Sauter, D. A., Eisner, F., Ekman, P., & Scott, S. K. (2015). Emotional vocalizations are recognized across cultures regardless of the valence of distractors. *Psychological Science, 26*(3), 354–356. doi:10.1177/0956797614560771

Sawyer, C., & Behnke, R. (2002). Behavioral inhibition and communication of public speaking state anxiety. *Western Journal of Communication, 66,* 412–422.

Sawyer, C., & Behnke, R. (1990). The role of self-monitoring in the communication of public speaking anxiety. *Communication Reports, 3,* 70–74.

Sawyer, C. R., Gayle, K., Topa, A., & Powers, W. G. (2014). Listening fidelity among native and nonnative English-speaking undergraduates as a function of listening apprehension and gender. *Communication Research Reports, 31*(1), 62–71. doi:10.1080/08824096.2013.844119

Scheerhorn, D., & Geist, P. (1997). Social dynamics in groups. In L. R. Frey & J. K. Barge (Eds.), *Managing group life: Communicating in decision-making groups* (pp. 81–103). Boston: Houghton Mifflin.

Schenck v. *United States*, 249 U.S. 47 (1919).

Scheufele, D., & Iyengar, S. (2012). The state of framing research: A call for new directions. *The Oxford Handbook of Political Communication Theories.* New York: Oxford University Press.

Scheufele, D. A., & Tewksbury, D. (2007). Framing, agenda setting, and priming: The evolution of three media effects models. *Journal of Communication, 57*(1), 9–20.

Schiesel, S. (2011, October 25). Best friends, in fantasy and reality. *New York Times,* p. C1.

Schmidt, M. S. (2015, January 15). State of the Union speechwriter for Obama draws on various inspirations. *The New York Times.* Retrieved from http://www.nytimes.com/2015/01/20/us/politics /cody-keenan-obamas-hemingway-draws-on-friends-empathy -and-a-little-whisky-for-state-of-the-union.html?_r=0

Schmidt, R. R., Morr, S., Fitzpatrick, P., & Richardson, M. (2012). Measuring the dynamics of interactional synchrony. *Journal of Nonverbal Behavior, 36*(4), 263–279.

Schofield, T., Parke, R., Castañeda, E., & Coltrane, S. (2008). Patterns of gaze between parents and children in European American and Mexican American families. *Journal of Nonverbal Behavior, 32*(3), 171–186.

Schradie, J. (2013, April 26). 7 myths of the digital divide. The Society Pages: Cyborgology. Retrieved from http://thesocietypages.org /cyborgology/2013/04/26/7-myths-of-the-digital-divide

Schrodt, P. (2009). Family strength and satisfaction as functions of family communication. *Communication Quarterly, 57*(2), 171–186.

Schrodt, P., & Wheeless, L. R. (2001). Aggressive communication and informational reception apprehension: The influence of listening anxiety and intellectual inflexibility on trait argumentativeness and verbal aggressiveness. *Communication Quarterly, 49,* 53–69.

Schroeder, L. (2002). The effects of skills training on communication satisfaction and communication anxiety in the basic speech course. *Communication Research Reports, 19,* 380–388.

Schroeder, M., & Berlinger, J. (2016, April 27). German city puts traffic lights on the ground—for you phone gazers. CNN. Retrieved from http://www.cnn.com/2016/04/27 /europe/germany-smart-phone-traffic-lights/

Schulman, P. R. (1996). Heroes, organizations, and high reliability. *Journal of Contingencies and Crisis Management, 4,* 72–82.

Schultz, B. (1982). Argumentativeness: Its effect in group decision-making and its role in leadership perception. *Communication Quarterly, 30,* 368–375.

Schultz, B. (1980). Communicative correlates of perceived leaders. *Small Group Behavior, 11,* 175–191.

Schuppe, J., & Alexander, P. (2016, January 12). State of the Union: Meet Cody Keenan, President Obama's speechwriter. *NBC News.* Retrieved from http://www.nbcnews.com/news /us-news/state-union-meet-cody-keenan-president-obama-s -speechwriter-n494816

Schwarz, R. (2016). 8 ground rules for great meetings. *Harvard Business Review.* Retrieved from https://hbr.org/2016/06/8 -ground-rules-for-great-meetings

Scott, W. R. (1981). *Organizations: Rational, natural, and open systems.* Englewood Cliffs, NJ: Prentice Hall.

Secret of the wild child [Transcript]. (1997, March 4). *Nova.* Public Broadcasting System. Retrieved March 25, 2008, from http://www.pbs.org/wgbh/nova/transcripts/2112gchild.html

Segrin, C., Hanzal, A., & Domschke, T. J. (2009). Accuracy and bias in newlywed couples' perceptions of conflict styles and the association with marital satisfaction. *Communication Monographs, 76,* 207–233.

Segrin, C., & Passalacqua, S. A. (2010). Functions of loneliness, social support, health behaviors, and stress in association with poor health. *Health Communication, 25*(4), 312–322.

Seidler, D. (2011, February 27). Acceptance speech presented at the 83rd Annual Academy of Motion Picture Arts and Sciences Awards, Hollywood, CA.

Selyukh, A. (2016, November 20). Postelection, overwhelmed Facebook users unfriend, cut back. NPR: All Tech Considered. Retrieved from http://www.npr.org/sections /alltechconsidered/2016/11/20/502567858/post-election -overwhelmed-facebook-users-unfriend-cut-back

Serban, A., & Roberts, A. J. (2016). Exploring antecedents and outcomes of shared leadership in a creative context: A mixed methods approach. *Leadership Quarterly, 27*(2), 181–199. doi:10.1016/j.leaqua.2016.01.009

Shafer, J. (2016, October 18). WikiLeaks and the oily Washington Press: A bunch of reporters got caught up in the Podesta flypaper. How bad is it, really? *Politico Magazine.* Retrieved from http://www.politico.com/magazine/story/2016/10/john-podesta-emails-wikileaks-press-214367

Shahani, A. (2015, July 13). On college campuses, suicide intervention via anonymous app. NPR: All tech considered. Retrieved from http://www.npr.org/sections/alltechconsidered/2015/07/13/422620195/on-college-campuses-suicide-intervention-via-anonymous-app

Shannon, C. E., & Weaver, W. (1949). *The mathematical theory of communication.* Urbana: University of Illinois Press.

Shannon, M., & Stark, C. (2003). The influence of physical appearance on personnel selection. *Social Behavior & Personality: An International Journal, 31*(6), 613.

Shattuck, S. (2016, May 2). 4 Powerful presentation lessons from apple. Prezi Blog. Retrieved from https://blog.prezi.com/4-powerful-presentation-lessons-from-apple/

Sheffield, R. (2016, April 25). Beyonce: Lemonade. *Rolling Stone.* Retrieved from http://www.rollingstone.com/music/albumreviews/beyonce-lemonade-20160425

Shehata, A., & Strömbäck, J. (2013). Not (yet) a new era of minimal effects: A study of setting at the aggregate and individual levels. *The International Journal of Press/Politics, 18*(2), 234–255.

Shen, C., Ratan, R., Cai, Y. D., & Leavitt, A. (2016). Do men advance faster than women? Debunking the gender performance gap in two massively multiplayer online games. *Journal of Computer-Mediated Communication, 21*(4), 312–329.

Shepherd, C. A., Giles, H., & LePoire, B. A. (2001). Communication accommodation theory. In W. P. Robinson & H. Giles (Eds.), *The new handbook of language and social psychology* (pp. 33–56). Chichester, UK: Wiley.

Sherif, C. W., Sherif, M. S., & Nebergall, R. E. (1965). *Attitude and attitude change.* Philadelphia: W. B. Saunders.

Sherif, M., & Sherif, C. W. (1967). Attitude as the individual's own categories: The social judgment-involvement approach to attitude and attitude change. In C. W. Sherif & M. Sherif (Eds.), *Attitude, ego-involvement, and change* (pp. 105–139). New York: Wiley.

Shin, D. (2016). Do users experience real sociability through social TV? Analyzing parasocial behavior in relation to social TV. *Journal of Broadcasting & Electronic Media, 60*(1), 140–159. doi:10.1080/08838151.2015.1127247

Sillars, A. L., & Canary, D. J. (2013). Conflict and relational quality in families. In A. L. Vangelisti (Ed.), *The Routledge handbook of family communication* (2nd ed., pp. 338–357). New York, NY: Routledge.

Shotter, J. (2009). Listening in a way that recognizes/realizes the world of "the other." *International Journal of Listening, 23*(1), 21–43.

Shultz, B. G. (1999). Improving group communication performance: An overview of diagnosis and intervention. In L. Frey, D. Gouran, & M. Poole (Eds.), *Handbook of group communication theory and research* (pp. 371–394). Thousand Oaks, CA: Sage.

Sides, C. H. (2000). Ethics and technical communication: The past quarter century. *Journal of Technical Writing and Communication, 30,* 27–30.

Sillars, A., Canary, D. J., & Tafoya, M. (2004). Communication, conflict, and the quality of family relationships. In A. L.

Vangelisti (Ed.), *Handbook of family communication* (pp. 413–446). Mahwah, NJ: Erlbaum.

Simonson, P., Peck, J., Craig, R. T., & Jackson, J. P. (Eds.). (2013). *The handbook of communication history.* New York: Routledge.

Sirolli, E. (2012, September). Want to help someone? Shut up and listen! *TED.com. Retrieved from*: http://www.ted.com/talks/ernesto_sirolli_want_to_help_someone_shut_up_and_listen

Sisavat, M. (2016, June 12). The 72 hottest bikini moments of 2016—so far! Popsugar.com. Retrieved from http://www.popsugar.com/celebrity/Best-Celebrity-Bikini-Pictures-2016-40566400#photo-40566400

Sisavat, M. (2016, January 1). The 49 hottest female celebrity selfies of 2015. Popsugar.com. Retrieved from http://www.popsugar.com/celebrity/Sexiest-Female-Celebrity-Selfies-Pictures-38522653#photo-39587470

Sixel, L. M. (2011, July 7). Manager claims boss asked her to dye gray hair. *The Houston Chronicle.* Retrieved from http://www.chron.com/business/sixel/article/Manager-claims-boss-asked-her-to-dye-gray-hair-2080057.php#ixzz1Rp5iRmra

Skovholt, K., Grønning, A., & Kankaanranta, A. (2014). The communicative functions of emoticons in workplace e-mails: :-). *Journal of Computer-Mediated Communication, 19*(4), 780–797. doi:10.1111/jcc4.12063

Slagle, M. (2009). An ethical exploration of free expression and the problem of hate speech. *Journal of Mass Media Ethics, 24*(4), 238–250. doi:10.1080/08900520903320894

Smit, C. (2015). *Uncertainty avoidance in international business: The complete guide.* Culturematters.com. Retrieved from https://culturematters.com/uncertainty-avoidance-in-international-business/

Smith, A. (2015). U.S. smartphone use in 2015. Pew Research Center. Retrieved from http://www.pewinternet.org/2015/04/01/us-smartphone-use-in-2015/

Smith, E. (2013). The truth won't always out: Tiger would still be burning bright if he hadn't crashed his car. *New Statesman, 142*(5142), 62.

Smith, M. (2015). Staying connected: Supportive communication during the college transition. In J. M. Vaterlaus, S. Tulane, & C. J. Bruess (Eds.), *Family communication in the digital age* (pp. 184–204). New York: Peter Lang.

Smith, P. (2005, February 11). Bullies incorporated. *Sydney Morning Herald.* Retrieved from http://www.smh.com.au

Smith, R. E. (1993). Clustering: A way to discover speech topics. *The Speech Teacher, 7*(2), 6–7.

Smith, S. W., Atkin, C. K., Martell, D., Allen, R., & Hembroff, L. (2006). A social judgment theory approach to conducting formative research in a social norms campaign. *Communication Theory, 16,* 141–152.

Smith, T. E., & Frymier, A. B. (2006). Get "real": Does practicing speeches before an audience improve performance? *Communication Quarterly, 54,* 111–125.

Smith-Lovin, L., Skvortz, J. K., & Hudson, C. (1986). Status and participation in six-person groups: A test of Skvoret's comparative status model. *Social Forces, 64,* 992–1005.

Snyder, M. (1974). Self-monitoring of expressive behavior. *Journal of Personality and Social Psychology, 30,* 526–537.

Snyder, M. (1979). Self-monitoring processes. In L. Berkowitz (Ed.), *Advances in social psychology* (Vol. 12, pp. 86–128). New York: Academic Press.

Snyder, M., & Klein, O. (2005). Construing and constructing others: On the reality and the generality of the behavioral confirmation scenario. *Interaction Studies, 6,* 53–67.

Sokol, R. I., Webster, K. L., Thompson, N. S., & Stevens, D. A. (2005). Whining as mother-directed speech. *Infant and Child Development, 14,* 478–486.

Soliz, J., & Giles, H. (2010). Language and communication. In C. R. Berger, M. E. Roloff, & D. R. Roskos-Ewoldsen (Eds.), *The handbook of communication science* (pp. 75–91). Thousand Oaks, CA: Sage.

Soliz, J., & Giles, H. (2014). Relational and identity processes in communication: A contextual and meta-analytical review of communication accommodation theory. In E. L. Cohen (Ed.), *Communication yearbook* (Vol. 38, pp. 107–143). New York: Routledge.

Solomon, D. H., & Vangelisti, A. L. (2010). Establishing and maintaining relationships. In C. R. Berger, M. E. Roloff, & D. R. Roskos-Ewoldsen, *The handbook of communication science* (pp. 327–344). Thousand Oaks, CA: Sage.

Sonnenfeld, J. (2011, January 23). The genius dilemma. *Newsweek.* Retrieved from http://www.newsweek.com/2011/01/23/the-genius-dilemma.html

Sonnentag, S., Unger, D., & Nägel, I. J. (2013). Workplace conflict and employee well-being: The moderating role of detachment from work during off-job time. *International Journal of Conflict Management, 24*(2), 166–183.

Sorenson, G. A., & McCroskey, J. C. (1977). The prediction of interaction in small groups. *Communication Monographs, 44,* 73–80.

Sosha, T. J. (1997). Group communication across the lifespan. In L. R. Frey & J. K. Barge (Eds.), *Managing group life: Communicating in decision-making groups* (pp. 3–28). Boston: Houghton Mifflin.

Span, P. (2013). Helping seniors learn new technology. Pew Research Center. Retrieved on May 2, 2014 from http://www.pewinternet.org/Media-Mentions/2013/Helping-Seniors-Learn-New-Technology.aspx

Speed dating at NYCC. New York Comic Con. Retrieved from http://www.newyorkcomiccon.com/Events/Events-R-Z/Speed-Dating-At-NYCC/

Spence, P. R., Westerman, D., Edwards, C., & Edwards, A. (2014). Welcoming our robot overlords: Initial expectations about interaction with a robot. *Communication Research Reports, 31*(3), 272–280.

Spillman, B. (2013, September 8). New headquarters for Zappos reflects company's growth, atmosphere. *Las Vegas Review-Journal.* Retrieved from http://www.reviewjournal.com/news/las-vegas/new-headquarters-zappos-reflects-companys-growth-atmosphere.

Spitzberg, B. H., & Cupach, W. R. (2008). Fanning the flames of fandom: Celebrity worship, parasocial interaction, and stalking (pp. 287–324). In J. R. Meloy, L. Sheridan, & J. Hoffman (Eds.), *Stalking, threatening, and attacking of public figures: A psychological and behavioral analysis.* New York: Oxford.

Spott, J., Pyle, C., & Punyanunt-Carter, N. M. (2010). Positive and negative nonverbal behaviors in relationships: A study of relationship satisfaction and longevity. *Human Communication, 13*(1), 29–41.

Sprague, J., Stuart, D., and Bodary, D. (2012). *The speaker's handbook.* Boston: Cengage Learning.

Sprain, L., & Boromisza-Habashi, D. (2013). The ethnographer of communication at the table: Building cultural competence, designing strategic action. *Journal of Applied Communication Research, 41*(2), 181–187.

Stafford, L. (2010). Geographic distance and communication during courtship. *Communication Research, 37*(2), 275–297.

Stamper, K. (2014, October 4). Slang for the ages. *The New York Times,* p. A19.

Stanley, A. (2012, April 13). There's sex, there's the city, but no Manolos. *The New York Times,* p. C1.

Stanley, A. (2014, 19 February). Tonight takes on tomorrow. *The New York Times,* p. C1.

Stars of YouTube share secrets of success. (2015, May). Think with Google. Retrieved from https://www.thinkwithgoogle.com/intl/en-gb/articles/stars-of-youtube-share-secrets-of-success.html

Steinberg, B. (2010). Swearing during family hour? Who gives a $#*! *Advertising Age, 81*(22), 2–20.

Stellar, J. E., Cohen, A., Oveis, C., & Keltner, D. (2015). Affective and physiological responses to the suffering of others: Compassion and vagal activity. *Journal of Personality and Social Psychology, 108*(4), 572–585. doi:10.1037/pspi0000010

Stephens, K. K., & Davis, J. (2009). The social influences on electronic multitasking in organizational meetings. *Management Communication Quarterly, 23*(1), 63–83.

Stern, J. (2012, April 9). Facebook buys Instagram for $1 billion. *ABC News.* Retrieved from http://abcnews.go.com/blogs/technology/2012/04/facebook-buys-instagram-for-1-billion/

Stevens, G. (2016, March 1). Following in Zappos footsteps: Is it time to shift to the holacratic workplace? Business.com. Retrieved from http://www.business.com/management/is-it-time-to-shift-to-the-holacratic-workplace/

Stewart, C. J., & Cash, W. B., Jr. (2014). *Interviewing: Principles and practices.* New York: McGraw-Hill.

Stewart, L. P., Cooper, P. J., & Steward, A. D. (2003). *Communication and gender.* Boston: Pearson Education.

Stiff, J. B., & Mongeau, P. (2003). *Persuasive communication.* New York: Guilford Press.

Stillion Southard, B. F., & Wolvin, A. D. (2009). Jimmy Carter: A case study in listening leadership. *International Journal of Listening, 23*(2), 141–152.

Stollen, J., & White, C. (2004). The link between labels and experience in romantic relationships among young adults. Paper presented at the International Communication Association, New Orleans Sheraton, New Orleans, LA, LA Online.

Stommel, W., & Koole, T. (2010). The online support group as a community: A micro-analysis of the interaction with a new member. *Discourse Studies, 12*(3), 357–378.

Stone, R. (2015, June 9). Beyond torture: The new science of interrogating terrorists. *Newsweek.* Retrieved from http://www.newsweek.com/2015/06/19/beyond-torture-new-science-interrogating-terrorists-340944.html

Strasburger, V. C., & Wilson, B. J. (2014). Television violence: Sixty years of research. In Gentile, D. A. (Ed.), *Media violence and children: A complete guide for parents and professionals.* Santa Barbara: ABC-CLIO.

Stroud, N. J. (2011). *Niche news: The politics of news choice.* New York, NY: Oxford University Press.

Stubbe, M. (2012). Sociolinguistics and intergroup communication. In H. Giles (Ed.), *The handbook of intergroup communication* (pp. 70–84). New York: Routledge/Taylor and Francis Group.

Suler, J. (2007). The psychology of cyberspace. Retrieved December 26, 2007, from http://www.usr.rider.edu/~suler/psycyber/psycyber.html (Original work published 1996)

Sullivan, L. (2006, July 26). In U.S. prisons, thousands spend years in isolation [Audio podcast]. In *All Things Considered.* Retrieved from http://www.npr.org/templates/story/story.php?storyId=5582144

Sullivan, P. J., Rickers, K., & Gammage, K. L. (2014). The effect of different phases of synchrony on pain threshold. *Group Dynamics, 18*(2), 122–128. doi:10.1037/gdn0000001

Sun, Y., Pan, Z., & Shen, L. (2008). Understanding the third-person perception: Evidence from a meta-analysis. *Journal of Communication, 58*, 280–300.

Sunstein, C. (2007). *Republic.com 2.0.* Princeton, NJ: Princeton University Press.

Sutzl, W. (2015). Street protests, electronic disturbance, smart mobs: Dislocations of resistance. *Brill Online.* Retrieved on August 12, 2016, from http://booksandjournals.brillonline.com/content /books/b9789004298774s013

Suzuki, B. H. (2002). Revisiting the model minority stereotype: Implications for student affairs practice and higher education. *New Directions for Student Services, 97,* 21.

Swenson-Lepper, T., Leavitt, M. A., Hoffer, M., Charron, L. N., Ballard, R. L., Bell McManus, L. M., & Tompkins, P. S. (2015). Communication ethics in the communication curriculum: United States, Canada, and Puerto Rico. *Communication Education, 64*(4), 472–490. doi:10.1080/03634523.2015.1041996

Tagliamonte, S. A. (2016). So sick or so cool? The language of youth on the internet. *Language in Society, 45*(1), 1–32. doi:10.1017 /S0047404515000780

Tajfel, H., & Turner, J. C. (1986). An integrative theory of intergroup conflict. In S. Worchel & W. Austin (Eds.), *Psychology of intergroup relations* (pp. 2–24). Chicago: Nelson-Hall.

Talwar, V., Renaud, S., & Conway, L. (2015). Detecting children's lies: Are parents accurate judges of their own children's lies? *Journal of Moral Education, 44*(1), 81–96.

Tamir, D. I., & Mitchell, J. P. (2012). Anchoring and adjustment during social inferences. *Journal of Experimental Psychology, 142*(1), 151–162.

Tandoc, E. C., Ferrucci, P., & Duffy, M. (2015). Facebook use, envy, and depression among college students: Is Facebooking depressing? *Computers in Human Behavior, 43*, 139–146.

Tannen, D. (2010). Abduction and identity in family interaction: Ventriloquizing as indirectness. *Journal of Pragmatics, 42*(2), 307–316.

Tannen, D. (2009). Framing and face: The relevance of the presentation of self to linguistic discourse analysis. *Social Psychology Quarterly, 72*(4), 300–305.

Tannen, D. (1992). *You just don't understand: Women and men in conversation.* London: Virago Press.

Tannen, D., Kendall, S., & Gorgon, C. (Eds.). (2007). *Family talk: Discourse and identity in four American families.* New York: Oxford University Press.

Taylor, P., & Keeter, S. (Eds.). (2010). Millennials: A portrait of generation next. Confident, connected, open to change. Pew Research Center. Retrieved from http://pewresearch.org/millennials

Team Rubicon. (2014, January 15). Our mission. Retrieved from http://teamrubiconusa.org/about

TED Prize. (2016). About programs & initiatives. TED.com. Retrieved from http://www.ted.com/about/programs-initiatives/ted-prize

TED Prize. (2013). About the TED prize. TED.com. Retrieved from http://www.ted.com/participate/ted-prize

Tekleab, A. G., Quigley, N. R., & Tesluk, P. E. (2009). A longitudinal study of team conflict, conflict management, cohesion, and team effectiveness. *Group and Organizational Management, 34*, 170–205.

Tell, C. (September 22, 2013). Step away from the phone! *New York Times,* p. ST1.

Teven, J. J. (2007a). Effects of supervisor social influence, nonverbal immediacy, and biological sex on subordinates' perceptions of job satisfaction, liking, and supervisor credibility. *Communication Quarterly, 55*(2), 155–177.

Teven, J. J. (2007b). Teacher caring and classroom behavior: Relationships with student affect, teacher evaluation, teacher competence, and trustworthiness. *Communication Quarterly, 55*, 433–450.

Teven, J. J. (2010). The effects of supervisor nonverbal immediacy and power use on employees' ratings of credibility and affect for the supervisor. *Human Communication, 13*, 69–85.

Teven, J. J. (2008). An examination of perceived credibility of the 2008 presidential candidates: Relationships with believability, likeability, and deceptiveness. *Human Communication, 11*, 383–400.

Teven, J. J., & Comadena, M. E. (1996). The effects of office aesthetic quality on students' perceptions of teacher credibility and communicator style. *Communication Research Reports, 13*(1), 101–108.

Teven, J. J., & Hanson, T. L. (2004). The impact of teacher immediacy and perceived caring on teacher competence and trustworthiness. *Communication Quarterly, 52,* 39–53.

Teven, J. J., & McCroskey, J. C. (1997). The relationship of perceived teacher caring with student learning and teacher evaluation. *Communication Education, 46,* 1–9.

Teven, J. J., McCroskey, J. C., & Richmond, V. P. (2006). Communication correlates of perceived Machiavellianism of supervisors: Communication orientations and outcomes. *Communication Quarterly, 54,* 127–142.

Teven, J. J., & Winters, J. L. (2007). Pharmaceutical sales representatives' social influence behaviors and communication orientations: Relationships with adaptive selling, sales performance, and job satisfaction. *Human Communication, 10,* 465–485.

Thacker, S., & Griffiths, M. D. (2012). An exploratory study of trolling in online video gaming. *International Journal of Cyber Behavior, Psychology and Learning (IJCBPL), 2*(4), 17–33.

TheoryOfReddit. (2016, June 11). Did the rise of various subreddits attract a lot of hateful people and the so-called "reactionary right" to Reddit? Retrieved from https://www .reddit.com/r/TheoryOfReddit/comments/4akbo8 /did_the_rise_of_various_subreddits_attract_a_lot/

Theiss, J. A., Knobloch, L. K., Checton, M. G., & Magsamen-Conrad, K. (2009). Relationship characteristics associated with the experience of hurt in romantic relationships: A test of the relational turbulence model. *Human Communication Research, 35*(4), 588–615.

Thibaut, J. W., & Kelley, H. H. (1959). *The social psychology of groups.* New York: Wiley.

Thompson, A. (2008, April 17). Scientist finds truthiness in "Colbert bump." Livescience.com. Retrieved from http://www.livescience .com/2451-scientist-finds-truthiness-colbert-bump.html

Thomas, D. C., Ravlin, E. C., & Wallace, A. W. (1996). Effect of cultural diversity in work groups. In P. Bamber, M. Erez, & S. Bacharach (Eds.), *Research in the sociology of organizations* (Vol. 14, pp. 1–33). Greenwich, CT: JAI.

Thomas, L. T., & Levine, T. R. (1994). Disentangling listening and verbal recall: Related but separate constructs? *Human Communication Research, 21,* 103–127.

Thompson, D., & Filik, R. (2016). Sarcasm in written communication: Emoticons are efficient markers of intention. *Journal of Computer-Mediated Communication, 21*(2), 105–120. doi:10.1111 /jcc4.12156

Thompson, W. (2016). The secret life of Tiger Woods. *ESPN the Magazine.* Retrieved from http://espn.go.com/espn/feature

/story/_/id/15278522/how-tiger-woods-life-unraveled-years-father-earl-woods-death

Tidwell, L. C., & Walther, J. B. (2002). Computer-mediated communication effects on disclosure, impressions, and interpersonal evaluations: Getting to know one another a bit at a time. *Human Communication Research, 28*(3), 317–348.

Tidwell, N. D., Eastwick, P. W., & Finkel, E. J. (2013). Perceived, not actual, similarity predicts initial attraction in a live romantic context: Evidence from the speed-dating paradigm. *Personal Relationships, 20*(2), 199–215.

Tierney, J. (2007, July 31). The whys of mating: 237 reasons and counting. *The New York Times,* p. F1.

Tiggemann, M. (2005). Television and adolescent body image: The role of program content and viewing motivation. *Journal of Social & Clinical Psychology, 24,* 361–381.

Tikkanen, S. A., & Frisbie, A. (2015). When bad timing is actually good: Reconceptualizing response delays. In D. S. Coombs & S. Collister (Eds.), *Debates for the digital age: The good, the bad, and the ugly of our online world* (p. 305). Santa Barbara: ABC-CLIO.

Tikkanen, S., Afifi, W., & Merrill, A. (2015). Gr8 textpectations: Parents' experiences of anxiety in response to adolescent mobile phone delays. In C. J. Bruess (Ed.), *Family communication in the age of digital and social media.* New York: Peter Lang.

Tillson, L. D. (2015). Spotlight on innovative communication courses in the commonwealth: Managing public speaking anxiety. *Kentucky Journal of Communication, 34*(2), 43–50.

Ting-Toomey, S., & Dorjee, T. (2015). Intercultural and intergroup communication competence: Toward an integrative perspective. In A. F. Hannawa & B. H. Spitzberg (Eds.), *Communication competence.* Berlin, Boston: De Gruyter Mouton.

Ting-Toomey, S., & Oetzel, J. G. (2002). Cross-cultural face concerns and conflict styles. *Handbook of International and Intercultural Communication, 2,* 143–164.

Tkaczyk, C. (2013, April 19). Marissa Mayer breaks her silence on Yahoo's telecommuting policy. *Fortune.* Retrieved from http://fortune.com/2013/04/19/marissa-mayer-breaks-her-silence-on-yahoos-telecommuting-policy/

Tolman, E. G. (2012). Observing cell phone use and enhancing collaborative learning using a wiki. *Communication Teacher, 4,* 1–5.

Toma, C. L. (2013, April). Feeling better but doing worse: Effects of Facebook self-presentation on implicit self-esteem and cognitive task performance. *Media Psychology, 16*(2), 199–220.

Tong, S. T., Van Der Heide, B., Langwell, L., & Walther, J. B. (2008). Too much of a good thing? The relationship between number of friends and interpersonal impressions on Facebook. *Journal of Computer-Mediated Communication, 13*(3), 531–549.

Tong, S. T., & Walther, J. B. (2015). The confirmation and disconfirmation of expectancies in computer-mediated communication. *Communication Research, 42*(2), 186–212. doi:10.1177/0093650212466257

Toussaint, L., & Cheadle, A. C. D. (2009). Unforgiveness and the broken heart: Unforgiving tendencies, problems due to unforgiveness, and 12-month prevalence of cardiovascular health conditions. In M. T. Evans & E. D. Walker (Eds.), *Religion and psychology.* New York: Nova Publishers.

Toussaint, L. L., Owen, A. D., & Cheadle, A. (2012). Forgive to live: Forgiveness, health, and longevity. *Journal of Behavioral Medicine, 35*(4), 375–386.

Tovares, A. V. (2012). Telling stories: Language, narrative, and social life by Deborah Schiffrin, Anna De Fina and Anastasia Nylund. *Journal of Sociolinguistics, 16*(3), 422–425. doi:10.1111/j.1467-9841.2012.00539_3.x

Tracy, J. L., & Robins, R. W. (2008). The nonverbal expression of pride: Evidence for cross-cultural recognition. *Journal of Personality & Social Psychology, 94*(3), 516–530.

Trepte, S., Reinecke, L., & Behr, K.-M. (2009). Creating virtual alter egos or superheroines? Gamers' strategies of avatar creation in terms of gender and sex. *International Journal of Gaming and Computer-Mediated Simulations, 1*(2), 52–76.

Triandis, H. C. (1986). Collectivism vs. individualism: A reconceptualization of a basic concept in cross-cultural psychology. In C. Bagley & G. Verma (Eds.), *Personality, cognition, and values: Cross-cultural perspectives of childhood and adolescence.* London: Macmillan.

Triandis, H. C. (1988). Collectivism vs. individualism. In G. Verma & C. Bagley (Eds.), *Cross-cultural studies of personality, attitudes, and cognition.* London: Macmillan.

Triandis, H. C. (2000). Culture and conflict. *The International Journal of Psychology, 35*(2), 1435–1452.

Triandis, H. C., Brislin, R., & Hul, C. H. (1988). Cross-cultural training across the individualism-collectivism divide. *International Journal of Intercultural Relations, 12,* 269–289.

Tripathy, J. (2010). How gendered is gender and development? Culture, masculinity, and gender difference. *Development in Practice, 20*(1), 113–121.

Tsa, W. C., Chen, C. C., & Chiu, S. F. (2005). Exploring boundaries of the effects of applicant impression management tactics in job interviews. *Journal of Management, 31*(1), 108–125.

Tse, M., Vong, S., & Tang, S. (2013). Motivational interviewing and exercise programme for community-dwelling older persons with chronic pain: A randomized controlled study. *Journal of Clinical Nursing, 22*(13/14), 1843–1856. doi:10.1111/j.1365-2702.2012.04317.x

Tuckman, B. W., & Jensen, M. A. C. (1977). Stages in small group development revisited. *Groups and Organizational Studies, 2,* 419–427.

Tufte, E. R. (2006). *The cognitive style of PowerPoint: Pitching out corrupts within* (2nd ed.). Cheshire, CT: Graphics.

Tufte, E. (2003, September). PowerPoint is evil: Power corrupts; PowerPoint corrupts absolutely. *Wired.* Retrieved from http://www.wired.com/wired/archive/11.09/ppt2.html

Turow, J., Hennessy, M., & Draper, N. A. (2015). *The tradeoff fallacy: How marketers are misrepresenting American consumers and opening them up to exploitation.* A report from the Annenberg School for Communication, University of Pennsylvania. Retrieved from https://ssrn.com/abstract=2820060; doi.org/10.2139/ssrn.2820060

Ubinger, M. E., Handal, P. J., & Massura, C. E. (2013). Adolescent adjustment: The hazards of conflict avoidance and the benefits of conflict resolution. *Psychology, 4*(1), 50–58.

The ubiquitous PowerPoint. (2013, April). Full text available. *Phi Delta Kappan, 94*(7), 7.

Uhl-Bien, M. (2006). Relational leadership theory: Exploring the social processes of leadership and organizing. *The Leadership Quarterly, 17,* 654–676.

Uhls, Y. T., Michikyan, M., Morris, J., Garcia, D., Small, G. W., Zgourou, E., & Greenfield, P. M. (2014). Five days at outdoor education camp without screens improves preteen skills with nonverbal emotion cues. *Computers in Human Behavior, 39,* 387–392.

U.S. Census Bureau. (2012). Census Bureau releases equal employment opportunity tabulation that provides a profile of America's workforce. Retrieved from http://www.census.gov/newsroom/releases/archives/employment_occupations/cb12-225.html

U.S. Department of Justice, Federal Bureau of Investigation. (2010, September). *Crime in the United States, 2009.* Retrieved from http://www2.fbi.gov/ucr/clus2009/index.html

U.S. Equal Employment Opportunity Commission. (n.d.). *Sexual harassment is against the law.* Retrieved on October 1, 2016, from https://www.eeoc.gov/youth/downloads/sexual_harassment.pdf

Uysal, N. (2016). Social collaboration in intranets: The impact of social exchange and group norms on internal communication. *International Journal of Business Communication, 53*(2), 181–199. doi:10.1177/2329488415627270

Valkenburg, P. M., & Peter, J. (2013). The differential susceptibility to media effects model. *Journal of Communication, 63,* 221–43.

Valkenburg, P., Peter, J., & Walther, J. B. (2016) Media effects: Theory and research. *Annual Review of Psychology, 67,* 315–38.

van den Heever, C. (2016, February 5). Move over Facebook: WeChat is set to become the only app African internet users need. *The World Post.* Retrieved from http://www.huffingtonpost.com/claire-van-den-heever/wechat-africafacebook_b_9149794.html

Van Dick, R., Tissington, P. A., & Hertel, G. (2009). Do many hands make light work? How to overcome social loafing and gain motivation in work teams. *European Business Review, 21*(3), 233–245.

Van Ouytsel, J., Van Gool, E., Walrave, M., Ponnet, K., & Peeters, E. (2016). Exploring the role of social networking sites within adolescent romantic relationships and dating experiences. *Computers in Human Behavior, 55,* 76–86. doi:10.1016/j.chb.2015.08.042

Van Swol, L. M., Braun, M. T., & Kolb, M. R. (2013). Deception detection, demeanor, and truth bias in face-to-face and computer-mediated communication. *Communication Research, 40*(5), 1–27.

Van Swol, L. M., Malhotra, D., & Braun, M. T. (2012). Deception and its detection: Effects of monetary incentives and personal relationship history. *Communication Research, 39*(2), 217–238.

Van Zandt, T. (2004). Information overload and a network of targeted communication. *RAND Journal of Economics, 35,* 542–561.

Vangelisti, A. L., & Hampel, A. D. (2009). Hurtful communication: Current research and future directions. In S. W. Smith & S. Wilson (Eds.), *New directions in interpersonal communication research* (pp. 221–241). Los Angeles, CA: Sage.

VanMeter, R. A., Grisaffe, D. B., & Chonko, L. B. (2015). Of "likes" and "pins": The affects of consumers' attachment to social media. *Journal of Interactive Marketing, 32,* 70–88.

Vela, L. E., Booth-Butterfield, M., Wanzer, M. B., & Vallade, J. I. (2013). Relationships among humor, coping, relationship stress, and satisfaction in dating relationships: Replication and extension. *Communication Research Reports, 30*(1), 68–75.

Villaume, W. A., & Brown, M. H. (1999). The development and validation of the vocalic sensitivity test. *International Journal of Listening, 13,* 24–45.

Visserman, M. L., & Karremans, J. C. (2014). Romantic relationship status biases the processing of an attractive alternative's behavior. *Personal Relationships, 21*(2), 324–334.

Vogel, D. R., Dickson, G. W., & Lehman, J. A. (1986). Persuasion and the role of visual presentation support: The UM/3M study (MISRC-WP-86-11), Minneapolis, MN: University of Minnesota, Management Information Systems Research Center.

Vogel, H. L. (2015). *Entertainment industry economics: A guide for financial analysis* (9th edition). New York: Cambridge University Press.

Vogt, N., & Mitchell, A. (2016, January 20). Crowdfunded journalism: A small but growing addition to publicly driven journalism.

Pew Research Center. Retrieved from http://www.journalism.org/2016/01/20/crowdfunded-journalism/

Von Raffler-Engel, W. (1983). *The perception of nonverbal behavior in the career interview.* Philadelphia: Benjamin.

Vrij, A. (2006). Nonverbal communication and deception. In V. Manusov & M. L. Patterson (Eds.), *The Sage handbook of nonverbal communication* (pp. 341–360). Thousand Oaks, CA: Sage.

Wade, N. (2010, January 12). Deciphering the chatter of monkeys and chimps. *The New York Times,* p. D1.

Waldron, V. R., & Applegate, J. A. (1998). Effects of tactic similarity on social attraction and persuasiveness in dyadic verbal disagreements. *Communication Reports, 11,* 155–166.

Waldron, V. R., & Kelley, D. L. (2005). Forgiving communication as a response to relational transgressions. *Journal of Social and Personal Relationships, 22,* 723–742.

Walker, H. (2015, February 26). 2 women are behind the viral dress that has everyone confused—Here's what they told us. *Business Insider.* Retrieved from http://www.businessinsider.com/origin-of-white-gold-or-black-blue-dress-2015-2

Wall, M. (2015). Citizen journalism: A retrospective on what we know, an agenda for what we don't. *Digital Journalism, 3*(6), 797–813.

Waller, M. J., Conte, J. M., Gibson, G., & Carpenter, A. (2001). The impact of individual time perception on team performance under deadline conditions. *Academy of Management Review, 26,* 586–600.

Walther, J. B. (1996). Computer-mediated communication: Impersonal, interpersonal, and hyperpersonal interaction. *Communication Research, 23,* 3–43.

Walther, J. B. (2006). Nonverbal dynamics in computer-mediated communication, or: :-(and the net :-('s with you, :-) and you :-) alone. In V. Manusov & M. L. Patterson (Eds.), *Handbook of nonverbal communication* (pp. 461–479). Thousand Oaks, CA: Sage.

Walther, J. B. (2011). Theories of computer-mediated communication and interpersonal relations. In M. L. Knapp & J. A. Daly (Eds.), *The SAGE handbook of interpersonal communication* (4th ed.) (pp. 443–479). Thousand Oaks, CA: Sage.

Walther, J. B., Hoter, E., Ganayem, A., & Shonfeld, M. (2015). Computer-mediated communication and the reduction of prejudice: A controlled longitudinal field experiment among Jews and Arabs in Israel. *Computers in Human Behavior, 52,* 550–558.

Walther, J. B., & Parks, M. R. (2002). Cues filtered out, cues filtered in: Computer-mediated communication and relationships. In M. L. Knapp & J. A. Daly (Eds.), *Handbook of interpersonal communication* (pp. 529–563). Thousand Oaks, CA: Sage.

Walther, J. B., & Ramirez, A., Jr. (2009). New technologies and new directions in online relating. In S. W. Smith & S. R. Wilson (Eds.), *New directions in interpersonal communication research* (pp. 264–284). Newbury Park, CA: Sage.

Walther, J. B., Van Der Heide, B., Kim, S. Y., Westerman, D., & Tong, S. T. (2008). The role of friends' appearance and behavior on evaluations of individuals on Facebook: Are we known by the company we keep? *Human Communication Research, 34*(1), 28–49.

Walther, J. B., Van Der Heide, B., Tong, S. T., Carr, C. T., & Atkin, C. K. (2010). Effects of interpersonal goals on inadvertent intrapersonal influence in computer-mediated communication. *Human Communication Research, 36*(3), 323–347.

Waltman, M., & Haas, J. (2011). *The communication of hate.* New York: Peter Lang.

Wang, C., Lee, M. K. O., & Hua, Z. (2015). A theory of social media dependence: Evidence from microblog users. *Decision Support Systems, 69,* 40–49.

Wang, D., Xiang, Z., & Fesenmaier, D. R. (2016). Smartphone use in everyday life and travel. *Journal of Travel Research, 55*(1), 52–63.

Wang, G., & Liu, Z. (2010). What collective? Collectivism and relationalism from a Chinese perspective. *Chinese Journal of Communication, 3*(1), 42–63.

Wang, Z., Irwin, M., Cooper, C., & Srivastava, J. (2015). Multidimensions of media multitasking and adaptive media selection. *Human Communication Research, 41*, 102–127.

Wanshel, E. (2016, April 13). Girls' school alums raise $180,000 for beloved security guard's retirement. Huffingtonpost.com. Retrieved from http://www.huffingtonpost.com/entry/kifleab-tekle-retirement-the-hockaday-school-gofundme_us_570d0d91e4b0885fb50e3843

Wanzer, M., Booth-Butterfield, M., & Gruber, K. (2004). Perceptions of health care providers' communication: Relationships between patient-centered communication and satisfaction. *Health Communication, 16*(3), 363–383.

Wayne, T. (2016, March 27). Holdouts of the social media age. *The New York Times.* Retrieved from http://www.nytimes.com/2016/03/27/fashion/not-on-facebook-twitter-social-media.html?_r=0

Ward, A.-K., Ravlin, E. C., Klaas, B. S., Ployhart, R. E., & Buchan, N. R. (2016, August 8). When do high-context communicators speak up? Exploring contextual communication orientation and employee voice. *Journal of Applied Psychology.* doi:10.1037/apl0000144

Ward, C. C., & Tracey, T. J. G. (2004). Relation of shyness with aspects of online relationship involvement. *Journal of Social and Personal Relationships, 21*, 611–623.

Wasserman, B., & Weseley, A. (2009). ¿Qué? Quoi? Do languages with grammatical gender promote sexist attitudes? *Sex Roles, 61*(9/10), 634–643.

Waters, S., & Ackerman, J. (2011). Exploring privacy management on Facebook: Motivations and perceived consequences of voluntary disclosure. *Journal of Computer-Mediated Communication, 17*(1), 101–115.

Watts, D. J. (2011). *Everything is obvious once you know the answer: How common sense fails us.* New York: Crown Publishing Group.

Way, N. (2011). *Deep secrets: Boys' friendships and the crisis of connection.* Cambridge, MA: Harvard University Press.

Webster, M. J., & Driskell, J. E., Jr. (1978). Status generalization: A review of some new data. *American Sociological Review, 42*, 220–236.

Webster, M. J., & Driskell, J. E., Jr. (1983). Beauty as status. *American Journal of Sociology, 89*, 140–165.

Wecker, C. (2012). Slide presentations as speech suppressors: When and why learners miss oral information. *Computers and Education, 59*(2), 260–273.

Weger, H., Jr., Castle, G. R., & Emmett, M. C. (2010). Active listening in peer interviews: The influence of message paraphrasing on perceptions of listening skill. *International Journal of Listening, 24*(1), 34–49.

Weisz, C., & Wood, L. F. (2005). Social identity support and friendship outcomes: A longitudinal study predicting who will be friends and best friends 4 years later. *Journal of Social and Personal Relationships, 22*, 416–432.

Welch, B. A., Mossholder, K. W., Stell, R. P., & Bennett, N. (1998). Does work group cohesiveness affect individuals' performance and organizational commitment? *Small Group Research, 29*, 472–494.

Welch, S. A., & Mickelson, W. T. (2013). A listening competence comparison of working professionals. *International Journal of Listening, 27*(2), 85–99.

Welles, B. F., Rousse, T., Merrill, N., & Contractor, N. (2014). Virtually friends: An exploration of friendship claims and expectations in immersive virtual worlds. *Journal of Virtual Worlds Research, 7*(2), 1–15.

Wells, T. M., & Dennis, A. R. (2015). To email or not to email: The impact of media on psychophysiological responses and emotional content in utilitarian and romantic communication. *Computers in Human Behavior, 54*, 1–9.

Werner, J. (2011, February 16). Bucks County teacher suspended for "lazy whiners" comments defends herself in new blog. *The Trentonian.* Retrieved from http://www.trentonian.com/article/TT/20110216/NEWS/302169990

Wertheim, L. J., & Keith, T. (2015). Stuck in the rough. *Sports Illustrated, 122*(15), 12–13.

What is the It Gets Better Project? (2013). It Gets Better Project. Retrieved on *November 1, 2013,* from http://www.itgetsbetter.org/pages/about-it-gets-better-project

Wheaton, S. (2012, October 13). Missouree? Missouruh? To be politic, say both. *The New York Times,* p. A1.

Whedon Studies Association. (2016). Latest issue of *Slayage* released. whedonstudies.tv. Retrieved from http://www.whedonstudies.tv/news/latest-issue-of-slayage-released1

Wheelan, S. A. (2012). *Creating effective teams: A guide for members and leaders* (4th ed.). Thousand Oaks: Sage.

Wheelan, S. A., & Burchill, C. (1999). Take teamwork to new heights. *Nursing Management, 30*(4), 28–31.

Weinman, J. J. (2015). The new king of late night. *Maclean's, 128*(48/49), 58–59.

Wiemann, J. M. (1977). Explication and test of a model of communication competence. *Human Communication Research, 3,* 195–213.

Wiemann, J. M., & Backlund, P. M. (1980). Current theory and research in communication competence. *Review of Educational Research, 50,* 185–189.

Wiemann, J. M., Chen, V., & Giles, H. (1986, November). Beliefs about talk and silence in a cultural context. Paper presented at the annual meeting of the Speech Communication Association, Chicago.

Wiemann, J. M., & Krueger, D. L. (1980). The language of relationships. In H. Giles, W. P. Robinson, & P. M. Smith (Eds.), *Language: Social psychological perspectives* (pp. 55–62). Oxford: Pergamon Press.

Wiemann, J. M., Takai, J., Ota, H., & Wiemann, M. O. (1997). A relational model of communication competence. In B. Kovačić (Ed.), *Emerging theories of human communication* (pp. 25–44). Albany, NY: State University of New York Press.

Wiemann, M. O. (2009). *Love you/hate you: Negotiating intimate relationships.* Barcelona, Spain: Editorial Aresta.

Wierzbicka, A. (2006). *English: Meaning and culture.* New York: Oxford.

Wiesenfeld, D., Bush, K., & Sikdar, R. (2010). The value of listening: Heeding the call of the Snuggie. *Journal of Advertising Research, 50*(1), 16–20.

Willard, G., & Gramzow, R. (2008). Exaggeration in memory: Systematic distortion of self-evaluative information under reduced accessibility. *Journal of Experimental Social Psychology, 44*(2), 246–259.

Willens, M. (2016, June 14). Sibling rivalry: The grown-up version. *The New York Times.* Retrieved from http://well.blogs.nytimes.com/2016/06/14/sibling-rivalry-the-grown-up-version/?_r=0

Williams, A. (2015, September 18). Move over, millennials, here comes generation Z. *The New York Times.* Retrieved from http:

//www.nytimes.com/2015/09/20/fashion/move-over-millennials -here-comes-generation-z.html?_r=0

Williams, D. E., & Hughes, P. C. (2005). Nonverbal communication in Italy: An analysis of interpersonal touch, body position, eye contact, and seating behaviors. *North Dakota Journal of Speech & Theatre, 18,* 17–24.

Williams, E. F., Dunning, D., & Kruger, J. (2013). The hobgoblin of consistency: Algorithmic judgment strategies underlie inflated self-assessments of performance. *Journal of Personality & Social Psychology, 104*(6), 976–994. doi:10.1037/a0032416

Williams, J. C. (2014). Women, work, and the art of gender judo. *Washington Post.* Retrieved from http://www.washingtonpost.com/opinions /women-work-and-the-art-of-gender-judo/2014/01/24/29e209b2 -82b2-11e3-8099-9181471f7aaf_story.html

Williams, K. D. (2001). *Ostracism: The power of silence.* New York: Guilford Press.

Williams, K. D., Govan, C. L., Croker, V., Tynan, D., Cruickshank, M., & Lam, A. (2002). *Group dynamics: Theory, research, and practice, 6*(1), 65–77.

Williams, K. D., & Sommer, K. L. (1997). Social ostracism by coworkers: Does rejection lead to loafing or compensation? *Personality and Social Psychology Bulletin, 23*(7), 693–706.

Williams, K. N., Herman, R., Gajewski, B., & Wilson, K. (2009). Elderspeak communication: Impact on dementia care. *American Journal of Alzheimer's Disease & Other Dementias, 24*(1), 11–20.

Williams, P. (1993). Surveillance hurts productivity, deprives employees of rights. *Advertising Age, 64,* 14.

Willoughby, B. J., Carroll, J. S., & Busby, D. M. (2012). The different effects of "living together": Determining and comparing types of cohabiting couples. *Journal of Social and Personal Relationships, 29*(3), 397–419.

Wilmot, W. W. (1987). *Dyadic communication* (3rd ed.). New York: Random House.

Wilson, B. J., Smith, S. L., Potter, W. J., Kunkel, D., Linz, D., Colvin, C. M., & Donnerstein, E. (2002). Violence in children's programming: Assessing the risks. *Journal of Communication, 52,* 5–35.

Wilson, G. L., & Hanna, M. S. (1993). *Groups in context: Leadership and participation in small groups* (3rd ed.). New York: McGraw Hill.

Wilson, R. (2015). Students' requests for trigger warnings grow more varied. *The Chronicle of Higher Education.* Retrieved from http: //chronicle.com/article/Students-Requests-for/233043

Winczewski, L. A., Bowen, J. D., & Collins, N. L. (2016). Is empathic accuracy enough to facilitate responsive behavior in dyadic interaction? Distinguishing ability from motivation. *Psychological Science, 27*(3), 394–404. doi:10.1177/0956797615624491

Winston, C. (2002, January 28). State of the Union stew. *The Christian Science Monitor.* Retrieved from https://www.csmonitor .com/2002/0128/p09s02-coop.html

Winston, C. N. (2014). Evaluating media's portrayal of an eccentric-genius: Dr. Sheldon Cooper. *Psychology of Popular Media Culture.* doi:10.1037/ppm0000060

Winter, J., & Pauwels, A. (2006). Men staying at home looking after their children: Feminist linguistic reform and social change. *International Journal of Applied Linguistics, 16*(1), 16–36.

Wittenbaum, G. M., Shulman, H. C., & Braz, M. E. (2010). Social ostracism in task groups: The effects of group composition. *Small Group Research, 41*(3), 330–353.

Wojciechowski, J., Stolarski, M., & Matthews, G. (2014). Emotional intelligence and mismatching expressive and verbal messages: A contribution to detection of deception. *PLoS ONE, 9*(3), 1–13. doi:10.1371/journal.pone.0092570

Wojcieszak, M., Bimber, B., Feldman, L., & Stroud, N. J. (2016). Partisan news and political participation: Exploring mediated relationships. *Political Communication, 33*(2), 241–260.

Wolfram, W., & Schilling-Estes, N. (2006). *American English: Dialects and variation* (2nd ed., p. 1). Malden, MA: Blackwell Publishing.

Wolvin, A. (2010). Response: Toward a listening ethos. *International Journal of Listening, 24*(3), 179–180.

Wolvin, A. D., & Coakley, C. G. (1991). A survey of the status of listening training in some *Fortune* 500 corporations. *Communication Education, 40,* 151–164.

Wong, E., & Cheng, M. (2013). Effects of motivational interviewing to promote weight loss in obese children. *Journal of Clinical Nursing, 22*(17/18), 2519–2530. doi:10.1111/jocn.12098

Woo, E. (2011, March 13). Sam Chwat dies at 57; actors lost, and learned, accents under dialect coach's tutelage. *Los Angeles Times.* Retrieved from http://articles.latimes.com/2011/mar/13/local /la-me-sam-chwat-20110313

Wood, B. (1982). *Children and communication: Verbal and nonverbal language development* (2nd ed.). Englewood Cliffs, NJ: Prentice Hall.

Wood, J. T. (2011). *Gendered lives: Communication, gender, and culture* (9th ed.). Boston, MA: Wadsworth Publishing.

Woods, S., Lambert, N., Brown, P., Fincham, F., & May, R. (2015). "I'm so excited for you!" How an enthusiastic responding intervention enhances close relationships. *Journal of Social & Personal Relationships, 32*(1), 24–40.

Woodzicka, J. (2008). Sex differences in self-awareness of smiling during a mock job interview. *Journal of Nonverbal Behavior, 32*(2), 109–121.

Worley, T. R., & Samp, J. (2016). Complaint avoidance and complaint-related appraisals in close relationships: A dyadic power theory perspective. *Communication Research, 43*(3), 391–413.

Wrench, J. S., McCroskey, J. C., & Richmond, V. P. (2008). *Human communication in everyday life: Explanations and applications.* Boston: Allyn & Bacon.

Wright, C. N., Holloway, A., & Roloff, M. E. (2007). The dark side of self-monitoring: How high self-monitors view their romantic relationships. *Communication Reports, 20*(2), 101–114.

Wright, K. B., Rosenberg, J., Egbert, N., Ploeger, N. A., Bernard, D. R., & King, S. (2013). Communication competence, social support, and depression among college students: A model of Facebook and face-to-face support network influence. *Journal of Health Communication, 18*(1), 41–57.

Xiang, W., Chen, S., Sun, L., Cheng, S., & Bove, V. M. Jr., (2016). Odor emoticon: An olfactory application that conveys emotions. *International Journal of Human-Computer Studies, 91,* 52–61. doi:10.1016/j.ijhcs.2016.04.001

Xu, F., Caldwell, C., Glasper, K., & Guevara, L. (2015). Leadership roles and transformative duties—preliminary research. *Journal of Management Development, 34*(9), 1061–1072. doi:10.1108 /JMD-12-2014-0156

Yaguchi, M., Iyeiri, Y., & Baba, Y. (2010). Speech style and gender distinctions in the use of *very* and *real/really*: An analysis of the Corpus of Spoken Professional American English. *Journal of Pragmatics, 42*(3), 585–597.

Yang Claire, Y., Boen, C., Gerken, K., Ting, L., Schorpp, K., & Harris, K. M. (2016). Social relationships and physiological determinants of longevity across the human life span. *Proceedings of the National Academy of Sciences of the United States of America, 113*(3), 578–583. doi:10.1073/pnas.1511085112

Yanping, T., & Soman, D. (2014). The categorization of time and its impact on task initiation. *Journal of Consumer Research, 41*(3), 810–822.

Yasui, E. (2009, May). Collaborative idea construction: The repetition of gestures and talk during brainstorming. A paper presented at the 59th meeting of the International Communication Association, Chicago, IL.

Yee, N., & Bailenson, J. (2007). The Proteus effect: The effect of transformed self-representation on behavior. *Human Communication Research, 33*(3), 271–290.

Yeo, S. K., Xenos, M. A., Brossard, D., & Scheufele, D. A. (2015). Selecting our own science: How communication contexts and individual traits shape information seeking. *The ANNALS of the American Academy of Political and Social Science, 658*(1), 172–191.

Yoo, C. Y. (2007). Implicit memory measures for Web advertising effectiveness. *Journalism & Mass Communication Quarterly, 84*(1), 7–23.

Yoo, S., & Noyes, S. (2016). Recognition of facial expressions of negative emotions in romantic relationships. *Journal of Nonverbal Behavior, 40*(1), 1–12. doi:10.1007/s10919-015-0219-3

Yook, E. (2004). Any questions? Knowing the audience through question types. *Communication Teacher, 18,* 91–93.

Yoon, K., Kim, C. H., & Kim, M. S. (1998). A cross-cultural comparison of the effects of source credibility on attitudes and behavioral intentions. *Mass Communication and Society, 1*(3–4), 153–173.

Young, S. L., Bippus, A. M., & Dunbar, N. E. (2015). Comparing romantic partners' perceptions of hurtful communication during conflict conversations. *Southern Communication Journal, 80*(1), 39–54.

Yukl, G. (1999). An evaluation of conceptual weaknesses in transformational and charismatic leadership theories. *Leadership Quarterly, 10,* 285–305.

Zabava Ford, W. S., & Wolvin, A. D. (1993). The differential impact of a basic communication course on perceived communication competencies in class, work, and social contexts. *Communication Education, 42*(3), 215–223.

Zacchilli, T. L., Hendrick, C., & Hendrick, S. S. (2009). The romantic partner conflict scale: A new scale to measure relationship conflict. *Journal of Social and Personal Relationships, 26*(8), 1073–1096.

Zappos.com. (2014, February 8). Introducing: Core values frog! Retrieved from http://about.zappos.com/jobs/why-work-zappos/core-values

Zarrinabadi, N. (2012). Self-perceived communication competence in Iranian culture. *Communication Research Reports, 29*(4), 292–298.

Zehir, C., Müceldili, B., Altindağ, E., Şehitoğlu, Y., & Zehir, S. (2014). Charismatic leadership and organization citizenship behavior: The mediating role of ethical climate. *Social Behavior & Personality: An International Journal, 42*(8), 1365–1375. doi:10.2224/sbp.2014.42.8.1365

Zeman, N. (2013, June). The boy who cried dead girlfriend. *Vanity Fair.* Retrieved from http://www.vanityfair.com/culture/2013/06/manti-teo-girlfriend-nfl-draft

Zhang, Q., & Andreychik, M. (2013). Relational closeness in conflict: Effects on interaction goals, emotion, and conflict styles. *Journal of International Communication, 19*(1), 107–116.

Zhang, Q., Oetzel, J. G., Ting-Toomey, S., & Zhang, J. (2015). Making up or getting even? The effects of face concerns, self-construal, and apology on forgiveness, reconciliation, and revenge in the United States and China. *Communication Research.* Advance online publication. doi:10.1177/0093650215607959

Zhou, W. (2016). When does shared leadership matter in entrepreneurial teams: The role of personality composition. *International Entrepreneurship and Management Journal, 12*(1), 153–169. doi:10.1007/s1136501403343

Ziebland S., & Wyke, S. (2012). Health and illness in a connected world: How might sharing experiences on the internet affect people's health? *Milbank Quarterly 90,* 219–249.

Zimbushka. (2008, May 27). *Mike Caro's 10 ultimate poker cues.* Retrieved from http://www.youtube.com/watch?v=QqF8m12JSDE

acknowledgments

Real Communicator Chapter 1.a: Adaptation of Natcom.org, Why Study Communication? Pathways to Your Future. Washington, D.C.: National Communication Association, 2016. Reprinted by permission of the National Communication Association.

Real Communicator Chapter 1.b: Adaptation of S. Morreale and A. Swickard-Gorman, eds., Pathways to Communication Careers in the 21st Century. Washington, D.C.: National Communication Association, 2006. Reprinted by permission of the National Communication Association.

What About You? Chapter 2: Adaptation of: VanMeter, R. A., Grisaffe, D. B., & Chonko, L. B. (2015). "Of 'Likes' and 'Pins': The Effects of Consumers' Attachment to Social Media." Journal of Interactive Marketing 32 (November 2015), 70–88. Copyright © 2015. Reprinted with permission from Elsevier.

What About You? Chapter 7: Adaptation of: Bodie, G. D., Worthington, D. L., & Gearhart, C. C. (2013). "The Revised Listening Styles Profile (LSP-R): Development and Validation," Communication Quarterly 61(1), 72–90, doi:10.1080/01463373.2012.720343. Copyright © 2013. Reprinted by permission of Taylor & Francis Ltd., http://www.tandfonline.com.

Speech 13.1: Sarah-Jayne Blakemore. "The Mysterious Workings of the Adolescent Brain," TED Talk, June 2012, retrieved from http://www.ted.com//talks/sarah_jayne_blakemore_the _mysterious_workings_of_the_adolescent_brain. Reprinted by permission.

Speech13.2: Ricky Martin. Remarks at the Vienna Forum. Reprinted by permission of the Ricky Martin Foundation. Ricky Martin, President and Founder.

index